INFORMATION TECHNOLOGY LAW

Cavendish
Publishing
Limited

London • Sydney

INFORMATION TECHNOLOGY LAW

Diane Rowland, Lecturer in Law,
University of Wales, Aberystwyth

Elizabeth Macdonald, Senior Lecturer in Law,
University of Wales, Aberystwyth
Both of the Centre for Computers, Technology and Law

Cavendish
Publishing
Limited

London • Sydney

First published in Great Britain 1997 by Cavendish Publishing Limited, The Glass House, Wharton Street, London WC1X 9PX.

Telephone: 0171-278 8000 Facsimile: 0171-278 8080

e-mail: info@cavendishpublishing.com

Visit our Home Page on http://www.cavendishpublishing.com

Macdonald, Elizabeth J

Information technology law: text, cases and materials

1. Computers – Law and legislation – Great Britain

2. Electronic data interchange – Law and legislation – Great Britain

I. Title II. Rowland, Diane

344.1'0378'004

1 85941 225 4

Printed and bound in Great Britain by
Biddles Ltd, Guildford and King's Lynn

PREFACE

Our impetus to produce this book arose out of our undergraduate and postgraduate teaching in information technology law. Although the number of texts in the area is now increasing, on being asked by students to recommend a casebook we were unable to do so. We have also found that one of the difficulties with a relatively new subject is that materials are not always readily accessible to students. Our aim was to include a range of materials sufficient to aid and enhance the student's study of this topic. In addition, in such a developing area, we felt it helpful to include a substantial element of our own texts, where the context required it.

The book is primarily aimed at undergraduate and postgraduate law students. Against that background, we hope that it will provide reassurance that a detailed knowledge of the technology is unnecessary to understand the legal issues. Where some rudimentary understanding is helpful, minimum technical explanations have been included. We think the book may also prove useful, and of interest, to computer scientists, who increasingly have to consider the wider implications of their discipline. They, of course, can skip the brief explanations of the technology!

We think that information technology provides exciting challenges and opportunities for the law and lawyers. We hope that we have communicated something of this to the reader.

We would particularly like to thank Michael Hirst for producing the chapter on evidence. His expertise in the area of evidence in general is well-established and the book has benefited from his contribution. We are also indebted to Jem Rowland for his advice on the more technical aspects of the text and to Michael Hirst, Reader in Law, University of Wales, Aberyswyth, for his contribution to Chapter 9.

We have attempted to state the law as at 1 April 1997.

Diane Rowland

Elizabeth Macdonald

ACKNOWLEDGMENTS

Grateful acknowledgment is made for permission to reprint copyright material, and in particular to the following to reprint material from the sources indicated.

Velasco, 'The copyrightability of non-literal elements of computer programs'. The article originally appeared at (1994) 94 Colum L Rev 242.

Tolley Publishing for permission to reproduce extracts from *Computer Law and Practice*.

International Bureau of World Intellectual Property Organisation (WIPO) for permission to reproduce WIPO Model Provisions on the Protection of Computer Software 1978 (Introduction).

Chris Reed for permission to reproduce extracts from Reed, C, 'Digital Information Law – Electronic Documents and Requirements of Form', 1996, Centre for Commercial Law studies, Queen Mary and Westfield College.

Extracts reprinted from *Reliability Engineering and System Safety*, Vol 32, Lloyd, pp 198–99, 1991, 'Liability for Defective Software' (1991), Computer Law and Security Report, Vol 12; Smith, G, 'EC Software Protection Directive: An Attempt to Understand Art 5(1), p 148, 1990–91, with permission from Elsevier Science Ltd, The Boulevard, Langford Lane Kidlington OX5 1GB, UK.

Decisions of Data Protection Tribunal, Reports of Patent Design and Trade Mark cases, Law Commission Consultation Paper No 138, 9th and 11th Reports of the Data Protection Registrar, Law Commission Report No 1982, Scottish Law Commission Report on Computer Crime, Cm 174, Law Commission Working Paper No 110, Law Commission Report on Computer Misuse Cm 819. Crown Copyright is reproduced with permission of the controller of Her Majesty's Stationary Office.

Institute of Electrical Engineers for permission to reproduce extracts from, *Safety Related Systems. A Professional Brief for the Engineer*.

Official Journal of the European Communities and *ECJ Reports*. Extracts reprinted with permission.

The Michigan Law Review for permission to reproduce extracts from Englund, SR, Note, 'Idea, Process or Protected Expression?: Determining the Scope of Copyright protection of the Structure of Computer programs' (1990) 88 Mich L Rev 866.

Rowland, D and Rowland, JJ, 'Competence and Legal Liability in the Development of Software safety-Related Applications' (1993) 2 *Information and Communications Technology Law* (previously *Law Computers and Artificial Intelligence*) 229 with permission of Carfax Publishing Limited, PO Box 25, Abingdon, Oxfordshire, OX14 3UE, UK.

LLP Limited for permission to reproduce extract from Faber, D, 'Electronic Bills of Lading' [1996] LMCLQ 23.

Incorporated Council for Law Reporting for England and Wales for permission to reproduce extracts from the *Law Reports* and the *Weekly Law Reports*.

Burton, 'Regulation and Control of the Internet: Is it Feasible? Is it Necessary?' (1995) 21 *Journal of Information Science*. Reprinted with the kind permission of Bowker-Saur, a division of Reed Elsevier (UK) Ltd and the Institute of Information Scientists.

West Publishing Co for permission to reproduce extracts from the *Federal Reporter*.

Cambridge Law Journal and Professor Brian Napier for permission to reproduce extracts from Napier, B, 'The Future of Information Technology Law' [1992] CLJ 46.

Butterworth & Co Ltd for permission to reproduce extracts from the *All England Law Reports*, Stapleton, *Product Liability*, 1994, and Aldhouse, 'UK Data Protection – Where are we in 1991?' (1991) 5 *Yearbook of Law, Computers and Technology* 180.

Stanford Law Review, Stanford, California 94305, USA and Fred B Rothman & Co, 10368 West Centennial Road, Littleton, Colorado 80127 for permission to reproduce extracts from Dunn, 'Defining the Scope of Copyright Protection for Computer Software' (1986) 38 Stanford LR 497 (© 1986 by the Board of Trustees of the Leland Stanford Junior University); Menell, 'An Analysis of the Scope of Copyright protection for Applications Programs' (1989) 41 Stanford LR 1045 (© 1989 by the Board of Trustees of the Leland Stanford Junior University).

Macmillan, for permission to reproduce extracts from Walden, 'EDI and the Law' in Edwards, Savage and Walden (eds), *Information Technology and the Law*.

Harvard Law Review and Professor AR Miller for permission to reproduce extracts from 'Copyright Protection for Computer Programs, Databases and Computer Generated Works' (1993) 106 Harv LR 510.

Harvard Law Review for permission to reproduce extracts from '*Computer Ass v Altai* (Casenote)' (1992) 106 Harvard L Rev 510.

IBC Business Publishing Ltd for permission to reproduce extracts from Bergsten and Goode, 'Legal Questions and Problems to be Overcome', in Thomsen and Wheble (eds), *Trading with EDI – The Legal Issues*, 1989.

Sweet & Maxwell Ltd for permission to reproduce extracts from the *Criminal Appeal Reports, Criminal Law Review, Law Quarterly Review, Fleet Street Reports, Journal of Business Law, European Intellectual Property Review, Commonwealth Law Reports, Encyclopedia of Data Protection*, 1995 Supplement; Rogers, WHV, *Winfield and Jolowicz on Tort*, 14th edn.

Fleming, G, *The Law of Torts*, 8th edn, The Law Book Company.

DTI for permission to reproduce extracts from *Implementation of the EC Directive on Product Liability*, November 1985, DTI.

Oxford University Press, Walton St, Oxford, OX2 6DP for permission to reproduce extracts from Carson, 'White Collar Crime and the Enforcement of Factory Legislation' (1970) 10 *British Journal of Criminology*. Stapleton, J, 'Three problems with the new product liability' in Cane and Stapleton (eds), *Essays for Patrick Atiyah*, 1991, Oxford University Press.

Poulet, 'Data Protection Between Property and Liberties' in Kaspersen and Oskamp (eds), *Among Friends in Computers*, 1990, Kluwer.

Every effort has been made to trace all the copyright holders but if any have been inadvertently overlooked the publishers will be pleased to make the necessary arrangement at the first opportunity.

CONTENTS

Preface v
Acknowledgments vii
Table of cases xv
Table of statutes xxiii
EC legislation and statutory instruments xxv

1 INTRODUCTION 1

SECTION A THE CHALLENGES OF COMPUTER SOFTWARE

2 PROTECTING AND EXPLOITING RIGHTS IN SOFTWARE – INTELLECTUAL PROPERTY RIGHTS 5
INTRODUCTION 5
THE SCOPE OF PROTECTION 28
The situation in the US 31
The situation in the UK 45
REVERSE ENGINEERING AND DECOMPILATION 54
THE 'SOFTWARE DIRECTIVE' 56
UK implementation of the software directive 60
Sui generis rights observed 63
PATENTS AND COMPUTER PROGRAMS 64

3 PROTECTING AND EXPLOITING RIGHTS IN SOFTWARE – CONTRACT 75
INTRODUCTION 75
Types of contract 75
Bespoke and standard software 75
The software licence 76
Goods or services or something else? 76
Scope of the chapter 77
SUITABILITY/QUALITY OF SOFTWARE 77
Pre-contractual statements 77
TERMS 83
DEVELOPMENT CONTRACTS 84
Delivery and further work 86
Acceptance tests 87
MODIFYING THE CONTRACTUAL OBLIGATIONS 88
Consideration 89
Duress 93
COPYRIGHT OWNERSHIP 96
THE LICENCE 98
Licence terms 98
EC DIRECTIVE 99
Basic use of software 99
Back-up copies 102
Error correction 103

THE 'SHRINK WRAP' LICENCE 106
Acquisition contract 107
Opening the envelope 109
A third possibility 112
Pragmatism 114
Damages 115
EXEMPTION CLAUSES 117
CONSTRUCTION 117
The Unfair Contract Terms Act 1977 119
Scope of the Act 126
The active sections 128
Definitions – 'deals as consumer' 130
Definitions – 'The requirement of reasonableness' 133

4 DEFECTIVE SOFTWARE – CONTRACT 151
INTRODUCTION 151
SALE OF GOODS 152
INFORMATION 154
INTELLECTUAL PROPERTY 158
SALE OF GOODS 160
HARDWARE AND SOFTWARE AND PRAGMATISM 161
Hardware and software 161
Pragmatism 163
SERVICES 166
The supply of software 170
SECTIONS 13–15 OF THE SALE OF GOODS ACT 1979 171
'By description' 172
SECTION 13 – SALE BY DESCRIPTION 172
What constitutes a 'description' for the purposes of s 13? 175
SATISFACTORY QUALITY 182
IMPLICATION OF THE TERM 183
Sale 'in the course of a business' 183
'Goods supplied under the contract' 185
Exceptions 185
WHAT CONSTITUTES SATISFACTORY QUALITY? 187
FITNESS FOR THE BUYER'S PARTICULAR PURPOSE – s 14(3) 190
Particular purpose 191
SALE BY SAMPLE 196
RELEVANCE OF THE IMPLIED TERMS 197

5 DEFECTIVE SOFTWARE – PRODUCT LIABILITY AND TORT 199
INTRODUCTION 199

CONSUMER PROTECTION ACT 1987 200
Is software a product? 200
Is there a defect? 205
Causation 207
The development risks defence 209
NEGLIGENCE 212

SECTION B THE CHALLENGES OF COMPUTER TECHNOLOGY

6 ELECTRONIC DATA INTERCHANGE 225
INTRODUCTION 225
EDI VS PAPER 225
Network provider 228
Network users 229
Contracting with the network provider and each user 230
Formalities 231
FORMATION OF A CONTRACT BY EDI 234
The symbolic function 240
Data protection 242
European Model EDI Agreement 242

7 PROTECTING THE PRIVATE INDIVIDUAL 249
INTRODUCTION 249
DATA PROTECTION 249
DATA PROTECTION ACT 1984 258
ENFORCEMENT MECHANISMS 267
INTERPRETATION BY THE DATA PROTECTION REGISTRAR 272
INTERPRETATION BY THE DATA PROTECTION TRIBUNAL 275
(a) Information shall be obtained fairly 275
(b) Information shall be processed fairly 279
Information shall be relevant and not excessive 286
INTERPRETATION BY THE COURTS 288
EXEMPTIONS 296
ASSESSMENT OF THE APPLICATION OF THE DATA PROTECTION ACT 297
DATA PROTECTION DIRECTIVE: DIRECTIVE 95/46/EC OF THE EUROPEAN PARLIAMENT AND OF THE COUNCIL 301
COMPARISON OF THE DIRECTIVE AND THE DATA PROTECTION ACT 303
Data protection principles 307
Rights of data subjects 308
Notification 311
Exemptions 311

Transborder data flows 313
IMPLEMENTATION IN THE UK 314
FURTHER ASPECTS OF DATA PROTECTION 315
DEFAMATION 318
Is it libel or slander? 319
Publication 320
Who is liable for the publication? 322

8 POLICING 'CYBERSPACE' 331
INTRODUCTION 331
COMPUTER FRAUD 333
THE OPERATION OF THE ACT 354
LEGAL PROBLEMS OF COMPUTER NETWORKS 358
EUROPEAN INITIATIVES 371

9 EVIDENTIAL ISSUES 375
INTRODUCTION 375
CRIMINAL CASES 376
Rules of admissibility 376
The hearsay rule 377
Automatic recordings 381
Computer evidence as admissible documentary hearsay 381
Computer evidence and proof of reliability 383
Proposals for reform 389
CIVIL CASES 390
Introduction 390
Hearsay and the Civil Evidence Act 1995 391
No special 'reliability' rules for computer evidence 392
Proving the contents of documents: originals, copies and business records 392
Contractual stipulations 394

Index 397

TABLE OF CASES

ACLU v Reno (1996) (unreported) 359–60, 363–67
Adams v Lindsell (1818) 1 B & Ald 681 235
Advent Systems Ltd v Unisys Corp 925 F 2d 670........ 159, 164
Ailsa Craig Fishing Co Ltd v Malvern Fishing Co Ltd [1983] 1 WLR 964 118
Alderslade v Hendon Laundry Ltd [1945] 1 KB 189 118
Alexander v Railway Executive [1951] 2 KB 882........ 109
Alphacell Ltd v Woodward [1972] AC 824 217
Anglia TV v Reed [1971] 3 All ER 690........ 115
Apple Computer Inc v Computer Edge Pty Ltd (1983) 50 ALR 581; [1984] FSR 246 .... 22, 23–27
Apple Computer Inc v Franklin Computer Corp 714 F2d 1240; 219 USPQ 762; 70 ALR Fed 153........ 21
Apple Computer Inc v Microsoft Corp (1994) 35 F3d 1435 (9th Cir) 41–42
Arcos Ltd v EA Ronaasen & Son [1933] AC 470 179
Ashington Piggeries v Christopher Hill [1972] AC 441........ 175–79, 181, 194
Ashley v London Borough of Sutton [1995] TR L Rep 350 .... 157, 170
Aswan Engineering v Lupdine [1987] 1 All ER 135 190
Atlantic Baron, The [1978] 3 All ER 1170 94
Atlas Express v Kafco (Importers and Distributors) Ltd [1989] 1 All ER 641
Attorney-General's Reference No 1 of 1991 [1992] WLR 432 349–50
Aztech Systems Pte Ltd v Creative Technology Ltd [1996] FSR 54........ 56

Baker v Selden 101 US 99 (1879) 25 LEd 891 .... 11, 31–32, 35
B & S Contracts and Designs Ltd v Victor Green Publications Ltd [1984] ICR 419 95
Bannerman v White (1861) 10 CBNS 844 78
Bartlett v Sydney Marcus Ltd [1965] 2 All ER 753 .... 183, 187
Barton v Armstrong [1976] AC 104 95
Beale v Taylor [1967] 1 WLR 1193 174
Bernstein v Pamson Motors (Golders Green) Ltd [1987] 2 All ER 220 183
Beta Computers (Europe) Ltd v Adobe Systems (Europe) Ltd [1996] FSR 371 .... 107, 112–14, 159, 165
Betts v Willmott (1871) LR 6 Ch App 239........ 110
Bevan Investments v Blackhall and Struthers (No 2) [1973] 2 NZLR 45........ 218
Biddell Bros Ltd v E Clemens Horst & Co Ltd [1911] KB 934........ 241
Birch v Paramount Estates Ltd (1956) 16 EG 396 79
Bissett v Wilkinson [1927] AC 177........ 81
Boardman v Phipps [1967] 2 AC 46........ 155
Bolam v Friern Hospital Management Committee [1957] 1 WLR 582 217–18
Brinkibon Ltd v Stahag Stahl und Stahlwarenhandelgesellschaft mbH [1982] 1 All ER 293 .... 237–38, 240
British Leyland Motor Corp Ltd v Armstrong Patents Co Ltd [1986] AC 577 105
British Westinghouse Electric and Manufacturing Co Ltd v Underground Electric Railways Co of London [1912] AC 673 116

Brogden v Metropolitan Railway Co (1877) 2 App Cas 666 109
Brown v Raphael [1959] 1 Ch 636 82
Brown Bag Software v Symanthec Corp (1992) 960 F2d 1465 (9th Cir) 43
Business Applications v Nationwide Credit Corp [1988] RTR 332 183
Byrne v Dean [1937] 1 KB 818. 321–22

Cammell Laird & Co Ltd v Manganese Bronze and Brass Co Ltd [1934] AC 402 195
Canada Steaship Lines Ltd v R [1952] AC 192. 118
C & P Haulage v Middleton [1983] 3 All ER 94. 115
Castle v Cross [1984] 1 WLR 1372 . . . . 381, 390
CCC Films (London) Ltd v Impact Quadrant Ltd [1984] 3 All ER 298 115
CCN Systems Ltd and CCN Credit Systems Ltd v Data Protection Registrar Case DA/90 25/49/9 279–81
Chapelton v Barry UDC [1940] 1 KB 532 108
Chappell & Co v Nestle Co [1960] AC 87. 90
Chester Grosvenor Hotel Co Ltd v Alfred McAlpine Management Ltd (1992) Build LR 115 128
Circle Freight International v Medeast Gulf Exports [1988] 2 Lloyd's Rep 427 83
Clarke v Dunraven [1897] AC 59 230
Collins v Godefroy (1831) 1 B & Ad 950. 90
Community Charge Registration Office of Rhondda BC v Data Protection Registrar Case DA/90 25/49/2. 287–88
Community Charge Registration Officers of Runnymede Borough Council v Data Protection Registrar Case DA/90 24/49/3, 4 and 5. 286–87
Computer Aided Design v Bolwell (1989) (unreported) 45, 48
Computer Associates v Altai (1994) 104 Yale LJ 435. . . . . 13, 30, 37–38, 40, 42–45, 47–51, 54

Conegate v HM Customs and Excise [1986] ECR 1007 372
Conopco Inc v McCreadie 826 F Supp 855. 159
Couchman v Hill [1947] 1 All ER 103 79
Cox v Riley [1986] CLR 460. . . . . 155, 339, 352
Credit and Marketing Services Ltd v Data Protection Registrar Case DA/90 25/49/10 283
Cubby Inc v Compuserve Inc 776 F Supp 135 (SDNY 1991). 323
CTN Casn and Carry v Gallaher [1994] 4 All ER 714. 96
Currie v Misa (1875) LR 10 Exch 153. 89
Curtis v Chemical Cleaning and Dyeing Co [1951] 1 KB 805 83

Darby v DPP (1994) *The Times*, 4 November 231
Darlington Futures Ltd v Delco Australia Property (1986) 68 ALR 385. 118
Data Protection Registrar v Amnesty International (British Section) (1994) *The Times*, 23 November. 290
Data Protection Registrar v Griffin (1993) *The Times*, 5 March. 289

Davies v Sumner [1984] 1 All ER 831 .... 130–31, 132
De Freitas v O'Brien [1995] 6 Med LR 108 221
Denco v Johnson [1992] 1 All ER 463 355
Derby & Co Ltd v Weldon [1991] 1 WLR 73 394
Devlin v Hall (1990) RTR 320 132
Dick Bentley Productions Ltd v Harold Smith (Motors) Ltd [1965] 2 All ER 65 .... 78, 79–80
Dimskal Shipping Co SA v International Transport Workers Federation (The Evia Luck) [1991] 4 All ER 871 96
Dodd v Wilson [1946] 2 All ER 691 .... 165, 166
Donaghue v Allied Newspapers Ltd [1938] Ch 106 50
DP Anderson & Co v Lieber Code Co [1917] 2 KB 469 21
DPP v McKeown [1997] 1 WLR 295 383
Dunlop Pneumatic Tyre Co v Selfridge & Co [1915] AC 79 .... 89, 107

Edgington v Fitzmaurice (1885) 29 Ch D 459 81
Edwards v National Coal Board [1949] 1 QB 704 207
Emmens v Pottle (1885) 16 QBD 354 322
Enimont Overseas v Rojugotanker Zadar (The Olib) [1991] 2 Lloyd's Rep 108 95
Entores Ltd v Miles Far Eastern Corp [1955] 2 QB 325–26 .... 235–38, 240
Equifax Europa Ltd v Data Protection Registrar Case DA/90 25/49/7 284–86
Esso Petroleum Co Ltd v Mardon [1976] QB 801 82
Eurodynamics Systems v General Automation Ltd (1988) (unreported) 158

Feist Publications Inc v Rural Telephone Service Co 113 LEd 2d 358 42
Flamar Interocean Ltd v Denmac Ltd [1990] 1 Lloyd's Rep 434 128
Fraser v Evans [1969] 1 QB 349 155
Frost v Aylesbury Dairy Co [1905] 1 KB 685 166
Fujitsu Ltd's Application [1996] RPC 511 71–72

Gale's Application, Re [1991] RPC 305 70–72
Geier v Kujawa, Weston and Warne Bros (Transport) [1970] 1 Lloyd's Rep 364 108
George Mitchell (Chesterhall) Ltd v Finney Lock Seeds Ltd [1983] 2 AC 803 .... 118, 133, 137
Gibson v Manchester City Council [1979] 1 WLR 294 107
Goodman v J Eban Ltd [1954] 1 QB 550 232–33
Gran Gelato Ltd v Richcliff (Group) Ltd [1992] 1 All ER 865 83
Grant v Australian Knitting Mills [1936] AC 85 173
Greaves & Co v Baynham Meikle [1974] 1 WLR 1261 218
Griffiths v Peter Conway Ltd [1939] 1 All ER 685 192–94

Hadley v Baxendale (1854) 9 EX 341 116
Harling v Eddy [1951] 2 All ER 212 79
Harlingdon & Leinster Enterprises v Christopher Hull Fine Art [1991] 1 QB 564 .... 173–74, 175, 188

Harris v Watson (1791) Peake 102 92
Hartley v Ponsonby (1857) 7 El & Bl 872 90
Havering LBC v Stevenson [1970] 3 All ER 609 .... 131, 132
Hawkes & Son (London) Ltd v Paramount Film Services Ltd [1934] Ch 593 28
Hedley Byrne & Co Ltd v Heller & Partners Ltd [1964] AC 465 213
Heilbut, Symons & Co v Buckleton [1913] AC 30 78
Hird v Wood (1894) 38 Sol J 235 329
Hitachi's Application [1991] RPC 415 69
Hollier v Rambler Motors Ltd [1972] 2 QB 71 118
Hollinrake v Truswell [1894] 3 Ch 420 .... 22, 23, 25
Hong Kong Fir Shipping Co Ltd v Kawasaki Kisen Kaisha [1962] 2 QB 26 172
Hood v Anchor Line [1918] AC 837 108
Houghton v Trafalgar Insurance Co [1954] 1 QB 247 117
Household Fire Insurance v Grant (1879) 4 Ex D 216 239
Household Fire Insurance v Hughes [1974] 1 All ER 261
Howard Marine & Dredging Co Ltd v A Ogden & Sons (Excavations) Ltd [1978] QB 574 83
Hyde v Wrench (1840) 3 Beav 334 234

IBA v EMI and BICC (1980) BLR 1 .... 214, 218, 219
Ibcos Computers Ltd v Barclays Mercantile Highland Finance Ltd [1994] FSR 275 .... 5, 51–53
IBM/Data Processor Network T06/83 [1990] EPOR 91 69
IBM/Semantically related expressions 69
Infolink Ltd v Data Protection Registrar Case DA/90 25/49/9 281–83
Innovations (Mail Order) Ltd v Data Protection Registrar Case DA/92 31/49/1 .... 276–78, 306
Interfoto Picture Library v Stiletto Visual Programmes [1988] 1 All ER 348 108

J Marcel (Furriers) Ltd v Tapper [1953] 1 WLR 49 169
Jacobs v Batavia and General Plantations Trust [1924] 1 Ch 287 80
John Richardson Computers v Flanders [1993] FSR 497 .... 28, 42, 45–48, 50, 53
Johnstone v Bloomsbury Health Authority [1991] 2 All ER 293 84
Jones v Daniel [1894] 2 Ch 332 107

Kendall v Lillico & Sons [1969] 2 AC 31 .... 83, 166, 190, 191, 196, 212
Kerrick and Co v Lawrence & Co (1890) 25 QBD 99 50
Koufos v Czarnikow Ltd [1969] 1 AC 350 116

Ladbrooke (Football) Ltd v William Hill (Football) Ltd [1964] 1 WLR 273 .... 23, 28, 46–50
Lady Gwendolen [1965] P 294 213
Lee v Griffin (1861) 1 B & S 272 .... 167, 168, 169
L'Estrange v F Graucob Ltd [1934] 2 KB 394 83

Linguaphone Institute Ltd v Data Protection Registrar Case DA/94 31/49/1 306
Liverpool City Council v Irwin [1976] 2 All ER 39 84
London and Globe Finance Corp Ltd, Re [1903] 1 Ch 732 336
Lotus v Borland Copyright and Computer Programs (1996) Tulane LR 2397 12

MacKenzie Patten & Co v British Olivetti Ltd (1984) (unreported) 77, 80
Manchester Liners Ltd v Rea Ltd [1922] AC 74 . . . . . 193, 194
Marcel v Metropolitan Police Commissioners [1992] Ch 225 250
Maskell v Horner [1915] 3 KB 106 95
McGregor v Procurator Fiscal of Kilmarnock (1993) (unreported) 295–96, 311
McGruther v Pitcher [1904] 2 Ch 306 100
Micron Computer Systems Ltd v Wang (1990) (unreported) 77, 84, 189, 192
Miller v California (1973) 413 US 15 365
Ministry of Housing and Local Government v Sharp [1970] 2 QB 223 . . . . . 1, 213
Mondial Shipping and Chartering BV v Astarte Shipping Ltd [1995] Comm LC 1011 239
Monson v Tussauds Ltd [1894] 1 QB 671 319
Moorcock, The (1889) 14 PD 64 84
Moore & Co and Landauer & Co, Re [1921] 2 KB 519 175
MS Associates v Power [1987] FSR 242 29
Myers v DPP [1965] 1 AC 1001 377–78

New Zealand Shipping Co Ltd v Satterthwaite [1974] 1 All ER 1015 109
Niblett Ltd v Confectioner's Materials Co Ltd [1921] 3 KB 387 112
Nichols v Universal Pictures Corp (1930) 45 F2d 119 (2nd Cir) 30
Norman v Bennett [1974] 1 WLR 1229 278
North Ocean Shipping v Hyundai Construction Co Ltd
(The Atlantic Baron) [1978] 3 All ER 1170 90

Occidental Worldwide Investment Corp v Skibs A/S Avanti
(The Siboen and the Sibotre) [1976] 1 Lloyd's Rep 293 94
Olib, The [1991] 2 Lloyd's Rep 108 95
Olley v Marlborough Court Hotel [1949] 1 KB 532 107
Oscar Chess Ltd v Williams [1957] 1 All ER 325 78–79
Oxford v Moss [1978] 68 Cr App Rep 183 . . . . . 155, 157

Parker v South Eastern railway Co Ltd [1877] 2 CPD 416
Parons (H) (Livestock) v Uttley Ingham & Co Ltd [1978] 1 All ER 525 116
Pau On v Lau Yiu Long [1980] AC 614 95
People v Esposito (1990) 553 NY Supp 2d 612 291
Pharmaceutical Society of Great Britain v Boots Cash Chemists [1953] 1 QB 401 1–7
Photo Production Ltd v Securicor [1980] AC 827 . . . . . 118, 136, 137
Preist v Last [1903] 2 KB 148 192

Prince Albert v Strange (1849) 1 Mac & G 25 154
ProCD v Zeidenberg US Ct of Appeals (1996) No 96–1139 (7th Cir), 20 June 108, 114

R v Bedworth (1993) (unreported) 356, 57
R v Brown [1996] 2 WLR 203 .... 260–61, 291–96
R v Burdett (1820) 4 B & Ald 95 321
R v Caldwell [1982] AC 341 289
R v Cochrane [1993] Crim LR 48 387
R v Coventry Justices Ex p Bullard (1992) 95 Cr App R 175 391
R v Fellows and Arnold [1997] 2 All ER 548 369
R v Fisher (1865) LR 1 CCR7 339
R v Gold & Shifreen [1988] AC 1063 337–38
R v Golizadeh [1995] Crim LR 232 388
R v Griffiths Ex p Attorney-General [1957] 2 All ER 379 326
R v Henderson and Battley (1984) (unreported) 339
R v Henn and Darby [1979] ECR 3795 372
R v Kopsch [1925] 19 Cr App Rep 50 357
R v Lawrence [1982] AC 510 .... 289, 290
R v Lawrence [1989] Crim L Rev 309 357
R v Munden (1996) (unreported) 336
R v Newbury (1995) (unreported) 387
R v Pettigrew [1980] 71 Cr App 39 .... 379, 381
R v Phipson [1984] 1 WLR 1372 390
R v Pile (1995) (unreported) 357–58
R v Ponting [1985] Crim L Rev 318 356
R v Poplar Coroner Ex p Thomas [1993] 2 WLR 547 216–17
R v R [1991] 3 WLR 767 272
R v Reid [1992] 3 All ER 673 289
R v Shephard [1993] AC 380 .... 375, 384–87
R v Spiby (1990) 91 Cr App R 186 .... 375, 381, 385–86
R v Thompson [1984] 1 WLR 962 333–35
R v Whiteley (1991) *The Times*, 6 February 155, 156–57, 340–41, 352
R v Wood (1982) 76 Cr App R 39 .... 375, 379–80
Raffles v Wichelhaus (1862) 2 H & C 906 235
R & B Custom's Brokers v United Dominion Trust [1988] 1 All ER 847 .... 130, 184, 186–87
Reardon Smith Line v Hansen Tangen [1976] 1 WLR 989 .... 175, 179–80
Rees Hough Ltd v Redland Reinforced Plastics Ltd [1985] 2 Con LR 109 133
Rindos v Hardwick (1994) (unreported) 319
Robinson v Graves [1935] 1 KB 579 .... 167, 168–69, 170
Robinson v Harman (1880) 5 App Cas 25 .... 82, 115
Roe v Naylor [1971] 1 KB 712 278
Rogers v Parish Ltd [1987] 1 QB 933 .... 183, 187–89

Routledge v Mackay [1954] 1 All ER 855 . . . 79, 83
Royscott Trust Ltd v Rogerson [1991] 3 All ER 294 . . . 82, 83

Saloomey v Jeppesen (1983) 707 F 2d 671 . . . 158
Salvage Association v CAP Financial Services Ltd [1995] FSR 654 . . . 116, 127, 128, 137, 138
Saphena Computing Ltd v Allied Collection Agencies Ltd [1995] FSR 616 . . . 85–86, 88–89, 97, 104, 170, 186, 196
Scotson v Pegg (1861) 6 H & N 295 . . . 90
Scruttons v Midland Silicones Ltd [1962] AC 446 . . . 109
Sega Enterprises Ltd v Accolade Inc 977 F2d 1510 . . . 13, 48, 55–56
Shevill v Presse Alliance SA Case C68/93 [1995] All ER (EC) 289 . . . 326–28
Siboen and the Sibotre [1976] 1 Lloyd's Rep 293 . . . 94
Slater v Finning [1996] 3 All ER 398 . . . 192
Smedley v Breed [1974] AC 839 . . . 212
Smith v Chadwick (1884) 9 App Cas 187 . . . 81
Smith v Eric S Bush (a firm) [1990] 1 AC 831 . . . 134–38
Smith v Land & House Property Corp (1884) 28 Ch D 7 . . . 81–82
Sophocleous v Ringer [1988] RTR 52 . . . 388
South Central Bell Telephone Co v Barthelemy (1994) 643 So 2D 1240 (La) . . . 156, 157
Spriggs v Sotheby Parke Bernet & Co [1986] 1 Lloyd's Rep 487 . . . 118
Spurling v Bradshaw [1956] 1 WLR 461 . . . 108
St Albans v ICL [1995] FSR 686 . . . 12, 86, 128, 137, 152–54, 155, 157, 161, 163, 164, 165, 171, 188, 197

StepSaver Data Systems Inc v Wyse Technology and Software Link Inc (1991) 939 F 2d 91 . . . 114
Stewart Gill Ltd v Horatio Myer & Co Ltd [1992] 2 All ER 257 . . . 133
Stilk v Myrick (1809) 2 Camp 317 . . . 91–93
Stratton Oakmont Inc v Prodigy Services Co (1995) NY Sup Ct Nassau Co; WL 323710; 63 USLW 2765 . . . 324
Sugar v LM & S Railway [1941] 1 All ER 172 . . . 109

T & J Harrison v Knowles & Foster [1918] 1 KB 608 . . . 175
Tehran Europe v ST Belton [1968] 2 QB 545 . . . 195
Thomas v Thomas (1842) 2 QB 851 . . . 90
Thompson v LM & S Railway [1930] 1 KB 41 . . . 83, 108
Thornett and Fehr v Beer & Son [1919] 1 KB 486 . . . 185
Thornton v Shoe Lane Parking [1971] 2 QB 163 . . . 107, 108
Toby Constructions products Pty Ltd v Computa Bar (Sales) Pty Ltd [1983] NSWLR 48 . . . 153, 161, 170–71
Total Information Processing Systems Ltd v Daman Ltd [1992] FSR 171 . . . 48–50
Tweddle v Atkinson (1861) 1 B & S 393 . . . 107

United Sattes v Thomas (1995) 74 F 3d 701 (6th Cir) 365
Universe Tankships Inc of Monrovia v International Transport Workers Federation [1983] 1 AC 366 94–95
University of London Press v University Tutorial Press Ltd [1916] 2 Ch 601 .... 5, 23

Vacwell Engineering Co Ltd v BDH Chemicals Ltd [1971] 1 QB 88 162
Vantage Navigation Corp v Suhail and Saud Bahwan Building Materials (The Alev) [1989] 1 Lloyd's Rep 138 95
Varley v Whipp [1900] 1 QB 513 172
Vicom/Computer-related invention: T208/84 [1987] EPOR 74 .... 68, 69, 73
Victoria Laundry (Windsor) Ltd v Newman Industries Coulson & Co Ltd [1949] 2 KB 528 116

Wang Laboratories Inc's Applications [1991] RPC 463 69
Ward v Byham [1956] 2 All ER 318 90
Whelan Associates v Jaslow Dental Laboratory Inc [1987] 797 F2d 1234 .... 31–40, 42–43, 45–46, 48, 53
White v Bluett (1853) 23 LJ Ex 36 90
White v John Warwick & Co Ltd [1953] 2 All ER 1021 118
Williams v Roffey Bros & Nicholls (Contractors) Ltd [1991] 1 QB 1 .... 90–91, 93
Wilson v Rickett, Cockerell & Co Ltd [1954] 1 QB 598 185
Wimpey Construction v Poole [1984] 2 Lloyd's Rep 499 221
Winter v GP Puttnam & Sons (1991) 938 F 2d 1033 (9th cir) 158
Wormell v RHM Agriculture Ltd [1986] 1 All ER 769 161–63

TABLE OF STATUTES

UK LEGISLATION

Banking Act 1979 393

Carriage of Goods by Sea Act 1992 241
Children and Young Persons (Harmful Publications) Act 1955 369
Civil Evidence Act 1968
s 5 . . . . 375, 392
Civil Evidence Act 1995 . . . . 375, 391–92
s 8 394
s 9 393–94
s 13 394
Communications Decency Act 1996 363
Companies Act 1985 231
Computer Misuse Act 1990 . . . . . . 341, 353–58
s 1 . . . . 346, 349
s 2 346–49
s 3 . . . . 348, 351–52
s 17 . . . . 347–48, 352
Consumer Protection Act 1987 199–212
s 1 202
Copyright (Computer Regulations) 1992 60
Copyright (Computer Software) Amendment Act 1985 27
Copyright Designs and Patents Act 1988 . . . . 27–28, 54, 56
s 1 76
s 17 99
s 3 76
s 21 . . . . 61, 62
s 29 . . . . 61, 63
s 50A 60–61, 102
s 50B 61–62
s 50C 60–61, 98, 101, 104, 106, 110
s 296A 63
Criminal Damage Act 1971 . . . . 157, 338, 340, 341, 352
s 1 339
s 10 . . . . 156, 339
Criminal Evidence Act 1965
s 1 382
Criminal Justice Act 1988
s 24 . . . . 381, 382, 385
s 25 382–83
s 27 382
Criminal Justice and Public Order Act 1994 . . . . 278–79, 368

Data Protection Act 1963 263
Data Protection Act 1984 . . . . 252, 256–318, 347
s 1 . . . . 259, 261–62, 279, 284, 295, 296
s 2 259
s 5 . . . . 268, 269, 275, 279, 288, 291, 293–95
s 7 286
s 10 268
s 11 268
s 12 268
s 13 275
s 20 269
s 21 269–70
s 22 . . . . 270, 272
s 23 270–72
s 24 271–72
s 27 . . . . 296, 305
s 28 285
s 29 296
s 32 296
s 33 296
s 34 296
s 36 . . . . 263, 267–68, 272
Sched 1 . . . . 262, 263, 275, 293
Defamation Act 1996
s 1 324–25
Deregulation and Contracting Out Act 1994 314

Finance Bill 1996 250
Food and Drugs Act 1955 212

Health and Safety at Work Act 1974 . . . . 207, 265
s 6 212

Law of Property (Miscellaneous Provisions) Act 1989
s 2 231

Malicious Communications Act 1988 320
Malicious Damage Act 1861 339
Misrepresentation Act 1967
s 2 82–83

Obscene Publications Act 1959
s 1 368
Official Secrets Act 1911 356
Occupiers' Liability Act 1957 128

Patents Act 1977 64–65
s 1 65
s 91 .... 65, 67
Police and Criminal Evidence Act 1984
s 68 382
s 69 .... 376, 383–85, 387, 388, 389, 390, 392
Sched 3 387–88
Protection of Children Act 1978 368
s 1 369
Public Order Act 1994 369

Sale and Supply of Goods Act 1994 .. 175, 182
s 4 171
Sale of Goods Act 1893 .... 162, 165
s 14 .... 190, 193
Sale of Goods Act 1979 .... 76, 86, 151, 152, 158, 160, 165, 166, 184
s 12 162
s 13 .... 83–84, 151, 166, 171–81
s 14 .... 83–84, 89, 130, 151, 153, 154, 161, 162, 164, 166, 171, 181–83, 185, 186, 187, 188, 189–96
s 15 .... 83–84, 151, 171, 196–97
s 15A 171
s 35 87–88
s 61 .... 153, 154, 183
Social Security Administration (Frauds) Bill 1996 250
Statute of Frauds 1677 231
Supply of Goods and Services Act 1982 .... 76, 160, 184, 216
s 8 .... 151, 197
s 9 .... 151, 197
s 10 .... 151, 197
s 13 .... 166, 229
s 18 153

Theatres Act 1968
s 4 320
Theft Act 1968
s 15 334–35
Trade Descriptions Act 1968 .... 130, 131, 184

Unfair Contract Terms Act 1977 .... 84, 88, 99, 117, 118, 119–38, 150, 152, 184, 185, 229
s 1 .... 119, 126, 127, 128
s 2 .... 119, 127, 134
s 3 .... 119–20, 127, 128, 129
s 4 .... 120, 127, 129
s 5 .... 120, 129–30
s 6 .... 121, 129, 134, 171
s 7 .... 121–22, 134
s 9 122
s 10 122
s 11 .... 122–23, 133, 134, 136
s 12 .... 123, 128, 129, 130, 172
s 13 .... 123, 129, 180–81
s 14 .... 123–34, 129
s 15 129
s 26 124
s 27 124–25
Sched 1 125–26
Sched 2 .... 126, 150
Unfair Terms in Consumer Contracts Regulations 1994 .... 90, 99, 117, 138–49

OVERSEAS LEGISLATION

Copyright Act (Singapore) ....
s 35 56
Copyright Act 1976 (United States) 21, 35, 59
s 117 63–64
Uniform Commercial Code (United States)
Art 2 .... 159, 160, 164

EC LEGISLATION AND STATUTORY INSTRUMENTS

EC Leglslation

Berne Convention for the Protection of Literary and Artistic Works 1886 57
Brussels Convention on Jurisdiction and Enforcement of Judgments in Civil and Commercial Matters 1968 327
Commercial Agents (Council Directive) Regulations 1993 77
Convention for the Protection of Individuals with regard to Automatic Processing of Personal Data 1981 (Council of Europe) 251, 257–58, 276, 281, 303, 311
Council Directive, 85/374 on the approximation of the laws, regulations and administrative provisions of the Member States concerning liability for defective products 204, 209, 210
Art 2 200
Art 6 205–06
Council Directive 91/250 on the legal protection of computer programs 54, 57, 59–60, 62, 99–106, 110, 159
Art 1 57
Art 4 . . . . 58, 99
Art 5 . . . . 58, 59, 63, 100, 101, 102, 110, 111
Art 6 58–60
Council Directive 87/54 on the legal protection of topographies of semiconductor products 12
Council Directive 95/46 on the protection of individuals with regard to the processing of personal data and on the free movement of such data 258, 291, 299–318
Art 1 . . . . 304, 313, 315
Art 2 . . . . 304, 307
Art 3 304–05
Art 6 . . . . 307, 312
Art 7 306
Art 8 305–06
Art 9 . . . . 312, 313
Art 10 308
Art 11 308–09
Art 12 309
Art 13 312
Art 14 310
Art 15 310
Art 18 311
Art 19 311
Art 18 311
Art 25 313–14
Art 26 314
Council Directive 93/13 on unfair terms in consumer contracts 141–49
Art 1 144
Art 2 144
Art 3 . . . . 144–45, 147–49
Art 4 145
Art 5 145
Art 6 145
Art 7 145–46

Art 8 146
Art 9 146
Art 10 146
Art 11 146
European Convention on Human Rights 1950 . . . . . 258, 302
Art 12 258
European Patent Convention 1973 64–65
Art 52 . . . . . 65, 67, 68
Lugano Convention on Jurisdiction and Enforcement of Judgments in Civil and Commercial Matters 1988 327
Single European Act 302
Strasbourg Convention on products liability in relation to physical injury and death 206–07, 209–11
Treaty on European Union
Art 189b 303
Vienna Convention on Treaties
Art 31 67

Statutory Instruments

Design Right (Semiconductor Topographies) Regulations 1989 SI 1989/1100 12

CHAPTER ONE

INTRODUCTION

The rapid development of information technology presents challenges for the law. Challenges which are not confined to any single one of the traditional legal categories but which arise in, for example, criminal law, intellectual property law, contract and tort. Even land law may not be untouched![1] Initially, these challenges manifested themselves at the micro, rather than the macro level, with questions such as the applicability of copyright protection for computer programs. More recently, with the accelerating growth of the Internet and the World Wide Web, some of these problems, such as privacy, have been exacerbated, and others, like the regulation of offensive material, have come to the fore. In effect, the questions posed for the law by the advancing technology are many and various but some idea of their scope can be gained by brief illustration:

- How does the law deal with computer hackers or those who introduce viruses?[2]
- Should a contract for the acquisition of software be categorised as one dealing with goods?[3]
- Similarly, should software be regarded as a product?[4]
- Can copyright subsist in a computer program? Would patent protection be more appropriate?[5]
- Does the widespread dissemination of text on networks herald the death of copyright?[6]
- Should the content of the material on the Internet be regulated and, if so, by whom?[7] What about freedom of information and expression?[8]
- How is the privacy of the individual to be protected amid the increasing capacity for storing, gathering and collating information?[9]

1 Through, for example, computerisation of the land registry raising the question of who could be liable if a defect in the software resulted in an inaccurate certificate. See *Min of Housing and Local Gov v Sharp* [1970] 2 QB 223 for consideration of a slightly different question (p 213).

2 See Chapter 8.

3 See Chapter 4.

4 See Chapter 5.

5 See Chapter 2.

6 For discussion of this question see, for example, Christopher Kervégant, 'Are copyright and droit d'auteur viable in the light of information technology?' (1996) 10 Int Review of Law, Computer and Technology 55.

7 See Chapter 8.

8 See Chapter 7.

9 See Chapter 7.

Concrete illustrations of these problems are regularly reported in the press. These cover a spectrum from the amusing and inconsequential to the highly significant. Recently in the news, was the 'points of view' problem, the *Shetland News* newspaper controversy and the millennium issue:

A hacker reportedly changed the message on the BBC 'Points of View' answer machine to the surprise of those attempting to leave legitimate comments for Ann Robinson.[10]

The Shetland News newspaper included on its World Wide Web site hypertext links to the Web pages of its rival, *The Shetland Times. The Shetland Times* took exception to this and claimed it was a breach of copyright. A Scottish court has, thus far, issued an interim interdict, pending full trial.[11]

Computers everywhere, from those in the home to those which are vital to commerce and industry, contain calendars. Commonly, these only refer to the last two digits of the year. Huge costs (and doubtless questions of liability) will be involved in attempting to prevent the chaos which would ensue if these machines register 00 as 1900 – a mere 100 years behind the times!

The point has already been made that the developments in information technology present challenges for many of the established categories of law. This leads to the question of whether information technology law should be regarded as a subject in its own right. Obviously, the initial reaction to attempt to deal with novel problems is to try to accommodate them within existing legal frameworks. This results in a fragmentary approach which may or may not be appropriate in the particular case. One of the important benefits of looking at the subject of information technology law as a whole is the opportunity to consider how apposite and coherent are piecemeal solutions which borrow from the different established legal areas. It may even lead to the recognition that there is a need for new legal concepts, transcending the traditional boundaries. The acknowledgment of information technology law as a subject worthy of study in its own right also produces a focus upon the issues which might not otherwise occur, with the risk that the particular problems generated by the scientific advances are otherwise merely regarded as footnotes to the established categories. Nonetheless, we have found it convenient to divide the discussion which follows in a way which largely reflects different established legal subjects and this also reflects the current state of the law. We have also found it useful to divide the book into two sections – the first of these concentrates on problems generated by the nature of computer software, whereas the second considers the impact of computer technology. However, the reader is invited to consider the aptness of the solutions arrived at and the desirability of a more integrated approach.

---

10 *Guardian* (1997) 31 March.

11 See, eg, *BNA's Electronic Information Policy and Law* (1996) Vol 1, p 723; *The Times* (1997) 21 January.

SECTION A

THE CHALLENGES OF COMPUTER SOFTWARE

PROTECTING AND EXPLOITING RIGHTS IN SOFTWARE – INTELLECTUAL PROPERTY RIGHTS

INTRODUCTION

Although it may be rather hackneyed to repeat the practical test of Petersen J in *University of London Press Ltd v University Tutorial Press Ltd*[1] that what is worth copying is *prima facie* worth protecting, the truth underlying this statement is demonstrated nowhere so strikingly as in the commercial exploitation of computer software. As the industry has developed there has been a trend towards general applications programs, rather than specific bespoke software, and a massive amount of research and development time and money is devoted to the creation of such new computer software. A further feature is the vulnerability of the medium to reproduction by individuals and the consequent threat of widespread copying and piracy. The commercial factors alone would suggest powerful reasons for protecting the intellectual property rights in such software, but when coupled with the ease of copying, make such protection imperative.

Despite these reasons and the fact that computers have now been in existence for almost half a century, protection of the intellectual property rights in computer programs has only really become an issue since the advent of microcomputers, a much more recent development. In the early stages of development of the industry, the problem was not particularly acute since computer systems were large, custom-built affairs. They were only used by large institutions, whether commercial, industrial or educational, and the public had no general access to them. In those cases where intellectual property rights might have been an issue, the software and programs written for them could be adequately protected by contract, supplemented by actions for breach of confidence. These methods may still provide a useful remedy in certain cases.[2] This situation changed dramatically as microprocessors and personal computers became commonplace; their use became widespread and was no longer confined to large institutions. At this point it was not possible to rely purely on contract and confidence to protect intellectual property rights in computer programs. As early as the beginning of the 1970s, the World Intellectual Property Organisation (WIPO) had begun to turn their attention to the issue, and, in 1978, produced model provisions for the

1 [1916] 2 Ch 601 at 610 *per* Petersen J.

2 The case of *Ibcos Computers Ltd v Barclays Mercantile Highland Finance Ltd* (1994) (discussed later at p 52), concerns an action for breach of confidence as well as an action for copyright infringement.

protection of intellectual property rights in computer software. The following extract summarises the desirability of legal protection for computer programs.

WIPO Model Provisions 1978 – Introduction Paragraph 6

Legal protection of computer software is desirable for the following reasons:

(a) *Investment and time required.* The investment in computer software is large: under a recent estimate based on the number of computers currently in use, and the past and expected increase in that number, together with estimates of the staff employed on programming activities and the cost of software, it is possible that a sum of the order of 13 billion US dollars is spent annually on the creation and maintenance of software systems. Although this must vary considerably, the time required for the planning and preparation of computer programs is long, often amounting to many man-months of total effort. The need for legal protection of computer programs should be seen not only in terms of the large-scale investment in computer software but also from the viewpoint of the small software enterprise or individual creator of software. The existence of strong legal protection would encourage the dissemination of their creations and enable such creators to avoid duplication of work. Without such dissemination, numerous programmers may spend considerable time and effort in order to accomplish, in parallel work, the same objective; although the programs created by them may be different, any one of those programs would probably fully accomplish the said objective. In any case, legal protection will encourage exploitation of software for purposes other than internal use.

(b) *Likely future developments.* Already, software is estimated to account for by far the greater part of the total cost of computer systems. The proportions of 70 per cent and 30 per cent representing the expenditure on software and hardware, respectively, would seem to be a reasonable estimate. In any case it can be expected that the software elements will, in the future, account for a substantial, if not a predominant, proportion of the expenditure and that the total expenditure on computer software will constantly increase. At present, the largest amount of expenditure on computer software seems to be devoted to the creation and maintenance of specific purpose user programs, not of general applicability; since such programs are not of direct interest to third parties, their misappropriation is relatively unlikely in view of the adaptation required. However, there is a trend towards the creation of computer programs that are of interest to more than one user or even of general and widespread utility and thus can help to save expenditures; such a trend towards standardised user software is likely to increase as computers become more accessible to the public and easier to operate and as the proportion of the cost of the hardware components in computer operations decreases. In the context of the increasing accessibility of computer software, reference should be made to two important developments: the creation of computer networks among nations aided by sophisticated telecommunications systems (a trend which highlights the need for *international* protection), and the move towards new programming techniques facilitating the use of computers by persons other than trained programmers.

(c) *Protection as an incentive to disclosure.* The importance of ensuring the ready accessibility of the important form of modern technology represented by computer software has been referred to on many occasions, particularly in the context of the needs of developing countries ... Although some computer programs would not be made publicly available in any event (for example, programs revealing a trade secret of an enterprise or those designed to complement computer hardware and transferred only with the corresponding computer), it is reasonable to suppose that many proprietors of the rights in other programs would at present rely primarily on secrecy either in order to exclude all others from using the software or to permit only selected persons to use it under a confidential disclosure contract. Where effective legal protection is available, the proprietors of rights could instead rely on that protection and disclose the software.

(d) *Protection as a basis for trade.* The lack of legal protection may be particularly harmful in the context of trade. Both the seller and the buyer of computer software are interested in legal protection because it increases the legal security of their relationship. A system of protection would also be of advantage to developing countries; such a system would encourage dissemination of software to those countries, not only because the publication of the software would not defeat protection but also the protection would eliminate the uncertainty of enforcing a confidential disclosure contract. Also, legal protection would enable dissemination on favourable terms in some cases; for example, the proprietor of the rights in computer software might be encouraged to license it in a developing country at an especially low royalty if he could be sure of being able to take action against users in other countries if his software were accidentally disclosed by the licensee in the developing country. Moreover, the greater disclosure in the advertisement of software which, it is hoped, will result from legal protection may help such countries to evaluate the alternatives on the international market.

(e) *Vulnerability of computer software.* Consideration should also be given to the vulnerability of some forms of computer software; for instance, a 'computer software package' consisting of a computer program and related descriptive and explanatory documentation, is expensive to prepare and easy to copy as soon as the prototype is available.

Although the WIPO document was prepared some 20 years ago and, therefore, has the status of a historical document as far as the computer industry is concerned, it shows that major problems were evident even at this early stage. The technology still had a long way to progress before it would be recognisable by present standards, but the trend towards standard application packages had been noted, together with the ease of copying and the global nature of the technology.

The purpose of the model provisions was to provide a framework which countries which were signatories to the agreement could use. Accepting that the legal protection of computer programs was desirable, the question that then had to be addressed was what was to be the most appropriate and effective method of protecting the intellectual property rights in computer software and programs.

WIPO Model Provisions 1978 – Introduction Paragraph 7

... Two forms of legal protection may be specifically directed to the results of the intellectual creativity in computer software: they are *patent protection* and *copyright protection*. In addition, there are *other branches of law* which can provide a means for protecting computer software, especially where it constitutes a trade secret.

(a) *Patent protection.* The patent would seem to be an appropriate form of legal protection of computer software since it covers new and inventive technical solutions. It can thus apply to programs embodying the same concept as a patented program, but in a completely different form; it can also be relied on to prevent others using the same program in a computer. However, in many countries, computer programs and other items of computer software, in particular algorithms, cannot be regarded as patentable inventions; the European Patent Convention, for example, contains an express provision to that effect (Article 52(2)(c)). In some countries, a computer program would seem to be at least *indirectly* protectable by, for example, a patent granted for a computer programmed in a new way or for a process relating to the use of a program as a means of operating a computer in a new manner or as a means of control in the manufacturing of articles. In most countries the question of patentability cannot be answered with any degree of certainty. Moreover, even if patent protection were generally available, it would probably cover only a minute proportion of computer programs since it is considered that only in a very few cases (perhaps 1 per cent) would a program have sufficient inventiveness to satisfy the requirements of patent law, although a large amount of time, effort and resources have been devoted to its creation. There are also serious practical difficulties to be taken into account: difficulties in conducting the examination relating to the novelty and inventiveness of a computer program, in establishing the documentation on the prior art and in finding qualified examiners. One further difficulty is that, under patent procedures, any person has access to a full disclosure of the invention enabling a person skilled in the art to make the patented product or use the patented process; in view of the relative difficulty of detecting misappropriations in a computer program, it could be argued that such an unrestricted disclosure to the public is not desirable; and yet, to make an exception in the case of computer programs might prejudice a fundamental principle of patent law: disclosure to the public.

(b) *Copyright protection.* Whereas patent law protects the technical idea underlying an invention, copyright law focuses on protecting the form in which ideas are expressed, although protection is not limited to that form. Thus, copyright protection would seem to be particularly appropriate for computer software as a whole (and not merely computer programs) since a large amount of computer software consists of descriptive or explanatory matter; even a computer program (consisting, for example, of magnetic tape) is a form of expression – of the ideas contained in the software leading up to the program. In most cases the intellectual creativity in computer software resides in the skill and effort used to make those ideas 'understandable' to a computer, as economically and effectively as possible. However, although some kinds of computer software (especially those in verbal form) are clearly protectable under copyright laws, experts disagree on whether other kinds (particularly a computer program on magnetic tape for example) can be considered a literary, artistic or scientific work, which are the traditional subjects of copyright protection. Moreover, such protection may be of very limited value since it essentially covers only copying (or related acts such as translation or adaptation); thus, in itself, the use of a program to operate a computer cannot be prevented by copyright law (just as the making of a cake cannot be an infringement of the copyright in the recipe). It is essential that use in a computer should be covered by the rights in computer software; it is, in fact, possible that copyright can provide a remedy in this case since it is probable that the use of a program always involves its copying in the computer memory, but the courts may not regard such internal reproduction as sufficient for the purposes of copyright law. The model provisions essentially adopt a copyright law approach which takes account of their subject matter's affinity with copyright protection and overcomes the possible limitations indicated above.

(c) *Other forms of protection.* The laws of certain countries provide a number of means of preventing the unauthorised disclosure or use of secret information. There are a number of laws, which directly penalise or provide civil law remedies against the misappropriation of a trade secret or of information obtained in breach of confidence. A common means of protecting information concerning computer software, which is provided by all laws, is by contract. Even in the absence of an express term in a contract, persons in a fiduciary relationship with a computer enterprise, such as its employees, can be prevented from disclosing secret information. Secret information can also be indirectly protected by certain provisions in criminal law, by general provisions in civil codes or by certain actions in the law of torts. Even in the absence of secrecy, the misappropriation of computer programs may, in certain circumstances, be actionable in the context of unfair competition law. However, even in countries where trade secrets can be protected directly, there is uncertainty or differences as to the scope of protection and as to the conditions (for example, whether disclosure to a licensee or to a restricted number of other third parties would prejudice the secrecy of the know-how protected). The disadvantage of protection under contract law is that in most cases it will be difficult to prevent persons outside the contractual relationship from disclosing or using a program. Moreover, one of the advantages of the establishment of clear and adequate legal protection for computer software is to encourage greater disclosure of information on computer software which would otherwise be vulnerable to misappropriation. The aim of such protection is therefore precisely to avoid any necessity to rely on secrecy and on laws and legal measures safeguarding secrecy.

In considering the various forms of protection available to computer software, this comparatively early document has identified with accuracy a number of issues which were to trouble the courts. The issues relating to patents are, as we shall see later, still substantially similar. With respect to the application of copyright principles, although we are probably no longer quite so concerned about programs on magnetic tape, the issue of whether a program could be regarded as a literary work is one which has been aired extensively in the courts in a number of jurisdictions.

The approach taken by the model provisions is essentially one of copyright drafted to protect the form of an original program, ie one that is the result of the creator's own intellectual effort, rather than the concepts on which it is based and this approach has proved to be very influential. Although the above extract does not enunciate in detail the reasons for this decision (and some of them are negative ones such as the unavailability of patent protection in many cases), it is clear that, in view of the huge commercial significance of software development, it might be necessary to amalgamate the reasons and rationale underlying the Continental and common law notions of copyright and take into account the encouragement of commercial innovation, the rights of the author as creator and also the public interest.

As can be seen, the resolution to use copyright and protect the intellectual property rights in software as if it was a literary work was, in many ways, a pragmatic response to an immediate problem. In formulating the model provisions, WIPO was not envisaging that they should be implemented as sui *generis* legislation but that the principles would be absorbed into the existing framework of protection. It was also hoped that the choice of copyright principles would lead to international protection based on the Berne Convention, although this clearly depends on whether a particular jurisdiction regards computer programs as appropriate subject matter for such protection.[3] But computer programs are sufficiently dissimilar to other literary works that this decision was not adopted without dissent and neither has this dissent been completely silenced by the application of current copyright law to computer programs. The following extract explains in more detail the reasons for the choice of copyright.

Copyright Protection of Computer Software in the United States and Japan
Part I
Dennis S Karjala
[1991] 6 EIPR 195–96

The decision to protect computer programs under copyright was in fact a radical departure from traditional intellectual property principles. The reason

3 See also WR *Cornish, Computer Program Copyright and the Berne Convention in Handbook of European Software Law* (1993) Part I, M Lehmann and CF Tapper (eds), Clarendon and later discussion in relation to the EC Software Directive at p 57.

is that computer software is functional – the technological means for using general purpose computing devices. Software is not art, music, or even literature. Software is developed with an end use in mind – an end use usually involving the performance of a task other than to please or inform human beings. Like all other technologies, software technology grows by incremental additions to the existing technological base. Programmers learn by studying existing programs, both at school and at their workplaces, and they adapt what they have learned to the new tasks that are placed before them.

... The famous case of *Baker v Selden* says that the functional aspects of works are properly the subject matter of patent law. Thus, under traditional intellectual property law, protected works of technology must show a considerable degree of inventiveness that is passed upon by an administrative review. Technological works that are insufficiently inventive to qualify for a patent are protected only for such time as they remain secret or invulnerable to reverse engineering.

Technology enjoys such limited protection, not because it is believed that technological creativity should go unrewarded. Rather, the law's contribution is limited because too much protection would impede technological progress rather than advance it, by restricting subsequent creators in what they could draw from the existing technological base. While not perfect, the traditional scheme for protecting technology under intellectual property law has worked tolerably well in balancing the tension between incentives (rewarding creators through legal protection) and technological advance that builds on past creations (limitation or denial of legal protection).

Notwithstanding this long and nearly uniform history of denying copyright protection to functional works, a conscious choice has been made to protect computer programs under copyright. The reasons were perfectly sound, but it is worth spelling them out explicitly because they have implications for interpreting the appropriate scope of copyright protection in a program. First, programs are easy to pirate, notwithstanding that their creation can require a large investment of time, money and energy. Yet, traditional patent law could cover at most a small percentage of programs, because most programs are simply an application of well-known techniques to a well-defined problem. If an incentive is to be supplied for the production of useful but complex programs, patent law will often not be up to the task. Moreover, in the absence of contractual restrictions, trade secret law does not protect against taking a program from a disk or tape that was lawfully acquired. It, too, therefore fails to protect programs that are widely distributed.

Traditional copyright protection, on the other hand, arises immediately on creation and in most countries requires little or no showing of 'inventiveness'. Moreover, copyright clearly protects against the one form of piracy that everyone agrees should be unlawful, namely, disk to-disk, ROM-to-ROM, and similar mechanical copying and translating from object code as well as line-by-line copying of source code. Copyright has the further advantage over a *sui generis* copyright-like statute in that protection against this kind of piracy is immediately international, without the need for formal action of any kind. When the problem to be solved is viewed as 'piracy' of this type, copyright law

> appears as a nearly obvious solution. It is hardly surprising, therefore, that so many countries have adopted it.

This seems to suggest that one of the most powerful arguments for copyright protection is a negative one,[4] that, if such protection were to be denied, the patent system would not be of use either since most programs are an application of well-known techniques often to well-known problems.[5] Another argument for the choice of copyright centres on the ease of copying: 'Because of the tremendous ease with which the creativity embodied in a program can be copied, copyright's originality standard, rather than patent's non-obviousness standard, better defines the level of creativity the law should require before it protects the typical computer program from copying.'[6] This, coupled with the ease of piracy would make innovations very vulnerable to having intellectual endeavour and investment in time and money abused. As we shall see, notwithstanding the objectives both philosophical and pragmatic for the choice of copyright for the protection of computer software, this choice can, at times, seem to raise as many problems as it solves and, in addition, the courts have not always approached the issue with a unanimity of purpose. For these reasons, there are still a number of academics and practitioners who advocate a *sui generis* protection for computer software.[7] Samuelson *et al*,[8] for instance, suggests that programs cannot be regarded merely as texts because 'a crucially important characteristic of programs is that they behave; programs exist to make computers perform tasks'. Since this attribute is central to the essential nature of programs, it gives them a 'dual character'; they can be regarded simultaneously as both 'writings and machines'. This means that, in their view, both copyright and patent law are not suitable for protecting software innovation. On the other hand, this view has been criticised as being

---

4 This argument can be compared with Scott Baker J's more recent comment in relation to software as goods in *St Albans v ICL* [1995] FSR 686 (see also discussion in Chapter 4) that 'if the supply of software is not the supply of goods, it is difficult to see what it can be other than something to which no statutory rules apply thus leaving the recipient unprotected in the absence of express agreement'.

5 See later discussion on p 64.

6 Glynn S Lunney, *'Lotus v Borland Copyright and Computer Programs'* (1996) Tulane Law Rev 2397 at 2431.

7 It should also be noted that there is a limited precedent for the use of *sui generis* protection for new technologies in respect of the protection available to the topography of semi-conductor chips. However, this is in the context of a market with a completely different structure, heavily dominated by the US which, therefore, found itself in a position to enforce its standards on the rest of the world. Basically, the US Semiconductor Chip Protection Act 1984 did not protect the design of non-US chips unless reciprocal protection was available in that state. In view of US dominance, a number of states legislated accordingly, including the EC in Council Directive 87/54/EEC on the legal protection of topographies of semiconductor products [1987] OJ L 24/36. The UK provisions are now contained in the Design Right (Semiconductor Topographies) Regulations 1989 SI 1989/1100. It is unlikely that consensus over the form of a *sui generis* protection for computer software would be achieved so easily.

8 'A Manifesto concerning the Legal Protection of Computer Programs' (1994) 94 Columbia Law Rev 2308.

overly pessimistic about the capabilities of existing legal regimes to accommodate new technological advances,[9] although the very evolution of existing law to take into account new developments has been likened to a form of *sui generis* protection.[10]

The two views expressed below perhaps summarise the opposite poles of the argument.

Is the Centre Beginning to Hold in US Copyright Law?
Richard H Stern[11]
[1993] 2 EIPR 39 at 40

> That courts are beginning to learn how to be more rational in applying copyright principles to computer software does not mean that copyright is a legal scalpel, after all, rather than a blunt instrument. When both the Second Circuit in *Altai*[12] and the Ninth Circuit in *Accolade* warned against 'forcing a square peg into a round hole', they meant that when one tries to apply ordinary principle of copyright law to computer software one gets very peculiar results – sometimes quite startling and unsatisfactory ones. Unless and until we devise a round peg for a round hole, we shall continue to lurch from one to another software law crisis ...
>
> We need a properly thought out utility model or petty patent type of law for computer software, treating it as the industrial property that it is, not as a species of poem or some other *belle lettre* or *beau art*. Copyright does not belong to the right one of Snow's cultures to do the job properly. Bridging the two cultures may be a noble idea, but there would be much less wear and tear on the industry if the experiment were carried out at some other experimental subject's expense ... We need a system that borrows appropriately from copyright law, patent law, and utility model law – perhaps slavish imitation law as well – and combines selected features of each, and new features where the nature of software dictates it, to provide a form of legal protection congruent to the subject matter, the commercial needs of industry, software professionals, and software users, and the interests of the public. The task of crafting such a system is not easy, but the alternative is perennial ineptitude and recurrent crisis.

In contrast, Miller warns against the 'false icon of *sui generis* protection':[13]

> ... seeking genre-specific limitations on particular program aspects or excluding them from copyright protection in favour of some – as yet undefined – form of *sui generis* protection is unnecessary and potentially mischievous. The

9 Jane C Ginsburg, 'Four Reasons and a Paradox: the Manifest Superiority of Copyright over *Sui Generis* Protection of Computer Software' (1994) 94 Columbia Law Rev 2559.

10 Duncan M Davidson, 'Common Law, Uncommon Software' (1986) 47 U Pittsburgh Law Rev 1037.

11 Maintaining an earlier view expressed in Stern, 'The Bundle of Rights suited to the New Technology' (1986) 47 U Pittsburgh Law Rev 1229.

12 See later discussion on p 37.

13 Arthur R Miller, 'Copyright Protection for Computer Programs, Databases and Computer-generated Works: Is anything new since CONTU?' (1993) 106 Harv L Rev 977 at 1034.

> effect would be to discard the growing experience under the present copyright law and the increasing certainty that it provides, in favour of something unknown, uncabined and unpredictable. This is especially dangerous given the dynamism of the software industry and the likelihood that today's restrictions will be ill-suited to tomorrow's innovations. Today's attempt to draw a bright defensive perimeter may produce tomorrow's Maginot line. Judgments as to the precise scope of copyright in the computer context are best left to judicial decision-making under a loosely textured and familiar statutory formula that can mature over time ...
>
> ... Courts always have had to struggle with the delicate questions of where the commonplace becomes originality and where legitimate imitation shades into infringement, especially in the environment of a new mode of expression. This process admittedly is even more difficult when it involves computer programs of the size, complexity, and sophistication of modern operating systems. But this difficulty is an inevitable aspect of fact-based determinations, which would not be easier under any genre-specific provisions that might be inserted in the copyright law or under some other – most assuredly less predictable – *sui generis* regime invented out of the whole cloth.
>
> It is a mistake to believe that creating highly refined legislative prescriptions or inventing an entirely new legal structure for software at this time will produce better results than carefully applying existing copyright principles to individual situations. As the case law involving the idea-expression dichotomy attests[14] the court decisions in this area are, by degree, crystallising into an understandable and sensible doctrinal matrix, obviating any need for a *sui generis* approach.

Doubtless, readers will formulate their own arguments about the most appropriate form of protection for the intellectual property rights in computer software, but whatever protection is developed needs to take into account the 'distinctive character of software programs'.[15]

Copyright has been chosen (even if by default) as the basis for protection but what is it about computer programs and computer technology that might cause problems for traditional copyright law? In simple terms, there are two broad areas which need to be considered. The first, and simplest in conceptual terms, if not in solution, is the mode of operation of computers and the ease of copying. Computer programs were made to be copied. It is impossible to run a computer program and avail oneself of its useful effects without copies being made, however transient, within the depths of the computer. Also, because programs may be corrupted or inadvertently erased, it is good computing practice to take and keep a back-up copy of each computer program. Whilst even this level of copying could constitute a technical breach of copyright unless express provision is made,[16] it is clear that such copying cannot be

14 See later at p 31.

15 Leo J Raskind, 'The Uncertain Case for Special Legislation protecting Computer Software' (1986) 47 U Pittsburgh Law Rev 1131.

16 See later at p 59.

construed as a threat to the commercial exploitation of that program. However, it is precisely the fact that the success of computer technology relies heavily on the ease with which programs can be copied that also makes it a trivial matter to produce multiple illicit copies, whether for private use, use within a commercial organisation or for selling on the open market. This is not an issue as far as the application of copyright law is concerned but causes significant problems for the enforcement of such law in relation to straight disk to disk copying and piracy of computer programs.[17] No special equipment is needed to make copies and multiple copies can be made quickly and for minimal capital outlay. These can then be marketed at much lower prices than the authentic version. The widespread copying of software within an organisation can also have a severely prejudicial effect on the rights of the copyright owner. This problem of enforcement in relation to straight copying has been further exacerbated by the growth of the Internet and the consequent ease with which software can be downloaded from remote sites.

It has proved much more difficult for traditional copyright rules to be applied to the actual process of copying at the stage at which the computer program is written by the programmer. Why should this be? Copyright was developed to protect the authors of literary, artistic and other works from those who might copy the way in which their ideas had been expressed, especially where this was done for commercial gain. On the face of it, therefore, it would seem to be an appropriate method for protecting the intellectual property rights in computer programs and, as we shall see, the way in which the law has developed in most jurisdictions, has been to protect programs as literary works. However, computer programs differ from conventional literary works in a number of important and fundamental ways, bringing into question the suitability of copyright for this purpose.

One important difference is that, in a computer program, the literary is combined with the technical,[18] causing technology to operate to produce a defined result, either within the computer system itself, or in the real world. Neither can programs, in their 'literary form', be readily understood other than by a person skilled in the particular programming language employed. Indeed, end users of the program, will often have no knowledge of the underlying program which is causing their computer to perform a particular task, nor will they have any need for such knowledge. Such characteristics are not shared by other literary works, even those of a utilitarian nature. The situation is further complicated by the fact that computer programs can be encapsulated in so many different media, ranging from hard-wired circuitry to transient impulses sent down telephone lines, neither of which, *prima facie,*

17 In an early note, now only of historical significance, it was nevertheless recognised that widespread piracy was likely to be a problem in the industry, even in an age when *only those large enough to own computers are well-established businesses* – see (1964) 64 Columbia Law Review 1274.

18 *Cf* Samuelson *et al's* discussion of the 'behavior' of software, above, n 8.

has much in common with a literary work. In between these two extremes, programs may be held on disks or tape that, perhaps, seem to have more in common with sound recordings, for instance. To appreciate the problems that computer programs have caused for intellectual property law, it will be instructive to examine both the nature of the beast and the problems encountered in applying some of the concepts of copyright law to computer programs.

The first issue to be dealt with is the manner in which computer programs are written and constructed; it is common for cases concerning these issues to contain some brief explanation of these mysteries.

John Richardson Computers Ltd v Flanders
[1993] FSR 497 at 503
High Court

Ferris J In order for a computer to be given the appropriate instructions it is necessary to communicate with it in some way. The only instructions which a computer can understand are those which consist of a series of 0s and 1s. Instructions set out in this way are said to be written in 'machine language' or machine code. (This may represent something of an oversimplification. I gather that at least in some cases the machine code which is fed into the computer will be translated by the machine into a more elaborate series of 0s and 1s. However this description will suffice for present purposes.) The machine code for one type of computer will usually be different from that for another type, although there may, of course, be compatibility between different manufacturers' products.

A suitably trained or skilled programmer will be able to write a program in machine code for a particular model of computer. But the process is slow and tedious and the program, although intelligible to the computer, will be virtually unintelligible to anyone except an equally skilled programmer. From the comparatively early days of computers, therefore, an alternative language for writing programs was devised. This was known as 'assembler language'. It used a variety of abbreviations more akin to ordinary language than machine code. A computer could not itself understand such a language directly but a program could be, and was, devised which enabled a computer to convert assembler language into the machine code which could be understood by the computer. The translation process is usually possible only in one direction. Assembler language can be translated into machine code, but not vice versa.

While assembler language has advantages over machine code it still requires many instructions to be written in order to achieve the simplest tasks. A variety of so-called high level languages has been devised in order to simplify the task of the programmer. These high level languages have been given names. They include such languages as Basic and derivatives of it, Fortran, Cobol and Pascal. The use of these languages enables the programmer to write a program in terms which more nearly resemble ordinary English than those used in lower level languages. They also permit what is, for the computer, quite a complex operation to be directed by a relatively compact command. Like assembler language, high level languages have to be translated into machine code before they can be understood and acted upon by a computer. The programs which have been devised to achieve this are called compilers. As with assembler language, the translation process is usually possible in one direction only. It is not generally possible to recreate a program in its higher language form from its translation into machine code.

In computer parlance the program as written in whatever language used by the programmer (whether machine code, assembler language or a high level language) is known as the source code. When this is converted by an assembler or a compiler into machine code it is known as the object code. In cases where the program is written in machine code the source code and the object code are the same. When computer programs are exploited commercially it is usual for the end user to be supplied only with the object code, this being all that the customer needs to load into his computer. The customer does not generally have access to the source code and, because of the difficulties concerning re-translation, cannot generally re-construct the source code from the object code.

This suggests that the computer programs themselves are rarely seen by the user, merely their effects, but in written form can be expressed as *source code* and *object code*. The source code is the program as written by the programmer and can be in any one of a whole host of different languages. Many of these are the so-called high-level programming languages that bear a certain resemblance to literary language and have their own rules of syntax and grammar. An example of part of a program written in the language C is shown below.

```
int bubblesort(int num_list[],int length)
{
int i,j,temp;
for (i=length-1;i>0;i—)
{
for (j=length-1;j>0;j—)
    if (num_list[j]<num_list[j-1])
    {
    temp = num_list[j];
    num_list[j] = num_list[j-1];
    num_list[j-1] = temp;
    };
};
return 0;
}
```

That there are similarities with literary language is clear. However, it is also evident that, without further specialist knowledge, the lay reader may get little further information. In fact, the purpose and function of this part of the program is to sort, in ascending order, an array of numbers. Readers with some knowledge of programming might have deduced this from the title 'bubblesort' and the fact that the variables have been given meaningful names, 'num_list' for number list, for instance. This represents a very simple routine which would be likely to be part of a more complex program. Due to its simplicity, it is unlikely that a programmer would annotate these lines of code any further. However, for longer and more elaborate programs, to assist understanding, comments are frequently added in literary language as markers to particular stages of the program. Thus the program above could, if required, be annotated as follows:

```
/* function bubblesort; takes an integer array, and its length,
and reorders its elements into ascending order. */
int bubblesort(int num_list[],int length)
{
int i,j,temp;
for (i=length-1;i>0;i—) /* iterate over whole array */
{
for (j=length-1;j>0;j—)
    if (num_list[j]<num_list[j-1]) /* compare adjacent elements */
    {
    temp = num_list[j];
    num_list[j] = num_list[j-1]; /* ...and swap if required */
    num_list[j-1] = temp;
    };
};
return 0;
}
```

Although this program is beginning to appear more intelligible to the lay person and certainly more understandable to a programmer, this version cannot be put into effect by the computer in its present form. In order that the function intended be performed, the source code has to be translated or *compiled* into the object code, a list of binary instructions which are represented on paper by a series of noughts and ones. It would be highly improbable for programmers to write directly in binary, most would select a suitable high-level language[19] which would then be compiled as described, by means of another program, the compiler. Some of the simpler programming languages such as machine and assembly code do approach simple binary form; these are much more difficult for even skilled programmers to follow but, nevertheless, are favoured by some programmers, as indeed was the case with Flanders in the previous extract.

19 Many are developed for specific applications, eg ADA is often used for safety-related programming.

In some respects, the explanation of Ferris J, above, oversimplifies the task of creating a workable computer program. When the source code is first compiled, the compiler translates the high level language into binary code, the so-called *relocatable object code* which is not quite the version which will produce the desired effect. Then, as the compilation proceeds, this relocatable object code will be linked to standard libraries of code which perform certain common functions and which would otherwise have to be written into the program from scratch, the PRINT command, for instance. The end result is the *executable object code* which will cause the computer to perform the desired function. As an illustration, those with Word for Windows on their computers will see examples of this if, in 'file manager',[20] they examine the files associated with the directory 'winword'. It will be noted that the whole package contains a large number of files, but, in particular, there are a number of files with the extension '.dll' such as 'spell.dll'. These are examples of the standard libraries referred to above, this one being for the spell-checker. Others can be found for the thesaurus and the grammar check. The file 'winword.exe' contains the executable object code for this word-processing package. A similar examination of the file associated with the directory 'windows' will reveal a host of files with the extension '.exe', representing the executable object code for the various applications and accessories associated with windows.

Thus a program is not created in a linear fashion, but has a particular structure at the level at which the computer operates. In addition to this, it will also have a certain structure at the higher level.

Ideas, process or protected experience?
Steven R Englund
(1990) 88 Michigan Law Review 866 pp 867–72 (footnotes omitted)

... A 'computer program' is defined in the 1976 Act as 'a set of statements or instructions to be used directly or indirectly in a computer in order to bring about a certain result'. Although, computers are only capable of *directly* executing 'computer instructions', which may be expressed as combinations of the binary digits zero and one, most programs are written in some sort of programming language that is more convenient to use. Such programs may only be *indirectly* executed by computer.

To understand how a computer program comes to have structure and why it is important that the processes implemented by programs and the ideas embodied may not be protected by copyright law, it is necessary to have some appreciation of computer programming. 'Computer programming' refers to the 'designing, writing and testing' of programs. Almost all programs are written with some concern for the efficient use of resources such as memory space and computer, programmer and user time. Since it will seldom, if ever, be possible to write a program minimising the use of all of these resources, programmers must choose some balance of these criteria appropriate to the nature of the particular program. There are as many ways to approach the task

20 Caution – this does not provide such a simple illustration for those with Windows 95!

> of writing a program to achieve certain efficiency objectives as there are programmers. It is, however, possible to make some generalisations about the techniques that most programmers use.
>
> A programmer begins the process of writing a program by precisely defining the program's 'function'. A program's function is what the program actually does, in contrast to its 'implementation', which is the method, including the instructions, that allow a program to accomplish that function. After the function of a program has been precisely defined, a programmer decomposes that function into simpler constituent problems or 'subtasks'. Subtasks, themselves may be decomposed similarly. This process of decomposition requires skill and judgment on the part of the programmer; decisions made at this stage of the programming process can profoundly affect the quality of the resulting program by determining whether a program will be more or less efficient in its use of computer and human resources. The resulting decomposition is determined both by the nature of the problem and by the approach of the programmer. Different programmers faced with the same problem would ordinarily be expected to produce somewhat different decompositions.
>
> Once the function of a program has been decomposed into subtasks, a programmer can determine how best to implement the functions of the subtasks and then write instructions in some programming language to do so. This Note refers to the portion of a program implementing a subtask as a 'module'. A module is thus nothing more than a relatively short sequence of instructions in some programming language that, when executed, performs some well-defined function that is one of the subtasks defined in the course of decomposing the ultimate function of the program. The functions of the modules in a program together with each module's relationship to other modules constitute the 'structure' of the program.
>
> The logic and instructions for implementing a subtask may often come from the work of others. The computer industry has long been characterised by the free sharing of programs and program parts among programmers. Not only does the borrowing of the implementation details eliminate the need to 'reinvent the wheel' with each new program, but borrowing and improving upon more general ideas is an important way in which the computer art progresses. This is important because, in order to ensure its decisions in copyright cases involving computer programs promote progress in the computer art, a court should have some understanding of the role of copyright law in promoting progress in that art.

Thus many aspects of a computer program may be copied, from straight line to line copying of both source and object code; so-called *literal copying,* to copying of the structure of the program, often referred to as *non-literal copying.* Should all these aspects of copying be subject to the law of copyright or only those which correspond to literal copying of the work, by analogy with a literary work? How far can computer programmers use the work done by others in their own creation of new programs, without infringing the original developer's rights? At what point does the code for a commonly used routine enter the public domain? These and other issues have resulted in discussion in many jurisdictions as to the extent of the scope of copyright protection for computer programs and the literature on the subject is now voluminous. As a number of these arguments continue to surface in discussions both in academic literature and in judicial deliberations, it is worth considering, in brief, the manner in which the arguments have developed thus far.

The first issue to be resolved was whether copyright could subsist in both source and object code. It has been accepted for a long time that copyright can subsist in code,[21] ie that a code could be construed as an original literary work.

DP Anderson & Co v Lieber Code Co
[1917] 2 KB 469

> **Bailhache J** ... it is contended that [the code] is not a literary work, either original or otherwise, and the ground upon which that contention is based is that the words in the code are not words in the ordinary sense at all, but are merely collections of letters which are in themselves meaningless and are made up in a merely mechanical way. I cannot accede to that argument. The words – I call them so for want of a better name – are for use for telegraphic purposes and to each of them a meaning can be attached by the person sending the message and also by the addressee.

Did this, by analogy, mean that copyright could subsist in both source code and object code? This question caused a debate that will be examined in some detail as it is highly illustrative of the way in which intellectual property law has been used to argue both for and against copyright protection for computer programs. US copyright law required the subject of copyright protection to be a 'writing' and also denied copyright protection to works of a utilitarian nature. This led to the suggestion that although there might be copyright in the source code, this could not be true of the object code which could not be construed as a 'writing'. Further credence was given to this view by the argument that object code was not created by a person but by a machine, referring to the process of compilation described above. On the other hand, computer programs are contained within the definition of literary work in the US Copyright Act 1976 and amendments, introduced in 1980, included the definition 'a set of statements or instructions to be used directly or indirectly in a computer in order to bring about a certain result', suggesting that the use of the word 'indirectly' must be taken to include object code. In addition, the US courts were beginning to recognise that object code was subject to copyright protection in cases such as *Apple Computer Inc v Franklin Computer Corp*.[22] These developments were mirrored in other jurisdictions, as for example in *SEGA Enterprises v Richards*.[23] Whilst the court was happy to accept in principle that computer programs could be the subject of copyright, there was some discussion as to whether copyright could subsist in both the source code and the object code.

21 *DP Anderson & Co v Lieber Code Co* [1917] 2 KB 469.

22 714 F2d 1240, 219 USPQ 762, 70 ALR Fed 153.

23 [1983] FSR 73.

The above argument both depends upon and presupposes that copyright protection will be extended to software because of the writing requirement or, in many jurisdictions, that a computer program is a form of 'literary work', as opposed to any other type of creation attracting copyright protection. Even this view was challenged by the Australian case of *Apple Computer v Computer Edge Pty Ltd*[24] in which it was said that the purpose of literary works was for enjoyment[25] and so the court declined to think that computer programs could be protected in this way. This decision was subsequently reversed, the Full Court of the Federal Court holding that the source programs were protected by copyright as new and original literary works and that the object programs were protected in consequence as adaptations of the source programs.[26] The issue was again considered on a further appeal to the High Court of Australia who concluded, although not without difficulty, that the *source* programs were protected as literary works. The court was divided, however, over whether protection could be afforded to the object code on any basis.

Computer Edge Pty Ltd v Apple Computer Inc
(1986) 161 CLR 171 at 187

> **Gibbs J** The questions involved in this case are of considerable difficulty, and they have given rise to differences of opinion in the writings on the subject. We were referred to some authorities which are contrary to the conclusions that I have reached. In the United Kingdom, the provisional opinion has been expressed by judges in interlocutory proceedings that a machine code program is either a reproduction or an adaptation of an assembly code program ... In Canada and South Africa it has been held that a program in an object code may be a literary work ... There are some differences between the language of the statutes considered in those cases and that of the Copyright Act, but I am not sure that the differences are material. In the United States the question has been considered in a number of cases and it has been held that an object code is entitled to copyright protection ... but the statute law in the United States is materially different from that of Australia. I have not found anything in those authorities that has persuaded me that a sequence of electrical impulses in a silicon chip, not capable itself of communicating anything directly to a human recipient, and designed only to operate a computer, is itself a literary work, or is the translation of a literary work within the Copyright Act.

The majority favoured the view that as the only manifestation of the object code at issue was as electrical impulses in a silicon chip which could neither be detected by, nor had any meaning for, humans, it could not be construed as a literary work.

24 (1983) 50 ALR 581; [1984] FSR 246.

25 A view which echoes the dictum of Davey LJ in *Hollinrake v Truswell* [1894] 3 Ch 420 at 428.

26 (1984) 53 ALR 225.

Computer Edge Pty Ltd v Apple Computer Inc
(1986) 161 CLR 171 at 201

Brennan J A literary work need not have literary merit ... The words 'literary work', as Peterson J pointed out in *University of London Press Ltd v University Tutorial Press Ltd,* 'cover work which is expressed in print or writing, irrespective of the question whether the quality or style is high'. A 'literary work', according to Davey LJ in *Hollinrake v Truswell,* is a work 'intended to afford either information and instruction, or pleasure, in the form of literary enjoyment' ... The observation is not unduly restrictive. If the print or writing in which the work is expressed conveys information or instruction, albeit to a limited group with special knowledge, it is immaterial that the information or instruction is not expressed in the form of words, phrases or sentences. Thus a telegraphic code has been held to be a literary work though the words of the code were meaningless in themselves ... The source programs were the product of substantial originality and skill, they were prepared as instructions for the manufacture of Apple II ROMS, they were in writing and they conveyed meaning at least to computer scientists and technicians. That is sufficient to bring them within the scope of literary copyright. The argument that a source program is not a literary work proposes a dichotomy between literary works and what are 'merely adjuncts to the operation of a mechanical device'. The dichotomy is false, for it cannot be said that every book of instructions for the operation of a machine is outside the scope of copyright protection. Copyright might not protect every minor direction for use of a machine or device, but that is not the present case. Here, the source programs are a set of complex and precise instructions for the manufacture of Apple II ROMs. The source programs are substantial original compilations. It would be an infringement of Apple's copyright in a source program to do in relation to that program in Australia without Apple's licence any of the acts prescribed in s 31(1)(a) of the Act.

The corresponding object programs, on the other hand, are not in writing. The electrical charges which constitute them may be represented in writing, using the conventional binary or hexadecimal notations. However, the written representation must not be confused with what is represented but not written. Copyright protection under Pt III of the Act is given only to works; under Pt IV of the Act it is given to subject matter other than works. The object programs do not come within Pt IV. To be a 'work' within Pt III, an object program must be one of the four classes of works as defined by s 101(1) – literary, musical, dramatic or artistic. To come within the scope of 'literary work' as that term was defined in the Act prior to the 1984 amendment, a literary work had to be in print or writing. Peterson J in *University of London Press* said:

> 'Copyright Acts are not concerned with the originality of ideas, but with the expression of thought, and in the case of "literary work", with the expression of thought in print or writing.'

And in *Ladbroke (Football) Ltd v William Hill (Football) Ltd* Lord Hodson regarded it as the undoubted truth that 'copyright is not concerned with the originality of ideas, but with the expression of thought, in the case of literary work with the expression of thought in print or writing'.

> Counsel for Apple nevertheless submitted that print or writing is not essential to the existence of a literary work, arguing that it is sufficient that the work be reduced to some material form. Some support for that submission may be found in s 22 of the Act which prescribes the time of the making of a 'literary, dramatic or musical work' as the time when 'the work was first reduced to writing or *to some other material form'*. It may be that the draftsman of s 22 regarded Braille as 'some other material form' rather than as 'writing', for writing is ordinarily read by sight but Braille is read by touch. It is unnecessary to speculate on that point. Section 22 implies that the form in which a literary work is expressed is writing or some other material form. A material form is a form which can be perceived by the senses. That is not to say that copyright subsists in a document on which the writing of an original literary work appears ... Copyright in a work is a right in respect of the form to which the work has been reduced, not a right of property in the object in or from which the form is perceptible. But a form from which the words, letters or figures of a literary work cannot be perceived by sight or touch (or, possibly, hearing) is not a material form to which the work has been reduced. The electrical charges which constitute the object programs cannot be seen or touched or heard or, if they can, they do not communicate the letters of the original literary work, the source programs. Nor, for that matter, do the electrical charges communicate the letters or figures by which an object program may be represented. The object programs are not literary works.

Neither, in the view of the majority, were they protected as adaptations of the source program.

***Computer Edge Pty Ltd v Apple Computer Inc* (1986) 161 CLR 171 at 204**

> **Brennan J** The action or process of turning the source program in '6502 Assembly Language' into the object program in what is called 'machine readable language' is said to be a translation. It strains the meaning of 'language' to include within its denotation the alphabetic symbols in which the source programs were written. Although the alphabetic symbols of the source programs may be classified as literary in form for the purposes of the Act, I would not describe those symbols as a language, the primary meaning of which is 'the whole body of words and of methods of combining them used by a nation, people or race' (Shorter *Oxford Dictionary*). It is difficult to divorce 'language' from human speech, and a means of communicating ideas which does not consist of words is not properly to be described as a language. A chemical formula or a mathematical equation are apt to communicate ideas, but I should not classify either as a language. '6502 Assembly Language' is not a language; it is a code. Even if the code were thought to be susceptible of 'translation' into another language, it was not so translated: the electrical charges which constitute the object programs are clearly not a language. To describe such electrical charges – no doubt helpfully enough for the purposes of computer science – as 'machine readable language' is to make metaphor serve as reality. The machine has no comprehension of thought which it is the essential purpose of language to convey, and the fact that a microprocessor is activated by a sequence of electrical charges in a predictable way does not mean that it has understood and executed some command.

The secondary meaning of translation comes closer to describing the connection between the sequences of electrical charges constituting the source programs and corresponding object programs. Like the messages sent by a morse telegraphist, the object programs might be regarded as an expression of the original text in a different medium: a translation of a written text into a sequence of electrical charges. The fact that an object program will so operate upon a suitably programmed computer as to cause it to print out either the original written text (the source program) or a binary or hexadecimal notation of the electrical charges (the object program) makes it arguable (I need put it no higher) that an object program is an expression of a source program in another medium and is a 'translation'. This approach, freed from the confusion arising from the metaphorical use of 'language', might command acceptance if it were not for the necessity of the 'adaptation' being itself a 'work'. In the Full Federal Court, the majority did not think it necessary to decide whether an 'adaptation' (that is, a 'translation') was a 'work' but I respectfully disagree. The language of s 31(l)(a)(vii) is clear, 'a work that is an adaptation'. We have seen that a sequence of electrical charges constituting an object program is neither a literary work nor any other kind of 'work'. An object program is therefore not 'a work that is an adaptation' of the source program in which copyright subsists

As we shall see, this view has not survived and does not represent the protection offered to computer programs in any jurisdiction. With the benefit of hindsight, it may be that the dissenting judgments of Mason J and Wilson J have turned out to be more influential, or, at least, to be a more accurate assessment of the current protection afforded to computer programs.

Computer Edge Pty Ltd v Apple Computer Inc
(1986) 161 CLR 171 at 193

Mason and Wilson JJ We have no hesitation in coming to the conclusion that each of the source programs was an original literary work ... Whether or not a literary work must be in writing, these programs were written. Although the substance of the program in each case was expressed in 6502 Assembly Code, this is a language which was readily intelligible to anyone versed in computer science. Each program was the product of skill, time and effort. It was a particular kind of vehicle for the communication of useful information to persons who may desire it. The fact that its creation was a step towards the goal of facilitating the operation of a computer does not warrant its dismissal by the appellants as no more than a mere adjunct to the operation of a mechanical device, by analogy with the sleeve which was the subject of the decision in *Hollinrake v Truswell*. On any view, in the form in which it was created and before it was transformed into another medium, each source program had an existence which was entirely independent of the machine. It was capable of conveying meaning as to the arrangement and ordering of instructions for the storage and reproduction of knowledge. In that form it was entitled to copyright protection.

The second submission of the appellants is that even if the source programs are the subject of copyright, the object programs are not. It is said that the members of the Full Court who formed the majority erred in holding each object program to be a 'translation' of the relevant source program and therefore an adaptation of a literary work within the meaning of that term as defined in s 10(1). The arguments advanced in support of the submission may be summarised as follows: (a) the object programs are merely sequences of electrical impulses within the computer; (b) a translation, in order to constitute an adaptation, must be a translation from one human language to another; (c) a translation of a literary work must itself be a literary work: (d) a translation of a literary work must convey a clear idea of the literary work to human beings. It is not correct to describe an object program as *merely* a sequence of electrical impulses within the computer. Electrical impulses there are, but those impulses serve to identify a set of instructions in machine readable language designed to guide the machine in its basic operations. They do not form part of the computer itself, notwithstanding that they may be embodied in a ROM or ROMs located permanently in silicon chips in a machine. They might equally well be contained in a magnetic disc or tape which can be inserted into or removed from the machine at will. The language may be recorded in visible form in binary or hexadecimal notation. The same result as is achieved by the use of an object program could be achieved by the manual operation of a computer in accordance with instructions written out in ordinary English and contained in a manual. The only problem would be that such a process would be impossibly tedious and therefore wholly impracticable.

The next question is whether the object program is a translation of the source program. The word 'translation' is not defined in the Act. One of the meanings given in the *Shorter Oxford English Dictionary* is 'the expression or rendering of something in another medium or form'. In the Federal Court, Sheppard J was of the opinion that a translation did not encompass something which could neither be seen nor heard. With all respect to his Honour, we are unable to share that view. True it is that the object program can be neither seen nor heard, but there can be no doubt that it exists and one knows where it can be found and how it can be activated. It seems to us that the conversion of a source code into an object code, albeit by the mechanical operation of a computer, is a process which effects a 'translation' of the source code from one language into another language. It is immaterial that the last-mentioned language takes a form which can only be read and understood in that form by a machine. It is an adaptation of a literary work. This conclusion finds support in the statement from the 1979 report of the United States National Commission on New Technological Uses of Copyright Works, p 21, n 109, which was cited by Fox J in his Honour's judgment in the Federal Court:

> 'A source code is a computer program written in any of several programming languages employed by computer programmers.
>
> An object code is the version of a program in which the source code language is converted or translated into the machine language of the computer with which it is to be used.'

We therefore reject the argument of the appellants that the only relevant translation is that which translates one human language into another human language. We also find no warrant for the argument that a translation must

> convey a clear idea of the literary work to human beings although, if it matters, there is no reason why an object program may not be reduced to writing and understood by those skilled in the art.
>
> The question whether an adaptation of a literary work must itself be a literary work is more difficult of resolution. Fox J considered it to be plain from the language of the Act itself that the question must be answered in the negative, and he did not find it necessary to consider whether the Apple II object codes could be regarded as literary works. Lockhart J did not address the question. His Honour, however, did confess to having considerable reservations about the correctness of the view that object programs are original literary works (a question which he did not have to decide), but we would understand that to be a different question from the one we are presently considering. Section 31(l)(a)(vii) provides that copyright, in relation to a literary work, is the exclusive right, *inter alia,* to reproduce in a material form a work that is an adaptation of that literary work. 'Work' is defined in s 10(l), unless the contrary intention appears, to mean *inter alia* a literary work. *Prima facie,* therefore, an adaptation of a literary work must itself satisfy the description of a literary work. Of course, one would expect that an adaptation, in this case a translation of the original literary work constituted by the source codes, would continue to display, in its new form, the characteristics which enabled the original work to satisfy that description. But it is argued for the appellants that that is not so in the present case because a literary work must be in writing. Ordinarily and traditionally it is no doubt true that a literary work would take a written form. But the Act does not require it to be so. Indeed, s 22(i) of the Act identifies the time when a work is made as the time when 'the work was first reduced to writing *or to some other material form* (our emphasis): see also s 21 of the Act. There seems to be no reason to doubt that a literary work is made and entitled to copyright protection from the time it is first recorded on tape, if that be the first material form that the work takes: In our opinion, an object code, although brought into existence by mechanical means, takes on the same literary character as is possessed from the source code from which it is derived. This conclusion seems necessarily to follow, if the protection secured by the Act to the source programs as original literary works is to be effective. If there is no copyright in the object programs which are a natural and necessary derivative of the source programs then there is no point in protecting the source programs.

Notwithstanding this dissenting view, the majority decision led to some consternation in the common law world as to the correct mode of application of copyright principles to computer programs. Some of this was based on theoretical argument, but some related to the practical issue of whether or not intellectual property rights in object code could be protected at all, if copyright was not deemed to be an appropriate medium for that protection. This confusion led directly to statutory action being taken in the UK, the Copyright (Computer Software) Amendment Act was passed in 1985 and its provisions have now been re-enacted in the Copyright, Designs and Patents Act (CDPA) 1988. Further amendments to this statute have now been incorporated by virtue of the Copyright (Computer Programs) Regulations 1992 and these will be discussed later.[27]

Copyright, Designs and Patents Act 1988 as amended

Section 3

(1) 'literary work' means any work which is written, spoken or sung and accordingly includes –

(a) a table or compilation

(b) a computer program

(c) preparatory design material for a computer program

Section 17

(1) The copying of the work is an act restricted by the copyright in every description of copyright work ...

(2) Copying in relation to a literary, dramatic, musical or artistic work means reproducing the work in any material form. This includes storing the work in any medium by electronic means.

Thus, *prima facie*, copyright law applies to both source code and object code and the owners of the copyright in the computer programs represented by this code have a legal remedy available in the case of unauthorised copying of those programs.

THE SCOPE OF PROTECTION

How much needs to be copied before an infringement occurs is defined differently in different jurisdictions. In the UK the concept is one of taking a substantial part (s 16(3) of the CDPA 1988), whilst the US considers unauthorised copying in terms of substantial similarity. While the detail of these may differ, they both require some assessment of what and how much has been copied in comparison with the whole. A consideration of the manner of constructing computer programs, to which reference has already been made, will reveal that many aspects of a program can be copied, from straight line by line copying of the source or object code (literal copying) to copying of the structure sequence and organisation (SSO) of the program (non-literal copying). It has been established, in relation to other areas of copyright law, that the test of substantial taking may be either quantitative or qualitative.[28] Thus, if part of a work is copied which is small in quantity but highly significant in terms of its overall contribution to the work, then an action will

27 See p 60.

28 See, eg, *Hawkes & Son (London) Ltd v Paramount Film Services Ltd* [1934] Ch 593 and *Ladbroke (Football) Ltd v William Hill (Football) Ltd* [1964] 1 WLR 273, in which Lord Pearce said 'whether a part is substantial must be decided by its quality rather than its quantity'. This latter case was relied upon by Ferris J in *John Richardson Computers v Flanders* [1993] FSR 497, see later discussion at p 45.

lie. It is common practice for programmers to include spurious lines of code which are not essential to the execution of the program but make the detection of copying easier. Other evidence may also raise a strong presumption of literal copying. Thus in *MS Associates v Power*[29] it was noted that there were a number of similarities in the names of the variables in the defendants' and plaintiffs' programs – names which would be expected to be decided quite arbitrarily. It was also noted that the function 'vtprs' appeared in both the defendants' and the plaintiffs' list of variables although the facts showed that the function was not used in the defendants' program.

Where there are similar errors in two programs, a strong presumption of copying may be raised, however, this may be capable of rebuttal because of another difference between computer programs and other forms of literary work. Whereas it is statistically improbable that if two authors independently have the same idea for a novel, they will write it in the same words and sentence construction, this is not such a remote possibility in the case of a computer program. If two programmers independently write a program to perform the same task, especially if this is a relatively simple task or subroutine, it may be very likely that they will write the same or similar program. It is also equally possible that they may make the same errors. If such programs contain the same errors then, although this may provide persuasive evidence, copying will not be a foregone conclusion as some errors are more frequent and obvious than others. Illustrations of these issues are again to be found in *MS Associates v Power* in which the same errors were noted in one part of the program but in relation to another part, it was perhaps possible to explain the observed similarities:[30]

MS Associates v Power
[1987] FSR 242 at 248

> In the plaintiffs' program the 'oct' function is arbitrarily grouped with the 'hex' function following it. In the defendant's B-tran, the 'oct' function similarly is grouped with the 'hex' function in the source file called 'hex c'. It is Mr Maskell's evidence that there is no obvious reason why it should be grouped with the 'hex' function, other than that the plaintiffs had so grouped them together, and indeed that it would have been better not to put it there but to allocate it to a separate source file of its own. However, on commenting on this point, the first defendants' evidence is that the 'hex' and 'oct' functions are commonly grouped together and are so in Microsoft BASIC.

Problems of this type create some fundamental difficulties in applying the law of copyright to computer programs. Copyright was developed to protect the form in which authors or artists create their work; to protect the expression of their idea rather than the idea itself. If, in the previous example, there is indeed only one way in which the program or part of the program can be

29 [1987] FSR 242.
30 [1987] FSR 242 at 248.

written, can this reasonably be treated as the expression of an idea, or has the expression merged with the idea, so that the whole cannot be protected by copyright? This issue, referred to as the idea/expression dichotomy, has now become central to some discussions on the scope of copyright protection for computer programs. Although the concept enjoyed a renaissance in connection with computer software, this is not a new idea for copyright law to accommodate and the boundaries of what is and is not copyrightable have been discussed elsewhere, particularly in the US, where the distinction has been given a statutory basis.[31] This has resulted in extensive discussion in the case law on the subject in the US, concerning the formulation of rules and tests to distinguish idea from expression. In particular, Learned Hand J, in *Nichols v Universal Pictures Corp*,[32] devised the 'levels of abstraction test':

> Upon any work, and especially upon a play, a great number of patterns of increasing generality will fit equally well, as more and more of the incident is left out. The last may perhaps be no more than the most general statement of what the play is all about, and at times might consist only of its title; but there is a point in this series of abstractions where they are no longer protected, since otherwise the playwright could prevent the use of his 'ideas' to which, apart from their expression, his property is never extended.

but went on to say, referring to the line between idea and expression that nobody 'has ever been able to fix that boundary and nobody ever can'.

The problems caused by the idea/expression dichotomy have been further exacerbated by the dispute surrounding the extent to which the non-literal elements of a program, the SSO, can be protected by copyright coupled with the extent to which elements of the structure form part of the expression of that program.

These non-literal elements are often referred to as the 'look and feel'[33] of a program and are often precisely those factors that are likely to give a particular program a competitive edge over its rivals, and, therefore, precisely those elements which the originators of the program will most want to protect. Thus the 'look' of a program may include elements of the user

31 US Copyright Act 1976, 17 USCS § 102(b), which provides that copyright protection does not extend to any 'idea, procedure, process, system, method of operation, concept, principle or discovery'.

32 45 F 2d 119 at 121 (2d Cir 1930) discussed in, eg, Steven R Englund, 'Idea, Process or Protected Expression?: Determining the Scope of Copyright Protection of the Structure of Computer Programs' (1990) 88 Mich L Rev 866, David WT Daniels, 'Learned Hand never played Nintendo: A Better Way to think about Non-literal, Non-visual Software Copyright Cases' (1994) 61 University of Chicago L Rev 613, Jon S Wilkins, 'Protecting Computer Programs as Compilations under *Computer Associates v Altai*' (1994) 104 Yale LJ 435.

33 A concept which originated in relation to greetings cards and childrens' books and entered the analysis of copyright infringement of computer programs in cases involving video games. See, eg, John WL Ogilvie, 'Defining Computer Program Parts under Learned Hand's Abstractions Tests in Software Copyright Infringement Cases' (1992) 91 Mich L Rev 526, Julian Velasco, 'The Copyrightability of Non-literal Elements of Computer Programs' (1994) 94 Col L Rev 242.

interface, such as the screen display, and determine the way in which the computer program appears to the user. The 'feel', on the other hand, includes those elements which determine the experience of using the program such as the keystroke sequences or other means of operating the program. The generic term 'look and feel' recognises that these concepts may frequently overlap or be interdependent.

The situation in the US

The extent to which this structure, sequence and organisation of a program can be regarded as the idea of the program or, alternatively, be protected by copyright law as part of the expression of that idea has, as already mentioned, been debated extensively by the courts in the US. Some of the arguments raised in these cases have been highly influential in stimulating the debate on the correct application of copyright principles to computer programs. The first such case was *Whelan Associates v Jaslow Dental Laboratory Inc*.[34] A computer program had been devised by an employee to keep records in a dental laboratory. The employee concerned subsequently left that employment and later created another software package to perform the same function. It was accepted that both packages provided the same service, ie the end product was the same, but that the coding was different, thus literal similarities were absent. It was argued, for the defendants, that the structure of a computer program must be the idea rather than the expression of that idea and therefore would be beyond the scope of copyright protection. The US Court of Appeals for the Third Circuit responded by trying to devise a rule for distinguishing idea from expression which they could then apply to the facts of the case.

Whelan Associates v Jaslow Dental Laboratory Inc
[1987] 797 F 2d 1222 at 1234

1. A rule for distinguishing idea from expression in computer programs

It is frequently difficult to distinguish the idea from the expression thereof. No less an authority than Learned Hand J, after a career that included writing some of the leading copyright opinions, concluded that the distinction will 'inevitably be *ad hoc*' ... Although we acknowledge the wisdom of Judge Hand's remark, we feel that a review of relevant copyright precedent will enable us to formulate a rule applicable in this case. In addition, precisely because the line between idea and expression is elusive, we must pay particular attention to the pragmatic considerations that underlie the distinction and copyright law generally. In this regard, we must remember that the purpose of the copyright law is to create the most efficient and productive balance between protection (incentive) and dissemination of information, to promote learning, culture and development ... We begin our analysis with the case of *Baker v Selden*, which, in addition to being a seminal case in the law of

34 [1987] FSR 1.

copyright generally, is particularly relevant here because, like the instant case, it involved a utilitarian work, rather than an artistic or fictional one. In *Baker v Selden*, the plaintiff Selden obtained a copyright on his book, '*Selden's Condensed Ledger, or Bookkeeping Simplified*', which described a simplified system of accounting. Included in the book were certain 'blank forms', pages with ruled lines and headings, for use in Selden's accounting system. Selden alleged that Baker had infringed Selden's copyright by making and selling accounting books that used substantially the same system as Selden's and that reproduced Selden's blank forms. No one disputed that Baker had the right to use and promulgate Selden's system of accounting, for all parties agreed that the system could not be copyrighted, although the court opined that it might be patentable. Nor did the parties dispute that the text of Baker's book on accounting did not infringe Selden's copyright. The dispute centred on whether Selden's blank forms were part of the method (idea) of Selden's book, and hence non-copyrightable, or part of the copyrightable text (expression). In deciding this point, the court distinguished what was protectable from what was not protectable as follows:

> [W]here the art [ie, the method of accounting] it teaches cannot be used without employing the methods and diagrams used to illustrate the book, or such as are similar to them, such methods and diagrams are to be considered as necessary incidents to the art, and given to the public.

Applying this test, the court held that the blank forms were necessary incidents to Selden's method of accounting, and hence were not entitled to any copyright protection. The court's test in *Baker v Selden* suggests a way to distinguish idea from expression. Just as *Baker v Selden* focused on the end sought to be achieved by Selden's book, the line between idea and expression may be drawn with reference to the end sought to be achieved by the work in question. In other words, *the purpose or function of a utilitarian work would be the work's idea, and everything that is not necessary to that purpose or function would be part of the expression of the idea* ... Where there are various means of achieving the desired purpose, then the particular means chosen is not necessary to the purpose; hence, there is expression, not idea. Consideration of copyright doctrines related to *scènes à faire* and fact-intensive works supports our formulation, for they reflect the same underlying principle. *Scènes à faire* are 'incidents, characters or settings which are as a practical matter indispensable ... in the treatment of a given topic' ... It is well-settled doctrine that *scènes à faire* are afforded no copyright protection. *Scènes à faire* are afforded no protection because the subject matter represented can be expressed in no other way than through the particular *scène à faire*. Therefore, granting a copyright 'would give the first author a monopoly on the commonplace ideas behind the *scènes à faire*' ... This is merely a restatement of the hypothesis advanced above, that the purpose or function of a work or literary device is part of that device's 'idea' (unprotectable portion). It follows that anything necessary to effecting that function is also, necessarily, part of the idea, too. Fact intensive works are given similarly limited copyright coverage ... Once again, the reason appears to be that there are only a limited number of ways to express factual material, and therefore the purpose of the literary work – telling a truthful story – can be accomplished only by employing one of a limited number of devices. Those devices therefore belong to the idea, not the expression, of the historical or factual work. Although the economic implications of this rule are necessarily somewhat speculative, we nevertheless believe that the rule would advance the basic purpose underlying the idea/expression distinction, 'the preservation of the balance between competition and protection reflected in the patent and copyright laws' ... As we stated above, among the more significant costs in computer programming are those attributable to developing the structure and logic of the program. The rule proposed here, which allows copyright protection beyond the literal computer code, would provide the proper incentive for programmers by protecting their most valuable efforts, while not giving them a stranglehold over the development of new computer devices that accomplish the same end. The principal economic argument used against this position – used, that is, in support of the position that programs' literal elements are the only parts of the programs protected by the copyright law – is that computer programs are so intricate, each step so dependent on all of the other steps, that they are almost impossible to copy except literally, and that anyone who attempts to copy the structure of a program without copying its literal elements must expend a tremendous amount of effort and creativity. In the words of one commentator: 'One cannot simply "approximate" the entire copyrighted computer program and create a similar operative program without the expenditure of almost the same amount of time as the original programmer expended.' Note, 68 Minn L Rev at 1290. According to this argument, such work should not be discouraged or penalised. A further argument against our position is not economic but jurisprudential; another commentator argues that the concept of structure in computer programs is too vague to be useful in copyright cases ... He too would therefore appear to advocate limiting copyright protection to programs' literal codes.

Neither of the two arguments just described is persuasive. The first argument fails for two reasons. In the first place, it is simply not true that 'approximation' of a program short of perfect reproduction is valueless. To the contrary, one can approximate a program and thereby gain a significant advantage over competitors even though additional work is needed to complete the program. Second, the fact that it will take a great deal of effort to copy a copyrighted work does not mean that the copier is not a copyright infringer. The issue in a copyrighted case is simply whether the copyright holder's expression has been copied, not how difficult it was to do the copying. Whether an alleged infringer spent significant time and effort to copy an original work is therefore irrelevant to whether he has pirated the expression of an original work.

As to the second argument, it is surely true that limiting copyright protection to computers' literal codes would be simpler and would yield more definite answers than does our answer here. Ease of application is not, however, a sufficient counterweight to the considerations we have adduced on behalf of our position.

Finally, one commentator argues that the process of development and progress in the field of computer programming is significantly different from that in other fields, and therefore requires a particularly restricted application of the copyright law. According to this argument, progress in the area of computer technology is achieved by means of 'stepping-stones', a process that 'requires plagiarising in some manner the underlying copyrighted work'. Note, 68 Minn L Rev at 1292. As a consequence, this commentator argues, giving computer programs too much copyright protection will retard progress in the field.

We are not convinced that progress in computer technology or technique is qualitatively different from progress in other areas of science or the arts. In balancing protection and dissemination, the copyright law has always recognised and tried to accommodate the fact that all intellectual pioneers build on the work of their predecessors. Thus, copyright principles derived from other areas are applicable in the field of computer programs.

2. Application of the general rule to this case

The rule proposed here is certainly not problem-free. The rule has its greatest force in the analysis of utilitarian or 'functional' works, for the purpose of such works is easily stated and identified. By contrast, in cases involving works of literature or 'non-functional' visual representations, defining the purpose of the work may be difficult. Since it may be impossible to discuss the purpose or function of a novel, poem, sculpture or painting, the rule may have little or no application to cases involving such works. The present case presents no such difficulties, for it is clear that the purpose of the utilitarian Dentalab program was to aid in the business operations of a dental laboratory. It is equally clear that the structure of the program was not essential to that task: there are other programs on the market, competitors of Dentalab and Dentcom, that perform the same functions but have different structures and designs.

This fact seems to have been dispositive for the district court:

The mere idea or concept of a computerised program for operating a dental laboratory would not in and of itself be subject to copyright. Copyright law protects the manner in which the author expresses an idea or concept, but not the idea itself ... There are many ways that the same data may be organised, assembled, held, retrieved and utilised by a computer. *Different computer systems may functionally serve similar purposes without being copies of each other. There is evidence in the record that there are other software programs for the business management of dental laboratories in competition with plaintiff's program. There is no contention that any of them infringe although they may incorporate many of the same ideas and functions.* The 'expression of the idea' in a software computer program is the manner in which the program operates, controls and regulates the computer in receiving, assembling, calculating, retaining, correlating, and producing useful information either on a screen, print-out or by audio communication.

... The conclusion is thus inescapable that the detailed structure of the Dentalab program is part of the expression, not the idea, of that program.

Our conclusion is supported by *SAS Institute, Inc v S&H Computer Systems, Inc*, the only other case that has addressed this issue specifically, in which the court found that a program's copyright could extend beyond its literal elements to its structure and organisation. In *SAS*, plaintiffs supported their allegation of copyright infringement of their computer program with evidence of both literal and organisational similarities between its program and the alleged infringer. The court found a copyright infringement, and although it did not discuss in detail its evaluation of the evidence, it is apparent that the organisational similarities of the programs were relevant to its decision. After a brief discussion of the programs' literal similarities, the court said:

> 'In addition, the copying proven at trial does not affect only the specific lines of code cited by Dr Peterson in his testimony. Rather, to the extent that it represents copying of the organisation and structural details of SAS, such copying pervades the entire S&H product.'

Although the SAS court did not analyse the point in great depth, we are encouraged by its conclusion.

The Copyright Act of 1976 provides further support, for it indicates that Congress intended that the structure and organisation of a literary work could be part of its expression protectable by copyright. Title 17 USC §103 (1982) specifically extends copyright protection to compilations and derivative works. Title 17 USC §101, defines 'compilation' as 'a work formed by the collection and assembling of pre-existing materials or of data that are selected, co-ordinated, or arranged in such a way that the resulting work as a whole constitutes an original work of authorship', and it defines 'derivative work', as one 'based upon one or more pre-existing works, such as ... abridgement, condensation, or any other form in which a work may be recast, transformed, or adapted' (emphasis added). Although the Code does not use the terms 'sequence', 'order' or 'structure', it is clear from the definition of compilations and derivative works, and the protection afforded them, that Congress was aware of the fact that the sequencing and ordering of materials could be copyrighted, ie that the sequence and order could be parts of the expression, not the idea, of a work.

Despite the reference to Learned Hand, this judgment does not build on his famous abstractions test but, instead, relies on another line of case law and also on statute to show that the structure, sequence and organisation of the program, the non-literal elements should be afforded copyright protection. In brief, the court found that the purpose of the program at issue was the organisation of the dental laboratory records and that the structure of the program was not necessary to that purpose following from the analogy with the reasoning in *Baker v Selden*. In consequence, the structure of Whelan's program was entitled to copyright protection.

One possible virtue of this approach is its simplicity but as Englund identifies below[35] this may generate its own problems.

> Perhaps the single virtue of the *Whelan* rule is that it is easy to apply. The widespread application of the rule is likely to have undesirable consequences. Given the court's broad conception of the purpose of a program as what a user might do with it rather than what the program actually does, almost any particular structure could be seen as not necessary to that purpose. The court failed adequately to consider the possibility that broad protection might allow

35 Steven R Englund, 'Idea, Process or Protected Expression?: Determining the Scope of Copyright Protection of the Structure of Computer Programs' (1990) 88 Michigan Law Review 866 at 881.

> *Whelan* to make it impossible for others to program a computer efficiently to perform the same function and employ the same process. Although the court purported to consider the need to 'create the most efficient and productive balance between protection (incentive) and dissemination of information to promote learning, culture and development', the court's rule may thus actually impair progress in the computer art.

Velasco[36] makes the point that the ideal test would be one which is both simple and accurate. In such a technically complex area as computer software, it has proved difficult to pursue either of these aims without compromising the other and it is unsurprising, therefore, that certain inadequacies have been identified in the simple test enunciated in *Whelan*. It can thus be criticised as being over-simplistic in its suggestion that it may be possible to both define and isolate a single purpose for a particular program. An obvious consequence of this is that if programmers are to be able to devise other programs that perform the same function but do not infringe copyright, then there have to be a number of other possible structures for the program which could, reasonably and efficiently, fulfil that same purpose. If not, the *Whelan* formulation is capable of conferring an almost patent-like protection on the first programmer to develop a suitable structure. In reality, most commercially important programs consist of a number of sub-routines and modules, each of which could, validly, be considered as an idea.[37] These problems were summarised accurately by Menell:[38]

> ... it is apparent that the emerging interpretation of copyright protection for application program code is quite far off the mark. Under the *Whelan* test, copyright extends to the structure, sequence and organisation of application code as long as the overall purpose of the entire program, broadly defined, can be implemented in another manner. Since many aspects of application code are dictated by basic principles of software engineering, the *Whelan* rule makes it difficult for others wishing to market programs performing the same task as the first comer to perform it as effectively. In effect, the *Whelan* test enables first comers to 'lock up' basic programming techniques as implemented in programs to perform particular tasks. This gives the first comer significant market power. In addition, since the programmer did not have to contribute novel and non-obvious programming techniques to our state of knowledge in order to get this legal protection, the monopoly power bestowed will not, in most cases, be justified on the basis of sound public policy analysis.
>
> Furthermore, in the light of the importance of sequential research in the application program industry, the *Whelan* test is likely to affect detrimentally the direction and cost of research and development. This can be seen clearly by

36 Julian Velasco, 'The Copyrightability of Non-literal Elements of Computer Programs' (1994) 94 Col L Rev 242.

37 A fact which was recognised by the Second Circuit in the later case of *Computer Associates v Altai* discussed later at p 37.

38 Peter S Menell, 'An Analysis of the Scope of Copyright Protection for Application Programs' (1989) 41 Stanford L Rev 1045 at 1082.

> analysing the set of options open to an application programmer who wishes to improve on an existing program that employs nothing more than good programming practice. In a world protecting only useful, novel and non-obvious programming elements, the programmer would be free to build upon the functional aspects of the first program. The *Whelan* test, however, prohibits the programmer from innovating in this way. The programmer would either have to: (1) secure a license for the original program (or its desired aspects) from the copyright owner; (2) circumvent the copyrighted material by expressing the desired functional aspects of the original program in a way that does not infringe its overall structure, sequence and organisation; or (3) independently develop the functional programming techniques. Plainly, all three of these options substantially raise the costs of innovative activity.

Karjala goes further and suggests that the reasoning based on the use of *scènes à faire* is inappropriate,[39] '... computer programs are literary works only in form ... In operation, they are pure works of function, that is of technology. The analogy with novels and plays ... is totally inapt for works of technology'. Although expressed as a criticism of the reasoning in *Whelan,* this could be regarded, more correctly, as a comment on the classification of computer programs as literary works for copyright purposes.

The US Court of Appeals, Second Circuit, recognised some of these problems in the later case of *Computer Associates v Altai,*[40] noting that the decision in Whelan had received a 'mixed reception' in the courts and that '*Whelan* has fared ... poorly in the academic community where its standard ... has been widely criticised for being overbroad',[41] and went on to use rather different reasoning. The case concerned the development of an 'operating system compatibility component' by Computer Associates which enabled a program to work with a number of different operating systems. One of the members of the team which developed this feature was later employed by Altai to develop a version of one of its own programs which could be used on various operating systems. Without the knowledge of Altai, the programmer based the program on the Computer Associates program including the literal copying of some 30% of the code. When Altai were made aware of this (by Computer Associates suing for copyright infringement!) they used different programmers to create a new version. Nonetheless, Computer Associates went on to sue for infringement of both programs alleging that even the second program made use of the non-literal elements of their original program.

Not surprisingly, at first instance, the court found that there had been infringement in relation to the first program. However, this court absolved Altai of liability in relation to the second program and Computer Associates

39 Dennis S Karjala, 'Copyright Protection of Computer Software in the US and Japan Part I' [1991] EIPR 195 at 198.

40 982 F 2d 693 (2nd Cir 1992).

41 *Ibid* at 705.

appealed, leading to the Second Circuit formulating what has become known as the 'abstraction – filtration – comparison' test as they struggled to formulate a suitable method for determining the copyrightability of the non-literal elements of a computer program. It was accepted in the case that copyright protection of computer programs extends beyond literal similarities in code and includes also similarities in structure. In contrast to the decision in *Whelan,* the judgment of the Second Circuit utilised Learned Hand's famous abstractions approach, at least for the first part of the test, and the *Whelan* formulation, that the overall purpose of the program can be equated with its idea, was roundly criticised on the basis that the majority of programs do not consist of a single 'idea' but are more accurately described as composites. Circuit Judge Walker therefore introduced a different test and in presenting this test the Second Circuit suggested that, when faced with this problem courts:[42]

> ... would be well-advised to undertake a three-step procedure based on the abstractions test utilised by the district court, in order to determine whether the non-literal elements of two or more computer programs are substantially similar. This approach breaks no new ground; rather it draws on such familiar copyright doctrines as merger, *scènes à faire* and public domain. In taking this approach, however, we are cognisant that computer technology is a dynamic field which can quickly outpace judicial decision-making. Thus in cases where the technology in question does not allow for a literal application of the procedure we outline below, our opinion should not be read to foreclose the district courts of our circuit from utilising a modified version.
>
> In ascertaining substantial similarity under this approach, a court would first break down the allegedly infringed program into its constituent structural parts. Then, by examining each of these parts for such things as incorporated ideas, expression that is necessarily incidental to those ideas, and elements that are taken from the public domain, a court would then be able to sift out all non-protectable material. Left with a kernel, or possibly kernels, of creative expression after following this process of elimination, the court's last step would be to compare this material with the structure of an allegedly infringing program. The result of this comparison will determine whether the protectable elements of the programs at issue are substantially similar so as to warrant a finding of infringement.

This was the source of what has become known as the abstraction – filtration – comparison test which was, subsequently, enlarged upon by the court.

> **Step One: Abstraction**
>
> ... As applied to computer programs, the abstractions test will comprise the first step in the examination for substantial similarity. Initially, in a manner that resembles reverse engineering on a theoretical plane, a court should dissect the allegedly copied program's structure and isolate each level of abstraction contained within it. This process begins with the code and ends

42 *Ibid* at 706.

with an articulation of the program's ultimate function. Along the way, it is necessary essentially to retrace and map each of the designer's steps – in the opposite order in which they were taken during the program's creation ...

At the lowest level of abstraction, a computer program may be thought of in its entirety as a set of individual instructions organised into a hierarchy of modules. At a higher level of abstraction, the instructions in the lowest-level modules may be replaced conceptually by the functions of those modules. At progressively higher levels of abstraction, the functions of higher-level modules conceptually replace the implementations of those modules in terms of lower-level modules and instructions, until finally, one is left with nothing but the ultimate function of the program. A program has structure at every level of abstraction at which it is viewed. At low levels of abstraction, a program's structure may be quite complex; at the highest level it is trivial ...

Step Two: Filtration

... This process entails examining the structural components at each level of abstraction to determine whether their particular inclusion at that level was 'idea' or was dictated by considerations of efficiency, so as to be necessarily incidental to that idea; required by factors external to the program itself; or taken from the public domain and hence is non-protectable expression ...

(a) Elements Dictated by Efficiency

... Copyrighted language may be copied without infringing when there is but a limited number of ways to express a given idea ... In the computer context, this means that when specific instructions, even though previously copyrighted, are the only and essential means of accomplishing a given task, their later use by another will not amount to infringement.

... In the context of computer program design, the concept of efficiency is akin to deriving the most concise logical proof or formulating the most succinct mathematical computation. Thus, the more efficient a set of modules are, the more closely they approximate the idea or process embodied in that particular aspect of the program's structure.

... Efficiency is an industry-wide goal. Since, as we have already noted, there may be only a limited number of efficient implementations for any given program task, it is quite possible that multiple programmers, working independently, will design the identical method employed in the allegedly infringed work. Of course, if this is the case, there is no copyright infringement.

... Thus, since evidence of similarly efficient structure is not particularly probative of copying, it should be disregarded in the overall substantial similarity analysis ...

(b) Elements Dictated by External Factors

... Professor Nimmer points out that 'in many instances it is virtually impossible to write a program to perform particular functions in a specific computing environment without employing standard techniques' ... This is a result of the fact that a programmer's freedom of design choice is often circumscribed by extrinsic considerations such as (1) the mechanical specifications of the computer on which a particular program is intended to run; (2) compatibility requirements of other programs with which a program is designed to operate in conjunction; (3) computer manufacturers' design standards; (4) demands of the industry being serviced; and (5) widely accepted programming practices within the computer industry ...

(c) Elements taken from the Public Domain

... Such material is free for the taking and cannot be appropriated by a single author even though it is included in a copyrighted work ... We see no reason to make an exception to this rule for elements of a computer program that have entered the public domain by virtue of freely accessible program exchanges and the like.

Step Three: Comparison

The third and final step of the test for substantial similarity that we believe appropriate for non-literal program components entails a comparison. Once a court has sifted out all elements of the allegedly infringed program which are 'ideas' or are dictated by efficiency or external factors, or taken from the public domain, there may remain a core of protectable expression. In terms of a work's copyright value, this is the golden nugget ...

The court then went on to discuss what it believed to be the relevant policy issues in drawing the line between idea and expression. In doing this, they recognised that assessing non-literal similarity in this way is far more favourable to the defendant than the method of assessing non-literal copying used in *Whelan* which the court in *Computer Associates* explicitly rejected. Nonetheless, they felt that a correct application of copyright principles was of overriding importance and were of the view that this would not have disastrous consequences for the industry.[43]

> ... we are unpersuaded that the test we approve today will lead to the dire consequences for the computer program industry that plaintiff and some amici predict. To the contrary, serious students of the industry have been highly critical of the sweeping scope of copyright protection engendered by the Whelan rule, in that it enables first comers to 'lock up' basic programming techniques as implemented in programs to perform particular tasks.
>
> While incentive based arguments in favour of broad copyright protection are perhaps attractive from a pure policy perspective, ultimately they have a corrosive effect on certain fundamental tenets of copyright doctrine. If the test we have outlined results in narrowing the scope of protection, as we expect it will, that result flows from applying, in accordance with Congressional intent, long-standing principles of copyright law to computer programs. Of course, our decision is also informed by our concern that these fundamental principles remain undistorted.

This judgment was generally well-received as demonstrating a good understanding of the way in which computer programs are designed and

43 *Ibid* at 712.

written. It was acknowledged, by some writers, that the decision was also able to deal with constraints of interoperability and compatibility;[44] 'together, *Altai* and *Sega* provide a method by which the courts can permit copying of internal interface elements necessary for compatibility while protecting elements not needed for compatibility'.[45] On the other hand, some reservations were expressed.

Case Note on *Computer Associates v Altai*
(1992) 106 Harvard L Rev 510

> Although the *Altai* court attempted to balance the interests involved in the protection of these basic elements, the court was unduly constrained by a uniquely literary view of the creative process and thus failed to recognise its own ability to 'keep pace' with technological change within the traditional copyright framework. Because the court protected more than the 'only and essential means' of accomplishing a programming task, its test will discourage innovative programming techniques and leave non-literal elements of computer programs under-protected.

Notwithstanding this criticism, the writer still found some positive features in the judgment which might form the basis of a workable test as long as certain provisos were taken into account:

> In certain cases, it may be necessary to limit the copyrightability of an 'essential means' of accomplishing a particular programming objective in order to allow continuing innovation but this will rarely preclude copyrightability. Even assuming, as the *Altai* court did, that 'efficiency' takes a lot of the creativity out of programming, the court did not assert that *no* creativity is involved. Rarely is there only one way to accomplish a given programming task.
>
> The 'abstraction – filtration – comparison' method of determining the copyrightability of a computer program's non-literal elements may be imperfect, but is arguably a 'practical necessity' in the computer program context. Abstracting and then filtering out unprotected elements 'eases the court's task of discerning the boundaries of protectable expression' by 'separating the program into manageable components'. However, the only elements – whether literal or non-literal – that should be filtered out are those that constitute the 'only and essential means' of accomplishing a given task. Although there is 'no statutory basis for treating computer programs differently from other literary work', courts should attempt to develop an approach to copyrightability that acknowledges the unique creative challenges posed by computer programming.

The decision in *Altai,* although taking more accurate recognition of the way in which computer programs are developed and written, cannot deal satisfactorily with the situations such as that which occurred in *Apple*

---

44 See also later discussion at p 54.

45 Timothy S Teter, 'Merger and the Machines: An Analysis of the Pro-compatibility Trend in Computer Software Copyright Cases' (1993) 45 Stanford L Rev 1061 at 1084.

Computer Inc v Microsoft Corp.[46] In this case applying the abstraction – filtration – comparison test would result in there being little to compare, because the program had been constructed from existing sub-routines already in the public domain or dictated by efficiency requirements, with a consequent denial of copyright protection.

Apple v Microsoft: Has the pendulum swung too far?
Steve S Moutsatsos and John C R Cummings
(1993) 9 CL&P 162

> It could be strongly argued that the decision in *Apple v Microsoft* simply turned on its facts and that the 'analytical approach' remains a sound legal process through which to examine software copyright issues. On the other hand, it is also possible to assert that the 'analytical approach' as it is applied to computer software, by its nature, may inevitably lead to the conclusion that the constituent elements of a computer program are not protectable under copyright law. The analytical dissection of a computer program, which is essentially a utilitarian work, is more likely to produce constituent parts that are found to be functional, as opposed to a movie or a novel ...

In such cases whether or not there is any copyright protection will depend on an assessment of the way in which they have been assembled and interlinked. It will be at this stage that the case law on the copyright of compilations may become very relevant.[47]

The discussion on the previous pages has focused exclusively on the cases of *Whelan and Altai*, largely because they have, subsequently, been the ones referred to in the UK cases, but also because they have generally proved to be influential and have both generated much debate. Also, in some ways, they can be viewed as two ends of the spectrum of copyright protection for computer programs. As noted by Moutsatsos and Cumming,[48] 'Both approaches are rooted in and use the language and legal precedent of copyright law but with vastly differing results'. *Whelan* with its almost patent-like protection operates in favour of the original developer of the program, whereas application of the test in *Altai* reduces considerably this protection. The opposing effects of these two judgments may be of significance for certain sectors of the industry. Thus in the appeal in *Altai,* the Software Publishers Association supported Computer Associates in opposing the lower court's decision and in support of the *Whelan* approach, whereas the American Committee for Interoperable Systems favoured rejection of the *Whelan* rationale.[49] Different commentators have both supported and opposed the

46 35 F 3d 1435 (9th Cir 1994).

47 In the US see *Feist Publications Inc v Rural Tel Serv Co* 113 L Ed 2d 358 cited in *Computer Associates v Altai,* in the UK. See discussion of *Richardson v Flanders,* p47.

48 Steve S Moutsatsos and John CR Cummings, '*Apple v Microsoft*: Has the pendulum swung too far?' (1993) 9 CL&P 162.

49 Lynda J Zadra-Symes, '*Computer Associates v Altai:* The Retreat from *Whelan v Jaslow*' [1992] EIPR 327.

decision in *Altai*, but Miller believes that *Altai* can be viewed as a further refinement of the approach begun in *Whelan* and suggests that the difference between the two has been overstated:[50] '... it seems more accurate to view *Altai* as adopting a series of modifications of *Whelan's* generalised statements and as using different terminology without deviating markedly from the *Whelan* court's fundamental reliance on the idea-expression dichotomy'.

Whatever view is taken of the relationship between the decisions in these two cases, the situation in the US courts has been more complex than the analysis above might suggest. As we have seen, both *Whelan and Altai* were decided in different circuits of the US Court of Appeals and, despite the criticisms of *Whelan* contained in the court's judgment in *Altai*, it was certainly not the case that the test in *Altai* immediately eclipsed that in *Whelan*. In addition, other Circuits devised other tests which might be based in part on either of these tests. This resulted, at times, in certain contradictions and confusions and in the words of the court in *Altai*[51] '... many of the decisions in this area reflect the courts' attempt to fit the proverbial square peg in a round hole'. The Ninth Circuit for instance developed its own test (the intrinsic – extrinsic test) for copyrightability of computer programs in *Brown Bag Software v Symanthec Corp*.[52] The proliferation of such tests and their subsequent modification led one commentator to state that 'The "look and feel" cases ... can fairly be characterised as a mess'.[53] The situation with regard to copyrightability of computer software in the US courts is thus more confused than is sometimes presented.[54]

Velasco has compared the various tests and has concluded that the test devised in *Computer Associates v Altai* is the best on offer from the courts.

The Copyrightability of Non-literal Elements of Computer Programs
Julian Velasco
(1994) 94 Columbia Law Review 242 at 284

... only the *Altai* test *explicitly* incorporates in a *systematic* way the Abstractions Test, the concept of merger, a very sophisticated understanding of the concept

50 Arthur R Miller, 'Copyright Protection for Computer Programs, Databases and Computer-generated Works: Is anything new since CONTU?' (1993) 106 Harv L Rev 977 at 1002.

51 982 F 2d 693 (2nd Cir 1992) at 712.

52 960 F 2d 1465 (9th Cir 1992).

53 David L Hayes, 'What's left of Look and Feel: A Current Analysis' (1993) 10 Computer Law 1.

54 A more detailed analysis is beyond the scope of this publication see, eg, David L Hayes, 'What's left of Look and Feel: A Current Analysis' (1993) 10 Computer Law 1, Arthur R Miller, 'Copyright Protection for Computer Programs, Databases and Computer-generated Works: Is anything new since CONTU?' (1993) 106 Harv L Rev 977, Julian Velasco, 'The Copyrightability of Non-literal Elements of Computer Programs' (1994) 94 Col L Rev 242, Dennis S Karjala, 'Recent US and International Developments in Software Protection (Part 2)' [1994] EIPR 58, Josef Drexl, 'What is Protected in a Computer Program? Copyright Protection in the US and Europe' IIC Studies in Industrial Property and Copyright Law, Vol 15, VCH 1994.

> of *scènes à faire*, and the concept of public domain materials. In short, from the perspective of copyright doctrine, the *Altai* test is superior to the others.

Despite this tribute, he nevertheless goes on to point out a failing and suggest an improvement:

> An inescapable failing of the *Altai* test is that its thoroughness in filtering out unprotectable elements of expression leads to underprotection ... Application of the compilations doctrine rectifies this failing ... works consisting entirely of uncopyrightable elements are often protected by the copyright law under the rubric of 'compilations'. Based on an analogy to compilations, copyright protection should subsist in computer programs even if they consist entirely of uncopyrightable elements if those elements were selected or arranged in an original manner. Therefore, an additional step should be added to Altai's 'Abstraction – Filtration – Comparison' test. After the court has completed the successive filtering of the second step of the *Altai* test, it should re-evaluate the elements that have been excluded as uncopyrightable to determine whether there are elements, or groupings of elements, that, in their selection, co-ordination or arrangement, are sufficiently original to merit copyright protection as a group in a manner analogous to compilations. This would be a 're-incorporating' stage since elements previously excluded from copyright protection are now reincorporated in the analysis, albeit as compilations ... The addition of the compilations doctrine expands the scope of the Altai test ... while simultaneously avoiding the overbreadth of 'total concept and feel'. It strikes the appropriate balance between the two, providing the substance needed for analysis while ensuring that only expression is protected.
>
> One final point should be made with regard to the proposed re-incorporating stage. In applying it, the court should recognise the fact that a work may be held to consist of *more than one* compilation, just as a work 'may consist of a mixture of numerous ideas and expressions' ...
>
> With the elimination of the unnecessary limitations imposed by the court and the addition of this re-incorporating stage, the *Altai* test becomes complete. In theory, at least, it should provide protection to *all* the elements and *only* to the elements of a computer program that deserve protection. Although decisions will still be 'ad hoc' to a certain extent, this Modified *Altai* Test provides the decision-maker with a framework for determining copyrightability that is solidly grounded in well-established copyright principles.

Despite dissent in some quarters and the evolution of different tests (as mentioned earlier, the Court of Appeals in *Altai*, itself, thought that modifications would be appropriate in some circumstances), the test was generally greeted with favour and the prevailing opinion seemed to be that this was likely to become the preferred approach:[55]

> Given the prestige of the Second Circuit and the considerable persuasiveness of the opinions, it is fair to conclude that *Computer Associates* has now become the analytical starting point for further analysis in the United States of the

55 Gary M Rinck, 'The Maturing US Law on Copyright Protection for Computer Programs: *Computer Associates v Altai* and other recent Case Developments' [1992] EIPR 351 at 356.

appropriate scope of copyright protection for computer programs ... The effects intended by the court in *Computer Associates*, of course, are greater competition, increased incremental innovation and a more public exchange or market in 'ideas'. Wherever United States' case law or legislation next turns, these should continue to be important objectives.

The situation in the UK

During the period in which the US courts were debating these issues, those involved in the UK waited impatiently for the first case to go to full trial. There was academic debate about how the approach of the UK courts might be influenced by the difficulties experienced by the US courts. There was also evidence provided by interlocutory hearings such as that of *Computer Aided Design v Bolwell*,[56] in which Hoffman J made reference to the decision in *Whelan v Jaslow*, that, at the least, the judiciary were taking cognisance of the American decisions. Computer Aided Design (CAD) were suppliers of both software and hardware. In particular, they marketed a software package called BUSNIX-FLEET. In a common scenario in this type of case, three employees including Bolwell left CAD to set up a rival business with the promise of both orders and financial assistance from a former customer of CAD who was dissatisfied with BUSNIX-FLEET. The defendants wrote a program using the 4th generation language, PROGRESS, and called the package the Towquest system. CAD then alleged that this had incurred both a breach of copyright and a breach of confidence. The respective programs used different codes and there was no allegation that the code itself was copied, rather that the overall design and structure, ie the *'look and feel'* of BUSNIX-FLEET had been substantially copied.

Although CAD failed to obtain an injunction because they were unable to satisfy the court that Towquest was *arguably* a substantial copy of BUSNIX-FLEET, Hofmann J said that the overall structure of a computer program was a form of literary expression in which copyright could exist and, in his express reference to the reasoning in *Whelan v Jaslow*, seemed to be condoning the approach in that case.

It was not until the end of 1992 that the High Court began to hear the case of *John Richardson Computers Ltd v Flanders*.[57] The facts of the case are complex but, in brief, both parties developed and marketed programs to print labels for prescriptions at pharmacists and keep details of the stock of drugs. Flanders, a self-taught programmer with a penchant for writing programs in machine code, had worked in the past for Richardson first as an employee and then as a self-employed consultant. After all ties with Richardson ceased, Flanders wrote a program in QuickBASIC for an IBM personal computer which he

56 High Court (1989) 23 August, unreported.

57 [1993] FSR 497.

marketed through a company, that he had established, called Chemtec. Richardson alleged that this program infringed his copyright in an earlier program written, with the help of Flanders, in assembler language for a BBC computer.

Ferris J identified a number of issues of which the most important and interesting for our purposes was 'what ought to be the approach of the court to the appraisal of an allegation of breach of copyright in a computer program where it is not claimed that the source code has itself been copied?'

John Richardson Computers Ltd v Flanders
[1993] FSR 497 at 519
High Court

6. Approach to be adopted by the court in this type of case

... it is apparent now that this is not a case where it can be said that any substantial parts of the source code of the BBC program have been copied in the Chemtec program. The two programs are, of course, written in different computer languages. This by itself would not avoid infringement if the Chemtec program could be said to be a translation of the BBC program, or a substantial part of it, into a different language (see section 1(2) of the 1985 Act, now section 21(4) of the 1988 Act). But this is not what is said to have happened. What is said is that the defendants have taken the general scheme of the BBC program, including the detail of certain routines of an idiosyncratic nature. The case was likened ... to one in which the plot of a book or other literary work has been taken ...

In making the analogy with novels and plays, this recalls the reasoning adopted in *Whelan v Jaslow*, and the argument continued to include both UK and US authorities. Ferris J then went on to discuss the proposition that the program could be protected as a compilation:

Mr Wilson, on behalf of JRC, also relied upon *Ladbroke (Football) Ltd v William Hill (Football) Ltd*. In that case Ladbrokes admitted having copied some parts of Hills fixed odds football betting coupons, but denied that Hills were entitled to copyright in those parts. They admitted that certain other parts of Hills coupons were protected by copyright, but they had not copied those parts. It was held by the House of Lords that the coupon had to be looked at as a single literary work and that, having regard to the skill and effort involved in working out certain parts of Hills coupon the coupon as a whole was an original compilation which was protected by copyright. I quote from the speech of Lord Pearce at page 291:

'In deciding therefore whether a work in the nature of a compilation is original, it is wrong to start by considering individual parts of it apart from the whole, as the appellants in their argument sought to do. For many compilations have nothing original in their parts, yet the sum total of the compilation may be original ...

In such cases the courts have looked to see whether the compilation of the unoriginal material called for work or skill or expense. If it did, it is entitled to be considered original and to be protected against those who wish to

> steal the fruits of the work or skill or expense by copying it without taking the trouble to compile it themselves.'

This approach, of course, gives rise to a further question where it is contended that what the defendant has copied is one or more of the unoriginal parts, not the compilation as a whole. As to this question, Lord Pearce said (at page 293):

> 'Whether a part is substantial must be decided by its quality rather than its quantity. The reproduction of a part which by itself has no originality will not normally be a substantial part of the copyright and therefore will not be protected. For that which would not attract copyright except by reason of its collocation will, when robbed of that collocation, not be a substantial part of the copyright and therefore the courts will not hold its reproduction to be an infringement. It is this, I think, which is meant by one or two judicial observations that "there is no copyright" in some unoriginal part of a whole that is copyright. They afford no justification, in my view, for holding that one starts the inquiry as to whether copyright exists by dissecting the compilation into component parts instead of starting it by regarding the compilation as a whole and seeing whether the whole has copyright. It is when one is debating whether the part reproduced is substantial that one considers the pirated portion on its own.'

In using the *William Hill* case by way of analogy, Ferris J found an English authority on which to base argument concerning the structure of the program, a process which begins to bear a resemblance to the assessment of substantial similarity required by US law. Having made reference to the non-literal elements in the fact that the compilation is itself an appropriate subject for copyright protection, Ferris J went on to apply the test from *Computer Associates v Altai.*

John Richardson Computers Ltd v Flanders
[1993] FSR 497 at 526
High Court

Ferris J In the test propounded in *Computer Associates* the discovery of a program's abstraction levels is the first step. The second step is to filter these abstractions in order to discover a 'core of protectable material'. In the process of filtration there are to be excluded from consideration (a) elements dictated by efficiency; (b) elements dictated by external factors; and (c) elements taken from the public domain. Each of these categories is explained at some length. The essence of the 'elements dictated by efficiency' is that if there is only one way to express an idea the idea and its expression are inseparable and copyright does not prevent the copying of the expression. The exclusion of 'elements dictated by external factors' arises from the fact that if two persons set about the description of the same event there may be a number of particular facts which can only be described in a particular way. The Court of Appeals cited with evident approval the observation of Professor Nimmer (a well-known academic commentator on United States copyright law) that:

> 'in many instances it is impossible to write a program to perform particular functions in a specific computing environment without employing standard techniques.'

> As to 'elements in the public domain':
>
> > 'plaintiffs may not claim copyright of an ... expression that is, if not standard, then commonplace in the computer software industry.'
>
> The third step in the process suggested in the *Computer Associates* case is to compare what is left of the 'abstractions' made from the plaintiff's case after filtering out these elements with the program which is said to be an infringement of that program.
>
> I have thought it right to deal at some length with the *Computer Associates* case because it explores the difficulties which arise in applying copyright law to computer programs to a greater extent than an English authority does. In the even more recent case of *Sega Enterprises Ltd v Accolade Inc*, the United States Court of Appeals for the Ninth Circuit approved the approach adopted by the Court of Appeals for the Second Circuit in *Computer Associates*. Not surprisingly neither of these decisions have yet been considered in an English case. There are references to *Whelan* in the judgments of Hoffmann J in *Computer Aided Systems v Bolwell*, and of Judge Paul Baker, QC in *Total Information Processing Systems Ltd v Daman Ltd* but both these references are very general and neither of them can be said to indicate a preference for the *Whelan* approach over the approach which has since been adopted on two federal circuits in the United States.
>
> There is thus nothing in any English decision which conflicts with the general approach adopted in the *Computer Associates* case. I think that in preference to seeking the 'core of protectable expression' in the plaintiff's program an English court will first decide whether the plaintiff's program as a whole is entitled to copyright and then decide whether any similarity attributable to copying which is to be found in the defendant's program amounts to the copying of a substantial part of the plaintiff's program. This was the approach which was held to be appropriate in the *William Hill* case. But at the stage at which the substantiality of any copying falls to be assessed in an English case the question which has to be answered, in relation to the originality of the plaintiff's program and the separation of an idea from its expression, is essentially the same question as the United States court was addressing in *Computer Associates*. In my judgment it would be right to adopt a similar approach in England. This means that consideration is not restricted to the text of the code, as Mr McEwen submitted that it was when putting the defendant's case at its highest level. Moreover the argument that consideration should be limited to the 'structure and organisation' of the program imports an unacceptable degree of uncertainty, because it is unclear at what level of abstraction (to use that term in the sense in which it was used in *Computer Associates*) the structure and organisation is to be discerned.

Despite the above analysis, when it came to applying the test to the facts of the case, there was no actual comparison of the BBC program code with the code of the Chemtec program, as might have been expected if the *Computer Associates* test had been used without modification. The expert witness had compared both codes in his report compiled for the court. One factor that seems to have had a bearing on the lack of such comparison in arriving at the final decision appears to be that Ferris J had trouble in understanding this part of the report and also that the situation was not made any clearer during cross-examination.

The test which was evolved in the case can perhaps be summarised by the following steps:

- Is the plaintiff's program as a whole is entitled to copyright protection?
- Are there similarities to the plaintiff's program in the defendant's program?
- Is any similarity attributable to copying?
- Do any such similarities amount to the copying of a substantial part of the plaintiff's program assessed by application of the abstraction – filtration – comparison test of *Computer Associates v Altai*?

The outcome of the case was that some infringement of Richardson's copyright was found, but this was fairly minor and in only a few limited respects. In writing the new program, it appeared that Flanders had not copied or translated all or a substantial part of the source code of the BBC program; instead he had created another program to fulfil a similar purpose and thus compete on the same market.

How are we to assess the first complete decision relating to copyright infringement of computer software in a UK court? In view of the length of time that such a case had been awaited, the judgment of Ferris J was perhaps subjected to more detailed scrutiny and analysis than is customarily awarded to decisions of the High Court. One aspect on which all seem to agree is that, in English law as has been determined in the US, copyright infringement does not only occur in cases of literal copying but may be found when copying of non-literal elements of the program can be established. The question is what is an appropriate test in such cases. It appears that, in starting from the judgment in *William Hill*, Ferris J does not believe that the abstraction – filtration – comparison test should be applied directly in an English case.

Although the abstraction process advocated in Altai based, as it is, on earlier US authorities, in particular the judgments of Learned Hand J, may not be compatible with the way in which copyright law has developed in the UK, neither does it mean that the attempt of Ferris J in formulating a suitable test is any more successful. In particular, an important consideration is the appropriateness of the analogy between a compilation and a computer program, on which the application of the *William Hill* authority depends. Such an analogy might be appropriate in the case where a program is assembled from existing subroutines, but it is questionable as to whether it is capable of more general application. A similar point was noted by Baker J in *Total Information Processing Systems Ltd v Daman Ltd*[58] who said that '(t)he mere linking of programs is not in my judgment itself an original, literary or artistic

58 [1992] FSR 171.

work in the way that the collective presentation of literary works by divers authorities is'. Nor could the compilation be regarded as a computer program separate from and in addition to the individual programs. However, this statement was later to be criticised by Jacob J in *Ibcos*[59] as not being capable of general application, although relevant to the facts in *Total Information*.

A second point is how far it is sensible to apply the three stage test, based as it is on the more rigidly imposed distinction between idea and expression embodied in US law. Whether or not it is articulated as such, the distinction does exist in the UK, albeit expressed in rather a different way. Thus in *Donoghue v Allied Newspapers Ltd*,[60] Farwell J said '... there is no copyright in an idea or ideas ... If the idea, however original, is nothing more than an idea, and is not put into any form of words, or any form of expression ... then there is no such thing as copyright at all'. This notion was also taken up by Baker J in *Total Information*,[61] '... stemming from the principle that copyright does not exist in ideas but in the expression of them, is the line of authorities commencing with *Kerrick and Company v Lawrence and Company*[62] that if there is only one way of expressing an idea that way is not the subject of copyright'.

The US basis for copyright infringement of substantial similarity requires much more wrestling with the idea/expression dichotomy than the UK test of establishing whether there has been copying of a substantial part, and the attempt by Ferris J to marry the US and UK approaches has also received a mixed reception. The above criticisms have been discussed by Arnold as follows.

Infringement of Copyright in Computer Software by Non-textual Copying: First Decision at Trial by an English Court
Richard Arnold
[1993] EIPR 250 at 253

So far as the analysis of the law is concerned, it is submitted that much of what Ferris J says is sound. In particular, he was plainly right to reject the submissions that a substantial part can only be reproduced if there is textual copying. Furthermore, there is force in the criticism of the *Whelan* approach, although the criticisms underplay the detail in which the court in that case did in fact compare the code structure. Equally, the judge was correct that the *Computer Associates* approach of extracting a 'core of protectable expression' is incompatible with English authority, and in particular the speeches of the House of Lords in *William Hill*.

Where the analysis may be questioned, however, is when Ferris J states that in considering substantiality it is right to adopt a similar approach to the approach set out in *Computer Associates.* Although Ferris J is not explicit about

59 See later at p 51.
60 [1938] Ch 106 at 109 and 110.
61 [1992] FSR 171 at 181.
62 (1890) 25 QBD 99.

> this, it appears that he has in mind the point made by Lord Pearce in the passage quoted above. It is submitted that what Lord Pearce envisaged was a different procedure however. This involves the following steps. (1) Decide whether copyright subsists in the plaintiff's work. (2) If so, decide whether there is a derivation. (3) If so, decide whether a substantial part has been reproduced; if the only part which has been reproduced is a part which by itself has no originality, then that part is not substantial. This is not the same thing as the filtering process described by the Court of Appeals in *Computer Associates*. It should be borne in mind that Lord Pearce was dealing with what was essentially a compilation case. At various places in the judgment Ferris J refers to a computer program as a compilation, but this does not seem to be correct except in the particular case where a program has been compiled from pre-existing sub-routines.
>
> Although *dicta* may be found in English cases to the effect that there is 'no copyright in ideas', the general trend of English authority is rather against attempts rigidly to distinguish between 'idea' and 'expression'. As Ferris J acknowledged, the position is different in the United States because the distinction has a statutory basis. Furthermore, as the judge has also acknowledged, reliance on the distinction can be dangerous. Despite this, Ferris J appears to have accepted that an English court should attempt to draw this distinction and moreover should engage in the *Computer Associates* filtering process in doing so. It is open to question whether this is the right approach under English law.

Even if the test is an appropriate one, it is difficult to apply; a fact which was recognised in the judgment itself and the result of the case was, in fact, more dependent on practical and pragmatic considerations relating to the comparison of the mode of operation of the two programs and an assessment of the opportunity for copying.

Richardson v Flanders was soon followed by another case, that of *Ibcos Computers Ltd v Barclays Finance Ltd*.[63] Again, the facts are rather complex, but the main features are as follows. In the 1970s, a programmer, Poole, wrote software for agricultural applications for a dealer, Clayton. Eventually, a company was set up in which both Poole and Clayton owned shares. Poole was the only employee of this company and continued to develop the software, now known as ADS. A deal between the company and a subsidiary of Barclays fell through but Poole, himself, was offered a two-year consultancy and parted company with Clayton. As a result, Poole and Clayton signed an agreement by which Poole was to return all company property and agreed not to modify or provide customer support for the ADS package. Poole acknowledged that the software and manuals were the sole property of the company whose assets were later transferred to Ibcos. Poole also agreed not to develop any agricultural software for two years.

63 [1994] FSR 275.

In 1986, Poole rewrote the ADS package but it was not marketed until the two years had expired in order to comply with the restrictive covenant. Poole received 10% of the licence fees.

The court agreed that there had been no breach of the restrictive covenant but also had to decide whether Poole's new version constituted a breach of copyright. Copyright infringement was claimed in the individual programs and sub-routines, the general structure and certain general features which were identified in the expert witnesses report.

Jacob J considered a number of the issues and, in particular directed attention to the idea/expression issue.

Ibcos Computers v Barclays Finance Ltd
[1994] FSR 275 at 290
High Court

Jacob J It was sometimes suggested in a general sort of way that because a particular program had a function, and especially if that function could only be achieved in one or a limited number of ways, there could be no copyright on it. The extreme form of this idea is expressed by Judge Baker in the *Total* case. He said:

> 'Secondly, stemming from the principle that copyright does not exist in ideas but in the expression of them is the line of authorities commencing with *Kenrick v Lawrence* that if there is only one way of expressing an idea that way is not the subject of copyright.'

That statement is in error in two ways. First, *Kenrick* (the case of the drawing of a hand showing voters which way to vote on a voting slip) did not decide that if there is only one way of expressing an idea then no copyright can subsist in it. What was held was that there was no copyright infringement in taking the idea of using a picture of a hand showing how to vote. Accordingly, a different picture embodying the same idea was not taking a substantial part of the copyright work. In that sense, only the principle that there is no copyright in an idea applied.

Secondly, there is, I think, danger in the proposition that, 'If there is only one way of expressing an idea that way is not the subject of copyright'. As Lord Hailsham observed in *LB Plastics v Swish:*

> 'But of course as the late Professor Joad used to observe it all depends on what you mean by "ideas". What the respondents in fact copied from the appellants was a mere general idea.'

It is of course true that copyright cannot protect any sort of general principle, such as the principle of drawing a hand to show how to vote, but it can protect a detailed literary or artistic expression ... The true position is that where an 'idea' is sufficiently general, then even if an original work embodies it, the mere taking of that idea will not infringe. But if the 'idea' is detailed, then there may be infringement. It is a question of degree.

Jacob's notion of a *detailed* idea that might be protected by copyright is, presumably, in the context of computer programs, that found when a number of sub-routines are put together to form one program. This would be the result of the intellectual effort, skill and judgment of the software writer, as opposed to a *general* idea, which would not be protected by copyright, and presumably might equate with the function, in the *Whelan* sense. He is thus not giving credence to the idea/expression dichotomy which has been much discussed in US law and, indeed, went on to discuss the use of US copyright principles in English cases. He pointed out that US copyright law is different from that in the UK, particularly in the fact that the idea/expression distinction has a statutory basis which has, necessarily, resulted in a different interpretation of that issue in the courts. On the question of judging substantial part he found it unnecessary to consider US authorities as he felt that it unnecessarily complicated the issue which could be resolved by applying the standard principles of UK copyright law.

Ibcos Computers v Barclays Finance Ltd
[1994] FSR 275 at 302
High Court

> **Jacob J** For myself I do not find the route of going via United States case law particularly helpful. As I have said, United Kingdom copyright cannot prevent the copying of a mere general idea but can protect the copying of a detailed 'idea'. It is a question of degree where a good guide is the notion of the overborrowing of the skill, labour and judgment which went into the copyright work. Going via the complication of the concept of a 'core of protectable expression' merely complicates the matter as far as our law is concerned. It is likely to lead to overcitation of United States authority based on a statute different from ours. In the end the matter must be left to the value judgment of the court. Having expressed this reservation, however, I thoroughly agree with what Ferris J went on to say: 'Consideration is not restricted to the text of the code ...'. That must be right: most literary copyright works involve both literal matter (the exact words of a novel or computer program) and varying levels of abstraction (plot, more or less detailed of a novel, general structure of a computer program).
>
> I therefore think it right to have regard in this case not only to ... 'literal similarities' but also to ... ' program structure' and 'design features'.

Thus, whether, or not there is agreement on the reasoning, it appears that there is agreement that non-literal elements can be protected by copyright in the UK, as well as in the US. Despite Jacob J's criticisms of the judgment in *Richardson v Flanders*, the *Ibcos* case was one in which there had been literal copying and so the assessment of a substantial part of the non-literal elements was not crucial to the case. It therefore remains to be seen how the test for copyright infringement of non-literal elements of computer programs will evolve in the UK.

REVERSE ENGINEERING AND DECOMPILATION

One feature which may be desirable in a computer program but which has no clear parallel in relation to more conventional literary works is the need for interoperability, ie the capacity of the computer program to be compatible with other computer programs or hardware elements in a system, such as a printer for instance. It will be remembered that the computer program at issue in *Computer Associates v Altai* had this property. If a computer program is to be interoperable with another, it may need to contain some of the same features, at least at the interface between the two. One way of producing a computer program which is interoperable with other programs is by decompiling (ie compiling in reverse), or reverse engineering, the object code of the program with which interoperability is desired, to obtain the source code in a high level language. This can then be used in the creation of the interface between the existing and the new or proposed program. Where the creator of the new program does not have the copyright in the other program, this can lead to allegations of copyright infringement as a result of the decompilation and subsequent development of the new program. Those sections of the industry that create software primarily for running on operating systems created by others, clearly have a vested interest in allowing decompilation to the maximum extent without fear of infringement, whereas other sectors of the industry, such as those who produce complete systems, are less likely to wish to permit decompilation or any other form of reverse engineering or analysis.

To what extent can copyright holders prevent decompilation for this purpose? Until the advent of the EC Software Directive and implementing legislation, such activity was likely to breach copyright unless it could be brought within the fair dealing exceptions contained in the Copyright, Designs and Patents Act 1988. Similar principles pertained in the US under the fair use doctrine which attempts to balance the author's right to exploit his or her work against the public interest in the widest possible dissemination of information. The relevant provisions are contained in s 107 of the US Copyright Act and allow what would otherwise be infringements for such purposes as criticism, comment, news reporting, teaching, scholarship or research, always provided that the use is non-commercial, does not affect the potential market or value of the work etc.

There was much discussion surrounding the application of these provisions to reverse engineering and decompilation, but with no unanimity of opinion. The opposing points of view are well explained in the following two extracts.

Defining the Scope of Copyright Protection for Computer Software
Susan A Dunn
(1986) 38 Stanford Law Review

Copyright law should not prohibit disassembly of computer programs. If disassembly leads to the creation of a final product that is not substantially similar to the original program, consumers will be enriched by a wider choice of programs. Their options are enhanced at the expense of the owner of the original copyright, who will find the scope of his monopoly is narrowed. But copyright law inevitably balances the proprietor's interest in protection against the public's interest in disclosure. For example, copyright law protects only expression and not ideas so that the public can profit by using the ideas in copyrighted works. If examining a copyrighted computer program through disassembly were illegal, the public could not take advantage of many of the ideas it contains. Replacing the substantial similarity test with evidence of the course of development would sharply alter the balance of competing rights in favour of copyright proprietors.

Copyright Protection for Computer Programs, Databases, and Computer-generated Works: Is anything new since CONTU?
Arthur R Miller
(1993) 106 Harvard Law Review 977 at 1026

The simple truth is that permitting decompilation allows a second comer to create a market substitute and reap the benefits of a successful program after others have incurred the risk and expense of its development – an especially inappropriate result given the extraordinary discrepancy between the cost of creating the software and the cost of duplicating it. If an exemption from copyright is permitted, the decompiler will be able to reproduce the entire program of competitor – appropriating in one relatively simple procedure what may represent years of creative effort and investment – and then electronically massage the copy until every trace of that illicit reproduction is obscured. Yet the resulting program may be no less a derivative work founded on the first program than is a motion picture based on the cleverest plot details and juiciest dialogue of a novel. Both works encroach on the copyright proprietor's statutory rights. Freedom to decompile also eliminates any incentive to produce an innovative or creative expression of one's own, thereby debilitating one of the basic objectives of the copyright regime.

In *SEGA Enterprises v Accolade*, one of the more recent cases on reverse analysis of computer programs in the US, the Court of Appeals for the Ninth Circuit, reversing the decision of the district court, seems to suggest that decompilation may be permissible in certain circumstances.[64] Although this

64 But compare the views of, eg, Miller (1993) 106 Harv L Rev 977 at 1014 *et seq* and Richard H Stern, 'An Ill-conceived Analysis of Reverse Engineering of Software as Copyright Infringement: *Sega Enterprises v Accolade*' [1992] EIPR 107 discussing the district court's decision and 'Reverse Engineering of Software as Copyright Infringement – An Update: *Sega Enterprises v Accolade*', following the judgment of the Court of Appeals. Hunter notes that the Australian courts would not arrive at the same conclusion: 'Reverse engineering computer software – Australia parts company with the world' (1993) 9 CL&P 122. See also Peter Waters and Peter G Leonard, 'The Lessons of Recent EC and US Developments for Protection of Computer Software under Australian Law' [1991] EIPR 125.

issue has not been discussed in the UK courts, making it difficult to ascertain whether or not the fair dealing provisions in s 29 of the Copyright, Designs and Patents Act 1988 apply to reverse engineering,[65] similar arguments have been aired before the High Court of Singapore concerning the fair dealing provisions in the Singapore Copyright Act.

Aztech Systems Pte Ltd v Creative Technology Ltd[66] concerned the development of computer sound cards which would be interoperable with the 'Sound Blaster' card – the market leader. Although it was alleged that this had been achieved by disassembly, the court found that there had been no actual decompilation but that the operation of the program had been studied using a logic analyser, a non-invasive operation, together with the use of program DEBUG, designed for fault-finding during program development and which can therefore be used to observe the operation of a program. Then by a 'process of trial, error and inference they worked out what features a sound card must have to be compatible with "Sound Blaster" and designed their card accordingly'. Did this come within the provisions contained in the s 35 of the Singapore Copyright Act, which allow for fair dealing for research and private study?

Research for industrial purposes or by companies was expressly excluded in the relevant legislation and so reliance was placed on fair dealing for private study. The court found that 'study' meant 'the devotion of time and attention to acquiring information and knowledge' and so the operations which had been carried out fell within this definition. As to the commercial aspect, it was held that the purpose had to be considered along with other relevant factors and that, in this case, there were public interest benefits in allowing this type of activity in terms of advantages to the consumer. However, notwithstanding this reasoning, the case was subsequently reversed by the Singapore Court of Appeal in November 1996[67] who found that there was sufficient evidence to find a breach of copyright within the terms of the Act.

THE 'SOFTWARE DIRECTIVE'

In parallel with the courts' development of the interpretation of the existing copyright law to copying of computer programs, changes in the legislation itself, to take into account the nature of computer programs, were imminent, precipitated by the need to implement the EC Directive on legal protection of

65 For a discussion of the application of the UK fair dealing provisions to copyright of computer programs see Chris Reed, 'Reverse Engineering Computer Programs without Infringing Copyright' [1991] EIPR 47.

66 [1996] FSR 54.

67 *Straits Times* (1996) 29 November.

computer programs[68] – the so-called 'software Directive'. This Directive was a recognition of the issues that had caused debate in relation to the protection of intellectual property rights in computer programs and also of the fact that, without harmonisation of these provisions, the completion and operation of the Single European Market in goods and services might be compromised. This was particularly necessary in view of the fact that different states had adopted quite different attitudes to the legal protection of computer programs. Thus, notwithstanding that many other jurisdictions both inside and outside Europe were basing their protection on copyright principles, this was not possible in Germany, for instance, where computer programs were viewed as technical and scientific products rather than literary works.[69] The fact that such states might be signatories to the Berne Convention was of little relevance as the issue was one of the categorisation of computer programs as copyright material. The Directive had a protracted gestation, not least because of a vociferous lobby from both sides of the industry relating to the scope of permissible decompilation contained in Article 6.[70] *Prima facie*, the agreed Directive extends copyright protection to computer programs as literary works and makes it clear that this protection is afforded to expression rather than idea.[71]

> **Article 1 Object of protection**
>
> 1. In accordance with the provisions of this Directive, Member States shall protect computer programs, by copyright, as literary works within the meaning of the Berne Convention for the Protection of Literary and Artistic Works. For the purposes of this Directive, the term 'computer programs' shall include their preparatory design material.
> 2. Protection in accordance with this Directive shall apply to the expression in any form of a computer program. Ideas and principles which underlie any element of a computer program, including those which underlie its interfaces, are not protected by copyright under this Directive.
> 3. A computer program shall be protected if it is original in the sense that it is the author's own original intellectual creation. No other criteria shall be applied to determine its eligibility for protection.

The rights permitted to copyright holders are defined by Articles 4–6.

---

68 Council Directive 91/250/EEC of 14 May 1991 on the legal protection of computer programs [1991] OJ L122/42.

69 See, eg, Andreas Wiebe, 'European Copyright Protection of Software from a German Perspective' (1993) 9 CL&P 79.

70 A detailed account of the extended discussions preceding adoption of the Directive is beyond the scope of this work but see, eg, Thomas Vinje, *The Legislative History of the EC Software Directive in Handbook of European Software Law* (1993) Part I, M Lehmann and CF Tapper (eds), Clarendon. Bridget Czarnota and Robert J Hart, *Legal protection of computer programs in Europe: a guide to the EC Directive* (1991) Butterworths.

71 For implementation in different Member States see *Handbook of European Software Law* (1995) Part II, M Lehmann and CF Tapper (eds), Clarendon. For the UK position see also later discussion at p 60.

Article 4 Restricted Acts

Subject to the provisions of Articles 5 and 6, the exclusive rights of the rightholder within the meaning of Article 2, shall include the right to do or authorise:

(a) the permanent or temporary reproduction of a computer program by any means and in any form, in part or in whole. Insofar as loading, displaying, running, transmission or storage of the computer program necessitates such reproduction, such acts shall be subject to authorisation by the rightholder;

(b) the translation, adaptation, arrangement and any other alteration of a computer program and the reproduction of the results thereof, without prejudice to the rights of the person whom alters the program;

(c) any form of distribution to the public, including the rental, of the original computer program or of copies thereof. The first sale in the Community of a copy of the program by the rightholder or with his consent shall exhaust the distribution right within the Community of that copy, with the exception of the right to control further rental of the program or a copy thereof.

Article 5 Exceptions to the restricted acts

1. In the absence of specific contractual provisions, the acts referred to in Article 4(a) and (b) shall not require authorisation by the rightholder where they are necessary for the use of the computer program by the lawful acquirer in accordance with its intended purpose, including for error correction.
2. The making of a back-up copy by a person having a right to use the computer program may not be prevented by contract insofar as it is necessary for that use.
3. The person having a right to use a copy of a computer program shall be entitled, without the authorisation of the rightholder, to observe, study or test the functioning of the program in order to determine the ideas and principles which underlie any element of the program if he does so while performing any of the acts of loading, displaying, running, transmitting or storing the program which he is entitled to do.

Article 6 Decompilation

1. The authorisation of the rightholder shall not be required where reproduction of the code and translation of its form within the meaning of Article 4(a) and (b) are indispensable to obtain the information necessary to achieve the interoperability of an independently created computer program with other programs, provided that the following conditions are met:

   (a) these acts are performed by the licensee or by another person having a right to use a copy of the program, or on their behalf by a person authorised to do so;

   (b) the information necessary to achieve interoperability has not previously been readily available to the persons referred to in subparagraph (a); and

(c) these acts are confined to the parts of the original program which are necessary to achieve interoperability.

2. The provisions of paragraph 1 shall not permit the information obtained through its application:

(a) to be used for goals other than to achieve the interoperability of the independently created computer program;

(b) to be given to others, except when necessary for the interoperability of the independently created computer program; or

(c) to be used for the development, production or marketing of a computer program substantially similar in its expression, or for any other act which infringes copyright.

3. In accordance with the provisions of the Berne Convention ... the provisions of this Article may not be interpreted in such a way as to allow its application to be used in a manner which unreasonably prejudices the rightholder's legitimate interests or conflicts with a normal exploitation of the computer program.

Notwithstanding the explicit reference to contract in Article 5(2), Article 9(1) further provides that 'Any contractual provisions contrary to Article 6 or to the exceptions provided for in Article 5(2) and (3) shall be null and void'. The provision regarding back-up copies was non-contentious. Taking a back-up copy of a program is good computing practice but without such a right being included explicitly in the licence to use the software (as is the usual practice) such a practice would be a technical infringement. In the US, amendments introduced in 1980 to the Copyright Act 1976 had served a similar purpose. However the rights, contained in a limited way in Article 5(3) and in more extensive form in Article 6, to undertake reverse analysis or decompilation under certain circumstances were to provoke much spirited debate both during the gestation of the Directive[72] and after its adoption,[73] in academic circles and also between representatives of different parts of the industry, in which the main protagonists took up positions similar to those evident in the extracts from Dunn and Miller above.

One problem in framing the terms of Article 6 was the need to reconcile the common law approach, in which reverse analysis might be permitted, in certain circumstances, under fair dealing or fair use exceptions, with a civil

72 See, eg, the debate between Cornish, Lake *et al* and Colombe and Meyer at [1989] EIPR 391, [1989] EIPR 43, [1990] EIPR 79, [1990] EIPR 129 and [1990] EIPR 325.

73 See, eg, Jérôme Huet and Jane C Ginsburg, 'Computer programs in Europe: A Comparative Analysis of the 1991 EC Software Directive' (1992) 30 Col J Transnatl L 327, Joseph Haaf, 'The EC Directive on the Legal Protection of Computer Programs: Decompilation and Security for Confidential Programming Techniques' (1992) 30 Col J Transnatl L 401, Paul G Hidalgo, 'Copyright Protection of Computer Software in the European Community: Current Protection and the Effect of the Adopted Directive' (1993) 27 International Lawyer 113, Peter Waters and Peter G Leonard, 'The Lessons of Recent EC and US Developments for Protection of Computer Software under Australian Law' [1991] EIPR 125, David Bainbridge, 'Computer Programs and Copyright: More exceptions to infringement' (1993) 56 MLR 591.

law tradition which looks for legal certainty in the legislation. The situation was made more complex by the view of different sectors of the industry, discussed further below, of the extent to which any type of reverse analysis should be permitted. The resulting provision covers the circumstances in which decompilation, in particular, is allowed to take place and also the purposes for which the information gained as a consequence can be used. The compromise arrived at in the Directive appears to be aimed at allowing products to be developed which are compatible with the original, rather than those which might be viewed as being in competition with the original.[74] This is a fine line to draw.

The EC has thus tried to use legislation to deal with issues which have previously been dealt with by the courts in a number of jurisdictions. Although the Directive has attempted to grapple with particular aspects of computer programs, its provisions do not necessarily assist in the problem of defining the scope of protection itself, which may still fall to be determined by the courts.

Scope of Protection in the European Community
From – Recent United States and International Developments in Software Protection (Part 2)
Dennis S Karjala
[1994] EIPR 58 at 63

The EC Software Directive, of course, fails almost completely to address either the scope-of-protection problem or the degree of copyright protection in user interfaces. Notwithstanding the Directive's purported goal of uniformity, therefore, one can expect courts in the various Member States to grope their way towards appropriate solutions much as do courts in the US federal system. In the long run, this is likely to lead to a better and more stable balance of the social policy tensions involved in software protection than detailed statutory coverage adopted in a highly charged political atmosphere. Perhaps the courts in Europe will benefit from the opportunity to observe the successes and failures of the American courts. Even so, one should expect a good deal of lurching, backtracking and zigzagging before a general consensus is reached.

UK implementation of the software directive

The UK implemented the software Directive by means of the Copyright (Computer Regulations) 1992[75] which amended the 1988 Act, particularly in relation to the new permitted acts; the creation of back-up copies, error correction and decompilation. The first two of these were covered by the introduction of new ss 50A and 50C.

74 See, eg, Jérôme Huet and Jane C Ginsburg, above, n 73.

75 SI 1992/3233.

Copyright, Designs and Patents Act 1988 as amended

Section 50A

(1) It is not an infringement of copyright for a lawful user of a copy of a computer program to make any back up copy of it which is necessary for him to have for the purposes of his lawful use.

(2) For the purposes of this section and sections 50B and 50C a person is a lawful user of a computer program if (whether under a licence to do any acts restricted by the copyright in the program or otherwise), he has a right to use the program ...

Section 50C

(1) It is not an infringement of copyright for a lawful user of a copy of a computer program to copy or adapt it, providing that the copying or adapting

(a) is necessary for his lawful use; and

(b) is not prohibited under any term or condition of an agreement regulating the circumstances in which his use is lawful.

(2) It may, in particular, be necessary for the lawful use of a computer program to copy it or adapt it for the purpose of correcting errors in it ...

This right to adapt, in so far as it is necessary for lawful use, extending even to the correction of errors, should be read in conjunction with the definition of 'adaptation' introduced by a new s 21(3)(ab) namely 'an arrangement or altered version of the program or translation of it'.

The manner of incorporating the decompilation right was to remove decompilation from the ambit of the fair dealing provisions relating to research and private study contained in s 29 and then introduce it as a new permitted act in s 50B. The provisions of s 29 will still apply to computer programs in relation to activities other than decompilation.

Copyright, Designs and Patents Act 1988 as amended

Section 29

4. It is not fair dealing

(a) to convert a computer program expressed in a low-level language into a version expressed in a higher level language; or

(b) incidentally in the course of so converting the program, to copy it ...

Section 50B

(1) It is not an infringement of copyright for a lawful user of a copy of a computer program expressed in a low-level language

(a) to convert it into a higher level language; or

(b) incidentally in the course of so converting the program, to copy it (that is to 'decompile it'), provided that the conditions in subsection (2) are met.

(2) The conditions are that

(a) it is necessary to decompile the program to obtain the information necessary to create an independent program which can be operated with the program decompiled or with another program ('the permitted objective'); and

(b) the information so obtained is not used for any purpose other than the permitted objective.

(3) In particular, the conditions in subsection (2) are not met if the lawful user

(a) has readily available to him the information necessary to achieve the permitted objective;

(b) does not confine the decompiling to such acts as are necessary to achieve the permitted objective;

(c) supplies the information obtained by the decompiling to any person to whom it is not necessary to supply it in order to achieve the permitted objective; or

(d) uses the information to create a program which is substantially similar in its expression to the program decompiled or to do any act restricted by copyright.

(4) Where an act is permitted under this section, it is irrelevant whether or not there exists any term or condition in an agreement which purports to prohibit or restrict the act ...

It is by no means clear that the definitions of decompilation contained in the Directive and the implementing regulations coincide. The regulations seem to confine decompilation exclusively to the situation in which the decompiler is working upwards from the low- to the high-level language. The Directive on the other hand refers to 'reproduction of the code and translation of its form' which appears to represent a much wider view of the scope of decompilation. The meaning of 'translation' of a computer program contained in s 21(4) of the 1988 Act, includes ' a version of the program in which it is converted into or out of a computer language or code or into a different computer language or code'. This corresponds more accurately with the terminology in the Directive but would not be included in the new definition of decompilation introduced by the Regulations.

The new s 50B(2) provides that decompilation will be allowed where it is 'necessary to create an independent program which can be operated with the program decompiled or another program'. This, taken together with s 50B(3), suggests that it may be lawful to create a competing program, provided it is not substantially similar to the original program but that it would be impermissible to devise modifications to an existing program to make it interoperable with another. This latter act would, apparently, be permitted under the terms of the Directive which allows decompilation where it is 'indispensable to obtain the information necessary to achieve the interoperability of an independently created computer program with other programs'.

The Directive, in Article 5(3) refers expressly to the right to 'observe, study or test the functioning of the program' this being done 'in order to determine the ideas and principles underlying any element of the program'. It might appear that this aspect has not been incorporated since the only reference to 'observation' is to be found in the new s 296A(1) making any contractual terms purporting to place limits on this process void. On the other hand, fair dealing for the purposes of research and private study is still permissible under s 29(1) and it may be that observation can legitimately be construed as such research or private study.

In implementing the Directive no express enactment relating to the idea/expression distinction referred to in Article 1 was included, so, in so far as this doctrine is a part of UK law, it remains on a case law basis rather than having a statutory basis as found in the US.

Sui generis rights observed

At the beginning of this chapter, the reasons for the choice of a copyright scheme rather than a *sui generis* right for the protection of the intellectual property rights in computer programs was discussed. As we have seen, the law in a number of jurisdictions has struggled with, and sometimes needed to modify, traditional copyright principles in order to apply them satisfactorily to computer programs. In the European Commission Green Paper 'Copyright and The Challenges of Technology – Copyright Issues requiring Immediate Action'[76] a *sui generis* right for computer programs was rejected under the influence of the observed case law trend towards copyright already formulated by the courts in a number of jurisdictions. Nonetheless, it could be argued that some of the modifications that were negotiated for inclusion in the software Directive, and that have led to the new derogations with respect to decompilation rights, modify traditional copyright principles to such an extent that the resulting protection is, more accurately, described as a *sui generis* right.[77] Goldstein[78] observes that *sui generis* protection for the intellectual property rights in computer programs is now less frequently advocated, and relates this to the protection which has evolved from the conventional copyright framework both in the US and in Europe.

> The principle reason in the decline in calls for *sui generis* legislation is that, in a very real sense, *sui generis* protection for computer programs is already being implemented throughout the world – albeit under the nominal auspices of copyright. Section 117 of the United States Copyright Act is specifically

76 COM (88) 172 final.

77 See, eg, the views expressed by Andreas Wiebe, 'European Copyright Protection of Software from a German Perspective' (1993) 9 CL&P 79.

78 Paul Goldstein, 'The EC Software Directive: A view from the USA' in *Handbook of European Software Law* (1993) Part I, M Lehmann and CF Tapper (eds), Clarendon.

tailored to the special features of computer programs; sections 102(b) and 107 of the Act have also been interpreted with particular attention to the particular nature of software. The EC Directive represents, to date, the most systematic tailoring of copyright to meet the special needs of computer programs. Indeed, apart from its relatively long term of protection, the Directive more closely resembles a *sui generis* law than it does copyright. Most important, the deliberations on the Software Directive have shown that the Berne Convention's rigorous standards, once thought to pose the most serious impediment to a copyright accommodation for computer programs, are sufficiently flexible to admit needed derogations from the reproduction and adaptation rights.

PATENTS AND COMPUTER PROGRAMS

Whereas it appears that, in the majority of cases, copyright will be the appropriate method of protecting the intellectual property in computer software, the question has also arisen as to whether patent protection might also, or alternatively, be available for computer programs. Certainly, if a patent could be obtained, it would be very valuable in providing the opportunity to those developing the programs to recoup their research and development costs. In recent years, therefore, a steady increase in the number of patent applications relating to computers and processing systems has been noted,[79] many of which have been for specific apparatus containing software which is, itself, novel or is used in a novel application, or for processes where the claimed invention is neither a pure mathematical algorithm nor a mental step. Clearly these will be highly specialised situations and to determine the conditions under which a patent might be available for such an invention, it is necessary to consider the relevant legal provisions in more detail.

In the UK, the Patents Act 1977 gave effect to the European Patent Convention of 1973 (EPC), the relevant provisions being Article 52 of the Convention and s 1 of the Act.

European Patent Convention 1973

Article 52 Patentable Inventions

(1) European patents shall be granted for any inventions which are susceptible of industrial application, which are new and which involve an inventive step.

(2) The following in particular shall not be regarded as inventions within the meaning of paragraph 1:

79 See, eg, RG Sterne, RE Sokohl and RR Axenfield, 'The Shifting Sands of Section 101 and Section 112 Requirements for Computer Program-related Inventions' [1994] Int Lawyer 29 at 30, Michael J Lenno, 'US Patent Rights in Financial Services Software' (1994) 10 CL&P 17.

(a) discoveries, scientific theories and mathematical methods; ...

(c) schemes, rules and methods for performing mental acts, playing games or doing business, and programs for computers;

(d) presentations of information.

(3) The provisions of paragraph 2 shall exclude patentability of the subject matter or activities referred to in that provision only to the extent to which a European patent application or European patent relates to such subject matter or activities as such.

Patents Act 1977

Section 1 Patentable Inventions

(1) A patent may be granted only for an invention in respect of which the following conditions are satisfied, that is to say

(a) the invention is new;

(b) it involves an inventive step;

(c) it is capable of industrial application;

(d) the grant of a patent for it is not excluded by subsection(s) (2) ...

(2) It is hereby declared that the following ... are not inventions for the purposes of this Act, that is to say, anything which consists of

(a) a discovery, scientific theory or mathematical method; ...

(c) a scheme, rule or method for performing a mental act, playing a game or doing business, or a program for a computer;

(d) the presentation of information;

but the foregoing provision shall prevent anything from being treated as an invention for the purposes of this Act only to the extent that a patent or application for a patent relates to that thing as such.

The Patents Act 1977, in recognition of its origins, directs that other legal rules will be of relevance:

Patents Act 1977

Section 91 Evidence of Conventions ...

(1) Judicial notice shall be taken of the following, that is to say

(a) the European Patent Convention, the Community Patent Convention and the Patent Co-operation Treaty ...

(b) any bulletin, journal or gazette published under the relevant convention ...

(c) any decision of, or expression of opinion by, the relevant convention court on any question arising under or in connection with the relevant convention.

Clearly the interpretation of *'as such'* in Article 52 EPC and s 1 of the Patents Act 1977 is a key issue in determining the patentability or otherwise of inventions in which the inventive step falls within a computer program. The crucial question would seem to be; is the claim for a patent for an invention involving a computer program an application for a patent for a program *'as such'* or, rather, is the effect to create an entirely new product or process within which the computer program can merely be regarded in the same light as any other component might be? Views on this matter in the US have, arguably, polarised more distinctly. Notwithstanding the existence of a similar statutory exclusion under 35 USC, s 101, many hold the view that claims for patents involving computer software should be treated in the same way as those concerning computer hardware. On the other hand, others advocate the opposite view[80] on the basis that software technology is significantly different from that which applies to hardware.[81]

In whichever jurisdiction they arise, such applications will, typically, fall into one of two basic categories:

(a) where the program embodies a procedure for performing a useful operation or a physical phenomenon forming part of the real world outside the computer;

(b) the program solves a technical problem in the operation of the system of which the computer on which it is running forms a part.

No patent can be granted where the application relates merely to the operation of the computer under the control of the program. This was emphasised as early as 1979, in Guidelines from the European Patent Office (EPO).[82]

> A computer program may take various forms, eg an algorithm, a flow-chart or a series of coded instructions which can be recorded on a tape or other machine-readable record-medium, and can be regarded as a particular case of either a mathematical method or a presentation of information. If the contribution to the known art resides solely in a computer program the subject matter is not patentable in whatever manner it may be presented in the claims. For example, a claim to a computer characterised by having a particular program stored in its memory or to a process for operating a computer under control of the program would be as objectionable as a claim to the program *per se* or the program when recorded on magnetic tape.

However because the statutory exclusions are well-known, it is unusual for a patent application to relate to a computer program without more, and there will always be an attempt to associate the application with some technical effect made possible by the novelty of the invention as a whole. The whole must therefore be examined for novelty and inventive step, taking into account the exclusions.

80 See, eg Sterne *et al*, above, n 79.

81 For a more philosophical discussion of the nature of technology and the purpose and application of both patents and exclusion from patentability see, eg, Axel Von Helfeld, 'Protection of Inventions Comprising Computer Programs by the European and German Patent Offices – A Confrontation' (1986) 2 CL&P 182.

82 Quoted in G Gall, 'European Patent Office Guidelines 1985 on the protection of inventions relating to computer programs' (1985) 2 CL&P 2.

European Patent Office Guidelines 1985 on the Protection of Inventions relating to Computer Programs
G Gall
(1985) 2 CL&P 1985

> Inventions which relate to computer programs or in which such programs constitute an essential element are subject to the general rules of patent law. Thus, in the case of inventions relating to programs for computers the relevant question is whether the invention is of a *technical* nature ... Guidelines make it clear that the basic test of whether there is an invention within the meaning of Article 52(1) EPC is 'separate and distinct from the question whether the subject matter is susceptible of industrial application, is new and involves an inventive step'. If the subject matter claimed is not excluded from patentability as 'non-technical subject matter' the invention must still pass *inter alia* the test whether the invention involved an inventive step (Article 56 EPC). Patent protection is reserved for such inventions which go beyond the capacities of the so-called 'ordinary men skilled in the art'.

Faced with making such decisions, therefore, both the Technical Board of Appeals of the EPO and the courts in the UK need to assess whether there is a *technical* contribution to known art. If this is found, then the fact that the best method of doing it is by computer is no bar to patentability. However, the precise meaning of technical contribution in this sense has proved elusive; Tapper[83] suggests that the 'concept of "technical effect" is not self-evident' and Lloyd[84] has remarked that the 'question what constitutes a technical advance is not always susceptible of ready or precise answer'.

The issue has been further complicated by the fact that different approaches to the interpretation of the exclusion are possible. Gall[85] further points out that the EPC is a multilateral international treaty and so should be construed in the light of the corresponding international law, in particular Article 31(1) of the Vienna Convention, which requires the provisions of a treaty to be interpreted in good faith, taking into account the meaning of the words in context and having regard to the object and purpose of the provisions in question. Evidence of such a purposive construction can perhaps be identified in some of the decisions made under the EPC. In contrast, the UK courts lean towards a more literal or technical interpretation of 'as such'. However, since decisions under the EPC have been both referred to and taken into account in judgments under the Patents Act 1977 (as would be expected taking into account s 91(1) of that Act) the situation is by no means clear cut. Without doubt, therefore, the test for patentability of inventions relating to computer technology has proved difficult both to apply and to explain, and

83 Colin Tapper in *Handbook of European Software Law* (1995) Part II, M Lehmann and CF Tapper (eds), Clarendon.

84 Ian Lloyd, 'Patenting Software – Humpty Dumpty Rules' [1995] SLT 163 at 164.

85 Above, n 82.

the most appropriate way of examining it is to consider some of the applications made and whether or not it proved possible to establish a case for patentability.

One of the leading cases in this area is the decision of the Technical Board of Appeal in *Vicom*.[86] The application concerned a claim for a method of digitally processing images in the form of a two-dimensional array which could be used to enhance or restore the technical quality of such images. It was the computer program that embodied the inventive idea which both controlled the process and gave it its value, but it was held that the application was not for the program *'as such'*, but for the invention it was used to perform. A decisive point was that the application was susceptible of industrial application since it could be used for investigating the properties of a real or simulated object or for designing an industrial article. The requisite technical effect could therefore be ascertained.

Vicom/Computer-related invention: T208/84
[1987] EPOR 74

12. The Board of Appeal is of the opinion that a claim directed to a technical process which process is carried out under the control of a program (be this implemented in hardware or software) cannot be regarded as relating to a program *as such* within the meaning of Article 52(3) EPC, as it is the application of the program for determining the sequence of steps in the process for which in effect protection is sought. Consequently, such a claim is allowable under Article 52(2) and (3) EPC ...

15. ... Generally, claims which can be considered as being directed to a computer set-up to operate in accordance with a specific program (whether by means of hardware or software) for controlling or carrying out a technical process cannot be regarded as relating to a computer program *as such* and thus are not objectionable under Article 52(2) and (3) EPC ...

16. ... Generally speaking, an invention which would be patentable in accordance with conventional patentability criteria should not be excluded from protection by the mere fact that, for its implementation, modern technical means in the form of a computer program are used. Decisive is what technical contribution the invention as defined in the claim when considered as a whole makes to the known art ... it would seem illogical to grant protection for a technical process controlled by a suitable programmed computer but not for the computer itself when set up to execute control.

In contrast the IBM/Semantically related expressions application[87] was found not to be patentable. The claim was for a method of generating a list of expressions semantically related to an input linguistic expression using a programmable data processing system. The semantic relationship was of

86 [1987] EPOR 74.

87 T52/85 [1989] EPOR 454.

abstract linguistic information content and did not relate to any physical entity.

It may be argued that the test is easier to apply to claims such as those of *Vicom* and *IBM/Semantically related expressions* which could be said to represent opposite ends of the spectrum.[88] However, the application, *IBM/Data Processor Network*[89] is, perhaps, more equivocal. It referred to a data processing system consisting of a plurality of data processors interconnected as nodes in a telecommunications network. Novel procedures enabled this network of computers to maintain concurrent connections between a terminal and more than one applications program and to provide simultaneous on-line processing using several data files located at remote processors. Notwithstanding that the end result, an enhancement of the range of practical steps which could be performed by linked computers, was achieved using software, it was said to solve a problem which was essentially technical, even though that technical effect was manifested within the computer itself.

In the UK both *Hitachi's Application*[90] and *Wang Laboratories Inc's Application*[91] failed to gain patent protection for their products. In the Hitachi case the application was for a particular type of compiler program which was able to increase the speed of operation significantly. Hitachi tried to rely on the *Vicom* decision saying that as the compiler was acting on a physical entity (the source program) this therefore could be regarded as constituting a technical process. The examiner found that just because a mathematical method operated on a physical entity it did not automatically follow that it was used in a technical process. The invention claimed amounted to a claim for the compiler program itself and therefore must be excluded.

Wang Laboratories Application was an attempt to patent a computer system shell and expert system. Expert systems are computer programs that have been constructed, using the knowledge from a human expert, in such a way that they are capable of functioning at the same standard (at least) of human experts in a given field. They are used as high-level intellectual aids to their users. Most expert systems contain of a set of facts describing a particular problem domain and a set of assertions or inference rules defining relationships between the facts and specifying how new facts can be deduced from existing facts by means of the assertions. These attributes being known as the knowledge base.

In this case the examining officer said that this was merely a claim for a computer program, *as such*, and should be excluded. The applicant's argument was that this was use of a computer program in a novel way, and

88 Compare also IBM/Computer-related invention T115/85 [1990] EPOR 107 and IBM/Text processing T65/86 [1990] EPOR 181 for instance.

89 T06/83 [1990] EPOR 91.

90 [1991] RPC 415.

91 [1991] RPC 463.

was not a claim for a program, *as such*. In addition, it was submitted that the words 'a scheme, rule or method for performing a mental act' in s 1(2)(c) were intended only to exclude those schemes which were intended to be and could be performed by a human mind. The Patents Court disagreed, this was not the correct interpretation of this phrase, a scheme etc for performing a mental act was excluded whatever steps or processes were involved, such a scheme was still excluded if the method was performed by computer whether or not the computer program adopted steps that would not ordinarily be used by a human mind. Accordingly, the claim relating to the expert system was a claim to a scheme or method for performing a mental act using a computer program and was not allowable. The claim relating to the computer system shell was a claim for a computer program and nothing more. The computer remained separate even when programmed and did not combine with the program to form a new machine. It is this last fact which seems to be the salient feature on which patentability of computer software depends.

The difficulty of applying the test can be seen in *Re Gale's Application*[92] which was a claim for a new method of calculating square roots, encapsulated in ROM (read only memory). This was first of all refused by the patents examiner on the ground that it was merely an application for a computer program. This decision was reversed by the Patents Court in which Aldous J argued that a distinction could be made between a disk containing a software program, which would not be patentable and the hard-wired ROM. This distinction could be made, in his view, because the ROM was used as a dedicated piece of apparatus to perform a particular task. This reasoning was not accepted by the Court of Appeal, in which Nicholls LJ acknowledged the importance of decisions made under the EPC in deciding such cases, and, referring to the *Vicom* claim, restored the original decision.

Re Gale's Application
[1991] RPC 305 at 327
Court of Appeal

> **Nicholls LJ** In the present case Mr Gale claims to have discovered an algorithm. Clearly that, *as such*, is not patentable. It is an intellectual discovery which, for good measure, falls squarely within one of the items, mathematical method, listed in section 1(2). But the nature of this discovery is such that it has a practical application, in that it enables instructions to be written for conventional computers in a way which will, so it is claimed, expedite one of the calculations frequently made with the aid of a computer. In my view the application of Mr Gale's formulae for the purpose of writing computer instructions is sufficient to dispose of the contention that he is claiming a mathematical method *as such*.
>
> That still leaves the difficulty that those instructions when written, and without more, are not patentable, because they constitute a computer program. Is there

92 [1991] RPC 305.

> something more? In the end I have come to the conclusion that there is not. The attraction of Mr Gale's case lies in the simple approach that, as claimed, he has found an improved means of carrying out an everyday function of computers. To that extent, and in that respect, his program makes a more efficient use of the computer's resources. A computer, including a pocket calculator with a square root function, will be a better computer when programmed with Mr Gale's instructions. So it may. But the instructions do not embody a technical process which exists outside the computer. Nor, as I understand the case as presented to us, do the instructions solve a 'technical' problem lying within the computer ... I confess to having difficulty in identifying clearly the boundary line between what is and what is not a technical problem for this purpose ... in the present case Mr Gale has devised an improvement in programming. What his instructions do, but it is all they do, is to prescribe for the cpu [central processing unit] in a conventional computer a different set of calculations from those normally prescribed when the user wants a square root. I do not think that makes a claim to those instructions other than a claim to the instructions as such. The instructions do not define a new way of operating the computer in a technical sense ...

Although there have been suggestions from time to time that the basic test of the 'technical contribution to the known art' might be subject to modification from time to time,[93] the centrality of the basic test was affirmed in *Fujitsu Limited's Application.*[94] The application was for a method and apparatus for modelling a synthetic crystal structure for designing inorganic materials. The applicant argued that, where there had been a technical contribution to known art, a patent should not be refused and, once a mental act had been tied to a technical application, it ceased to be merely a mental act and could, therefore, become the subject matter of a patent. The examiner distinguished a manipulation of the technical quality of the data (as in *Vicom*) and the manipulation of the content of the information in this application. The question then was whether the fact that the image represented, ie the crystal structure was a 'technical artefact', gave the whole application a technical character. The examiner found that, on the evidence, the application was not only for a computer program, but was, in substance, a scheme or method for performing a mental act and was therefore unpatentable. This decision was upheld on appeal in which Laddie J summarised the requirements for patentability of computer programs.

Fujitsu Limited's Application
[1996] RPC 511 at 530
Patents Court

> **Laddie J** It seems to me that the relevant provisions of the Act and the EPC ... produce the following principles:

93 See, eg, Tim Press, 'Patent Protection for Computer-related Inventions' in Chris Reed (ed), *Computer Law* (1996) 3rd edn, Blackstone Press.

94 [1996] RPC 511.

1. The types of subject matter referred to in section 1(2) are excluded from patentability as a matter of policy. This is so whether the matter is technical or not.
2. The exclusion from patentability is a matter of substance not form. Therefore the exclusion under section 1(2) extends to any form of passive carrier or recording of excluded subject matter. Thus, merely because a piece of paper is in principle patentable (save to the extent that it lacks novelty), it is not permissible, for example, to record a literary work (section 1(2)(b)) or a computer programs (section 1(2)(c)) on a piece of paper and then seek patent monopoly for the paper bearing the recorded work. Similarly, it is not permissible, without more, to seek protection for a computer program when it is stored on a magnetic medium or *merely* loaded into a computer.
3. *Prima facie* a computer running under the control of one program is a different piece of apparatus from the same computer when running under the control of another program. It follows that a claim to a computer when controlled by a program or to a method of controlling a computer by a program or to a method of carrying out a process by use of a computer so controlled *can* be the subject of patent protection. However, because the court is concerned with substance not form, it is not enough for the designer of a new program to seek protection for his creation merely by framing it in one of these terms. The court or patent office must direct its attention not to the fact that the program is controlling the computer but to what the computer, so controlled, is doing.
4. Therefore a data processing system operating to produce a novel result would not be deprived of protection on the ground that it was a program as such. On the other hand, even if the effect of the program is to make the computer perform in a novel way, it is still necessary to look at precisely what the computer is doing, ie at the nature of the process being carried out. If all that is being done, as a matter of substance, is the performance of one of the activities defined under section 1(2) as unprotectable, then it is still unprotectable.

In accordance with these principles, just as it would be possible to obtain a patent, considerations of novelty aside, for a faster chip or a more effective storage medium, there is no reason in principle or logic why modification of the computer to achieve the same speed or storage increase by means of software should be excluded from protection. The fact that the advance is achieved in software rather than hardware should not affect patentability. To use in a slightly different context Nicholls LJ's words from *Gale's Application*, that would be to exalt form over substance. Similarly, if a new process achieved by mechanical means would be patentable, there is no reason why the same process achieved by computer means should be any less patentable. If that is so, it does not matter whether the patent claims are drafted in terms of a process controlled by a computer, a computer when programmed in particular way or a method of controlling a computer. In each case the substance of the invention is the same.

... Is it enough for [counsel for the applicant] to demonstrate that his client's

> advance is of a technical character and relates to a technical field? The answer depends on what is meant by the word 'technical'. [He] appeared to me to use it as if it covered all areas of practical development which were not associated with the liberal arts. That is not what I understand to have been the way in which it was used in the decided cases. In particular in *VICOM* and *IBM* it is only processes or methods which do not fall foul of the express exclusions from patentability under section 1(2) which are treated as suitably 'technical'. Therefore use of the word 'technical', the meaning of which takes its colour from its context, is apt to confuse. What counts in this area is whether the method or process controlled by the program or the computer running it is one which itself is excluded from patentability.

The problems surrounding the application of the test for patentability of computer programs are unlikely to deter the large producers of computer systems from seeking patents for their products where they feel this is appropriate. This may, perhaps, be given additional impetus in the light of some of the uncertainty surrounding the application of copyright principles to computer programs. If a computer program can be granted a patent then the producer will enjoy the monopoly that goes with it and will cease to be concerned about issues of decompilation, adaptation and so on. Given the commercial importance of many software products and products containing software, it is not surprising that patent applications are filed in instances where designers/developers perceive novelty and inventiveness.

CHAPTER THREE

PROTECTING AND EXPLOITING RIGHTS IN SOFTWARE – CONTRACT

INTRODUCTION

Types of contract

There are numerous different types of contract which can relate to computer hardware and software: contracts for the sale or lease of hardware, or of a hardware and software package; contracts licensing software; contracts for the maintenance of hardware or software (which may be called support contracts); distribution agreements between manufacturers and distributors of software or hardware; bureau services contracts under which one party, which has computer hardware and software, supplies computer services or facilities to a party which does not have its own hardware or software. These are just some examples of the different types of contract dealing with computer hardware and software which may be encountered. It is not the purpose of this chapter to set out in detail the terms which might occur in each type of contract, rather it will deal with some of the issues which may arise in relation to contracts concerned with computer software. The focus is on software. Hardware clearly constitutes goods and contracts dealing with goods are familiar from other contexts. It is software which principally poses the significantly different questions. The point should also be made that, although the term 'software' can be used widely, to mean anything which is not hardware, unless otherwise indicated, it will be used here to mean computer programs. This is the type of software which raises significant issues for information technology law.

Bespoke and standard software

Discussion of contracts dealing with software requires a distinction to be made between different basic types of software. At one end of a spectrum is 'bespoke' software. That is software written for a particular user. At the other end of the spectrum, is mass produced software which is simply bought 'off the shelf' by many users. Somewhere in between will be modified standard software for which the basic programme will be the same in each case, but it will then be modified to some extent to meet the needs of the individual user. This division may be relevant, for example, in considering whether a contract for the supply of software should be regarded as a contract for the sale of goods or the supply of services (or something else).

The software licence[1]

When computers first began to be sold the software was merely something to be supplied with them. It simply was not seen as something to be separately exploited. The focus was on the hardware. It was in the early 1970s that serious consideration began to be given to software as a resource to be protected and exploited and the practice grew up of using licences to do so. The licence would set out what the acquirer could, and could not, do with the software. Despite initial uncertainly, it has become clear that licensing does, indeed, provide an appropriate approach to the exploitation of software. With the recognition that copyright can exist in software,[2] the licence has become the vehicle by which the acquirer is given rights to use the software. In so doing, it provides the means by which those who develop software can recoup the large costs of that development, make a profit, and find encouragement to further development.

There are difficulties in licensing software when the developer does not deal directly with the end user and with the trend away from bespoke, to 'off the shelf' software, this has become a common situation. If the end user does not deal with the developer how is his, or her, use to be licensed? There may be a chain of contracts. The end user may be a sub-licensee of a distributor who obtained a licence from the developer – the distributor's licence including the right to create sub-licenses. However, the mass production of standard software has posed its own legal difficulties. How are licences to be 'mass produced' when someone can acquire software simply by walking into a shop, selecting software from a display, and paying for it at a till. The attempt to create licences in this type of case by means of what has been called the 'shrink wrap' licence will be returned to below.[3]

Goods or services or something else?

One problem which is of particular conceptual and practical significance is the legal nature of software. Obviously, a programme is, at bottom, information and it is protected by intellectual property rights in the form of copyright. However, could software also be regarded as 'goods'? Should the supply of software be regarded as a service? On a practical level, these questions arise in the context of the applicability of the legislation such as the Sale of Goods Act 1979, the Supply of Goods and Services Act 1982 and the Commercial Agents

1 Freed, 'The Protection of Computer Software in the USA' (1982) Computers and Law 6, 'Legal Interests' Relation to Software Programs', Computer Law and Practice, May/June 1986, 141, 'The Birth, Life and Death of Computer Law' (1990–91) 7 Comp Law and Security Rep 107, 155, (1992) 8 Comp Law and Security Rep 19.

2 See now ss 1 and 3. of the Copyright, Designs and Patents Act 1988.

3 See p 107.

(Council Directive) Regulations 1993. The issue of classification will be returned to in the next chapter when the question of liability for defective software is addressed.

Scope of the chapter

A single chapter in a book on information technology law cannot deal, in depth, with all aspects of contract law. Instead, the discussion will focus on some aspects of contract law which are particularly relevant in the context of software transactions.

SUITABILITY/QUALITY OF SOFTWARE

Pre-contractual statements

The consumer who wants software will either simply walk into a shop and purchase it 'off the shelf' or select and purchase it through a mail-order catalogue. Businesses may acquire hardware and software in the same way if all that is required is, for example, a straightforward word-processing package. However, if a business wants software which is tailored to its particular needs, it will contract for 'bespoke' software, to be written for it, or for standard software to be modified to meet its particular circumstances, and those circumstances might relate not only to the type of business but also to the need for new software to be compatible with an existing system.

In any of the above situations, but particularly in relation to bespoke or modified standard software, there may be discussions between the supplier and the acquirer as to the needs of the acquirer and whether the software will fulfill them. If, after the acquisition, the acquirer is unhappy with the software, disputes may arise as to what was said about it and the legal effect of any such statements. The acquirer may claim that the supplier is liable on the basis that the pre-contractual statements became terms or that they were misrepresentations and such claims have occurred in relation to the acquisition of software and computer systems in, for example, *Micron Computer systems Ltd v Wang*[4] and *Mackenzie Patten & Co v British Olivetti Ltd*.[5] These two possible bases of liability should be considered.

(i) Pre-contractual statements becoming terms

The question of whether a pre-contractual statement has become a term is often put in terms of whether the statement was a mere representation or a

4 (1990) 9 May, unreported.

5 (1984) 11 January, unreported.

warranty.[6] The basic test for whether a pre-contractual statement became a term of the contract is the intention of the parties[7] and that intention is objectively ascertained.[8] It is not easy to apply a test dependent upon the ascertainment of intention. However, certain indicators of the parties' intention have been focused on by the courts, such as the situation where it is clear to both parties that the statement in question is key to the decision to contract.[9] However, in the context of software contracts, the indicators which are most likely to be relevant are reliance and the relative expertise of the parties. This relates to the situation in which one party relies on the statements of the other party and that other party possesses the greater expertise. This can be illustrated by the contrasting cases of *Oscar Chess Ltd v Williams*[10] and *Dick Bentley Productions Ltd v Harold Smith (Motors) Ltd.*[11]

Oscar Chess Ltd v Williams [1957] 1 All ER 325

The defendant sold a Morris car to the plaintiff car dealer. The dealer was familiar with the car and had been given lifts in it. The defendant innocently described the car as a 1948 model and produced the registration book ('log-book') which stated it to be a 1948 car. At some time before the defendant became the owner of the car, its registration book had been tampered with and the car was actually a 1939 model. There was no difference in appearance between a 1948 and a 1939 model and the plaintiff did not discover the truth until eight months after the purchase. The plaintiff took action to recover the difference between what he paid for the car and what he would have paid for a 1939 model. He claimed that it had been a term of the contract that the car was a 1939 model. His claim failed – no such term was found.

Denning LJ The material distinction here is between a statement which is a term of the contract and a statement which is only an innocent misrepresentation. This distinction is best expressed by the ruling of Holt CJ, 'Was it intended as a warranty or not?' using the word 'warranty' there in its ordinary English meaning; because it gives the exact shade of meaning required. It is something to which a man must be taken to bind himself.

In applying this test, however, some misunderstanding has arisen by the

6 Warranty can be used in more than one sense. In this context it is used simply to mean a term. It may also be used in contrast with conditions and innominate terms to designate a particular type of term, the breach of which leads to specific consequences. Breach of a warranty gives rise only to a right to damages. Breach of a condition gives a right to damages and also to terminate the contract. Breach of an innominate term gives a right to damages but only gives a right to terminate if the breach substantially deprives the injured party of all the benefit which they were intended to derive from the contract. See Koffman & Macdonald, *The Law of Contract* (1995) 2nd edn, pp 111–26, Tolley.

7 *Heilbut, Symons & Co v Buckleton* [1913] AC 30.

8 For a case which clearly shows the need for an objective approach, see *Thake v Maurice* [1986] 1 All ER 497.

9 *Bannerman v White* (1861) 10 CBNS 844. See further Koffman & Macdonald, *op cit,* pp 89–93.

10 [1957] 1 All ER 325.

11 [1965] 2 All ER 65.

use of the word 'intended'. it is sometimes supposed that the tribunal must look into the minds of the parties to see what they themselves intended. That is a mistake ... The question whether a warranty was intended depends on the conduct of the parties, on their words and behaviour, rather than on their thoughts. If an intelligent bystander would reasonably infer that a warranty was intended that will suffice ...

It is instructive to take some recent instances to show how the courts have approached this question. When the seller states a fact which is or should be within his own knowledge and of which the buyer is ignorant, intending that the buyer should act on it and he does so, it is easy to infer a warranty: see *Couchman v Hill* ([1947] 1 All ER 103), where a farmer stated that a heffer was unserved, and *Harling v Eddy* ([1951] 2 All ER 212), where he stated that there was nothing wrong with her. So also if the seller makes a promise about something which is or should be within his own control; see *Birch v Paramount Estates Ltd* ((1956) 16 Estates Gazette 396), decided on Oct 2, 1956 in this court, where the seller stated that the house would be as good as the show house. If, however, the seller when he states a fact, makes it clear that he has no knowledge of his own but has got his information elsewhere, and is merely passing it on, it is not easy to imply a warranty. Such a case was *Routledge v Mackay* ([1954] 1 All ER 855), where the seller stated that a motor cycle combination was a 1942 model, and pointed to the corroboration of that statement to be found in the registration book, and it was held that there was no warranty.

Turning now to the present case, much depends on the precise words that were used. If the seller says, 'I believe that the car is a 1948 Morris. Here is the registration book to prove it', there is clearly no warranty. It is a statement of belief, not a contractual promise. If, however, the seller says: 'I guarantee that it is a 1948 Morris. This is borne out by the registration book, but you need not rely solely on that. I give you my own guarantee that it is', there is clearly a warranty. The seller is making himself contractually responsible, even though the registration book is wrong.

... What is the proper inference from the known facts? it must have been obvious to both that the seller himself had no personal knowledge of the year when the car was made. He only became owner after a great number of changes. He must have been relying on the registration book. It is unlikely that such a person would warrant the year of manufacture. The most that he would do would be to state his belief, and then produce the registration book in verification of it. In these circumstances the intelligent bystander would, I suggest, say that the seller did not intend to bind himself so as to warrant that the car was a 1948 model. If the seller was asked to pledge himself to it, he would at once have said 'I cannot do that. I have only the log-book to go by, the same as you' ...

***Dick Bentley Productions Ltd v Harold Smith (Motors) Ltd* [1965] 2 All ER 65**

DB asked the car dealer S to find him a 'well vetted' Bentley car. S found a car and showed it to DB. He told DB that it had only been driven 20,000 miles since a new engine had been fitted and that was the mileage shown on the odometer. DB purchased the car and had numerous problems with it. It was discovered that it had done a far greater mileage than 20,000 since the new engine had been fitted. DB sued on the basis that the mileage had become a term of the contract – his claim was successful.

Lord Denning MR Looking at the cases once more, as we have done so often, it seems to me that if a representation is made in the course of dealings for a contract, for the very purpose of inducing the other party to act on it, and it actually induces him to act on it by entering into the contract, that is *prima facie* ground for inferring that the representation was intended as a warranty ... Suffice it that the representation was intended to be acted on and was in fact acted on. But the maker of the representation can rebut this inference if he can show that it was an innocent misrepresentation, in that he was innocent of fault in making it, and that it would not be reasonable in the circumstances for him to be bound by it. In the *Oscar Chess* case the inference was rebutted ... Whereas in the present case it is very different. The inference is not rebutted. Here we have a dealer, Mr Smith, who was in a position to know, or at least to find out, the history of the car. He could get it by writing to the makers. He did not do so. Indeed it was done later. When the history of this car was examined, his statement turned out to be quite wrong. He ought to have known better. There was no reasonable foundation for it.

These cases illustrate that the courts regard the expertise of one party as relevant to the question of whether a statement has become a term. In the context of a software contract, the point can be further illustrated by *Mackenzie Patten & Co v British Olivetti Ltd*.[12] In that case a solicitors' practice purchased hardware and software. The purchasers had no expertise or knowledge of computers and relied on the seller's statements as to its suitability for their needs and as to the functions it could perform. It proved unsuitable and could not perform one of the functions which the solicitors had wanted. The solicitors sued, claiming both breach of a term and misrepresentation. They succeeded on the basis that the seller's statements had become terms of the contract. The judge emphasised the purchasers' lack of expertise and reliance on that of the seller.[13] The remedy, as is usually the case for breach of contract, was damages.

Before leaving the question of whether a pre-contractual statement has become a term, some consideration should be given to the 'parol evidence rule'. This becomes relevant when, for example, there is a document recording contract terms but it does not include the contents of a pre-contractual statement which, it is being argued, became a term. It has been said that 'it is firmly established as a rule of law that parol evidence cannot be used to add to, vary or contradict a deed or other written document'.[14] In other words, where there is a contractual document, it might be argued that the 'parol

12 (1984) 11 January, unreported.

13 The alternative claim, based on misrepresentation was not addressed by the judge once he had found for the purchasers on the basis of a breach.

14 *Jacobs v Batavia and General Plantations Trust* [1924] 1 Ch 287, Lawrence J at p 295.

evidence rule' prevented any evidence being brought that a pre-contractual statement furnished an additional term. However, the status of the so-called 'parol evidence rule' is doubtful. It may be nothing more than a presumption that if there is a written agreement which looks like a complete contract, it is the complete contract. But that presumption can be rebutted if it is shown that there were intended to be other terms. Once looked at in this light the 'rule' ceases to have much force. In addition, whilst taking the view of the 'rule' indicated here, the Law Commission also concluded that even if it was, properly speaking, a rule of law, there were so many exceptions to it that it was unlikely to work injustice.[15]

(ii) Pre-contractual statements as misrepresentations[16]

A misrepresentation requires a statement of existing or past fact by the misrepresentor, to the misrepresentee, which induces the misrepresentee to contract with the misrepresentor. In other words, what is needed is a pre-contractual statement of fact by one party, to the other, which that other party relies upon in deciding to contract.[17] As has already been suggested, reliance may well be present where there is an imbalance of knowledge or expertise, as there often will be in the acquisition of software. The point which needs to be considered here, because of its particular relevance to the situation where advice is being given on the suitability of software, is the division between statements of opinion and statements of fact.

It has already been stated that, for a misrepresentation to be found, there must be a statement of fact. Statements of opinion, intention, or law will not suffice.[18] However, in some situations, the courts have been willing to find statements of fact where, at first sight, there is merely a statement of opinion or intention or law. That is obviously the case where what is stated to be one party's intention or opinion simply is not that party's intention or opinion – clearly there is a misrepresentation that the party has that intention[19] or holds that opinion. Less obviously, the courts have also been willing to find statements of fact where what is, apparently, merely a statement of opinion, is made by an expert or the person who is simply in the best position to assess the situation. So, for example, in *Smith v Land & House Property Corporation*[20] the court was concerned with a statement in the sale particulars of a hotel that

15 Law Com 154 (1986). Marston [1986] CLJ 192.

16 On misrepresentation generally see Koffman & Macdonald, *op cit*, Chapter 13.

17 *Smith v Chadwick* (1884) 9 App Cas 187. It is disputed whether there is a requirement of 'materiality', ie that the reasonable person would have relied on the statement. See Koffman & Macdonald, *op cit*, pp 251–52.

18 *Bissett v Wilkinson* [1927] AC 177.

19 *Edgington v Fitzmaurice* (1885) 29 Ch D 459.

20 (1884) 28 Ch D 7.

it was occupied by a 'most desirable tenant' for a term of 272 years. The tenant in question had not been paying his rent on time and Bowen LJ said:[21]

> if the facts are not equally known to both sides, then a statement of opinion by the one who knows the facts best involves very often a statement of material fact, for he impliedly states that he knows facts which justify his opinion.

The court concluded that stating that the occupier was a 'desirable tenant' was not merely a statement of opinion. There was also a misrepresentation. Similarly, this type of argument might prove relevant in relation to a software contract. In that context, it is likely to be the statement of an expert which is in question and the implied statement of fact there would seem to be that the expert has properly used his, or her, expertise in forming his, or her, opinion.[22]

A misrepresentation makes a contract voidable and so the contract can be rescinded provided one of the bars to rescission is not operative.[23] Damages can also be claimed for misrepresentation. If the case is one where the misrepresentation involves fraud, the tort action for deceit can be used. Alternatively, damages may be available because the situation is covered by the tort action for negligent misstatement,[24] or because it falls within the ambit of s 2(1) of the Misrepresentation Act 1967. All of the actions for damages, including that under s 2(1)[25] will result in damages being calculated on the tortious, rather than the contractual, basis – they will put the injured party in the position he, or she, would have been in had the misrepresentation not occurred, ie their pre-contractual position.[26]

The action under s 2(1) will normally be the most favourable of the actions for damages. Obviously, the common law action for negligent misstatement merely requires the injured party to prove negligence, rather than the fraud which has to be established for the action for deceit, although the action for negligent misstatement will also require proof of a duty of care. However, the action under s 2(1) is generally the easiest for the injured party to use. Under s 2(1) it is for the person who made the misrepresentation to prove that he, or she, reasonably believed in the truth of what was being asserted, ie it is for the

21 At p 15. See also *Brown v Raphael* [1958] 1 Ch 636.

22 *Esso Petroleum Co Ltd v Mardon* [1976] QB 801.

23 The common law bars are (i) *restitutio in integrum* has become impossible (ie it is impossible to return the parties to their pre-contractual position), (ii) third party rights (eg a *bona fide* third party has acquired a proprietary interest in the goods which were the subject matter of the contract), (iii) affirmation of the contract by the injured party, after he, or she has acquired knowledge of the misrepresentation, (iv) lapse of time. Misrepresentation Act, s 2(2), is sometimes referred to as a 'statutory bar' since it allows the courts to prevent or undo rescission if it would be 'equitable so to do'. See further Koffman & Macdonald, *op cit*, pp 263–68.

24 *Hedley Byrne & Co Ltd v Heller & Partners Ltd* [1964] AC 465.

25 *Royscott Trust Ltd v Rogerson* [1991] 3 All ER 294.

26 Contractual damages for breach will put the injured party in the position he, or she, would have been in had the contract not been breached, ie the position the injured party would have been in had the contract been performed (*Robinson v Harman* (1880) 5 App Cas 25, Parke B at p 35).

misrepresentor to disprove negligence under this action – reversing the burden of proof from that applicable under the action for negligent misstatement[27] – and, of course, no duty of care is required.

TERMS

When software is in question, some of the most significant terms will be those licencing its use and licence terms will be considered below. Here we should briefly consider sources of contractual terms other than the pre-contractual statements looked at above and give some further consideration to the problem of the acquisition of suitable software, particularly in the context of development contracts.

If the injured party signed a contractual document its contents will provide contractual terms whether he, or she, has any knowledge of them or not.[28] If such a document is not signed, then, in the absence of actual knowledge of its contents, its effectiveness to import terms into the contract will depend upon whether there has been reasonably sufficient notice of it.[29] That is an objective test, requiring sufficient notice for the reasonable person, rather than the particular individual concerned.[30] Even if clauses have not been appropriately introduced into a particular transaction, they may be imported if there has, previously, been a consistent course of previous dealings between the parties, involving those terms.[31] There is a considerable degree of artificiality in the way in which clauses can become terms of a contract. It means that written contractual terms, particularly standard terms, may be seen as having very little to do with the agreement of the parties in any subjective sense.

Contract terms may be implied[32] as well as express. They may be implied by statute as for example with the terms implied by the ss 13–15 of the Sale of

27 A factor which was vital to the success of the injured party in *Howard Marine & Dredging Co Ltd v A Ogden & Sons (Excavations) Ltd* [1978] QB 574. (The absence of any need to establish a duty of care under s 2(1) was also of significance.) The action under s 2(1) also has the benefit of at least some of the rules applicable to the tort action based on fraud rather than negligence such as the laxer remoteness test – *Royscott Trust Ltd v Rogerson (but see Gran Gelato Ltd v Richcliff (Group) Ltd* [1992] 1 All ER 865 in relation to the question of contributory negligence.

28 *L'Estrange v F Graucob Ltd* [1934] 2 KB 394. There are limited exceptions. If the contents of the terms has been misrepresented then the part misrepresented will not be enforced (*Curtis v Chemical Cleaning and Dyeing Co* [1951] 1 KB 805). Signed terms are also subject to a claim of *non est factum*.

29 *Parker v S E Ry Co Ltd* [1877] 2 CPD 416. See generally Koffman & Macdonald, *op cit*, pp 135–41. See further p 108.

30 *Thompson v L M & S Ry* [1930] 1 KB 41.

31 See eg *Kendall v Lillico & Sons* [1969] 2 AC 31, *Circle Freight International v Medeast Gulf Exports* [1988] 2 Lloyd's Rep 427. See generally Macdonald (1988) 8 Legal Studies 48, Koffman & Macdonald, *op cit*, pp 141–47.

32 See generally Koffman & Macdonald, *op cit*, pp 96–106.

Goods Act 1979, which are considered in the next chapter. Otherwise, at common law, they may be implied in fact, in law, or by custom. Terms are implied in fact on the basis of the parties' intention, but within very narrow confines. The tests applied are whether it is necessary to imply the term to give the contract 'business efficacy'[33] and also the 'officious bystander' test, ie whether the term was so obvious that, had an officious bystander approached the contracting parties and suggested it, they would have said that of course the term in question was included.[34] The implication of terms in law is not based on the intention of the parties, but upon necessity and the type of contract,[35] ie the term must be one which it is 'necessary' to imply into the type of contract in question and not merely the particular contract. Intention is relevant only to the extent that a term will not be implied in the face of a contrary term.[36]

DEVELOPMENT CONTRACTS

The trend is away from bespoke software but contracts to develop software, or a computer system, for a particular business are still of some significance and they may create the most difficult problems in relation to the contents of the contract. One particular difficulty with such contracts is identifying exactly what the acquiring party requires. As part of the contracting process, the parties should draw up a detailed functional specification, which then becomes part of the contract. This should state, in detail, what the proposed software will do. It may not be easy to draw up such a document – the software developer is an expert in software and what can be done with it but he, or she, is not an expert in the acquirer's business, whatever that may be, and it is obvious that problems may arise from this information gap. The acquirer may end up with a system which does not do some of what he, or she, needed it to do because those needs have not been explained to the software developer. In *Micron Computer Systems Ltd v Wang (UK) Ltd*[37] the purchaser of a system had expected the system to perform what he termed 'transaction logging'. It did not do so. It was found that that did not mean that the system was in breach of a term that it should be reasonably fit for the buyer's particular purpose. The buyer had never made known to the seller that 'transaction logging' was required.

33 *The Moorcock* (1889) 14 PD 64.

34 *Shirlaw v Southern Foundries Ltd* [1939] 2 KB 206, Mackinnon LJ at p 227.

35 *Liverpool City Council v Irwin* [1976] 2 All ER 39.

36 *Johnstone v Bloomsbury Health Authority* [1991] 2 All ER 293 – the Court of Appeal indicated that an express contrary term might be treated as an exclusion clause falling within the Unfair Contract Terms Act 1977 in appropriate circumstances (see Macdonald (1992) 12 Legal Studies 277).

37 (1990) 9 May, unreported.

It is difficult to draw up specifications of what the software should do. However, once that is done, the difficulty for the developer is the technical one of designing software which will do what is required. Once a program has been written, it will need to be tested and, as a far as possible, 'debugged'. An interesting view of this process, and of what would not amount to a breach was taken in *Saphena Computing*.

***Saphena Computing Ltd v Allied Collection Agencies Ltd* [1995] FSR 616**

Staughton LJ ... software is not necessarily a commodity which is handed over or delivered once and for all at one time. It may well have to be tested and modified as necessary. It would not be a breach of contract at all to deliver software in the first instance with a defect in it. That seems to be confirmed in a passage in the expert report of Mr Larner, a witness called by the suppliers, dealing with the nature of the commodity. He said this:

> 'Just as no software developer can reasonably expect a buyer to tell him what is required without a process of feedback and reassessment, so no buyer should expect a supplier to get his programs right first time. He too, needs feedback on whether he has been successful. This is why the buyer needs to run acceptance tests using typical business transactions to ensure that each works correctly. Inevitably, though, some will not. This may be the supplier's fault but it is equally possible that the buyer may have got his requirements wrong, have expressed them badly or unwittingly have used terms which were open to different interpretations. Whatever the cause, the programs have to be modified and then retested until the correct result is achieved.'

We were told that there was no dispute as to that passage, although there was or may have been a dispute as to what acceptance tests there were. It seems to show in my judgment, as I have already said, that software is not a commodity which is delivered once, only once, and once and for all, but one which will necessarily be accompanied by a degree of testing and modification. Naturally it could be expected that the supplier will carry out those tasks. He should have both the right and duty to do so. For somebody else to modify another person's software would necessarily, as the judge found in another connection, involve a degree of learning time.

So I conclude that it was part of the contract that the suppliers in this case should have the right and the duty to test and modify as necessary the software they supplied. No doubt there was a time limit for that purpose – a reasonable time is that which the law would ordinarily supply.

Saphena Computing raises a number of issues which need to be considered here – the idea of delivery followed by further work to bring software up to standard, and acceptance tests.

Delivery and further work

When goods are sold, there is a point at which the property in the goods and the risk, passes to the purchaser. The 'property' in goods is, basically, their ownership. It can be distinct from delivery and there is no necessary connection between the passing of property and delivery. 'Risk' normally passes to the buyer at the same time as property passes.[38] The 'risk' in question is not defined by the Sale of Goods Act 1979, but it would seem to be the risk that goods will be wholly, or partly, destroyed or damaged, or lost by theft, without the fault of either party.[39] The point to be made here is that it is the time at which risk passes that consideration needs to be given to the question of compliance with the statutory implied terms,[40] such as whether the goods are reasonably fit for the buyer's particular purpose. If the same approach is taken to software then, in asking whether the software is reasonably fit for the acquirer's purpose, what should be focused on is not delivery, but the passing of risk. It is at the point that risk passes that the question of whether the software is of the appropriate quality should be asked. The notion that risk and property could pass in the software and yet that there would remain an extended period over which the software could be brought up to standard is inconsistent with the analytical framework suggested by the approach taken to sale of goods contracts. It might be taken to suggest that software should not be regarded as goods.[41] However, whether software is goods, there must be a point in time at which it has to comply with the standard specified. In *St Albans City and District Council v ICL*,[42] in dismissing submissions based on the line taken by Staughton LJ in *Saphena*, Nourse LJ said:

> 'Parties who respectively agree to supply and acquire a system recognising that it is still in the course of development cannot be taken, merely by virtue of that recognition, to intend that the supplier shall be at liberty to supply software which cannot perform the function expected of it at the stage of development at which it is supplied.'

It would seem that, rather than viewing the situation as one in which there would be a breach but for the fact that the software is still being worked on, as seems to have been the case in *Saphena*, greater consideration should be given to the appropriate point in time at which the contract requires compliance with the relevant standard.

---

38 Section 20 of the Sale of Goods Act 1979.

39 Sealy & Hooley, *Text and Materials in Commercial Law* (1994) p 242.

40 See *Benjamin's Sale of Goods*, 4th edn, AG Guest (ed), para 11–056.

41 See p 152 ff.

42 [1996] 4 All ER 481.

Acceptance tests

One further factor to be considered here is that of 'acceptance'. In the context of the sale of goods, acceptance is defined by ts 35 of the Sale of Goods Act 1979.

35. Acceptance

(1) The buyer is deemed to have accepted the goods subject to subsection (2) below

(a) when he intimates to the seller that he has accepted them; or

(b) when the goods have been delivered to him and he does any act in relation to them which is inconsistent with the ownership of the seller.

(2) Where goods are delivered to the buyer, and he has not previously examined them, he is not deemed to have accepted them under subsection (1) above until he has had a reasonable opportunity of examining them for the purpose

(a) of ascertaining whether they are in conformity with the contract; and

(b) in the case of a contract for sale by sample, of comparing the bulk with the sample.

(3) Where the buyer deals as consumer or (in Scotland) the contract of sale is a consumer contract, the buyer cannot lose his right to rely on subsection (2) above by agreement, waiver or otherwise.

(4) The buyer is also deemed to have accepted the goods when after the lapse of a reasonable time he retains the goods without intimating to the seller that he has rejected them.

(5) The questions that are material in determining for the purposes of subsection (4) above whether a reasonable time has elapsed include whether the buyer has had a reasonable opportunity of examining the goods for the purpose mentioned in subsection (2) above.

(6) The buyer is not by virtue of this section deemed to have accepted the goods merely because

(a) he asks for, or agrees to, their repair by or under an arrangement with the seller; or

(b) the goods are delivered to another under a sub-sale or other disposition.

(7) Where the contract is for the sale of goods making one or more commercial units, a buyer accepting any goods included in a unit is deemed to have accepted all the goods making the unit; and in this subsection 'commercial unit' means a unit division of which would materially impair the value of the goods or the character of the unit.

The significance of acceptance, in the context of sale of goods, is that, if goods are 'accepted' within the meaning of s 35(1), the right to reject for breach of a condition is lost, and the breach will be treated merely as a breach of warranty.[43] The question which must be asked is whether, if 'acceptance tests' are specified in a contract for the supply of software they are to be understood as having the same effect as 'acceptance' under the Sale of Goods Act 1979? Do they show that the acquirer of software has 'intimated' his acceptance to the supplier[44] and thereby lost the right to reject the goods, but retaining the right to claim damages? At common law, affirmation of a contract by the injured party, and the loss thereby of the right to terminate the contract for breach of condition, can only occur once the injured party knows of the breach, although, in limited circumstances, an injured party might also be prevented from terminating by waiver or estoppel.

Obviously, it will be important to determine if the contract is one for the sale of goods,[45] but the contract itself might make clear the impact of the successful completion of the acceptance tests. However, it can be suggested that, particularly if the contractual provision is more restrictive of the acquirer's remedies than would otherwise be the case, either on the basis of the 1979 Act or the common law, the relevant contractual provision could be treated as an exemption clause, the effectiveness of which could be subject to the Unfair Contract Terms Act 1977.[46]

MODIFYING THE CONTRACTUAL OBLIGATIONS

The point has been made that, at the time when a contract is made, it may be difficult for the parties to accurately define the software required, particularly when a development contract is in question. Additionally, the software developer may encounter greater difficulties in producing the software required than was anticipated when the contract was made. These factors mean that software development contracts may well need to be modified before their performance is completed and a number of particular difficulties can arise in relation to contractual modifications. The more generally recognised ones of consideration and duress will be looked at below, but first, a brief look should be taken at the way in which the difficulties of initially defining the software to be created was dealt with in *Saphena Computing Ltd v Allied Collection Agencies Ltd*.[47]

In *Saphena* the acquirer was in business as a debt collecting agency. It made two contracts for the acquisition of software from the supplier. The first

43 Section 11(4).

44 See s 35(1)(a).

45 See p 150.

46 On the 1977 Act generally see below p 126. The Act requires the drawing of a difficult borderline between clauses which exclude liability and those which define obligations and it is not one that can simply depend upon the form of the clause see s 13 and s 3 and see generally Macdonald (1992) 12 Legal Studies 277.

47 [1995] FSR 616.

for the supply of software and hardware which would computerise its accounts and allow access to them through printouts and the second for the extension of the system to make it 'on-line'. An 'on-line' system would have meant that the accounts could be viewed on a screen and that what was seen there would be up to date as soon as any new information (such as payment) was entered into the system. The first stage was completed satisfactorily in itself, but the attempt to bring the system 'on-line' created problems with the software already installed and these were not easily remediable. The second contract had been made in August 1985 but the system was not satisfactory by February 1986, at which point the acquirers lost patience and agreed with the suppliers to end the contract. The case raised questions in relation to copyright and the acquirer's rights to remedy defects in the program. What should be noted in this context is the view of the court as to the contents of the implied term that the system would be reasonably fit for the buyer's particular purpose.[48] Havery QC (Off Ref) said:[49]

> it was an implied term of each contract for the supply of software that the software would be reasonably fit for any purpose which had been communicated to the plaintiff's before the contract was made and for any purpose subsequently communicated, provided in the latter case that the plaintiffs accepted the defendant's instructions to make the relevant modifications. The making of the modifications constitutes or implies acceptance of the instructions ...

Havery QC regarded the contract as envisaging the modification of the content of the term that the goods should be reasonably fit for the acquirer's particular purpose. This evidences the problems of drawing up the functional specification at the start of the contract: the acquirer may be unclear as to what is required or may not fully explain it to the supplier. The case also illustrates the fact that contracts for bespoke or modified standard software may need to be modified. Problems may arise from that need and the alteration of contracts should now be examined.

Consideration

Unless it is embodied in a deed, an agreement requires the presence of consideration if it is to be legally binding as a contract. Consideration is basically some benefit to the promisee or detriment to the promisor and, obviously, the requirement applies to both parties.[50] The benefit or detriment should be of some financial significance, rather than, for example, some

48 The basis of the implication is not clear in this case but a term requiring goods to be reasonably fit for the buyer's particular purpose is implied by s 14(3) of the Sale of Goods Act 1979 (see also Supply of Goods and Services Act 1982). See below pp 190.

49 [1995] FSR 616 at p 644.

50 *Currie v Misa* (1875) LR 10 Exch 153. Consideration is the 'price of the promise' (*Dunlop Pneumatic Tyre Co v Selfridge & Co* [1915] AC 79).

emotional benefit,[51] but the level of financial benefit or detriment is, generally, irrelevant.[52] In other words, the law does not, in general, examine whether the parties have arrived at a 'fair' contract price.[53] This is usually expressed by saying that the law does not consider the adequacy of consideration and in *Thomas v Thomas*,[54] for example, it meant that the adequacy of paying £1 a year rent for a valuable property was not regarded as legally relevant.

However, the law does label some consideration as insufficient and that is what must be focused on here. The point in relation to modifications of contracts is that, traditionally, a promise by X, to Y, to perform what is already required by another contract between X and Y, has not been regarded as sufficient consideration.[55] However, a more recent approach indicates that there will be sufficient consideration in this situation if there is some practical benefit to Y in obtaining performance, rather than merely being left with the right to sue X for breach of the first contract.[56] Of course, in such a case, X may be 'extorting' a promise to pay more for the performance already contracted for, but some protection is afforded to Y in such a situation by the doctrine of duress, which will be considered below. Here the case of *Williams v Roffey Bros* should be considered – the case which introduced the more modern approach to the question of further payment for performance of an existing contractual duty.

***Williams v Roffey Bros & Nicholls (Contractors) Ltd* [1991] 1 QB 1**

The defendant building contractors had contracted to do building work on a block of 27 flats. They sub-contracted the carpentry work to the plaintiff. Before the plaintiff had completed the carpentry work he found that he was in financial difficulties. The contract price had turned out to be a 'bad deal', from his perspective. The defendants were under pressure to complete on time because of clauses stating that certain sums were to be paid if completion was late. The defendants met with the plaintiff and offered him additional remuneration, to be paid as he completed the work on each flat. The defendants did not maintain the additional payments and the plaintiff sued for the extra sums promised. The question was whether the plaintiff had provided any consideration for the defendants' promise to pay the additional sums, when he was merely doing what he was already bound to do under the existing contract. The Court of Appeal found that there was consideration in

51 *White v Bluett* (1853) 23 LJ Ex 36 but see *Ward v Byham* [1956] 2 All ER 318.

52 *Thomas v Thomas* (1842) 2 QB 851, *Chappell & Co v Nestle Co* [1960] AC 87.

53 But see the Unfair Terms in Consumer Contracts Regulations 1994, below p 149.

54 (1842) 2 QB 851.

55 The same applied, and still applies, where the promised performance is of the carrying out of a public duty (*Collins v Godefroy* (1831) 1 B&Ad 950), but not where the existing contractual obligation is to a third party (*Scotson v Pegg* (1861) 6 H&N 295). There is no difficulty in finding consideration in any of the cases if some further consideration is supplied, going beyond the existing duty (*Hartley v Ponsonby* (1857) 7 El & Bl 872).

56 This has been held not to extend to the situation where a debtor offers to pay only part of the money owed (*Re Selectmove* [1995] 2 All ER 531).

the practical benefit that the defendants gained in the flats being completed on time.

Glidewell LJ In his address to us counsel for the defendants outlined the benefits to the defendants which arose from their agreement to pay the additional £10,300 as (i) seeking to ensure that the plaintiff continued to work and did not stop in breach of the sub-contract, (ii) avoiding the penalty for delay and (iii) avoiding the trouble and expense of engaging other people to complete the carpentry work.

However, counsel submits that, though the defendants may have derived, or hoped to derive, practical benefits from their agreement to pay the 'bonus', they derived no benefit in law, since the plaintiff was promising to do no more than he was already bound to do under his sub-contract, ie continue with the carpentry work and complete it on time. Thus there is no consideration for the agreement.

Counsel for the defendants relies on the principle of law which, traditionally, is based on the decision in *Stilk v Myrick* (1809) 2 Camp 317 ...

There is, however, another legal concept of relatively recent development which is relevant, namely that of economic duress. Clearly, if a sub-contractor has agreed to undertake work at a fixed price, and before he has completed the work declines to continue with it unless the contractor agrees to pay an increased price, the sub-contractor may be held guilty of securing the contractor's promise by taking unfair advantage of the difficulties he will cause if he does not complete the work. In such a case an agreement to pay an increased price may well be voidable because it was entered into under duress. Thus the concept may provide another answer in law to the question of policy which has troubled the courts since before *Stilk v Myrick* and no doubt led at the date of that decision to a rigid adherence to the doctrine of consideration.

... [T]he present state of the law on this subject can be expressed in the following proposition: (i) if A has entered into a contract with B to do work for, or to supply goods or services to, B, in return for payment by B and (ii) at some stage before A has completely performed his obligations under the contract B has reason to doubt whether A will, or will be able to, complete his side of the bargain and (iii) B thereupon promises A an additional payment in return for A's promise to perform his contractual obligations on time and (iv) as a result of giving his promise B obtains in practice a benefit, or obviates a disbenefit, and (v) B's promise is not given as a result of economic duress or fraud on the part of A, then (vi) the benefit to B is capable of being consideration for B's promise so that the promise will be legally binding.

As I have said, counsel for the defendants accepts that in the present case by promising to pay the extra £10,300 the defendants secured benefits. There is no finding, and no suggestion, that in this case the promise was given as a result of fraud or duress.

If it be objected that the propositions above contravene the principle in *Stilk v Myrick*, I answer that in my view they do not: they refine and limit the application of the principle, but they leave the principle unscathed, eg where B secures no benefit by his promise. It is not in my view surprising that a principle enunciated in relation to the rigours of seafaring life during the Napoleonic wars should be subjected during the succeeding 180 years to a process of refinement and limitation in its application in the present day.

It is therefore my opinion that on his findings of fact in the present case, the judge was entitled to hold, as he did, that the defendants promise to pay the extra £10,300 was supported by valuable consideration, and thus constituted an enforceable agreement ...

Russell LJ ... In the late twentieth century I do not believe that the rigid approach to the concept of consideration to be found in *Stilk v Myrick* is either necessary or desirable. Consideration there must still be but in my judgment the courts nowadays should be more ready to find its existence so as to reflect the intention of the parties to the contract where the bargaining powers are not unequal and where the finding of consideration reflects the true intention of the parties.

... The plaintiff has got into financial difficulties. The defendants, through their employee Mr Cottrell, recognised that the price that had been agreed originally with the plaintiff was less than what Mr Cottrell himself regarded as a reasonable price. There was a desire on Mr Cottrell's part to retain the services of the plaintiff so that the work would be completed without the need to employ another sub-contractor. There was further a need to replace what had hitherto been a haphazard method of payment by a more formalised scheme involving the payment of a specified sum on the completion of each flat. These were all advantages accruing to the defendants which can fairly be said to have been in consideration of their undertaking to pay an extra £10,300. True it was that the plaintiff did not undertake to do any work additional to that which he had originally undertaken to do but the terms on which he was to carry out the work were varied and, in my judgment, that variation was supported by consideration which a pragmatic approach to the true relationship between the parties readily demonstrates.

For my part I wish to make it plain that I do not base my judgment on any reservation as to the correctness of the law long ago enunciated in *Stilk v Myrick*. A gratuitous promise, pure and simple, remains unenforceable unless given under seal. But where, as in this case, a party undertakes to make a payment because by so doing it will gain an advantage arising out of the continuing relationship with the promisee the new bargain will not fail for want of consideration.

Purchas LJ The point of some difficulty which arises on this appeal is whether the judge was correct in his conclusion that the agreement reached on 9 April failed for lack of consideration within the principle established by the old cases of *Stilk v Myrick*, approving *Harris v Watson* (1791) Peake 102. Counsel for the plaintiff was bold enough to submit that ... this court was bound by neither authority. I feel I must say at once that, for my part, I would not be prepared to overrule two cases of such veneration involving judgments of judges of such distinction except on the strongest possible

> grounds since they form a cornerstone of the law of contract which has been observed over the years and is still recognised in principle in recent authority ... Although this rule has been the subject of some criticism it is still clearly recognised in current textbooks of authority ...
>
> In my judgment, therefore, the rule in *Stilk v Myrick* remains valid as a matter of principle ... The modern cases tend to depend more on the defence of duress in a commercial context rather than lack of consideration ...
>
> The question must be posed: what consideration has moved from the plaintiff to support the promise to pay the extra £10,3000 added to the lump sum provision? In the particular circumstances ... there was clearly a commercial advantage to both sides from a pragmatic point of view in reaching the agreement of 9 April. The defendants were at risk that as a result of the bargain they had struck the plaintiff would not or indeed possibly could not comply with this existing obligation without further finance. As a result of the agreement the defendants secured their position commercially. There was, however, no obligation added to the contractual duties imposed on the plaintiff under the original contract. Prima facie this would appear to be a classic *Stilk v Myrick* case. It was, however, open to the plaintiff to be in deliberate breach of the contract in order to 'cut his losses' commercially. In normal circumstances the suggestion that a contracting party can rely on his own breach to establish consideration is distinctly unattractive. In many cases it obviously would be and if there was any element of duress brought on the other contracting party under the modern development of this branch of the law the proposed breaker of the contract would not benefit.

Duress[57]

When a contract has been made, and performance commenced, the parties may become heavily dependent upon each other. If only one party becomes dependent, then the situation is ripe for the other party to ask for further payment to perform what he, or she, is already bound to do by the terms of their existing contract.[58] A partly developed software system might well give rise to such a situation, for example, and the enforceability of any new agreement might come into question. As has been indicated, since the decision in *Williams v Roffey Bros*[59] consideration has ceased to be the important factor in looking at the enforceability of any such new agreement. The main question

57 See generally Halson, 'Opportunism, Economic Duress and Contractual Modifications' (1991) 107 LQR 649, Koffman & Macdonald, *op cit*, pp 273–83.

58 See, for example, *Atlas Express v Kafco (Importers and Distributors) Ltd* [1989] 1 All ER 641, *North Ocean Shipping v Hyundai Construction Co Ltd (The Atlantic Baron)* [1978] 3 All ER 1170.

59 See above p 90.

is now clearly identified as whether the new agreement was made under duress.

The concept of duress requires the law to distinguish between acceptable hard bargaining and the use of unacceptable pressure which will render a contract voidable. It is a difficult line to draw and it is only relatively recently that English law has been prepared to recognise duress in all but the most extreme of cases, such as a threat of physical violence to the person. In fact, the principle that a contract could be voidable on the basis of economic duress was not recognised until Mocatta J did so, *obiter*, in *The Siboen and The Sibotre (Occidental Worldwide Investment Corp v Skibs A/S Avanti)*.[60] Some of the difficulties in determining what should amount to economic duress are illustrated in the judgments in *Universe Tankships Inc of Monrovia v International Transport Workers Federation.*

Universe Tankships Inc of Monrovia v International Transport Workers Federation [1983] 1 AC 366

A Liberian corporation owned a ship which sailed under a flag of convenience, thereby avoiding many requirements beneficial to its seamen. When the ship docked at Milford Haven, it was 'blacked' by the ITF in an effort to obtain improved conditions for the crew. The owners paid various sums to enable their vessel to leave port, including a 'contribution' to the ITF welfare fund. Once the ship was clear of port, the owners sued to recover their 'contribution' as money paid under duress, and succeeded.

Lord Diplock

> It is, however, in my view crucial to the decision of the instant appeal to identify the rationale of this development of the common law. It is not that the party seeking to avoid the contract which he has entered into with another party, or to recover money that he has paid to another party in response to a demand, did not know the nature or the precise terms of the contract at the time he entered into it or did not understand the purpose for which the payment was demanded. The rationale is that his apparent consent was induced by pressure exercised upon him by that other party which the law does not regard as legitimate, with the consequence that the consent is treated in law as revocable unless approbated either expressly or by implication after the illegitimate pressure has ceased to operate on his mind. It is a rationale similar to that which underlies the voidability of contracts entered into and the recovery of money exacted under colour of office, or under undue influence or in consequence of threats of physical duress.
>
> Commercial pressure, in some degree exists wherever one party to a commercial transaction is in a stronger bargaining position than the other party ...

60 [1976] 1 Lloyd's Rep 293.

Lord Scarman

> It is, I think already established law that economic pressure can in law amount to duress ...: *Barton v Armstrong* [1976] AC 104 and *Pau On v Lau Yiu Long* [1980] AC 614. The authorities upon which these two cases were based reveal two elements in the wrong of duress: (1) pressure amounting to compulsion of the will of the victim; and (2) the illegitimacy of the pressure exerted. There must be pressure, the practical effect of which is compulsion or the absence of choice. Compulsion is variously described in the authorities as coercion or the vitiation of consent. The classic case of duress is, however, not the lack of will to submit but the intentional submission arising from the realisation that there is no other practical choice open to him. This is the thread of principle which links the early law of duress (threat to life or limb) with later developments when the law came also to recognise as duress first the threat to property and now the threat to a man's business or trade ...
>
> The absence of choice can be established in various ways, eg by protest, by the absence of independent advice, or by declaration of intention to go to law to recover the money paid or the property transferred: see *Maskell v Horner* [1915] 3 KB 106. But none of these evidential matters goes to the essence of duress. The victim's silence will not assist the bully, if the lack of any practicable choice but to submit is proved. The present case is an excellent illustration. There was no protest at the time, but only a determination to do whatever was needed as rapidly as possible to release the ship. Yet nobody challenges the judge's finding that the owner acted under compulsion ...
>
> The real issue in the appeal is therefore as to the second element in the wrong of duress: was the pressure applied by the ITF in the circumstances of this case one which the law regards as legitimate? For as Lord Wilberforce and Lord Simon of Glaisdale said in *Barton v Armstrong* [1976] AC 104, 121D: 'the pressure must be one of a kind which the law does not regard as legitimate.'
>
> As the two noble and learned Lords remarked at p 121D, in life, including the life of commerce and finance, 'many acts are done under pressure, sometimes overwhelming pressure': but they are not necessarily done under duress. That depends on whether the circumstances are such that the law regards the pressure as legitimate ...

Lord Scarman indicated two tests for the existence of economic duress and a two stage test has gained support. However, it differs somewhat from that stated by Lord Scarman. It is now put in terms of:[61]

(i) the lack of a reasonable alternative to agreeing, for the person threatened; and

(ii) the illegitimacy of the threat.

61 See, eg, *Enimont Overseas v Rojugotanker Zadar (The Olib)* [1991] 2 Lloyd's Rep 108 at p 114. *B & S Contracts and Designs Ltd v Victor Green Publications Ltd* [1984] ICR 419. *Vantage Navigation Corp v Suhail and Saud Bahwan Building Materials (The Alev)* [1989] 1 Lloyd's Rep 138.

In other words, it is Lord Scarman's reference to 'pressure amounting to compulsion of the will of the victim' which no longer accurately states the test. Rather, the test now reflects what he referred to as the 'classic case of duress'. This is clearer than Lord Scarman's original test as it makes it obvious that the person against whom the threat is made, makes a choice. It makes it clear that duress is not concerned with the person threatened being rendered incapable of making a choice because his, or her, 'will' is not functioning normally, but rather that duress is concerned with someone having to make a decision in circumstances that the law regards as unacceptable.[62]

However, the lack of a reasonable alternative to agreeing is not, in itself, sufficient to constitute duress. The second part of the test indicates that the circumstances of the decision will not be unacceptable unless the threat was 'illegitimate'. Pressure would, generally,[63] seem to be illegitimate where what is threatened is unlawful, in that it is a criminal or civil wrong (including the threat to breach a contract) or where the threat itself is such a wrong (eg blackmail). In the recent case of *CTN Cash and Carry v Gallaher*[64] the Court of Appeal indicated, obiter, that this might be extended to threats to do something which is not unlawful (eg a threat not to make a contract), but which took place in circumstances where the person making the threat was not acting *bona fide* and the relationship between the parties was a 'protected' one. The ambit of the category of 'protected relationships' was not made clear, but the court obviously did not think the two businesses in the instant case fell within it – the contrast was made between 'protected relationships' and a 'purely commercial context'.

COPYRIGHT OWNERSHIP

When software is acquired, the copyright interest in it is not usually acquired as well, merely a right to use it under the terms of a licence. However, there will be some cases in which the acquirer also becomes the copyright holder. This might happen in relation to software which the acquirer commissioned the developer to devise for him or her. However, the ownership of copyright, particularly under a development contract, may be disputed and such a dispute will be considered below. First, the desirability of copyright ownership for both such parties is put in context by Chappatte.

62 See Atiyah (1982) 98 LQR

63 See the discussion in *Dimskal Shipping Co SA v International Transport Workers Federation (The Evia Luck)* [1991] 4 All ER 871.

64 [1994] 4 All ER 714.

Philip Chappatte, 'Specific problems in the licensing of software' [1995] Comp Law & Practice 16

The ownership of software is not normally an issue in commercial transactions except where one person (the software house) has agreed to develop application software for another (the user) involving either the developing of a complete software system or developing additions and improvements or adaptations to an existing system.

Let us take an example. If a manufacturer of heavy machinery asks a software house to develop application software to suit its specific needs and business environment, the software house may be able to suggest a standard software package which is 30 or 40 per cent fit for the user's requirements. The rest of the software system will have to be specifically developed by the software house for the user.

Benefits of ownership for user

The user may acquire substantial benefits by obtaining ownership. I will mention three benefits:

(i) The user will be able to avoid all restrictions on use and transferability and the problems associated with a revocable licence if he acquires ownership;

(ii) If the software house uses the whole or part of the software developed for the user for the benefit of other persons, the user may be able to extract royalties from the software house for subsequent use and sub-licences;

(iii) Ownership of the software means control over software. What can often be the most important benefit for the user is that ownership will enable the user to ensure that none of his competitors will be able to obtain the right to use the software developed for him.

Disadvantages for the software house

If the user acquires proprietary rights, the software house will obviously lose the corresponding benefits acquired by the user. For example, the software house will not freely be able to use certain software routines developed for the user in our example for the benefit of another person or to incorporate those routines in one of its standard software packages. But the software house may also face real practical difficulties if a user does acquire proprietary rights.

It may be administratively burdensome for the software house to develop an internal register dividing software it has developed in which it has a proprietary right and other software it has developed owned by its customers. It may be difficult for the software house to prevent its programmers and designers from drawing on their previous experience which may unwittingly involve the copying of customised software developed for and owned by a particular user.

In *Saphena Computing Ltd v Allied Collection Agencies Ltd*[65] the ownership of the intellectual property rights in the software was disputed. The acquirers argued that the beneficial interest in the copyright should vest in them as they had commissioned the software. Havery QC (Off Ref) took the line that the

65 [1995] FSR 616.

starting point should be that the copyright, and the beneficial interest in it, belonged to the developer unless there was something to displace that assumption. He arrived at that conclusion because s 4(3) of the Copyright Act 1956 expressly provided that the person who commissioned a photograph, or the painting or drawing of a portrait, should be entitled to the copyright in it but, in contrast, there was no such allocation of copyright to the commissioner of a literary work and software is treated as a literary work for the purposes of the copyright legislation. In addition, in the instant case, there was nothing to displace the assumption that the commissioning party did not acquire copyright – no express or implied term and no implied or resulting trust.

THE LICENCE

Licence terms

The software licence will deal with such matters as:

- to whom the licence is granted;
- the equipment on which, and location at which, it may be used;
- the use to which the software can be put[66] (eg sub-licensing is usually forbidden);
- whether the source code or object code is supplied (normally the acquirer only receives the object code);
- whether the licence is exclusive or non-exclusive (normally it will be non-exclusive unless it is being granted to a distributor who is to exploit the software through sub-licensing it);
- whether the licensee can transfer the licence;[67]
- the duration of the licence which may be for a fixed or indefinite period. It will normally state that it is to terminate on the occurrence of certain breaches by the licencee or on the licencee's insolvency;[68]
- confidentiality – the licence may state that the 'software' is confidential information which should not be disclosed, if the licensor is attempting to gain the protection afforded to such information;
- exemption clauses – the licensor will insert an exemption clause in an

66 Defining the use rendered 'lawful' by the licence may be particularly important in the light of s 50C of the Copyright, Designs and Patents Act 1988, which bases its limited 'right' to, for example, copy, adapt or correct errors in software, on what is necessary for the software's 'lawful' use.

67 The copyright holder may wish to prevent a licence being transferred to a rival.

68 Such termination has serious potential consequences for a licencee whose business is organised around the use of the software. The purchaser of such a business may require a check to see that the relevant software licences have not been infringed.

attempt to exclude or restrict any liability he, or she, might incur to the licensee.

The effectiveness of exemption clauses must be considered in the light of the Unfair Contract Terms Act 1977 which is considered below.[69] In addition, the 1994 Regulations on Unfair Terms in Consumer Contracts will subject to a test of 'fairness' many non-individually negotiated terms in contracts between sellers or suppliers of goods or services and consumers. The Regulations are also considered below.[70]

EC DIRECTIVE

Basic use of software

It is generally said that using software will be in breach of copyright unless the user has a licence. This is because its use almost inevitably requires it to be copied onto hardware and, in the absence of a licence, such copying has generally been said to entail a breach of copyright.[71] However, what must be considered is the effect on this of Article 5(1) of the EC Directive on the Protection of Computer Programs. This might be seen as providing the acquirer with a right to make the copy required for the basic use of software.

> **Article 5(1) states:**
>
> In the absence of specific contractual provisions, the acts referred to in Article 4(a) and (b) shall not require authorisation by the rightholder where they are necessary for the use of the computer program by the lawful acquirer in accordance with its intended purpose, including for error correction.

The 'acts' referred to in Article 4(a) and (b) are, *inter alia*, the 'permanent or temporary reproduction of computer programs' and 'the translation, adaptation, arrangement and any other alteration of a computer program and the reproduction thereof'.[72] This means that the Directive might be seen as providing the right to make the copy of software which its basic use requires. However, any such right would be limited and what must be considered is the extent to which the copyright owner could prevent any such right being acquired by including an express contrary term. In other words, what is the meaning of the first part of Article 5(1), ie '[I]n the absence of specific contractual provisions ...'. Two possibilities were considered by Graham Smith.

69 See p 119.

70 See p 138.

71 See ss 17(1), (2), and (6) of the Copyright, Designs and Patents Act 1988.

72 See above p 58.

Graham Smith, 'EC Software Protection Directive – An Attempt to Understand Article 5(1)' [1990–91] 7 Computer Law and Security Report 148

An immediate question which arises in relation to Article 5(1) is what is meant by the words 'in the absence of specific contractual provisions ...'? It would seem that these words could bear at least one of the following two meanings:

1. **'In the absence of any specific contractual provisions which expressly permit those act, the acts referred to ...'**

   On this interpretation, Article 5(1) deals with the situation where no express licence is granted by the rightholder to the user in respect of the use of the program. Since the use of the program would constitute an infringement of copyright, because it would involve reproduction and/or translation of the program, Article 5(1) in effect grants a statutory licence to the acquirer to use the program in accordance with its intended purpose. Any right given by Article 5(1) that is not granted by a contractual provision would be granted by the Article. If there is no contract, Article 5(1) will apply in its entirety; if there is a contract the Article would fill in any gaps in the contractual provisions as to use. On this interpretation, however, a provision that excluded any or all of the acts referred to in Articles 4(a) and (b) would fall outside the scope of the Article. The validity of such provision would have to be determined by reference to the other provisions of the Directive.

2. **'In the absence of specific provisions to the contrary, the acts referred to ...'**

   On this interpretation Article 5(1) may be excluded by express words but will apply to the extent not excluded, even where there is an express provision dealing with the user's rights to use the program. To that extent it is similar to the first interpretation. More controversially, however, on this interpretation an express provision excluding any of the acts specified in Article 5(1) or even any use at all would be valid.

At this point it is necessary to look at other parts of the Directive itself, to see what light they may shed on the interpretation of Article 5(1). The first provision to note is Article 9(1) which provides that 'any contractual provisions contrary to Article 6 or to the exceptions provided for in Article 5(2) and (3) shall be null and void'. This Article does not say anything about Article 5(1), which suggests that excluding it will be valid. However, if one then refers to the recitals, the opposite appears to be the case. Recitals 16 and 17 provide as follows:

> 'Whereas the exclusive rights of the author to prevent the unauthorised reproduction of his work have to be subject to a limited exception in the case of a computer program to allow the reproduction technically necessary for the use of that program by the lawful acquirer;
>
> *Whereas this means the acts of loading and running necessary for the use of a copy of a program which has been lawfully acquired, and the act of correction of its errors, may not be prohibited by contract;* whereas in the absence of specific contractual provisions, including when a copy of the program has been sold, any other act necessary for the use of the copy of program may be

> performed in accordance with its intended purpose by a lawful acquirer of that copy.'
>
> The second of the above recitals states first of all that the acts of loading and running necessary for the use of a copy of a program, and the act of correction of errors, may not be prohibited by contract. No provision to that effect, however, appears in the text of the Directive. In particular, as we have seen, Article 9 does not so specify. The rest of the second of the above recitals uses the same words as Article 5(1), namely 'in the absence of specific contractual provisions' but adds the interesting words 'including when a copy of the program has been sold ...'. This appears to be designed to cover the situation where mass marketed software is sold without a signed licence agreement and would therefore support the first of the interpretations suggested above, that Article 5(1) is meant to fill in gaps in the contractual rights of use. This recital also uses the words 'any other act necessary for the use of the copy of a program ...' which appears to be a reference to the acts referred to in Articles 4(a) and (b) other than loading and running, ie displaying, transmission, storage, translation, adaptation, arrangement or other allocation of a computer program.

After additionally considering the history of the provision, Smith argues that there are rights to load, run, and correct errors in software, even if there is an express contrary term. In other words, on this interpretation, the Directive provides the 'lawful acquirer' of software with a basic right to use software that cannot be removed by contract. However, this was not the approach adopted in the legislation introduced to implement the Directive ('Mass marketed software' will be returned to below – it raises the question of the effectiveness of the 'shrink wrap' licence[73]).

What is now s 50C of the Copyright, Designs and Patents Act 1988 states:

> (1) It is not an infringement of copyright for the lawful user of a copy of a computer program to copy or adapt it, provided that the copying or adapting
>
> (a) is necessary for his lawful use; and
>
> (b) is not prohibited under any term or condition of an agreement under which his use is lawful.
>
> (2) It may, in particular, be necessary for the lawful use of a computer program to copy or adapt it for the purpose of correcting errors in it ...

As can be seen, this clearly makes any copying or adapting by the acquirer, subject to contrary contractual agreement. This is not in keeping with an interpretation of Article 5 which would make the basic right to use the software irremovable by agreement.[74] It should also be noted that the section seems generally restrictive of any notion of a right to make basic use of

73 See p 106.

74 It should be noted that s 50C would require a contrary contract term. If the Directive is construed so that there is no right under Article 5(1) where there is a contrary agreement, it does not seem to require any such agreement to be contractual.

software. There is an important difference to be noted between the Directive's references to 'lawful acquirer' and use of the software in accordance with its 'intended purpose', and the statutory references to 'lawful user' and 'lawful use'. It would seem that someone might well be argued to be a 'lawful acquirer' although they lacked the rights to make them a 'lawful user' and the same point can be made in relation to 'lawful use' and 'intended purpose' ('lawful user' is defined in s 50A(2)). These points will be returned to below in considering the 'shrink wrap' licence problem.[75]

Back-up copies

The making of back-up copies of software is commonly regarded as sound practice. A disk can be affected, and the program corrupted, by a number of factors, such as a faulty disk drive, heat, or an electro-magnetic field. Some copyright holders even put instructions in the manual that before the software is put to any other use it should be copied and a copy put in a safe place to be used in the event of the other becoming corrupted. However, some copyright holders do not want any copies of this type made, perhaps for security reasons, but consideration should now be given to ts 50A of the 1988 Act which states that it is not an infringement of copyright for a 'lawful user'[76] of a copy of a computer program to make any back up copy of it 'which it is necessary for him to have for the purposes of his lawful use' (s 50A(1)). This 'right' to make a necessary back-up copy cannot be removed by any contrary agreement. Section 50A(3) states that where an act is permitted by the section, 'it is irrelevant whether or not there exists any term or condition in an agreement which purports to prohibit or restrict the act'. Any such term is void under s 296A.

Section 50A is based on Article 5(2). Both are of limited scope. The right to make a back-up copy, irrespective of contrary agreement, is limited to cases where it is 'necessary' to make such a copy. If 'necessary' is strictly construed, this would be of very limited application. In most cases a back-up copy will be highly desirable, but not strictly necessary, in the sense of 'essential to', the actual use of the program. However, 'necessary' may be understood in its context. In a commercial context it might be taken to mean 'necessary' for the commercial use of the software. It might then be found that having a readily accessible back-up copy would often be necessary for its commercial use. The business user being, effectively, unable to use it if it could become unavailable to him, or her, for a time, through corruption of the disc, for example. Obviously, it was this, latter, type of approach to necessity which was envisaged by Susan Singleton in her consideration of how a copyright holder

75 See p 110.

76 See below.

who wished to avoid back-up copies being made might redraft his, or her, licences appropriately.

Susan Singleton, 'Computer Software Agreements and the Implementation of the EC Directive' (1993) 9 Computer Law and Practice 50

Although many licences do permit the making of back-up copies, in which case there is no need to amend licence provisions, some companies do not want a back-up copy [to be made] for security or other reasons. Indeed, they may make devices on the software which prevent the making of a back-up copy. How are they affected by the new law? If it is necessary for the user to make a back-up copy for his lawful use then he is allowed to do so and any condition prohibiting it is void. There are no restrictions on placing copyright protection devices on software. Those wanting to restrict copying can continue to use such devices ...

The question will be 'what is necessary?'. Licensors should consider adding words such as the following, provided they reflect the true facts:

> 'The licensor has available a 24 hour service for the provision of duplicate software to that licensed under this agreement in the event that the licensee requires a back-up copy, whether through total destruction of the software licensed, or its corruption. Given such availability there is no necessity for the licensee to have a right to make such copies of the software for any purpose, including without prejudice to the foregoing generality, for back-up purposes and therefore such right is prohibited in accordance with the provisions of section 50A of the Copyright, Design and Patents Act 1988.'

If 24-hour facilities cannot be provided then a copy could be made available to a bank or other organisation under terms providing for release of the program when designated disaster circumstances arise.

Error correction

Error correction will normally require the use of the source code, rather than merely the object code. It will not normally be undertaken by the acquirer of software. In particular, a maintenance agreement will often be made in relation to software, coming into effect once acceptance has occurred and encompassing error correction.[77] The question may arise as to whether the error in question amounts to a breach of the supply contract and that will depend upon the express and implied terms of that contract.

However, the point which should be focused on here is whether the acquirer can correct errors in the software and this question is affected by the

77 There will be difficulties for the acquirer of software if access to the source code for necessary error correction is denied because the copyright holder becomes insolvent or otherwise ceases to function. To deal with these situations 'source code escrow' is sometimes used ie the source code is held by a third party, to be released to the acquirer on the happening of certain specified events, such as the copyright holder's insolvency. There may, however, be difficulties with this under insolvency law (see *Encyclopaedia of Information Technology Law*, pp 6–138).

EC Directive and, what is now s 50C of the 1988 Act. Article 5 of the Directive includes 'error correction' within the acts which are not in breach of copyright when they are necessary for the intended purpose of a program[78] (see above). Similarly, s 50C states that, subject to contrary agreement, the copying or adapting which is necessary for the lawful use of a program is not a breach of copyright and s 50C(2) makes it clear that 'it may, in particular, be necessary for the lawful use of a computer program to copy or adapt it for the purpose of correcting errors in it'. Some of the difficulties in interpreting these provisions were outlined above in the general context of the discussion of the basic use of software. It should be noted that, whatever the extent of the 'right' conferred by the Directive, and whether or not the Act appropriately makes it removable by contrary agreement, it is not the acquirers 'right' to have errors corrected, merely to correct them without being in breach of copyright. In addition, it would seem that there is no obligation, in these provisions, for the seller to supply the source code which is generally needed for error correction. The contractual obligation is normally only to supply the object code but it may provide for the supply of the source code. The Directive and the legislation would not seem to make the source code, as such, available to any greater extent to the acquirer. Under these provisions, it would seem to be a matter of acquirers merely being enabled to attempt to adapt (translate) the object code and use that for error correction, without being in breach of copyright.

In *Saphena Computing Ltd v Allied Collection Agencies*[79] the availability and use of source codes for error correction was considered. The case was concerned with an attempt to provide an 'on-line' computer system for a debt collecting agency. The plaintiff suppliers experienced difficulties in trying to make the software function as required. The time they spent in attempting to deal with the problems eventually led the defendant acquirers to agree to a termination of the contract and they then called in a third party to deal with the problems. The particular point which needs to be considered here is the question of whether the defendants were entitled to possession of the source code, and to use it to remedy the defects in the software. Havery QC (Off Ref) considered the question in general terms under the original supply agreement and in the more specific situation of the agreement to terminate an incomplete supply contract. In general he thought there was no right to the source code but he was prepared to imply a term[80] to give business efficacy to the termination agreement.

78 It has been argued, to the contrary that, on its wording, Article 5(1) does not only encompass error correction which is necessary for the intended purpose of the program, but rather treats error correction as an intended purpose: see Mark Sherwood-Edwards 'Seven Degrees of Separation: the Software Directive and UK implementation' (1993) 9 Computer Law and Practice 169.

79 [1995] FSR 636.

80 See above p 83.

[The] fact that source programs remain the property of the plaintiffs must entail two propositions: first, that once the plaintiffs have completed the supply of the software that has been agreed to be supplied, ie the object programs, they are entitled to remove the source program from the defendants computer. The only way of doing that is by deleting them. Secondly, it entails that the defendants are not entitled to copy the source programs if they do remain in their possession, since the source programs remain the property of the plaintiffs ... and no licence is granted for their reproduction or adaptation.

In my judgment, this conclusion is not affected by the decision in *British Leyland Motor Corporation Ltd v Armstrong Patents Co Ltd* [1986] AC 577. The factual basis of that case was that during its expected lifetime a car supplied by the plaintiffs and originally fit for its purpose would require, in order to continue to be fit for its purpose, to have its exhaust pipe replaced by a new one, the manufacture of which would involve the reproduction of the plaintiff's copyright drawings. The ultimate purchaser would have no remedy against the person who supplied the car to him or against anyone else (subject, no doubt, to competition law) if he, the purchaser, could obtain no replacement exhaust pipe.

In the present case, on the other hand, once the software is fit for its purpose, it stays fit for its purpose. If by any chance a flaw is discovered showing that it is unfit for its purpose (which is hardly likely after prolonged use) there is a remedy in damages against the supplier, if solvent, until the expiry of the period of limitation. It may well nevertheless be that the effect of *British Leyland* is that if the software supplied by the plaintiffs to the defendants in the present case turns out to be unfit for its purpose, and the defendants at the time have access to the source code, the plaintiffs cannot restrain reproduction of the source code for the purpose of rendering the software fit for its purpose. But that does not mean either that the defendants can retain the source code against that eventuality, or that they are entitled to require the plaintiffs to supply it to them in that event.

... In the present case, I am satisfied from the evidence ... that at any rate in the case of ready written programs, unlike the case of motor cars, the purchaser is not normally in a position, and therefore cannot reasonably expect, either to repair them or improve them. The factual basis for restricting what would otherwise be the plaintiff's rights in their source code does not therefore exist.

But the position so far as completion of the software originally agreed to be supplied ... is different. At the time that the relationship came to an end, the plaintiff was in the course of ... removing bugs from it in order to make it fit for the purposes communicated to the plaintiff ... It was not entirely fit for those purposes on [the termination date]. In my judgment, it cannot reasonably be held to have been the intention of [the defendants] and [the plaintiffs] when they determined their business relationship, that the software should remain with its bugs and though usable, not entirely fit for the purposes I have mentioned. Although [the plaintiff] was no longer to be involved, it must in my judgment, have been implicit that he would let the defendants have the use of the source programs which were necessary to put the software into a state where it was fit for those purposes. It was indeed accepted by counsel for the

> plaintiffs that the defendants were entitled to reproduce source programs for that purpose ...
>
> ... the defendants would be entitled to copy the source programs to the extent necessary to complete the software ... to make it reasonably fit for the purposes specified ... In my judgment implied terms to that effect are necessary to give business efficacy to the agreement to bring the relationship between the parties to an end.

Of course, if the source program is available to the acquirer, s 50C(2) will now be relevant to the question of whether it can be copied in order to correct errors. The additional point to be made is that the Directive and s 50C only extend to error correction. They do not cover enhancement of software. A maintenance agreement will often cover updates.

THE 'SHRINK WRAP' LICENCE[81]

The problem of the effectiveness of the shrink wrap licence can be epitomised by the purchase of software 'off the shelf' from a shop. The purchaser will, for example, take his, or her, newly acquired software home, open the box containing it and discover that it is contained in an envelope on which it is stated that opening the envelope will constitute acceptance of the copyright holder's licence terms, which are also included in the box. It may well also state that if the purchaser does not want to accept the licence terms, the software may be returned to the shop from which it was purchased, for a full refund.[82]

There are numerous variations on the fact situation indicated above. The packaging arrangements may vary, but all raise the same type of issues. It may also be that the software is not acquired from a shop but by mail order or by telephone order. Again many of the same issues arise as under the above fact situation. Primary consideration will be given to the purchase in a shop with comments on other situations where that is required. One basic question in each situation is whether the shrink wrap licence is effective in contract,[83] and there are two basic possibilities to consider. It might be argued to be part of the contract, made between the supplier, S, and the acquirer, A, for the acquisition of the software (ie the supply in the shop) or part of a contract

81 See generally, Lemley, 'Intellectual Property and Shrink Wrap Licences' (1995) 68 So Cal LR 1239, Stern, 'Shrink Wrap Licences of Mass Marketed Software: Enforceable Contracts or Whistling in the Dark?' (1985) 11 Rutgers Computer Law & Tech L J 51, Millard, 'Shrink Wrap Licensing' 4 Comp Law & Security Report (Nov-Dec) 8, Smith, 'Tear Open Licences – Are They Enforceable in England?' (1986) Comp Law & Practice 128.

82 There may be difficulties in finding that the supplier is under an obligation to the acquirer to take back the software and return the price paid – see below p 112.

83 By analogy with patent law, it has been argued that the licences might be partially effective as non-contractual 'limited licences', providing the acquirer with restricted rights to use the software. See p 110.

formed when the envelope is opened, between A and the copyright holder, C. A third possibility, combining elements of these two, will also be considered below, in the context of a recent decision of the Scottish Court, *Beta v Adobe*.[84]

Acquisition contract

In considering the acquisition of software from a shop, the first point to consider is whom the acquirer, A, contracts with. *Prima facie* at that stage there is simply a contract between the shop, S, and A. The transaction certainly looks like a simple sale of the software by S to A. On this basis, the contract made in the shop is of no assistance to the copyright holder, C, in enforcing the licence terms. There are two reasons for this. Firstly, the licence terms, the existence of which is not even indicated until the box is opened, are introduced too late to be part of the contract made in the shop. Secondly, the doctrine of privity of contract, although presently under review,[85] currently means that only those who are parties to contracts can enforce their terms and C is not a party to the contract between A and S.[86] These points can be expanded on.

The first point to be made is simply that new terms cannot be introduced into a contract once it has been made.[87] If the licence terms are not introduced into the transaction until after the contract in the shop has been made, they cannot be part of the contract between A and S.

Contract formation is normally analysed in terms of offer and acceptance. An offer expresses a willingness to be contractually bound by certain terms,[88] if the other party accepts them. An acceptance occurs when the other party agrees to the same terms.[89] In a shop, the offer is normally made by the customer when the goods are taken to the till and it is accepted by the assistant at the till.[90] If the existence of licence terms does not become apparent until after the box has been opened, and that does not take place before offer and acceptance have occurred, obviously they have been introduced too late, after the contract was made, and cannot be part of it. This was recognised in the Scottish case of *Beta v Adobe*.[91] The same point can also be made in relation to the mail order, or telephone order, of software. In those cases, the contract

84 See below p 112.

85 Law Com Rep No 242 – 'Privity of Contract: Contracts for the Benefit of Third Parties'.

86 *Tweddle v Atkinson* (1861) 1 B & S 393, *Dunlop Pneumatic Tyre Co Ltd v Selfridge & Co Ltd* [1915] AC 847. On privity generally see Koffman & Macdonald, *op cit*, Chapter 18.

87 *Olley v Marlborough Court Hotel* [1949] 1 KB 532. *Thornton v Shoe Lane Parking* [1971] 2 QB 163.

88 See, eg, *Gibson v Manchester City Council* [1979] 1 WLR 294.

89 *Jones v Daniel* [1894] 2 Ch 332.

90 *Pharmaceutical Society of Great Britain v Boots Cash Chemists* [1953] 1 QB 401.

91 See below p 112.

will normally be made when the acquirer's order (the offer) is accepted by despatch of the goods (in the case of mail order) or by express acceptance on the telephone, in the case of a telephone order. If not even the existence of the licence was indicated prior to A's opening of the box, it cannot form part of the contract terms.

The situation also has to be considered in which the licence terms are referred to on the outside of the box.[92] Clauses may be incorporated into contracts from unsigned documents on the basis of reasonably sufficient notice.[93] It should also be noted that incorporation by reference is possible, ie the document providing notice does not have to contain the terms but can merely refer to where they can be found.[94] The test is objective[95] and whether incorporation by notice occurs is basically[96] a question of fact in each case,[97] dependent upon such matters as the legibility and prominence of the relevant writing. One factor which has been seen as relevant to the test generally is whether the place where the notice is to be found is the type of place in which the reasonable person would expect to find a contractual term. One reason why the clause on the deck chair ticket in *Chapelton v Barry UDC*[98] did not provide reasonably sufficient notice of an exemption clause was that the ticket was seen as something which the reasonable person would view merely as a method of proving that the deck chair hire charge had been paid, rather than as a document containing contract terms. One question is whether people normally expect to find contract terms referred to on the back of a box containing software. The size and position of any such notice on the box would also be relevant and it would, for example, be ineffective if the shop

---

92 This fact seems to have been emphasised by the US court in the recent case of *ProCD v Zeidenberg* US Ct of Appeals (7th Circuit) No 96–1139 (June 20, 1996). See below p 114.

93 *Parker v South Eastern Railway Co* [1877] 2 CPD 416. The 'red hand rule' has been added to this, so that the more unreasonable or unusual a clause the greater the degree of notice required to provide reasonably sufficient notice – *Thornton v Shoe Lane Parking* [1971] 1 QB 163, *Interfoto Picture Library v Stiletto Visual Programmes* [1988] 1 All ER 348. (The name of the rule stems from a famous dictum of Denning LJ, as he then was, in *Spurling v Bradshaw* [1956] 1 WLR 461. He said (at p 461) 'the more unreasonable a clause is, the greater the notice which must be given of it. Some clauses which I have seen would need to be printed in red ink on the face of the document with a red hand pointing to [them] before the notice could be held to be sufficient'). On incorporation by notice generally see Koffman & Macdonald, *op cit*, pp 135–41.

94 *Thompson v L M & S Railway* [1930] 1 KB 41. It would seem that a copy of the terms should be accessible before A contracts.

95 In *Thompson v L M & S Railway* [1930] 1 KB 41 it was indicated that it was irrelevant that the passenger in question was illiterate. The reasonable person was to be presumed to be able to read English. The situation would be otherwise where the party seeking to incorporate the terms knew, or should, as a reasonable person, have known, that the other party, or the group to which he, or she, belongs, was, in some way, less able to read or understand the notice (*Richardson, Spence & Co v Rowntree* [1894] AC 217, *Geier v Kujawa, Weston and Warne Bros (Transport)* [1970] 1 Lloyd's Rep 364).

96 But note the 'red hand rule' (see n 93).

97 *Hood v Anchor Line* [1918] AC 837 at 834.

98 [1940] 1 KB 532.

had stuck a price tag, or some other label, over it.[99] It should be easier for such incorporation to take place as acquirers, in general, begin to assume that the acquisition of software will involve licence terms.[100]

However, even if the licence is incorporated by notice into the contract between S and A, under the present law,[101] this is not of direct assistance to C, because of the second point indicated above – privity of contract. The doctrine of privity of contract currently[102] prevents C from enforcing terms in a contract to which he, or she, is not a party. C would have to rely on indirect enforcement through, possibly, a chain of sub-licences, culminating in the contract between S and A. This might be overcome by arguing that S had contracted not only on his, or her, own behalf, but also as agent for C, making C a party to the contract.[103] However, it should be emphasised that this argument would only be of any use if the licence terms were not introduced too late to form part of the contract made in the shop. Additionally, it must be recognised that finding that S was acting as C's agent would be a very artificial construction to put upon events and it is probably not one which would be readily compatible with the parties' own views of the situation. Of course, the privity problem does not arise if the software is acquired directly, by mail order or telephone order, from C. The problem of the timing of the introduction of the licence remains, unless it is sufficiently referred to in the mail order advertisement or by C's telephone order taker, before the contract is concluded.

Opening the envelope

If there are difficulties in finding that the licence is part of the contract under which the software is acquired in the shop, can a separate contract be found which is made when A opens the packet containing the software? The argument would be that the offer is made by C and A accepts by performing the stated act of opening the envelope. Acceptance of an offer normally requires communication but it is possible to have acceptance by conduct.[104] However, that conduct would have to be unequivocal and another explanation of the opening of the envelope may be possible. It could be argued that A may not be responding to C's offer of a licence, but rather exercising a right already acquired. The contention would be that, at the time

99 *Sugar v L M & S Railway* [1941] 1 All ER 172.

100 *Alexander v Railway Executive* [1951] 2 KB 882 at p 886.

101 But see Law Com Rep No 242 – 'Privity of Contract: Contracts for the Benefit of Third Parties'.

102 See n 101.

103 *New Zealand Shipping Co Ltd v Satterthwaite* [1974] 1 All ER 1015, but see *Scruttons v Midland Silicones Ltd* [1962] AC 446.

104 *Brogden v Metropolitan Ry Co* (1877) 2 App Cas 666.

that the software was acquired from S, A also acquired certain basic rights to use it. Such rights might stem from the legislation implementing the EC Directive on the Protection of Computer Programs, from a common law licence, or from terms implied into the contract between S and A.

As was indicated above, Article 5(1) of the EC Directive on the Protection of Computer Programs provides the 'lawful acquirer' of software with a right to, *inter alia*, copy it, where such copying is necessary for its use 'in accordance with its intended purpose'. The reference to 'lawful acquirer' might well be seen as encompassing the person who buys software in a shop and as providing him, or her, with a right which would explain the opening of the software packet as something other than an acceptance of the licence. However, as has already been indicated, what is now s 50C of the Copyright, Designs and Patents Act 1988, the provision intended as an implementation of Article 5(1), does not refer to the 'lawful acquirer' of software but rather to its 'lawful user' and also refers to 'lawful use' rather than 'intended purpose'. It seems doubtful whether, without using an implied term (considered below) or some such device, the acquirer of the software in the shop can be seen as a 'lawful user' unless the licence is effective. Certainly, that would seem to be the case on any natural construction of 'lawful user', but the point should be made that something other than a natural construction of the section may be required, if it is to be seen as a proper implementation of the Directive. In addition, as it stands, any natural interpretation of the reference to 'lawful user' in s 50C is open to the criticism of circularity.[105]

Another possible explanation for the opening of the envelope is that the common law provides a 'limited licence' for the acquirer of software so that the acquisition is not rendered pointless. An analogy with patent law might lead to such a conclusion.[106] Unless it occurs with the consent of the patentee, the sale or use of a patented article is an infringement of the patent. This led the courts to hold that if a patented item is sold without any restrictions being placed on it, the purchaser obtains an implied licence to use and resell the item.[107] By analogy, this might provide a basic right to use software if the acquirer has not been granted a licence by the copyright holder. There might also be some benefit to the copyright holder in this analogy. The sale of a patented item is subject to any licence restrictions of which notice is given at the time of the sale and the patentee can directly enforce such restrictions.[108] In the absence of a contract the copyright holder may, by this analogy be able to provide the acquirer of software with a limited licence, but it would seem that the copyright holder would not thereby gain the benefit of the exemption

105 'Lawful user' is defined in s 50A(2). For criticism of the phrase see Mark Sherwood-Edwards, 'Seven Degrees of Separation: the software Directive and UK implementation' (1993) 9 Computer Law and Practice 169.

106 Graham P Smith, 4 Int Jo Law and Info Technology 131 at pp 140–41.

107 *Betts v Willmott* (1871) LR 6 Ch App 239. Smith, *op cit*.

108 *McGruther v Pitcher* [1904] 2 Ch 306. Smith, *op cit*.

clause which would probably have been included in a contractual licence. The point must also be made that it is, in any event, now unclear to what extent this analogy is still possible in the face of Article 5(1) of the EC Directive. That Article provides for the basic use of software in the absence of contractual provision. Certainly, it would seem that a non-contractual[109] implied licence should not provide a means to reduce an acquirer's rights below the level provided for by Article 5 and, the impetus for non-contractual rights to be implied may not survive the Directive at all.

The final possibility to be considered here is that the opening of the software envelope, was not based on acceptance of the licence, but a right to use the software derived from an implied term in the contract under which the software was acquired (ie the contract made in the shop, with S, in our primary example). Certainly, in *Saphena Computing Ltd v Allied Collection Agencies Ltd*[110] where software was supplied to the defendants for the purposes of their business as a debt collecting agency, the court regarded it as 'perfectly clear' that there had to be an implied term 'that the defendants should have a copyright licence to enable them to use the software for that purpose'.[111] Courts may well be reluctant to find that a supply of software is quite pointless because the acquirer has no right to use the software. They may be willing to imply a term in law giving a basic right to use the software on the basis that such a term is necessary in that type[112] of contract.[113] Of course, there are difficulties with the idea of an implied term, conferring rights to do what would otherwise be a breach of copyright, if the contract is not between the acquirer and the copyright holder. A chain of implied terms might be suggested, although such a chain would be vulnerable to the insertion of an express contrary term in the first contractual link between the copyright holder and the person to whom he, or she, supplies.[114]

Obviously, there are considerable hurdles in the way of finding that there were two effective contracts – the supply contract and the licence. It should also be noted that the two contract analysis was considered, and rejected, by the Scottish court in *Beta Computers (Europe) Ltd v Adobe Systems (Europe) Ltd*[115]

109 But note that s 50C, 'implementing Article 5(1)', merely refers to contrary agreement, without specifying that it must be contractual.

110 [1995] FSR 617.

111 Havery QC, Off Ref at p 637.

112 The argument here would seem to apply whether the transaction is a sale of the disk or merely a hiring of it (as may sometimes be argued to be the case) – in either situation, its acquisition is completely undermined if it cannot be used.

113 See above p 84.

114 Even a term which would otherwise be implied in law will not be implied in the face of an express contrary term. Although sometimes the express contrary term might be rendered ineffective, and the implication therefore allowed, under the Unfair Contract Terms Act 1977 (*Johnstone v Bloomsbury Health Authority* [1991] 2 All ER 293). See also s 3 of the 1977 Act and Macdonald (1992) 12 Legal Studies 277.

115 [1996] FSR 371.

because of the difficulties which might ensue. If the situation was construed as one which could give rise to two distinct contracts, with S, the supplier, not being a party to any second, licence, contract, Lord penrose was concerned that A, the acquirer, might not be able to recover the purchase price of the software, or refuse to pay it, if A did not wish to accept the licence terms. Any statement on the packaging that A can recover the purchase price if the licence is unacceptable, will not be contractually enforceable by A, against S, unless it has been properly incorporated into the contract between A and S.[116] However, A might be able to claim that S's supply was in breach of contract.[117] It might be argued that the supply of software which, without further agreement with C, could not be used without infringing C's copyright, would be in breach of the term implied by the s 12 of the Sale of Goods Act 1979,[118] that the seller has a right to sell the goods. In *Niblett Ltd v Confectioner's Materials Co Ltd*[119] a breach of that implied term was found when the sellers supplied tins of condensed milk which were labelled in such a way as to infringe a third party's trade mark.

The problem considered by Lord Penrose, and outlined above, obviously arises if the view is taken that A cannot use the software without accepting the licence terms. However, Lord Penrose's other concern with the two contract analysis was in relation to the possibility that C's attempt to create a licence with A would be ineffective but A would nevertheless be able to use the software. He was concerned that S might be liable to C, through a breach of the contract under which C supplied the software to S, and, more significantly, that the position of C, as the copyright owner, would be undermined, a point which will be returned to below.[120]

A third possibility

A third possible analysis of the shrink wrap licence situation was identified by the Scottish Court in *Beta Computers (Europe) Ltd v Adobe Systems (Europe) Ltd*.[121] However, the court's reasoning which led to the conclusion that the licence was effective, has its roots in the principle of *ius quaesitum tertio* which is not present in English law and there are limitations on the significance of the decision for English law as it stands, at present, because of the doctrine of privity of contract. However, it should be borne in mind that changes may be

116 See above p 108.

117 A restitutionary claim might also be made but it would prove problematic to argue that a total failure of consideration had occurred when A had, technically received title to the disk – see the approach taken in *Rowland Divall* [1923] 2 KB 500.

118 If the contract is not one for the sale of goods, then it can be argued that an analogous term has been breached, see p 165.

119 [1921] 3 KB 387.

120 See p 114.

121 [1996] FSR 371.

made to the doctrine of privity in the light of the recent report of the Law Commission.[122]

In *Beta v Adobe*, A placed an order with S for certain standard software. S obtained the software from Informix. Variously described as the manufacturer of the software, or its author, Informix was undoubtedly the holder of the copyright in the software, C. S delivered the software to A. A attempted to return the package and refused to pay for it. The case was concerned with S's claim for payment. A's defence was based on a document which Informix, C, included in the packaging of its software. The document was labelled as containing 'End User Licence Conditions' and it stated 'Opening the Informix SI software Package indicates your acceptance of its terms and conditions'. A claimed that these licence conditions gave them a right to return the software without payment. The court agreed.

Lord Penrose considered that there were two possible ways in which the transaction might be viewed:

(i) The contract of supply was formed when the order was made and accepted. The licence conditions would be irrelevant to such a contract as they would have been introduced too late, after offer and acceptance had occurred. The licence conditions would have merely provided terms of a contract to be made directly between A and Informix, which A would have accepted on opening the packaging.

(ii) The licence conditions were relevant to the contract of supply. Either there was no concluded contract between A and S until the licence conditions had been introduced into the transaction and accepted by A, or there was a concluded contract of supply which was suspensive prior to A's acceptance of the licence.

As has already been indicated, Lord Penrose rejected the first possibility, in favour of the second.

Lord Penrose's unease with the first possibility has already been looked at.[123] He recognised that the second exposed suppliers to the risk of end users rejecting software because they were not prepared to be bound by the licence terms of the copyright holder. Nevertheless, he viewed it as serving the interests of the industry as a whole through ensuring that licence terms were effective. However, he noted that the second possibility itself encompassed two alternative analyses which had to be considered:

(a) There was no contract between A and S unless, and until, the licence terms were agreed to.

(b) There was a contract made when S agreed to supply A with what was ordered, but it was suspensive until the conditions were accepted.

122 Law Com Rep No 242 – 'Privity of Contract: Contracts for the Benefit of Third Parties'.
123 See p 112.

Lord Penrose thought that the former analysis was to be preferred. He viewed the right to use the software, which was only acquired under the licence, as so important to the contract that the parties could not be regarded as having concluded it until the licence terms were introduced and agreed to. As has already been indicated, the explanation of the usefulness of the contract so concluded was dependant upon Scots law, which allows enforcement of some obligations by third parties through *ius quaesitum tertio*. On that basis, although the licence conditions were analysed as part of the contract between S and A they could, nevertheless, be enforced against A, by C, Informix, the copyright holder. In other words, under Scots law, the problem of privity of contract, identified above, does not arise even though C is not a party to the contract encompassing the licence terms. It has been noted that the Law Commission has recently made recommendations in relation to the English doctrine of privity of contract and contractual benefits for third parties.

Pragmatism

The reliance upon the principle of *ius quaesitum tertio*, makes *Beta v Adobe* of limited value outside of its Scottish context. However, the court's desire not to undermine the position of the holder of the copyright was noted above, and it is also worth noting Lord Penrose's statement that:[124]

> There is little doubt, in my mind, that the interests of the industry as a whole in the efficient and sensible management of transactions requires that effect should be given to the [licence] conditions if possible.

There may be an impetus to find a means of holding shrink wrap licences to be effective because that result is viewed as being of practical benefit.[125] Something of this approach is also to be found in the recent US case of *ProCD Inc v Mathew Zeidenberg and Silken Mountain Web Services Inc.*[126] In that case, unlike the earlier *Step Saver* case,[127] the licence was held to be effective against a background of the court's view of the benefits of such a conclusion.

In *ProCD v Zeidenberg*, ProCD used different licence terms to differentiate consumer and commercial purchases of its database. The consumer was charged $150 for the purchase, which was much less than the commercial buyer, but was also authorised to do much less with the database than the commercial buyer. The court took that the view that it was beneficial to both consumers and commercial buyers that ProCD should take such an approach, which was obviously dependent on the effectiveness of the licence terms.

124 At p 379.

125 But see Graham P Smith, 4 Int Jo Law and Info Technology 131.

126 US Ct of Appeals (7th Circuit) No 96–1139 (20 June, 1996)

127 *Step-Saver Data Systems Inc v Wyse Technology and Software Link Inc* (1991) 939 F 2d 91 (US Ct of Appeals (3rd Circuit)).

Damages[128]

A software 'bug' can cause considerable losses to a business when its effects are felt. The potential scope of the losses which a 'bug' can cause are graphically illustrated by what occurred when one affected A T & T's long distance telephone network. Within 10 minutes, 50% of calls were failing to get through and a day's telephone traffic was lost before software 'patches' could be installed to avoid the 'bug'. The direct cost of the day's lost traffic to A T & T was between sixty and seventy-five million dollars and obviously losses would also have been made by A T & T's customers, and, additionally, there were long-term effects on A T & T through loss of confidence. It had been a company whose advertising had concentrated on its reliability to justify its pricing being higher than that of its competitors.[129]

Of course, the potential for losses caused by defective software will vary from business to business and the extent to which the business is dependent on the software, as well as the specific defect. It will also depend on the type of contract. The point has already been made as to the difficulties involved in drafting and performing a software development contract, for example.[130] However, the damages recovered, under contract law, for any loss, no matter how large or small, depend upon the same basic rules. The basic principle on which an award of contractual damages is made is that damages should place the injured party in the position he, or she, would have been in had the contract been properly performed,[131] ie the position he, or she, would have been in had there been no breach. This means that when a contract is breached the injured party can recover for the profits he, or she, would have made had the contract been performed. In other words, in contract, the injured party can recover his, or her, expectation loss. It is, of course, possible for an injured party merely to claim expenditure wasted because of the breach.[132] That party will not, however, be able to evade the basic principle by so doing. He, or she, will not recover any expenditure which the party in breach can establish would have been lost even if the contract been performed.[133] Claiming for wasted expenditure does not allow the injured party to recover more than he, or she, would have obtained had the contract been performed, ie an award of damages does not relieve the injured party from the consequences of having made a bad bargain.

128 See generally Koffman & Macdonald, *op cit*, pp 408–32.

129 See David Davies, 'Anatomy of a Disaster' (1990) 6 Comp Law and Security Report 27.

130 See p 84.

131 *Robinson v Harman* (1880) 5 App Cas 25, Parke B at p 35.

132 *Anglia TV v Reed* [1971] 3 All ER 690.

133 *CCC Films (London) Ltd v Impact Quadrant Films Ltd* [1984] 3 All ER 298, *C & P Haulage v Middleton* [1983] 3 All ER 94.

There are certain limitations on awards of damages made under the above basic principle. For example, the injured party will not recover for a loss which is too remote. This means that he, or she, will not recover for a loss which, at the time the contract was made, was not within the reasonable contemplation of the parties as liable to result from the breach.[134] This rule prevented recovery of some of the losses claimed in *Victoria Laundry (Windsor) Ltd v Newman Industries Coulson & Co Ltd*.[135] The case was concerned with the late delivery of a boiler to a laundry at a time when there was a shortage of laundry facilities. The laundry could recover for the loss of ordinary laundry business which it could have undertaken had it had the boiler on time, but it could not recover for the loss of an unusually profitable dyeing contract which it would have undertaken had the boiler not been delivered late. The second loss was too remote to be encompassed within the damages awarded.

An award of damages may also be circumscribed by the duty to mitigate. This, so called, 'duty' means that the injured party will not be able to recover for any loss which he, or she, could have avoided by behaving reasonably after the breach.[136] In *Salvage Assn v CAP Financial Services Ltd*[137] the question arose as to the damages recoverable when a system development contract had been terminated by SA because of CAP's inability to successfully complete the system. It would seem to have been with the duty to mitigate in mind that the judge commented that:[138]

> I am satisfied that SA's decision to abandon the CAP system altogether and start afresh was entirely reasonable ... CAP was not able to complete the system satisfactorily and there was no point in getting another software house to redesign and rebuild a discredited system. It was much more sensible to start afresh. The upshot was that the project to computerise SA's head office accounting with a system designed and developed by CAP had failed and SA's expenditure on that system had been wasted.

The injured party, SA was able to recover all the money it had expended on the CAP system. Had it been found that the reasonable course was not to abandon the CAP system entirely, but to contract with another company for its completion, then the duty to mitigate would mean that SA's recovery would not have encompassed any expenditure on the CAP system which would not have been wasted had that system been salvaged.[139]

134 *Hadley v Baxendale* (1854) 9 Ex 341, *Koufos v Czarnikow Ltd* [1969] 1 AC 350, *Parsons (H) (Livestock) v Uttley Ingham & Co Ltd* [1978] 1 All ER 525.

135 [1949] 2 KB 528.

136 *British Westinghouse Electric and Manufacturing Co Ltd v Underground Electric Railways Co of London* [1912] AC 673, Lord Haldane at p 689.

137 [1995] FSR 654.

138 At p 680.

139 Obviously, in those circumstances, the cost of salvaging the system would have been recoverable – this is the other side of the duty to mitigate.

EXEMPTION CLAUSES[140]

Exemption clauses are basically clauses which exclude or restrict, or appear to, exclude or restrict, liability for breach of contract or other liability arising through tort, bailment, or statute. They may be aimed at totally excluding liability ('exclusion clauses') or merely restricting or limiting it ('limitation clauses') by, for example, limiting the sum recoverable in damages.

To be effective in relation to contractual liability, an exemption clause must have been incorporated into the contract, it must be appropriately worded to cover the breach which occurred and it must not be rendered ineffective by legislation – basically either the Unfair Contract Terms Act 1977 or the Unfair Terms in Consumer Contracts Regulations 1994. The question of incorporation of clauses into contracts has been looked at.[141] Brief consideration should be given to the construction of the contract (ie interpreting it, or more specifically, asking if the clause is appropriately worded to cover the breach), and the legislation must be looked at.

CONSTRUCTION

A strict approach is taken to the interpretation of exemption clauses and the contra proferentem rule is applied, which means that if there is any ambiguity in the clause, it will be construed in the way which is least favourable to the party seeking to rely upon it. This can be illustrated by *Houghton v Trafalgar Insurance Co.*[142]

In *Houghton,* H had insured his car with T. H had an accident and tried to claim on his insurance policy for the damage to his car. The policy excluded liability where 'Loss, damage, and/or liability caused or arising whilst any car is involved in racing, pace making ... or is conveying any load in excess of that for which it was constructed'. When the accident occurred there were six people in the car instead of the five which it was designed to carry. The extra person had been sitting on the lap of one of the rear seat passengers. The insurers contended that they were not liable because of the exclusion dealing with conveyance of an excess 'load'. The Court of Appeal held that the insurers were liable. Whilst the first part of the exclusion clearly could relate to passenger vehicles, they interpreted the reference to a 'load' as relating to the situation where a vehicle, such as a lorry or van, has a specified 'load weight'. The clause was not regarded as sufficiently clear and unambiguous to

140 See Koffman & Macdonald, *op cit*, Chapters 9 and 10.

141 See pp 83, 108.

142 [1954] 1 QB 247.

remove the insurance company's liability for the accident to H's ordinary private car.

One particular aspect of the *contra proferentem* rule occurs in relation to liability for negligence[143] (eg a negligent breach or negligence in tort). If a clause expressly refers to liability for negligence,[144] obviously it will cover that liability. The difficulties arise where there is no express reference to negligence as such, but a widely worded general clause is used, which it is argued encompasses liability for negligence (eg a clause referring to 'any liability'). In these circumstances, the courts have taken an approach which means that the clause is more likely to be construed as covering liability for negligence if there is no other liability for it to cover[145] and less likely to be construed as covering negligence if there is other, strict, liability for it to cover.[146] The idea would seem to be that it is unlikely that the injured party would have accepted a clause covering the other party's liability in the event of negligence and, if there is other liability, the clause can be assigned a purpose without the need for it to be understood as covering negligence.

Prior to the enactment of the Unfair Contract Terms Act 1977 the courts were apt to take an extreme approach to construction to prevent exemption clauses from being effective. In *Hollier v Rambler Motors Ltd*[147] for example, they construed a clause as not covering liability based on negligence when there could be no breach in the absence of negligence – leaving the clause with no real role in the contract. Since the advent of the 1977 Act, it has been said that 'strained construction' should not be used.[148] It has also been indicated that the rules of construction should not be applied in 'their full rigour' to limitation clauses (in contrast with exclusion clauses).[149] However, this distinction does not seem justifiable in the extensive form envisaged. As the High Court of Australia said, in refusing to adopt the distinction, 'a limitation clause may be so severe in its operation as to be virtually indistinguishable from that of an exclusion clause'.[150]

143 *Canada Steamship Lines Ltd v R* [1952] AC 192, Lord Morton, delivering the judgment of the Privy Council, at p 208.

144 For example, *Spriggs v Sotheby Parke Bernet & Co* [1986] 1 Lloyd's Rep 487.

145 For example, *Alderslade v Hendon Laundry Ltd* [1945] 1 KB 189.

146 *White v John Warwick & Co Ltd* [1953] 2 All ER 1021.

147 [1972] 2 QB 71.

148 *Photo Production Ltd v Securicor* [1980] AC 827, *George Mitchell (Chesterhall) Ltd v Finney Lock Seeds Ltd* [1983] 2 AC 803.

149 *Ailsa Craig Fishing Co Ltd v Malvern Fishing Co Ltd* [1983] 1 WLR 964, *George Mitchell (Chesterhall) Ltd v Finney Lock Seeds Ltd* [1983] 2 AC 803.

150 *Darlington Futures Ltd v Delco Australia property* (1986) 68 ALR 385 at p 391.

The Unfair Contract Terms Act 1977

PART I

1. Scope of Part I

(1) For the purposes of this Part of this Act, 'negligence' means the breach

(a) of any obligation, arising from the express or implied terms of a contract, to take reasonable care or exercise reasonable skill in the performance of the contract;

(b) of any common law duty to take reasonable care or exercise reasonable skill (but not any stricter duty);

(c) of the common duty of care imposed by the Occupiers' Liability Act 1957 or the Occupier's Liability Act (Northern Ireland) 1957.

(2) This Part of the Act is subject to Part III; and in relation to contracts, the operation of sections 2 to 4 and 7 is subject to the exceptions made by Schedule 1.

(3) In the case of both contract and tort, sections 2 to 7 apply (except where the contrary is stated in section 6(4)) only to business liability, that is liability to breach of obligations or duties arising

(a) from things done or to be done by a person in the course of a business (whether his own business or another's); or

(b) from the occupation of premises used for business purposes of the occupier; and references to liability are to be read accordingly but liability of an occupier of premises for breach of an obligation or duty towards a person obtaining access to the premises for recreational or educational purposes, being liability for loss or damage suffered by reason of the dangerous state of the premises, is not a business liability of the occupier unless granting that person such access for the purposes concerned falls within the business purposes of the occupier.

(4) In relation to any breach of duty or obligation, it is immaterial for any purpose of this Part of this Act whether the breach was inadvertent or intentional, or whether liability for it arises directly or vicariously.

2. Negligence liability

(1) A person cannot by reference to any contract term or to a notice given to persons generally or to particular persons exclude or restrict his liability for death or personal injury resulting from negligence.

(2) In the case of other loss or damage, a person cannot so exclude or restrict his liability for negligence except in so far as the term or notice satisfies the requirement of reasonableness.

(3) Where a contract term or notice purports to exclude or restrict liability for negligence a person's agreement to or awareness of it is not of itself to be taken as indicating his voluntary acceptance of any risk.

3. Liability arising in contract

(1) This section applies as between contracting parties where one of them deals as consumer or on the other's written standard terms of business.

(2) As against that party, the other cannot by reference to any contract term

(a) when himself in breach of contract, exclude or restrict any liability of his in respect of the breach; or

(b) claim to be entitled

(i) to render a contractual performance substantially different from that which was reasonably expected of him, or

(ii) in respect of the whole or any part of his contractual obligation, to render no performance at all,

except in so far as (in any of the cases mentioned above in this subsection) the contract term satisfies the requirement of reasonableness.

4. Unreasonable indemnity clauses

(1) A person dealing as consumer cannot by reference to any contract term be made to indemnify another person (whether a party to the contract or not) in respect of liability that may be incurred by the other for negligence or breach of contract, except in so far as the contract term satisfies the requirement of reasonableness.

(2) This section applies whether the liability in question

(a) is directly that of the person to be indemnified or is incurred by him vicariously;

(b) is to the person dealing as consumer or to someone else.

5. 'Guarantee' of consumer goods

(1) In the case of goods of a type ordinarily supplied for private use or consumption, where loss or damage

(a) arises from the goods proving defective while in consumer use; and

(b) results from the negligence of a person concerned in the manufacture or distribution of the goods,

liability for the loss or damage cannot be excluded or restricted by reference to any contract term or notice contained in or operating by reference to a guarantee of the goods.

(2) For these purposes

(a) goods are to be regarded as 'in consumer use' when a person is using them, or has them in his possession for use, otherwise than exclusively for the purposes of a business; and

(b) anything in writing is a guarantee if it contains or purports to contain some promise or assurance (however worded or presented) that defects will be made good by complete or partial replacement, or by repair, monetary compensation or otherwise.

(3) This section does not apply as between the parties to a contract under or in pursuance of which possession or ownership of the goods passed.

6. Sale and hire-purchase

(1) Liability for breach of the obligations arising from

(a) section 12 of the Sale of Goods Act 1979 (seller's implied undertakings as to title etc);

(b) section 8 of the Supply of Goods (Implied Terms) Act 1973 (the corresponding thing in relation to hire-purchase),

cannot be excluded or restricted by reference to any contract term.

(2) As against a person dealing as consumer, liability for breach of the obligations arising from

(a) sections 13, 14 or 15 of the 1979 Act (seller's implied undertakings as to conformity of goods with description or sample, or as to their quality or fitness for a particular purpose);

(b) sections 9, 10 or 11 of the 1973 Act (the corresponding things in relation to hire-purchase),

cannot be excluded or restricted by reference to any contract term.

(3) As against a person dealing otherwise than as consumer, the liability specified in subsection (2) above can be excluded or restricted by reference to a contract term, but only in so far as the term satisfies the requirement of reasonableness.

(4) The liabilities referred to in this section are not only the business liabilities defined by section 1(3), but include those arising under any contract of sale of goods or hire-purchase agreement.

7. Miscellaneous contracts under which goods pass

(1) Where the possession or ownership of goods passes under or in pursuance of a contract not governed by the law of sale of goods or hire-purchase, subsections (2) to (4) below apply as regards the effect (if any) to be given to contract terms excluding or restricting liability for breach of obligation arising by implication of law from the nature of the contract.

(2) As against a person dealing as consumer, liability in respect of the goods' correspondence with description or sample, or their quality or fitness for any particular purpose, cannot be excluded or restricted by reference to any such term.

(3) As against a person dealing otherwise than as consumer, that liability can be excluded or restricted by reference to such a term, but only in so far as the term satisfies the requirement of reasonableness.

(3A) Liability for breach of the obligations arising under section 2 of the Supply of Goods and Services Act 1982 (implied terms about title etc in certain contracts for the transfer of the property in goods) cannot be excluded or restricted by reference to any such term.

(4) Liability in respect of

(a) the right to transfer ownership of the goods, or give possession; or

(b) the assurance of quiet possession to a person taking goods in pursuance of the contract, cannot (in a case to which subsection (3A) above does not apply) be excluded or restricted by reference to any such term except in so far as the term satisfies the requirement of reasonableness.

(c) This section does not apply in the case of goods passing on a redemption of trading stamps within the Trading Stamps Act 1964 or the Tradings Stamps Act (Northern Ireland) 1965.

9. Effect of breach

(1) Where for reliance upon it a contract term has to satisfy the requirement of reasonableness, it may be found to do so and be given effect accordingly notwithstanding that the contract has been terminated either by breach or by a party electing to treat it as repudiated.

(2) Where on a breach the contract is nevertheless affirmed by a party entitled to treat it as repudiated, this does not of itself exclude the requirement of reasonableness in relation to any contract term.

10. Evasion by means of secondary contract

A person is not bound by any contract term prejudicing or taking away rights of his which arise under, or in connection with the performance of, another contract, so far as those rights extend to the enforcement of another's liability which this Part of this Act prevents that other from excluding or restricting.

11. The 'reasonableness' test

(1) In relation to a contract term, the requirement of reasonableness for the purposes of this Part of this Act, section 3 of the Misrepresentation Act 1967 and section 3 of the Misrepresentation Act (Northern Ireland) 1967 is that the term shall have been a fair and reasonable one to be included having regard to the circumstances which were, or ought reasonably to have been, known to or in the contemplation of the parties when the contract was made.

(2) In determining for the purposes of section 6 or 7 above whether a contract term satisfies the requirement of reasonableness, regard shall be had in particular to the matters specified in Schedule 2 to this Act; but this subsection does not prevent the court or arbitrator from holding, in accordance with any rule of law, that a term which purports to exclude or restrict any relevant liability is not a term of the contract.

(3) In relation to a notice (not being a notice having contractual effect), the requirement of reasonableness under this Act is that it should be fair and reasonable to allow reliance on it, having regard to all the circumstances obtaining when the liability arose or (but for the notice) would have arisen.

(4) Where by reference to a contract term or notice a person seeks to restrict liability to a specified sum of money, and the question arises (under this or any other Act) whether the term or notice satisfies the requirement of reasonableness, regard shall be had in particular (but

without prejudice to subsection (2) above in the case of contract terms) to

(a) the resources which he could expect to be available to him for the purpose of meeting the liability should it arise; and

(b) how far it was open to him to cover himself by insurance.

(5) It is for those claiming that a contract term or notice satisfies the requirement of reasonableness to show that it does.

12. 'Dealing as consumer'

(1) A party to a contract 'deals as consumer' in relation to another party if

(a) he neither makes the contract in the course of a business nor holds himself out as doing so; and

(b) the other party does make the contract in the course of a business; and

(c) in the case of a contract governed by the law of sale of goods or hire-purchase, or by section 7 of this Act, the goods passing under or in pursuance of the contract are of a type ordinarily supplied for private use or consumption.

(2) But on a sale by auction or by competitive tender the buyer is not in any circumstances to be regarded as dealing as consumer.

(3) Subject to this, it is for those claiming that a party does not deal as consumer to show that he does not.

13. Varieties of exemption clause

(1) To the extent that this Part of this Act prevents the exclusion or restriction of any liability it also prevents

(a) making the liability or its enforcement subject to restrictive or onerous conditions;

(b) excluding or restricting any right or remedy in respect of the liability, or subjecting a person to any prejudice in consequence of his pursuing any such right or remedy;

(c) excluding or restricting rules of evidence or procedure; and (to that extent) sections 2 and 5 to 7 also prevent excluding or restricting liability by reference to terms and notices which exclude or restrict the relevant obligation or duty.

(2) But an agreement in writing to submit present or future differences to arbitration is not to be treated under this Part of this Act as excluding or restricting any liability.

14. Interpretation of Part I

In this Part of the Act

'business' includes a profession and the activities of any government department or local or public authority;

'goods' has the same meaning as in the Sales of Goods Act 1979;

'hire-purchase agreement' has the same meaning as in the Consumer Credit Act 1974;

'negligence' has the meaning given by section 1(1);

'notice' includes an announcement, whether or not in writing, and any other communication or pretended communication; and

'personal injury' includes any disease and any impairment of physical or mental condition.

Part II

[Deals with Scotland]

PART III

26. International supply contracts

(1) The limits imposed by this Act on the extent to which a person may exclude or restrict liability by reference to a contract term do not apply to liability arising under such a contract as is described in subsection (3) below.

(2) The terms of such a contract are not subject to any requirement of reasonableness under section 3 or 4: and nothing in Part II of this Act should require the incorporation of the terms of such a contract to be fair and reasonable for them to have effect.

(3) Subject to subsection (4), that description of contract is one whose characteristics are the following–

(a) either it is a contract of sale of goods or it is one under or in pursuance of which the possession or ownership of goods passes, and

(b) it is made by parties whose places of business (or, if they have none, habitual residences) are in the territories of different States (the Channel Islands and the Isle of Man being treated for this purpose as different States from the United Kingdom).

(4) A contract falls within subsection (3) above only if either

(a) the goods in question are, at the time of the conclusion of the contract, in the course of carriage, or will be carried, from the territory of one State to the territory of another; or

(b) the acts constituting the offer and acceptance have been done in the territories of different States; or

(c) the contract provides for the goods to be delivered to the territory of a state other than that within whose territory those acts were done.

27. Choice of law clauses

(1) Where the law applicable to a contract is the law of any part of the United Kingdom only by choice of the parties (and apart from that choice would be the law of some country outside the United Kingdom) sections 2 to 7 and 16 to 21 of this Act do not operate as part of the law applicable to the contract.

(2) This Act has effect notwithstanding any contract term which applies or purports to apply the law of some country outside the United Kingdom, where (either or both)

(a) the term appears to the court, or arbitrator or arbiter to have been imposed wholly or mainly for the purpose of enabling the party imposing it to evade the operation of this Act; or

(b) in the making of the contract one of the parties dealt as consumer, and he was then habitually resident in the United Kingdom, and the essential steps necessary for the making of the contract were taken there, whether by him or by others on his behalf.

28 ...

29 ...

SCHEDULES

SCHEDULE 1

SCOPE OF SECTIONS 2 TO 4 AND 7

1. Sections 2 to 4 of this Act do not extend to

(a) any contract of insurance (including a contract to pay an annuity on human life);

(b) any contract so far as it relates to the creation or transfer of an interest in land, or to the termination of such an interest, whether by extinction, merger, surrender, forfeiture or otherwise;

(c) any contract so far as it relates to the creation or transfer of a right or interest in any patent, trade mark, copyright, registered design, technical or commercial information or other intellectual property, or relates to the termination of any such right or interest;

(d) any contract so far as it relates

(i) to the formation or dissolution of a company (which means any body corporate or unincorporated association and includes a partnership), or

(ii) to its constitution or the rights or obligations of its corporators or members;

(e) any contract so far as it relates to the creation or transfer of securities or of any right or interest in securities.

2. Section 2(1) extends to

(a) any contract of marine salvage or towage;

(b) any charter-party of a ship or hovercraft; and

(c) any contract for the carriage of goods by ship or hovercraft; but subject to this sections 2 to 4 and 7 do not extend to any such contract except in favour of a person dealing as consumer.

3. Where goods are carried by ship or hovercraft in pursuance of a contract which either

(a) specifies that as the means of carriage over part of the journey to be covered; or

(b) makes no provision as to the means of carriage and does not exclude that means, then sections 2(2), 3 and 4 do not, except in favour of a person dealing as consumer, extend to the contract as it operates for and in relation to the carriage of the goods by that means.

4. Section 2(1) and (2) do not extend to a contract of employment, except in favour of the employee.
5. Section 2(1) does not affect the validity of any discharge and indemnity given by a person, on or in connection with an award to him of compensation for pneumoconiosis attributable to employment in the coal industry, in respect of any further claim arising from his contracting the disease.

SCHEDULE 2

'GUIDELINES' FOR APPLICATION OF REASONABLENESS TEST

The matters to which regard is to be had in particular for the purposes of sections 6(3), 7(3) and (4) ... are any of the following which appear to be relevant

(a) the strength of the bargaining positions of the parties relative to each other, taking into account (among other things) alternative means by which the customer's requirements could have been met;

(b) whether the customer received an inducement to agree to the term, or in accepting it had an opportunity of entering into a similar contract with other persons, but without having to accept a similar term;

(c) whether the customer knew or ought reasonably to have known of the existence and extent of the term (having regard, among other things, to any custom of the trade and any previous course of dealing between the parties);

(d) where the term excludes or restricts any relevant liability if some condition is not complied with, whether it was reasonable at the time of the contract to expect that compliance with that condition would be practicable;

(e) whether the goods were manufactured, processed or adapted to the special order of the customer.

Scope of the Act

Despite its name, the Unfair Contract Terms Act 1977 does not deal with 'unfair terms' as such. For the most part, the Act applies to clauses which 'exclude or restrict liability'.[151] It can, basically, be said that the Act applies to 'exemption clauses'. Of course, it does not apply to all exemption clauses, and the scope of the Act should be considered.

Basically, the Act applies to 'business liability' (s 1). However, certain contracts are excluded from its operation in whole, or in part (Schedule 1). The important exclusion to consider here is that to be found in para 1(c) of

151 There is provision in it, most notably in s 3(2)(b) and s 13, to prevent it being evaded by the redrafting of clauses to avoid its scope by avoiding the use of clauses in the form of exclusions or restrictions of liability.

Schedule 1, which removes from the scope of ss 2 to 4 of the Act, contracts in so far as they relate to the creation, transfer or termination of intellectual property rights. The scope of this ouster from the operation of the Act was considered in *The Salvage Assn v CAP Financial Services Ltd*.

The Salvage Assn v CAP Financial Services Ltd [1995] FSR 654[152]

Judge Thayne Forbes (Off Ref)

The use of the words '... any contract so far as it relates to ...' in subparagraph (c) shows clearly that the subparagraph is strictly limited in its application and that it does not necessarily extend to all the terms of a relevant contract. That is to be contrasted with the wording of paragraph 1(a) of Schedule 1 of the 1977 Act which provides that sections 2 to 4 do not extend to 'any contract of insurance ...' ie the entire contract of insurance is excepted from the operations of sections 2 to 4, not just certain provisions of the contract: see *Micklefield v S A C Technology Ltd* [1990] 1 WLR 1002 at page 1008.

I agree with Mr Blunt's submission that paragraph 1(c) applies only to those provisions of a contract which deal with the creation or transfer of a *right or interest* in the relevant intellectual property. It does not extend generally to all the terms of a contract simply because the contract is concerned overall with the provision of a service, performance of which will result in a product to which the law affords the protection of one or more of the specified intellectual property rights. The individual terms of the contract in question have to be considered. Any term which is concerned with the creation or transfer of a right or interest in the intellectual property which attaches to the product will form part of the contract to which paragraph 1(c) applies ... On the other hand if a term is one which is concerned with aspects of the contract between the parties other than the creation or transfer of rights in the intellectual property attaching to the product, then paragraph 1(c) does not apply.

In my opinion, the terms of the two contracts out of which the issues in this action primarily arise are not concerned with the creation or transfer of any right or interest in the intellectual property rights which attach to the System, its programs and documentation. This action is principally concerned with the contractual terms as to the competence of CAP's staff, the quality of their performance, the quality of the subject matter of each contract, the time of completion of the System and the construction and application of terms which exclude or limit CAP's liability for breach of contract or negligence. In my judgment therefore, paragraph 1(c) of Schedule 1 of the 1977 Act does not apply to the provisions of the two contracts which deal with such matters, because contractual terms such as these do not relate to the creation or transfer of an interest in any relevant intellectual property either in the System or its documentation.

This takes a restrictive approach to the para 1(c) exclusion.

If the exemption clauses in question are capable of falling within the 1977 Act, it must be decided which, if any, of the 'active sections' is relevant. These

152 The facts are given above, p 104.

are the sections which state that something is to happen to a certain exemption clause, ie either that it is automatically ineffective or that it is effective only if it 'satisfies the requirement of reasonableness'. There are also 'definition sections' which assist in determining the scope of the 'active sections' and these will be looked at once the 'active sections' have been considered.

The active sections

Section 2 deals with liability arising from negligence.[153] Section 2(1) renders automatically ineffective clauses which 'exclude or restrict liability' for negligently caused death or personal injury. Such terms are 'black listed'. Their reasonableness or otherwise is irrelevant. Section 2(2) deals with clauses excluding or restricting any other sort of negligently caused loss or damage and renders them ineffective except in so far as they satisfy the 'requirement of reasonableness'. The section deals not only with contractual clauses, but also covers, for example, non-contractual disclaimers which may be used to try to exclude or restrict such liability in tort.

Section 3 deals with the situation in which one party 'deals as consumer' or on the other party's 'written standard terms of business'. Contracts may come within both of the situations covered. Someone who deals as consumer may well contract on the other party's written standard terms of business. The meaning of 'deals as consumer' is dealt with by s 12 and is considered below.[154] There is no statutory definition of 'written standard terms of business'. Whether a party has a set of 'written standard terms' should depend upon the pattern and degree of usage of the relevant terms.[155] If the relevant party clearly has 'written standard terms of business', the question may arise as to whether the alterations of them in the instant case are such that the contract cannot be regarded as having been made on that party's written standard term of business. Determining that should be a matter of the extent of alteration of the original terms and also of which terms are altered (some terms in a set of standard terms being intended to be particularised to individual contracts).[156] One further point to be made is that what is required by s 3 is not merely that written standard terms of business be used but that they should be the written standard terms of the relevant party. Should terms used throughout a particular trade, and commonly used by the party in

153 Section 1(1) makes it clear that this covers the situation where there is a breach of the duty to take reasonable care or exercise reasonable skill arising under the contract or in tort or under the Occupiers' Liability Act 1957.

154 See p 130.

155 *Flamar Interocean Ltd v Denmac Ltd* [1990] 1 Lloyd's Rep 434, *Chester Grosvenor Hotel Co Ltd v Alfred McAlpine Management Ltd* (1992) 56 Build LR 115, *The Salvage Association v CAP Financial Services Ltd* [1995] FSR 654, *St Albans City and District Council v International Computers Ltd* [1995] FSR 686.

156 *St Albans City and District Council v International Computers Ltd* [1995] FSR 686.

question, be regarded as that party's 'written standard terms of business' for the purposes of s 3?

Once it is determined that the contract in question falls within s 3, then it should be noted that the scope of the section extends beyond terms which, in form, 'exclude or restrict liability'. Such terms are covered by s 3(2)(a) and are rendered ineffective unless they 'satisfy the requirement of reasonableness'. However, s 3(2)(b) extends the scope of the section beyond terms in the form of exclusions or restrictions of liability. It is one of the provisions of the Act which prevents its easy evasion by drafting which avoids those forms. Section 3(2)(b)(i), for example, extends the reasonableness test to terms under which the party who contracts on his own written standard terms of business, or who contracts with someone who deals as consumer, claims to render a performance substantially different from that which was reasonably expected of him.

Section 6 covers exemption clauses dealing with the terms implied into contracts for the sale or hire-purchase of goods.[157] There are analogous provisions in s 7 dealing with other contracts under which possession or ownership of goods passes. Section 6(1)(a) renders automatically ineffective any term excluding or restricting liability in relation to the terms implied by s 12 of the Sale of Goods Act 1979. Section 6(2)(a) does the same in relation to the exclusion or restriction of liability for breach of the terms implied by the 1979 Act, ss 13–15, provided the buyer 'deals as consumer'. These are the other terms 'black listed' by the 1977 Act. However, if the buyer does not 'deal as consumer', liability for breach of the terms implied by ss 13–15 of the Sale of Goods Act 1979 can be excluded or restricted by a clause which satisfies the 'requirement of reasonableness'.[158] Section 6 also contains analogous provisions dealing with exemptions of the terms implied into hire-purchase contracts.[159] Obviously, the question of whether the buyer 'deals as consumer' is very important in the context of s 6 and this will be returned to.[160]

Unlike most of the other active sections, s 4 does not refer to terms which 'exclude or restrict liability'. It deals with terms under which someone who 'deals as consumer' has to indemnify the other party in relation to that other party's liability for negligence or breach of contract. Such clauses are ineffective unless they satisfy 'the requirement of reasonableness'.

Section 5 of the Unfair Contract Terms Act 1977 is of very limited application. It was enacted to deal with a very specific problem – that of manufacturers or distributors of goods attempting to remove their liability for goods which proved defective 'in consumer use' due to the negligence of the

157 See p 171.

158 Section 6(3).

159 On the terms implied by ss 12–15 of the Sale of Goods Act 1979, see p 171.

160 See p 130.

manufacturers or distributors. The relevant clause would be found in a 'guarantee' which also stated that the consumer had certain rights. This section does not apply between parties to a contract under, or in pursuance of which, possession or ownership of goods passes (s 5(3)). It does not cover clauses in contracts between sellers and buyers of goods.

Section 10 deals with one of the ways in which the other sections of the Act might have been avoided. It prevents a term being used in a second contract to achieve the exclusion or restriction of liability which the Act would prevent in a first contract.

Definitions – 'deals as consumer'

'Deals as consumer' is dealt with by s 12. It is vital to the question of whether someone deals as consumer to determine whether they contract 'in the course of a business'. The approach taken to this question can be seen in the case of *R & B Customs' Brokers v United Dominion Trust.*

***R & B Custom's Brokers v United Dominion Trust* [1988] 1 All ER 847**

The plaintiff company was in business as a freight forwarding agent. It purchased a car, on credit terms, for the use of its two directors and sole shareholders. The car proved to be defective and did not comply with the terms implied by s 14(3) of the Sale of Goods Act 1979. There was, however, a clause purporting to exclude the implied term unless the buyer 'dealt as consumer' within the meaning of s 12 of the Unfair Contract Terms Act 1977.

Dillon LJ

Under the Trade Descriptions Act 1968 any person who in the course of a trade or business applies a false trade description to goods is, subject to the provisions of that Act, guilty of an offence. It is a penal Act, whereas the 1977 Act is not, and it is accordingly submitted that decisions on the construction of the 1968 Act cannot assist on the construction of s 12 of the 1977 Act. Also the legislative purposes of the two Acts are not the same. The primary purpose of the 1968 Act is consumer protection, and the course of business referred to is the course of business of the alleged wrongdoer. But the provisions as to dealing as a consumer in the 1977 Act are concerned with differentiating between two classes of innocent contracting parties (those who deal as consumers and those who do not) for whom differing degrees of protection against unfair terms are afforded by the 1977 Act. Despite these distinctions, however, it would in my judgment, be unreal and unsatisfactory to conclude that the fairly ordinary words 'in the course of a business' bear a significantly different meaning in, on the one hand, the 1968 Act and, on the other, s 12 of the 1977 Act. In particular I would be very reluctant to conclude that these words bear a significantly wider meaning in s 12 than in the 1968 Act. I turn therefore to *Davies v Sumner* [1984] 1 All ER 831. That case was not concerned with a company, but with an individual who had used the car for the purposes of his business as a self-employed courier. When he sold the car by trading it in part exchange for a new one, he had applied a false trade description to it by falsely representing the mileage the car had travelled to be far less than it actually was. Lord Keith who delivered the only speech in the House of Lords, commented that it was clear that the transaction ... was reasonably incidental to the carrying on of the business, but he went on to say ([1984] 3 All ER 831 at pp 833–34):

> 'Any disposal of a chattel held for the purposes of a business may, in a certain sense, be said to have been in the course of that business, irrespective of whether the chattel was acquired with a view to resale or for consumption or as a capital asset. But in my opinion s 1(1) of the 1968 Act is not intended to cast such a wide net as this. The expression "in the course of a trade or business" in the context of an Act having consumer protection as its primary purpose conveys the concept of some degree of regularity, and it is to be observed that the long title of the Act refers to "misdescription of goods, services, accommodation and facilities provided in the course of trade". Lord Parker CJ in the *Havering* case [*Havering LBC v Stevenson* [1970] 3 All ER 609] clearly considered that the expression was not used in the broadest sense. The reason why the transaction there in issue was caught was that in his view it was "an integral part of the business carried on as a car hire firm". That would not cover the sporadic selling off of pieces of equipment which were no longer required for the purposes of a business. The vital feature of the *Havering* case appears to have been, in Lord Parker's view, that the respondent business *as part of its normal practice* bought and disposed of cars. The need for some degree of regularity does not, however, involve that a one-off adventure in the nature of trade, carried through with a view to profit, would not fall within s 1(1) because such a transaction would itself constitute a trade.'

Lord Keith then held that the requisite degree of regularity had not been established on the facts of *Davies v Sumner* because a regular practice of buying and selling cars had not yet been established at the time of the alleged offence. He pointed out for good measure that the disposal of the car was not a disposal of stock in trade of the business, but he clearly was not holding that only a disposal of stock in trade could be a disposal in the course of a trade or business.

Lord Keith emphasised the need for some degree of regularity, and he found pointers to this in the long title of the 1968 Act. I find pointers to a similar degree of regularity in the 1977 Act, where matters merely incidental to the carrying on of a business are concerned, both in the words I would emphasise, 'in the course of' in 'in the course of a business' and in the concept, or legislative purpose, which must underlie the dichotomy under the 1977 Act between those who deal as consumers and those who deal otherwise than as consumers.

This reasoning leads to the conclusion that, in the 1977 Act also, the words 'in the course of a business' are not used in what Lord Keith called 'the broadest sense'. I also find helpful the phrase used by Lord Parker CJ and quoted by Lord Keith, 'an integral part of the business carried on'. The reconciliation between that phrase and the need for some degree of

> regularity is, as I see it, as follows: there are some transactions which are clearly integral parts of the business concerned and these should be held to have been carried out in the course of those businesses; this would cover, apart from much else, the instance of a one-off adventure in the nature of trade where the transaction itself would constitute a trade or business. There are other transactions, however, such as the purchase of the car in the present case, which are at the highest only incidental to the carrying on of the relevant business; here a degree of regularity is required before it can be said that they are an integral part of the business carried on and so entered into in the course of that business.
>
> Applying the test thus indicated to the facts of the present case, I have no doubt that the requisite degree of regularity is not made out on the facts. Mr Bell's evidence that the car was the second or third car acquired on credit terms was, in my judgment, and in the context of the case, not enough. Accordingly, I agree with the judge ... the company was 'dealing as consumer' ...

A company can 'deal as a consumer'. Simply because he, she, or it, is in business does not prevent the relevant party from 'dealing as consumer'. It is a matter of whether the transaction was integral, in itself, to that person's business or occurring with sufficient 'regularity'. The point should also be made that despite the emphasis on 'regularity', it would seem that an element of frequency is also required. Some further thought should be given to the two categories of transactions which are 'in the course of a business'.

Although the *Havering* case is referred to above as one in which the transaction was 'integral' to the business, it would seem that it should be regarded as a case falling within the merely incidental but sufficiently regular category.[161] *Havering* was concerned with a car hire business with a fleet of 24 cars. It was run on the basis that each car was changed after it had been used for about two years. In other words, there was a sale, on average, about once a month and it was against that pattern of dealing that it was held the sale of a particular car had occurred 'in the course of a business'. The sale in itself, would seem to be no more 'integral to the business' than that of the courier selling his car in *Davies v Sumner* or the sale of a car by a taxi business in *Devlin v Hall*.[162] In both cases, the transactions were held not to have been made 'in the course of a business' because there was not a sufficient pattern of dealings, ie the regularity of the transactions was the important factor – the transactions were not regarded as integral in themselves.

Additionally, it should be noted that where the contract involves the supply of goods, there is a further requirement[163] for the acquirer to be 'dealing as consumer'. It is required that the goods be of 'a type ordinarily

161 It may be that it should then be regarded as 'integral' to the business, although not integral in itself, but because of its regularity.

162 (1990) RTR 320.

163 Section 12(1)(c).

supplied for private use or consumption'. This could affect the approach taken to a transaction involving software if it is found to be 'goods'[164] and it raises a number of problems. What is a 'type' of goods? What about software which can be supplied either as a program intended for domestic use or as a larger program, intended for commercial use? Will the two programs constitute different 'types' of goods? Will either be 'goods' 'ordinarily' supplied for private use or consumption?[165]

Definitions – 'The requirement of reasonableness'

The 'requirement of reasonableness' is a key feature of the Act, with the effectiveness of exemption clauses often depending on whether they can satisfy the test. Section 11(5) places the burden of proving 'reasonableness' on the person seeking to use the clause. The assessment of 'reasonableness' does not occur in the light of the actual breach which occurred, but on the basis of what was known, or should reasonably have been contemplated, at the time of contracting[166] and that is very significant – a point which is illustrated by the outcome in *Stewart Gill Ltd v Horatio Myer & Co Ltd*.[167] In that case, the clause failed to satisfy the requirement of reasonableness not because of the breach to which it would have applied in the instant case, but because of the other situations which it could potentially cover. This means that there will be a greater possibility of a clause being effective if it is of narrow application and it would seem advisable to draft several clauses to cover different aspects of liability, rather than one wide one. In that way, at least some of the exemptions may be effective.[168]

Before considering the factors relevant to the 'requirement of reasonableness', the courts' approach to appeals in relation to the application of this test should be noted. In *George Mitchell Ltd v Finney Lock Seeds Ltd*[169] Lord Bridge took the view that there could be legitimate differences of opinion on the reasonableness test and that:[170]

> when asked to review such a decision on appeal, the appellate court should treat the original decision with the utmost respect and refrain from interference with it unless satisfied that it proceeded upon some erroneous principle or was plainly and obviously wrong.

164 See p 152.

165 See Kidner (1987) 38 NILQ 46, Brown [1988] JBL 386, Pearce [1989] LMCLQ 371.

166 Section 11(1).

167 [1992] 2 All ER 257.

168 *Rees Hough Ltd v Redland Reinforced Plastics Ltd* [1985] 2 Con LR 109.

169 [1983] 2 AC 803.

170 At p 816.

Decisions on the 'reasonableness' of a clause in one case are of limited precedent value.[171]

Consideration should now be given to the working of the test and it should be noted that Schedule 2 contains guidelines as to its operation.[172] These guidelines are a non-exhaustive list of relevant factors and that, in itself, is indicative of the functioning of the test which, basically, involves a weighing of the relevant factors in each case. This can be seen through considering the House of Lords' decision in *Smith v Bush.*

***Smith v Eric S Bush (a firm)* [1990] 1 AC 831**

The case was concerned with the liability of a surveyor for a negligent valuation of a house, which had been carried out for mortgage purposes. The valuation was paid for by the intending house purchaser, but the surveyor's contract was with the building society and the action by the house purchaser arose out of tort rather than contract. The question was whether the surveyor could rely upon a disclaimer to avoid liability to the house purchaser. The disclaimer fell to be considered under s 2 of the 1977 Act, the requirement of reasonableness had to be applied, and it was held that it was not satisfied. The disclaimer was ineffective. (Although the action was a tortious one, the comments on the reasonableness test are generally applicable.)

Lord Griffiths

I believe that it is impossible to draw up an exhaustive list of factors that must be taken into account when a judge is faced with this difficult decision [ie the application of the 'reasonableness' test]. Nevertheless, the following matters should in my view, always be considered.

(1) Were the parties of equal bargaining power? If the court is dealing with a one-off situation between parties of equal bargaining power the requirement of reasonableness would be more easily discharged than in a case such as the present where the disclaimer is imposed on the purchaser who has no effective power to object.

(2) In the case of advice, would it have been reasonably practicable to obtain the advice from an alternative source taking into account considerations of costs and time? In the present case it is urged on behalf of the surveyor that it would have been easy for the purchaser to have obtained his own report on the condition of the house, to which the purchaser replies that he would then be required to pay twice for the same advice and that people buying at the bottom end of the market, many of whom will be young first-time buyers are likely to be under considerable financial pressure without the money to go paying twice for the same service.

---

171 But see Lord Griffiths comments on future cases in *Smith v Bush*, below.

172 By s 11(2) these guidelines are relevant to the reasonableness test when applied under s 6 or s 7. However, they are the type of factors which are likely to be relevant, simply on the facts, in many cases and will then be looked at on that basis (eg *Phillips Products Ltd v Hyland* [1987] 2 All ER 620 at p 628).

(3) How difficult is the task being undertaken for which liability is excluded? When a very difficult or dangerous undertaking is involved there may be a high risk of failure which would certainly be a pointer towards the reasonableness of excluding liability as a condition of doing the work. A valuation, on the other hand, should present no difficulty if the work is undertaken with a reasonable skill and care. It is only defects which are observable by a careful visual examination that have to be taken into account and I cannot see that it places any unreasonable burden on the valuer to require him to accept responsibility for a fairly elementary degree of skill and care involved in observing, following up and reporting on such defects. Surely it is work at the lower end of the surveyor's field of professional expertise.

(4) What are the practical effects of the decision of the question of reasonableness? This must involve the sums of money potentially at stake and the ability of the parties to bear the loss involved, which in its turn, raises the question of insurance. There was once a time when it was regarded as improper even to mention the possible existence of insurance cover in a lawsuit. But those days are long past. Everyone knows that all prudent, professional men carry insurance, and the availability and cost of insurance must be a relevant factor when considering which of two parties should be required to bear the risk of a loss. We are dealing in this case with a loss which will be limited to the value of a modest family house and against which it can be expected that the surveyor will be insured. Bearing the loss will be unlikely to cause significant hardship if it is borne by the surveyor but it is, on the other hand, quite possible that it will be a financial catastrophe for the purchaser who may be left with a valueless house and no money to buy another. If the law in these circumstances denies the surveyor the right to exclude his liability, it may result in a few more claims but I do not think so poorly of the surveyor's profession to believe that the floodgates would be opened. There may be some increase in surveyor's insurance premiums which will be passed on to the public, but I cannot think that it will be anything approaching the difference between the [building society's] offer of a valuation without liability and a valuation with liability discussed in the speech of my noble and learned friend Lord Templeman. The result of denying a surveyor, in the circumstances of this case, the right to exclude liability will result in distributing the risk of his negligence among all house purchasers through an increase in his fees to cover insurance, rather than allowing the whole of the risk to fall on the one unfortunate purchaser.

I would not, however, wish it to be thought that I would consider it unreasonable for professional men in all circumstances to seek to exclude or limit their liability for negligence. Sometimes breathtaking sums may turn on professional advice against which it would be impossible for the adviser to obtain adequate insurance cover and which would ruin him if he were to be held personally liable. In these circumstances it may indeed be reasonable to give the advice upon a basis of no liability or possibly of liability limited to the extent of the adviser's insurance cover ...

> It must, however, be remembered that this is a decision in respect of a dwelling house of modest value in which it is widely recognised by surveyors that purchasers are in fact relying on their care and skill. It will obviously be of general application in broadly similar circumstances. But I expressly reserve my position in respect of valuations of quite different types of property ...

There will obviously be a variety of factors to be considered in each case and their importance will have to be assessed in the context of the particular case. The parties' relative bargaining powers may be relevant, as may the question of whether the party against whom the clause is being used, knew its contents, or had ample opportunity to ascertain them.[173]

However, although the application of the test is a weighing process and any factor is merely one indicator, some factors may be more significant than others. The existence, or otherwise, of an alternative, to the particular contract, has been important in some cases[174] and it was referred to by Lord Griffiths in *Smith v Bush*. The comment there was put in terms of whether or not the advice could have been obtained elsewhere, as advice was the commodity that the case was concerned with, but the availability of an alternative contract has been seen as generally relevant. It may be easier for a party to establish that his, or her, exemption clause is reasonable if it can also be established that he, or she, also offered an alternative higher priced contract which did not contain the exemption clause.[175] However, as the judgment of Lord Griffiths indicates, the court will consider not merely the existence of an alternative but also its reality. In *Smith v Bush*, cost was the factor making the alternative unrealistic, but insufficiently drawing an alternative to the attention of the other party might also adversely affect the court's view of it.

However, it may be that the most generally significant factor is that of insurance. As we have seen, it was considered in *Smith v Bush*, and particular reference is made to it in s 11(4), in the context of determining the reasonableness of limitation clauses. The basic questions will be as to which party was in the best position to insure, and at what cost. That was considered by the House of Lords in *Photo Production Ltd v Securicor Ltd*.[176] In that case, the contract was for the provision of security services, which included periodic nightly visits to PP's factory by S's employees. On one visit, one employee of S decided to start a fire. The factory was burnt down. The question was whether S could rely upon an exemption clause in relation to its liability for the

173 For example, *Singer Co (UK) Ltd v Tees and Hartlepool Port Authority* [1988] 2 Lloyd's Rep 164, *Stag Line Ltd v Tyne Ship Repair Group Ltd (The Zinnia)* [1984] 2 Lloyd's Rep 211.

174 *R W Green Ltd v Cade Bros Farms* [1978] 1 Lloyd's Rep 602, *Woodman v Photrade Processing Ltd* (unreported) but see (1981) 131 NLJ 935 and Miller & Harvey, *Consumer and Trading Law Cases and Materials.*

175 *Woodman v Photrade Processing Ltd* (unreported) but see (1981) 131 NLJ 935 and Miller & Harvey, *Consumer and Trading Law Cases and Materials.*

176 [1980] AC 827.

destruction of the factory. Because of the date when it was made, the contract was not one to which the Unfair Contract Terms Act 1977 applied. However, having answered the construction question in S's favour, and obviously aware of the test in the 1977 Act, the House of Lords commented that the clause was 'reasonable'. The parties were of roughly equal bargaining power, the risk of fire damage had been allocated to the party best able to insure against it, and S was providing a cheap service. PP had to insure its factory against fire damage in general and S could not have provided such a cheap service if it had needed to insure (even if it could have obtained such insurance).

In contrast with *Photo Productions*, the insurance factor was one indicator of the unreasonableness of the clause in *Salvage Assn v CAP*,[177] where the clause was being used against a party which, effectively, could not insure by the party which had insurance. Similarly, in *Mitchell v Finney Lock Seeds*[178] the insurance factor was one indicator of the clause lack of reasonableness. The seed sellers, who sought to rely on a limitation clause, could have insured without needing to materially increase their price.

Further light is shed on the insurance factor by *Smith v Bush*. As we have seen, in that case, the disclaimer was held to be unreasonable even though it was clear that if it was ineffective the surveyors would have to increase their prices to pay for further insurance. There was a pointer to reasonableness which was to be found in the correlation of a low price for a service hedged round by a limitation of liability and the need for surveyors to increase their prices, to cover increased insurance costs, if the limitation was not effective. However, in the circumstances, this pointer to reasonableness was outweighed by the consequences to individuals if the limitation was effective.

The potential consequences of allowing the disclaimer to be effective in *Smith v Bush* were extreme and arguably make it an unusual case, indicative of an approach which should not be followed too often. It should be noted that it was, however, followed in the case of *St Albans City and District Council v ICL*,[179] with the position of the council being equated with that of the house purchaser in *Smith v Bush*, which would seem to be considerable extension of the approach taken in the latter case. It seems that, more generally, and particularly in the commercial sphere, the question of the reasonableness of an exemption clause should, more usually, be determined by whether there was a correlation between the contract price and the use of an exemption clause, ie whether the party accepting the exemption clause thereby had only to pay a relatively cheap price. Although, of course, this might well be overridden if the exemption clause transferred the burden of the loss onto the party which

177 [1995] FSR 654.

178 *George Mitchell (Chesterhall) Ltd v Finney Lock Seeds Ltd* [1983] 2 AC 803.

179 [1995] FSR 686.

was unable to insure, as in *Salvage Assn v CAP*.[180] However, in both that case and the *St Albans* case it was indicated that when a limitation clause is in question it will be important to consider whether the precise level of the limit can be justified by some correlation to some other factor, such as the level of insurance cover available to the party seeking to rely on the clause.

In relation to software supplied in a commercial context it would certainly seem that there should be a strong argument for accepting an exemption clause as reasonable in a contract for the development of software, provided that there is an appropriate correlation between the price, the availability of insurance and the exemption clause. The development of software is not a dangerous task but it might well be seen as a difficult one with a significant risk of failure or, at least, of problems (bugs are notoriously difficult to eradicate). In that light, Lord Griffiths' third factor in *Smith v Bush* could be seen as indicating the reasonableness of an exemption clause in such a contract. It should be remembered that it was clearly key to the finding that the clause was unreasonable in the *Salvage Assn* case that CAP themselves had decided that £25,000 was too low a limit in the type of contract in question.

Unfair Terms in Consumer Contracts Regulations 1994[181]

UNFAIR TERMS IN CONSUMER CONTRACTS REGULATIONS 1994

(SI 1994, No 3159)

1. Citation and commencement

   These Regulations may be cited as the Unfair Terms in Consumer Contracts Regulations 1994 and shall come into force on 1st July 1995.

2. Interpretation

   (1) In these Regulations

   'business' includes a trade or profession and the activities of any government department or local or public authority;

   'the Community' means the European Economic Community and the other States in the European Economic Area;

   'consumer' means a natural person who, in making a contract to which these Regulations apply, is acting for purposes which are outside his business;

   'court' in relation to England and Wales and Northern Ireland means the High Court, and in relation to Scotland, the Court of Session;

   'Director' means the Director General of Fair Trading;

   'EEA Agreement' means the Agreement on the European Economic Area signed at Oporto on 2 May 1992 as adjusted by the Protocol signed at Brussels on 17 March 1993;

   'Member State' shall mean a State which is a contracting party to the

180 [1995] FSR 654.

181 See Koffman & Macdonald, *op cit*, Chapter 11.

EEA Agreement but until the EEA Agreement comes into force in relation to Liechtenstein does not include the State of Liechtenstein;

'seller' means a person who sells goods and who, in making a contract to which these Regulations apply, is acting for purposes relating to his business; and 'supplier' means a person who supplies goods or services and who, in making a contract to which these Regulations apply, is acting for purposes relating to his business.

3. Terms to which these Regulations apply

(1) Subject to the provisions of Schedule 1, these Regulations apply to any term in a contract concluded between a seller or supplier and a consumer where the said term has not been individually negotiated.

(2) In so far as it is in plain, intelligible language, no assessment shall be made of the fairness of any term which

(a) defines the main subject matter of the contract; or

(b) concerns the adequacy of the price or remuneration, as against the goods or services sold or supplied.

(3) For the purposes of these Regulations, a term shall always be regarded as not having been individually negotiated where it has been drafted in advance and the consumer has not been able to influence the substance of the term.

(4) Notwithstanding that a specific term or certain aspects of it in a contract has been individually negotiated, these Regulations shall apply to the rest of a contract if an overall assessment of the contract indicates that it is a pre-formulated standard contract.

(5) It shall be for any seller or supplier who claims that a term was individually negotiated to show that it was.

4. Unfair terms

(1) In these Regulations, subject to paragraphs (2) and (3) below, 'unfair term' means any term which contrary to the requirement of good faith causes a significant imbalance in the parties' rights and obligations under the contract to the detriment of the consumer.

(2) An assessment of the unfair nature of a term shall be made taking into account the nature of the goods or services for which the contract was concluded and referring, as at the time of the conclusion of the contract, to all circumstances attending the conclusion of the contract and to all the other terms of the contract or of another contract on which it is dependent.

(3) In determining whether a term satisfies the requirement of good faith, regard shall be had in particular to the matters specified in Schedule 2 to these Regulations.

(4) Schedule 3 to these Regulations contains an indicative and non-exhaustive list of the terms which may be regarded as unfair.

5. Consequence of inclusion of unfair terms in contracts

(1) An unfair term in a contract concluded with a consumer by a seller or supplier shall not be binding on the consumer.

(2) The contract shall continue to bind the parties if it is capable of continuing in existence without the unfair term.

6. Construction of written contracts

A seller or supplier shall ensure that any written term of a contract is expressed in plain, intelligible language, and if there is doubt about the meaning of a written term, the interpretation most favourable to the consumer shall prevail.

7. Choice of law clauses

These Regulations shall apply notwithstanding any contract term which applies or purports to apply the law of a non-Member State, if the contract has a close connection with the territory of the Member States.

8. Prevention of continued use of unfair terms

(1) It shall be the duty of the Director to consider any complaint made to him that any contract term drawn up for general use is unfair, unless the complaint appears to the Director to be frivolous or vexatious.

(2) If having considered a complaint about any contract term pursuant to paragraph (1) above the Director considers that the contract term is unfair he may, if he considers it appropriate to do so, bring proceedings for an injunction (in which proceedings he may also apply for an interlocutory injunction) against any person appearing to him to be using or recommending use of such a term in contracts concluded with consumers.

(3) The Director may, if he considers it appropriate to do so, have regard to any undertakings given to him by or on behalf of any person as to the continued use of such a term in contracts concluded with consumers.

(4) The Director shall give reasons for his decision to apply or not to apply, as the case may be, for an injunction in relation to any complaint which these Regulations require him to consider.

(5) The court on an application by the Director may grant an injunction on such terms as it thinks fit.

(6) An injunction may relate not only to use of a particular contract term drawn up for general use but to any similar term, or a term having like effect, used or recommended for use by any party to the proceedings.

(7) The Director may arrange for the dissemination in such form and manner as he considers appropriate of such information and advice concerning the operation of these Regulations as may appear to him to be expedient to give to the public and to all persons likely to be affected by these Regulations.

SCHEDULE 1

CONTRACTS AND PARTICULAR TERMS EXCLUDED FROM THE SCOPE OF THESE REGULATIONS

These Regulations do not apply to

(a) any contract relating to employment;

(b) any contract relating to succession rights;

(c) any contract relating to rights under family law;

(d) any contract relating to the incorporation and organisation of companies or partnerships; and

(e) any term incorporated in order to comply with or which reflects

(i) statutory or regulatory provisions of the United Kingdom; or

(ii) the provisions or principles of international conventions to which the member States or the Community are party.

SCHEDULE 2

ASSESSMENT OF GOOD FAITH

In making an assessment of good faith, regard shall be had in particular to

(a) the strength of the bargaining positions of the parties;

(b) whether the consumer had an inducement to agree to the term;

(c) whether the goods or services were sold or supplied to the special order of the consumer; and

(d) the extent to which the seller or supplier has dealt fairly and equitably with the consumer.

SCHEDULE 3

INDICATIVE AND ILLUSTRATIVE LIST OF TERMS WHICH MAY BE REGARDED AS UNFAIR

[See annex of Directive – below.]

EC Directive on Unfair Terms in Consumer Contracts

Having regard to the Treaty establishing the European Economic Community, and in particular Article 100A thereof,

Having regard to the proposal from the Commission,

In co-operation with the European Parliament,

Having regard to the opinion of the Economic and Social Committee,

Whereas it is necessary to adopt measures with the aim of progressively establishing the internal market before 31 December 1992; whereas the internal market comprises an area without internal frontiers in which goods, persons, services and capital move freely;

Whereas the laws of Member States relating to the terms of contract between the seller of goods or supplier of services, on the one hand, and the consumer of them, on the other hand, show many disparities, with the result that the national markets for the sale of goods and services to consumers differ from each other and that distortions of competition may arise amongst the sellers and suppliers, notably when they sell and supply in other Member States;

Whereas, in particular, the laws of Member States relating to unfair terms in consumer contracts show marked divergences;

Whereas it is the responsibility of the Member States to ensure that contracts concluded with consumers do not contain unfair terms;

Whereas, generally speaking, consumers do not know the rules of law which, in Member States other than their own, govern contracts for the sale of goods or services; whereas this lack of awareness may deter them from direct transactions for the purchase of goods or services in another Member State;

Whereas, in order to facilitate the establishment of the internal market and to safeguard the citizen in his role as consumer when acquiring goods and services under contracts which are governed by the laws of Member States other than his own, it is essential to remove unfair terms from those contracts;

Whereas sellers of goods and suppliers of services will thereby be helped in their task of selling goods and supplying services, both at home and throughout the internal market; whereas competition will thus be stimulated, so contributing to increased choice for Community citizens as consumers;

Whereas the two Community programmes for a consumer protection and information policy underlined the importance of safeguarding consumers in the matter of unfair terms of contract; whereas this protection ought to be provided by laws and regulations which are either harmonised at Community level or adopted directly at that level;

Whereas in accordance with the principle laid down under the heading 'Protection of the economic interests of the consumers', as stated in those programmes: 'acquirers of goods and services should be protected against the abuse of power by the seller or supplier, in particular against one-sided standard contracts and the unfair exclusion of essential rights in contracts';

Whereas more effective protection of the consumer can be achieved by adopting uniform rules of law in the matter of unfair terms; whereas those rules should apply to all contracts concluded between sellers or suppliers and consumers; whereas as a result *inter alia* contracts relating to employment, contracts relating to succession rights, contracts relating to rights under family law and contracts relating to the incorporation and organisation of companies or partnership agreements must be excluded from this Directive;

Whereas the consumer must receive equal protection under contracts concluded by word of mouth and written contracts regardless, in the latter case, of whether the terms of the contract are contained in one or more documents;

Whereas, however, as they now stand, national laws allow only partial harmonisation to be envisaged; whereas, in particular, only contractual terms which have not been individually negotiated are covered by this Directive; whereas Member States should have the option, with due regard for the Treaty, to afford consumers a higher level of protection through national provisions that are more stringent than those of this Directive;

Whereas the statutory or regulatory provisions of the Member States which directly or indirectly determine the terms of consumer contracts are presumed not to contain unfair terms; whereas, therefore, it does not appear to be necessary to subject the terms which reflect mandatory statutory or regulatory provisions and the principles or provisions of international conventions to which the Member States or the Community are party; whereas in that respect the wording 'mandatory statutory or regulatory provisions' in Article 1(2) also covers rules which, according to the law, shall apply between the contracting parties provided that no other arrangements have been established;

Whereas Member States must however ensure that unfair terms are not included, particularly because this Directive also applies to trades, businesses or professions of a public nature;

Whereas it is necessary to fix in a general way the criteria for assessing the unfair character of contract terms;

Whereas the assessment, according to the general criteria chosen, of the unfair character of terms, in particular in sale or supply activities of a public nature providing collective services which take account of solidarity among users, must be supplemented by a means of making an overall evaluation of the different interests involved; whereas this constitutes the requirement of good faith; whereas, in making an assessment of good faith, particular regard shall be had to the strength of the bargaining positions of the parties, whether the consumer had an inducement to agree to the term and whether the goods or services were sold or supplied to the special order of the consumer;

Whereas the requirement of good faith may be satisfied by the seller or supplier where he deals fairly and equitably with the other party whose legitimate interests he has to take into account;

Whereas, for the purposes of this Directive, the annexed list of terms can be of indicative value only and, because of the cause of the minimal character of the Directive, the scope of these terms may be the subject of amplification or more restrictive editing by the Member States in their national laws;

Whereas the nature of goods or services should have an influence on assessing the unfairness of contractual terms;

Whereas, for the purposes of this Directive, assessment of unfair character shall not be made of terms which describe the main subject matter of the contract nor the quality/price ratio of the goods or services supplied; whereas the main subject matter of the contract and the price/quality ratio may nevertheless be taken into account in assessing the fairness of other terms; whereas it follows, *inter alia*, that in insurance contracts, the terms which clearly define or circumscribe the insured risk and the insurer's liability shall not be subject to such assessment since these restrictions are taken into account in calculating the premium paid by the consumer;

Whereas contracts should be drafted in plain, intelligible language, the consumer should actually be given an opportunity to examine all the terms and, if in doubt, the interpretation most favourable to the consumer should prevail;

Whereas Member States should ensure that unfair terms are not used in contracts concluded with consumers by a seller or supplier and that if, nevertheless, such terms are so used, they will not bind the consumer, and the contract will continue to bind the parties upon those terms if it is capable of continuing in existence without the unfair provisions;

Whereas there is a risk that, in certain cases, the consumer may be deprived of protection under this Directive by designating the law of a non-Member country as the law applicable to the contract; whereas provisions should therefore be included in this Directive designed to avert this risk;

Whereas persons or organisations, if regarded under the law of a Member State as having a legitimate interest in the matter, must have facilities for initiating proceedings concerning terms of contract drawn up for general use in contracts concluded with consumers, and in particular unfair terms, either before a court or before an administrative authority competent to decide upon complaints or to initiate appropriate legal proceedings; whereas this possibility does not, however, entail prior verification of the general conditions obtaining in individual economic sectors;

Whereas the courts or administrative authorities of the Member States must have at their disposal adequate and effective means of preventing the continued application of unfair terms in consumer contracts,

HAS ADOPTED THIS DIRECTIVE:

Article 1

1. The purpose of this Directive is to approximate the laws, regulations and administrative provisions of the Member States relating to unfair terms in contracts concluded between a seller or supplier and a consumer.
2. The contractual terms which reflect mandatory statutory or regulatory provisions and the provisions or principles of international conventions to which the Member States or the Community are party, particularly in the transport area, shall not be subject to the provisions of this Directive.

Article 2

For the purposes of this Directive:

(a) 'unfair terms' means the contractual terms defined in Article 3;

(b) 'consumer' means any natural person who, in contracts covered by this Directive, is acting for purposes which are outside his trade, business or profession;

(c) 'seller or supplier' means any natural or legal person who, in contracts covered by this Directive, is acting for purposes relating to his trade, business or profession, whether publicly owned or privately owned.

Article 3

1. A contractual term which has not been individually negotiated shall be regarded as unfair if, contrary to the requirement of good faith, it causes a significant imbalance in the parties' rights and obligations arising under the contract, to the detriment of the consumer.
2. A term shall always be regarded as not individually negotiated where it has been drafted in advance and the consumer has therefore not been able

to influence the substance of the term, particularly in the context of a pre-formulated standard contract.

The fact that certain aspects of a term or one specific term have been individually negotiated shall not exclude the application of this Article to the rest of a contract if an overall assessment of the contract indicates that it is nevertheless a pre-formulated standard contract.

Where any seller or supplier claims that a standard term has been individually negotiated, the burden of proof in this respect shall be incumbent on him.

3. The Annex shall contain an indicative and non-exhaustive list of the terms which may be regarded as unfair.

Article 4

1. Without prejudice to Article 7, the unfairness of a contractual term shall be assessed, taking into account the nature of the goods or services for which the contract was concluded and by referring, at the time of conclusion of the contract, to all the circumstances attending the conclusion of the contract and to all the other terms of the contract or of another contract on which it is dependent.
2. Assessment of the unfair nature of the terms shall relate neither to the definition of the main subject matter of the contract nor to the adequacy of the price and remuneration, on the one hand, as against the services or goods supplied in exchange, on the other in so far as these terms are in plain intelligible language.

Article 5

In the case of contracts where all or certain terms offered to the consumer are in writing, these terms must always be drafted in plain, intelligible language. Where there is doubt about the meaning of a term, the interpretation most favourable to the consumer shall prevail. This rule on interpretation shall not apply in the context of the procedures laid down in Article 7(2).

Article 6

1. Member States shall lay down that unfair terms used in a contract concluded with a consumer by a seller or supplier shall, as provided for under their national law, not be binding on the consumer and that the contract shall continue to bind the parties upon those terms if it is capable of continuing in existence without the unfair terms.
2. Member States shall take the necessary measures to ensure that the consumer does not lose the protection granted by this Directive by virtue of the choice of the law of a non-Member country as the law applicable to the contract if the latter has a close connection with the territory of the Member States.

Article 7

1. Member States shall ensure that, in the interests of consumers and of competitors, adequate and effective means exist to prevent the continued

use of unfair terms in contracts concluded with consumers by sellers or suppliers.

2. The means referred to in paragraph 1 shall include provisions whereby persons or organisations, having a legitimate interest under national law in protecting consumers, may take action according to the national law concerned before the courts or before competent administrative bodies for a decision as to whether contractual terms drawn up for general use are unfair, so that they can apply appropriate and effective means to prevent the continued use of such terms.
3. With due regard for national laws, the legal remedies referred to in paragraph 2 may be directed separately or jointly against a number of sellers or suppliers from the same economic sector or their associations which use or recommend the use of the same general contractual terms or similar terms.

Article 8

Member States may adopt or retain the most stringent provisions compatible with the Treaty in the area covered by this Directive, to ensure a maximum degree of protection for the consumer.

Article 9

The Commission shall present a report to the European Parliament and to the Council concerning the application of this Directive five years at the latest after the date in Article 10(1).

Article 10

1. Member States shall bring into force the laws, regulations and administrative provisions necessary to comply with this Directive no later than 31 December 1994. They shall forthwith inform the Commission thereof. These provisions shall be applicable to all contracts concluded after 31 December 1994.
2. When Member States adopt these measures, they shall contain a reference to this Directive or shall be accompanied by such reference on the occasion of their official publication. The methods of making such a reference shall be laid down by the Member States.
3. Member States shall communicate the main provisions of national law which they adopt in the field covered by this Directive to the Commission.

Article 11

This Directive is addressed to the Member States.

Done at Luxembourg, 5 April 1993.

ANNEX

TERMS REFERRED TO IN ARTICLE 3(3)

1. Terms which have the object or effect of
   - (a) excluding or limiting the legal liability of a seller or supplier in the event of the death of a consumer or personal injury to the latter resulting from an act or omission of that seller or supplier;
   - (b) inappropriately excluding or limiting the legal rights of the consumer *vis-à-vis* the seller or supplier or another party in the event of total or partial non-performance or inadequate performance by the seller or supplier of any of the contractual obligations, including the option of offsetting a debt owed to the seller or supplier against any claim which the consumer may have against him;
   - (c) making an agreement binding on the consumer whereas provision of services by the seller or supplier is subject to a condition whose realisation depends on his own will alone;
   - (d) permitting the seller or supplier to retain sums paid by the consumer where the latter decided not to conclude or perform the contract, without providing for the consumer to receive compensation of an equivalent amount from the seller or supplier where the latter is the party cancelling the contract;
   - (e) requiring any consumer who fails to fulfil his obligation to pay a disproportionately high sum in compensation;
   - (f) authorising the seller or supplier to dissolve the contract on a discretionary basis where the same facility is not granted to the consumer, or permitting the seller or supplier to retain the sums paid for services not yet supplied by him where it is the seller or supplier himself who dissolves the contract;
   - (g) enabling the seller or supplier to terminate a contract of indeterminate duration without reasonable notice except where there are serious grounds for doing so;
   - (h) automatically extending a contract of fixed duration where the consumer does not indicate otherwise, when the deadline fixed for the consumer to express this desire not to extend the contract is unreasonably early;
   - (i) irrevocably binding the consumer to terms with which he had no real opportunity of becoming acquainted before the conclusion of the contract;
   - (j) enabling the seller or supplier to alter the terms of the contract unilaterally without a valid reason which is specified in the contract;
   - (k) enabling the seller or supplier to alter unilaterally without a valid reason any characteristics of the product or service to be provided;
   - (l) providing for the price of goods to be determined at the time of delivery or allowing a seller of goods or supplier of services to increase their price without in both cases giving the consumer the

corresponding right to cancel the contract if the final price is too high in relation to the price agreed when the contract was concluded;

(m) giving the seller or supplier the right to determine whether the goods or services supplied are in conformity with the contract, or giving him the exclusive right to interpret any term of the contract;

(n) limiting the seller's or supplier's obligation to respect commitments undertaken by his agents or making his commitments subject to compliance with a particular formality;

(o) obliging the consumer to fulfil all his obligations where the seller or supplier does not perform his;

(p) giving the seller or supplier the possibility of transferring his rights and obligations under the contract, where this may serve to reduce the guarantees for the consumer, without the latter's agreement;

(q) excluding or hindering the consumer's right to take legal action or exercise any other legal remedy, particularly by requiring the consumer to take disputes exclusively to arbitration not covered by legal provisions, unduly restricting the evidence available to him or imposing on him a burden of proof which, according to the applicable law, should lie with another party to the contract.

2. Scope of subparagraphs (g), (j) and (l)

(a) Subparagraph (g) is without hindrance to terms by which a supplier of financial services reserves the right to terminate unilaterally a contract of indeterminate duration without notice where there is a valid reason, provided that the supplier is required to inform the other contracting party or parties thereof immediately.

(b) Subparagraph (j) is without hindrance to terms under which a supplier of financial services reserves the right to alter the rate of interest payable by the consumer or due to the latter, or the amount of other charges for financial services without notice where there is a valid reason, provided that the supplier is required to inform the other contracting party or parties thereof at the earliest opportunity and that the latter are free to dissolve the contract immediately.

Subparagraph (j) is also without hindrance to terms under which a seller or supplier reserves the right to alter unilaterally the conditions of a contract of indeterminate duration, provided that he is required to inform the consumer with reasonable notice and that the consumer is free to dissolve the contract.

(c) Subparagraphs (g), (j) and (l) do not apply to: transactions in transferable securities, financial instruments and other products or services where the price is linked to fluctuations in a stock exchange quotation or index or a financial market rate that the seller or supplier does not control; – contracts for the purchase or sale of foreign currency, traveller's cheques or international money orders denominated in foreign currency;

(d) Subparagraph (l) is without hindrance to price-indexation clauses, where lawful, provided that the method by which prices vary is explicitly described.

The 1994 regulations, which came into force on 1 July 1995, implemented the EC Directive on Unfair Terms in Consumer Contracts.[182] They do not simply apply to exemption clauses. The Regulations apply a fairness test to non-individually negotiated terms in contracts between consumers and sellers or suppliers, with certain 'core' terms being exempted from the test provided they are in plain, intelligible language. Certain contracts are excluded from the scope of the Regulations,[183] but there is no equivalent of Schedule 1, para 1(c) of the 1977 Act, with its reference to intellectual property rights.

The definition of 'consumer' is in Regulation 2. It is restricted to 'natural persons', which means that a company cannot be a consumer for the purposes of the regulations. This differs from the category of those who 'deal as consumers' under the Unfair Contract Terms Act 1977 and in general a mechanistic approach to the categorisation under the regulations seems likely, with businesses simply being excluded from its protection, without any consideration of how central the contract in question is to the operation of the business.[184]

The fairness test is applied to terms which have not been individually negotiated. Most such terms will be contained in standard form contracts but the category does not seem to be solely limited to such terms. Regulation 3(3) states that:

> a term shall always be regarded as not having been individually negotiated where it has been drafted in advance and the consumer has not been able to influence the substance of the term.

The exclusion of certain 'core' terms from the fairness test is covered by Regulation 3(2). It would seem to cover terms defining the main subject matter of the contract or stating the price, its exact scope is, however, problematic,[185] and it should be emphasised that it is restricted to cases in which the 'core' terms are in 'plain, intelligible language'. In any event, it would seem that the 'core' terms should always be taken into account in assessing the fairness of other terms.[186]

Regulation 4(1) states that an unfair term is one which:

> contrary to the requirement of good faith causes a significant imbalance in the parties' rights and obligations to the detriment of the consumer.

182 (1993) OJ L 95/29 – made under Article 100A on the basis that it is concerned with the establishment of an internal market.

183 Schedule 1.

184 Contrast the approach to 'deals as consumer' under the 1977 Act. See p 130.

185 Macdonald [1994] JBL 441.

186 See recital 19 of the Directive.

Like 'reasonableness' under the 1977 Act this is assessed against the background of the circumstances at the time of contracting.[187] Looking for a significant imbalance in the parties' rights and obligations would seem to require a weighing of the rights and obligations of the two parties. There are guidelines on 'good faith' in Schedule 2, which for the most part, are familiar from the guidelines to the reasonableness test under the 1977 Act.[188] They differ, however, in expressly making relevant to the question of good faith, 'the extent to which the seller or supplier has dealt fairly and equitably with the consumer'. Further assistance in determining which terms will be unfair can be found in Schedule 3, which contains a non-exhaustive list of terms which 'may be regarded as unfair'.

The consumer can use the Regulations in the same way as someone can use the Unfair Contract Terms Act 1977 against an exemption clause. An unfair term will not bind the consumer,[189] and the consumer can rely on this when in dispute with a seller or supplier. However, the Regulations also provide for a different form of attack on unfair terms. The Director General of Fair Trading has the power to, *inter alia*, obtain injunctions to prevent the use of unfair terms more generally.[190]

187 Regulation 4(2).

188 In Schedule 2 of the 1977 Act.

189 Regulation 5(1).

190 Regulation 8.

CHAPTER FOUR

DEFECTIVE SOFTWARE – CONTRACT

INTRODUCTION

This chapter is concerned with contractual liability for defective software, principally computer programs which raise questions unique to the area of information technology law and, unless otherwise indicated, the references to software should be understood accordingly. Obviously, such liability may well stem from an express term of the contract (see Chapter 4) but this chapter will focus on whether one of the statutory regimes, implying terms into certain types of contract, can apply to a contract for the supply of software. The Sale of Goods Act 1979, for example, implies terms that goods must correspond with their description (s 13) and sample (s 15), and that they should be of satisfactory quality (s 14(2)) and reasonably fit for the buyer's particular purpose (s 14(3)). Sections 8–10 of the Supply of Goods and Services Act 1982 imply similar terms into contracts for the hire of goods and s 13 implies a term into a contract for services, that the services will be carried out with reasonable care and skill. Obviously, if applicable, such terms could be very helpful to someone seeking damages for defects in a program but, before the content and application of those terms is considered, there is a major issue to be addressed – the classification of contracts for the supply of software. Can a contract for the supply of software constitute a contract for the sale of goods? Even if software can be described as 'goods', would a contract for its supply be better classified as a contract for services? These are the type of issues which will, initially, be considered in this chapter.

However, before addressing the question of whether software can be 'goods', some points should be made to clarify the discussion. Programs are most commonly supplied on a disk or other such medium and the focus will be on that method of supply. Unless otherwise indicated, references to software will be to programs on disks. It will be made clear when what is being looked at is the treatment of any program which has been downloaded over a telephone line, or using some other such link.

SALE OF GOODS

In *St Albans City and District Council v International Computers Ltd*[1] Sir Iain Glidewell stated that software could constitute goods. That case should be looked at before embarking on a more general discussion of the question of that categorisation. His comments were *obiter* and the issue requires full consideration.

St Albans City and District Council v International Computers Ltd [1996] 4 All ER 481

This case was concerned with the sale of a computer and software, by ICL, to the local authority, which wanted the computer to deal with the introduction of the Community Charge and its finances generally. A defect in the program led to an overstatement of the population figure for the council's area and a consequent loss of revenue from central government and from the Community Charge itself (the rate was set too low for the smaller number of people from which the Community Charge would actually be collected), and also meant that the council had to pay a larger sum to the County Council by way of precept. The loss to the council was something in excess of £1.3m. The question was whether this was recoverable from ICL. It was found that there was a breach of an express term. ICL claimed to rely upon a limitation clause to restrict this liability to £100,000 but Scott Baker J found that was ineffective under the Unfair Contract Terms Act 1977[2] and the local authority recovered. The Court of Appeal basically agreed with the decision of Scott Baker J, except that the sum recoverable by the council from ICL was reduced to take account of the fact that the loss of revenue from the community charge itself had, rightly, been claimed from charge payers the following year. However, what is important here is that it was considered whether terms could be implied by the Sale of Goods Act 1979 into contracts for software.

Sir Iain Glidewell

> [Was] the contract between the parties subject to any implied term as to quality or fitness for purpose, and if so, what was the nature of that term? Consideration of this question during argument led to discussion of a more general question, namely: 'Is software goods?' To seek to answer this question, it is necessary first to be clear about the meaning of some of the words used in argument.
>
> In his judgment, Scott Baker J ([1995] FSR 686 at 698) adopted a description of a computer system which contains the following passage which I have found helpful:
>
>> By itself hardware can do nothing. The really important part of the system is the software. Programs are the instructions or commands that tell the hardware what to do. The program itself is an algorithm or formula. It is of necessity contained in a physical medium. A program

1 [1996] 4 All ER 481.

2 [1995] FSR 686.

> in machine readable form must be contained on a machine readable medium, such as paper cards, magnetic cards, magnetic tapes, discs, drums ...

In relation to COMCIS the property in the program, ie the intangible 'instructions or commands', remained with ICL. Under the contract, St Albans was licensed to use the program. This is a common feature of contracts of this kind. However, in order that the program should be encoded in the computer itself, it was necessarily first recorded on a disk, from which it could be transferred to the computer. During the course of the hearing the term 'software' was used to include both the (tangible) disk onto which the COMCIS program had been encoded and the (intangible) program itself. In order to answer the question, however, it is necessary to distinguish between the program and the disk carrying the program.

In both the Sale of Goods Act 1979, s 61, and the Supply of Goods and Services Act 1982, s 18, the definition of goods includes 'all personal chattels other than things in action and money'. Clearly, a disk is within this definition. Equally clearly, a program, of itself, is not.

If a disk carrying a program is transferred, by way of sale or hire, and the program is in some way defective, so that it will not instruct or enable the computer to achieve the intended purpose, is this a defect in the disk? Put more precisely, would the seller or hirer of the disk be in breach of the terms as to quality and fitness for purpose implied by s 14 of the 1979 Act and s 9 of the 1982 Act? Mr Dehn QC, for ICL, argues that they would not. He submits that the defective program in my example would be distinct from the tangible disk, and thus that the 'goods' – the disk – would not be defective.

There is no English authority on this question ... We were referred as was Scott Baker J, to a decision of Rogers J in the Supreme Court of New South Wales, *Toby Constructions Products Pty Ltd v Computa Bar (Sales) Pty Ltd* [1983] NSWLR 48. The decision in that case was that the sale of a whole computer system, including both hardware and software, was a sale of 'goods' within the New South Wales legislation, which defines goods in similar terms to those in the English statute. That decision was in my respectful view clearly correct, but it does not answer the present question. Indeed Rogers J specifically did not answer it. In expressing an opinion I am therefore venturing where others have, no doubt wisely, not trodden.

Suppose I buy an instruction manual on the maintenance and repair of a particular make of car. The instructions are wrong in an important respect. Anybody who follows them is likely to cause serious damage to the engine of his car. In my view, the instructions are an integral part of the manual. The manual including the instructions, whether in book or video cassette, would in my opinion be 'goods' within the meaning of the 1979 Act, and the defective instructions would result in a breach of the implied terms in s 14.

If this is correct, I can see no logical reason why it should not also be correct in relation to a computer disk onto which a program designed and intended to instruct or enable a computer to achieve particular functions has been encoded. If the disk is sold or hired by the computer manufacturer, but the program is defective, in my opinion there would *prima facie* be a breach of the terms as to quality and fitness for purpose implied by the 1979 Act or the 1982 Act.

Some unease may be generated by the idea of treating an error in the instructions in a manual as a defect in goods that could constitute a breach of the terms implied by s 14 of the Sale of Goods Act 1979. Someone exercising professional expertise is normally only required to do so with due care and would not usually be subject to strict liability, such as that embodied in the implied terms. However, whatever the situation in relation to an instruction manual, there may be a stronger argument for characterising software as goods because of its functional nature, a point which will be returned to below.[3]

It should be emphasised that Sir Iain Glidewell's comments were *obiter*. There was an express term which covered the situation and, in any event, the case could not be one for the sale, or even hire, of goods, no matter what the characterisation of software. The disks containing the program were not supplied to the Council, rather a representative of ICL installed the program onto the Council's computers and the Council did not come into possession of the disks as such. The case is an important one, but the question of categorising software should now be addressed generally.

The starting point, for considering whether software can be goods, should be the statutory definition of goods. Section 61 of the Sale of Goods Act 1979 states:

> 'Goods' includes all personal chattels other than things in action and money ...

One argument is that a computer program cannot be goods as it is, in nature, information and not a 'personal chattel'. Another is that it is intellectual property and so is covered by the exclusion, from the definition, of 'things in action'. These two arguments should be considered.

INFORMATION

The argument that a program is information and so cannot be goods is put forward by Scott.

Andrew Scott, 'Software as Goods: nullum simile est idem' [1987] Comp Law & Practice 133

> The starting point in determining whether to classify software as goods or services must be the definition of 'goods' in s 61 of the Sale of Goods Act 1979. This defines 'goods' as including all personal chattels other than things in action and money. A personal chattel is a chose in possession, which is a form of personal property, that is, a thing in which a person has property rights.
>
> Software, since it is simply coded information, is altogether different in nature from personal property. In *Prince Albert v Strange* (1849) 1 Mac & G 25, however, Lord Cottenham LC held that the plaintiff could restrain the

3 See p 157.

publication of copies of etchings made by the plaintiff, on the basis of the existence of property rights in those etchings. His Lordship stated:

> 'The property in an author or composer of any work of literature, art or science, such work being unpublished and kept for his private use or pleasure, cannot be disputed.'

However, this proposition can no longer be considered good law. In *Fraser v Evans* [1969] 1 QB 349 Lord Denning MR stated that in proper circumstances the courts will restrain the publication or use of confidential information; but that the jurisdiction of the court to do so was not based on the existence of property rights or contract, but on the duty of good faith. The existence of property rights in information has been repudiated by high authority. In *Boardman v Phipps* [1967] 2 AC 46 Lord Upjohn stated:

> 'In general information is not property at all. It is normally open to all who have eyes to read and ears to hear ... [C]onfidential information is often and for many years has been described as the property of the donor ... But in the end the real truth is that it is not property in any normal sense but equity will restrain its transmission to another if in breach of some confidential relationship.'

Therefore rights with respect to information concern control over its use. It was this proposition which formed the basis of the decision of the stipendiary magistrate in *Oxford v Moss* [1978] 68 Cr App Rep 183, which was upheld on appeal. The defendant, who was an engineering undergraduate, was charged with the theft of confidential information from the senate of his university. This information consisted of the questions set for an examination. On appeal by the prosecutor, the Divisional Court held that confidential information was not 'property' within the meaning of s 4 of the Theft Act 1968, and therefore could not be appropriated.

Information, although not property, has value in itself. The courts recognise and protect this intrinsic value by permitting the author or donor control over its use. When information is recorded on some medium, that medium is then invested with the value of the information. Information, and therefore software, cannot be considered as 'goods' within the definition contained in s 61.

However, when a program is embodied on a computer disk or other such medium, the argument that it is simply information can be met from two perspectives – (a) the physical and (b) the functional.

(a) Physical

The physical argument, that the program has physical form on the disk or other such medium, was recognised in the *St Albans* case.[4] It was also used in the criminal case of *R v Whitely*[5] where the question was whether the alteration and deletion of computer files by a 'hacker' could constitute criminal damage

4 In the *St Albans* case, Sir Iain Glidewell recognised that a program, 'of itself' was not goods but concluded that it could be when embodied in a disk – see above.

5 [1991] *The Times*, 6 February. See also *Cox v Riley* [1986] CLR 460.

within s 1(1) of the Criminal Damage Act 1971. Additionally, it has been focused on by the US courts, for example, by the Supreme Court of Louisiana in *South Central Bell Telephone Co v Barthelemy*.[6] In considering whether the software Bell had acquired constituted 'tangible personal property' for the purposes of a New Orleans sales and use tax. It was said:

> South Central Bell argues that the software is merely 'knowledge' or 'intelligence', and as such is not corporeal and thus not taxable. We disagree with South Central Bell's characterisation. The software at issue is not merely knowledge but rather knowledge recorded in a physical form which has physical existence, takes up space on the tape, disk or hard drive, makes physical things happen and can be perceived by the senses ...

R v Whitely (1991) 33 Cr Rep 25

Lord Lane LCJ gave the opinion of the Court of Appeal.

> The principle ground of the defence which has formed the basis of the appeal to this Court was that a distinction had to be made between the disc itself and the intangible information held upon it which, it was contended, was not capable of damage as defined in law. The argument put before the court of trial and repeated here was as follows:
>
> The computers and the disc cannot be damaged by the sort of interference performed by the appellant. They were designed to perform a particular function and, despite the appellants actions, they were still capable of performing that function. Neither the computers nor the discs suffered any physical damage at all. Any destruction or alteration of the information on a disc, or the writing of information to a disc, only affects information on the disc and does not damage or impair the usefulness of the disc itself ...
>
> Section 10(1) of the Criminal damage Act 1971, so far as material to the present case, defines 'property' as 'property of a tangible nature', whether real or personal ...
>
> The evidence before the jury was that discs are so constructed as to contain upon them thousands, if not millions, of magnetic particles. By issuing commands to the computer, impulses are produced which magnetise or demagnetise those particles in a particular way. By that means it is possible to write data or information on the discs and to program them to fulfil a variety of functions. By the same method it is possible to delete or alter data, information or instructions which have previously been written on the disc. The argument advanced on behalf of the appellant when reduced to its essence seems to us to be this. That since the state of the magnetic particles on the disc is not perceptible by the unaided human senses, for instance sight or touch, the appellant's activities only affected the 'intangible information contained' on the disc itself even if the absence of such a perceptible change is not fatal to the prosecution, goes on the submission, interference with particles cannot amount to damage in law.

6 643 So 2d 1240 (1994 La).

> It seems to us that the contention contains a basic fallacy. What the Act requires to be proved is that intangible property has been damaged, not necessarily that the damage itself should be tangible. There can be no doubt that the magnetic particles upon the metal disc were part of the discs and if the appellant was proved to have intentionally and without lawful excuse altered the particles in such a way as to cause an impairment of the value or usefulness of the disc to the owner, there would be damage within the meaning of s 1. The fact that the alteration could only be perceived by operating the computer did not make the alterations any the less real, or the damage ...

It should be noted that the type of situation which was considered in *Whitely* was taken outside the scope of the Criminal Damage Act 1971 by the Computer Misuse Act 1990, following the recommendations of the Law Commission.[7] The basic approach remains of interest here. It emphasises the physical embodiment of the program on the computer disk or other such medium.[8]

(b) Functional

The second point to be raised, against the argument that software cannot be goods because it is information, is that based on its functional aspect. In the *South Central Bell* case (above) reference was made to the fact that the software is used to make a computer (ie hardware) 'perform a desired function' and this aspect of software should now be considered.

It should be asked whether a program, embodied on a disk and ready to be fed into a computer, is merely information? Is it distinguishable from the exam paper in *Oxford v Moss*[9] which was referred to by Scott?[10] If a program is likened to a literary work, which is the categorisation applied to it to provide it with the protection of copyright, then it is most like an instruction manual or 'how to' book, which was the analogy made by Sir Iain Glidewell in *St Albans v ICL*. Certainly, software is not like a novel! However, a program differs from even an instruction manual. It does not simply tell the individual what to do. The software interacts directly, with the hardware. In *St Albans City and District Council v International Computers Ltd*,[11] at first instance, Scott Baker J was of the opinion that software 'is not simply abstract information like information passed by word of mouth. Entering software alters the contents of the hardware'. This may not be an entirely accurate view of the effect of software on hardware but the general idea is clear enough – software

7 Report on Computer Misuse, No 186 (1989). See further Chapter 8.

8 But see *James Ashley v The London Borough of Sutton* [1995] TR L Rep 350.

9 (1978) 68 Cr App Rep 183.

10 See p 155.

11 [1995] FSR 686 at p 699.

is not mere information, it has a direct effect on hardware. Another point can also be made, following on from this. If there is a defect in software, there may well not be a point at which an individual has an opportunity to exercise judgment, assess what is occurring, and intervene to prevent some unexpected, and unwanted, result. Software may be information, but it is not simply information.

An analogy can be made here with the US case of *Winter v G P Puttnam & Sons*.[12] In that case, the question arose as to the applicability of product liability laws to a book on collecting and cooking mushrooms. It was held that the information contained in the book was not a product. What is of interest here is that, in coming to that conclusion, the court contrasted the situation before it with one involving software. It was indicated that software would be a product. The software was seen as something more than just information.[13] It can be contended that the functional aspect of software strengthens the case for the 'goods' categorisation to cover both a disk and the program embodied on it.

INTELLECTUAL PROPERTY

As we have seen, the definition of goods in the 1979 Act excludes 'things in action' and it might be argued that programs are covered by this exclusion and therefore are not goods. However, the program is not, itself, copyright; it is protected by copyright. This was recognised by Steyn J in *Eurodynamics Systems v General Automation Ltd*.[14] He said, 'Although the ideas and concepts involved in software remained [the defendants'] intellectual property, the reality of the transaction is that there has been the transfer of a product'. When there is a contract for the supply of a program, it is not simply an assignment of intellectual property rights. In fact, as has been indicated,[15] in most cases there will not be an assignment of the copyright in a program, although licenses are normally granted. Properly identified, the problem is whether, when intellectual property rights are in question, they dominate the

12 (1991) 938 F 2d 1033 (9th cir).

13 See further Saxby (ed) *Encyclopaedia of Information Technology Law* (1990) p 7084, Sweet & Maxwell. In fact, this type of distinction has been made in relation to US product liability laws in a way which might be used to argue that a program supplied as a written source code could constitute goods. In *Saloomey v Jeppesen* (1983) 707 F 2d 671 airline charts were not treated like other printed information. When a chart failed to show a mountain which was in the vicinity of an airport, it was held to be a defective product. Such information is relied on more automatically, and with less scope for assessment, than most information and the analogy with a computer program can be made. For discussion of the question of product liability see Chapter 5.

14 (1988) 6 September, unreported.

15 See p 96.

transaction to prevent the disk, with the program embodied in it, from being regarded as goods. Copyright restrictions are not seen as preventing a book, video tape or compact disc from being goods, but such items do not have a functional use in the way that software does, and that difference in use is not only noteworthy in itself, but also makes a considerable difference to the impact of intellectual property rights. Intellectual property rights impact upon the enjoyment of books and videos to a very much more limited extent than upon the enjoyment of software.[16] A book can be read or a video watched without any need for the purchaser to obtain a licence to avoid being in breach of copyright. In contrast, the use of software will entail copying it onto hardware which, in the absence of a licence, would, *prima facie,* be in breach of copyright,[17] although the impact of the EC Directive on this must now be borne in mind.[18] In other words, the basic purpose for which a book or video is purchased can be fulfilled without any need for the purchaser to consider intellectual property rights. The same is not true of software. Indeed the view has been taken that software cannot be likened to books or other such goods, but must be regarded as *sui generis*.[19]

> The analogy with a printed book is, in my opinion, false. Even if one considered the wider field of printed material, there would be no true analogy. A book typically is intended to be read, not copied, as a way of enjoying or using the object ... there are no limitations on accessing the information which affect readers generally ... In the case of software there is no possibility of accessing the information without copying it. In my opinion the only acceptable view is that the supply of proprietary software for a price is a contract *sui generis.*

However, the argument, that software cannot be goods because of the intellectual property rights involved, was considered by the US Court of Appeal for the Third Circuit in *Advent Systems Ltd v Unisys Corp*.[20] The court had to determine the applicability of Article 2 of the Uniform Commercial Code to a contract under which Advent agreed to supply hardware and 'license software' to Unisys.[21] Weiss J, delivering the opinion of the court, said:

> That a computer program may be copyrightable as intellectual property does not alter the fact that once in the form of a floppy disk or other medium, the program is tangible, movable and available in the marketplace.

---

16 See *Beta v Adobe* [1996] FSR 387.

17 Section 17(1) of the Copyright, Designs and Patents Act 1988.

18 See p 99 in relation to the impact of the EC Directive on the Protection of Computer Programs.

19 *Beta Computers (Europe) Ltd v Adobe Systems (Europe) Ltd* [1996] FSR 387.

20 925 F 2d 670. But see *Conopco Inc v McCreadie* 826 F Supp 855. The argument was not considered, as such, in *Beta v Adobe* but some support for it may be found in the approach there taken.

21 Article 2 applies to goods and intellectual property is outside the Code. See generally Rodau, 'Computer Software: Does Article 2 of the Uniform Commercial Code Apply' (1986) Emory LJ 853.

The court emphasised the physical embodiment of the program in a disk or other such medium in concluding that it was goods, and not merely intellectual property, and fell within Article 2. This same approach could be taken to indicate that a program embodied on a disk would be goods under the Sale of Goods Act 1979. However, some further, related, points must be considered in relation to whether a contract for the supply of a disk containing a program can be a contract for the sale of goods within the 1979 Act.

SALE OF GOODS

Section 2(1) of the Sale of Goods Act 1979 states that a contract of sale of goods is:

> a contract by which the seller transfers or agrees to transfer the property in goods to the buyer for a money consideration called the price.

The 'property in goods' is not the physical object but, basically the ownership of the goods.[22] The person to whom a disk is supplied will take it subject to the restrictions of copyright and a licence will normally be involved. The question is whether those restrictions are sufficient to prevent that person acquiring the 'property' in the goods? Certainly, copyright restrictions are not seen as preventing there from being a sale of a book, video tape or compact disc, but as has been indicated, such restrictions impact rather differently on books than on software. However, if a disk with a program on it is classified as goods, it may be doubted whether this type of argument would prevail.

Of course, if there is clearly no transfer of the ownership even of the disk or other such medium (which may well occur where non-standard software is in question), but a mere supply under an agreement that the disk will be returned when the program licence terminates, then the contract will not fall within the 1979 Act. However, it should be remembered that similar terms to those implied by the Sale of Goods Act 1979 are implied into contracts for the hire of goods by the Supply of Goods and Services Act 1982.

---

22 See generally Atiyah, *Sale of Goods* (1995) 9th edn, J Adams (ed) p 265 *et seq.*

HARDWARE AND SOFTWARE AND PRAGMATISM

Consideration has been given to the arguments that a program is information or copyright and so cannot constitute goods. Some arguments in favour of that classification have been indicated, but we should now consider two further such arguments. One relates to the situation where software is sold with hardware but another, based on pragmatism, is more general.

Hardware and software

In *St Albans v ICL*[23] Scott Baker J, and subsequently Sir Iain Glidewell in the Court of Appeal[24] adopted the description of a computer system used in the Australian case of *Toby Constructions Products Ltd v Computer Bar Sales Pty Ltd*:[25]

> By itself hardware can do nothing. The really important part of the system is the software. Programs are the instructions or commands that tell the hardware what to do.

On this basis, where software is supplied with hardware, it is possible to draw an analogy, with other cases falling within the Sale of Goods Act 1979, to argue that a problem in the program could lead to a breach of one of the implied terms as to quality or fitness for purpose in s 14. In *Wormell v RHM Agriculture Ltd*[26] consideration was given to whether there was a breach of the term implied by s 14(3) of the Sale of Goods Act 1979 through the supply of weedkiller with misleading instructions. There was nothing wrong with the weedkiller as such, it would have been effective if properly used.

***Wormell v RHM Agriculture Ltd* [1986] 1 All ER 769**

Piers Ashworth QC

> [*Willis v FMC Machinery and Chemicals Ltd* (1976) 68 DLR (3d) 127] was a case where the defendants sold a weedkiller which, when used on its own, was safe and effective, but when mixed with an insecticide reacted with that insecticide (the insecticide was also perfectly safe), was dangerous and destroyed the crop. The weedkiller taken by itself was certainly fit for its purpose. Nicholson J said this (at 148):
>
>> 'Having determined that there was in this contract an implied condition as to fitness of the product for a particular purpose, it becomes necessary to decide whether or not there was a breach of that condition. It is clear, without doubt, that Dacthal W-75 was fit for controlling weed infestation

23 [1995] FSR 686.
24 [1996] 4 All ER 481.
25 [1983] 2 NSWLR 48.
26 [1986] 1 All ER 769.

> in the growing of turnips. However, it is also clear in the circumstances of this case that the use of the material Dacthal W-75 in combination with certain insecticides and under certain climatic conditions causes severe damage to the turnip plants. The evidence in this case establishes to my satisfaction that Dacthal W-75 is potentially dangerous to turnip plants and consequently cannot be said to be reasonably fit for use in the control of weeds because it cannot safely be applied in conjunction with certain insecticides under certain climatic conditions (not unusual in PEI). Where information of the potential danger is not given to a buyer as it was not in this case, there was a breach of the condition of fitness as set out in s 16(1) of the Sale of Goods Act.'

> That condition was similar to the condition of fitness in the Sale of Goods Act 1893.

> That is in some respects the converse of the present case. It was a case where a warning of danger to the crops was not given. Certainly a warning of danger to the crops was given here. However, it does establish that in considering whether or not goods are fit for a purpose, instructions or warnings contained on the container must be taken into account or at any rate can properly be taken into account, and Rees J came to the same conclusion.

> My view is that the instructions here were misleading. I appreciate that they are approved by the Advisory Council and by the schemes run within the industry. I appreciate that they cannot be changed without permission. Nevertheless, the onus must be firstly on the manufacturer to ensure that his instructions are clear. These in my view, were not clear, indeed I think they were positively misleading.

> If a retailer then sells the goods (that is the chemical together with its container and instructions) and those instructions make the goods not reasonably fit for their purpose, in my view there is a breach of s 14(3) of the 1979 Act. Furthermore, it is a breach by the retailer, ie the seller, even though the seller himself may not have sufficient technical knowledge to know whether or not these instructions are accurate. He of course would have his remedy against the manufacturer, and in this case it has been made clear to me that Shell are standing behind the retailer.

In the *Wormell* case, the Court of Appeal reversed the finding of a breach of s 14(3) by Piers Ashworth QC.[27] However, they did so on the basis that, in the instant case, the instructions were not misleading. They did not cast doubt on the idea that a breach could occur if instructions were absent or misleading.[28] There is some support here for the idea that a defective program could lead to a breach of the terms implied by s 14 if it was supplied in a package, with hardware.[29] However, some unease might be generated if the treatment of

27 [1987] 3 All ER 75.

28 See also *Vacwell Engineering Co Ltd v BDH Chemicals Ltd* [1971] 1 QB 88; Brown [1988] LMCLQ 502.

29 The argument would seem to be not that the software, or the instructions, are themselves goods but rather that their deficiencies can nevertheless lead to a breach of the terms implied by s 14 in relation to the undoubted goods – the hardware.

software packaged with hardware was divorced from that of software acquired alone.

Pragmatism

In the *St Albans* case, both Scott Baker J and Sir Iain Glidewell did not confine their comments to a program supplied with hardware. They indicated that a program supplied on a disk or other such medium, but without any hardware, should also be treated as 'goods'. Scott Baker J's reasoning was basically pragmatic. He took the view that otherwise no statutory regime would apply and the recipient would be unprotected in the absence of express terms. This type of pragmatic argument was seen as persuasive by Brian Napier in his article 'The Future of Information Technology Law' [1992] CLJ 46.

Napier, 'The future of Information Technology Law' [1992] CLJ 46

... we must first acknowledge the problem of knowing what software is in legal terms. When we acquire software, we acquire structured and coded information of a highly specialised nature. Software is of course protected by the law of intellectual property, but it is not itself intellectual property. It is essentially information, and as Lord Upjohn stated many years ago, information as such is generally not property. The law recognises its value by allowing restrictions on its use, not by bringing it within the realm of ownership. Information cannot be stolen and it would appear that it can be the subject of criminal damage only in so far as it is recorded on a physical storage medium. Thus it would seem to follow inexorably that no 'goods' within the meaning of the Sale of Goods Act 1979 are involved if a pure software transaction takes the form of a sale – though judges in England have hesitated to say so. When we buy pure software (ie structured information) we acquire the intellectual achievement of the individual who by his work has produced the information. But that is not all. In almost all cases such purchase of information is accompanied by the acquisition of the medium – such as a floppy disc or chip – on which it is recorded. We normally acquire title to that medium – at least when we buy the whole product in the shops. But when software is captured on a physical medium do we have, by *specificatio,* creation of a new thing, capable of constituting a 'good' ...? If the answer is 'yes', as some have suggested then it might be objected that we have allowed the physical medium to dictate the legal message. But if we say 'no' we face a much greater evil – a flat contradiction between our commonsense expectations and legal analysis. Most consumers would be surprised, and rightly so, at the suggestion that the retailer from whom their software was bought guaranteed only the floppy disc and the system documentation (the handbook) – not the performance and quality of the programs recorded on it. The view that recorded software is 'goods' has recently been affirmed in the USA by a Court of Appeals considering the scope of Article 2 of the Uniform Commercial Code.

Napier's comments are in the context of protection for the consumer. The practical benefits of transactions in software being encompassed in an established category of contracts might be seen as more far reaching. In *Advent v Unisys*,[30] in deciding that Article 2 of the Uniform Commercial Code applied, Weis J said:

> Applying the UCC to computer software transactions offers substantial benefits to litigants and the courts. The Code offers a uniform body of law on a wide range of questions likely to arise in computer disputes ... The importance of software to the commercial world and the advantages to be gained by the uniformity inherent in the UCC are strong policy arguments favoring inclusion.

The Sale of Goods Act 1979 does not provide a complete code. Even in relation to contracts falling within it, there are times when the general law of contract has to be considered.[31] Nevertheless, it covers many issues[32] and, certainly, it is not confined to providing protection for consumers.

However, even though there are undoubted attractions in finding software to be included in a well-established legal category, it must be considered whether that is appropriate. The law may say that, henceforth, elephants are to be called mice but the law cannot say that elephants are mice. Is software too unlike other things which are categorised as goods for the label to be appropriate? The goods which software is most akin to are books, music CDs, and video tapes but one of the factors, used to indicate that software is not just information, its functional aspect, also makes it very different from those types of goods. Additionally, despite the comment of Scott Baker J in the *St Albans* case,[33] it should be noted that programs are not always transferred using a disk or some other such medium. Could a program transferred down a telephone line constitute goods? That seems unlikely,[34] but, if it cannot, then a problem with the pragmatic argument arises. The 'goods' categorisation might provide an existing legal framework for consideration of some transactions involving computer programs but certainly not all. Would categorising as goods a program embodied, and transferred, on a disk, or other such medium, inappropriately divorce its legal categorisation from that

30 925 F 2d 670.

31 See generally PS Atiyah, *op cit*.

32 There are, for example, provisions dealing with payment (s 8), time (s 9), passing of property (ss 16–20B), delivery (ss 27–34), remedies (ss 38–54).

33 [1995] FSR at p 699.

34 It seems doubtful that such a contract could be considered as a contract for the sale of goods. Such a categorisation would seem contrary to an approach which emphasises the importance of the embodiment of the program in a disc or other such medium. However, it has been indicated that it is uncertain whether electricity can constitute goods (*Benjamin's Sale of Goods*, 4th edn, AG Guest (ed) 1–084) and, if it could be so treated, it could similarly be argued that a program supplied by downloading could be goods (see 'Computer Programs as Goods under the UCC' (1979) 77 Mich LR 1149).

of programs transferred without the use of such a medium?[35] In *Beta Computers (Europe) Ltd v Adobe Systems (Europe) Ltd*,[36] a Scottish case, dealing with the question of the effectiveness of a 'shrink wrap' licence,[37] Lord Penrose, *obiter*, considered the contention that software should be regarded as goods. He said:

> This reasoning [that software is goods] appears to me to be unattractive, at least, in the context with which this case is concerned. It appears to emphasise the role of the physical medium and to relate the transaction in the medium to sale or hire of goods. It would have the somewhat odd result that the dominant characteristic of the complex product, in terms of value or the significant interests of the parties, would be subordinated to the medium by which it was transmitted to the user in analysing the true nature and effect of the contract.

The final point to be made here relates to Scott Baker J's concerns, in the *St Albans* case, that if the supply of software is not a supply of goods it will be 'something to which no statutory rules apply, thus leaving the recipient unprotected in the absence of express agreement.'[38] The Sale of Goods Act 1979 is largely based on the 1893 Act of the same name. Legislation covering other contracts dealing with goods occurred much later (eg Supply of Goods and Services Act 1982). However, prior to the existence of wider legislation, the common law proved capable of often implying the same or similar terms into contracts dealing with goods which did not fall within the Sale of Goods Acts.[39] Similarly, it would not be impossible for the court to find that the common law implied terms that programs should be of 'satisfactory quality' and 'reasonably fit' for the purchaser's 'particular purpose' even if, in all cases or some cases, software is not categorised as goods. When the Court of Appeal considered the *St Albans* case, Sir Iain Glidewell thought that, in the absence of an express term requiring the program to be fit for its purpose, one could have been implied at common law.[40]

As will be seen, when consideration is given to the terms implied by s 14 of the Sale of Goods Act 1979, those terms, requiring the goods to be of 'satisfactory quality' and 'reasonable fitness' for the buyer's 'particular purpose', are flexible in their content and similar terms, dealing with the functioning of the program, may be appropriate, generally, in contracts for the

35 And of some cases where such a medium was used but not delivered to the recipient of the program, as in *St Albans v ICL*.

36 [1996] FSR 387.

37 See p 106.

38 [1995] FSR 686. There was an express term that the computer system would be reasonably fit for the buyer's purpose in the *St Albans* case.

39 For example, *Dodd v Wilson* [1946] 2 All ER 691. See generally PS Atiyah, *op cit*, pp 21–23.

40 [1996] 4 All ER 481 at p 494. The implication envisaged would appear to have been one made 'in fact', but such an implied term might be found more generally, 'in law'. For the implication of terms at common law see p 83.

supply of programs. It is worthwhile considering the terms implied by the Sale of Goods Act 1979 not only because software may be categorised as goods in some cases but also because, even if that is not seen as appropriate in any case, the common law may imply the same or similar terms.

SERVICES

Even if software can be goods and ownership of the disk passes, it may still be argued that it is inappropriate that its supply should be categorised as a sale of goods. It may be argued that the transaction should be regarded as a contract for work and materials (or, more broadly, for 'services') rather than for goods. Of course, there may well be found to be a contract for services if no goods are in question. However, what is of particular note here is the distinction between a contract for services which also involves goods and one that is simply for the sale of goods. The line between such contracts for services and contracts for the sale of goods has been one which the courts have attempted to draw in many different contexts and it has never proved an easy categorisation to make.[41] Nevertheless, it may be a very important distinction. If a contract for the supply of software is one for the sale of goods, then, subject to the possibility of their inapplicability, or of the effectiveness of an exemption clause, the software will have to comply with the statutory implied terms as to description (s 13 of the Sale of Goods Act 1979), satisfactory quality (s 14(2)) and reasonable fitness for the buyer's particular purpose (s 14(3)). Whilst the terms implied by s 14 set standards by reference to the 'reasonable person' (s 14(2)) or require 'reasonable fitness' (s 14(3)), they are all nevertheless strict. The seller cannot escape liability for their breach by proving that the problem with the goods was not due to any fault on his, or her, part.[42] In contrast, if what is in question is the provision of a service then the relevant implied term stems from s 13 of the Supply of Goods and Services Act 1982, which merely requires that, where the supplier of a service acts in the course of a business, he, or she, should do so with due care. The strict terms, requiring goods to be, *inter alia*, of satisfactory quality, would apply only to goods supplied incidentally to the service.[43] (It is possible for there to be additional terms which are either express, or implied at common law, which impose stricter obligations in relation to what is produced by the

41 See, eg, Samek 'Contracts for Work and Materials' (1962) 36 ALJ 66.

42 *Kendall v Lillico* [1969] 2 AC 31, *Frost v Aylesbury Dairy Co* [1905] 1 KB 685.

43 In *Dodd v Wilson* [1946] 2 All ER 691 the contract was for the services of a vet. He was strictly liable when a vaccine with which he inoculated a cow was not reasonably fit for its purpose. Of course, had the problem been with the way the injection was given, for example, he would only have been liable in the absence of due care.

services,[44] but here we are primarily concerned with the terms implied by statute.)

In the context of contracts concerned with software and the statutory regimes, the impact of a contract being for services, rather than goods, can be illustrated. If there is a contract to write a bespoke program, which is categorised as a contract for services, then the strict liability would seem only to apply to the fabric of the disk.[45] The content of the program would be the outcome of the services and the relevant statutorily implied term would simply be that requiring the services to be performed with due care. In other words, the strict liability terms would not apply to the product of the services, only to goods transferred to the other party incidentally to those services. A more complex problem might arise where the contract is for the supply and installation into the purchaser's system of an 'off the shelf' program. If such a contract was characterised as being one for services, because of the work involved in the installation, then it would seem that any aspect of the program adapted by that installation would only be covered by the requirement that the work should be carried out with due care. However, if the 'off the shelf' software was goods then any defect in the program which was not caused by the installation, would seem to be subject to the strict requirements of the statutorily implied terms as to fitness for purpose and satisfactory quality.[46]

Two basic approaches to distinguishing contracts for the sale of goods and contracts for the supply of services can be found. These can be seen in the cases of *Lee v Griffin*[47] and *Robinson v Graves*.[48] *Lee v Griffin* was concerned with a contract made by a dentist to supply a set of false teeth, made to fit the individual patient. On appeal, that was concluded to be a contract for the sale of goods. In *Robinson v Graves* a contract was made with an artist for a portrait of a particular individual and the Court of Appeal concluded that it was a contract for the services of the artist, rather than one for the sale of goods.

---

44 For example, *Greaves & Co (Contractors) v Beynham Meikle and Partners* [1975] 3 All ER 99. An additional term implied at common law, that the software would be reasonably fit for its purpose may be the explanation of the assumption in *Saphena Computing Ltd v Allied Collection Agencies* [1995] FSR 616 that it made no difference whether the contract was one for goods or services.

45 But see the assumption in *Saphena Computing Ltd v Allied Collection Agencies* [1995] FSR 616 that it made no difference, to the applicability of the strict liability terms as to quality, whether the contract was characterised as being for goods or services (Staughton LJ at p 652). See also n 44 above. See also *St Albans City and District Council v International Computers Ltd* [1995] FSR 686 at p 698 and n 46.

46 Could this provide, on the facts of the case, a justification for the odd assumption of Scott Baker J in *St Albans City and District Council v International Computers Ltd* [1995] FSR 686 at p 698 that it made no difference to the implied terms whether the contract was characterised as being for goods or services?

47 1 B&S 272.

48 [1935] 1 KB 579.

Lee v Griffin **1 B & S 272**

Crompton J

...The main question which arose at the trial was whether the contract ... could be treated as one for work and labour, or whether it was a contract for goods sold and delivered. The distinction between these two causes of action is sometimes very fine; but, where the contract is for a chattel to be made and delivered, it clearly is a contract for the sale of goods. There are some cases in which the supply of materials is ancillary to the contract, as in the case of a printer supplying the materials on which a book is printed. In such a case an action might perhaps be brought for work and labour done, and materials provided, as it could hardly be said that the subject matter of the contract was a sale of a chattel; perhaps it is more in the nature of a contract merely to exercise skill and labour ... I certainly do not agree to the proposition that the value of the skill and labour, as compared to that of the material supplied, is a criterion by which to decide whether the contract be for work and labour or for the sale of a chattel. Here however, the subject matter of the contract was the supply of goods. The case bears a strong resemblance to that of a tailor supplying a coat, the measurement of the mouth and fitting of the teeth being analogous to the measurement and fitting of the garment.

Blackburn J

... the question is whether the contract was one for the sale of goods or for work and labour. I think that in all cases, in order to ascertain whether the action ought to be brought for goods sold and delivered, or for work and labour done and materials provided, we must look at the particular contract entered into between the parties. If the contract be such that, when carried out, it would result in the sale of a chattel, the party cannot sue for work and labour; but, if the result of the contract is that the party has done work and labour which ends in nothing that can be the subject of a sale, the party cannot sue for goods sold and delivered. The case of an attorney employed to prepare a deed is an illustration of this latter proposition. It cannot be said that the paper and ink he uses in preparation of the deed are goods sold and delivered. The case of a printer printing a book would most probably fall within the same category ... In the present case, the contract was to deliver a thing which, when completed, would have resulted in the sale of a chattel; in other words, the substance of the contract was for goods sold and delivered. I do not think that the test to apply to these cases is whether the value of the work exceeds that of the materials used in its execution; for if a sculptor were employed to execute a work of art, greatly as his skill and labour, supposing it to be of the highest description, might exceed the value of the marble on which he worked, the contract would, in my opinion, nevertheless be a contract for the sale of a chattel.

Robinson v Graves **[1935] 1 KB 579**

Greer LJ

I can imagine that nothing would be more surprising to a client going to a portrait painter to have his portrait painted and to the artist who was accepting the commission than to be told that they were making a bargain about the sale

> of goods. It is, of course, possible that a picture may be ordered in such circumstances as will make it an order for goods to be supplied in the future, but it does not follow that that is the inference to be drawn in every case as between the client and the artist. Looking at the propositions involved from the point of view of interpreting the words in the English language it seems to me that the painting of a portrait in these circumstances would not, in the ordinary use of the English language, be deemed to be the purchase and sale of that which is produced by the artist. It would, on the contrary, be held to be an undertaking by the artist to exercise such skill as he was possessed of in order to produce for reward a thing which would ultimately have to be accepted by the client. If that is so, the contract in this case was not a contract for the sale of goods.
>
> ... If you find as they did in *Lee v Griffin* that the substance of the contract was the production of something to be sold by the dentist to the dentist's customer, then that is a sale of goods. But if the substance of the contract, on the other hand, is that skill and labour have to be exercised for the production of the article and that it is only ancillary to that that there will pass from the artist to his client or customer some materials in addition to the skill involved in the production of the portrait, that does not make any difference to the result, because the substance of the contract is the skill and experience of the artist in producing the picture.
>
> ... For these reasons I am of opinion that in this case the substance of the matter was an agreement for the exercise of skill and it was only incidental that some materials would have to pass from the artist to the gentleman who commissioned the portrait. For these reasons I think that this was not a contract for the sale of goods

The Court of Appeal in *Robinson v Graves* attempted to argue that its approach was consistent with the line taken in *Lee v Griffin*, but it is clear that there are two different approaches operating.

In *Lee v Griffin*[49] the basic approach was that if the services produced goods, the ownership of which the supplier transferred to the other party, there was a contract for the sale of goods. This line was mitigated only in the situation where the transfer of ownership of any goods could be regarded as relatively insignificant, as in the example of the solicitor drawing up the deed. Clearly, Blackburn J's references to the 'substance' of the contract were not intended to be taken any further than that.

Robinson v Graves takes an approach which allows much more scope for a contract to be characterised as one for services (or, work and materials). It is a matter of looking for the dominant element in the contract – the end product or the skill and expertise of the person providing the services. This is commonly described as looking for the 'substance of the contract' but, as has already been indicated, this should not be confused with the line taken by Blackburn J in *Lee v Griffin*.

---

49 See also, eg, *J Marcel (Furriers) Ltd v Tapper* [1953] 1 WLR 49.

The supply of software

Obviously, the acquisition of bespoke software provides the strongest case for arguing that a contract for the supply of software must be regarded as one for services rather than goods. However, even then the categorisation, should not be assumed in every case. Two particular examples can be suggested where a contract for bespoke software might nevertheless be characterised as one for goods. The first example relates to the case in which, although the software is being written because it was requested by one particular company, the suppliers realise that there will be a market to supply it to other companies and intend to do so.[50] It might be argued that the intent to, subsequently, 'mass supply' the software, could effect the characterisation of a contract to supply what was, at that stage, bespoke software, making it appropriate to characterise it as being for goods, rather than services. The other example concerns the 'turn key contract'. Even where goods are to be manufactured by a seller it is possible for that seller to contract simply in relation to a result (the goods), rather than the manufacture and delivery of the goods. The former case may be argued to be one for the sale of goods rather than the supply of services and this argument would seem to apply to the so-called 'turn key' contract. That is the type of contract where a complete system is installed and then simply handed over to the party to whom it is being supplied. (The name 'turn key contracts' stemming from those cases where the acquirer is 'locked out' until the system is completed, only at that point being given access to it.) In such contracts, the way in which the supplier arrives at the completed product seems to be irrelevant to the other party. It is a contract purely concerned with results and a 'goods' rather than 'services' categorisation may be appropriate, even where what is in question is bespoke software.

After considering bespoke software, modified standard (or, modified 'off the shelf') software should be looked at. The approach taken in *Robinson v Graves*[51] could provide a strong argument in favour of the services classification where some modified standard software is in question, depending upon the extent and novelty of the modification.

At the other end of the spectrum from bespoke software is standard, or 'off the shelf', software. There seems to be little scope for an argument that, even if such software is goods, a contract for its supply must nevertheless be characterised as one for services.[52] In *Toby Constructions Products Ltd v Computer Bar Sales Pty Ltd* where the contract was for the supply of a computer system, composed of hardware and 'off the shelf' software, Rogers J

50 This was the fact situation in *Saphena Computing Ltd v Allied Collection Agencies Ltd* [1995] FSR 616 which led to a dispute as to the ownership of copyright.

51 See above.

52 But see *James Ashley v The London Borough of Sutton* [1995] Tr L Rep 350.

concluded that he was dealing with a contract for goods and dismissed the argument that it was services which were in question. He said:[53]

> Whilst representing the fruits of much research work, [the software] was in current jargon, off the shelf, in a sense, mass produced. There can be no comparison with a one off painting. Rather is the comparison with a mass produced print of a painting.

SECTIONS 13–15 OF THE SALE OF GOODS ACT 1979

These sections imply terms into contracts for the sale of goods. They may prove very useful to the purchaser of defective software if such software is categorised as goods. However, as has been suggested, even if software is not characterised as goods the courts may imply similar terms at common law.[54] The value of examining these terms does not solely lie in the possibility that software will be construed as goods.

As has already been indicated,[55] the possibility of excluding or restricting liability for breaches of the terms implied by ss 13–15 is restricted by the s 6 of the Unfair Contract Terms Act 1977. The status of the implied terms should also be noted. They are conditions and breach of a condition normally gives the injured party the right to reject the goods, as well as claim damages, no matter how trivial the breach. However, the effect of a breach of these conditions has been modified by the 1994 Sale and Supply of Goods Act 1994.[56] Section 15A of the Sale of Goods Act 1979 now states:

> (1) Where in the case of a contract of sale
>
> (a) the buyer would, apart from this subsection, have the right to reject goods by reason of a breach on the part of the seller of a term implied by sections 13, 14, or 15 above; but
>
> (b) the breach is so slight that it would be unreasonable for him to reject them, then, if the buyer does not deal as consumer, the breach is not to be treated as a breach of condition but may be treated as a breach of warranty.
>
> (2) This section applies unless a contrary intention appears in, or is to be implied from, the contract.
>
> (3) It is for the seller to show that a breach fell within subsection (1)(b) above.

53 [1983] 2 NSWLR 48 at p 51.

54 *St Albans City and District Council v ICL* [1996] 4 All ER 481 see p 165.

55 See p 129.

56 Section 4 of the Sale and Supply of Goods Act 1994, following the recommendations of the Law Commission (Law Com No 160, Cmnd 137, 1987).

This means that (subject to contrary intention) if the buyer does not 'deal as consumer',[57] then he, or she, has no right to reject the goods for a breach which is so trivial that it would be unreasonable to do so.[58]

SECTION 13 – SALE BY DESCRIPTION

The Sale of Goods Act 1979, s 13(1) states:

> Where there is a contract for the sale of goods by description, there is an implied term that the goods will correspond with their description.

Two basic questions arise under the section; when is a sale 'by description' and what constitutes 'a description' for the purposes of s 13.

'By description'

Obvious examples will immediately spring to mind of situations in which there will clearly be a sale 'by description'. It would seem inevitable that there will be a sale by description when the contract is for unascertained goods, for example (ie goods not identified when the contract is made, such as a contract for purely generic goods – 5,000 tons of coal). In relation to specific goods (ie goods identified and agreed upon at the time the contract is made) the obvious example of a sale by description is where buyer has not seen the goods before the contract is made.[59] However, it is clear that sale by description is not restricted to such cases. There may be a sale by description where goods are seen, and even selected, by the buyer. Section 13(3) states:

> A sale of goods is not prevented from being a sale by description by reason only that, being exposed for sale or hire, they are selected by the buyer.

This means that goods displayed in a shop and selected from the shelf by the buyer may still be sold by description. However, the emphasis here is on

57 This phrase is taken from the Unfair Contract Terms Act 1977, where it is defined in s 12 (s 61(5A) Sale of Goods Act 1979). See p 130.

58 This innovation is analogous to the common law innominate term. However, when a term is innominate, rather than a condition or warranty, the right to terminate the contract for breach, or, in the language of the Sale of Goods Act 1979, the right to reject the goods, depends upon whether the injured party has been substantially deprived of all the benefit which he, or she, was intended to derive from the contract (*Hong Kong Fir Shipping Co Ltd v Kawasaki Kisen Kaisha* [1962] 2 QB 26). In other words, when a term is innominate the right to reject is only present if the breach has very serious consequences. In contrast, s 15A means that rejection for breach of one of the terms implied by ss 13–15 is always available except where the breach is trivial. Section 15A does not equate the implied terms with innominate terms but it is in keeping with their development. Both prevent a trivial breach being used opportunistically, by the injured party, to escape from a contract which has simply become a bad bargain from that party's perspective. See Koffman & Macdonald, *op cit*, pp 114–17.

59 *Varley v Whipp* [1900] 1 QB 513.

'may'. The question still arises as to when the goods involved in such sales, or other types of sales, are sold by description. In *Grant v Australian Knitting Mills* [1936] AC 85 Lord Wright said, at p 100:

> a thing is sold by description though it is specific, so long as it is sold not merely as the specific thing but as the thing corresponding to a description.

In other words, the question is whether the parties were merely contracting about the thing in front of them (for example) or that thing as something corresponding to a description.[60] In the latter case, the sale is 'by description'. This was seen in terms of reliance by the Court of Appeal in *Harlingdon & Leinster Enterprises v Christopher Hull Fine Art*.[61]

Harlingdon & Leinster Enterprises v Christopher Hull Fine Art
[1991] 1 QB 564

> The defendant had two paintings for sale which had been described in a 1980 sale catalogue as the work of Gabrielle Munter, an artist of the German expressionist school. The defendant telephoned the plaintiff, telling him that he had two Munter's for sale. When the plaintiff came to the defendant's gallery, the defendant made it clear that he had no expertise in German expressionist painting. The plaintiff saw the paintings and bought one for £6,000. The invoice described the painting as being by Munter. The painting was discovered to be a fake and the plaintiff claimed, *inter alia*, that there was a breach of the term implied by the Sale of Goods Act 1979, s 13(1). The majority of the court, with Stuart-Smith dissenting, held that there had not been a sale by description.
>
> **Nourse LJ**
>
> Section 13(l) of the Sale of Goods Act 1979 is in these terms:
>
> > Where there is a contract for the sale of goods by description, there is an implied condition that the goods will correspond with the description.
>
> The sales to which the subsection is expressed to apply are sales 'by description'. Authority apart, those words would suggest that the description must be influential in the sale, not necessarily alone, but so as to become an essential term, ie a condition, of the contract. Without such influence a description cannot be said to be one by which the contract for the sale of the goods is made.
>
> I think that the authorities to which we were referred are consistent with this view of s 13(1) ...
>
> ... It is suggested that the significance which some of these authorities attribute to the buyer's reliance on the description is misconceived. I think that that criticism is theoretically correct. In theory it is no doubt possible for a description of goods which is not relied on by the buyer to become an essential term of a contract for their sale. But in practice it is very difficult,

60 See also *Beale v Taylor* [1967] 1 WLR 1193.

61 [1991] 1 QB 564.

> and perhaps impossible, to think of facts where that would be so. The description must have a sufficient influence in the sale to become an essential term of the contract and the correlative of influence is reliance. Indeed, reliance by the buyer is the natural index of a sale by description. It is true that the question must, as always, be judged objectively and it may be said that previous judicial references have been to subjective or actual reliance. But each of those decisions, including that of Judge Oddie in the present case, can be justified on an objective basis. For all practical purposes, I would say that there cannot be a contract for the sale of goods by description where it is not within the reasonable contemplation of the parties that the buyer is relying on the description.

Slade LJ

> While some judicial dicta seem to support the view that there can be no sale by description unless there is actual reliance on the description by the purchaser, I am not sure that this is strictly correct in principle. If a party to a contract wishes to claim relief in respect of a misrepresentation as to a matter which did not constitute a term of the contract, his claim will fail unless he is able to show that he relied on this representation in entering into the contract; in general, however, if a party wishes to claim relief in respect of a breach of a *term* of the contract (whether it be a condition or warranty) he need prove no actual reliance.
>
> Nevertheless, where a question arises as to whether a sale of goods was one by description, the presence or absence of reliance on the description may be very relevant in so far as it throws light on the intentions of the parties at the time of the contract. If there was no such reliance by the purchaser, this may be powerful evidence that the parties did not contemplate that the authenticity of the description should constitute a term of the contract – in other words, that they contemplated that the purchaser would be buying the goods as they were. If, on the other hand, there was such reliance (as in *Varley v Whipp* [1900] 1 QB 513, where the purchaser had never seen the goods) this may be equally powerful evidence that it was contemplated by both parties that the correctness of the description would be a term of the contract (so as to bring it within section 13(l)).

Note the different degrees of reliance which Slade and Nourse LJJ referred to. Nourse LJ referred to sufficient reliance for the description to be an 'essential term', a condition. Whilst Slade LJ seems to have considered that sufficient reliance to make it a term will suffice. As we shall see, there is only a very limited scope for a descriptive term to be the appropriate type of description to fall within s 13. The greater reliance indicated by Nourse LJ is in keeping with that.[62]

62 But see *Beale v Taylor* [1967] 1 WLR 1193.

What constitutes a 'description' for the purposes of s 13?

At first sight it might seem obvious what is referred to when s 13 says that goods must correspond with their description. However, not everything which would be regarded as a description of the goods in everyday terms will constitute a 'description' for the purposes of s 13. In fact, the modern case law takes a very restrictive view of which descriptions fall within s 13.

It has already become clear that only descriptions which are also terms of the contract in their own right can constitute 'descriptions' for the purposes of s 13. In other words, s 13 does not alter the balance between terms and representations.[63] However, not even all descriptive terms will now constitute 'descriptions' for the purposes of s 13.

In the past, in cases like *Re Moore & Co and Landauer & Co*[64] a very wide approach was taken to which descriptive terms were capable of falling within s 13. In that case, there was a contract for the sale of Australian tinned fruit packed in cases containing 30 tins each. The correct overall number of tins was delivered but some of them were packed in cases of 24 tins. The arbitrator found that it made no difference to the market value of the goods whether they were packed in cases of 24 or 30 tins. The Court of Appeal, nevertheless, held that there was a breach of the term implied by s 13. Bankes LJ stated that it was irrelevant whether the trade viewed such matters as important or whether they affected the market value of the goods if, on the face of the contract, they were part of the description of the goods.[65] However, the decision attracted criticism. As the implied term is a condition, this wide approach to s 13 meant that, at that time,[66] the buyer could have a right to reject the goods for trivial breaches. To avoid rejection of goods for trivial breaches the courts developed the modern approach to the scope of the implied term – they could not take the alternative course of altering the status of the term as that was dictated by statute.[67] The most significant case in considering the more modern, and narrower, approach to s 13 is *Ashington Piggeries v Christopher Hill*.[68]

Ashington Piggeries v Christopher Hill [1972] AC 441

> The appellants (Udall) had approached the respondents (Hill), who were animal food compounders, to mix mink food for them. The respondents knew

63 *Harlingdon & Leinster Enterprises v Christopher Hull Fine Art* [1991] 1 QB 564, *T & J Harrison v Knowles & Foster* [1918] 1 KB 608. See further, below, p 180 in relation to what purpose is served by s 13 in the light of this.

64 [1921] 2 KB 519.

65 At p 523.

66 The Sale and Supply of Goods Act 1994 amended the effect of the 'condition' classification (see above p 171).

67 *Reardon Smith Line v Hansen Tangen* [1976] 1 WLR 989, Lord Wilberforce at p 998.

68 [1972] AC 441.

nothing about mink but the appellants supplied them with the formula to be used. One of the ingredients in the formula was herring meal. The respondents supplied the appellants with the compounded mink food which was known as 'King Size'. However, they made up a quantity of 'King Size' using a batch of Norwegian herring meal. Unfortunately, the preservative in the meal had reacted, during its manufacture, to produce a chemical, dimethylnitrosamine (DMNA), which was poisonous to mink. The result was that the batch of 'King Size' made from Norwegian herring meal caused the death of some mink. The appellants claimed against the respondents on several bases. Their claim under s 13 was based on the argument that what had been used in the feed could not be described as 'herring meal' because of the DMNA. The respondents claimed, in turn, against the third party ('the Norwegians') who had supplied them with 'herring meal'. Their claim under s 13 was on the basis that the substance had been stated to be 'Norwegian herring meal. Fair average quality of the season' and that there was a breach of s 13 as it was not 'herring meal' and it was not 'fair average quality'. The description 'herring meal' was found to identify the goods and it fell within s 13 but there was no breach as the goods complied with that 'description', despite the DMNA. The descriptive words, 'fair average quality' did not identify the goods and so did not form part of the 'description' for the purposes of s 13.

Lord Diplock

Not all statements about the characteristics of goods which are the subject matter of a contract of sale form part of the 'description' by which they are sold. Sections 13 and 14 draw a distinction between the description by which goods are sold, on the one hand, and their fitness for the particular purpose for which they are required and their quality, on the other. Section 14(4) recognises that a contract for the sale of goods may contain an express statement about the fitness of the goods for a particular purpose or their quality which does not form part of the description by which they are sold but constitutes a separate stipulation in the contract which may be either a condition or warranty depending upon the construction of the contract (see section 11(1)(b)).

A contract for the sale of goods is one whereby the property in goods which have been physically identified is transferred from the seller to the buyer (see sections 1(1) and 16). But a contract may be made for the sale of unascertained goods before the actual goods in which the property is to be transferred are physically identified and agreed upon. At the time of making such a contract the kind of goods which are its subject matter can only be identified verbally and/or by reference to a sample. The 'description' by which unascertained goods are sold is, in my view, confined to those words in the contract which were intended by the parties to identify the kind of goods which were to be supplied. It is open to the parties to use a description as broad or narrow as they choose. But ultimately the test is whether the buyer could fairly and reasonably refuse to accept the physical goods proffered to him on the ground that their failure to correspond with that part of what was said about them in the contract makes them goods of a different kind from those he had agreed to buy. The key to section 13 is identification.

Udall bases his claim against Hill in the first instance on section 13 of the Act. The goods, he submits, did not correspond with the description by which they were sold. The contract was oral. The subject matter was unascertained goods, and it is common ground that the description by which they were sold was contained in Udall's formula which set out in detail the ingredients of the feeding-stuff to be compounded by Hill. One of the described ingredients was 'herring meal' ...

DMNA was not an ingredient referred to in the formula. Milmo J, following the cases about the sale of 'copra cake' which was contaminated with castor seed, held that a feeding-stuff which contained DMNA in quantities which rendered it toxic to mink did not correspond with the description by which the goods were sold.

I agree with your Lordships and the Court of Appeal that this is not so. Udall's formula was commercial not chemical. The ingredient described as 'herring meal' did not cease to comply with that description because it was manufactured from herrings to which a preservative had been added to prevent them from deteriorating. The most usual preservative is common salt (sodium chloride) but the evidence showed that another salt of sodium, sodium nitrite, had been used in Norway for several years before 1961. In certain conditions which can occur during the normal process of manufacture of herring meal the amino-acids naturally present in the herring break down into an organic chemical, dimethylsamine, which can react with sodium nitrite to form DMNA (dimethylnitrosamine). The occurrence of this reaction may affect the quality of the meal. It does not alter its identity as 'herring meal' ...

So I come once more to section 13 of the Sale of Goods Act 1893, upon which Hill in turn founds his claim against the Norwegians. Since the contract was in writing the description by which the goods were sold must be determined by construing the words used by the parties in the contract. What the contract said about the goods was 'Norwegian herring meal, fair average quality of the season, expected to analyse not less than 70% protein, not more than 12% fat and not more than 40% salt'. I agree with your Lordships that the description by which the goods were sold is limited to the words 'Norwegian herring meal'. That is what identifies the subject matter of the contract. Where a contract contains an express statement about the quality of the goods to be supplied the *prima facie* inference is that this was intended by the parties not as an identification of the kind of goods that are alone the subject matter of the contract, but as an express stipulation as to the standard of quality to which goods of that kind supplied under the contract shall conform. Such an express stipulation may be intended as a condition or as a warranty. Which it is, depends upon the construction of the contract.

Lord Wilberforce

The question is whether the compound mink food sold by the respondents (under the name 'King Size') corresponded with the description. The appellants' case was that the food was to be made up according to a formula which identified generically the ingredients and specifically the

> chemical additives, quantifying precisely the proportions of each ingredient. One of these ingredients was herring meal. The food delivered in certain relevant months, it was claimed, did not correspond with the description because it contained a significant quantity of DMNA. The proposition is that 'King Size' made partly of herring meal which contains DMNA does not correspond with the description 'King Size'. This can be reduced to the proposition that the herring meal ingredient did not correspond with the description because it contained DMNA. The analogy was invoked, inevitably, by the appellants of copra cake with castor seed; the respondents invoked that of oxidised iron. The learned judge accepted the former, the Court of Appeal the latter.
>
> Whether in a given case a substance in or upon which there has been produced by chemical interaction some additional substance can properly be described or, if one prefers the word, identified, as the original substance qualified by the addition of a past participle such as contaminated or oxidised, or as the original substance plus, or intermixed with, an additional substance, may, if pressed to analysis, be a question of an Aristotelian character. Where does a substance with a quality pass into an aggregate of substances? I do not think that it can be solved by asking whether the chemical interaction came about by some natural or normal process, eg, preservation by the addition of salt (sodium chloride), or by some alien intrusion by the production of DMNA from sodium nitrite through a heating effect. I cannot see any distinction in principle in this difference. Further I do not believe that the Sale of Goods Act was designed to provoke metaphysical discussions as to the nature of what is delivered, in comparison with what is sold. The test of description, at least where commodities are concerned, is intended to be a broader, more common sense, test of a mercantile character. The question whether that is what the buyer bargained for has to be answered according to such tests as men in the market would apply, leaving more delicate questions of condition, or quality, to be determined under other clauses of the contract or sections of the Act. Perhaps this is to admit an element of impression into the decision, but I think it is more than impression which leads me to prefer the answer, if not all of the reasoning, of the Court of Appeal that the defect in the meal was a matter of quality or condition rather than of description. I think that buyers and sellers and arbitrators in the market, asked what this was, could only have said that the relevant ingredient was herring meal and, therefore, that there was no failure to correspond with description. In my opinion, the appellants do not succeed under section 13.

From *Ashington Piggeries* the test for whether the relevant descriptive terms constitute 'descriptions' for the purposes of s 13 could be said to be that of 'identity', ie only descriptions which identify the goods fall within the scope of s 13.[69] Although Lord Diplock referred to unascertained goods, the test can be regarded as a general one for specific and unascertained goods – he was adopting an approach previously indicated in relation to specific goods. Note

69 For an interesting discussion of this see Coote (1976) ALJ 17.

should also be made of Lord Wilberforce's test for determining if the implied term has been breached – the 'men in the market place test'.[70]

However, what needs to be considered further here is the meaning of the 'identity test'. It would seem that s 13 covers descriptions which identify the goods in the sense that they indicate the 'kind' of goods with which the contract is concerned or that which is 'essential' about them. At this point, a philosophical discussion could be embarked upon as to the nature of identity and whether it is distinguishable from attributes. However, we should remember the context in which it has become necessary to consider the meaning of a test based upon identity and the way in which the courts are treating the test. Certainly they do not seem concerned with the nature of goods in a metaphysical, or abstract, sense, rather it is question of whether the description relates to that which is essential about the goods in the eyes of the parties as reasonable people. Further assistance in understanding the 'identity test' can be gleaned from *Reardon Smith v Hansen Tangen*.[71]

***Reardon Smith v Hansen Tangen* [1976] 1 WLR 989**

A contract was made to charter a ship on which construction had not been commenced at the time of the contract. By the time the charter came to be fulfilled, the charter market had changed radically and the contract had become very costly to the charterers. The ship met the very detailed contract specifications but it was also stated in the contract that it was '354 Osaka', which would normally have indicated that it would be the 354th ship to be built at the Osaka shipyard. However, it was not built at the Osaka yard, as it was too large, but rather at a new yard, Oshima, and at that yard it was known as 004 Oshima. Throughout the documents dealing with its chartering and sub-chartering the ship had been referred to as '354 Osaka'. In order to escape from the costly contract the charterers alleged they had a right to repudiate the contract as the ship was not '354 Osaka'. They were arguing by analogy with sale of goods contracts that there was a breach of condition as the ship did not comply with its description. The House of Lords found that they had no right to reject the vessel because it was '004 Oshima'.

Lord Wilberforce

> In my opinion the fatal defect in their argument consists in their use of the words 'identity' or 'identification' to bridge two meanings. It is one thing to say of given words that their purpose is to state (identify) an essential part of the description of the goods. It is another to say that they provide one party with a specific indication (identification) of the goods so that he can find them and if he wishes sub-dispose of them. The appellants wish to say of words which 'identify' the goods in the second sense, that they describe them in the first ... I can only read the words in the second sense.

70 Contrast the stricter approach in *Arcos Ltd v E A Ronaasen & Son* [1933] AC 470.

71 [1976] 1 WLR 989.

> The difference is vital. If the words are read in the first sense, then, unless I am right in the legal argument above, each element in them has to be given contractual force. The vessel must, as a matter of contract, and as an essential term, be built by Osaka and must bear their Yard No 354 – if not the description is not complied with and the vessel tendered is not that contracted for.
>
> If in the second sense, the only question is whether the words provide a means of identifying the vessel. If they fairly do this, they have fulfilled their function. It follows that if the second sense is correct, the words used can be construed much more liberally than they would have to be construed if they were providing essential elements of the description.
>
> The appellants at one time placed great stress on the yard no provision. They contended that by using it the 'owners' assumed an obligation that the vessel should bear a number which would indicate that it would be constructed in the yard, where that number was appropriate, in sequence after vessels bearing earlier yard numbers (350–53). But this argument broke down in face of the fact, certainly known to Sanko which used and introduced the number into the charter-parties, that the sequence through 354 was the sequence used at Osaka Shipbuilding Company's yard at Osaka, which yard could not construct the vessel. Thus the use of the yard no. for the contracted vessel must have had some other purpose than indicating construction at a particular yard. This turns the argument against the appellants – for it shows the words to be 'labelling' words rather than words creating an obligation.

Note Lord Wilberforce's two meanings of 'identity' and 'identification'. The court also considered whether it was vitally important that the ship was built at the Osaka yard because, for example, of the expertise available at that yard. Their consideration of whether '354 Osaka' 'identified' the ship was relative to the views of the parties. It was not based on the abstract nature of a tanker (there was no search for what constitutes 'essence of tanker'!).

Care is required in applying the identity test to distinguish which descriptive terms constitute 'descriptions' for the purposes of s 13. Only descriptive terms which state what is 'essential' about the goods, in the eyes of the parties, fall within s 13 and, in the light of *Ashington Piggeries*, it is clear that 'essential' has to be understood restrictively. In other words, the scope of the term implied by s 13 is very narrow. It would also seem that s 13 does very little. The older approach meant that s 13 had the role of giving all descriptive terms the status of conditions (converting at least some of them from the status of mere warranties). In contrast, if the modern approach only includes descriptive terms which state that which is essential about the goods, it would seem that such terms would be conditions in their own right. This might be seen as making s 13 irrelevant and unnecessary. However, the impact of s 6 of the Unfair Contract Terms Act 1977 must be borne in mind. That section provides significant protection against the exclusion or restriction of liability for breach of the statutorily implied terms. Certainly those who deal as consumers acquire greater protection against a clause exempting liability for breach of one of the terms implied by the Sale of Goods Act 1979 than for breach of a simple express term of the contract.[72]

In the context of software, questions relevant to the 1979 Act, s 13, might arise in relation to the statement that, for example, what was being supplied was a 'word-processing program suitable for office use'. Provided that the entire statement is part of the contract terms, the question of the scope of s 13 might become relevant. A number of examples can be considered.

- Section 13 might merely cover the statement that what was being supplied was a 'program'. If there was some defect in its functioning, the question would then arise (following Lord Wilberforce in *Ashington Piggeries*) as to whether that defect would affect the characterisation of it by 'the men in the market place' – would they still regard it as a 'program'?
- It seems more likely that the situation would be one in which it would be found to be essential to the parties that the program should be a 'word-processing program'. In this case, there would be a clear breach if what was supplied was not a word-processing program but a spreadsheet program. In the industry these are clearly distinct types of program and are commonly advertised, and referred to, as such. In that context, the effect of the men in the market place test seems clear. However, if what has been supplied is a program which would be an efficient word-processor but for the defects in it, there seems less likely to be a breach (a merely defective program is still likely to be regarded as a word-processing program by the 'men in the market place', although it should depend upon the extent of the problems).
- The final possibility raised by the statement above is that the scope of s 13 extends to the statement that the word-processing program is for 'office use'. As Lord Diplock indicated in *Ashington Piggeries* (see above), there is no easy distinction to be made between quality and description. Words indicating the quality of the goods may be part of the 'description' for the purposes of s 13, but that will not usually be the case. They will usually merely be of relevance to the terms implied by s 14(2) and s 14(3) or in their own right, as express conditions, warranties or innominate terms. However, the basic test must be applied in each case. What is important is the perceptions of the parties. It must be asked whether such a descriptive term 'identified' the goods in the relevant sense. If the statement that the program was for 'office use' was found to fall within s 13 then the 'men in the market test' should be applied to the particular complaint, eg that the program could not handle the integration of different documents well enough.

72 See p 129.

SATISFACTORY QUALITY

Section 14 implies a term that the goods are of satisfactory quality.

(2) Where the seller sells goods in the course of a business, there is an implied term that the goods supplied under the contract are of satisfactory quality.

(2A) For the purposes of this Act, goods are of satisfactory quality if they meet the standard that a reasonable person would regard as satisfactory, taking account of any description of the goods, the price (if relevant) and all other relevant circumstances.

(2B) For the purposes of this Act, the quality of goods includes their state and condition and the following (among other things) are in appropriate cases aspects of the quality of goods

(a) fitness for all the purposes for which goods of the kind in question are commonly supplied;

(b) appearance and finish;

(c) freedom from minor defects;

(d) safety; and

(e) durability.

(2C) The term implied by subsection (2) above does not extend to any matter making the quality of the goods unsatisfactory

(a) which is specifically drawn to the buyer's attention before the contract is made;

(b) where the buyer examines the goods before the contract is made, which that examination ought to reveal; or

(c) in the case of a contract for sale by sample, which would have been apparent on a reasonable examination of the sample.

The Sale and Supply of Goods Act 1994 substituted the term that goods should be of satisfactory quality for an older term which required goods to be of 'merchantable quality'. The statutory definition of merchantability was somewhat different from that of the new term. What was then s 14(6) of the 1979 Act said:

> Goods of any kind are of merchantable quality within the meaning of subsection (2) above if they are as fit for the purpose or purposes for which goods of that kind are commonly bought as it is reasonable to expect having regard to any description applied to them, the price (if relevant) and all the other relevant circumstances.

Whilst there are some similarities with the basic definition of satisfactory quality in s 14(2A) (in the references to description and price), on the whole, this looks very different from the new term. The definition of merchantability focused upon goods being reasonably fit for at least one of the purposes for which they were commonly supplied. However, in its application it may not have been very different from what is required by the new term. Certainly, despite the emphasis on fitness for purpose in what was then s 14(6), the courts' interpretation of what was required for merchantability did not allow the term to be regarded as a simple requirement that the goods should function. A car might have been required to do more than simply get from A to B. It might have been required to do so with a degree of comfort, style and reliability, depending upon such factors as the price paid and the description of it.[73] In addition, the aspects of quality listed in what is now s 14(2B) are all matters which had been identified in the case law as relevant to the question of merchantability.[74] At the end of the day, the results arrived at in applying the new term may not be very different from those which would have resulted from requiring goods to be merchantable. However, the old case law should be considered with caution. Analogies will be appropriate in some cases but that will not always be so. The new term, requiring goods to be of satisfactory quality should be applied as such and the basic test in s 14(2A) should be emphasised. It is a matter of what the reasonable person would regard as satisfactory. Of course, the reasonable person does not make the assessment in a vacuum, but against a background of 'any description of the goods, the price (if relevant) and all other relevant circumstances' and the assessment is also assisted by the list in s 14(2B) of 'aspects of the quality of goods'.

IMPLICATION OF THE TERM

Before the test of satisfactory quality is addressed, the background factors to the implication of the term will be considered (eg the term is implied where the contract was made 'in the course of a business') as well as the situations identified in s 14(2C) in which there will not be a breach of the term requiring goods to be of satisfactory quality.

Sale 'in the course of a business'

For the term requiring goods to be of satisfactory quality to be implied by s 14(2), the seller must contract 'in the course of a business'. The same applies to the term implied by s 14(3) and it also applied to the term previously implied by s 14(2) (merchantability).

Section 61(1) tells us that 'business' includes 'a profession and the activities of any government department or local or public authority' but there is no

73 See *Rogers v Parish Ltd* [1987] 1 QB 933 below.

74 'Appearance and finish' – *Rogers v Parish* [1987] 1 QB 933, *Bernstein v Pamson Motors (Golders Green) Ltd* [1987] 2 All ER 220. Minor defects – *Bernstein v Pamson Motors. Safety* – *Bartlett v Sydney Marcus Ltd* [1965] 2 All ER 753, *Bernstein v Pamson Motors*. Durability – *Business Applications v Nationwide Credit Corp* [1988] RTR 332.

further definition, of 'business' or the phrase 'in the course of a business'. The phrase is relatively new to the sale of goods legislation, having been substituted by the Supply of Goods (Implied terms) Act 1973. Prior to the 1973 Act, merchantability was implied where goods were bought from a seller 'who deals in goods of that description'. The change to the requirement that the sale be 'in the course of a business' made the implication much more widely occurring but it is not clear just how much more widely. Emphasis could be placed upon the fact that the reference is to a business and not the business and the phrase could be taken simply to refer to any sale by a business, however tenuous the connection between the sale and the nature of the business, for example any sale by a solicitor of an old office typewriter could be covered. However, the phrase also occurs in the Trade Descriptions Act 1968 and the Unfair Contract Terms Act 1977 and in the context of those Acts it has been considered by the courts.[75] Upon the basis of the case law on those Acts, a seller basically contracts in the course of a business if the sale is 'an integral part' of the seller's business or if it is incidental to it but occurring with sufficient regularity.[76] In other words, the sale must either be of something which it is the business of the seller to sell (eg sale of a car by someone in the car sale business) or, when the sale is merely incidental to the business, the seller must sell such items with sufficient regularity (eg the seller uses the goods in his business and regularly sells them when they need to be replaced, as in the frequent sale of a car by someone in the car-hire business[77]). Of course, this construction of 'in the course of a business' was not made in the context of the Sale of Goods Act 1979 and, it is by no means certain that the same construction will be adopted for the purposes of that Act. Under the 1979 Act the courts could still give the phrase its full potential width and arguably that is the more appropriate line to take. However, in *R & B Customs Brokers v United Dominion Trust*,[78] in applying the approach taken under the Trade Descriptions Act 1968 to the phrase 'in the course of a business' in the context of the Unfair Contract Terms Act 1977, Neill LJ also referred to the occurrence of the phrase in the Sale of Goods Act 1979 and the Supply of Goods and Services Act 1982 and he concluded that:[79]

> it would be unsatisfactory ... if, when dealing with broadly similar legislation, the courts were not to adopt a consistent construction of the same or similar phrases.

---

75 See *Havering London Borough Council v Stevenson* [1970] 3 All ER 609, *Davies v Sumner* [1984] 3 All ER 831, *R&B Customs Brokers v United Dominion Trust* [1988] 1 All ER 847. See further p 130.

76 It might also be a 'one off adventure in the nature of trade'. See p 132.

77 *Havering LBC v Stevenson* [1970] 3 All ER 609. Contrast *Devlin v Hall* where there was not yet an established pattern of sales and the sale in question was held not to be 'in the course of a business'.

78 [1988] 1 All ER 847.

79 At p 859.

He seems to have regarded the four statutes as 'broadly similar legislation' on the basis that they are all 'dealing with the protection of consumers'. However, this approach can be doubted under the Unfair Contract Terms Act 1977[80] and its extension to the Sale of Goods Act 1979 would seem to be unduly restrictive of the applicability of the implied terms.

'Goods supplied under the contract'

This seems to mean 'goods delivered in purported pursuance of the contract'[81] so that if the problem is something added to the goods contracted for the seller cannot avoid liability simply by saying that there is nothing wrong with the contract goods themselves. In *Wilson v Rickett, Cockerell & Co Ltd*[82] there was a contract for the sale of coalite but, unfortunately, what was supplied was not merely coalite. Added to it was an explosive substance which detonated when the coalite was put in a fire. The seller was unsuccessful in his argument that there was no breach of the implied term as there was nothing wrong with the coalite, the contract goods, as such.[83] In the context of software this type of argument might be raised if a virus had been added to the disk on which a program was supplied.

Exceptions

Sub-section 14(2C) contains exceptions. If it applies, the buyer will not be able to claim that there has been a breach of the implied term. We are here concerned with the exceptions in s 14(2C)(a) and (b).[84] Sub-section (a) refers to the situation where a matter which would otherwise have made the goods of unsatisfactory quality does not do so because it was drawn to the buyers attention before the contract was made. Sub-section (b) deals with the situation where a matter which would have made the goods of unsatisfactory quality does not do so because, before contracting, the buyer examined the goods and 'that examination' should have revealed the matter in question. As the reference is to 'that' examination the exception should only relate to matters which should have been revealed by the examination actually made, however cursory, and not a 'reasonable examination'. However, in *Thornett and Fehr v Beer & Son*[85] the buyer had seen the outside of the barrels of glue which he was purchasing but, through lack of time, he had not opened any of

80 *Kidner* (1987) 38 NILQ 46, *Brown* [1988] JBL 386, *Pearce* [1989] LMCLQ 371.

81 *Wilson v Rickett, Cockerell & Co Ltd* [1954] 1 QB 598, Denning LJ at p 607.

82 [1954] 1 QB 598.

83 See also *Geddling v Marsh* [1920] 1 KB 668.

84 Section 14(2C)(c) refers to the situation where a sale is by sample. See p 196.

85 [1919] 1 KB 486.

them. The defect would only have been discovered had he opened the barrels, but the examination made prevented a claim. The case seems to relate the exception to a 'reasonable examination' but it need cause us no difficulties now as it was decided under an older version of the statutory provision dealing with merchantability, which referred to 'such examination' rather than 'that examination'. We are not now concerned with 'merchantability' and, in any event, as with the later provision dealing with merchantability, the reference now is to 'that examination'. It should be emphasised that there is no obligation on the buyer to make any examination at all. In fact, odd as it may seem, given the presence of the exception in s 14(2C)(b), it may be argued that it is better for the buyer not to examine the goods.[86]

When software is in question, even a very detailed examination will not bring every 'bug' in the program to light and it should be emphasised that the exception should only relate to matters which should have been discovered by the examination actually made by the buyer. In addition, the point can be made that for the exception in s 14(2C)(b) to apply, the buyer's examination will have to have been of 'the goods'. If software is purchased, it will often not have been the 'the goods' sold which were examined, but another copy, used for demonstration purposes. However, even if the exception will not technically apply, any difficulty revealed by an examination of another copy might affect what the reasonable person would regard as satisfactory – ie it might affect the application of the basic test of satisfactory quality (see s 14(2A)).[87] In addition, the exception in s 14(2C)(a) is not restricted to matters drawn to the buyer's attention using 'the goods' sold to the buyer. Some limitation of the software sold to the buyer might be drawn to the buyer's attention using another copy of that software.

There may be some difficulty with the exceptions where some matter which, but for the exceptions, would make the goods of unsatisfactory quality becomes known to the buyer prior to the contract of sale but it is reasonably believed to be unimportant and rectifiable and it subsequently proves to be neither. This sort of situation might arise in relation to software which must be fitted into an existing system.[88] It arose in the context of the purchase of a car in *R & B Customs Brokers v United Dominion Trust* and was given some consideration by the Court of Appeal in the context of exception (b). In that case R & B decided to purchase a Colt Shogun car and it was allowed to take possession of the car before the contract of sale was completed. Before the contract was made, R & B discovered that the car roof leaked. After the sale

86 Unless the sale is by sample. See s 14(2C)(c).

87 The case would be inappropriate to be a sale by sample. See s 15 below.

88 In *Saphena Computing Ltd v Allied Collection Agencies Ltd* [1995] FSR 616 Staughton LJ said (at p 652) '... it is important to remember that software is not necessarily handed over or delivered once and for all at one time. It may well have to be tested and modified as necessary ...'.

was completed there were repeated, but unsuccessful, attempts to repair the leak and the upholstery became 'sodden with water, mouldy and evil-smelling'. When R & B brought an action, the defendant argued that the car was merchantable, despite the leak, because it was known about before the contract was made. The Court of Appeal did not have to decide upon that question as they found for R & B on the basis that, in this climate, a car with a leaking roof was not reasonably fit for its purpose under s 14(3) of the Sale of Goods Act 1979. However, Neill LJ did not find himself 'persuaded' that merchantability was excluded as regards a defect which had come to light before contracting 'if at the time the contract is made the buyer is reasonably of the opinion that the defect can be, and will be rectified, quite easily at no cost to himself'.[89]

WHAT CONSTITUTES SATISFACTORY QUALITY?

As we have seen, the basic test of satisfactory quality is set out in s 14(2A). It refers to the standard that 'a reasonable person would regard as satisfactory, taking account of any description, the price (if relevant) and all other relevant circumstances'. The reference to the standard of a reasonable person makes the test very flexible and able to encompass the vastly different types of goods to which the Act applies. The disadvantage of flexibility is that it makes it difficult to apply the term. There is some further assistance in the identification of certain 'aspects of the quality of goods' in s 14(2B).

Some idea of how the standard set by s 14(2A) may be applied may be gleaned from *Rogers v Parish Ltd*,[90] although the court was applying the old implied term of merchantability. It is worth noting the way in which the court used the description and price of the goods to decide if the goods had complied with the standard required. (It should be remembered that, despite the focus in the definition of merchantability on the goods' fitness for their common purpose, the court did not regard the mere basic functioning of the car as sufficient to render it merchantable.)

***Rogers v Parish Ltd* [1987] QB 933**

The case was concerned with the purchase of a new Range Rover which proved to have faulty oil seals and problems with the engine, gear box and bodywork. The Court of Appeal found that it was not merchantable.

Lord Mustill

> Starting with the purpose for which 'goods of that kind' are commonly bought, one would include in respect of any passenger vehicle not merely

89 [1988] 1 All ER 847 at 856, Dillon LJ at 851. See also *Bartlett v Sidney Marcus* [1965] 1 WLR 1013, Salmon LJ at 1018 and Danckwerts LJ at 1017.

90 [1987] QB 933.

> the buyer's purpose of driving the car from one place to another but of doing so with the appropriate degree of comfort, ease of handling and reliability and, one may add of pride in the vehicles outward and interior appearance. What is the appropriate degree and what relative weight is to be attached to one characteristic of the car rather than another will depend on the market at which the car is aimed.
>
> To identify the relevant expectation one must look at the factors listed in the subsection. First the description applied to the goods. In the present case the vehicle was sold as new. Deficiencies which might be acceptable in a second hand vehicle were not to be expected in one purchased as new. Next the description 'Range Rover' would conjure up a particular set of expectations, not the same as those relating to an ordinary saloon car, as to the balance between handling, comfort and reliability. The factor of price was also significant. At more than £14,000 this vehicle was, if not at the top end of the scale, well above the level of the ordinary family saloon.

The problems with the car rendered it unmerchantable when they were weighed against the reasonable expectations of the fitness of a passenger vehicle described as a 'new Range Rover' and for which the price charged was well above that of the ordinary family saloon. Similarly, when considering whether goods are of the standard that a reasonable person would regard as satisfactory, it should be a matter of balancing the problems with the goods against the standard suggested by such matters as description and price. In relation to software, a program might be of unsatisfactory quality if it was so difficult to use that doing anything with it would take the average consumer an inordinate length of time. That would particularly be the case if the program was marketed as one which was easy to use by the average consumer.

In the light of the above discussion, it may seem odd that the reference to price in s 14(2A) is qualified by the phrase 'if relevant'. The immediate reaction to this may well be that the price must always be relevant. However, it is a factor over which care must be taken. It would not be relevant to set the standard for goods generally which were sold in, for example, the 'January sales' if the goods were not presented as 'seconds' or in any way 'shop soiled' or 'defective'.[91] In addition, the price factor may need to be treated with some care in relation to novel software. When a novel program is first put on the market it will be expensive but it will have problems which have not yet come to light. Later versions will resolve the problems. It would seem that, despite the expense of a novel program when it is first put on the market, the reasonable person could nevertheless regard it as being of a satisfactory standard even though there were some problems with it.[92] Obviously, whether

91 Price would also seem to be less directly significant if the purchase was in some sense a 'risk'. This would seem to provide the best explanation of why the price was seen as irrelevant to the question of the merchantability of the painting in *Harlingdon & Leinster Enterprises v Christopher Hull Fine Art* [1991] 1 QB 564.

92 But see *St Albans City and District Counsel v ICL* [1996] 4 All ER 481.

it is of satisfactory quality would be a matter of the number and extent of the problems. Lloyd makes a similar point on the relevance of price. His comment was made in the context of merchantability but it seems that it should still be valid.

Lloyd (1991) 32 Reliability Engineering and System Safety 193

> In *Rogers* the court went on to point out that the price charged for a motor car would influence the level of quality required from it. Although this factor will normally be relevant in determining the acceptability of manufactured products it may be of less utility in relation to computer programs. Here, the cost of raw materials constitutes a fraction of the total value of the software and, on the basis that it is easier to emulate than to innovate, the costs of a company making a derivative version of an existing program should be lower. On this basis, the purchaser of a 'look alike' or 'cloned' version of a program should not be obliged to accept any significant lowering of standards.

One further, and general, question which should be asked is whether the reasonable person's assessment of what is a 'satisfactory standard' will take account of the normal standards of the computer industry as the court did in *Micron Computer Systems Ltd v Wang*[93] in relation to the question of merchantability. Against the background of the industry norm, it was decided that the time taken by the system to 'back-up' did not make it unmerchantable and neither did the failure of the hard disk after one year. That was regarded as normal and to be expected. Such references to industry norms could be used to lower the requirements of the implied term. However, although there were some dicta which might have raised concern that such a situation could occur in relation to merchantability,[94] a similar argument was firmly rejected by the Court of Appeal in *Rogers v Parish*.[95]

After looking at the basic test of satisfactory quality, some consideration should also be given to the 'aspects' of quality identified in s 14(2B). Depending on the circumstances, they may be relevant to the reasonable persons assessment of what constitutes a satisfactory standard for the type of goods in question. As has already been indicated, the courts had identified these 'aspects' of satisfactory quality as relevant to the question of merchantability.[96] However, there is likely to be some difference in the treatment of the first aspect of quality – the fitness of the goods for all of the purposes for which goods of the kind sold are commonly supplied – and the way in which fitness for common purpose was treated in considering merchantability. The first point to be made is that 'purpose' is likely to be construed more narrowly now than when it provided the focus for the

93 (1990) 9 May, unreported.

94 For example, *Bernstein Pamson Motors (Golders Green) Ltd* [1987] 2 All ER 220 Rougier J at pp 228–29.

95 [1987] 2 All ER 232 at p 237.

96 See n 74 above.

definition of merchantability. In the context of s 14(6) purpose had to be treated widely if merchantability was not to become a matter of whether the goods simply functioned. That impetus for a broad approach to 'purpose' is no longer present. 'Purpose' may now be regarded as referring to the mere functioning of the goods. In the context of a car it may now be seen as merely referring to whether the car will get from A to B, without any requirement of a degree of style, comfort and reliability. Questions of style, comfort and reliability can now fall under other aspects of quality identified in s 14(2B) or could simply be encompassed within the general test of what a reasonable person would regard as satisfactory. The second point which should be made is that goods were merchantable if they were reasonably fit for one of their common purposes.[97] However, this change in the law must be treated with some care. The statutory reference to fitness for all the purposes for which goods of the kind in question are commonly supplied is a change in the law which provides a further impetus for the narrowing of the meaning of purpose. It is also likely to lead to careful consideration of what 'kind' of goods a contract is concerned with. This question arose in relation to merchantability[98] but the 'kind' of goods in question is likely to be more narrowly identified now that what is relevant is fitness for *all* of the purposes for which goods of the kind in question are commonly supplied and not merely fitness for one of those purposes.[99] In relation to software, different versions of the same program may be supplied for home and office use. Provided it was clear at the time of purchase that what was being bought was the version intended for home use, it would seem that the 'kind' of goods would not be ones which were commonly supplied for office use. Under those circumstances, the aspect of quality identified by s 14(2B)(a) would not indicate that the software was of unsatisfactory quality if it was not reasonably fit for office use, provided it was reasonably fit for home use.

FITNESS FOR THE BUYER'S PARTICULAR PURPOSE – S 14(3)

The implied term dealing with fitness for the buyer's purpose was originally dealt with by s 14(1) of the Sale of Goods Act 1893. An amended provision is now contained in s 14(3) of the Sale of Goods Act 1979 which states:

> Where the seller sells goods in the course of a business and the buyer, expressly or by implication, makes known
>
> (a) to the seller; or

97 *Kendall v Lillico* [1969] 2 AC 31, *Aswan Engineering v Lupdine* [1987] 1 All ER 135.

98 See, eg, *Beecham v Francis Howard* (1921) VLR 428, *Brown v Craiks* [1970] 1 All ER 823,

99 It seems likely, for example, that the kind of goods would now be more narrowly construed in a case like *Aswan Engineering v Lupdine* [1987] 1 All ER 135.

(b) where the purchase price or part of it is payable by instalments and the goods were previously sold by a credit broker to the seller, to that credit broker,

any particular purpose for which the goods are being bought, there is an implied obligation that the goods supplied under the contract are reasonably fit for that purpose, whether or not that is a purpose for which such goods are commonly supplied, except where the circumstances show that the buyer does not rely, or that it is unreasonable for him to rely, on the skill or judgment of the seller or credit-broker.

The implied term that the goods should be of 'satisfactory quality' sets a general standard for the goods. It is not a standard which relates to the buyer's intended use of the goods. In contrast, the term implied by s 14(3) may result in the seller guaranteeing that the goods are reasonably fit for the buyer's purpose. Of course, the seller should not be required to provide goods fit for some unusual and unknown purpose of the buyer and the term is restricted to the situation where the particular purpose has been expressly or impliedly made known to the seller and the buyer has reasonably relied on the skill or judgment of the seller. In addition, the term only requires *reasonable* fitness for the buyer's particular purpose and the standard thereby set for the goods will depend upon how broadly or narrowly the particular purpose has been made known to the seller. These points will be considered further below in looking at the specific elements of s 14(3).[100]

Particular purpose

It has already been indicated that the importance of s 14(3) lies in the fact that it requires the goods to be fit for the buyer's particular purpose. The reference to 'particular' does not mean that the purpose must be very narrow, it merely means specified. A particular purpose may be very general[101] but whether it is wide or narrow, it must be expressly or impliedly made known to the seller.

In some cases it will be easy to establish that the particular purpose has been impliedly made known. It will not be difficult, for example, to find that the buyer of a hot water bottle impliedly made known to the seller that her

100 Like satisfactory quality the term here is only implied if the seller 'sells the goods in the course of a business'. We have already considered this requirement in the context of s 14(2) (see p 183). Similarly, the meaning of 'goods supplied under the contract' was also looked at above (see p 185). A point not looked at above, and which should be briefly explained here is the reference in s 14(3) to 'credit broker'. The reference to the buyer making his purpose known to a credit broker is to cover the situation where a purchaser wishes to pay the purchase price of the goods in instalments and the original owner, the credit broker, arranges this by selling the goods to a finance house which then sells them to the buyer on such terms. The reference to credit broker in s 14(3) ensures that the person who sells the goods to the buyer cannot escape the requirements of the implied term on the basis that the buyer's purpose was not made known to him but only to the original owner.

101 *Kendall v Lillico* [1969] 2 AC 31, Lord Pearce at p 114.

particular purpose was to fill it with hot water.[102] However, if the buyer's actual intended use of the goods is very specialised, or unusual, then it will have to be expressly brought to the seller's attention if the buyer is to gain the protection of the implied term. In *Micron Computer Systems Ltd v Wang*[103] the buyers failed to make it known to the sellers that they wanted a system which would perform 'transaction logging'. The failure of the system to do this therefore did not mean that it was not reasonably fit for the buyer's particular purpose. A more general example is provided by *Griffiths v Peter Conway Ltd.*[104]

Griffiths v Peter Conway Ltd [1939] 1 All ER 685

The sellers made a Harris tweed coat for the buyer. When she wore it an adverse skin reaction was provoked which induced dermatitis. The buyer claimed that there was a breach of the term implied by s 14(1), which was the subsection which then covered the term now implied by s 14(3), as the coat was not reasonably fit for her to wear. The court found that the dermatitis had been caused because she had unusually sensitive skin and that a similar effect would not have been produced on normal skin. On that basis there was no breach of the implied term. Her 'abnormal' particular purpose had not been made known to the sellers.

Sir Wilfred Greene MR

> He says that the buyer, Mrs Griffiths, expressly made known to the defendants the particular purpose for which the coat was required, that is to say, for the purpose of being worn by her, Mrs Griffiths, when it was made. Once that state of affairs is shown to exist, Mr Morris says that the language of the section relentlessly and without any escape imposes upon the seller the obligation which the section imports.
>
> It seems to me that there is one quite sufficient answer to that argument. Before the condition as to reasonable fitness is implied, it is necessary that the buyer should make known, expressly or by implication, first of all the particular purpose for which the goods are required.
>
> The particular purpose for which the goods were required was the purpose of being worn by a woman suffering from an abnormality. It seems to me that, if a person suffering from such an abnormality requires an article of clothing for his or her use, and desires to obtain the benefit of the implied condition, he or she does not make known to the seller the particular purpose merely by saying: 'The article of clothing is for my own wear.' The essential matter for the seller to know in such cases with regard to the purposes for which the article is required consists in the particular abnormality or idiosyncrasy from which the buyer suffers. It is only when he has that knowledge that he is in a position to exercise his skill or judgment, because how can he decide and exercise skill or judgment in relation to the suitability of the goods that he is selling for the use of the

102 *Preist v Last* [1903] 2 KB 148.

103 (1990) 9 May, unreported.

104 [1939] 1 All ER 685. See also *Slater v Finning* [1996] 3 All ER 398.

particular individual who is buying from him unless he knows the essential characteristics of that individual? The fact that those essential characteristics are not known, as in the present case they were not known, to the buyer does not seem to me to affect the question. When I speak of 'essential characteristics,' I am not, of course, referring to any variations which take place and exist within the class of normal people. No two normal people are precisely alike, and, in the 'matter of sensitiveness of skin', among people who would be described as normal their sensitiveness must vary in degree.

This does not mean that there is a line which it is the function of the court, or of a medical witness, to draw with precision, so as to define all cases where normality ceases and abnormality begins. The impossibility of drawing such a line by reference to some scientific formula or something of that kind does not mean that, for the present purpose, the difference between normality and abnormality is a thing that must be disregarded, cannot be ascertained. It is a question that no judge and no jury would have any real difficulty in deciding on the evidence in any particular case. In this particular case, the judge has found the existence of abnormality, and, that being so, it seems to me impossible to say that the seller here had the particular purpose pointed out to him so as to show that the buyer relied on his skill or judgment. After all, the object of that is to enable the seller to make up his mind whether or not he will accept the burden of the implied condition, and the effect of the argument addressed to us would be to impose that implied condition upon the seller without his having the opportunity of knowing the vital matter which would affect his mind.

One or two cases were referred to. The only one which I find it necessary to mention, and that for the purpose of distinguishing it, is *Manchester Liners, Ltd v Rea, Ltd* [1922] AC 74]. That was a case where shipowners ordered from the defendants, who were coal merchants, 500 tons of South Wales coal for the bunkers of their steamship, the Manchester Importer. It so happened that, owing to the control of the coal trade that was in existence at that time, the supply of bunkering coal was very much restricted, and the defendants, having secured the right to a cargo through the coal controller, proceeded to supply bunker coal out of that cargo to the plaintiffs in satisfaction of the contract. It so happened that the coal so supplied was not suitable for the bunkering of that steamer, which was a natural draught steamer, and, as a consequence, she was obliged to return to port. The owners sued the coal merchants for damages, and relied upon the Sale of Goods Act 1893, s 14(1). It was held by the House of Lords that, on the facts of the case, the implication of the statutory warranty was not rebutted. The ground on which it was said that it was rebutted was connected with the coal control, which limited the source of supply available to the merchants for the purpose of fulfilling their contract. That was negatived. The important matter for the present purpose is that the House of Lords held that, by ordering bunker coal for that particular steamship, the buyer was making known to the seller the particular purpose for which the coal was required. Lord Buckmaster said:

> 'It then remains to be considered whether in the circumstances there was any warranty that the coal was suitable for the purpose for which it was required. It is plain that the order was expressed for the use of a particular steamship, and it must, therefore, be assumed that the respondents knew the nature of her furnaces and the character of the coal she used, for it was this coal they contracted to supply.'

> Mr Morris relies on that passage, and says that this coat was for the use of a particular individual. However, there is all the difference in the world between a case such as that and a case like the present. Steamships differ in types – and some of them have one kind of furnace and some another, and so forth, and the coal which is suitable for one is not necessarily suitable for another. That was a matter which would be within the knowledge of coal merchants.

In *Griffiths* all that had been made known to the sellers was that the coat was to be worn by the purchaser. That was not sufficient to bring into play the term implied by what is now s 14(3). Her wearing of the coat was regarded as 'abnormal'. The situation would have been different had she informed the sellers that her skin was unusually sensitive and that she was relying on them to make her a coat which she could wear without skin problems arising. The situation should also be different where the goods are of a type which are known to have to be particularised to the user in relation to the relevant aspect of their use and that point provided the basis of the distinction made with the earlier case of *Manchester Liners Ltd v Rea Ltd*.[105] It was known in the trade that ships' boilers varied in the type of coal which they used. When the buyer stated the name of the ship, it was made clear to the seller that the buyer's particular purpose was to use the coal in boilers of the type on the ship specified.

It will often be clear what the buyer's general purpose is in buying software. A word-processing program will usually be purchased to word-process. However, if the buyer's purpose is a more specialised one, and if s 14(3) is to apply, that specialised purpose may well have to have been drawn specifically to the seller's attention. It may be that, for example, the software has to be compatible with an existing system. Sometimes incompatability with an existing system would make it a case analogous to *Griffiths*. On other occasions, if the software is such that it is normally used as a supplement to various systems, then the analogy would be with the *Manchester Liners* case. In more general terms, the test which was put in terms of 'abnormality' in *Griffiths* has been put in terms of whether the buyer's actual purpose was 'reasonably foreseeable',[106] eg if a buyer just asks for a particular type of program, the applicability of s 14(3), to the question of compatibility, depends

105 [1922] AC 74.

106 *Ashington Piggeries v Christopher Hill* [1972] AC 441 at p 477, *Kendall v Lillico* [1969] 2 AC 31 at p 91.

upon whether it is reasonably foreseeable that the buyer's actual purpose is to use the software as part of a system so that he, or she, needs compatible software.

Another issue in relation to the different uses to which software may be put and the scope of s 14(3) is raised by Lloyd.

Lloyd, 'Liability for defective software' (1991) 32 Reliability Engineering and System Safety 193

> Under the Act, whilst a purchaser is obliged to inform the seller if he intends to put a product to an unusual purpose, no specific intimation is required in respect of normal usage. As in many other respects, the application of this provision to computer software raises difficult issues. The development of cheap personal computers has led to the marketing of cut down versions of programs intended for commercial use. Although these may be adequate for domestic purposes they may prove incapable of coping with the more extensive demands of a business user.
>
> Whilst the distinction between business and domestic use is not a new one, novelty does lie in the fact that, with a computer program, any design limitations are not as transparent as those pertaining to a more tangible product. Thus, for example, it will normally be apparent whether the features present in an electric drill render it suitable for home or for commercial use. This may face sellers with a dilemma. Given that the question whether a customer is obliged to give specific notice of an intended purpose is determined in large part by the seller's claim in respect of the product, the latter may be well advised to make clear the design limits to which the product is subject. However, this may reveal the fact that the product is an inferior version of a species program. Although this may be justified by reason of a lower selling price it would not constitute a compelling marketing feature.

It should be emphasised that for the term to be implied, not only must the buyer rely upon the seller to provide goods which are reasonably fit for the buyer's particular purpose, but it must be reasonable for the buyer to so rely. Reliance can be partial provided that it relates to the aspect of the goods fitness which is relevant to the buyer's claim.[107] Reliance may not exist, or may not be reasonable, if the buyer has the greater expertise or is in much the best position to make an assessment of the goods suitability.[108]

However, even if the particular purpose has been expressly or impliedly made known to the seller and the buyer reasonably relied on the seller, the question still has to be asked whether the implied term has been breached. Where the particular purpose that is made known is a general purpose, the fact that the goods are not fit for the buyer's more specific, actual, purpose only means that they are not fit for part of the buyer's particular purpose. Being unfit for only part of the particular purpose does not necessarily mean

107 *Cammel Laird & Co Ltd v Manganese Bronze and Brass Co Ltd* [1934] AC 402.

108 For example, *Tehran Europe v S T Belton* [1968] 2 QB 545.

that they are not *reasonably* fit for the particular purpose as a *whole*. The 'width of the [particular] purpose is compensated, from the seller's point of view, by the dilution of his responsibility'.[109] More generally, 'reasonable fitness for the buyer's particular purpose' will depend upon the seriousness of the problem with the goods and the proportion of the 'particular purpose' which is affected. Lord Pearce considered an example in *Kendall v Lillico* [1969] 2 AC 31:

> I would expect a tribunal of fact to decide that a car was reasonably fit for touring even though it was not well adapted for conditions in a heat wave: but not if it could not cope adequately with rain. If, however, it developed some lethal and dangerous trick in very hot weather I would expect it to be found unfit ... the rarity of the unsuitability would be weighed against the gravity of its consequences. Again if food was merely unpalatable or useless on rare occasions, it might well be reasonably suitable for food. But I should certainly not expect it to be held reasonably suitable if even on very rare occasions it killed the consumer.

In addition, the point can be made that the implied term may be breached by an accumulation of smaller difficulties. In *Saphena Computing Ltd v Allied Collection Agencies Ltd*[110] Havery QC (Official Referee) said:[111]

> ... its main problems were those which are evidence of a lack of tuning – principally slow operation and poor design of input and output procedures ... it is clear to me that on the evidence [these defects] represent a shortfall of the system below the standard required of fitness for its purpose.

SALE BY SAMPLE

Section 15 provides for implied conditions where the sale is by sample. Like s 13, and unlike s 14(2) and s 14(3) there is no requirement that the sale should be 'in the course of a business' although other sales are unlikely to be 'by sample'. Section 15 states:

> (1) A contract of sale is a contract for sale by sample where there is an express or implied term to that effect in the contract.
>
> (2) In the case of a contract for sale by sample there is an implied term
>
> (a) that the bulk will correspond with the sample in quality;
>
> (c) that the goods will be free from any defect, making their quality unsatisfactory, which would not be apparent on reasonable examination of the sample.[112]

109 *Ashington Piggeries v Christopher Hill* [1972] AC 441, Lord Wilberforce at p 497.

110 [1995] FSR 616.

111 At p 644.

112 See also s 14(2C)(c) which prevents s 14(2) being relied upon when the sample has not been inspected and the problem, rendering the goods unsatisfactory, would have been discoverable on a reasonable examination.

A sample serves much the same purpose as a description of the goods. In *Drummond v Van Ingen* Lord Macnaghten said:[113]

> The office of a sample is to present to the eye the real meaning and intention of the parties with regard to the subject of the contract which, owing to the imperfections of language, it may be difficult or impossible to express in words. The sample speaks for itself.

However, the mere fact that a small part of the goods was present at the time of contracting does not necessarily indicate that the sale is 'by sample' within s 15. The goods may have been displayed simply to provide a basic idea of the goods being offered. Under s 15(1), it is a matter of determining the parties' intention as embodied in an express or implied term. The question is whether the parties contracted for goods which corresponded with a sample.

Section 15 seems unlikely to have much application in relation to the sale of software. Software will seldom be bought under circumstances which mean that there is provision of a sample from a larger bulk of goods. If a disk is supplied with a 'cut down' version of a program on it to encourage the purchase of the full program, in every day terms that may well be described as 'a sample', but it would seem that it should not be regarded as part of the 'bulk' (ie the full program). It is a copy of part of it. The term would be apposite if there was a purchase of multiple disk copies of a particular program and one of the copies had been tested before the purchase.

RELEVANCE OF THE IMPLIED TERMS

The implied terms considered above deal with the situation where there is a sale of goods. It has already been pointed out that similar terms are implied if the goods are not sold but hired out.[114] However, the larger question remains as to the classification of software. Can it be goods? It was suggested above, that this question might not be fundamental to the implication of these or similar terms. The same or similar terms might be implied at common law[115] even if software is regarded as *sui generis*.

113 (1887) 12 App Cas 284 at p 297.

114 Sections 8–10 of the Supply of Goods and Services Act 1982.

115 See *St Albans v ICL* [1996] 4 All ER 481 above p 152.

CHAPTER FIVE

DEFECTIVE SOFTWARE – PRODUCT LIABILITY AND TORT

INTRODUCTION

The liability for defective software arising out of contract has already been discussed in Chapter 4. As computer control becomes usual for many, if not most, applications it becomes apparent that the failure of systems containing software may well have an impact on many people who are not a party to the contract to supply that software. They may suffer economic loss or physical injury.[1] One of the most highly publicised system failures of this type was that of the Computer Aided Despatch (CAD) system of the London Ambulance Service (LAS) in October and November 1992. The Report of the Inquiry into the incident[2] demonstrates a number of the difficult issues which may arise when attempting to apportion liability in an incident such as this. In contrast, more and more common domestic appliances are controlled by means of programmable devices. Unlike some of the other areas of law considered in this book, liability for defective software has no dedicated statutes to examine and no case law of significance to assist in predicting how existing legal principles might be applied to such situations. Some cases founded in contract have now come before the UK courts but these are a long way from answering some of the fundamental questions posed by such circumstances. There have, as yet, been no cases based in tort although there has been much speculation as to how tortious principles should be applied. What follows is, therefore, an attempt to review and distil a number of the arguments that have been discussed into a coherent framework and to suggest how the law might move forward in this area. The case law which will be cited has been chosen in an attempt to provide suitable analogies with other situations, many of these are favourites of other commentators, but where they make a useful point, no excuse should be needed for a re-examination. It must be remembered though, that such cases can only be useful by way of analogy and some will perform this task rather better than others.

In the event of a system containing defective software failing there may be liability in negligence and also, for cases of physical injury or damage, under the Consumer Protection Act 1987.

1 For examples see D Rowland, 'Liability for Defective Software' [1991] Camb LR 78, Ian Lloyd, 'Liability for Defective Software' (1991) 32 Reliability Engineering and System Safety 193.

2 Report of the Inquiry into the London Ambulance Service, South West Thames Regional Health Authority, February 1993.

CONSUMER PROTECTION ACT 1987

Whilst it is not the purpose or function of this work to assess the rationale and philosophy underlying the introduction of the product liability regime introduced in the UK by the Consumer Protection Act 1987, a consideration of some of the debate surrounding the genesis of this statute is, necessarily, incidental. The 1987 Act was passed to implement the EC product liability Directive,[3] a document which had been some years in gestation. Article 1 of the Directive provides, quite simply, that '[t]he producer shall be liable for damage caused by a defect in his product'. 'Product' is then further defined in Article 2 to include '... all movables ... even though incorporated into another movable or into an immovable'. This can be compared with the relevant section of the Consumer Protection Act,[4] '... "product" means any goods or electricity and ... includes a product which is composed in another product, whether by virtue of being a component part or raw material or otherwise; ...'. In theory, the effect of product liability legislation, for those situations in which it applies, is to eliminate the necessity to show negligence and, instead, replace it with the requirement to demonstrate a causal link between the defect in the product and the damage caused. This is often referred to as a type of strict liability on the grounds that the culpability of the producer in relation to the defect is not a relevant factor.

Is software a product?

Can computer software fall within this definition of product? This question has stimulated much debate, some of the arguments are, essentially, a reflection of the tangibility/intangibility debate discussed in relation to software as goods and will not be repeated here,[5] but other arguments are inextricably linked with the concept of product and the underlying premises on which the Act and Directive are based.[6] The realisation that there might be problems with the categorisation of computer software had dawned prior to implementation of the Directive.

3 Council Directive 85/374/EEC of 25 July 1985 on the approximation of the laws, regulations and administrative provisions of the Member States concerning liability for defective products (1985) OJ L 210/29.

4 Section 2(1).

5 See Chapter 4.

6 See, eg, Jakob Hirschbaeck, 'Is software a product?' (1989) 5 CL&P 154, Ian Lloyd, 'Liability for Defective Software' (1991) 32 Reliability Engineering and System Safety 193, D Rowland, 'Liability for Defective Software' [1991] Camb LR 78.

Implementation of the EC Directive on Product Liability
DTI November 1985

Paragraph 47. Special problems arise with those industries dealing with products concerned with information such as books, records, tapes and computer software ... It does not appear that the Directive is intended to extend liability in such situations. On the other hand, it is important that liability is extended to the manufacturer of a machine which contains defective software and is thereby unsafe ... the line between those cases may however not be easy to draw, particularly in the field of new technology where the distinction between hardware and software is becoming increasingly blurred.

This suggests that even though software can be regarded as pure information in some respects, the development of technology, together with the way in which it might be used to control systems and apparatus, may conspire to make an apparently logical boundary indistinct. However, it appeared that, by the time of implementation this issue had officially disappeared and the advice following implementation was that, in the event of a defect in software leading to physical damage, liability would rest with the producer of the complete system,[7] implicitly rejecting the notion of software as a product in its own right.

Predictably this did not silence the academic debate and there is still a considerable divergence of views on the answer to the question. These differing approaches are now found, not only in specialist works, but also in standard texts on the law of tort: '[i]t is unclear whether books and computer software, which may endanger persons if they contain inaccuracies, fall within the definition of "products".'[8] Compare also the following two views.

The Law of Torts, 8th edn, p 501
John G Fleming
Law Book Company 1992

Products comprise 'any goods and electricity', including component parts. Presumably, however, not information contained in publications, however hardbound. Nor pure services: a designer is not liable unlike a producer of a defectively designed product. Misleading or inadequate warnings may make an accompanying product defective, but defective software instructions addressed to the computer, are not 'goods'.[9] What is the reason for drawing this distinction between goods and services, seeing that the rationale for the former – consumer protection – seems to apply equally to the latter? The distinction is doctrinally difficult to justify, seeing that the human element, albeit masked, is as much involved in the creation of products as is services and that the accident-preventive rationale necessarily targets human behaviour. The reasons are accidental and pragmatic. Foremost is the

7 *Guide to the Consumer Protection Act 1987* (1987) DTI, para 11.

8 KM Stanton, *The Modern Law of Tort* (1994) p 222, Sweet & Maxwell.

9 Relying on Jane Stapleton 'Software, Information and the Concept of Product' (1989) 9 Tel Aviv U Stud L 147.

provenance of warranties attached to the sale of goods, from which the seminal American tort liability derived. More fundamental may be the fact that professional services are excluded because their product is furnished for one client at a time so that the cost of liability cannot be spread as widely as over a whole line of tangible products ...

Winfield and Jolowicz on Tort, 14th edn, p 271
WVH Rogers
Sweet & Maxwell 1994

It seems that information is not within the Act even though it is incorporated in tangible form in a book but the same may not be true of computerised information, where the line between 'software' and 'hardware' may be difficult to draw sensibly. If an airline crashes because a component in an automatic landing device fails above a certain temperature there is clearly a defective product within the Act. Can the position really be so different if it is programmed so that it simply does not operate in certain foreseeable conditions or if it gives the pilot a misleading indication?

A number of issues are raised in these two extracts, the 'pure information' theory fatal to a classification of software as product, the goods/services distinction and the pragmatic approach which considers the end result of the defect rather than its location. If the first of these is to be argued successfully, it is important that all the attributes of computer software are fully taken into account.

Three Problems with the New Product Liability
Jane Stapleton
Essays for Patrick Atiyah, Chapter 11
Peter Cane and Jane Stapleton (eds)
Oxford University Press 1991

My suggestion that the reform focus on defective products may have been strengthened by a doomed attempt to shift attention away from human conduct and make the imposition of stricter liability more palatable, gains some support from the attitude of reformers to computer software. Some years ago I argued that software, being mere information, is not a 'good'[10] for the purposes of the UK law of supply of goods; and that were defective navigational software to cause a plane to crash or a heart-lung machine to cut out, those thereby injured might at first seem to have problems establishing a cause of action under the CPA which defines the 'product' in terms of 'goods'. But the CPA s 1(1) requires UK courts to construe its provisions to accord with the Directive which defines 'product' in terms of 'movables'. This might not seem to help much, but some commentators suggest that defective software may fall under the Directive, and that the European Court of Justice might take a 'flexible' attitude to the notion of 'product' which will allow it to be expanded more widely than 'goods' to allow in phenomena which, in policy terms, are 'like' defective goods. But what is it about defective software that suggests that it might be like defective goods? Is it like goods because,

10 See n 9, above.

> although it is a service, the human origin of errors in a program is less obvious than the human origin of most pure services?. Is their human origin masked in a way that facilitates imposition of liability?. Perhaps; but it should be noted that the masking characteristic is a variable. Suppose that the designer (A) of a navigational software program incorrectly enters the height of a mountain, causing a plane to crash. If the software package is to be a 'product' for the purposes of the Directive, is a map incorrectly drawn by B, which carries the identically incorrect information to the pilot also to be a product?. If so, what about where the same information is conveyed to the pilot orally by an on-board navigator (C) – is he the supplier of a 'product'? ...
>
> In deciding if 'defective software' is to be a 'defective product' within the Directive, the ECJ has to identify what it is about defective 'goods' which makes claims arising out of the injuries they cause special. The warranty origin of the focus on defective goods does not provide the answer. Nor does the fact that many goods are mass-produced, because liability under the Directive is not confined to mass-produced goods and, in any case, non-goods such as software and maps can be mass-produced and cause physical injury. For the same reasons, the complexity of some goods and their sophisticated production techniques do not provide the key. Nor can the reason be that the focus on defects in goods in the Directive eliminates the necessity to evaluate conduct: it does not.

Although the fact of inputting inaccurate data may result in a malfunction which, in turn, produces certain adverse consequences, this is a gross simplification of both the nature and the function of computer control in most systems. The potential defects that are likely to give rise to the severest problems are errors in coding or logic that cause the mode of operation of the computer controlled system to depart from its specification. This may not be traceable to any particular human error as such, but, instead may be due to a 'design error' in the software. This is, arguably, the point at which software begins to diverge from 'pure information'; although capable of reduction to written format, the program is designed to be a working entity and is 'engineered' in the true sense of the word, just as much as a more conventional control system might be. This suggests that the more accurate view is to consider a defect in the software as a design fault and this argument can also take into account the more pragmatic approach suggested in the above extract from Winfield and Jolovicz.

The final issue raised is that of the goods vs services[11] debate, the extent to which the categorisation of the contract to supply software can be described in terms of a contract for goods or a contract for services and the impact that this categorisation might have on the boundaries of the definition of product. Whittaker, in supporting the division of software into the two categories of mass-produced package and specialist bespoke software finds assistance in the American approach.

11 See discussion in Chapter 4.

European Product Liability and Intellectual Products
Simon Whittaker
(1989) 105 LQR 125 at 135

> Should computer software be included as a product for the purposes of the Directive? ... English commentators in the specialist journals have merely raised the question of the application of the Directive to the area. The American materials are more helpful, although, somewhat surprisingly, there appears to be no American case decided specifically on the question whether computer software is a product for the purposes of its strict liability. However, American commentators agree that this issue should be determined by deciding whether the reasons for imposing strict liability apply to software. Prince, for example, sees the placing of the product into the 'stream of commerce', the producer's better position to control risks and his ability to spread the cost of accidents as the three rationales most commonly used by American courts considering the expansion of the scope of strict liability beyond chattels. He distinguishes two broadly different types of software: software which is specially designed for the needs and to the order of the consumer, and software which is a standard marketed package. Prince concludes that the reasons for strict liability do not apply to the specially designed computer program as it:
>
>> 'is not really placed in the stream of commerce because it is distributed to only one customer. Also, because the program is only sold to one user, the supplier is not in a better position than the user to bear the costs. Since the supplier is not selling the product *en masse*, he cannot spread the cost of a defect over a number of consumers. Finally, the supplier may have more expertise and knowledge regarding the tailored program because the supplier wrote the program. However, in these situations, the user is normally very heavily involved in the design stage of the program because the user must tell the supplier what the program is to do.'
>
> On the other hand he considers that these same reasons do apply to 'ready to use software' as to any other product which is distributed *en masse.*

Ultimately, it will be for the courts to decide to which of these interpretations of the nature of software they choose to give effect. Evidence of the Commission's view of the intention of the Directive, if not necessarily of the logic of classifying software as a product, was illustrated in the answer to the following question asked in the European Parliament[12] – 'Does the EEC Directive on product liability also cover ... computer software?' The answer to this was unequivocal on the basis that, as the term product was defined as all movables even though incorporated into another movable or into an immovable, the Directive also applied to software. Returning to the distinction between bespoke and mass-produced software, Whittaker raises a further issue for interpretation of European Community law and the potential harmonisation of services.

12 Written Question 706/88 (1989) OJ C 114/42.

European Product Liability and Intellectual Products
Simon Whittaker
(1989) 105 LQR 125 at 130

In the case of computer software a broad distinction should be drawn between the situations where it is made to a standard design for mass distribution ('off the peg') and where it is composed specially to order for a particular purpose for a particular client ('made to measure'). In the former case, software packages circulate within the Community in very little different ways from other, manufactured goods and the arguments from competition and freedom of movement of goods would apply to the same extent. However, in the case of made to measure software, these arguments lose their force. Such programmes do not circulate in the market at all, whether within the Member State or within the Community. It is true that different liability rules would affect competition between software engineers of the Member States in question, but here it can be seen that we have strayed into the freedom of movement of services rather than of goods. This, of course, is also an important aspect of the common market and, moreover, the European Court has frequently taken the 'context of all the provisions establishing a common organisation of the market' into account in interpreting Community provisions.

Is there a defect?

If, indeed, computer software can be construed as a product, how is a defect in that software to be identified? This may raise practical as well as legal problems. Lloyd has remarked that '[t]he quest for perfect software has proved as successful as the hunt for the Loch Ness monster'.[13] In fact, the relevant issue may be not so much a question as to whether the sought after goal exists, but rather whether it is possible to demonstrate how far the search is from the target. The degree of complexity of most computer programs, creating manifold combinations and permutations, means that most computer software is impossible to test exhaustively for all foreseeable conditions. Comprehensive testing is therefore out of the question. Many faults will be discovered by routine testing but, as far as identifying defects that will compromise safety is concerned, these are more likely to be discovered by the testing of boundary conditions than the testing of normal operating conditions. It is usual to assume that in any piece of software some residual 'bugs' will remain but not all of these will give rise to 'defects; only those that could lead to damage.

Defect was defined in Article 6 of the Directive as follows:

13 Ian Lloyd, *Information Technology Law* (1993) Butterworths, see also similar comments in Ian J Lloyd and Moira Simpson, *Law on the Electronic Frontier: Hume Papers on Public Policy 2(4)* (1994) Edinburgh University Press.

Article 6

1. A product is defective when it does not provide the safety which a person is entitled to expect, taking all circumstances into account, including:
   (a) the presentation of the product;
   (b) the use to which it could reasonably be expected that the product would be put;
   (c) the time when the product was put into circulation.
2. A product shall not be considered defective for the sole reason that a better product is subsequently put into circulation.

This was implemented in the Consumer Protection Act, s 3(1) which provides that '... there is a defect in a product ... if the safety of the product is not such as persons generally are entitled to expect; and for those purposes "safety" in relation to a product, shall include safety with respect to products comprised in that product ...'.

Basing the definition of defect on a safety standard that 'persons are entitled to expect' implies an objective assessment of 'defect'. This is in accordance with the commentary on the Strasbourg Convention.[14]

Commentary on the Strasbourg Convention
Paragraph 35

... the committee [of experts] formulated a definition of defect taking as the basic elements 'safety' and 'legitimate expectancy'.

This, however, does not involve the safety or expectancy of any particular person. The use of the words 'a person' and 'entitled' clearly shows that a product's safety must be assessed according to an objective criterion. The words 'a person' do not imply any expectation on the part of a victim or a given consumer. The word 'entitled' is more general than the word 'legally' (entitled); in other words, mere observance of statutory rules and rules imposed by authorities do not preclude liability.

The committee did not wish to use the word 'reasonably'. Such expression ... could diminish the consumer's rights, since it could include considering economic factors and assessing expediency which ought not to be taken into account in determining the safety of a product.

It is arguable whether, in fact, this is the standard which has survived the Directive and the 1987 Act and there have been suggestions that, instead, reformers 'have seized on the ill-defined concept of a product 'defect' which required the benefits of the product as they were at the time of circulation to be balanced against its costs'.[15] If it is this latter concept that has held sway, then the resultant effect is more akin to a negligence standard than one of

14 Strasbourg Convention on products liability in relation to physical injury and death – text and commentary in Law Commission Report No 82 on Liability for Defective Products 1977 (Scottish Law Commission Report No 45).

15 Jane Stapleton, 'Products Liability Reform – Real or Illusory?' (1986) 6 OJLS 392.

strict liability. Moreover, the apparent decision, recorded above, not to employ a standard of reasonableness in the consideration of a safety issues is, itself, an interesting one when compared with the standards expected by other comparable legislation. The standard of safety for employees at work is governed primarily by the qualification 'as far as reasonably practicable'[16] which imports precisely the risk-benefit analysis that is purported to be excluded in the product liability regime envisioned under the Strasbourg Convention.

How then is the standard to be assessed in systems containing software? It has been suggested both that '... in those more complex situations where modern tort liability also operates, eg cases of foreseeable misuse or complex design systems where the standard is neither agreed nor obvious, the "expectations test" is misleading and inadequate'[17] and also that '[t]he "consumer expectations" test for legal defectiveness ... has had limited appeal as an operational rule for complex design defect cases. Primarily this is because the consumer simply does not have adequate information to know what to expect'.[18] A comparison can be made with the situation for 'conventional' products, where the general safety record may have a particular relevance in ascertaining whether the product was defective. This is unlikely to be the case for systems involving computer software where failure free operation in the past is not necessarily an indication of failure free operation in the future, especially for products that are likely to be used in different situations and conditions. In such circumstances, a fault could remain hidden for some time until triggered by a particular combination of inputs that may not have occurred before. In addition, the operative time at which a diagnosis of defectiveness needs to be made is the moment of supply. It is possible that the software may have been updated, modified or otherwise upgraded, making it difficult to assess the defectiveness of the original version, but in the absence of such changes software does not 'wear out' in the same way as hardware.

Causation

The final factor which has to be established is that the defect caused the damage. This may be difficult to prove depending on the nature and type of software involved. It goes without saying that any physical damage will always be inflicted by hardware and so a causal link has to be established between the apparently defective software instructions, their effect on the

16 See especially in this context s 6 of the Health and Safety at Work Act 1974 and *Edwards v National Coal Board* [1949] 1 QB 704 *per* Lord Asquith.

17 Jane Stapleton, *Product Liability* (1994) p 235, Butterworths.

18 Nicholas P Terry, *State of the Art Evidence: From logical construct to judicial retrenchment* (1991) 20 Anglo-Amer LR 285.

hardware and the consequence to the victim. Such observations highlight perhaps the difference between software and pure information; once computer software has commenced giving instructions to the system under its control, it may activate an inevitable sequence of events which becomes difficult to interrupt.[19]

It may be difficult to establish causation if there has also been some human input or intervention. In so-called fly-by-wire aircraft, such as the Airbus A320 (now being superseded by the A330 and A340), the pilot flies the plane not directly but by means of a joy stick connected to the appropriate mechanisms via a computer.[20] The presence of the computer allows for intelligent control of the aircraft which should be able to compensate for both malfunctions and pilot error. The role of the pilot (or indeed the operator/controller of other computerised systems) often only becomes crucial in the event of failure of the normal operating system. What is the situation if defective software causes such a malfunction and the pilot is unable to land the plane safely. What was the cause of the accident? Clearly each case will hinge on its particular circumstances but there are a number of general observations which can be made. There will be appropriate procedures which should be carried out in the event of a failure and, if the pilot fails to carry these out, there may be a break in the chain of causation and the accident may be put down to 'pilot error'. However, the danger with human intervention being confined to abnormal cases can mean that there is very little opportunity to practice and become proficient in such skills.[21] In addition, it is entirely possible that a situation could arise where the computer would 'not allow' the pilot to take corrective action or, alternatively, that the back-up system of control provided was inadequate to land the plane safely, especially in adverse weather conditions, even for an expert pilot. Although the root cause of the mishap might be the defective software, at least some of these elements would qualify as a *novus actus interveniens*, sufficient to break the chain of causation.

In the mid-1980s, defects in the software controlling the Therac-25 radiotherapy machine[22] resulted in substantial overdoses of radiation being administered to several patients with resulting injury, illness and death in some cases. Conceptually, this appears to be an example where it is easier to

19 Details and discussions of a number of software failures and near-failures can be found in the newsgroup comp.risks, available also at http://catless.ncl.ac.uk/Risks/ – these include reports of the circumstances of some of the Airbus A320 accidents and reports of the incidents involving the Therac 25 radiotherapy machine.

20 In fact the A320 has five on-board computers some of which are back-ups designed to switch into use if a fault is detected in the operational computer.

21 Apparently human error is involved in about 60% of all aircraft accidents. Although this does not necessarily indicate 'pilot error' it does show that human factors are also a relevant consideration. See, eg, Neil Storey, *Safety-critical Computer Systems* (1996) Addison-Wesley.

22 For further details see Nancy G Leveson, *Safeware: System Safety and Computers* (1995) Appendix A, Addison-Wesley. Medical Devices: The Therac-25 story.

accept the link between the defective software and the damage. Suppose, instead, that the software error had resulted in an underdose of radiation with the result that patients died, not from the effects of the radiation, but from the cancer for which they were supposedly being treated.[23] In this scenario, the damage would be the result of the original disease, ie it would not be caused by the radiotherapy machine, which could not, therefore, be classed as 'legally defective'.[24]

The development risks defence

Notwithstanding the label of 'strict liability' applied to the products liability regime introduced by the EC Directive and Consumer Protection Act, it is possible for producers to escape liability if they can avail themselves of the so-called 'development risks' defence contained in Article 7(e) of the Directive 'that the state of scientific and technical knowledge at the time when he put the product into circulation was not such as to enable the existence of the defect to be discovered'. This is a controversial defence and the Member States were given the choice as to whether to include it in their implementing legislation. Interestingly, it had not been included in the Strasbourg Convention for the reasons given below.

Commentary on the Strasbourg Convention
Paragraphs 39–40[25]

> Some experts maintained that 'development risks' should be a ground for exclusion of liability in the case of technically advanced products. Any stipulation to the contrary might discourage scientific research and the marketing of new products.
>
> Against this opinion it was argued that such an exception would make the convention nugatory since it would reintroduce into the system of liability established by the convention the possibility for the producer to prove the absence of fault on his part. Exclusion of liability in cases of 'development risks' would also invite the use of the consumer as a 'guinea-pig'.
>
> In conclusion the committee considered that the problem was one of social policy, the main question being whether such risks should be borne by the consumer of the producer and/or, in whole or in part, by the community.
>
> The committee considered that, as insurance made it possible to spread risk over a large number of products, producers' liability, even for development

23 A similar situation arose in relation to a radiotherapy device at a North Staffordshire hospital, although not as a result of a error on the software.

24 See also later discussion in relation to negligent designs at p 212.

25 Strasbourg Convention on products liability in relation to physical injury and death – text and commentary in Law Commission Report No 82 on Liability for Defective Products 1977 (Scottish Law Commission Report No 45).

> risks, should not be a serious obstacle to planning and putting into circulation new and useful products.
>
> The committee therefore decided that development risk should not constitute an exception to producers' liability.

Despite criticisms both over the use of the defence as such and the change in wording from that supplied in the Directive,[26] the UK included the defence in the 1987 Act, s 4(1)(e), 'that the state of scientific and technical knowledge at the relevant time was not such that a producer of products of the same description as the product in question might be expected to have discovered the defect if it had existed in his products while they were under his control'. The emphasis of this defence is rather different and refers to a comparison with other producers, ie a negligence-type test whereas the Directive implies an obligation to consider the available knowledge in the world at large.[27] Thus in relation to the UK defence, Reed[28] suggests that, given the practice in the industry, 'it is arguable that a software producer who failed to discover a quite serious defect in his software would nevertheless be able to take advantage of the defence, so long as the defect is not in an area of the program that would be tested as a matter of course by others in the industry'.

A number of commentators have discussed the various possible combinations envisaged by the defence.[29] The two outer extremes are those where the defect is either unknown and undiscoverable or known and discoverable. In the former there will be no liability whereas there will always be liability in the latter case. In between these two extremes are the situations where the defect is either known but undiscoverable or, conversely, unknown but discoverable. The latter is, arguably, the usual position and one in which it is incumbent on the producer to utilise the current state of knowledge to uncover the defect. The former is more difficult to rationalise but is, perhaps, the one which best describes the position with respect to potential defects in software. It is never possible to provide assurance that any software is free from error and such errors are capable of becoming defects if they compromise the safety of the system. Techniques used to develop software for use in safety-critical systems take this fact into account by starting from the premise that such software is bound to contain errors. The use of the definite article in the wording of the defence seems to indicate that it refers to a specific defect. Such a concept is difficult to apply to software development and, based on this, the use of the defence appears problematic. On the other

26 Hansard (Lords) Vol 485 Cols 848–55 (9/3/87) and Hansard (Lords) Vol 487 Col 784 (14/5/87).

27 Christopher Newdick, 'Risk, Uncertainty and "Knowledge" in the Development Risks Defence' (1991) 20 Anglo-Amer LR 309.

28 Chris Reed (ed) *Computer Law* (1996) 3rd edn, Blackstone Press.

29 See, eg, Newdick, above, n 27 and also in 'The Development Risk Defence of the Consumer Protection Act 1987' (1988) 47 CLJ 455, Christopher Hodges *Product Liability; European Laws and Practice* (1993) Sweet & Maxwell.

hand, if we start from the presumption of the presence of a defect, it may be that the situation is accurately represented by the phrase 'known but undiscoverable'. It has been suggested that where the danger is known but science has not developed a means of eliminating the danger, then it would be open to the manufacturer to argue that the product is not defective instead of pleading a defence of development risks.[30] In relation to defective software though, the view has also been expressed that,[31] 'the argument that a software producer could not be expected to discover his own mistakes is not a compelling one'. Since software is developed by human ingenuity, any faults should be regarded as introduced rather than inherent. Neither is it clear how all of these factors affect or are affected by the question of resource allocation for research. Stapleton[32] points out that the full pre-circulation screening test for some defects, including bugs in complex software would be 'astronomically expensive', but suggests also that, '[t]o give the defence substance then it must protect in cases of defects which could only be discovered, if at all, by extraordinary means'. It is plain that testing cannot be carried on for ever, but when should a producer stop testing? Does this, necessarily, entail a comparison with the behaviour of the 'reasonable' producer?

It is also important to note that the issue of when knowledge becomes available is crucial – the defence is unavailable after the date at which the existence of the defect could have been discovered. This may be especially pertinent for non-research based industries (this market is becoming increasingly relevant as increasing numbers of domestic appliances contain software) for which it is likely that there will be a lapse in time before the requisite information concerning the defect is available to the producer.

It is difficult to assess how important the availability of a development risks defence might be to the software industry. An argument that was advanced at the time of the Strasbourg Convention,[33] albeit unsuccessfully, was that technically advanced industries needed a development risks defence if innovation and progress were not to be stifled. This was the primary reason for including it within the UK legislation. Nonetheless, a number of other Member States have chosen not to include the defence and producers exporting to those countries will need to take responsibility for their own development risks even though this is unnecessary in relation to the domestic market. In addition, there is no similar defence in contract where liability is

30 Ewan McKendrick, 'Product Liability and the Development Risks Defence' [1990] Law for Business 252 but compare Newdick's view that the defence cannot be available once the possibility of a defect has been foreseen ('The Development Risk Defence of the Consumer Protection Act 1987' (1988) 47 CLJ 455).

31 Ian Lloyd, 'Liability for Defective Software' (1991) 32 Reliability Engineering and System Safety 193.

32 Jane Stapleton, *Product Liability* (1994) Butterworths.

33 Above, p 209.

imposed when a defect would not be able to be detected even by the 'utmost skill and judgment on the part of the seller'.[34]

Some other statutory systems impose a much stricter standard. A case frequently referred to in this connection, by way of analogy, is that of *Smedley v Breed*,[35] decided under the Food and Drugs Act 1955. The case arose out of a caterpillar in a tin of peas. The salient facts for comparison are that a stringent system of inspection had been instigated, the success of which was evidenced by the fact that there were only four complaints out of a total of 3.5m tins, despite the fact that the caterpillars were difficult to detect being of similar shape, size and colour to the peas themselves. So, even though the particular 'defect' might be difficult to discover, there was ample evidence that the defendant had taken steps to ensure that the number of such defects was minimised. Nonetheless, the court found that, under the strict liability scheme contained in the relevant statute, the only possible defence for the presence of extraneous matter was where this was 'an unavoidable consequence of the process itself'. Although the court accepted that the system was as good as reasonable skill and diligence could make it, this could only go to mitigation and the fact that in any commercial process, however well-managed, some failures are statistically predictable, was irrelevant. Interestingly, the observed failure rate of four out of 3.5m was clearly viewed as excellent by the court at the time; it is a moot point as to whether this would be an acceptable failure rate for safety-critical software for which probability of failure rates demanded are typically of the order of 10^{-8} and 10^{-9}.

In contrast, s 6 of the Health and Safety at Work Act 1974 which imposes requirements on those who manufacture 'articles for use at work' utilises a standard of 'as far as reasonably practicable', as referred to earlier[36] but also includes a positive duty to arrange for testing and examination to ensure safe design and construction, together with a duty to arrange for research to discover and hence eliminate or minimise risks.[37]

NEGLIGENCE

Whether or not the Consumer Protection Act 1987 can ever be said to apply to systems containing software, there will always be some situations involving defects in software where the regime is inappropriate, either because of the nature of the software at issue or the nature of the damage. In such cases,

34 *Henry Kendall and Son Ltd v William Lillico* [1969] 2 AC 44 at 84 *per* Lord Reid.

35 [1974] AC 839.

36 Above, p 207.

37 See further D Rowland, 'Liability for Defective Software' [1991] Camb LR 78, Bott, Coleman, Eaton and Rowland, *Professional Issues in Software Engineering* (1995) 2nd edn, UCL Press.

potential liability will be determined by the principles of negligence. Even then there have been suggestions that negligence will not be capable of founding liability. It was suggested in *Ministry of Housing and Local Government v Sharp*, a case concerning an inaccurate land certificate that, due to the likelihood of computerisation of the Land Registry, the Registrar's absolute statutory duty of care should be held to exist independently of negligence since '[c]omputers might produce an inaccurate certificate without negligence on the part of anyone'.[38] It might be supposed that the average person (and even the average judge!) now has a greater general understanding of computing, at least to the extent of realisation that computers can only be as accurate as the person who wrote the program, input the data or interpreted the output made them. Nonetheless, there is still some truth in Tapper's assertion that, '[i]t is common experience that computer systems do malfunction without any negligence on anyone's part, just because they are so complicated, and exhaustive testing in all possible situations in which they might be used is impossible'. The challenge is to distinguish the failures that are due to negligence from those that are not.

Where the loss generated as a result of a defect in software is purely economic then, if there is no remedy available in contract, the only possibility will be to consider liability for negligent misstatement, the operative principles for which were set out in *Hedley Byrne v Heller*.[39] In order to limit the class of potential plaintiffs, a special relationship is required between the parties plus evidence of reliance on the statement. This test for liability could be appropriate when the loss is a consequence of relying on the output of the software[40] – unless the act of reliance on the output can, itself, be construed as negligent. Such an approach might be suitable when considering the potential liability for artificial intelligence and expert systems, as it can be argued that diagnostic expert systems are tools to 'aid' professionals in making their diagnoses. They should not be relied on absolutely as they are no substitute for intelligent thought but merely a useful pointer to a particular course of action. This could also be the case where the output is accurate but insufficient by itself.[41] It has also been suggested that, given the problems with the intangible nature of software, the tort of negligent misstatement might have more general application in relation to computer software in that the program instructions are 'relied upon' by the computer to attain the relevant result.

In the case of bespoke software which, being categorised as the provision of services, is unlikely to fall within the ambit of product liability legislation, it will be necessary to show that the system was designed negligently.

38 [1970] 2 QB 223 at 275 *per* Salmon LJ.

39 [1964] AC 465.

40 See also Barry B Sookman, 'The Liability of Information Providers in Negligence' (1989) 5 CL&P 141.

41 *Cf* the situation in 'The Lady Gwendolen' [1965] P 294 cited in Chris Reed *Computer Law* (1996) 3rd edn, Blackstone Press, for example.

Product Liability, p 251
Jane Stapleton
Butterworths 1994

> ... claims relating to the inadequate design of products can be made in negligence. There may well be practical reasons why such claims were in the past less often made than were claims for manufacturing errors but the propriety of such claims in negligence is without doubt. Many past negligence cases rested on a plaintiff's complaint that her predicament was made worse by the negligence of the defendant in relation to the design ... The highly publicised Thalidomide litigation of the late 1960s and early 1970s was a classic example in the UK of a negligent design and R & D allegation, yet it was never challenged as being outside the realm of *Donoghue v Stevenson* negligence liability. A number of other UK design cases can be found typically focusing on the inadequacy of R & D or failure to warn [cites cases]. Moreover in recent years UK appellate courts have clearly confirmed manufacturer liability in negligence for the design condition of products. Although the issues raised on appeal in *Lambert v Lewis* did not focus on the trial judge's finding of liability against the manufacturer of a towing hitch on the basis of negligent design both the Court of Appeal and the House of Lords expressly accepted that finding.

The House of Lords in *IBA v EMI* and *BICC*[42] could have found liability for negligent misstatement as certain assurances were given concerning the efficacy of the design, but they equally found negligence in the design itself, which Lord Fraser regarded as 'a distinct and sufficient reason for imposing liability'. How is the negligence of a designer of software systems to be judged; by what criteria should the achievements and failures of software engineers be assessed? It is clear that the individuals in question possess, or should possess, special expertise and one area of law that has developed to examine the achievements of those professing a particular expertise is that of professional negligence. There have, as yet, been no cases which have had to consider the role of software engineer as designer or the status of software engineer as a 'professional'. Could such a person be construed as coming within this latter category? Jackson and Powell[43] refer to the four attributes which are deemed to be necessary characteristics of professions namely, the nature of the work, the moral aspect, collective organisation and status. Thus the nature of the work is expected or presumed to be of high intellectual content requiring particular study and qualifications, professionals are expected to have some moral commitment to the community at large, they are expected to be governed by an organisation that sets the standards for and regulates the conduct of its members and there should be evidence that they are accorded a particular status by the community. How far do these factors pertain to software engineers?

42 (1980) 14 BLR 1 and see later discussion at p 219.

43 Rupert Jackson and John Powell, *Jackson and Powell on Professional Negligence* (1992) 3rd edn, Sweet & Maxwell.

Where the work undertaken is of a safety-critical nature these factors are becoming increasingly pertinent. Many transport systems, particularly air and rail, rely on computer control, as do major hazard installations such as nuclear reactors and chemical plants. Failure of such systems is likely to result in disaster such that it seems inconceivable that persons designing the software for those applications would not be cognisant of their duty to the public at large. The 'profession' is governed by two professional organisations, the Institution of Electrical Engineers (IEE) and the British Computer Society (BCS) who together have considered the entry qualifications and continuing professional development necessary for those engaged on such work. Both organisations create standards and codes of conduct to which their members are expected to adhere.[44] Of particular relevance in this context is the following definition of competence from the IEE's professional brief on safety-related systems.[45]

> Competence requires the possession of qualifications, experience and qualities which include:
>
> - such theoretical training as would ensure acquisition of the necessary knowledge of the field in which they are required to work;
> - a thorough knowledge of the hazards and failure of the equipment for which they are responsible;
> - an understanding and detailed knowledge of the working practices used in the organisation for which they work, as well as a general knowledge of the working practices in other establishments of a similar type;
> - a detailed working knowledge of all statutory provisions, approved codes of practice, other codes of practice, guidance material and other information relevant to their work, and an awareness of legislation and practices, other than those which might affect their work;
> - the ability to give advice to others;
> - the calibre and personality to enable them to communicate effectively with their peers, any staff working under their supervision, and their own supervisors;
> - an awareness of current developments in the field in which they work;
> - an appreciation of their own limitations, whether of knowledge, experience, facilities, resources, etc, and a preparedness to declare any such limitation.

The status of such engineers in the wider community is uncertain as, arguably, is the status of a number of other branches of engineering that, nevertheless, have been considered as professions by the courts. It is certainly clear from the documentation of the relevant professional organisations that

---

44 Much of this activity had its genesis in joint IEE/BCS consultative document *Software in Safety-related Systems* (1989) published by the IEE.

45 *Safety-related Systems. A professional brief for the engineer* (1992) IEE, now superceded by *Safety-related systems. Guidance for engineers* (1995) Hazards Forum.

they feel they have the attributes of a profession, so would presumably expect their members to reach the standard that the law requires of a professional.

In any case, where the software engineer has contracted to design specialist bespoke software, the Supply of Goods and Service Act 1982 will imply a term that 'reasonable care and skill' will be used in the performance of the contract. It is submitted that such a term will, in any case, require a similar level of competence as that appropriate to the professional in negligence. Nonetheless, in negligence there will not necessarily be a duty of care towards all those who might be affected by the failure of the software. It is clear that there is a very different range of foreseeable plaintiffs in relation to defects in the design of a radiotherapy machine, as compared with a fly-by-wire aircraft, for instance. There are policy considerations which may pull in either direction and the dividing line may not be easy to draw. There may be such potential for damage that it may be considered unjust to hold the designer liable, but, equally, both contractor and client may have their own particular knowledge and expertise about the system such that an apportionment of liability may be more appropriate.

There will also again be the necessity to show causation. Returning to the example of the radiotherapy machines,[46] although an arguable case of negligence might be made out in relation to the overdose, because of the problems with proving causation, a claim of negligence might, again, be difficult to substantiate where the software fault resulted in an underdose. If a design standard was mandated for the design of the equipment and was not adhered to in either case, it is difficult to support the conclusion that the designer in the one instance is less culpable than the other. Similar issues were raised in a case involving the decision of a coroner's court not to hold an inquest on the death of an asthmatic after an ambulance was delayed, on the basis that she did not die an 'unnatural' death. Coincidentally, this case was heard around the time of the failure of the London Ambulance Service computer system and, although, this was not the cause of the delay in this case, the court was clearly aware of the implications.

R v Poplar Coroner, ex p Thomas
[1993] 2 WLR 547 at 552
Court of Appeal

> **Dillon LJ** ... it is easy to think of a variety of different scenarios as a result of which an ambulance could have arrived too late to save a patient who had suffered a severe attack of asthma like Miss Thomas's, eg (i) the distance from the ambulance centre to the patient's home was too great for there to have ever been any chance of the ambulance arriving in time to save the patient; (ii) there was much more traffic than normal in the locality and so the ambulance was delayed and arrived just too late; (iii) the ambulance was diverted on its journey and had to take a much longer route because of flooding caused by a

46 See above p 208.

> burst water main, which may have been due to lack of proper maintenance by the water company; (iv) a newly installed computer installed by the ambulance service to handle emergency calls more efficiently malfunctioned, as newly installed computers are prone to; or (v) the ambulance came late because the ambulance crew were inefficient and the management was slack.
>
> I do not suggest that any of these scenarios actually fits the facts of Miss Thomas's case. I do not know what the cause of delay was. But in each of these scenarios common sense indicates that what caused the patient's death was, on Lord Salmon's test in *Alphacell Ltd v Woodward* [1972] AC 824, 847, the asthmatic attack, not the congestion of the traffic, the bursting of the water main, the malfunction of the computer or the inefficiency of the ambulance service.

Although the court was not charged with any assessment of civil liability, the causation issue is set out in very plain terms. As to the existence of a duty of care, it does not seem unreasonable, that if someone is contracted to write software for an ambulance despatch system, then they might have in their contemplation the likely effect on a patient in the event of a system failure. Although agreeing with Dillon LJ as to the outcome of this case on the facts, Simon Brown LJ took a rather more circumspect view of the causation issue, especially as it might affect a negligence claim.

R v Poplar Coroner, ex p Thomas
[1993] 2 WLR 547 at 554
Court of Appeal

> **Simon Brown LJ** I do not find the question of causation in this context susceptible of quite the same sort of robust approach that the House of Lords advocated in a very different context in cases such as *McGhee v National Coal Board* [1973] 1 WLR 1. The question arising there was: can the court properly infer, in the absence of a provable direct link, that one particular state of affairs caused or contributed to another. In those cases the possibility of there being more than one cause was immaterial. Indeed courts often find there to have been several different causes of a given eventuality. Take this very case: can it really be doubted that if an action was brought in respect of Miss Thomas's death, whatever the court found regarding negligence it would certainly find the death to have been caused at least in part by the late arrival of the ambulance?

Assuming that there are no problems in respect of causation the standard of care required of a professional is that of the ordinarily competent member of that profession as set out by McNair J in *Bolam v Friern Hospital Management Committee*:[47]

> When you get situations which involve the use of some special skill or competence, then the test as to whether there has been negligence or not, is not the test of the man on the top of the Clapham Omnibus, because he has not got that special skill. The test is the standard of the ordinary skilled man exercising

47 *Bolam v Friern Hospital Management Committee* [1957] 1 WLR 582 at 586.

> and professing that special skill. A man need not possess the highest expert skill; it is well established law that it is sufficient if he exercises the ordinary skill of an ordinary competent man exercising that particular art.

This basic test has then been refined in relation to different professions taking note of the fact that professions can be divided into two groups, those who cannot guarantee the results of their labour and those who could be said to impliedly warrant to produce a particular result.[48] Engineers are likely to fall into the latter category as noted by Lord Scarman in *IBA v EMI and BICC*[49] '[i]n the absence of any terms (express or implied) negating the obligation, one who contracts to design an article for a purpose made known to him undertakes that the design is reasonably fit for the purpose'. This can be construed as requiring a higher standard than that of the basic *Bolam* test.[50]

A number of facets of the standard of care required of the emerging profession of the software engineer have been identified,[51] but, of these, some are of particular concern to this discipline. The first is on whom does the duty fall to identify the system as safety-related? Whereas it might be thought that the procurer would be in the best position to make this assessment, it cannot necessarily be assumed that the procurer is aware that safety-critical applications require design and implementation procedures that are any different from those used for 'normal' computer systems. This may be especially pertinent for systems for which the safety connection is not immediately obvious.[52] However, neither can it be assumed that the software engineer is likely to be in a better position to make this assessment.

A common measure of the standard of care is provided by adherence to relevant standards and codes of practice[53] and there is no reason why this should be any different for the software engineer. Although there are a number of standards laid down for specific industry sectors such as defence and the aircraft industry,[54] there are as yet no widely accepted standards for the development of safety-critical software, other than a general acceptance that the usual practices of software development for non-safety-related applications are inadequate for safety-related systems. It is to be expected that there will be a relationship between the level of competence required of a software engineer and the integrity required of the design. Given that the

48 D Rowland and JJ Rowland, 'Competence and Legal Liability in the Development of Software for Safety-related Applications' (1993) 2 LCAI 229.

49 (1980) 14 BLR 1 and see later discussion at p **.

50 *Greaves & Co v Baynham Meikle* [1974] 1 WLR 1261 at 1269, aff'd [1975] 1 WLR 1095.

51 See further Rowland and Rowland, above, n 48 and John Cooke, 'Architects and Engineers: Practising in the Public Interest' (1991) 14 UNSW Law Journal 73.

52 See E Geake, 'Did Ambulance Chiefs Specify Safety Software?' [1992] New Scientist, Vol 136, 7 November, p 5.

53 *Bevan Investments v Blackhall and Struthers No 2* [1973] 2 NZLR 45.

54 See further Bott, Coleman, Eaton and Rowland Professional Issues in Software Engineering (1995) 2nd edn, Chapter 11, UCL Press.

latter increases with the level of safety required it is here that an awareness of the standard of care becomes paramount.

Competence and Legal Liability in the Development of Software for Safety-related Applications
D Rowland and JJ Rowland
(1993) 2 Law, Computers and Artificial Intelligence 229 at 233

At present, safety-critical practitioners seem to divide into three groups:

1. Those who are aware in general of the problems raised by safety-critical software development and are striving to adjust their working practices so as to produce software of what they consider to be an adequate quality.
2. Those who are attempting to follow, and where possible do better than, the emerging standards.
3. Those who are developing safety-critical systems and yet are not aware that there are special problems.

The first of these probably most accurately reflects what can be described as the ordinarily competent safety-critical practitioner, whilst a growing number of specialists fall into the second category. It is widely suspected that a significant proportion of companies producing safety-related software belong in the third category ...

An important consideration for a technologically advanced industry, such as the software industry, is the legitimate concern that innovation should not be stifled by legal rules. Designs for systems that are 'at the cutting edge of technology' may not have been tried and tested in the same way as a more pedestrian project, and the industry owes its success to its ability to create and market new methods of control or new systems and products. Nonetheless, where there are safety implications in a design, the law has not shied away from requiring the highest consideration of the safety factors as evidenced in the case of *IBA v EMI and BICC*[55] concerning the collapse of the Emley Moor television transmitter in 1969. The defendants, BICC, argued vigorously that a finding of negligence would be likely to stifle innovation and inhibit technological progress, they produced evidence that there was neither any available source of empirical knowledge nor agreed practice; they were 'both at and beyond the frontier of professional knowledge'.

Competence and Legal Liability in the Development of Software for Safety-related Applications
D Rowland and JJ Rowland
(1993) 2 Law, Computers and Artificial Intelligence 229 at 238

In view of the potentially catastrophic consequences of collapse of the mast, the House of Lords were agreed that it would have been necessary for BICC to exercise a high degree of care. By applying standard principles of negligence Lord Edmund-Davies deduced:

55 (1980) 14 BLR 1. For a more detailed consideration of this case see, eg, KM Stanton and AM Dugdale, 'Design Responsibility in Civil Engineering Work' (1981) 131 NLJ 583.

> 'The graver the foreseeable consequences of failure to take care, the greater the necessity for special circumspection ... The project may be alluring. But the risks of injury to those engaged in it, or to others, or to both, may be so manifest and substantial, and their elimination may be so difficult to ensure with reasonable certainty that the only proper course is to abandon the project altogether ... The law requires even pioneers to be prudent.'

It was found that the cause of the collapse was due to a combination of vortex shedding and asymmetric icing on the stays, which would be likely to cause problems at even relatively low wind velocities. The House of Lords unanimously agreed that these factors could reasonably have been foreseen and the fact that the project was at the forefront of knowledge at the time was no excuse. It was foreseeable that large quantities of ice might be deposited on the stays and that this was likely to be asymmetric, but that the resultant stresses would be exacerbated by vortex shedding had never been considered by BICC whose design was therefore held to be negligent.

The behaviour that the law expects of the reasonably competent professional who is operating at the frontiers of knowledge at the time can be inferred from this statement of Lord Edmund-Davies:

> 'Justice requires that we seek to put ourselves in the position of BICC when first confronted by their daunting task, lacking all empirical knowledge and adequate expert advice in dealing with the many problems awaiting solution. But those very handicaps created a clear duty to identify and to think through such problems, including those of static and dynamic stresses, so that the dimensions of the "venture into the unknown" could be adequately assessed and the ultimate decision as to its practicality arrived at.'

The power of software arises principally from the relative ease with which highly complex systems can be created and changed. There is a consequent temptation to undertake development without adherence to appropriate engineering principles and to quite readily undertake a 'venture into the unknown'; after all, software can be changed easily and it is tempting to think that any faults can be corrected easily. However, unless software is designed very carefully a seemingly simple change can have an unexpected side effect that may not become apparent for some considerable time afterwards, so that any departure from strict quality assurance procedures during development almost certainly becomes another 'venture into the unknown'. In the case of software the 'dimensions' of such ventures are not readily assessed, so that departure from established methods can be particularly risky.

Finally, what is the standard that can be expected if the client requests (and pays for) the services of an acknowledged expert? Is the expertise of such a person to be judged by reference to the standards of the 'ordinarily competent practitioner'. It seems reasonable to suggest that the standard of such individuals should, instead, be assessed by reference to a more limited class of those with specialist knowledge. This might create problems where the class is small such that the general or accepted standard is difficult to determine, but it has been confirmed that even a small number of specialists can constitute a reasonable body of opinion, the question is one of quality not quantity.[56] In any event if the specialist is in possession of actual knowledge that might not be possessed by the general body of that profession then he or she is under a duty to make use of that actual knowledge.[57]

Thus, although there may be a number of possible causes of action which could be pursued in the event of the defective software which resulted in damage, there is considerable uncertainty about the scope and boundaries of liability and also about those on whom liability might fall. Modern technology relies extensively on software and it is perhaps surprising that there has been little activity in the courts as yet. Neither does this seem to be due to the excellence of the software; Hatton[58] points out that, '[a]n explosion in the volume of software would not be a cause for concern if software quality was improving at the same rate proportionately. Unfortunately the plain truth is that software is simply not getting much better'. Given these concerns it may only be a matter of time before the judiciary are called upon to decide some of the issues raised in this chapter.

56 *De Freitas v O'Brien* [1995] 6 Med LR 108 at 115 *per* Otton LJ.

57 See, eg, *Wimpey Construction v Poole* [1984] 2 Lloyds Rep 499.

58 Les Hatton, *Software failures, follies and fallacies* (1997) IEE Review, p 49.

SECTION B

THE CHALLENGES
OF
COMPUTER TECHNOLOGY

CHAPTER SIX

ELECTRONIC DATA INTERCHANGE

INTRODUCTION

Electronic Data Interchange (EDI) has been defined as 'the computer to computer transmission of business data in a standard format'.[1] It is a means of business communication which replaces paper with structured electronic messages.[2] It is more secure than simply using e-mail.

It would be possible for a business to set up dedicated EDI links with each of its trading partners but that is unlikely to be economic. The common way for businesses to communicate using EDI is through a Value Added Network Service (VAN) so that the sender routes the message to its recipient through the network, rather than by a direct line between the sender's and the recipient's computer.

EDI is more secure than simple e-mail. Its security is obtained through such matters as the technical procedures used, the protocols for message formats, data storage logs and acknowledgments of messages and confirmations of their content.

The purpose of this chapter is simply to provide an introduction to some of the challenges to the law which may be raised by the use of EDI. It does not deal, individually, with the many specialised areas of commerce on which EDI may impact but rather attempts to provide an overview of the basic legal problems which may be encountered. Consideration of, for example, Electronic Fund Transfers are left to more specialist works.[3]

EDI VS PAPER

EDI has been seen to be of considerable significance:[4]

> In international trade, EDI introduces changes facilitating the evolution of a global economy ... Geographic distances, time requirements and language barriers fade into the background as national barriers become transparent and a 'borderless world' emerges.

1 The United Nations Trade Interchange Directory (UNTDID), TRADE/WP. 4/R.721.

2 See *The Encyclopaedia of Information Technology Law*, p 5009.

3 For example, *Cross Border Electronic Banking* (1995), Lloyd's of London press, Norton, Reed & Walden, *Electronic Banking and the Law* (1993) Arora, *Encyclopaedia of Information Technology Law*.

4 AH Boss and JB Ritter, *Electronic Data Interchange Agreements – A Guide and Sourcebook* (1993), p 9.

However, its more immediate significance is that it is 'paperless trading' and, although this is something of an overstatement, it conveys the basic idea of what is involved and indicates its most immediate advantage – the efficiency gains and reductions in the costs which stem from the time taken to produce, and process, the numerous pieces of paper otherwise required for trade.

I Walden and N Savage, 'The Legal Problems of Paperless Transactions' [1989] JBL 102

> Paper transfers can cause business hold-ups, with the documentation often moving more slowly than the goods. In international trade, the absence of the right documentation can cause delays at the port of entry and expose the goods to the risk of deterioration and damage and may account for high demurrage costs.
>
> Within a sophisticated business environment, the more complex the production process the more paper is needed. Paper is required internally for evidence of agreed pricing, quantities and other contract terms, and for proof of delivery. The longer the supply chain the more paper you need in order to communicate quantities from the supplier to the main producer. Such communications can take time where the relationship is a continuing one and hence modifications to orders and cancellations are more likely to generate claims.
>
> The use of third parties, such as agents for carrying goods and the insurance arrangements creates further documentation in order to lay down the limits of authority, and the scope of cover ...
>
> The major advantage of EDI is through reduction in administration costs:
>
> > 'Any company that can reduce the time and money spent on costly trade documentation will have an immediate competitive advantage. The cost saving goes well beyond more efficient processing of orders and faster invoicing, to strategic priority areas like reducing inventories and setting up just in time delivery systems.'

Of course, the savings may not simply lie in the removal of the paper element as such. Stock control may be carried out automatically through a computer which then, itself, dispatches appropriate orders to the computers of the relevant suppliers.

However, if EDI transactions are faster than paper based ones, the question should be asked as to whether paper has advantages which EDI cannot emulate. The different types of messages for which EDI might be used should be considered.

E Bergsten and R Goode, 'Legal Questions and Problems to be Overcome' in Thomsen & Wheble, Trading with EDI – The Legal Issues

> (i) Communications having no legal significance
>
> Many trade communications are designed purely to inform and have no legal significance. They are not a prelude to contract, a part of the contract or the performance of a contractual obligation; they create no legal commitment and they are not prescribed by any rule of public law.

Examples are statistical information, information about markets, details of export and import formalities, and so on. Such data is passed between sender and recipient purely for their mutual convenience ...

(ii) Communications having contractual significance

Other types of communication are contractually significant in that they constitute or evidence a contract or are sent in fulfilment of a contractual obligation. Examples are an offer, an acceptance, a notice of appropriation of goods under a contract of sale, the delivery of a bill of lading or a certificate of insurance, a certificate of quantity, quality, or origin. In principle, it is for the parties themselves to agree on the mode of communication, and the law may need change only to the extent that it prescribes mandatory formalities of contract or rules of evidence and proof that do not accommodate EDI;

(iii) Communications operative to transfer ownership, control or contract rights

... If we take the bill of lading as the paradigm of a documentary communication falling within this category, we find it fulfills a variety of functions. It is a receipt for the goods; it evidences or constitutes the terms of carriage; it is a document of title, the delivery of which confers on each successive holder constructive possession of the goods (assuming these to be identified by the bill) ...

(iv) Communications required by law

A prime example is the customs declaration ...

The first type of message, the purely informational, does not pose any particular problems if EDI is used rather than some other form of communication. However, there may be difficulties in relation to the others.[5] The types of problems are highlighted by Walden.

Ian Walden, 'EDI and the Law' in Information Technology & The Law (1990), 2nd edn, Edwards, Savage & Walden

Paper-based documents have three basic functions which could be required in any replacement system: an informative function, an evidential function and a symbolic function. It is within the last two functions that potential legal problems arise.

A disadvantage of electronic messaging systems is their 'fleeting' nature. It can be difficult to produce an acceptable record of what has occurred between trading parties, in the event of a dispute. In 1985, the United Nations

5 A fifth category was also identified, which overlaps with the other four.

'(v) Communications requiring legal authority or licence

In many countries the transfer of data across national boundaries requires legal authorisation or licence, for example where it involves the use of a public telecommunications service or the transfer of data which is sensitive in terms of national security or the protection of national economic interests. This is necessarily a matter within the domain of public law and the exercise of executive discretion. The data involved may fall within any of the other four types of message.'

Commission on International Trade Law (UNCITRAL) published a report that considered the legal value of computer records. It concluded:

> 'Almost all countries that replied to the questionnaire appeared to have legal rules which were at least adequate to permit the use of computer evidence and to permit the court to make an evaluation necessary to determine the proper weight given to data.' [A/CN 9/265]

The key evidential issue is the weight that a court gives to electronic records, once they have been admitted, and will involve satisfying the court of the integrity of any record. This will primarily be a question of agreeing to, and implementing, adequate security procedures.

The symbolic function of paper documents raises the most difficult legal issues for EDI: where physical possession of a document invests the holder with certain legal rights. The bill of lading and the bill of exchange are two primary examples in UK law. With a bill of lading, transfer of the paper document represents the legal transfer of title to the goods; whereas a bill of exchange, enables a transferable deferred payment obligation to arise. At the moment, such 'negotiable instruments' cannot be replicated in EDI, however, attempts to create an electronic alternative are being considered within various international fora.

Administrative rules and regulations is another area which can impede the use of EDI. The range of documents that are required by various governmental authorities is vast, for example, health certificates and certificates of origin. To allow for such submissions to be made electronically will require not only changes in the terminology of certain regulations but also the installation of the necessary equipment ...

Evidential matters as such are looked at in Chapter 9. Further consideration will be given, below, to the question of whether EDI can comply with legal requirements for documents, or writing, or signature.[6] The question of the 'symbolic' function of paper will also be addressed in looking at documents, such as bills of lading, where the piece of paper itself confers rights.[7]

Network provider

It has been indicated that EDI is normally carried out through a network provided by a third party. This means that the use of EDI basically involves consideration of two types of issues. Those between the network provider and its users and those between the users themselves. Initial consideration will be given to the position of the network provider.

The responsibilities of the network provider were identified by Moteshar as:[8]

---

6 See p 231.

7 See p 240.

8 'Liability issues of EDI' in *EDI and The Law*, Walden (ed), p 49.

- Conveyance of the message in the correct format and protocol.
- Safeguarding against corruption of the message.
- Securing that the message is conveyed to the recipient.
- Preserving the confidentiality and security of the message.

However, what the network provider is supplying is, basically, a service, and his or her obligations in relation to that service are likely to be merely to take due care. In the absence of an express term, s 13 of the Supply of Goods and Services Act 1982 would imply a term to that effect. Section 13 states:

> In a contract for the supply of a service where the supplier is acting in the course of a business, there is an implied term that the supplier will carry out the service with reasonable care and skill.

The network provider's liability is likely to be further confined by an exemption clause, but, of course, the Unfair Contract Terms Act 1977 may render that ineffective[9] and, at least in relation to the privacy and confidentiality of the messages conveyed, the licences under which VAN's operate will require all reasonable steps to be taken to protect them.[10]

Network users

Interchange agreements

Parties using EDI to contract with one another may well first enter into an interchange contract to govern their relationship. The interchange agreement will usually not deal with the substance of any trading contracts they will want to make,[11] rather it provides the structure for using EDI to make those contracts. An interchange agreement will cover, for example, complying with the VAN network provider's User Handbook, the protocol for the message, the need for any acknowledgment of messages and confirmation of content, allocation of responsibility for the completeness and accuracy of the messages, and the keeping of data logs and storage of messages.[12] The International Chamber of Commerce has produced Uniform Rules of Conduct for the Interchange of Trade Data by Teletransmission (the UNCID rules) and the EC has adopted a Model Interchange Agreement[13] which is set out at the end of this chapter.

9 See p 119 for discussion of the 1977 Act.

10 Condition 7.1, Value Added Data Services Licence, Telecommunications Act 1984. See generally Moteshar, 'Liability issues of EDI' in *EDI and The Law*, Walden (ed).

11 The practice is different in the US where networks have been developed to serve the needs of particular large businesses in dealing with their suppliers etc.

12 *Computer Law*, Reed (ed), 2nd edn, p 263, Blackstone Press, *EDI and the Law* (1989) Walden (ed), Chapters 5 and 6, Blenheim Online.

13 (94/820/EC) OJ L338/98 – 28 December 1994.

Contracting with the network provider and each user

An interchange agreement will normally place an obligation on both parties to comply with the technical procedures of the network provider. However, even if such an agreement, or such a term, was not expressly present between particular users, it could be argued that it would be implied into their relationship because each of them will have contracted with the network provider to comply with those requirements. The argument is based on *Clarke v Dunraven*, a case which is normally only referred to, in contract textbooks, as providing an example of a contract formation which does not fit within the usual offer and acceptance analysis. Nevertheless, it is a case which could be of importance in the context of EDI networks.

***Clarke v Dunraven* [1897] AC 59**

The Mudhook Yacht Club had organised a regatta. Each of the entering yachtsmen had agreed with the club to abide by the rules. During a race, the yacht *Satanita,* breaching the rules, ran into and sank the yacht *Valkyrie.* Under the rules, the *Satanita* was liable and the court that held the *Satanita* was so liable on the basis that those rules formed a contract between each of the individual yachtsman.

Lord Halsbury

> No doubt the persons who drew up the terms on which the different competitors were to race were different persons from those who are now litigants at your Lordships' Bar; but I think it cannot be doubted that the substance of it is that the persons who are going to race agree to race upon those terms with each other.

Lord Herschell

> I cannot entertain any doubt that there was a contractual relation between the parties to this litigation. The effect of their entering for the race, and undertaking to be bound by these rules to the knowledge of each other, is sufficient, I think, where those rules indicate liability on the part of the one of the other, to create a contractual obligation to discharge that liability. That being so, the parties must be taken to have contracted that a breach of any of these rules would render the party guilty of that breach liable, in the language of rule 24, to 'pay all damages' ...

The analogy with the situation where each network user has agreed, with the network provider, to abide by his, or her, rules is clear.

Formalities[14]

In English law, most contracts do not require any formalities such as writing or signature. However, some contracts do. Contracts for the sale or other disposition of an interest in land, for example, must be made in writing,[15] and contracts of guarantee must be evidenced in writing.[16] In addition, other formalities may be required by a particular business situation. There are, for example, requirements for the keeping and production of certain company 'documents'.[17] Brief consideration should be given to the question of whether any formality requirements can be met by the use of EDI messages. In any specific case, it will be a matter of construing the particular, applicable, statutory requirement, but some general comments can be made.

Document

It can be argued that, in general, there is nothing to prevent requirements in statutes, or statutory instruments for a 'document' being fulfilled by information in a digital form, as such, 'because the essential feature of a document is that it conveys information'.[18] However, in some cases, the focus may be on the medium of storage of the information – the physical 'document' – rather than the information as such,[19] and EDI message might not then be found to be appropriate.[20]

Writing

In relation to 'writing', it would seem that an EDI message would not normally fulfill a requirement for writing. Schedule 1 of the Interpretation Act 1978 states:

> 'Writing' includes typing, printing, lythography, photography and other modes of representing or reproducing words in a visible form, and expressions referring to writing are construed accordingly.

This definition will apply in the absence of any other, specific to the legislation in question, and the reference to 'visible form' would seem to preclude EDI. The situation may be different, however, where it is merely required that the transaction be 'evidenced' in writing, rather than that it be undertaken in

---

14 See generally Reed, *Digital Information Law – Electronic Documents and Requirements of Form* (1996) Centre for Commercial Law Studies, Queen Mary and Westfield College, University of London.

15 Section 2 of the Law of Property (Miscellaneous Provisions) Act 1989.

16 Section 4 of the 1677 Statute of Frauds.

17 For example, Companies Act 1985.

18 Reed, *op cit*, p 288.

19 *Darby v DPP* (1994) *The Times*, 4 November.

20 Reed, *op cit*, pp 285–89.

writing. It would seem that the 'evidence' could be produced by creating a hard copy of the EDI message.[21]

Signature

A signature can be seen as performing various functions:[22]

- it identifies the source of the document, that is, the writer;
- it confirms the information on the document; and
- it constitutes proof of the signatory's responsibility for the correctness and/or completion of the information on the document.

It can be argued that these functions could be carried out by a 'digital signature'. A 'digital signature' can be achieved using cryptography.[23] Three numbers can be used – perhaps encoded on 'smart cards'. One number forms the sender's 'private key' which is used to encrypt his, or her, messages. The others make up the 'public key' which is used to decipher the messages but which cannot re-encrypt them. The size of the numbers involved can make this a secure system. They cannot determine, of course, who is using any particular private key,[24] but then signatures can be forged and the sender will have to maintain the security of that 'key'. It is also worth noting that the cryptography process is such that the message cannot be altered once the signature has been added to it, for example by the receiver.

However, even if a 'digital signature' can be achieved, is it capable of constituting a signature when that is required? The meaning of 'signature' has been considered by the courts in the context of various statutes. In the absence of any definition, on the whole, a wide approach has been taken. In *Goodman v J Eban Ltd*[25] the use of a rubber stamp which contained a facsimile of the firm's ordinary signature was held to be sufficient to comply with the requirement of signature in the Solicitor's Act 1932.

Goodman v J Eban Ltd [1954] 1 QB 550

Romer LJ

> It is stated in *Stroud's Judicial Dictionary* (3rd edn) under the title 'Signed; signature' that 'speaking generally a signature is the writing or otherwise affixing, a person's name, or a mark to represent his name, by himself or by his authority with the intention of authenticating a document as being that of, or

21 See Reed, *op cit*, pp 289–92.

22 HB Thomsen 'Background' in *Trading with EDI – The Legal Issues* (1989), p 23 Thomsen & Wheble, IBC Financial.

23 See generally, C Davies, 'Legal Aspects of Digital Signatures' (1995) 11 Comp Law & Practice 165, B Wright, 'Alternatives for Signing Electronic Documents' [1995] 11 Comp Law and Security Rep 139 (May-June).

24 *Computer Law*, Reed (ed), 2nd edn, p 268, Blackstone Press.

25 [1954] 1 QB 550.

> as binding on, the person whose name or mark is so written or affixed.' This statement appears to me to be in accordance with the authorities, and, in my opinion, Mr Goodman's letter was 'signed' within this formula. The letter was typewritten and concludes with the words (also typed) 'Yours faithfully Goodman, Monroe and Company'. This was immediately followed by a repetition of the firm name, in a form which at first sight looks as though it had been written by hand, but which in reality was impressed by Mr Goodman through the medium of a rubber stamp. This repetition would plainly be otiose were it merely intended to repeat the typed name of the firm; and the obvious intention of Mr Goodman was that it should be regarded as a signature for the purposes of authenticating the letter. If, in fact, his clients entertained any doubt as to the authenticity of the letter, nothing could be easier than to ask him, by telephone or letter, to confirm it. A manual signature is not necessary either for a will (which is at least as solemn a document as a solicitor's bill of costs) or to satisfy the Statute of Frauds; and provided that affixing of a name by a rubber stamp complies in other respects with the definition in Stroud to which I have already referred, I see no reason why it should not be sufficient for the purposes of section 65 of the Solicitor's Act 1932 ...

Printing or typewriting the relevant name can also be sufficient and this type of approach could be seen as encompassing a digital signature, in the absence of any contrary indication in the specific statute.[26]

There is scope for at least some of the existing formality requirements to be satisfied when EDI is used. However, where there are no overriding reasons for requiring hard copy, it has been suggested that new definitions be introduced to make it clear that EDI can be used.

Chris Reed, *Digital Information Law – Electronic Documents and Requirements of Form* (1996) Centre For Commercial Law Studies, Queen Mary and Westfield College, University of London

> The most obvious way of reforming the law's requirements of form is to create new definitions, and apply them to existing legislation unless there are overriding reasons why the Law should continue to insist on hard copy. Under this approach three definitions would be needed:
>
> 'Document' should be defined as any recording of information on any medium of information storage including temporary or transient recordings. This is already the most common definition of the term, and emphasises the fact that it is the information content of the document which is important, not the information storage medium.
>
> 'Writing' should be defined as any permanent recording of information on any medium of information storage. This definition is likely to be the most controversial ...
>
> 'Signature' should be defined as any process performed on a document by

26 However, the point has been made that there is an emphasis in the case law on the 'marking' of the relevant physical document and such an emphasis can be seen as contrary to the recognition of an electronic signature as sufficient – Reed, *Digital Information Law – Electronic Documents and Requirements of Form*, p 300.

> or under the authority of a person ('the signatory') which (a) alters the information content of that document, and (b) is intended to identify the signatory and evince his adoption of the contents of the document.
>
> ... there will be circumstances where the adoption of these definitions would defeat the law's purpose ...
>
> ... where the law is designed to protect individuals who may not have access to the equipment necessary to perceive digital or other non-directly perceptible information, eg:
>
> - requirements to publish information;
> - requirements to give notices to individuals;
> - requirements that individuals supply information in a prescribed form.
>
> ...
>
> Where the law currently requires certain contracts to be made in writing, with the intention of protecting individuals against entering onerous contracts without understanding the seriousness of the obligations involved, it will not always be necessary to prescribe hard copy writing. An equally effective method of protecting the individual would be to permit the contract to be made in any form, but to insist on the individual option of withdrawing from the contract.

FORMATION OF A CONTRACT BY EDI

The parties may have set out many of their own rules for contract formation in an interchange agreement. However, if they have not made such an agreement, or if it does not cover such matters, it will be necessary to consider the common law.

As has been indicated,[27] the question of whether or not two parties have made a contract is normally analysed in terms of offer and acceptance, ie a contract is formed when one party, the offeror, has made an offer which the other party, the offeree, has accepted. A purported acceptance which changes the terms of the offer, is not an acceptance but a counter offer and the original offer can no longer be accepted.[28] One situation which should be considered here is that of an EDI offer which is 'damaged' in transit.

When using EDI, if a message is damaged in transit, it is likely to be received as a meaningless scramble of letters and numbers, but what of the situation where an offer is damaged in transit in such a way that it appears to be a sensible message? If the offeree states that he accepts the offer, will a contract have been formed? If neither party realises, or should have realised, what has occurred, and the differences are material, then it would seem that

27 See p 107.

28 *Hyde v Wrench* (1840) 3 Beav 334.

there should be no contract. Even objectively, no agreement can be found and the situation would seem to be analogous to the case of an ambiguous offer, which is understood by the offeree in a different sense from that intended by the offeror.[29]

The case of the damaged, but apparently sensible offer, seems likely to be rare. A problem which is more likely to require consideration is that of the acceptance which is 'lost'[30] in transit. The general rule is that acceptance is only effective once it has been communicated to the offeror. However, when something other than simple face to face communication has been used between the parties, the question has often arisen as to whether that rule should apply. The 'postal rule' is well-known and it means that, normally, a posted acceptance will be effective on posting,[31] although that will not be the case if it goes astray because the acceptor has not addressed it properly,[32] or if the offeror has specified that any acceptance will only be effective once he, or she, has received it.[33] However, the postal rule has not been applied in the context of messages sent by telex machines. What approach should be taken to an offer and acceptance made using EDI? Should the normal rule, or the postal rule, be used? This may be dealt with by an interchange agreement but, if it is not, what approach should the law take? Some guidance may be found in considering the line taken by the courts in relation to acceptance sent by telex.

***Entores Ltd v Miles Far Eastern Corporation* [1955] 2 QB 326**

The plaintiffs, in London, made an offer by telex to the agents of the defendant corporation, in Holland. This was accepted by a telex which was received on the plaintiff's telex machine in London. The relevant issue was whether the contract was made in England. If it was, that would provide a basis for the plaintiffs to serve a writ on the defendant corporation outside of the jurisdiction. The court held that the contract was made in London.

Denning LJ

> When a contract is made by post it is clear law throughout the common law countries that the acceptance is complete as soon as the letter is put into the post box, and that is the place where the contract is made. But there is no clear rule about contract made by telephone or by Telex. Communications by those means are virtually instantaneous and stand on a different footing.
>
> The problem can only be solved by going in stages. Let me first consider the case where two people make a contract by word of mouth in the presence of one another. Suppose for instance that I shout an offer to a man

29 *Raffles v Wichelhaus* (1862) 2 H & C 906.

30 Or damaged so that it is unintelligible.

31 *Adams v Lindsell* (1818) 1 B & Ald 681.

32 *Household Fire Insurance v Grant* (1879) 4 Ex D 216.

33 *Holwell Securities v Hughes* [1974] 1 All ER 161.

across a river or a courtyard but I do not hear his reply because it is drowned by an aircraft flying overhead. There is no contract at that moment. If he wishes to make a contract, he must wait till the aircraft is gone and then shout back his acceptance so that I can hear what he says. Not until I have his answer am I bound ...

Now take the case where two people make a contract by telephone. Suppose, for instance, that I make an offer to a man by telephone and, in the middle of his reply, the line goes 'dead' so that I do not hear his words of acceptance. There is no contract at that moment. The other man may not know the precise moment when the line failed. But he will know that the telephone conversation was abruptly broken off: because people usually say something to signify the end of the conversation. If he wishes to make a contract he must therefore get through again to make sure that I heard. Suppose next, that the line does not go dead, but is nevertheless so indistinct that I do not catch what he says and I ask him to repeat it. He then repeats it and I hear his acceptance. The contract is made, not on the first time when I do not hear, but only on the second when I do hear. If he does not repeat it there is no contract. The contract is only complete when I have his answer accepting the offer.

Lastly, take the Telex, Suppose a clerk in a London Office taps out on the teleprinter an offer which is immediately recorded on a teleprinter in a Manchester office, and a clerk at that end taps out an acceptance. If the line goes dead in the middle of the sentence of acceptance, the teleprinter motor will stop. There is then obviously no contract. The clerk at Manchester must get through again and send his complete sentence. But it may happen that the line does not go dead, yet the message does not get through to London. Thus the clerk at Manchester may tap out his acceptance and it will not be recorded in London because the ink at the London end fails or something of that kind. In that case, the Manchester clerk will not know of the failure but the London clerk will know of it and will immediately send back a message 'not receiving'. Then, when the fault is rectified, the Manchester clerk will repeat his message. Only then is there a contract. If he does not repeat it there is no contract. It is not until the message is received that the contract is complete.

In all the instances I have taken so far, the man who sends the message of acceptance knows that it has not been received or he has reason to know it. So he must repeat it. But, suppose he did not know that his message did not get home. He thinks it has. This may happen if the listener on the phone does not catch the words of acceptance, but nevertheless does not trouble to ask for them to be repeated: or the ink on the teleprinter fails at the receiving end, but the clerk does not ask for the message to be repeated: so that man who sends an acceptance reasonably believes an acceptance has been received. The offeror in such circumstances is clearly bound, because he will be estopped from saying that he did not receive the message of acceptance. It is his own fault that he did not get it. But if there should be a case where the offeror without any fault on his part does not receive the message of acceptance – yet the sender of it reasonably believes it has got home when it has not – then I think there is no contract.

> My conclusion is that the rule about instantaneous communication between the parties is different from the rule about the post. The contract is only complete when the acceptance is received by the offeror: and the contract is made at the place where the acceptance is received.

Brinkibon Ltd v Stahag Stahl und Stahlwarenhandelgesellschaft mbH **[1982] 1 All ER 293**

The parties negotiated the sale of a quantity of steel bars. The buyers, an English company, accepted by telex sent from London to Vienna. The relevant question was whether the contract was made in England, allowing service out of the jurisdiction. The court held that the contract was made in Vienna.

Lord Wilberforce

> In this situation, with a general rule covering instantaneous communication inter praesentes or at a distance, with an exception applying to non-instantaneous communication at a distance, how should communication by telex be categorised? In *Entores Ltd v Miles Far Eastern Corp* the Court of Appeal classified them with instantaneous communications. Their ruling, which has passed into the textbooks ... appears not to have caused either adverse comment, or any difficulty to businessmen. I would accept it as a general rule.
>
> Since 1955 the use of Telex communication has been greatly expanded, and there are many variations on it. The senders and the recipients may not be the principals to the contemplated contract. They may be servants or agents with limited authority. The message may not reach, or be intended to reach, the designated recipient immediately: messages may be sent out of office hours, or at night, with the intention, or on the assumption, that they will be read at a later time. There may be some error or default at the recipient's end which prevents receipt at the time contemplated and believed in by the sender. The message may have been sent and/or received through machines operated by third persons. And many other variations may occur. No universal rule can cover all such cases, they must be resolved by reference to the intentions of the parties, by sound business practice, and in some cases by a judgment where the risk should lie ...

Lord Fraser

> I wish only to add a comment on the subject of where a contract is made when it is accepted by telex between parties in different countries. The question is whether acceptance by telex falls within the general rule that it requires to be notified to the offeror in order to be binding, or within the exception of the postal rule whereby it becomes binding when (and where) it is handed over to the Post Office. The postal rule is based on considerations of practical convenience, arising from the delay that is inevitable in delivering a letter. But it has been extended to apply to telegrams sent through the Post Office, and in strict logic there is much to be said for applying it also to telex messages sent by one business firm directly to another. There is very little, if any, difference in the mechanics of transmission between a private telex from one business to another and a telegram sent through the Post Office, especially one sent from one large

> city to another. Even the element of delay will not be greatly different where the operator of the recipient's telex is a clerk with no authority to conclude contracts, who has to hand it to his principal. In such a case a telex message is not in fact received instantaneously by the responsible principal. I assume that the present case is a case of that sort.
>
> Nevertheless, I have reached the opinion that, on balance, an acceptance sent by telex directly from the acceptor's office should be treated as if it were an instantaneous communication between the principals, like a telephone conversation. One reason is that the decision to that effect in *Entores v Miles* seems to have worked without leading to serious difficulty or complaint from the business community. Secondly, once the message has been received on the offeror's telex machine, it is not unreasonable to treat it as delivered to the principal offeror, because it is his responsibility to arrange for the prompt handling of messages within his own office. Thirdly, a party (the acceptor) who tries to send a message by telex can generally tell if his message has been received on the other party's (the offeror's) machine, whereas the offeror, of course, will not know if an unsuccessful attempt has been made to send an acceptance to him. It is therefore convenient that the acceptor, being in the better position, should have the responsibility for ensuring that his message is received. For these reasons, I think that it is right in the ordinary simple case, such as I take this to be, the general rule and not the postal rule should apply. But I agree ... that the general rule will not cover all the many variations that may occur in telex messages.

In asking the question whether the normal rule should apply, requiring acceptance to be received, or the postal rule, it is common to focus on whether the method of communication was 'instantaneous'. This has become the point which is commonly emphasised from the above cases. However, it can be argued that such a focus is misconceived. In *Entores,* Denning LJ's survey of the problem primarily dealt with situations in which one party should have known that a message had not arrived. Under those circumstances, the answer to whether or not there has been an effective acceptance seems self-evident. It is obvious, for example, that there should not have been an effective acceptance if the acceptor knew, or should have known that his, or her, message had not arrived on the offeror's telex. The more difficult situation is where the message is not received on the offeror's machine and neither party is at fault, or should have known that it had not arrived. In that situation, what is required is a rule which allocates the risk that the message will not be received without either party having been in a position to know of that non-arrival, or being at fault in the non-arrival. In effect, Denning LJ chose the normal rule, rather than the postal rule, to allocate that risk. However, his choice on that issue does not seem to have anything to do with whether the method of communication is instantaneous or not, and that point is made by Lord Fraser in *Brinkibon* in making his analogy between telexes and telegrams.

In any event, acceptance telexes are generally only effective once received, but a brief clarificatory point should be made. In *Brinkibon*, Lord Fraser suggests that receipt of a telex should be taken to occur when it arrives on the offeror's machine 'as it is his responsibility to arrange for the prompt handling of messages in his own office'. It would seem to be a commercially acceptable practice, and in keeping with the generally objective approach to contract, that the telex should be taken to have been received when it is printed on the telex of the offeror, rather than requiring the offeror actually to read it. However, a qualification should be placed on this where a telex arrives on the offeror's machine outside of normal office hours. In that case, the better approach would seem to be[34] that a message which arrives on the machine outside of office hours should only be effective once office hours have resumed.[35]

So far discussion of when, and if, an acceptance is effective, has been confined to telexes, but that provides necessary background for consideration of EDI. In the context of EDI, when there is a direct link between the parties, then the situation could be argued to be directly akin to that of a telex and then, subject to fault on the part of the offeror, an acceptance would only be effective when received.[36] It is when the parties are using a VAN, as will normally be the case, that the argument is likely to arise that the situation is akin to that of entrusting a letter (or telegram) to the post office, and that the 'postal rule' should apply. If the postal rule applied then acceptance would normally[37] be effective as soon as it was received by the network provider.

However, the approach taken to telexes would seem to indicate that the postal rule should not be more widely used than at present – that acceptances should, generally, only be effective when received, unless the non-receipt, or faulty receipt, is due to the fault of the offeror. This would result in an EDI acceptance being effective only when it is received on the offeror's computer, or, if that is the system, when it is placed in some sort of electronic letter box, or pigeon hole, by the network provider, for collection by the offeror. This would also be subject to the qualification noted above in relation to messages received outside of normal office hours.

The approach that an EDI acceptance is only effective once received might be justified on the, arguably spurious, basis that it can be an instantaneous method of communication and that therefore the postal rule does not apply. However, it has already been suggested that speed of communication should

34 In *Mondial Shipping and Chartering BV v Astarte Shipping Ltd* [1995] Commercial Law Cases 1011 Gatehouse J took this approach to the question of when a notice of withdrawal of a ship became effective. For discussion of the case see Haslam, 'Contracting by Electronic Means' (1996) 146 NLJ 549.

35 A reasonable period for the office in question to 'start the day' should be allowed.

36 In the sense indicated above.

37 It should not be effective at that point, for example, if it does not arrive at the offeror's computer because the acceptor misaddressed it – such a qualification applies in the context of the postal rule. *Household Fire Ins v Grant* (1879) 4 Ex D 216.

not be a key element in determining the applicable rule. The better approach would seem to be to recognise that communicating electronically, via a third party, requires the allocation of the risk that a message will go astray without the fault of either offeror or acceptor. There are two possibilities. Firstly, the normal rule could apply (ie no effective acceptance until it is received by the offeror), with the acceptor taking the risk that no contract has been formed when he, or she, thinks it has been. Secondly, the postal rule could apply, with the offeror taking the risk of being contractually bound without being given an opportunity to know that the contract has been formed. It may be that the better explanation of the non-extension of the postal rule to telexes is not that the telex is instantaneous, but rather that it is better to expect one party to take the risk of no contract being in existence, when he, or she, thinks it is, rather than the other party having to take the risk of being bound without knowing that the contract has been made.

It is possible to construct an argument for the application of the postal rule in relation to acceptance by EDI, but the better approach may well be to require receipt of acceptance by the offeror. Of course, if either party is at fault in the non-receipt of the message, or should have known of it, then the risk of non-receipt should be allocated to that party accordingly – as was indicated in relation to telexes in *Entores*.

The above discussion has focused on when a contract is made. However, as was the case in both *Entores* and *Brinkibon*, the question may also arise as to where it was made. If, as has been suggested, an EDI acceptance should, generally, only be effective on receipt, then the contract will be made where receipt occurs. If, however, the postal rule applied, it would seem that the contract would be made wherever it is received by the network provider – the equivalent of a letter being put into a post box.

One further point should be considered here in relation to the message which is lost or damaged in transit. If the message was lost or damaged through the fault of the network provider then there might be scope for an action against him, or her, by the injured party, or parties. However, the network provider is likely to seek to rely upon an exemption clause to meet any such claim.[38]

The symbolic function

It was indicated above that paper can have a symbolic function and one example of this is the bill of lading. When goods are shipped the shipowner (carrier) delivers a bill of lading to the shipper (consignor). It is used to

38 On exemption clauses see p 117.

represent the goods so that it is transferred[39] to the person who makes an agreement to buy the goods, giving him, or her, the right to their possession or control. 'In law and in fact [the bill of lading] represents the goods. Possession of the bill of lading places the goods at the disposal of the purchaser'.[40] It is also accepted as security by banks, who will lend money on it. The bill of lading 'symbolises' the goods to which it relates and has come to be seen as something of value in itself. Can an EDI message take on this role?

Traditionally, the bill of lading has been a signed paper document and there must be doubts as to whether an EDI substitute will be recognised as effective without some form of legislation.[41] This is supported by the approach taken in the Carriage of Goods by Sea Act 1992 which contains provision for regulations to be made to extend its application to cases in which telecommunications systems are used.[42] Two types of schemes have been seen as possible means of bringing about an effective EDI substitute for the paper bill of lading, but any such scheme will require international recognition to be effective. These schemes are described by Faber.

D Faber, 'Electronic Bills of Lading' [1996] LMCLQ 232

> The speed and convenience of electronic communication have led to efforts to introduce systems for electronic production of negotiable bills. These can broadly be categorised into two types: the depository system and the notification system. The first ... involves the deposit of the paper bill with a registry which receives notification as the right to possession of the goods is changed by electronic transfer; the carrier can refer to the register to ensure that delivery is made to the correct party. A number of similar schemes have been devised but all rely on the existence of a bill of lading, whether paper or, as in one case, programmable plastic rather like a credit card. The second system, which is the type contemplated in the Rules for Electronic Bills of Lading produced by the Comite Maritime International (CMI) in 1990, is one of notification to the carrier. It is entirely electronic and does not require the existence of a paper bill of lading. Using electronic messages the carrier issues an electronic bill to the shipper, together with a private code or 'key', possession of which entitles the holder to control the goods. The right of control is passed to other interests after notification by the shipper to the carrier, who cancels the original key and gives a new private key to the person entitled to control the goods. It is intended that the key holder should have the same rights as a bill of lading holder ...

There is an impetus to finding an electronic substitute for the paper bill of lading. In 1986, the Sea Docs scheme tried out a deposit type approach, but it

39 It can be transferred by mere transfer or endorsement and, because of this, it is sometimes described as 'negotiable' but it is not negotiable in the technical sense of providing an innocent transferee with good title despite the transferor's lack of good title.

40 *Biddell Bros Ltd v E Clemens Horst & Co Ltd* [1911] KB 934 at p 956.

41 Faber 'Electronic Bills of Lading' [1996] LMCLQ 232.

42 Faber, p 236.

did not attract widespread support and was not financially viable.[43] The Bolero project is an attempt to use the second type of scheme.[44]

Data protection

Although EDI is basically concerned with commercial dealings, there is still the potential for some messages to come within the ambit of the Data Protection Act 1984, as 'personal data', and its restrictions and requirements should be borne in mind in this context. It may require the security of certain messages or prevent their export from the jurisdiction, for example. Data protection is dealt with in Chapter 000.

European Model EDI Agreement

This European Model Electronic Data Interchange (EDI) Agreement is concluded by and between:

....

and

....

hereinafter referred to as 'the parties'.

Article 1 Object and scope

1.1 The 'European Model EDI Agreement', hereinafter referred to as 'the Agreement', specifies the legal terms and conditions under which the parties, conducting transactions by the use of electronic data interchange (EDI), operate.

1.2 The Agreement consists of the legal provisions set out in the following and shall be completed by a Technical Annex.

1.3 Unless otherwise agreed by the parties, the provisions of the Agreement are not intended to govern the contractual obligations arising from the underlying transactions effected by the use of EDI.

Article 2 Definitions

2.1 For the purpose of the Agreement, the following terms are defined as follows:

2.2 EDI:

Electronic Data Interchange is the electronic transfer from computer to computer, of commercial and administrative data using an agreed standard to structure an EDI message.

2.3 EDI message:

An EDI message consists of a set of segments, structured using an agreed

43 Faber, p 242.

44 Faber, pp 242–43.

standard, prepared in a computer readable format and capable of being automatically and unambiguously processed.

2.4 UN/Edifact:

As defined in the UN/ECE,[45] the United Nations rules for electronic data interchange for administration, commerce and transport comprise a set of internationally agreed standards, directories and guidelines for the electronic interchange of structured data and in particular, interchange related to trade in goods and services, between independent computerised information systems.

2.5 Acknowledgment of receipt:

The acknowledgment of receipt of an EDI message is the procedure by which, on receipt of the EDI message, the syntax and semantics are checked, and a corresponding acknowledgment is sent by the receiver.

Article 3 Validity and formation of contract

3.1 The parties, intending to be legally bound by the Agreement, expressly waive any rights to contest the validity of a contract effected by the use of EDI in accordance with the terms and conditions of the Agreement on the sole ground that it was effected by EDI.

3.2 Each party shall ensure that the content of an EDI message sent or received is not inconsistent with the law of its own respective country, the application of which could restrict the content of an EDI message, and shall take all necessary measures to inform without delay the other party of such an inconsistency.

3.3 A contract effected by the use of EDI shall be concluded at the time and place where the EDI message constituting acceptance of an offer reaches the computer system of the offeror.

Article 4 Admissibility in evidence of EDI messages

To the extent permitted by any national law which may apply, the parties hereby agree that in the event of dispute, the records of EDI messages, which they have maintained in accordance with the terms of the Agreement, shall be admissible before the Courts and shall constitute evidence of the facts contained therein unless evidence to the contrary is adduced.

Article 5 Processing and acknowledgment of receipt of EDI messages

5.1 EDI messages shall be processed as soon as possible after receipt, but in any event within the time limits specified in the Technical Annex.

5.2 An acknowledgement of receipt is not required unless requested.

5.3 Where an acknowledgment is required, the receiver of the EDI message to be acknowledged shall ensure that the acknowledgment is sent within one business day of the time of receipt of the EDI message to be acknowledged, unless an alternative time limit has been specified in the Technical Annex.

A business day means any day except a Saturday, Sunday or any declared public holiday in the place of receipt of an EDI message.

45 United Nations Economic Commission for Europe.

The receiver of an EDI message requiring an acknowledgment shall not act upon the content of the EDI message until such acknowledgment is sent.

5.4 If the sender does not receive the acknowledgment of receipt within the time limit, he may, upon giving notification to the receiver to that effect, treat the EDI message as null and void as from the expiration of that time limit or initiate an alternative recovery procedure as specified in the Technical Annex, to ensure effective receipt of the acknowledgment.

In case of failure of the recovery procedure, within the time limit, the EDI message will definitely be treated as null and void, as from the expiration of that time limit, upon notification to the receiver.

Article 6 Security of EDI messages

6.1 The parties undertake to implement and maintain security procedures and measures in order to ensure the protection of EDI messages against the risks of unauthorised access, alteration, delay, destruction or loss.

6.2 Security procedures and measures include the verification of origin, the verification of integrity, the non-repudiation of origin and receipt and the confidentiality of EDI messages.

Security measures and measures for the verification of origin and the verification of integrity in order to identify the sender of an EDI message and to ascertain that any EDI message received is complete and has not been corrupted, are mandatory for any EDI message. When required, additional security procedures and measures may be expressly specified in the Technical Annex.

6.3 If the use of security measures and procedures results in the rejection of, or in the detection of an error in an EDI message, the receiver shall inform the sender thereof, within the specified time limit.

The receiver of an EDI message which has been rejected, or which contains an error shall not act upon the EDI message before receiving instructions from the sender. When a rejected or erroneous message is retransmitted by the sender, the EDI message should clearly state that it is a corrected EDI message.

Article 7 Confidentiality and Protection of Personal Data

7.1 The parties shall ensure that EDI messages containing information specified to be confidential by the sender or agreed mutually to be confidential between the parties, are maintained in confidence and are not disclosed or transmitted to any unauthorised persons nor used for any purposes other than those intended by the parties.

When authorised, further transmission of such confidential information shall be subject to the same degree of confidentiality.

7.2 EDI messages shall not be regarded as containing confidential information to the extent that such information is in the public domain.

7.3 The parties may agree to use a specific form of protection for certain messages such as a method of encryption to the extent permitted by the law in either of their respective countries.

7.4 Where EDI messages which contain personal data are sent or received in countries where no data protection law is in force, and until a relevant Community legislation is implemented, each party agrees as a minimum standard, to respect the provisions of the automatic processing of personal data.[46]

Article 8 Recording and Storage of EDI Messages

8.1 A complete and chronological record of all EDI messages exchanged by the parties in the course of a trade transaction shall be stored by each party, unaltered and securely, in accordance with the time limits and specifications prescribed by the legislative requirements of its own national law, and, in any event, for a minimum of three years following the completion of the transaction.

8.2 Unless otherwise provided by national laws, EDI messages shall be stored by the sender in the transmitted format and by the receiver in the format in which they are received.

8.3 Parties shall ensure that electronic or computer records of the EDI messages shall be readily accessible, are capable of being reproduced in a human readable form and being printed, if required. Any operational equipment required in this connection shall be retained.

Article 9 Operational requirements for EDI

9.1 The parties undertake to implement and maintain the operational environment to operate EDI according to the terms and conditions of this Agreement, which includes but is not limited to the following:

9.2 Operational equipment

The parties shall provide and maintain the equipment, software and services necessary to transmit, receive, translate, record and store EDI messages.

9.3 Means of communication

The parties shall determine the means of communication to be used, including telecommunication protocols and, if required, the choice of third party service providers.

9.4 EDI message standards

All EDI messages shall be transmitted in accordance with the UN/Edifact standards, recommendations and procedures as approved by the United Nations Economic Commission for Europe (UN/ECE-WP 4) and with European standards.

9.5 Codes

Data element code lists referred to in EDI messages shall include UN/Edifact maintained code lists, international code lists issued as ISO international standards and UN/ECE or other officially published code lists.

46 Convention No 108 of the Council of Europe of 28 January 1981.

Where such code lists are not available, preference shall be given to the use of code lists published, maintained and ensuring correspondences with other coding systems.

Article 10 Technical specifications and requirements

The Technical Annex shall include the technical, organisational and procedural specifications and requirements to operate EDI according to the terms of this Agreement, which includes but is not limited to the following:

- operational requirements for EDI, as referred to in Article 9, including operational equipment, means of communication, EDI message standards and codes;
- processing and acknowledgment of EDI messages;
- security of EDI messages;
- recording and storage of EDI messages;
- time limits;
- procedures for tests and trials to establish and monitor the adequacy of the technical specifications and requirements.

Article 11 Liability

11.1No party to this Agreement shall be liable for any special, indirect or consequential damages caused by a failure to perform its obligations of this Agreement.

11.2No party to this Agreement shall be liable for any loss or damages suffered by the other party caused by any delay or failure to perform in accordance with the provisions of this Agreement, where such delay or failure is caused by an impediment beyond that party's control and which could not reasonably be expected to be taken into account at the time of conclusion of the Agreement or the consequences of which could not be avoided or overcome.

11.3If a party engages any intermediary to perform such services as the transmission, logging or processing of an EDI message, that party shall be liable for damage arising directly from the intermediary's acts, failures or omissions in the provision of said services.

11.4If a party requires another party to use the services of an intermediary to perform the transmission, logging or processing of an EDI message, the party who required that use shall be liable to the other party for damage arising directly form the intermediary's acts, failures or omissions in the provision of said services.

Article 12 Dispute Resolution

Alternative 1[47]

Arbitration Clause

Any dispute arising out of or in connection with this Agreement, including any

47 A choice is to be made by the parties between alternative 1 'Arbitration clause' or Alternative 2 'Jurisdiction clause'.

question regarding its existence, validity or termination, shall be referred to and finally resolved by the arbitration of a (or three) person(s) to be agreed by the parties, or failing agreement, to be nominated by ....,[48] in accordance with and subject to the rules of procedure of ....[49]

***Alternative* 2**

Jurisdiction Clause

Any dispute arising out of or in connection with this contract shall be referred to the courts of ....[50]

Article 13 Applicable Law

Without prejudice to any mandatory national law which may apply to the parties regarding recording and storage of EDI messages or confidentiality and protection of personal data, the agreement is governed by the law of ....[51]

Article 14 Effect, Modifications, term and severability

14.1Effect

The Agreement shall be effective from the date on which it is signed by the parties.

14.2Modifications

Where required, additional or alternative provisions to the Agreement, agreed in writing by the parties, will be considered as part of the Agreement as from their signature.

14.3Term

Any party may terminate the Agreement by giving not less than one month's notice either by registered post or by any other means agreed between the parties. Termination of the Agreement shall only affect transactions after that date.

Notwithstanding termination for any reason, the rights and obligations of the parties referred to in Articles 4, 6, 7, and 8 shall survive termination.

14.4Severability

Should any article or part of an Article of the Agreement be deemed invalid, all other Articles shall remain in full force and effect.

48 An 'appointing authority' has to be completed by the parties.

49 A 'choice of procedure of commercial arbitration' has to be completed by the parties.

50 A 'country' has to be completed by the parties.

51 *Ibid.*

CHAPTER SEVEN

PROTECTING THE PRIVATE INDIVIDUAL

INTRODUCTION

Since time immemorial, information has been collected and exchanged about individuals at many levels of society. In the words of Earl Ferrars: 'The collection of personal data is as old as society itself. It may not be the oldest profession but it is one of the oldest habits.'[1] Such activities range from the collection and storage of personal information by government, for a multitude of reasons and purposes, to the gossip exchanged at local meeting places. Apart from the fact that increasing computerisation has facilitated the collection and storage of such data, the much-used phrase 'the global village' itself encompasses the notion that exchange of information can now take place on a worldwide scale.

This chapter is devoted to a consideration of the way in which the law is able to deal with abuses of the global information infrastructure in so far as this relates to information about individuals, whether true or false. This will involve a study of whether and in what manner increasing computerisation can compromise an individual's privacy or facilitate acts which threaten the individual's reputation or integrity and may be actionable by the tort of defamation.

DATA PROTECTION

Prior to the so-called information revolution, information and data held on individuals would only be kept in traditional filing cabinets or the equivalent. Not only would these be accessed only relatively infrequently, perhaps, by the holder of the data, but it would be difficult for other users of similar information or those with information about the same individual to gain access. The ease with which computers can store and manipulate data has caused a dramatic change in this respect and has made it a simple matter for information about particular individuals held in a number of places to be correlated. Indeed, a whole industry has arisen out of the operation referred to as 'data matching' whereby a profile of a particular individual is assembled from data held at a number of sources. Such profiles are used extensively for marketing purposes and lists of those with similar profiles form a commodity

1 Earl Ferrars, HL Debates (Hansard) 11 October 1993, col 37.

which is, itself, traded to businesses to enable selective targeting of a particular sector of the market. This process need not, however, be confined to business use as pointed out succinctly by Browne-Wilkinson VC: 'If the information obtained by the police, the Inland Revenue, the social security services, the health service and other agencies were to be gathered together in one file, the freedom of the individual would be greatly at risk. The dossier of private information is the badge of the totalitarian state.'[2] This describes, not only the phenomenon of data matching, but also highlights the dangers to individual rights and liberties and is indicative of some of the fears which surround the storage of personal data on computer systems. These fears have been voiced for some time[3] and even as far back as 1975, a significant amount of information about identifiable individuals was already kept on computer by central government.[4] Such anxieties were exacerbated as industry and commerce also began to rely on the use of computers to such an extent that it is now impossible to imagine business being conducted without them. But this very reliance by business on the increased use of networks, both internally and externally to the enterprise, creates the tension between business needs and the individual's right of privacy.

REPORT OF COMMITTEE ON DATA PROTECTION PARAGRAPHS 2.09–2.11[5]

2.09 In the use that is made of personal data, the interests of the individual and the interests of society may conflict and need to be resolved in the same way as in the context of individual liberty. With data protection the solution must take the same form: a balance must be found between the interests of the individual and the interests of the rest of society, which include the efficient conduct of industry, commerce and administration. But, as with our liberties, it is not a single point of balance which must be established. There are cases, for example with regard to religious and political beliefs, where the right balance will preserve the individual's freedom to adhere to his beliefs and will deny to society, and to particular institutions within it such as government departments or commercial enterprises, the opportunity to interfere with that freedom. At the other extreme the maintenance of national security and of law and order in society may require the balance to be struck at a point where the interests of society are given a far higher value than those of the individual.

2 *Marcel v Metropolitan Police Commissioner* [1992] Ch 225 at 240. Compare this prediction with the likely outcome if the Finance Bill and Social Security Administration (Fraud) Bills of 1996 are enacted. These Bills contain provisions that facilitate data matching between government departments to aid in identification of fraudulent social security claims.

3 These fears have not yet abated – see for instance HC Debates (Hansard) 30 January 1984, col 86 (Paddy Ashdown) and Eighth Report of the Data Protection Registrar HMSO 1992, Appendix 1 quoting the above comment of Browne-Wilkinson VC.

4 For details see *Computers: Safeguards for Privacy* Cmnd 6354 HMSO 1975, Tables 1 and 2, further updated in *Report of the Committee on Data Protection* Cmnd 7341 HMSO 1978, Appendix 6.

5 Cmnd 7341 HMSO 1978.

Between these extremes there is a wide spectrum, and the balance for a particular use of personal data may be established differently in different cases. It may also be settled differently in different societies, and may shift within the same society with changes, for example, in its political climate or institutional structures.

2.10 The means by which the balances are struck, and the conditions under which the agreements between data subjects and data users are reached, are of great importance. Where the agreement is voluntary, the result will not be fair unless each party fully understands the requirements of the other, and there is a clear understanding of what data are to be provided, and for what purposes they will be used. Fairness requires openness in such dealings and it also requires that no advantage should be taken of any disparities in bargaining power.

2.11 But there are many cases where these conditions for fairness cannot exist. Data users cannot always be expected, or even be able, to appreciate fully the requirements of data subjects. Even less can data subjects be expected to appreciate fully the requirements of data users, let alone the relevant technicalities of information handling. In many cases, especially where the relationship is between the government and the governed, there can be no question of equal bargaining power; in yet others it may turn out that agreement simply cannot be reached. In all such cases, only an independent third party can fairly weigh all the interests involved – those of the data subject, the data user and society at large – and determine the best point of balance.

Whereas it is accepted that civil liberties and human rights cannot be absolute and unfettered, this extract illustrates how difficult it may be to achieve an acceptable balance between the competing rights of those involved. It is the Herculean task of legislation on data protection to achieve that balance. In particular, the passage quoted cites, by way of example, the protection of religious and political beliefs – as the legislation has developed, this is part of a wider issue that has not yet been tackled effectively and will be discussed in more detail later.[6]

Nonetheless, identification of these competing needs together with pressure from the international community[7] have forced the law to respond. This raises issues of particular interest in the UK where, historically, there has been no constitutionally protected right of privacy as such. Although it is beyond the scope of this book to assess the extent to which the law in the UK is capable of protecting individual privacy in general,[8] the issues surrounding data protection clearly impinge on and are related to the right to privacy.

6 See p 299.

7 In agreements such as Council of Europe Convention for the Protection of Individuals with regard to Automatic Processing of Personal Data 1981.

8 For further discussion see, eg, the Consultation Paper *Infringement of Privacy Lord Chancellor's Department* 1993, Raymond Wacks, *Personal Information: Privacy and the Law* (1993) Clarendon.

Indeed, the origins of the Data Protection Act 1984 can be traced back to the Younger Committee on Privacy appointed on 13 May 1970. This Committee was established in response to growing concerns during the 1960s in respect of the amount of personal information kept by various organisations and to which the individuals concerned had no right of access. Its terms of reference were: 'To consider whether legislation is needed to give further protection to the individual citizen and to commercial and industrial interests against intrusion into privacy by private persons and organisations or by companies and to make recommendations.' Although, at this time, the use of computers was still comparatively novel and largely confined to large commercial and educational institutions, the potential for the problems identified earlier in the use of computer systems for these purposes had already been identified and one chapter of the Younger Report[9] concentrated on this perceived threat to privacy.

REPORT OF THE COMMITTEE ON PRIVACY
Paragraph 581

> We attempted to identify the various aspects of this alleged threat which were raised by computerised personal information stores and seemed to distinguish such stores in the public mind from others kept by traditional methods. We found that the computer's facility to store, link, manipulate, and provide access to information gave rise to suspicions that complete personal profiles on a great number of people could be compiled; that information could be used for a purpose for which it was not initially collected; that some information could be inaccurate; that it facilitated access to confidential information by many people scattered over a wide area; that its powers of correlation were so superior to traditional methods that it made practicable what had hitherto been impracticable; and that it encouraged the growth on an entirely new scale of information gathering and of organisations to do it. Others feel that there is a danger of information emanating from a computer being thought to be free from human error.

The Committee thus concentrated on three particular areas of concern; the use of computers to compile personal profiles, their capacity to correlate information and the ease with which unauthorised access to data could be obtained. Although the Report came to the conclusion that '[w]e cannot on the evidence before us conclude that the computer as used in the private sector is at present a threat to privacy, but we recognise that there is a possibility of such a threat becoming a reality in the future'[10] it, nevertheless, did formulate ten principles which were suggested as forming a guide for the use of computers which manipulated personal data and that, subsequently, were to

9 Cmnd 5012 HMSO 1972.

10 But note that around this time some of these fears had been identified as a reality in the US see, eg, Arthur R Miller, 'The Assault on Privacy: Computers Data Banks and Dossiers' in The *New Technology's Threat to Personal Privacy* (1971) Chapter 2, University of Michigan Press.

be the basis for the Data Protection Principles. These are reproduced below together with the rationale for their formulation.

REPORT OF THE COMMITTEE ON PRIVACY[11]
Paragraphs 592–600

There could be an incentive to cover the cost of acquisition and recording of the information by using it for purposes additional to that for which it was originally collected. For example, a computerised record of subscribers to a trade publication might well prove useful to the manufacturers of certain products advertised therein. The situation could be a clear breach of privacy in so far as it could be held that private information (a name and address) given solely for the purpose of receiving a magazine is passed on without the authority of the originator. Therefore:

1. Information should be regarded as held for a specific purpose and should not be used without appropriate authorisation for other purposes.
2. Access to information should be confined to those authorised to have it for the purpose for which it was supplied.

Furthermore, because it is often cheaper to collect all available information in one operation and because computers have the capacity to store it, there could be a double incentive for the owners of the computers to hoard large amounts of information, some of which, though not essential now, might prove useful at some later date. We believe that:

3. The amount of information collected and held should be the minimum necessary for achievement of a specified purpose.

A great deal of personal information is acquired to provide statistics to assist planning and other research, or is acquired for some other purpose and subsequently adapted to a form suitable for such ends. Planners and researchers, however, rarely need to know identities of individuals. Therefore:

4. In computerised systems handling information for statistical purposes, adequate provision should be made in their design and programs for separating identities from the rest of the data.

.... While we do not think that a printout should automatically be supplied {of the information held about individuals in a computerised record} we think that every system should be so designed that in situations where printout is appropriate an individual can on request be told of the contents of the record. Therefore:

5. There should be arrangements whereby the subject could be told about the information held concerning him.

We are not convinced that considerations of privacy are at present sufficiently in the minds of computer users and we think that more regard should be paid to such considerations than is the case now. Therefore:

6. The level of security to be achieved by a system should be specified in advance by the user and should include precautions against the deliberate abuse or misuse of information.

11 Cmnd 5012 HMSO 1972.

... A security system would be incomplete, however, if it did not include provision for the detection of an irregularity. Therefore:

7. A monitoring system should be provided to facilitate the detection of any violation of the security system.

There are three further principles of only marginal relevance to privacy which we feel we should put forward for consideration alongside the seven we enumerate above. Computers have the capacity to retain information in effect indefinitely so that it is occasionally stored ... with little regard to a time limit. Therefore:

8. In the design of information systems, periods should be specified beyond which the information should not be retained.

Private sector computer users usually have a commercial interest in ensuring the accuracy and up-to-dateness of information and protecting it from corruption during processing. There are at present, however, no procedures in general use for dealing quickly with inaccuracies. Therefore:

9. Data held should be accurate. There should be machinery for the correction of inaccuracy and the updating of information.

The coding of the subjective judgments often entails the loss of shades of meaning and emphasis. For example, a numeral; indicating 'fair' in evaluating an employee's performance is capable of wide interpretation. In such cases it would be preferable to refer the interrogator of the computer to a more detailed report. Therefore:

10. Care should be taken in coding value judgments.

Although three years later in the White Paper 'Computers and Privacy',[12] it appeared that legislation was imminent: 'In the government's view the time has come when those who use computers to handle personal information, however responsible they are, can no longer remain the sole judge of whether their own systems adequately safeguard privacy ... The government have therefore decided that the right course is to introduce legislation ...', conflicting political, commercial and individual factors resulted in the legislation being a long time in gestation. A further Committee was established under Sir Norman Lindop to look exclusively at the issue of data protection and, perhaps, to reassure those who were concerned about the introduction of what could be regarded as privacy legislation, the Lindop Report[13] was at pains to distinguish privacy and data protection.

REPORT OF THE COMMITTEE ON DATA PROTECTION[14]
Paragraphs 2.03–2.07

The concept of data privacy

2.03 There are aspects of privacy which have no immediate connection with the handling of personal data in information systems, such as intrusion into

12 Cmnd 6353 and Supplement Cmnd 6354. *Computers: Safeguards for Privacy* HMSO 1975.

13 *Report of the Committee on Data Protection*, Cmnd 7341 HMSO 1978.

14 *Ibid.*

the home, powers of entry and search, and embarrassing publicity in the media. There are also aspects of data protection which have no immediate connection with privacy. For example, the use of inaccurate or incomplete information for taking decisions about people is properly a subject for data protection, but it may not always raise questions of privacy.

2.04 The Younger Committee had to deal with the whole field of privacy. Our task has been to deal with that of data protection. In fact, the two fields overlap, and the area of overlap can be called 'information privacy' or, better, 'data privacy'. It is an important area, and we have a good deal to say about it in this Report. But it is not by itself the whole field of data protection, and we have had to consider some matters which do not directly raise questions of privacy. However, we found it useful to examine the concept of data privacy, and its implications and consequences. For this purpose we have used the term data privacy to mean the individual's claim to control the circulation of data about himself.

'Private' data

2.05 There is wide variation in what data about themselves people regard as 'private'. Such variations exist between one individual and another, between different sections of society, between societies in different countries, and between different periods of time in the same society.

2.06. Some people are willing to allow more to be known about themselves than others. Differences of age, personality, temperament, views and beliefs all have a part to play. Variations in social and cultural mores account for variations between different sectors of the same society; variations in institutions, cultures and traditions, and in the style and political characteristics of government, account for variations between different societies. Changes in attitude in the same society are related to many factors such as its economic development, changing educational standards, social conventions, and opportunities for self-determination.

2.07 'Privateness' is clearly not an attribute of data themselves, for the same data may be regarded as very private in one context and not so private, or not private at all, in another. Equally, when data are regarded as private, that does not mean that they are, or should be, known only to the individual to whom they refer: rather it means that he wants them to be known only to him and to those others who he agrees should know them. There are many ways in which such agreements are established. In the simplest case the individual gives the data directly to another party; this may be a quite voluntary act or it may be an obligation entered into as part of a commercial contract. At the other extreme, the agreement may be made on his behalf by Parliament enacting legislation which requires him to provide the data to someone. One cannot judge such agreements, however they are reached, without taking a view of the purposes for which the data are to be used, and the conditions under which they are to be applied to those purposes.

The Lindop Report suggested a Data Protection Authority and separate Codes of Practice, having the force of law, for different sectors of industry. In the event, these particular proposals were not acted upon and it was pressure brought about by the need to ratify the Council of Europe Convention in 1981, and the consequent threat to business in the UK if this did not occur, that led, eventually, to the passing of the Data Protection Act 1984. In the White Paper 'Data Protection. The Government's Proposals for Legislation',[15] it was stated that the suggested provisions would 'safeguard privacy, protect our trading interests and enable the UK to ratify the Council of Europe Convention'. In order to do this, certain of the proposals of Lindop, referred to above, were rejected and the substance of the legislation was based on the earlier principles articulated in the Younger Report and which had been influential in shaping the contents of the Council of Europe Convention itself.

The first Bill was lost because of the dissolution of Parliament and an amended version eventually received the Royal Assent on 12 July 1984. Despite the loss of the first Bill, the debates which marked the motion for second reading of that Bill provide a useful illustration of the perceived objectives of the legislation that remains unaltered by the passing of the second Bill.

Parliamentary Debates (Commons) 11 April 1983

William Whitelaw

Wherever we look, the information technology revolution is having its effect in the banks and the building societies, in the retail trade and mail order business, throughout commerce and industry, and increasingly in Government. Thanks to computers the use, transmission and communication of information is becoming daily both more complex and more proficient. The developments have been considerable even in the short time since Sir Norman Lindop's committee published its report on data protection in 1978; still more is this true of the period since the subject of privacy was last fully debated in this House, back in 1973, following the report of the committee under Sir Kenneth Younger in the previous year.

These developments have undoubtedly brought substantial benefits, more efficient business transactions and the rapid movement of information needed, for example, for proper decision-taking in matters of health, social welfare, and so on. The great majority of computer systems are, as they say in the trade, 'subject friendly' – that is, they benefit those about whom information is stored.

If we are to continue to improve efficiency and productivity, maintain our trading competitiveness, and keep up the service that Governments supply to the citizen, we must ensure that the information technology industry flourishes. And that is the purpose of the Bill. To achieve that purpose the Bill must do two things: reassure the public that the holding of personal information on computers is properly controlled, so dispelling any lingering unease that might otherwise inhibit their use; and, secondly, protect our

15 Cmnd 8539 HMSO 1982.

international trading position by bringing us into step with the increasing number of European countries which already have data protection legislation in force. Companies operating on a multinational basis – and thousands of jobs are involved – depend increasingly on the international interchange of computerised data, including personal data. If the flow of data to this country were interrupted, the operations of many of those companies here would be threatened.

Last April's White Paper on data protection said that there had been few reported instances in this country of the misuse of information held on computers. That remains the position, but that does not mean that there is no potential for abuse. Nor should it blind us to the real concern that that potential could become reality if suitable controls are not introduced. In view of some of the criticisms of this Bill that I have read and listened to during the last few days, let me make one thing absolutely clear from the outset. The Bill provides the individual for the first time with a general right of access to data held about him and it requires the registration of the holding and use of data. It gives no new powers to the police or to any public authority other than the data protection registrar.

Before I turn to the details of the scheme, there are two further points that I would make. The first relates to the committee under Sir Norman Lindop, to which I referred in passing earlier. I want to pay tribute ... to the substantial and painstaking report which that committee produced, and from which the Government have greatly benefited in the formulation of the present proposals. We have not followed the committee in all its recommendations, but I hope that the members of the committee will note the various points at which their recommendations and ours do coincide. I hope also that, where we have diverged, they will come to appreciate why we have gone in the direction that we have.

Secondly, I draw attention to the European dimension. In January 1981, the Council of Europe Convention on data protection was opened for signature. Together with the guidelines on privacy protection of the OECD, the convention offers an international standard for data protection. This has provided us with a yardstick against which to measure our own proposals. Our intention is to ratify the Council of Europe convention, and we have kept its provisions firmly in mind in drafting the Bill.

With the convention now widely accepted as setting a necessary standard, we shall find increasingly a division between those countries with data protection, and those without. The latter will be more and more at risk of action from countries determined to prevent the undermining of their own data protection laws by the export of personal data to countries without protection. We must not allow any excuse for sanctions against the United Kingdom. That is what makes it imperative that we legislate without delay. Even if we were not already convinced of the rightness of legislation in this field, we should be compelled by this consideration to bring ourselves into line with European practice.

It is clear from this that the Council of Europe Convention was a major catalyst to the actual introduction of the legislation. Although this agreement is, *prima facie*, aimed at protecting individuals, one consequence of ratification is the requirement to prevent transfer of data to jurisdictions that do not provide the same level of protection for personal data. The Convention attempts, *inter alia*, to reconcile the notion of effective data protection with the ideal of free flow of information as set out in Article 10 of the European Convention on Human Rights. In pursuance of this, Article 12 of the Convention on automatic processing of data contains provisions allowing restriction of transborder data flows 'except where the regulations of the other Party provide an equivalent protection [for the personal data]'. It was this fact which precipitated action in the UK since it was clear that, without such ratification, the UK would, itself, become a country to which data transfer was likely to be prohibited, thus isolating domestic business from European and possibly other international markets. Clearly, therefore, the needs of the commercial sector were paramount, but a persistent theme in many quarters was the protection of privacy in the wider sense. There has been an on-going debate about the extent to which privacy is protected by legislation on data protection, which shows no sign of abating, and which has recently been reactivated by the provisions of the EC Directive on data protection.[16] The *modus operandi* of the statute itself will reveal the extent to which its provisions acknowledge the existence of a right to privacy and the extent to which the legislation is able to satisfy the competing requirements of the data user and data subject already identified.

DATA PROTECTION ACT 1984

The structure of this statute is rather different from most other UK statutes. Stallworthy suggests that this has arisen because the main provisions follow the Council of Europe Convention and are, therefore, influenced by principles of statutory draftsmanship which are more usually associated with civil law systems.[17] The view of Aldhouse is that 'the Data Protection Act is unprecedented. Even the black letter criminal provisions make use of new concepts ...'.[18] Before discussing the requirements of the Act, a further controversial issue has been the relationship between the words 'data' and 'information'. Although these words are often used interchangeably in colloquial speech, they do have distinct definitions, but this has not always

16 Directive 95/46/EC of the European Parliament and of the Council of 24 October 1995 on the protection of individuals with regard to the processing of personal data and on the free movement of such data. OJ 1995 L281/31 discussed at p 301.

17 M Stallworthy, 'Data Protection: Regulation in a Deregulatory State' [1990] Statute Law Review 130.

18 FGB Aldhouse, 'UK Data Protection – Where are we in 1991' (1991) 5 YLCT 180.

been acknowledged in the provisions of the Data Protection Act 1984. Dictionary definitions suggest a degree of organisation differentiating 'data' from 'information', which is a rather more nebulous concept. Interestingly, for these purposes, the Oxford dictionary suggests that data is information from which inferences may be drawn. It is, nonetheless, clear that the two concepts are related in that data, whether or not recorded on a computer, will be derived from information obtained from the subject of the data or elsewhere. This is reflected in some of the definitions in s 1 of the Act.

DATA PROTECTION ACT 1984

Section 1

(2) 'Data' means information recorded in a form in which it can be processed by equipment operating automatically in response to instructions given for that purpose.

(9) 'Disclosing' in relation to data, includes disclosing information extracted from the data ...

In contrast the offences created in s 5 refer explicitly to 'data' rather than 'information'. Thus s 5(2) :

A person ... shall not –

(a) hold personal data ...

(b) hold any such data, or use any such data ...

(c) obtain such data, or information to be contained in such data ...

(d) disclose such data ...

(e) directly or indirectly transfer such data ...

Despite this, the restriction in the definition of data in s 1(2) to include 'information recorded in a form in which it can be processed by equipment operating automatically in response to instructions given for that purpose', ie only that which is held on computer, surely precludes the possibility that the Act only protects data. As far as the individual is concerned the data itself, in machine readable form, is likely to be unintelligible and what will concern that individual is the release or mismanagement of information. In this respect, the long title of the Data Protection Act may be revealing – 'An Act to regulate the use of automatically processed information relating to individuals and the provision of services in respect of such information'. Such difficulties of definition and application have been discussed by the House of Lords in the recent case of *Brown*. The case itself was concerned with the interpretation of the word 'use' in relation to data[19] but the argument for the Crown depended on the definition of data in s 1(2).

19 See later discussion at p 291.

R v Brown
[1996] 2 WLR 203
House of Lords

Lord Hoffman

That definition is wide enough to include information capable of being processed by equipment other than the normal computer. But for practical purposes it means information recorded in computer-readable form. To be in a form capable of being processed by the police national computer, the information has to be stored electronically in binary code. Only in this form can it be processed by the syntax of a digital computer. So the Crown says that 'data' (and therefore also 'personal data') meant, in this case, information recorded in binary code.

In its binary form, however, the information is incomprehensible to the human mind. 'Data' as defined is therefore something different from what one ordinarily understands by 'information'. It is, in fact, wholly uninformative. The Act, says Mr Langdale for the Crown, draws a clear distinction between data and information in the ordinary sense of that word. In the present case, the defendant did not use information but he used data. Mr Langdale reinforces his argument by reference to the definition of 'disclosing' in section 1(9). This says that disclosing in relation to data 'includes disclosing information extracted from the data'. So it is argued that information is not data; it is something which you extract from data.

Pursuing this argument to its logical conclusion, Mr Langdale said that the only way in which data could be 'used' was through the instrumentality of a computer, which can convert the binary digits into conventional symbols, pictures or sound. Therefore the 'use' of data can mean only the processing of that data in a computer. It cannot mean the use of the information derived from the computer, because once it has been called to the video screen or printed out, it is no longer in computer-readable form.

There is a certain formal elegance about this argument but for a number of reasons I think it is unsound. First, the purpose of the Act, as declared in the long title, is to 'regulate the use of automatically processed information relating to individuals'. It is to restrict the use which can be made of computerised information about them. It would be strange if the Act was concerned only with what happened unseen in the computer and not with what happened when the information became accessible to the human user. This is not making the tail wag the dog; it is all tail and no dog ...

I said that the argument depended almost entirely upon the terms of the definition because I have not forgotten that Mr Langdale also relied upon the reference to 'information extracted from the data' in section 1(9). But I do not think that this really helps him either. One should compare this phrase with the definition of 'processing' in section 1(7):

'"Processing", in relation to data, means amending, augmenting, deleting or re-arranging the data or extracting the information constituting the data and, in the case of personal data, means performing any of those operations by reference to the data subject.'

There, the phrase 'extracting the information constituting the data' clearly describes the process of causing the computer to convert the binary-coded information into readable form. But what has been extracted is 'the information constituting the data'. In other words, what has been extracted is still data. It has not ceased to be data as a result of the process of extraction.

What, then, is meant by 'information extracted from the data?' One can expand this phrase by substituting for 'data' a paraphrase of its definition in section 1(2). It then reads: 'information extracted from information recorded in computer-readable form'. This is something different from simply converting information from binary code to intelligible form. It contemplates information extracted from information. In my view, what it has in mind is the processing of raw data in a computer to obtain other forms of useful information. For example, a computer may contain nothing more than raw accounting data: the prices and quantities of goods purchased by a business, expenses, prices for which the finished products were sold and so forth. From this raw information, the application of a computer programme can produce information which was not previously recorded, such as the profit or loss, the gross and net margins and various ratios. This, in my view, illustrates what is meant by 'information extracted from the data'.

The fallacy in the Crown's argument is, I think, one common among lawyers, namely to treat the words of an English sentence as building blocks whose meaning cannot be affected by the rest of the sentence. Only by this process can it be claimed that because the Act defines 'data' as being information in computer-readable form, every statement about data in the Act must be a reference to the information in that form. This is not the way language works. The unit of communication by means of language is the sentence and not the parts of which it is composed. The significance of individual words is affected by other words and the syntax of the whole. An ancient historian, for example, may say that some interesting inscriptions concerning the Greek corn trade have been discovered in an archaeological excavation. In that sentence, 'inscriptions' means writings on stone. This, no doubt, is how the word would be defined in a dictionary. But the historian may then say that he has used the inscriptions as the basis of an article. This does not necessarily mean that he has examined the stones himself. He could have seen photographs or transcripts. It would still be correct for him to say that he has made use of the inscriptions. In this context, the statement is true if the information which the historian used was derived from the writings on stone. Likewise one can say that one has made use of information in computer-readable form even if one did not use the information in that form.

Further, what is protected by the Act is 'personal data' defined as:

Section 1

(3) 'Personal data' means data consisting of information which relates to a living individual who can be identified from that information (or from that and other information in the possession of the data user), including any expression of opinion about the individual but not any indication of the intentions of the data user in respect of that individual.

A more pertinent question to ask is whether information relating to individuals and from which they can be identified equates to the meaning of 'personal information' as understood in everyday parlance? Wacks suggests that personal information[20] 'consists of those facts, communications or opinions which relate to the individual and which it would be reasonable to expect him to regard as intimate or sensitive and therefore to want to withhold or at least restrict their collection, use or circulation'. Arguably, this does not include as much material as would be covered by the statutory definition, since it relies on some objective assessment of the information over which it would be reasonable for individuals to retain control. As we shall see, it is precisely this type of information which may not be protected to the extent the individual considers desirable.[21]

The Act applies to all those who hold personal data and these are known as data users.

Section 1

(5) 'Data user' means a person who holds data, and a person 'holds' data if

(a) the data form part of a collection of data processed or intended to be processed by or on behalf of that person ...; and

(b) that person (either alone or jointly or in common with other persons) controls the contents and use of the data comprised in the collection; and

(c) the data are in the form in which they have been or are intended to be processed ... or are in a form into which they have been converted after being so processed and with a view to being further so processed on a subsequent occasion.

(4) 'Data subject' means an individual who is the subject of personal data.

(7) 'Processing' in relation to data, means amending, augmenting, deleting and re-arranging the data or extracting the information constituting the data and, in the case of personal data, means performing any of those operations by reference to the data subject.

Once it is clear that the Act applies, the central requirement is one of registration – data users are required to register with the Data Protection Registrar and to process data in accordance with the principles of good data management contained in the Act. These 'data protection principles', whose origin can be traced to the Younger Report, are contained in a Schedule to the Act rather than in the body of the statute itself. The Act provides certain rights for individuals with regard to the processing of information held about themselves on computer and provides for enforcement mechanisms and compensation in certain situations. These aspects of the Act will be considered in turn.

20 Raymond Wacks, *Personal Information: Privacy and the Law* (1993) p 26, Clarendon and note also the comments of the Lindop Committee, p 254

21 See p 299.

The Data Protection Principles – Data Protection Act 1984 Schedule 1

1. The information to be contained in personal data shall be obtained and the personal data shall be processed, fairly and lawfully.
2. Personal data shall be held only for one or more specified and lawful purposes.
3. Personal data held for any purpose or purposes shall not be used or disclosed in any manner incompatible with that purpose or those purposes.
4. Personal data held for any purpose or purposes shall be adequate, relevant and not excessive in relation to that purpose or those purposes.
5. Personal data shall be accurate and, where necessary, kept up to date.
6. Personal data held for any purpose or purposes shall not be kept any longer than is necessary for that purpose or those purposes.
7. An individual shall be entitled:
   (a) at reasonable intervals and without undue delay or expense:
      (i) to be informed by any data user whether he holds personal data of which that individual is the subject; and
      (ii) to access to any such data held by the data user; and
   (b) where appropriate, to have such data corrected or erased.
8. Appropriate security measures shall be taken against unauthorised access to, or alteration, disclosure or destruction of, personal data and against accidental loss or destruction of personal data.

The remedies available for the consequences of breach of the data protection principles are contained in the body of the statute itself and include individual remedies such as compensation for unauthorised disclosure in the event of damage and criminal penalties for non-registration and unauthorised use of the data. Although the Data Protection Act 1963 has been on the statute book for more than 10 years, its provisions have not yet seen much interpretation by the courts. It could be that this is due to the excellence of its drafting[22] but a more significant and more likely factor may be the sheer magnitude of the policing and enforcement task and the difficulties of detecting and locating breaches. The Act provides a number of enforcement mechanisms, considered in more detail below, and, in particular, the office of the Data Protection Registrar, created by the Act, is charged with the duties of maintaining a register of data users and considering applications for registration, promoting observance of the data protection principles, upholding the rights of data subjects and arranging for dissemination of information about the Act.[23]

22 See, eg, Bainbridge, *Introduction to Computer Law* (1993) Pitmans.

23 Section 36 of the Data Protection Act 1984.

Encyclopaedia of Data Protection[24]
Paragraphs 1-041–1-042

The Data Protection Registrar and the Register

The Registrar

The Registrar's functions may be broadly classified as:

(a) administrative, in relation to establishment and maintenance of the register of users of personal data and of computer bureau operators;

(b) supervisory, in relation to compliance with the Act; and

(c) promotional, in relation to the data protection principles, dissemination of information about the operation of the Act and, where appropriate, development of codes of practice for guidance in complying with the principles.

The Registrar's obligation to promote observance of the data protection principles is an overriding duty applied to the performance of all his functions under the Act, so underlying the quasi-ethical nature of the principles. The Registrar has direct responsibility for promotion of the principles, and the term 'promotion', though not defined in the Act, implies something wider than enforcement. Enforcement of the principles, without any direct obligation on data users to observe them, would be an inappropriate term to describe the Registrar's function, and development of a body of jurisprudence based on the principles through codes of practice, empirical experience and judgment is as important an aspect of the Registrar's function as is enforcement of the resulting rules.

In order to promote the principles, the Registrar develops, interprets and applies them, both in general terms and in particular circumstances, and where disputes and uncertainty arise, exercises an ombudsman role. This role, and mediating between the conflicting interests of data users and data subjects, may prove to be the most important of the Registrar's subsidiary functions, although it is not expressly stated in the Act. Appeals from the Registrar's decisions, including decisions on interpretation and application of the principles, lie to the Data Protection Tribunal and thence, on a point of law, to the courts, but the initial responsibility for developing a practical jurisprudence based on the principles lies with the Registrar. In the introduction to the second issue of his Guideline 4 ... the Registrar states that 'Whether there is a contravention of a principle is a question of fact for the Registrar to decide in the first place'. This potentially onerous duty, in combination with his other functions, puts the Registrar into the position of being lawgiver, policeman, judge and jury at the lowest level of enforcement.

There is clear potential for a conflict of interests when so many roles need to be combined, but the government of the day were quite clear as to the rationale behind it.

24 Sweet & Maxwell, 1995 supplement.

Parliamentary Debates (Commons) 11 April 1983

William Whitelaw

We have made compliance with these principles enforceable through the medium of the registrar, so establishing a single authority on the subject who can consult, advise and negotiate before taking action. A vital feature of the scheme is his capacity to use his discretionary powers to tailor his response to the circumstances in each case. This flexibility of approach, we believe, is much preferable to any scheme in which, say, a user collecting data unfairly or holding inaccurate data is directly liable to criminal prosecution.

We have gone for a single registrar rather than a multimember authority for positive reasons. We see it as by far and away the most economic use of resources. Since the scheme will be funded by data users themselves, that is of particular importance to them. We believe that an individual registrar will be able to act more rapidly, authoritatively and consistently in this complex and infinitely varied field than could a committee. His interpretation of the principles, and determination of what in particular circumstances constitutes contravention of the principles, will place a premium on consistency and the kind of build-up of understanding and expertise that an individual can best achieve. Because of the variety of cases that will arise, we think that a registrar who is able to look for and accept advice from wherever he sees fit in the special circumstances that he faces will be better equipped than a committee representing an inevitably incomplete range of interests ...

In providing for a registrar with a supervisory function of this kind we have had to strike a delicate balance. On the one hand, there is the risk of setting up a cumbersome bureaucracy, continuously at the heels of legitimate business activity and impeding technological developments. On the other hand, we must guard against the registrar being ineffective, lacking the powers and resources to give any teeth to the legislation. The Government do not want some vast new quango that will jeopardise efficiency in every area of national life: thus we have gone for a compact organisation which will not interfere unnecessarily. The burdens on law-abiding data users will be kept to a minimum. On the other hand, it is nonsense to suggest that the registrar will be ineffective when the need for action arises.

The extent to which the combination of roles is successful is a moot point – although the Act merges these roles in the person of the Registrar, it does not always provide the means to fulfil them all efficiently. Thus, there is a policing function but the Act provides no real powers of investigation. This combination of responsibilities at the primary enforcement level is common to a number of other regulatory regimes, however, it is rare to have one individual responsible for such a range of activities. Similarly, some of these other regimes make use of criminal sanctions for some contraventions, causing questions to be raised about the role of the criminal law in this context. A comparison can be made, for instance, with inspectors appointed under the Health and Safety at Work Act 1974 who act as both police, prosecutor and have the power to serve notices requiring compliance with the relevant statutory provisions. In comparison, the Data Protection Registrar has similar powers relating to notices, has a power to refuse registration and, as highlighted in the above extract, is charged also with *promoting* the observance of the data protection principles – suggesting not only overseeing and enforcement but also education and guidance. In comparison to the area of occupational health and safety which has been regulated for more than 150 years in the UK, it is still rather early to make any assessment of how the differing roles of the Registrar and their interdependence might affect the manner and effectiveness of the enforcement. Any assessment of the success with which the roles can be combined will likely be influenced by the view that is taken of regulatory or white-collar crime in comparison with other criminal activities.

White Collar Crime and the Enforcement of Factory Legislation
WG Carson
(1970) 10 British Journal of Criminology 383

> ... The crucial component in this motivational background is the inspector's interpretation of his own function, since it is from this that his decisions about how to enforce the law derive their immediate contextual meaning ... the inspectors ... did not see themselves as members of an individual police force primarily concerned with the apprehension and subsequent punishment of offenders. Rather, they perceived their major function to be that of securing compliance with standards of safety, health and welfare required and thereby achieving the ends at which the legislation is directed ... Concerned with securing the offender's compliance rather than his punishment they tended to choose methods of enforcement as much for their functional efficiency in attaining this objective as for their appropriateness as punitive responses.

Carson went on to suggest that the legal proceedings were themselves used for a rather different purpose than was the case in the rest of the criminal justice system.

> [Legal proceedings had] a functional role ... in relation to the enforcement process as a whole; whether utilised for their predicted effect upon an individual occupier or upon other employers in their area, they were seen as a means to an end rather than an end in themselves.

Whatever the conflicts between the varying roles of the Registrar, the primary function is, arguably, one of enforcement, with other duties, such as dissemination of information, being ancillary to this. This is in contrast with Data Protection Commissioners in some other jurisdictions whose role can be likened more to that of an Ombudsman.

UK Data Protection – Where are we in 1991?
FGB Aldhouse
(1991) 5 Yearbook of Law, Computers and Technology 180

Registrar's Role

... The United Kingdom Registrar has the power to prosecute and to serve supervisory notices. He has a duty to consider complaints and he has certain limited investigatory powers such as the ability to obtain search warrants. In that respect the Registrar is a classic UK enforcing authority. Although his status of independence and reporting to Parliament is akin to that of the Parliamentary Commissioner, he does not have the decision-making role of an ombudsman.

That is distinctly not the case with officials such as the Federal German Data Protection Commissioner of the Canadian Federal Privacy Commissioner. Their jurisdiction is limited to the public sector. They have an audit role and their sanction is principally publicity rather than the use of classic enforcement measures.

This distinction has consequences for the political role of data protection officials. The ombudsman-type commissioners see an important part of their task as promoting political debate about data protection and privacy issues, commenting on those issues and indeed campaigning for a particular viewpoint. On the other hand those officials such as the Irish Commissioner and the United Kingdom Registrar, who are authorities enforcing a legal sanction and are cast much more in the role of policemen, are considerably more circumspect in commenting on these general contentious issues. This is perhaps in part a matter of political culture, but it is undoubtedly in large part a consequence of the distinct role of these officials.

ENFORCEMENT MECHANISMS

One of the primary tasks of the Registrar is the upkeep of the Register and so she[25] will consider applications for registration. In addition, there are a number of avenues of enforcement possible under the Act, depending on the nature and type of the irregularity and, in the first instance, ensuring compliance with the provisions of the Act is also a job for the Registrar as discussed above.

DATA PROTECTION ACT 1984
Duties of the Registrar relating to enforcement

Section 36

(1) It shall be the duty of the registrar so to perform his functions under this Act as to promote the observance of the data protection principles by data users and persons carrying on computer bureaux.

25 The current Data Protection Registrar is Elizabeth France, who succeeded Eric Howe on his retirement on 31 August 1994.

(2) The Registrar may consider any complaint that any of the data protection principles or any provision of this Act has been or is being contravened and shall do so if the complaint appears to him to raise a matter of substance and to have been made without undue delay by a person directly affected; and where the Registrar considers any such complaint he shall notify the complainant of the result of his consideration and of any action which he proposes to take.

To assist the Data Protection Registrar in carrying out these duties, the Act gives her a number of powers of entry and inspection[26] and also the power to issue one of three types of notice; an enforcement notice, a de-registration notice or a transfer prohibition notice. Once the Registrar is satisfied that a 'registered person has contravened or is contravening any of the data protection principles'[27] then, taking into account whether the contravention has caused or is likely to cause distress,[28] an enforcement notice may be served. Such a notice will detail the steps required to produce compliance with the relevant principles. Note that registration is a pre-requisite for the service of such a notice – in the event of mismanagement of data by an unregistered data user then the correct procedure is to bring a charge under s 5(1) (see p 288). A de-registration notice is a more severe form of notice resulting in the user's entry being removed from the register but, in this case, the Registrar must be satisfied that 'compliance with the principle or principles in question cannot be adequately secured by the service of an enforcement notice'.[29] Finally, the purpose of transfer prohibition notices is to prevent transfer of data outside the jurisdiction unless the rights of the data subject are adequately safeguarded.[30]

In the early days of the Act, the main thrust of the work of the Registrar was in creating the register, a mammoth task when the potential number of

	1991/2	**1992/3**	**1993/4**	**1994/5**	**1995/6**
No of charges under the DPA	27	71	36	66	47
For non-registration	26	63	29*	54*	25

*Also includes offences under s 6(5) for failure to amend details of registration, one in 1993–94 and two in 1994–95.

entries is considered. It is still considered that there is massive under-registration, it has been estimated that the UK register should contain half a million entries, whereas the actual number of registrations is only of the order

26 Contained in Schedule 4 to the Act.

27 Section 10 (1) of the Data Protection Act 1984.

28 Section 10(2) of the Data Protection Act 1984.

29 Section 11(2) of the Data Protection Act 1984.

30 Section 12 of the Data Protection Act 1984.

of 200,000.[31] The first cases which came to court were for non-registration, a strict liability offence under s 5(1) (or s 5(4) for computer bureaux).

Although such cases still form a significant part of the case load as shown by the figures above,[32] there is now an emergent body of case law that is not merely rubber stamping the requirement for registration, but is seeking to interpret the provisions and key concepts in the Act. At the first level, the Registrar is able to clarify and influence the interpretation of the statutory provisions and, in particular, of the Data Protection Principles as made clear in the previous section. This process may be continued by the Data Protection Tribunal and thence in the courts if there is a point of law at issue. A number of sections of the Act create offences which may be tried in the criminal courts, examples include s 5 which creates offences of non-registration and aspects of data mismanagement and s 20 which relates to the criminal liability of directors and other corporate servants. It is also a criminal offence, by virtue of s 10 to fail to comply with the terms of any of the notices described above.

The individual also has a role to play in enforcement when exercising the rights contained in Part III of the Act.

DATA PROTECTION ACT 1984

Rights Of Data Subjects

Section 21 Right of access to personal data

(1) Subject to the provisions of this section, an individual shall be entitled

(a) to be informed by any data user whether the data held by him include personal data of which that individual is the data subject; and

(b) to be supplied by any data user with a copy of the information constituting any such personal data held by him;

and where any of the information referred to in paragraph (b) above is expressed in terms which are not intelligible without explanation the information shall be accompanied by an explanation of those terms.

(2) A data user shall not be obliged to supply any information under subsection (1) above except in response to a request in writing and on payment of such fee (not exceeding the prescribed maximum) as he may require; but a request for information under both paragraphs of that subsection shall be treated as a single request and a request for information under paragraph (a) shall, in the absence of any indication to the contrary, be treated as extending also to information under paragraph (b).

(3) In the case of a data user having separate entries in the register in respect of data held for different purposes a separate request must be made and a separate fee paid under this section in respect of the data to which each entry relates.

31 11th report of the Data Protection Registrar, Chapter 4, HMSO 1995.

32 Compiled from details extracted from the 8th–12th Reports of the Data Protection Registrar HMSO 1992–96.

(4) A data user shall not be obliged to comply with a request under this section

(a) unless he is supplied with such information as he may reasonably require in order to satisfy himself as to the identity of the person making the request and to locate the information which he seeks; and

(b) if he cannot comply with the request without disclosing information relating to another individual who can be identified from that information, unless he is satisfied that the other individual has consented to the disclosure of the information to the person making the request.

The remaining subsections of s 21 outline the necessary administrative requirements.

Section 22 Compensation for inaccuracy

(1) An individual who is the subject of personal data held by a data user and who suffers damage by reason of the inaccuracy of the data shall be entitled to compensation from the data user for that damage and for any distress which the individual has suffered by reason of the inaccuracy.

(2) In the case of data which accurately record information received or obtained by the data user from the data subject or a third party, subsection (1) above does not apply if the following requirements have been complied with

(a) the data indicate that the information was received or obtained as aforesaid or the information has not been extracted from the data except in a form which includes an indication to that effect; and

(b) if the data subject has notified the data user that he regards the information as incorrect or misleading, an indication to that effect has been included in the data or the information has not been extracted from the data except in a form which includes an indication to that effect.

(3) In proceedings brought against any person by virtue of this section it shall be a defence to prove that he had taken such care as in all the circumstances was reasonably required to ensure the accuracy of the data at the material time.

(4) Data are inaccurate for the purposes of this section if incorrect or misleading as to any matter of fact.

Section 23 Compensation for loss or unauthorised disclosure

(1) An individual who is the subject of personal data held by a data user or in respect of which services are provided by a person carrying on a computer bureau and who suffers damage by reason of

(a) the loss of the data;

(b) the destruction of the data without the authority of the data user or, as the case may be, of the person carrying on the bureau; or

(c) subject to subsection (2) below, the disclosure of the data, or access having been obtained to the data, without such authority as aforesaid, shall be entitled to compensation from the data user or, as the case may be, the person carrying on the bureau for that damage and for any distress which the individual has suffered by reason of the loss, destruction, disclosure or access.

(2) In the case of a registered data user, subsection (1)(c) above does not apply to disclosure to, or access by, any person falling within a description specified pursuant to section 4(3)(d) above in an entry in the register relating to that data user.

(3) In proceedings brought against any person by virtue of this section it shall be a defence to prove that he had taken such care as in all the circumstances was reasonably required to prevent the loss, destruction, disclosure or access in question.

Section 24 Rectification and erasure

(1) If a court is satisfied on the application of a data subject that personal data held by a data user of which the applicant is the subject are inaccurate within the meaning of section 22 above, the court may order the rectification or erasure of the data and of any data held by the data user and containing an expression of opinion which appears to the court to be based on the inaccurate data.

(2) Subsection (1) above applies whether or not the data accurately record information received or obtained by the data user from the data subject or a third party but where the data accurately record such information, then

(a) if the requirements mentioned in section 22(2) above have been complied with, the court may, instead of making an order under subsection (1) above, make an order requiring the data to be supplemented by such statement of the true facts relating to the matters dealt with by the data as the court may approve; and

(b) if all or any of those requirements have not been complied with, the court may, instead of making an order under that subsection, make such order as it thinks fit for securing compliance with those requirements with or without a further order requiring the data to be supplemented by such a statement as is mentioned in paragraph (a) above.

(3) If a court is satisfied on the application of a data subject

(a) that he has suffered damage by reason of the disclosure of personal data, or of access having been obtained to personal data, in circumstances entitling him to compensation under section 23 above; and

(b) that there is a substantial risk of further disclosure of or access to the data without such authority as is mentioned in that section,

the court may order the erasure of the data; but, in the case of data in respect of which services were being provided by a person carrying on a computer bureau, the court shall not make such an order unless such steps as are reasonably practicable have been taken for notifying the person for whom those services were provided and giving him an opportunity to be heard.

This also means, therefore, that the civil courts will need to consider interpretation of the Act when making orders for compensation for inaccuracy, loss or unauthorised disclosure or for rectification and erasure as allowed for in ss 22–24 above.

INTERPRETATION BY THE DATA PROTECTION REGISTRAR

Further to the general duty, referred to already, to promote observance of the data protection principles, the Data Protection Registrar interprets and applies the provisions of the Act both in the official Guidelines produced to comply with the duties concerned with dissemination of information under s 36(3) and also in the publication of the Data Protection Registrar's Annual Reports as required by s 36(5). Below is an example of the suggested interpretation of 'lawful' for the purposes of the first and second data protection principles.

From the Ninth Report of the Data Protection Registrar June 1993[33]

4. Determining the Meaning of the Law
Lawfulness in the First and Second Data Protection Principles

No interpretation of the term 'lawful' is provided in the Act. Therefore, it has to be interpreted in accordance with the normal rule, which is that a word must be given its ordinary meaning unless the context in which it is used shows another intention. There is nothing in the Data Protection Act to suggest that the term should be given other than its normal meaning.

Lawfulness was considered in a House of Lords case in 1991[34] and in that case 'unlawful' was held to mean:

> ... something which is contrary to some law or enactment or is done without lawful justification or excuse.

This is a broad definition; it applies equally to the public and the private sectors and it applies both to those breaches of the law which can be punished by criminal penalties and those which are dealt with by the civil courts.

The effect of this broad definition is that a data user must comply with all relevant rules of law in relation to the purposes for which he holds personal data, and the ways in which he obtains and processes it. So, for example, it seems to me that information which is obtained by theft or in breach of an enforceable contractual agreement is likely to be unlawfully obtained ...

The Registrar also suggested certain areas for concern that might provide fertile ground for breaches of the First and Second Data Protection Principles.

33 See also Data Protection Registrar's Guidelines: Third Series, November 1994 Guideline 4.
34 *R v R* [1991] 3 WLR 767 at p 775 *per* Lord Keith of Kinkel.

(i) Confidentiality

There are circumstances where an obligation of confidence arises between a data user and a data subject. This may flow from a variety of circumstances or in relation to different types of information. Examples might occur in respect of medical information or banking procedures. An obligation of confidence gives the data subject the right not to have his information used for other purposes or disclosed without his permission unless there are other over-riding reasons in the public interest for this to happen.

Where an obligation of confidence arises it is unlawful for a data user to use the information for a purpose other than that for which it was provided. Where such a use involves the processing of the personal data, then this may entail unlawful processing within the meaning of the First Principle. This is important for those who hold and process ...

The law of confidence applies to government and statutory organisations just as it applies to private persons. Many such bodies obtain confidential information in order to carry out their duties ... Public bodies may obtain much of the information they hold under statutory powers. Such powers are given to these data users specifically to carry out their statutory functions. Where a data user obtains information of a confidential quality in pursuance of its statutory functions and that information is then used or disclosed other than in pursuance of those functions, it is my view that a breach of confidence is likely unless there is some other statutory authority or just cause or excuse for the unauthorised uses and disclosures. If such uses or disclosures entail the processing of the personal data then this is likely to be unlawful processing.

(ii) The *Ultra Vires* Rule

... The *ultra vires* rule is a rule of law which states that those vested with statutory powers are only able to do those things that Parliament has allowed them to do by statute. This includes doing things that are reasonably necessary to allow them to fulfil their primary functions. It follows, therefore, that a statutory body which obtains, processes or holds personal data for a purpose for which it has no statutory authority will be acting *ultra vires* and therefore unlawfully in holding, obtaining and processing those data.

(iii) Excess of Delegated Powers

The rules applying to Crown bodies are similar in effect although technically different in law. Where a particular activity is covered by a statutory scheme, for example the payment of benefits, then the Secretary of State and government agency dealing with that area have to follow the rules laid down in the statute in order to act lawfully. If they do not do so they may be acting unlawfully. Even where there is no detailed specific law dealing with an area and it is dealt with under executive powers then those powers will be defined either expressly or implicitly.

A government body which deals with personal data should therefore ensure it is aware of the relevant statutory scheme governing the activity and the extent of the powers given by the scheme. This is particularly important in so far as there may be specific restrictions on the use or disclosure of data. If the body goes outside the powers to obtain, process or hold personal data it will be doing so unlawfully.

(iv) The Concept of Legitimate Expectations

.... there is a continuing, firm, majority belief that government agencies can be trusted to keep and use information in a responsible way. It is within this context of the expectations of individuals that the concepts of legitimate expectation fall to be considered.

In essence this means that in some circumstances an individual who will be adversely affected by a decision of a public body will be entitled to be notified of or consulted about such a decision before it is made. This could apply, for example, if it has been the case that a particular set of information obtained from individuals has not been made public or disclosed and the individual had no reason to think there would be any alteration in this situation. In such circumstances a proposal to disclose this information, where this may have an adverse effect on the individual, may be unacceptable unless the individual has been consulted and given an opportunity to voice his or her position. The individual has a legitimate expectation of consultation which should be respected and complied with. Failure to comply with a legitimate expectation may render unlawful any holding or processing of personal data associated with the proposed alteration in information practices.

It is clear, here, that the Data Protection Registrar is calling on established legal principles to suggest the likely interpretation of the terms at issue.[35] In contrast, in both the Annual Reports and other occasional reports the Registrar also suggests how the statutory provisions might be applied to new advancements in technology, for instance.[36] This type of preliminary report by the Data Protection Registrar may subsequently be very influential, as seen in relation to the problems raised by direct marketing, discussed below.

35 See also, in this context Rosemary Jay 'Current Legal Issues in UK Data Protection' (1995) 1 CTLR 152.

36 See, for example, Tenth Report of the Data Protection Registrar HMSO 1994 referring to the application of the Act to, *inter alia*, Calling Line Identification, Teleworking, Smart Cards, Document Image Processing and the Internet.

INTERPRETATION BY THE DATA PROTECTION TRIBUNAL

The Data Protection Tribunal is empowered to hear appeals against notices served by the Data Protection Registrar and also against refusal to register.[37] A number of these cases have led to clarification of some of the provisions of the Act and, on occasions, have provided confirmation of some of the preliminary views of the Registrar.

The first data protection principle requires that 'information to be contained in personal data shall be obtained and personal data shall be processed, fairly and lawfully'. With the exception of obtaining of data or information from sources not included in the Register,[38] violations of this principle do not have corresponding offences defined in the body of the statute and so application, enforcement and interpretation is, initially, a matter for the Registrar and thence the Tribunal. There have been appeals against notices served by the Registrar relating to both fair obtaining and fair processing of data which have led to the Tribunal considering both of these issues.

(a) Information shall be obtained fairly[39]

Some of the factors to be taken into account in the decision as to whether information has been obtained *fairly* came before the Tribunal as a consequence of a notice served on the mail order company, Innovations Ltd. As well as supplying goods mail order, this firm derived a significant amount of its income by trading in lists of customer names and addresses and making these lists available to other companies for direct marketing purposes (so-called 'list rental').

The whole area of direct marketing and trading in customer details had, for some time, been a concern for those seeking to regulate data management in response to the fact that customer data had become a commodity in its own right. In 1985, a Council of Europe Recommendation[40] had suggested that '[t]he collection of data from an individual for any reason other than normal customer or contributor relations should be permissible for direct marketing purposes only on condition that this has been expressly stated at the time of collection'. This Recommendation further suggested that customers should have rights to refuse to allow their data to be included on lists, to have the lists transmitted to third parties and to have data removed from lists. The same

37 Section 13 of the Data Protection Act 1984.

38 Note also s 5(2) of the Data Protection Act.

39 For the statutory guidance on interpretation of fair obtaining see Schedule 1, Part II of the Data Protection Act 1984.

40 Council of Europe Recommendation No R(85) 20 1985.

view had been taken by the Registrar, that individuals should be notified of the likelihood of their personal details being used for list rental before, or at the time of, obtaining the relevant data if that data were to be deemed to be *fairly* obtained. There was evidence that this had been generally accepted as it was included in the British Code of Advertising Practice[41] which included the stipulation that customers should be given the opportunity to object at the time of data collection and also should be advised if the purposes for which the data were to be used changed subsequently. However, in contrast there had also been a strong lobby from a sector of the industry during the draft stages of the EC Directive on data protection against the requirement that the data subject be informed of the purposes of the intended processing.[42]

It was against this background that a notice was served on Innovations Ltd. The enterprise obtained its custom by orders from its catalogues and in response to advertisements placed in the media. Customers ordering directly from the catalogues were advised of the possibility of their details being made available for other purposes, but those responding to the advertisements did not receive such advice until after they had placed an order, ie after they had supplied their personal details in response to the advertisement. The company argued that it was not practicable to provide notice of this practice in all other media advertisements, because of time and space constraints, and that later notification was more appropriate, as it would allow customers to be given more choice over the potential use of their information. The Registrar, on the other hand, argued that, if the obtaining was to be fair, the customer had to be aware of all the potential uses of personal details at the time that the order was made. The company appealed against the notice.

Innovations (Mail Order) Limited v Data Protection Registrar
Case DA/92 31/49/1

28. Certain interpretation of the data protection principles is provided in part II of the first schedule of the Data Protection Act, 1984. Paragraph 1(1) provides '... in determining whether information was obtained fairly regard should be had to the method by which it was obtained, including in particular whether any person from whom it was obtained was deceived or misled as to the purpose or purposes for which it is to be held, used or disclosed'. Our attention was also drawn to paragraph 7, relating to use for historical, statistical or research purposes. We have taken account of this aid to interpretation. We do not find an intention to mislead, what we do find is that some at least of those the advertising reaches may, from the absence of a warning as to the purpose of list trading, conclude that supplying a name and address will not result in it being traded. Such members of the public will in this sense therefore have been misled. In

41 Rules for Direct Marketing including List and Database Management see, eg, *Encyclopaedia of Data Protection*, paras 5-419–5-437, Sweet & Maxwell.

42 This lobby was not successful and the final Article 10 of Directive 95/46/EC has evolved from a right of the data subject to be informed to a duty on the data user to inform.

reaching this conclusion we take account of the factors established by specimen advertisements and the code of practice to which we have referred. We are satisfied that advertisers who list trade do now very commonly give a warning. We accept that the appellant's witness, Mr Swabey, has no knowledge of any complaint from customers that they were not warned until after their names and addresses had been obtained that a purpose was to list trade them. Furthermore we took account of the fact that the only evidence of a complaint that the onus should not be placed upon the data subject to object to the inclusion of his name and address in a list, was in 1989. The Registrar accepted that he had no evidence of distress or damage at the time he issued the enforcement notice.

29. We are satisfied from the above facts that it is established that when customers place orders together with their names and addresses the appellant 'obtains' personal information within the meaning of the first data protection principle. We are further satisfied that the appellant has two purposes and intentions at that time, namely to supply goods to its customers and to trade in names and addresses. Thus we conclude that a general purpose of the time of obtaining is to trade in personal information even if, thereafter, selected names may be excluded. We reject the argument at one time advanced by the appellant that there was no such general purpose at the time that personal information was obtained as it was only thereafter that a decision was made whether to trade a particular name and address or not.

30. We have reached a conclusion that the words 'fairly obtained' in the first data protection principle direct attention to the time of obtaining, not to a later time. We do not ignore the facts and circumstances of what happens thereafter. They may provide evidence of the purpose or purposes for which the data was in fact obtained and may provide evidence of the intention of the data user when he has sought, received, collected and obtained the personal information. We conclude in the facts and circumstances of this case that a purpose for which personal information is obtained, namely, list trading, is not obvious, unless clearly stated, before it is obtained. The purpose that is obvious is the supply of goods. We conclude the personal information will not be fairly obtained unless the data subject is so told of the non-obvious purpose before the information is obtained. We have taken into account that many advertisers give notice in ordinary language in their advertisements that they may trade in names and addresses. Many give prospective customers the option to order without having their names and addresses traded. We do not have to decide whether the absence of such a choice may in certain circumstances, for example, with a monopoly supplier, result in unfair obtaining. What the enforcement notice seeks to achieve is that each advertisement should warn that trading in personal information may result if the name and address is supplied. Many traders are likely to incorporate choice for the customer as to whether to have his name list traded or not in order to avoid loss of trade. It may also assist those to whom the lists are traded since it will remove from the lists those who are unlikely to be interested in

such direct mail. The fact that many advertisers currently give notice in their advertisements where they trade in personal information makes it more likely that the absence of such a warning, where there is nonetheless a general purpose to list trade, increases the risk that members of the public will be misled.

31. We conclude that a later notice may be a commendable way of providing a further warning, but whether it does so or not, we conclude that the law requires in the circumstance we have here that when possible the warning must be before the obtaining. This can best be done by including the warning in the advertisement itself. Where it may not be possible (eg the use of existing names for a new purpose) we consider that the obligation to obtain the data subject's positive consent for the non-obvious use of their data falls upon the data user.

In order to ensure compliance with the first data protection principle, the most frequent practice engaged in by companies who participate in list rental is to provide an 'opt-out' box in their order form or advert to enable customers to indicate if they do not wish their data to be used in this way. The scope of fair obtaining was returned to in the later case of *Linguaphone Institute Ltd v Data Protection Registrar*.[43] The Data Protection Tribunal confirmed the decision in Innovations and drew attention to the fact that it could equally be a violation of the first data protection principle if the opt-out box was not clearly positioned and/or it was in such minute typeface that it could not be regarded as putting customers on notice of the potential use of their data[44] – '... we are concerned that the opt-out box appears in minute print at the bottom of the order form. In the Tribunal's view the position, size of print and wording of the opt-out box does not amount to a sufficient explanation to an enquirer that the company intends or may wish to hold use or disclose that personal data provided at the time of enquiry for the purpose of trading in personal information ...'.[45]

Concern about the effects of the growing market in personal data were recognised both by the Data Protection Registrar[46] and also the Audit Commission[47] and, eventually, resulted in certain amendments being introduced into the 1984 Act by the Criminal Justice and Public Order Act

43 Case DA/94 31/49/1.

44 The courts have, of course, taken a similar approach in relation to disclaimers and trade descriptions: 'To be effective any such disclaimer must be as bold, precise and compelling as the trade description itself and must be as effectively brought to the notice of any person to whom the goods may be supplied' (*Norman v Bennett* [1974] 1 WLR 1229 at 1232 *per* Ld Widgery). Compare also cases on incorporation of contractual terms see, eg, the reasoning advanced in *Roe v RA Naylor* [1917] 1 KB 712 *per* Bailhache J.

45 Since the decisions in *Innovations* and *Linguaphone,* the Registrar has produced a revised Guideline detailing the requirements for list and database management in relation to direct marketing available in pdf format at http://www.open.gov.uk/dpr/guidance.htm.

46 Ninth Report of the Data Protection Registrar HMSO 1993.

47 *Opportunity makes a thief: An analysis of computer abuse* HMSO 1994.

1994. This legislation inserted new subsections into s 5[48] creating offences relating to the sale or offering for sale of personal data in circumstances where the data has been obtained as a result of procuring disclosure in contravention of the Act.[49] The first convictions for procuring the disclosure of personal data and of selling the procured information contrary to the new ss 5(6) and 5(7) were recorded recently after a private investigator obtained confidential information by deception from the Driver and Vehicle Licensing Agency.[50]

(b) Information shall be processed fairly

Unlike fair obtaining, there is no statutory guidance on what constitutes fair processing, although some limited guidance is provided by the Data Protection Registrar in Guidelines No 2 (on definitions) and No 4 (on the principles). Taken together these suggest that any assessment of whether processing is fair will need to take into account the purposes of processing, the type of processing and the consequences to the data subject. Consideration of this question by the Tribunal arose out of a number of appeals against enforcement notices served against certain credit reference agencies because of the Registrar's belief that these agencies were violating the requirement contained in the first Data Protection Principle to *process* personal data fairly. The definition of *processing* contained in s 1(7) of the Act includes the extracting of information and, although the precise methods of extraction varied between the agencies, the important fact in each case was that the method of extraction was too wide, by address, for instance, rather than by name, resulting in persons being judged to be bad credit risks on the basis of another person's record. This was illustrated, by what was agreed to be a representative complaint, in the case of *CCN Systems Ltd and CCN Credit Systems Ltd v Data Protection Registrar*. J had bought a house from W. Three years later, J applied for a cheque guarantee card but was refused and was told that CCN had provided the credit reference. A copy of his file (obtained under s 158 of the Consumer Credit Act 1974) showed a judgment against W. The only connection between J and W was that they had, at separate times, lived at the same address.

A number of points of clarification of interpretation come from the arguments and judgments in the cases involving these credit reference agencies.

48 For interpretation and enforcement of s 5 see p 288, below.

49 See Martin Wasik, 'Dealing in the Information Market: Procuring, Selling and Offering to Sell Personal Data' 1995, Vol 9, p 193, International Yearbook of Law, Computers and Technology.

50 See, eg, *Computing* (1996) p 2, (1996) 146 NLJ 1178.

CCN Systems Ltd and CCN Credit Systems Ltd v Data Protection Registrar
Case DA/90 25/49/9

Fairness

48. We now come to the crucial question whether the processing that we have described may be said to be unfair. It was urged on us by Mr Donaldson that we should not judge the question of fairness by considering simply whether what was done was fair or unfair in relation to the individual. Fairness, he said, involves a balancing of competing interests, so that in judging whether processing was fair we should set against any possible unfairness to the individual the advantages gained by other individuals, the benefits to the grantors of credit, and the public welfare. It is necessary to say something about these counterbalancing considerations.

49. We heard evidence from CCN's witnesses of what they thought would be the consequences of upholding the enforcement notice. They said that the absence of third party information would make it more difficult to predict the creditworthiness of applicants for credit. With less information available the judgments of credit grantors would be less reliable. It would be necessary to do one of two things. Either the number of applicants accepted for credit would remain the same and the number of defaulters would rise, or in an attempt to keep the number of defaulters constant it would be necessary to refuse credit to more applicants, many of whom would have turned out to be good payers. In either case, a consequence would be higher interest rates or reduced profits. One witness hinted that if the enforcement notice were upheld his company might well depart the consumer credit field to be replaced, he suggested, by less reputable lenders. Thus if it is thought unfair to the individual to classify him or her by reference to third party information, some individuals who now obtain credit would be denied credit, or some would pay more. We should not, argued Mr Donaldson, decide that the extraction of third party information was unfair without taking account of the present benefits to other applicants – and, indeed, perhaps the applicant himself who might not get credit in the absence of third party information – and to the credit grantors, as well as to the public interest in securing a supply of credit as widely available as possible.

50. We are very conscious of the benefits of reliable credit reference and credit scoring systems in preventing over-commitment by debtors, a measure very much for their benefit and that of the community, and in ensuring a well-managed credit system for the benefit of potentially sound debtors and of the credit and supply industries. We have no doubt that credit scoring systems work for the public good, but they must operate in a way that extracts information fairly.

51. The word 'fairly' in the first principle is not defined in the Act, and no guidance is given as to its interpretation. In determining its meaning we must have regard to the purpose of the Data Protection Act. It is quite clear, from the Act as a whole and in particular from the data protection principles set out in Schedule 1, that the purpose of the Act is to protect the rights of the individual about whom data is obtained, stored, processed or supplied, rather than those of the data user. The Act was the result of

concerns about the use of computer data, concerns voiced in Parliament and in the reports of a number of representative official committees and widely held throughout Europe (hence the Council of Europe's Convention for the Protection of Individuals with regard to Automatic Processing of Personal Data opened for signature on January 28, 1981 referred to in sections 37 and 41 of the Act).

52. In our view, in deciding whether the processing we have described is fair we must give the first and paramount consideration to the interests of the applicant for credit – the 'data subject' in the Act's terms. We are not ignoring the consequences for the credit industry of a finding of unfairness, and we sympathise with their problems, but we believe that they will accept that they must carry on their activities in accordance with the principles laid down in the Act of Parliament.

53. Having taken due account of the evidence we have heard and the considerations urged upon us we have come to the clear conclusion that it is unfair for a credit reference agency, requested by its customers to supply information by reference to a named individual, so to program the extraction of information as to search for information about all persons associated with a given address or addresses notwithstanding that those persons may have no links with the individual the subject of the enquiry or may have no financial relationship with that individual. We believe this to be so even if the customer has requested address-based information and notwithstanding what is said to be its predictive value. We reject the notion that an organisation like CCN, with its wide specialist knowledge of and experience in credit reference and credit scoring, is a mere 'conduit pipe'. We believe the sort of processing carried out in this case is the very sort of activity at which the Act is aimed. We think it right to say that we accept that CCN did not intend to process data unfairly, and did not believe itself to be acting unfairly. But it is necessary to determine the question of fairness objectively, and in our view the case of unfairness has been made out.

Two important points are made here, firstly, in relation to the purpose of the Act in protecting the rights of the individual and, secondly, in relation to the fact that the standard is one of objective fairness and the irrelevance, therefore, as to whether or not the data user had the motive or intention to breach the Data Protection Principles. In the next case, a number of arguments were advanced concerning the interpretation of the term processing in relation to whether or not extraction of the information had actually taken place at the material time.

Infolink Ltd v Data Protection Registrar
Case DA/90 25/49/9
Processing

55. The word 'processing' is defined in section 1(7) of the Data Protection Act as follows:

'Processing' in relation to data, means amending, augmenting, deleting or rearranging the data or extracting the information constituting the data and, in the case of personal data, means performing any of those operations by reference to the data subject.

56. There was no real dispute that the crucial part of the definition in the present case was 'extracting the information constituting the data', but there was disagreement as to what precisely was involved in extracting information. One view was that this meant that the computer was operated so as to produce one of three things: information in the form of sheet of paper: information revealed on a screen; or information – perhaps data would be a better word – fed into a scoring program. Mr Pumfrey did not accept that this amounted to the extraction of information. He argued that extraction does not take place until the information was used for its purpose, and asked whether extraction took place at a stage when the information extracted was seen by no human being and had no objective effect. He used two striking metaphors; until the information was put to use it had no reality, it was an unopened book; and he likened extraction without use to someone shouting in an empty room – you could not say that he had said anything if no one had heard it. Information, he said, is something that informs, and it does not inform until it is used by the credit grantor for the purpose of granting credit.

57. In our view, the metaphors equally support a contrary argument. An unopened book contains as much, and the same, information as the same book opened, and we are in the realm of metaphysics if we deny that someone has spoken because no one has heard. We believe that it is perfectly possible to say that information is extracted at a stage before a human being looks at the screen of the video display unit or the sheet of paper and, as far as credit scoring is concerned, the information extracted is used without any human being seeing it. We are plainly concerned, in the definition in section 1(7) of the Act, with the 'performing [of) operations' by a machine, and extracting for present purposes leads to what is produced by the machine at the end of the extraction process.

In addition to a consideration of the competing interests of the data subject and the data user, referred to in the first paragraph of the extract from the judgment in the CCN decision, the Tribunal also clarified certain issues in relation to fairness.

Infolink Ltd v Data Protection Registrar
Case DA/90 25/49/6

64. In the CCN case we came to the conclusion that 'in deciding whether the processing we have described is fair we must give the first and paramount consideration to the interests of the applicant for credit – the "data subject" in the Act's terms'. We added that we were not ignoring the consequences for the credit industry of a finding of unfairness, and that we sympathised with their problems. Later we added the following: 'Although we have concluded that fairness is to be judged primarily by reference to the data subject, we have taken account of the interests of CCN and of their customers, the credit industry, in considering whether the Registrar has exercised his discretion properly.'

65. In the present case, Mr Pumfrey referred to our ruling in the CCN case that we must give the first and paramount consideration to the interests of the applicant for credit. He took this to mean that the applicant's interests prevailed over all other interests and argued that if this was intended by the Act it would not have introduced the concept of fairness at all. We do not think this adequately sums up our finding in the earlier case. We do not think 'paramount' bears the meaning that it is the only consideration, but rather the most important single consideration. In other words, we are to weigh the various considerations, and do so, but are entitled to give more weight to the interests of the individual about whom the credit reference enquiry is being made.

66. Mr Pumfrey made a number of other points. He argued that since information such as county court judgments is made public, it is the policy of the government (he used the expression 'public policy') that such information should be publicly available, and that Infolink advances this public policy by making the information accessible. We certainly accept that there is a public interest in having access to records of county court and other judgments and other public information, and we do not quarrel with the making of public information available to Infolink's customers. Objection is taken to a much narrower activity: the alleged unfairness of extracting information for the purpose of credit reference about third parties not financially linked with the individual seeking credit.

67. Mr Pumfrey went on to argue that since Infolink's customers could themselves search public records, for example of county court judgments, it could not be said that the extraction of such public information could be unfair. We do not agree with this. Collecting all the public information on Infolink's database admittedly serves the public purpose of making the information accessible, but it is unrealistic to suggest that Infolink's customers might have been able to spend the time to research the public files to discover, not only information about the individual in whom they are interested ('the subject of the search') but also about other individuals whose only feature is the sharing of an address with the subject of the search. This use of computers to extract a large body of information – which may or may not be relevant is one of the activities the Act is, in our view, intended to regulate.

A further argument in relation to processing was advanced in *Equifax Europa Ltd v Data Protection Registrar* and related to the requirement in s 1(7) that processing in the case of personal data (ie as defined in s 1(3)) should be by reference to the data subject. In this case, it was argued that, as the data was extracted by reference to the address and not to the name, the Act did not even apply – there was no processing by reference to the data subject.[51]

51 Another case involving a credit reference agency was decided on substantially similar reasoning: *Credit and Marketing Services Ltd v Data Protection Registrar* Case DA/90 25/49/10.

Equifax Europa Ltd v Data Protection Registrar
Case DA/90 25/49/7

The 'no-processing' argument

43. The 'no-processing' argument rests on section 1(7) of the Act. It will be recalled that the essential part of the first data protection principle in this case, extracted from the words in Schedule 1, reads: 'personal data shall be processed fairly.' 'The meaning of "processed" is to be derived from section 1(7).' '"Processing", in relation to data, means amending, augmenting, deleting or re-arranging the data or extracting the information constituting the data and, in the case of personal data, means performing any of those operations *by reference* to the data subject.' 'Personal data' is defined in section 1(3) as follows: "'Personal data" means data consisting of information which relates to a living individual who can be identified from that information (or from that and other information in the possession of the data user)'.

44. In the CCN decision we identified the relevant activity of processing as 'extracting the information constituting the data', but no argument was directed to the closing words of subsection (7). Mr Chalton now argues that in the present case personal data is not processed, and hence the first principle, which imposes standards for the processing of personal data, has no application. This proposition is based on the definition of processing just cited. We have personal data, such as information relating to named individuals concerned with matters such as court judgments or credit agreements. That information is extracted from the database for the purpose of credit reference. But processing, according to the last words of the definition, means extracting the information *by reference to the data subject*, and according to Mr Chalton that is not how Equifax extracts data. It extracts data by reference to address, not by reference to name, even though the sole purpose of the extraction is to enable a credit grantor to decide whether to grant credit to an individual. It is of course that very activity, extraction by an address-based search rather than by name search, which produces details of entries relating to all persons at the address whether or not they are, or are connected with, the appellant for credit, that the Registrar objects to as being unfair. Mr Chalton contrasted the phrase 'by reference to' with the different phrase 'with regard to' used elsewhere in the Act.

45. What did Parliament mean when it used the words 'by reference to?' As a definition of 'processing', it would seem that the passage is quite adequate without the addition of the last phrase: processing means amending, augmenting, deleting or re-arranging the data or extracting the information constituting the data.

46. Why, then, did Parliament add the words 'and, in the case of personal data, means performing any of those operations by reference to the data subject'. (We should add that 'Data subject' means an individual who is the subject of personal data, so that both the applicant for credit, if there is any data about him on the database, and the other persons whose details are extracted, are all data subjects, though not perhaps 'the' data subject.)

Both Mr Carr and Mr Chalton agreed that the purpose of the added words was to limit the scope of application of the Act, to relieve the burden of supervision imposed on the Registrar, and to reduce the cost of compliance with the Act. But they disagreed on how those words were to be interpreted. As we have seen, Mr Chalton equated the phrase to a description of how the data user accessed the data, whether by name or in some other way. Mr Carr, on the other hand, would have regard to the intention and purpose of the processing.

47. We found two examples given by Mr Chalton helpful. He instanced the Driver and Vehicle Licensing Centre computer in Swansea. It is, he said, possible to access the database by reference to the vehicle number; this, he said, would not be processing by reference to data subjects even if the computer extracted a list of past and present keepers of the vehicle. One might, he said, be interested in the vehicle itself, such as the date it was manufactured.

48. His other example was the Land Registry computer. One could, he said, access the computer's database either by reference to the names of individuals, such as registered owners, or by reference to title number – in other words, by reference to the land. The first means of access would involve processing, the second, according to Mr Chalton, would not.

49 We find this particular example helpful for this reason. Mr Chalton is looking at the phrase 'by reference to the data subject' as linked to the mode of input into the computer system in order to conduct an operation such as amending data or extracting information. But it is difficult to believe that Parliament, or the draftsman, was looking at the issue through a computer-operator's eyes. What Parliament had in mind, we think, is the difference between approaching the database to conduct operations that had nothing to do with the data subject, and operations that focused on the data subject. Thus using the Land Registry's computer to change the boundaries of a plot of land, or perhaps to extract a copy of a restrictive covenant, would in no way concern the individual identity or attributes of a data subject, and need not attract the control over processing. On the other hand, using the computer to extract the name of a data subject, whether the computer was approached by typing in the name of the data subject or by retrieving his name in some other way, would constitute processing.

50. If we are right in this, it seems to us not to matter whether the search on Equifax's database was initiated by typing in the name of the subject of the enquiry or typing in the description of a piece of land associated with the subject of the enquiry. In both cases the object of the exercise is to learn something about individuals, not about the land. The data is processed in a way linked to the data subject, and hence by reference to the data subject. (For another use of 'by reference to' where it does not mean the way the computer is operated see section 28(4).) Equifax emphasised that it did not in most cases even know the name of the individual seeking credit, as if this confirmed that the extraction could not be by reference to the data subject. But Equifax is a credit reference agency, one of its registered

> purposes is 'the provision of information relating to the financial status of individuals' and it knows perfectly well that its customers have in mind particular individuals with whom it is contemplating entering into credit transactions ... We therefore find that the extraction of information constituting personal data by Equifax's address-based search is performed by reference to the data subject and so constitutes processing.

Information shall be relevant and not excessive

The fourth data protection principle requires that personal data held for any purpose or purposes shall be adequate, relevant and not excessive in relation to that purpose or those purposes. During the existence of the short-lived Community Charge or 'poll tax', a number of complaints were received that information required by those administering the Act was in excess of that needed. The task of compiling and maintaining the register of those who were subject to the charge was the duty of the Community Charge Registration Officers (CCROs) in each area. In order to comply with the fourth data protection principle, the Registrar had suggested[52] that data users should establish the minimum amount of information they could hold which was compatible with their intended purposes. On advice from the Registrar, a number of CCROs modified their requests, but a number did not comply and, accordingly, the Registrar refused applications to register on this basis in accordance with s 7(2)(b). The CCROs appealed. Three of these appeals were heard together as they all concerned the gathering of information concerning the type of property inhabited.

Community Charge Registration Officers of Runnymede Borough Council, South Northamptonshire District Council and Harrow Borough Council v Data Protection Registrar

Cases DA/90 24/49/3, 4 and 5

> Having concluded that property type information was personal data we had to consider whether we were satisfied that the holding of such data infringed the 4th Data Protection Principle that the data should be adequate, relevant and not excessive for the purposes for which it was held by the CCRO ... We considered the duty to maintain the register could properly include the obtaining and holding of at least some additional information on the computer database ... The appellant submitted that we should not take a very restrictive view of the discretion that a particular CCRO might exercise as to the amount of additional information he considered should be held to assist him to carry out his statutory duty. While there may be some force in the argument that what is judged to be excessive should not in some circumstances be too strictly construed we concluded that it could not be decisive where the issue is whether a wide class of data such as property type information should be held without any kind of limitation as to the extent of what was held ...

52 See Guideline 4 para 4.2.

> We were referred in the course of the hearing to the Guideline booklet Number 4 issued by the Data Protection Registrar entitled 'The Data Protection Principles'. Paragraph 4.2 relating to the 4th Principle advises that data users should seek to identify the minimum amount of information about each individual which is required in order properly to fulfil their purpose and that they should try to identify the cases where additional information will be required and seek to ensure that such information is only collected and recorded in those cases. We endorse this general guidance for those wishing to have a test to apply to answer the question whether personal data is adequate, relevant and not excessive for the purposes for which it is held. We find that the appellants held on database a substantial quantity of property type information obtained from voluntary answers on the canvass forms or from other sources. It was established that in holding such information, the appellants were holding far more than was in fact necessary for their purposes ...
>
> We find, and the appellants appear to accept, that it is not relevant and would be excessive to hold wide classes of data merely on the ground that future changes in the law may in remote and uncertain future circumstances require further property types to be added to the existing exceptions identified by the Data Protection Registrar.

A further case considered a similar question, this time in relation to the gathering of information on dates of birth. It was accepted by the Registrar that it might, on occasion, be necessary to hold dates of birth in relation to certain categories of person, such as those who were almost 18, students etc, and, subject to these exceptions, the majority of CCROs removed any reference to date of birth for other individuals. However, the CCRO for Rhondda did not comply and alleged, *inter alia,* that the information required was necessary because holding dates of birth provided a useful method of distinguishing between people in an area in which many had both surnames and given names in common.

Community Charge Registration Officer of Rhondda Borough Council v Data Protection Registrar

Case DA/90 25/49/2

> There was evidence before us that nationally less than one per cent of households contained persons with the same surname and the same first name. There was no evidence before us as to percentages applying within the area of Rhondda Borough Council, although it was probable that they were greater than the national figure. We approached the question of whether the information was irrelevant and excessive without taking too restrictive a view of the discretion that a particular CCRO might exercise as to the amount of information he considered would assist him to carry out his statutory duties. We found that it was established that the Appellant held and wished to continue holding dates of birth information on as many as possible. The information was to be obtained from answers voluntarily given on canvass forms. We found that the Appellant did not seek to limit the information to be

held on his database to those who would shortly attain the age to become charge payers or to identify persons living at the same address with identical names. The information as to dates of birth was personal data and was to cover persons generally at least insofar as the information had been voluntarily provided. We find that the information the Appellant wishes to hold on database concerning individuals exceeds substantially the minimum amount of information which is required in order for him to fulfil the purposes for which he has sought registration namely to fulfil his duty to compile and maintain the Community Charges Register ... We are satisfied by the evidence before us that the wide and general extent of the information about dates of birth is irrelevant and excessive.

INTERPRETATION BY THE COURTS

Some violations of the data protection principles, for which enforcement is primarily a matter for the Registrar, are supplemented by criminal offences created in the body of the Act. Thus s 5 creates, *inter alia*, offences relating to registration and to a number of other aspects of data mismanagement, that may also be, incidentally, breaches of the Data Protection Principles.

DATA PROTECTION ACT 1984

Section 5

(1) A person shall not hold personal data unless an entry in respect of that person as a data user, or as a data user who also carries on computer bureau, is for the time being contained in the register.

(2) A person in respect of whom such an entry is contained in the register shall not

(a) hold personal data of any description other than that specified in the entry;

(b) hold any such data, or use any such data held by him, for any purpose other than the purpose or purposes described in the entry;

(c) obtain such data, or information to be contained in such data, to be held by him from any source which is not described in the entry;

(d) disclose such data held by him to any person who is not described in the entry; or

(e) directly or indirectly transfer such data held by him to any country or territory outside the United Kingdom other than one named or described in the entry.

(4) A person shall not, in carrying on a computer bureau, provide services in respect of personal data unless an entry in respect of that person as a person carrying on such a bureau, ... is for the time being contained in the register.

(5) Any person who contravenes subsection (1) above or knowingly or recklessly contravenes any of the other provisions of this section shall be guilty of an offence.

Insofar as the Act only applies to personal data processed by a data user, the courts have, on occasions, had to discuss these preliminary issues in advance of the substantive offences contained in s 5. Thus the scope of the definition of data user was considered in *Data Protection Registrar v Griffin*.[53] Griffin was an accountant who kept his client's accounts on computer. The requisite information was obtained in written form from invoices and other records. This was then entered onto spreadsheets held on the computer that facilitated the subsequent preparation of the statement of accounts. Griffin was charged with the s 5(1) offence of non-registration and, in his defence, he pleaded that he was not a data user and so had no need to register. The definition of *data user* in the Act includes a requirement to 'control the contents and use' of the data. He based his argument, therefore, on the fact that, although he manipulated the data, he did not control the contents and use as this was limited both by codes of professional conduct and by the client's instructions. The argument was thus that controlling the contents and use, necessarily, implied the freedom to treat the data at will. This succeeded at trial and the Registrar appealed by way of case stated. The Divisional Court reversed the decision, finding that even though there might be constraints placed on the extent to which Griffin could control and use the data, nevertheless he had control over the manner in which the raw data was manipulated and choice over the precise way in which the accounts were constructed. He was therefore a data user as defined.

The offence in s 5(1) with which Griffin was charged, requires no *mens rea*, but for the other offences created in s 5, it is necessary to show that they were committed either *knowingly* or *recklessly*. It is accepted that recklessness may be used in either a subjective or objective *(Caldwell)* sense in the criminal law. Subjective recklessness refers to the conscious taking of an unjustified risk[54] whereas objective recklessness may arise when either no thought has been given as to the existence of an obvious risk, or there has been recognition of the risk but it has been ignored. This definition was first expounded in the cases of *Caldwell and Lawrence*.[55] The use of *Caldwell* recklessness has largely been restricted to statutory offences containing the word 'reckless' or 'recklessly', although it is not invariably applied to such offences but it appeared that the courts had confined its use to cases under the Criminal Damage Act 1971 (such as *Caldwell*) and cases of reckless driving (such as *Lawrence* and, more recently, *Reid*[56]). In which sense should recklessly in s 5(5) of the Data Protection Act be used?

In an early case, the Halifax Building Society was charged with knowingly or recklessly holding or using personal data for purposes other than those

53 *The Times* (1993) 5 March.

54 See, eg, *Cunningham* [1957] 2 QB 396.

55 *Caldwell* [1982] AC 341, *Lawrence* [1982] AC 510.

56 [1992] 3 All ER 673.

described in the register, contrary to s 5(2)(d). This case arose out of an investigation into a refusal to meet a subject access request. The person concerned had asked for details concerning withdrawals from cash machines, times of these withdrawals, his Halifax card number and balance enquiries. This was refused by the Society on the grounds that it was not personal data but operating systems data belonging to the Society. It considered that it was 'not obliged to disclose information which is likely to prejudice the prevention or detection of fraud or crime', however, it was found to be not registered for the purpose of crime prevention. If there had been a registration for this purpose then an exemption from the subject access provisions could have been claimed under s 28.[57] The Data Protection Registrar served notices[58] relating to a breach of the seventh data protection principle relating to individual's rights of access and also instigated proceedings. It was found, however, that there was no case to answer, as the evidence was that there was an honest belief that the purpose of crime prevention was merely ancillary to the other registered purposes and, when advised that additional registration was required, the entry in the register was amended accordingly. The court, therefore, was denied the opportunity to discuss the issue of recklessness (and neither was there any judicial pronouncement on the scope of the meaning of 'personal data' which would have been central to the case if it had continued).

More recently, the Divisional Court has had cause to consider the meaning of recklessness in s 5(5). In *Data Protection Registrar v Amnesty International (British Section)*,[59] Amnesty was charged under both s 5(2)(b) and (d) in relation to two offences of trading in and disclosure of personal information for purposes and to persons not described in the Register. At first instance, the court found that the relevant factor was foreseeability of harm, rather than whether or not the user had been reckless as to the management of the data in a manner incompatible with the registration. As the outcome of Amnesty's action was merely an unsolicited mailing, it was held, using this test, that Amnesty had not been reckless. On appeal to the Divisional Court by way of case stated, it was held that the seriousness of the consequences of the breach had been confused with the breach itself. In ruling that the appropriate definition of recklessness for s 5 was the objective definition found in *Lawrence*, Rose LJ said:

> ... The particular sensitivity of a person about whom data was released was unlikely to be in the knowledge of the holder of the data and it would be wrong if criminal liability were to be determined by reference to a factor outside the knowledge of the holder or discloser ...
>
> ... in order for the prosecution to prove the necessary element of recklessness in s 5 it had to show

57 For exemptions generally see p 296 below.

58 Subsequently revoked after negotiations with the Society.

59 *The Times* (1994) 23 November.

1. That there was something in the circumstances that would have drawn the attention of the ordinary prudent individual to the possibility that his act was capable of causing the kind of mischief that section 5(2) and (5) were intended to prevent and that the risk of those mischiefs occurring was not so slight that the ordinary prudent individual would justifiably treat it as negligible; and
2. That before doing the act the defendant either failed to give any thought to the possibility of any such risk or, having recognised the possibility, nevertheless went on to do it.

The meaning of *use* in s 5(2)(b), and hence in the Third Data Protection Principle, was at issue in a recent decision of the House of Lords – the first time they have been called upon to interpret the provisions of this statute. The case concerned a police officer, Brown, who checked the registration numbers of vehicles owned by persons being pursued by a debt collecting business operated by a friend of his. These checks were made on the police computer by other officers on his behalf. Brown was charged with use for an improper purpose, contrary to s 5(2)(b). In his defence, he said that the inquiries had been made for legitimate policing purposes, (there was an appropriate entry for policing purposes in the Register) and it was coincidental that the persons who owned the vehicles were also of interest to his friend's business. He was convicted, but his appeal against conviction was allowed by the Court of Appeal[60] and the Crown appealed to the House of Lords.

Both the Court of Appeal and the House of Lords agreed that the case hinged on the meaning of use. Although Brown had read information concerning the vehicles on the computer screen, there was no evidence brought that he had taken any action in response to the information he had gained.[61] The House of Lords upheld the majority view of the Court of Appeal that use should be given its natural and ordinary meaning and that, accordingly, Brown had not used the information.[62]

R v Brown [1996] 2 WLR 203
House of Lords

Lord Goff of Chieveley

I approach the matter as follows. I accept that, since the word 'use' is not defined in the Act, it must be given its natural and ordinary meaning. Synonyms of the verb 'use' are to 'make use of', or to 'employ for a purpose'. Here the word is used in relation to 'data', and data means information recorded in a computer-readable form. I must confess that at first sight I would

60 *R v Brown* [1994] QB 547.

61 Note that 'retrieval' is included in the definition of processing now contained in Directive 95/46/EC see p 307.

62 A New York court (*People v Esposito* 553 NY Supp 2d 612 (1990)) also dismissed the case against a police officer charged with using the New York Police Information System, for reasons not connected with an authorised criminal justice purpose, on the grounds that there was no evidence that the access had not been for personal benefit or profit.

not have thought that simply retrieving such information from the database in which it is stored, so that it appeared on a screen or a printout and could therefore be read by a human being, could properly be described as 'using' the information so recorded. Of course, the computer would be used to retrieve it; but the retrieval of the information would not of itself be 'using' the information so retrieved. It would simply be transferring the information into a different form. This to my mind underlines the fact that the definition of data as information in a computer-readable form does not mean that such information is only data while it is so recorded. It means rather that, if information is so recorded, it becomes data for the purposes of the Act; and if such information from that source is thereafter made use of it is used within the meaning of the Act. So if for example a police constable with the Kent Constabulary operates the police computer to retrieve personal data from the database so that he becomes aware of its contents, and then proceeds to make use of that information, he uses the personal data within the meaning of the statute. In such a case, the retrieval is not the use; it is simply a prerequisite of the use. Moreover if the police officer, who is the servant or agent of the data user, the Chief Constable, knowingly or recklessly puts the information to an improper use, he will be guilty of an offence under the Act. This may occur not only where the police officer retrieves the personal data from the database and then puts the information to an improper use, but also where, for example, he improperly makes use of personal data which has come to his knowledge when he operated the police computer innocently on a previous occasion, or where the data has been communicated to him by a colleague who had innocently operated the computer.

The same principles apply to disclosure as they do to use. Although there is a particular reference to the meaning of 'disclosing' in section 1(9) of the Act, to which I shall shortly refer, disclosure as such is not defined in the Act, and the word 'disclose', like the word 'use', should where it appears in the Act be given its natural and ordinary meaning. Subject to exceptional circumstances, information which is recorded in computer-readable form cannot be disclosed unless it has first been retrieved from the database and changed into a form in which it can be communicated to that person. I do not consider that section 1(9) places any obstacle in the way of that simple proposition. It provides:

> '"Disclosing", in relation to data, includes disclosing information extracted from the data; and where the identification of the individual who is the subject of personal data depends partly on the information constituting the data and partly on other information in the possession of the data user, the data shall not be regarded as disclosed or transferred unless the other information is also disclosed or transferred.'

It is apparent from reading the whole of this provision that it is concerned with the particular case of disclosing information extracted from data, ie information extracted from the information recorded in computer-readable form, and with the particular situation which arises where such an extract does not of itself reveal the identity of the person who is the subject of the data (as the whole of the data would if it fell within the definition of personal data in section 1(3)). I cannot see how this special provision can have any impact on the conclusion that the word 'disclose', being undefined in the Act, should be

> given its natural and ordinary meaning. Indeed, if the purpose of this provision had been to provide that exceptionally disclosure may occur after the information has been retrieved from the database, it would surely have been drafted in a different form; and a similar provision would have been made in respect of use.
>
> I add in parentheses that a question may arise whether the unauthorised transfer of data from the database of one computer to the database of another within the United Kingdom (*cf* section 5(2)(e)) could of itself amount to disclosure of data contrary to section 5(2)(d) of the Act. No such question arises for decision in the present case. I however incline to the view that such a transfer would not of itself amount to disclosure of data 'to any person who is not described in the entry' contrary to section 5(2)(d), although it may readily be inferred that the person effecting the transfer was inevitably thereby disclosing the data to another person or persons who, as he well knew, would retrieve the information from the second database and so have the information disclosed to him. On this basis, I cannot see that this exceptional case detracts from the approach to the construction of the Act which I favour.
>
> Confirmation of the approach which I favour can be found elsewhere in the Act. Useful examples can be seen in Schedule 1 to the Act, which is concerned with the Data Protection Principles. The Third Principle (set out in paragraph 3 of Part I of the Schedule) is that 'Personal data held for any purpose or purposes shall not be used or disclosed in any manner incompatible with that purpose or those purposes'. Such a principle cannot, as I read it, be concerned only with information while it is in computer-readable form. It is concerned with use or disclosure by a person of the relevant information as such. Further confirmation of the correctness of this approach is to be found in paragraph 7 of Part II of Schedule 1, which refers to personal data 'held for historical, statistical or research purposes and not used in such a way that damage or distress is, or is likely to be, caused to any data subject'. Such a use would be inconceivable if data could only be used by its being retrieved from the database.
>
> It seems to me that the above reading of the statute accords not only with the natural and ordinary meaning of the word 'use' in its statutory context, but also with the statutory purpose of protecting personal data from improper use (or disclosure). It is a startling fact that, if the construction urged upon your Lordships by the prosecution were correct, a police officer who idly operated the police computer, retrieving personal data onto the screen without putting it to any use, would not merely be subject to disciplinary action (where appropriate) but would be guilty of a criminal offence; whereas another police officer who learned from a colleague of certain information constituting personal data stored in the database of the police computer and then, knowing of its source, used the information for business purposes, would not. This surely cannot be the statutory intention; indeed if it were so, it could give rise to justifiable concern on the part of individuals who are the subject of personal data.

This is an extremely literal interpretation of the statue but, arguably, any suggestion that merely causing the information to be displayed on the screen is use of that information is, perhaps, to confuse the use of the data with the use of the database itself. By analogy, a telephone directory (a database) is 'used' to find a phone number and then one uses the information contained within it to make the phone call, illustrating, in agreement with Lord Goff, that the retrieval is not itself the use, but the pre-requisite to that use. However, a rather different interpretation was evident in the dissenting judgment of Lord Griffiths who looked, instead, at the purpose of the Act and the UK's obligations in ratifying the Council of Europe Convention.

***R v Brown* [1996] 2 WLR 203**
House of Lords

Lord Griffiths:

Whilst I have found this to be a difficult question I have come to the conclusion that 'use' should be given a broad construction as otherwise the purpose of the Act will not be achieved, there will be a serious lacuna in the protection it provides, and there will be difficulties in its enforcement.

The Act of 1984 was enacted to implement the obligations that this country accepted as a signatory to the Convention for the Protection of Individuals with regard to Automatic Processing of Personal Data (1981) (Cmnd 8341). The Act should therefore be construed so far as permissible to accord with the Convention.

Article 1 of the Convention sets out the object and purpose of the Convention in the following language:

> 'The purpose of this Convention is to secure in the territory of each party for every individual, whatever his nationality or residence, respect for his rights and fundamental freedoms, and in particular his right to privacy, with regard to automatic processing of personal data relating to him ("data protection").' (My emphasis.)

To read the personal data about an individual displayed on a computer screen or in a printout is an invasion of that person's privacy, if there is no legitimate purpose for doing so. I therefore prefer the construction that forbids the illegitimate display of personal data and this is achieved by giving a wide construction to use in section 5(2)(b) so that it covers not only applying the information in the data for an illegitimate purpose but also the invasion of privacy involved in the illegitimate display of the information.

It is not straining the meaning of language to say that a person is using the information stored in a computer if he informs himself of its contents. Whether or not he then goes on to apply the information for a particular purpose, and to use it in that sense, will depend on the value of the information to him: but whether or not he applies the information does not alter the fact that he has wrongly invaded the privacy of the individual, and now has the information available to apply at any time in the future.

Once information has entered the public domain it is impractical to attempt to place any restraints on its use or further dissemination. The Act therefore concentrates its protective provisions in section 5 upon the conduct of those who hold or have access to personal data, in an attempt to ensure that they do

> not abuse the data, and confine it to the proper purpose for which it is required.
>
> The purpose of the offences created by section 5 of the Act is clearly to protect the integrity and security of the data. A servant or agent of the holder of data is guilty of an offence if he uses data for any purpose not described in the register, if he discloses it to any person not described in the register, if he obtains it from a source not described in the register, and if he transfers it to a territory outside the United Kingdom not described in the register. So what would be the position of a police officer who deliberately falsified personal data held in the computer? He undoubtedly processed the data within the meaning of section 1(7); but if he was not 'using' the data by processing it he committed no offence. I cannot believe that in the Data Protection Act it was intended that wrongful interference with the data by those with access to it should not be an offence. But such is the result if 'use' is given the limited meaning adopted by the Court of Appeal.
>
> This police officer had no business to be reading the personal data on the police computer for debt-collecting purposes, and I see no hardship in adopting a construction of the section that creates an offence if he does so. If on the other hand an obligation is laid on the prosecution to prove not only that illegitimate access to the information in the computer was obtained, but also how that information was subsequently applied I can see great practical difficulties in the enforcement of the Act and the protection of personal data that the Convention and the Act intended to achieve.

This is a much more radical interpretation and, in concentrating on privacy aspects, Lord Griffiths was taking an unusual step for a UK court, especially as this case was not concerned with infringement of privacy *per se*. It will be interesting to see whether, as the EC Directive[63] is implemented, this approach becomes more influential in the future.

The case of *Brown* can be compared with another case involving a police officer, that of *McGregor v Procurator Fiscal of Kilmarnock*.[64] The neighbour of a police officer was concerned about the man with whom his 18 year old daughter was living and asked the police officer, McGregor, if he could find out any information for him. McGregor obtained certain information about the man in question from both the Police National computer and the Scottish Criminal records computer and communicated some of this to the daughter in a telephone call, with the intention of trying to persuade her to return to her father. He was found to have used the information for a purpose other than that for which registration had been made and appealed, on the basis that, as he was seeking to maintain law and order and was concerned for the girl's welfare, he had used the information for policing purposes. According to the terms of registration, policing purposes includes the protection of life and

63 See p 301, below.

64 22 June 1993, see March 1994 update of *Encyclopaedia of Data Protection* (1988) Sweet & Maxwell.

property, the maintenance of law and order and the rendering of assistance to the public. Whilst the court accepted that the McGregor's motives were undoubtedly humanitarian, his action was not for a policing purpose within the terms of the register and his appeal was dismissed. Clearly this decision is entirely compatible with the House of Lords judgment in *Brown* in that, in this case, something further had been done with the information once it had been retrieved from the computer.

EXEMPTIONS

In principle, the Data Protection Act 1984 applies to all data users, whether in the public or private sectors but, for some activities and purposes, Part IV of the Act contains exemptions from all or part of the provisions. Many of these were introduced in order to ameliorate the apparently heavy burden being placed on business and commerce by the new regulatory regime. An exemption may arise for a number of reasons. It may be that the activity is considered to raise no real issue of privacy such that subjecting the user to the full force of the provisions is considered unnecessarily onerous. Thus domestic use is exempted under s 33. At the other end of the spectrum, exemptions will apply where there are interests of national security (s 27) although it is left very much to the discretion of government departments as to when this should apply.

The extent of the exemptions[65] was criticised extensively during the lifetime of the first Bill and when the Bill was re-introduced the scope of some of the exemptions had been amended. In particular, there is no longer an exemption for immigration records which had been a feature of the first Bill and the introduction of s 1(8) has ensured that the use of computers purely for the preparation of text cannot be construed to be 'processing' within the meaning of s 1(7) – the so-called word-processing exemption. Exemptions from some or all of the data protection provisions now apply in connection with health and social work (s 29), regulation of financial services (s 30), judicial appointment and legal professional privilege (s 31), payroll and accounting purposes (s 32) and examination marks (s 33). Disclosure or publication of data may also be required by virtue of the application of other statutory provisions and exemptions will also apply in these cases (s 34).

65 See also late????? exemptions in the Data Protection Directive, p 311.

ASSESSMENT OF THE APPLICATION OF THE DATA PROTECTION ACT

After the passing of the 1984 Act, the Registrar began the publication of the first series of Guidelines designed to educate and inform data subjects and users alike about the new statute. Whilst pointing out that the Act established new legal rights for individuals it was also said that '[t]he Act does not seek to prevent data users using personal data for legitimate purposes providing that they are appropriately registered and they operate in accordance with the principles'. In that this was written soon after the Act was passed, it is illuminating in its attitude. One of the paramount concerns seemed to be to make it clear that the intention, at the time, was not to introduce unnecessary burdens on business, or to prevent the processing of personal data, provided that processing took place within the framework of the data user's registration. So far as the data subject is concerned, the protection given is clearly circumscribed by the fact that the extent and scope of registration itself is primarily determined by the data user. At registration, users must supply information related to the purpose for which the data will be held, the sources from which it is obtained and the persons to whom disclosure will be made. As these are specified by the data users themselves, the terms of the registration, subject to the Registrar's approval, are largely self-determined. As long as the subsequent processing of personal data takes place within the framework of the registration, as defined by the registration document, and within the terms of the data protection principles, then it is unlikely that an individual who nevertheless feels that his or her privacy has been compromised will have any recourse to law.

Thus the potential role of data protection in safeguarding privacy was sidelined at the inception of the legislation and an assessment of the extent to which it is able to perform this function has been further complicated by the multifaceted meaning of privacy. During the introduction of the first Data Protection Bill, Geoffrey Dickens MP considered three forms of privacy right:

> First we have what can be regarded as general rights, usually specified as protection from intrusion into domestic affairs and from surveillance, harassment, exposure and embarrassment. Secondly, there are specific legal rights which touch on privacy, such as those protected by the laws on confidence, defamation, trespass or contract. Thirdly, we have what are best described as procedural rights such as the duties governing the use of personal information, especially that required compulsorily by governments, banks, insurance companies, credit card agencies ...

Data protection was identified as falling within the third category, immediately suggesting that its capacity to protect privacy in the wider sense will be limited. It is also not always apparent, in any analysis of the application and function of the Act, in which sense the term privacy is being used. The Lindop report, in common with many other writers in the field referred to the following definition of Westin[66] that '[p]rivacy is the claim of individuals, groups or institutions to determine for themselves when, how and to what extent information about them is communicated to others ...' and also that of Miller,[67] namely, 'the individual's ability to control the circulation of information relating to him'. Westin's definition, in particular, is based on the right of self-determination that may be placed at particular risk by the practice of data matching made so simple by modern information technology.[68]

When applying any definitions of privacy to issues of data protection, one again encounters the dichotomy between personal information and personal data and the related issue of who is entitled to exert control over each category. It is possible to consider that personal information should be under the control of the person to whom it refers whereas, it may be claimed that, insofar as personal data arises from information which may have been recorded and/or processed in a particular way, the data user should be able to exert rights over the use of such data. Thus, competing interests although often a reflection of the conflict between the individual and the state, may equally well refer to a balancing of the right of individuals to privacy and control over the use of their own information with the right of other individuals or organisations to use that same information, which they may have compiled and processed, to the best commercial effect.

Whilst in upholding a general right to privacy, civil libertarians might tip this balance in favour of the right of individuals to control data concerning themselves, this may not be an automatic or obvious result.

Yves Poullet, 'Data Protection between Property and Liberties' in *Among Friends in Computers and Law* (1990) Kaspersen and Oskamp (eds), Kluwer

The individual is not the owner of data that concerns him, not even the bearer towards it of a right close to a real right. An individual projects a certain image of himself spontaneously upon society, which image may be precisely captured by another. Coupled with other information, it then takes shape in the eyes of the person who is processing it. There can be no question of *a priori* denying to another the use of an image of me which I myself have given him. My liberty is opposed to his, which is that of freedom of association within the framework of data systems operated by a union, of religious liberty in the framework of processing undertaken by a religious authority, or more frequently, the liberty to do business in the case of companies. This conflict should resolve itself by the balance of interests method, by which the authority

66 Alan F Westin, *Privacy and Freedom* (1967) Bodley Head.

67 Arthur R Miller, *The Assault on Privacy: Computers, Databanks and Dossiers* (1971) University of Michigan Press.

68 See also,Yves Poullet, 'Data Protection between Property and Liberties' in *Amongst Friends in Computers and Law* (1990) HWK Kaspersen and A Oskamp (eds), Kluwer Law and Taxation.

> charged with deciding the conflict takes into account the respective legitimate interests expressing the liberty of each party.
>
> ... a number of legislative rulings foresee an exception for certain data or certain types of processing. Thus it is easy to justify that legislation should forbid the processing of philosophical, trade union or religious data, because, *a priori*, the processing of such data imperils my religious, political or philosophical liberty. With reference to the same data, the same legislations exempt precisely such religious associations, trade unions and the press from this very prohibition, which can be explained as the desire to affirm the freedom of association and the freedom of the press above individual liberties. As we can observe from these limited examples, recording of the same nominative data my be limited, regulated or free, according to the liberties put into question by its being recorded. There is certainly a debate between liberties and the necessity of appreciating, with regard to the interests of society, the weight accorded to each of them.
>
> Particularly in the context of the freedom of the holder of the file to do business, beyond the limits imposed with regard to certain data which characterise, in an immediate way, such recognised constitutional liberties as freedom of opinion, of religion or association, may we admit that legislation, in defining the file holder's right to information also defines the limit of that right? Should not the principle of the holder of the file's right to collect data be affirmed as such, even if, *a posteriori*, certain abuses must be decided *in casu* by the judge? In other words, should data protection legislation intervene in the private sector other than by providing for the right of access ... should it rule on the contents and limits of private processing?

This raises the issue, not only of the control of processing of personal information, as such, but also of the nature of the personal data which is being processed. The conflict over who has the right of control over personal data reaches its height in relation to so-called 'sensitive data'. This is precisely the type of information which is likely to fall within the boundaries referred to by Wacks, who refers to those facts, communications or opinions which it would be reasonable to expect an individual to regard as intimate or sensitive.[69]

In this respect, the Council of Europe Convention recognised that, whilst the potential harm resulting from processing personal data may depend more on context than contents, the risk of damage will undoubtedly increase in respect of certain categories of information. Thus Article 6 in acknowledging the existence of 'special categories of data' provides that '[p]ersonal data revealing racial origin, political opinions or religious or other beliefs, as well as personal data concerning health or sexual life, may not be processed automatically unless domestic law provides appropriate safeguards ...'. However, no guidance was given as to what appropriate safeguards might include. This provision of the Convention was acknowledged in the White

69 Raymond Wacks, *Personal Information: Privacy and the Law* (1993), p 26, Clarendon: see earlier discussion at p **.

Paper preceding the Data Protection Act and a general power to make regulations under the Act was included on the basis that '[t]he power to make regulations will be needed to deal, amongst other things, with the processing of categories of data where it is not sufficient to rely on the general principles alone ...'. Again, there was no suggestion as to the situations in which this might occur. Why should sensitive data be treated differently? Some of the characteristics referred to in this category are open for all to see, such as race, ethnic origin and even religion in some cases. In some cases, these attributes may also be revealed merely by a person's name. Ardent trade unionists and political activists may not wish to hide their allegiances. It may be that such data should be protected less for reasons of privacy than fear of arbitrary discrimination. Whatever protection is required there has been remarkably little debate on this issue in the UK, in contrast to that in some other jurisdictions.[70] When the second reading of the Bill was introduced to the House, Leon Britton merely noted that:[71] '... it is remarkably difficult to separate personal information into sensitive and non-sensitive categories. Sensitivity is a subjective concept. What is mundane to one person may be highly private to another'.

As yet, no regulations have been made under the power given in the Act and, in UK law, the same provisions apply to all types of personal data. Aside from the lack of protection afforded to individual privacy, it is questionable whether the law as it stands complies with the Council of Europe Convention, especially as the data subject has no right to prevent the processing of their personal data provided that the data user adheres to the provisions of the Data Protection Act 1984. This situation may be forced to change as the EC Directive on data protection is implemented.[72]

The ability of the Data Protection Act to protect individual privacy is further restricted by the fact that the Act does not apply to manual records. Notwithstanding the long title of the Council of Europe Convention – 'for the protection of the individual with regard to automatic processing of data' – which demonstrates the paramount concern of the Convention, provision is made for the extension of protection to records held manually. Article 3(2) allows that '[a]ny State may ... give notice ... that it will also apply this convention to personal data files which are not processed automatically'.

Unlike the problem of sensitive data, the question of the application of the Act to manual records was aired much more extensively during the Bill's passage through Parliament. Although, it was accepted that personal data kept in manual records could equally pose a threat to privacy, the view was that this paled into insignificance in comparison with the threat posed by

70 See, eg, M Stallworthy *Data Protection: Regulation in a Deregulatory State* [1990] Statute Law Review 130.

71 HC Debates (Hansard) 30 January 1984, col 33.

72 See p 301, below.

computers. The massive administrative and bureaucratic burden which would be imposed if the scope of the Act were to be extended in this way could not be justified. Although this provoked criticism from certain quarters at the time of enactment, it was, nevertheless, in line with the emergent legislation on data protection in a number of other jurisdictions.

Given that the application of the 1984 Act is confined to material stored on computer, it is difficult to view it as human rights legislation rather than a new regulatory regime for business made necessary by the nature of computers and instigated to redress the imbalance between data user and data subject which might occur otherwise. In the words of Burkett,[73] '[d]ata protection legislation seeks to introduce normatively what information technology has taken away technologically'. These flaws in the legislation, if it is to be taken seriously as privacy legislation, have been noted by the Registrar's Office; in 1994, Rosemary Jay, legal advisor in the Office of the Data Protection Registrar suggested[74] that the Act was a 'rather tentative effort to address the emergent issues of information use ... arbitrarily confined to computerised information' and which 'failed to deal adequately with the concept of individual rights in information ...'. She concluded, therefore, that '... we are a long way from achieving a reconciliation of the competing interests which exist in this area'. It is interesting to note that, even before these comments, the Data Protection Act 1984 had come to be regarded by the Office of the Registrar much more as privacy legislation, in intent and philosophy, if not in practice, than merely business regulation: 'Data protection is a human rights matter rather than any question of the technical regulation of computers.'[75]

DATA PROTECTION DIRECTIVE: DIRECTIVE 95/46/EC OF THE EUROPEAN PARLIAMENT AND OF THE COUNCIL

Of those European states that have legislation on data protection the majority provide similar protection, in essence, because of its origins in the Council of Europe Convention. Nevertheless, it was perceived by the European Community that the discrepancies between different jurisdictions were sufficient to warrant further harmonisation between the Member States. In addition, despite the Convention, by the end of the 1980s, some Member States still had no appropriate legislation and a further concern was that any

73 Comparing data protection legislation with general access legislation in H Burkett, 'Data Protection and Access to Data' in *From Data Protection to Knowledge Machines. The Study of Law and Information* (1990), P Seipel (ed), Kluwer.

74 *Data Protection: A Current Perspective* Lecture given at Hull University 7 March 1994 text available at http://www.hull.ac.uk/Hull/Law_Web/complaw/dplect.html.

75 9th Report of the Data Protection Registrar HMSO 1993.

differences in the protection afforded to data in each Member State might lead to restrictions on transborder data flow from those countries with a higher level of protection. This would obviously impede the functioning of the internal market, a crucial factor in the wake of the date of 31 December 1991 set by the Single European Act for the completion of the Single European Market. Accordingly, in 1990, a proposal for a Directive on the protection of individuals with regard to the processing of personal data and on the free movement of such data was published.[76]

The foregoing might suggest that a primary reason was business efficacy and the facilitation of free movement of data, but the competing interests endemic in this area are strongly represented in the preamble to the original proposal which refers, not only to transborder data flows but also the importance of protecting the right of privacy. Although the European Union has no Bill of Rights, as such, the European Court of Justice has, on many occasions, taken the opportunity to point out that Community law protects fundamental rights, and has looked both to the constitutions of the Member States and the European Convention on Human Rights for guidance. It is thus entirely in accordance with this tradition that this Directive should seek to protect privacy. In the event, the final version was to be a long time in gestation – one problem was to devise legislation which would both ensure a high level of protection and yet not compromise that already in place in some Member States. In view of the different interpretations put on the various concepts in the different jurisdictions, the Economic and Social Committee were particularly concerned as to whether the proposal actually increased the level of protection or merely accentuated the differences between Member States. An amended proposal was published in 1992[77] but, although this was debated by the European Parliament and approved subject to amendments,[78] forward progress then seemed to come to a halt. Action was eventually precipitated by activity in a related area, namely the Recommendations to the European Council from the High Level Group on the Information Society (the 'Bangemann Report'). This report initiated by the European Council in December 1993 and produced for the Corfu Summit in 1994 looked at all facets of the so-called Information Society. Chapter 3 of the Bangemann Report 'Completing the Agenda' contains reference to those provisions which will need to be taken into account if the full benefit of the new era is to be realised without any risk of consequent damage and disadvantage. These include, *inter alia*, a consideration of privacy issues.

> The demand for the protection of privacy will rightly increase as the potential of the new technologies to secure (even across national frontiers) and to manipulate detailed information on individuals from data, voice and image

76 COM (90) 314 final – SYN 287 [1990] OJ C 277/3.

77 COM (92) 422 final – SYN 287 [1992] OJ C 311/30.

78 [1992] OJ C 94/198.

> sources is realised. Without the legal security of a Union-wide approach, lack of consumer confidence will certainly undermine rapid development of the information society.
>
> Europe leads the world in the protection of the fundamental rights of the individual with regard to personal data processing. The application of new technologies potentially affects highly sensitive areas such as those dealing with the images of individuals, their communication, their movements and their behaviour. With this in mind, it is quite possible that most Member States will react to these developments by adopting protection, including trans-frontier control of new technologies and services.
>
> Disparities in the level of protection of such privacy rules create the risk that national authorities might restrict free circulation of a wide range of new services between Member States in order to protect personal data.
>
> The Group believes that without the legal security of a Union-wide approach, lack of consumer confidence will certainly undermine the rapid development of the information society. Given the importance and sensitivity of the privacy issue, a fast decision from Member States is required on the Commission's proposed Directive setting out general principles of data protection.

This recommendation, from such an eminent source, proved the necessary boost to revive the proposed Directive. In the period between the original proposal and the Bangemann report, new legislative procedures had been adopted following the Treaty on European Union and the proposed Directive had become subject to the co-decision procedure under the new Article 189b EC. In pursuance of this process, the Council adopted a common position early in 1995[79] and, following the decision of the Parliament,[80] the final Directive was published in October 1995.[81] The adopted Directive was a much amended and augmented version of the original 1990 proposal and contains a total of 72 recitals in the preamble. However, it is an indication of the general agreement between Parliament and the Council on this issue that the final text exhibits only very minor changes from that of the common position.

COMPARISON OF THE DIRECTIVE AND THE DATA PROTECTION ACT

Given that both the 1984 Act and the recent Directive are grounded in and influenced by the Council of Europe Convention, it is not at all surprising that, on the whole, their provisions appear similar. Nonetheless, there are a number of important points of distinction. Firstly and fundamentally, the Directive

79 [1995] OJ C 93/1.

80 [1995] OJ C 166/80 and 105.

81 Directive 95/46/EC of the European Parliament and of the Council of 24 October 1995 on the protection of individuals with regard to the processing of personal data and on the free movement of such data [1995] L 281/31.

refers to the protection of privacy, signalling that, even though limited, data protection is part of the fundamental right of privacy.

Article 1 Object of the Directive

1. In accordance with this Directive, Member States shall protect the fundamental rights and freedoms of natural persons, and in particular, their right to privacy with respect to the processing of personal data.

In view of this object, the Directive, unlike the Act, is not confined to automatic processing.

Article 3 Scope

1. This Directive shall apply to the processing of personal data wholly or partly by automatic means, and to the processing otherwise than by automatic means of personal data which form part of a filing system or are intended to form part of a filing system.

and

Article 2 Definitions

(c) 'personal data filing system' ('filing system') shall mean any structured set of personal data which are accessible according to specific criteria, whether centralised, decentralised or dispersed on a functional or geographic basis;

Thus so-called 'manual data' are included within the ambit of the Directive, closing the gap which omission of this category of records created in the protection of individuals under the Data Protection Act 1984. There are limits to the application of the Directive to manual data as can be inferred from the definition above and from recital 27:

> ... as regards manual processing, this Directive covers only filing systems, not unstructured files; whereas, in particular, the content of a filing system must be structured according to specific criteria relating to individuals allowing easy access to personal data; whereas in line with the definition in Article 2(c), the different criteria for determining the constituents of a structured set of personal data, and the different criteria governing access to such a set, maybe laid down by each Member State; whereas files or sets of files as well as their cover pages, which are not structured according to specific criteria, shall under no circumstances fall within the scope of this Directive.

The UK expressed some disquiet over the inclusion of manual records in this way, and a derogation was negotiated allowing manual records which predated the Directive a period of 12 years before compliance by Member States was required, subject to the provision that if they were subjected to further manual processing in the interim, they should be brought into conformity at that time (Article 32(2) and recital 69).

The Directive does not apply to the processing of data outside the scope of Community competence.

Article 3 Scope

2. This Directive shall not apply to the processing of personal data:

in the course of an activity which falls outside the scope of Community law, such as those provided for by Titles V and VI of the Treaty on European Union and in any case to processing operations concerning public security, defence, state security (including the economic well-being of the state when the processing operation relates to state security matters) and the activities of the state in areas of criminal law.

There has been some debate over what is intended to be encompassed by this requirement. Presumably it includes all areas of economic and business activity which the Community has competence to regulate. The Data Protection Act includes exemptions from its requirements for certain of the areas referred to above, eg s 27 in relation to national security. In relation to others the exemption is only partial, eg data relating to crime are exempted from the subject access provisions. The Directive refers to the 'activities of the state' – it is clear that there is not a general prohibition on the processing of records relating to crime since this is further governed by Article 8(5) referring to sensitive data.[82]

Article 8 makes provision for all types of sensitive data. As has already been discussed, no regulations regarding sensitive data have been made under the power given to the Secretary of State under the Data Protection Act 1984. The Directive, however, places a general prohibition on the processing of such data.

Article 8 The processing of special categories of data

1. Member States shall prohibit the processing of personal data revealing racial or ethnic origin, political opinions, religious of philosophical beliefs, trade-union membership, and the processing of data concerning health or sex life.

Subsequent paragraphs of Article 8 provide for certain occasions when such processing will be allowed subject to appropriate safeguards, eg in relation to employment (Article 8(2)(b)). Some of these are susceptible to a number of interpretations eg:

Article 8(2) Paragraph 1 shall not apply where:

(c) processing is necessary to protect the vital interests of the data subject or to another person where the data subject is physically or legally incapable of giving his consent; ...

(e) the processing relates to data which are manifestly made public by the data subject or is necessary for the establishment, exercise or defence of legal claims.

82 In this context there may be potential for conflict with the government's proposals for access to criminal records for employment and related purposes. See the White Paper *On the Record* Cmnd 3308 HMSO 1996 and Appendix 2 10th Report of the Data Protection Registrar 1995.

Clearly there is room for debate over the precise meaning of the terms 'vital interest' and 'manifestly made public'. However, a more general exception to the ban on processing sensitive data is contained in:

Article 8(2) Paragraph 1 shall not apply where:

(a) the data subject has given his explicit consent to the processing of those data, except where the laws of the Member State provide that the prohibition referred to in paragraph 1 may not be lifted by the data subject's giving his consent.

Article 7 provides the general standard for lawful processing of non-sensitive personal data.

Article 7 Criteria for making data processing legitimate

Member States shall provide that personal data may be processed only if:

(a) the data subject has unambiguously given his consent; or

(b) processing is necessary for the performance of a contract to which the data subject is party or in order to take steps at the request of the data subject prior to entering into a contract; or

(c) processing is necessary for compliance with a legal obligation to which the controller is subject; or

(d) processing is necessary in order to protect the vital interests of the data subject; or

(e) processing is necessary for the performance of a task carried out in the public interest or in the exercise of official authority vested in the controller or in a third party to whom the data are disclosed; or

(f) processing is necessary for the purpose of the legitimate interests pursued by the controller …

Thus where none of (b)–(f) apply, as in list rental for instance, the consent required from the data subject must be 'unambiguous', in contrast to the 'explicit' consent needed to process sensitive data. Clearly, if consent is to be construed as unambiguous then there must be no room for doubt, but explicit consent suggests a higher standard of proof in which the consent is distinctly stated and cannot be implied, however unequivocal the implication. Even for non-sensitive data, the standard expected under the Data Protection Act is not one of unambiguous consent but is related to the absence of objection in the presence of notice of intended processing.[83] It seems that the Directive may require more positive action to legitimise processing of personal data, so that the presumption is changed, from one in which further processing is permitted unless a contrary indication is notified, to one in which it is not unless there is definite evidence of consent.

83 See Case DA/92 31/49/1 *Innovations (Mail Order) Limited v Data Protection Registrar* and Case DA/94 31/49/1 *Linguaphone Institute Ltd v Data Protection Registrar*, see p 276.

Data protection principles

In common with the Data Protection Act 1984, the Directive lays down principles of good data management. The Directive apparently replaces the eight of the Act with five, but matters such as subject access and security, for instance, which are referred to in the data protection principles in the Act, are dealt with elsewhere in the Directive.

Article 6 Principles relating to data quality

1. Member States shall provide that personal data must be:
   (a) processed fairly and lawfully;
   (b) collected for specified, explicit and legitimate purposes and not further processed in a way incompatible with those purposes. Further processing of data for historical, statistical or scientific purposes shall not be considered as incompatible provided that Member States provide appropriate safeguards;
   (c) adequate, relevant and not excessive in relation to the purposes for which they are collected and/or further processed;
   (d) accurate, and where necessary, kept up to date; every reasonable step must be taken to ensure that data which are inaccurate or incomplete, having regard to the purposes for which they were collected or for which they are further processed, are erased or rectified;
   (e) kept in a form which permits identification of data subjects for no longer than is necessary for the purposes for which the data were collected or for which they are further processed. Member States shall lay down appropriate safeguards for personal data stored for longer periods for historical, statistical or scientific use.

The first principle set out in Article 6(1)(a) is, in fact, more extensive than that of the first principle in the Data Protection Act 1984 as a consequence of the wider definition of 'processing' contained in the Directive.

Article 2 Definitions

(b) 'processing of personal data' ('processing') shall mean any operation or set of operations which is performed upon personal data, whether or not by automatic means, such as collection, recording, organisation, storage, adaptation or alteration, retrieval, consultation, use, disclosure by transmission, dissemination or otherwise making available, alignment or combination, blocking, erasure or destruction.

The Directive distinguishes between the 'controller' and the 'processor' of data, the latter being merely one who processes data on behalf of the controller. The 'controller' is the one (whether alone or jointly with others) who 'determines the purposes and means of processing personal data'. All controllers of personal data in the areas covered by the Directive will be required to adhere to the principles,[84] even if they are subject to exemption from notification.[85] This is in contrast to the Act where registration is a prerequisite for the need for compliance.

Rights of data subjects

It is in defining the scope of individual rights that there is, perhaps, greater divergence from the provisions of the 1984 Act. The Directive commences by referring, expressly, to the right of privacy in relation to the processing of personal data, which is then amplified by the more detailed rights set out in Chapters IV, V and VII. The scope of some of the rights, also provided by the Data Protection Act, may be broader under the Directive because of the wider definition of processing and the inclusion of manual records, for example. On the other hand, as the Directive only applies to areas within Community competence, this may lead to a diminution of rights in other areas. The rights set down in the Directive can be divided, loosely, into the right of access, the right to information and the right to object. These are then reinforced and supplemented by provisions relating to compensation and judicial remedies.

INFORMATION TO BE GIVEN TO THE DATA SUBJECT

Article 10 Information in cases of collection of data from the data subject

Member States shall provide that the controller or his representative must provide a data subject from whom data relating to himself are collected with at least the following information, except where he already has it:

(a) the identity of the controller and of his representative, if any;

(b) the purposes of the processing for which the data are intended;

(c) any further information such as

- the recipients or categories of recipients of the data;
- whether replies to the questions are obligatory or voluntary, as well as the possible consequences of failure to reply;
- the existence of the right of a access to and the right to rectify the data concerning him.

in so far as such further information is necessary, having regard to the specific circumstances in which the data are collected, to guarantee fair processing in respect of the data subject.

Article 11 Information where the data have not been obtained from the data subject

1. Where the data have not been obtained from the data subject, Member States shall provide that the controller or his representative must at the time of undertaking the recording of personal data or if a disclosure to a

84 See also Recital 51 of Directive 95/46/EC.

85 See p 311, below.

third party is envisaged, no later than the time when the data are first disclosed provide the data subject with at least the following information, except where he already has it:

(a) the identity of the controller and of his representative, if any;

(b) the purposes of the processing;

(c) any further information such as

- the categories of data concerned,
- the recipients or categories of recipients,
- the existence of the right of access to and the right to rectify the data concerning him

in so far as such further information is necessary, having regard to the specific circumstances in which the data are processed, to guarantee fair processing in respect of the data subject.

2. Paragraph 1 shall not apply where, in particular for processing for statistical purposes or for the purposes of historical or scientific research, the provision of such information proves impossible or would involve a disproportionate effort or if recording or disclosure is expressly laid down by law. In these cases Member States shall provide appropriate safeguards.

THE DATA SUBJECT'S RIGHT OF ACCESS TO DATA

Article 12 Right of access

Member States shall guarantee every data subject the right to obtain from the controller:

(a) without constraint at reasonable intervals and without excessive delay or expense:

- confirmation as to whether or not data relating to him are being processed and information at least as to the purposes of the processing, the categories of data concerned, and the recipients or categories of recipients to whom the data are disclosed,
- communication to him in an intelligible form of the data undergoing processing and of any available information as to their source,
- knowledge of the logic involved in any automatic processing of data concerning him at least in the case of the automated decisions referred to in Article 15(1);

(b) as appropriate the rectification, erasure or blocking of data the processing of which does not comply with the provisions of this Directive, in particular because of the incomplete or inaccurate nature of the data;

(c) notification to third parties to whom the data have been disclosed of any rectification, erasure or blocking carried out in compliance with (b), unless this proves impossible or involves a disproportionate effort.

DATA SUBJECT'S RIGHT TO OBJECT

Article 14 The data subject's right to object

Member States shall grant the data subject the right:

(a) at least in the cases referred to in Article 7(e) and (f), to object at any time on compelling legitimate grounds relating to his particular situation to the processing of data relating to him, save where otherwise provided by national legislation. Where there is a justified objection, the processing instigated by the controller may no longer involve those data;

(b) to object, on request and free of charge, to the processing of personal data relating to him which the controller anticipates being processed for the purposes of direct marketing, or to be informed before personal data are disclosed for the first time to third parties or used on their behalf for the purposes of direct marketing, and to be expressly offered the right to object free of charge to such disclosures or uses.

Member States shall take the necessary measures to ensure that data subjects are aware of the existence of the right referred to in the first subparagraph of (b).

Article 15 Automated individual decisions

1. Member States shall grant the right to every person not to be subject to a decision which produces legal effects concerning him or significantly affects him and which is based solely on automated processing of data intended to evaluate certain personal aspects relating to him, such as his performance at work, creditworthiness, reliability, conduct, etc.
2. Subject to the other Articles of this Directive, Member States shall provide that a person may be subjected to a decision of the kind referred to in paragraph 1 if that decision:
   (a) is taken in the course of the entering into or performance of a contract, provided the request for the entering into or the performance of the contract, lodged by the data subject, has been satisfied or that there are suitable measures to safeguard his legitimate interests, such as arrangements allowing him to put his point of view; or
   (b) is authorised by a law which also lays down measures to safeguard the data subject's legitimate interests.

Assuming that processing is carried out within the terms of the Data Protection Principles, the 1984 Act provides no right to object, as such. The Directive, in contrast, provides such a right in the two situations described in Article 14, although these are somewhat limited in scope. Article 14(a) refers to processing in connection with the exercise of official authority vested in the controller, tasks carried out in the public interest or the purposes of the legitimate interests pursued by the controller. In this case it is possible for this right to be overridden by national legislation. The right to object to the use of personal data for direct marketing, contained in Article 14(b) would, arguably, arise from a combination of other provisions, such as the need for unambiguous consent and the principle of fair processing but, in view of the depth of feeling on this matter, an expressly stated right is welcome.

Notification

The Directive replaces the concept of registration with one of notification. Registration under the Data Protection Act concentrates on the purpose of processing, so that, even where a user is registered, contraventions may arise if data are processed for purposes outside the terms of the registration.[86] In contrast, the requirement of notification contained in the Directive focuses on the fact of processing, which, it will be remembered, is broadly defined, although this will necessarily include a consideration of the purpose of that processing.

Article 18 Obligation to notify the supervisory authority

1. Member States shall provide that the controller or his representative, if any, must notify the supervisory authority ... before carrying out any wholly or partly automatic processing operation or set of such operations intended to serve a single purpose or several related purposes.

Article 19 Contents of notification

1. Member States shall specify the information to be given in the notification. It shall include at least:
   (a) the name and address of the controller and of his representative, if any;
   (b) the purpose or purposes of processing;
   (c) a description of the category or categories of the data subject and of the data or categories of data relating to them;
   (d) the recipients or categories of recipient to whom the data might be disclosed;
   (e) proposed transfers of data to third countries;
   (f) a general description allowing a preliminary assessment to be made of the appropriateness of the measures taken ... to ensure security of processing.

It is open to Member States to simplify the notification process or exempt from notification in certain circumstances specified in further parts of Article 18, or to extend any aspects of the notification process to non-automatic processing operations (Article 18(5)).

Exemptions

The Council of Europe Convention allows exemptions from data protection provisions, where such exemptions are deemed necessary in a democratic society to protect certain interests of the state, the protection of the data subject or the rights and freedoms of others. It appears that the exemptions provided in the Directive are capable of a wider construction than those of the Convention.

86 See eg, *McGregor v Procurator Fiscal of Kilmarnock* discussed at p 295.

Article 13 Exemptions and restrictions

1. Member States may adopt legislative measures to restrict the scope of the obligations and rights provided ... when such a restriction constitutes a necessary measure to safeguard:

   (a) national security;

   (b) defence;

   (c) public security;

   (d) the prevention, investigation, detection and prosecution of criminal offences, or of breaches of ethics for regulated professions;

   (e) an important economic or financial interest of a Member State or of the European Union, including monetary, budgetary and taxation matters;

   (f) a monitoring, inspection or regulatory function connected, even occasionally, with the exercise of official authority in cases referred to in (c), (d), and (e);

   (g) the protection of the data subject or of the rights and freedoms of others.

Some of the reasoning behind allowing exemptions was discussed by the Registrar in 'Questions to Answer: Paper 9 – The Exemptions'.

> ... exemptions should only be permitted in limited circumstances. Broadly, these are the circumstances where achieving the 'right' balance of interests requires the data protection rule to be disapplied. What is meant by the 'right' balance will vary according to the particular circumstances ... it may be that the balance, for example, favours the public interest whereas in others it favours the individual data subject or another individual ... the balance may require safeguarding the privacy of third parties at the expense of individuals' subject access rights by removing information identifying third parties when responding to a subject access request. What is meant by the 'rule' will also vary. It may, for example, be withholding information in response to a subject access request where provision of the information would be likely to prejudice the prevention of detection of crime in that particular case: a very narrow exemption applying to only one area of data protection regulation.

As well as the exemptions expressly referred to in Article 13, there are other limitations on the application of the Directive, such as the permissible derogations from the obligation to notify, referred to above. The provisions of the Directive are not to be applied to processing for exclusively domestic and personal reasons (Recital 12 and Article 3(2)), and the fact that the Directive only applies to areas within Community competence will, inevitably, exempt certain other categories of processing. It also appears, from Recital 29 and Article 6(1)(e), that the exemption currently provided, in relation to length of time, for storage of personal data used for historical and statistical purposes can continue. A further exemption is contained in Article 9.

Article 9 Processing of personal data and freedom of expression

Member States shall provide for exemptions or derogations ... for the processing of personal data carried out solely for journalistic purposes or the purpose of artistic or literary expression only if they are necessary to reconcile the right to privacy with the rules governing the freedom of expression.

Where the protection of one fundamental right may impinge on the enjoyment of another right, the problem of achieving a satisfactory balance is never amenable to easy solution. The Directive leaves it to Member States to achieve an appropriate balance in this context. The Data Protection Act contains no parallel provision to Article 9, although processing purely for the creation of text is excluded from its application. Thus, there is no general exemption in relation to journalism, and the potential scope of such an exemption may prove to be a contentious issue which needs to be viewed within the wider debate of press freedom and privacy.[87]

Transborder data flows

In the discussion of individual rights, it must not be forgotten that the Directive, in common with other data protection regulation, has the dual objective of both safeguarding privacy in relation to processing of personal data and facilitating transborder data flow.

Article 1 Object of the Directive

2. Member States shall neither restrict nor prohibit the free flow of personal data between Member States for reasons connected with the protection afforded under paragraph 1 [the right of privacy with respect to the processing of personal data].

The importance of the free flow of such data is further underlined by the first sentence of Recital 56 'Whereas cross-border flows of personal data are necessary for the expansion of international trade'. Thus there are no grounds for restricting the free flow of data provided the appropriate safeguards are in place. Indeed, it is the very necessity referred to in Recital 56 which makes protection of the individual so vital.

TRANSFER OF DATA TO THIRD COUNTRIES

Article 25 Principles

1. The Member States shall provide that the transfer to a third country of personal data which are undergoing processing or are intended for processing after transfer may take place only if, without prejudice to compliance with the national provisions adopted pursuant to the other

87 See, eg, *Review of Press Regulation* Cmnd 2135 HMSO 1993, *Infringement of Privacy* Consultation Paper of the Lord Chancellor's Department, The Scottish Office 1993, Raymond Wacks, *Privacy and Press Freedom* (1995) Blackstone Press.

provisions of this Directive, the third country in question ensures an adequate level of protection.

2. The adequacy of the level of protection afforded by a third country shall be assessed in the light of all the circumstances surrounding a data transfer operation or set of data transfer operations; particular consideration shall be given to the nature of the data, the purpose and duration of the proposed processing operation or operations, the country of origin and country of final destination, the rules of law, both general and sectoral, in force in the third country in question and the professional rules and security measures which are complied with in that country.
3. The Member States and the Commission shall inform each other of cases where they consider that a third country does not ensure an adequate level of protection ...
4. Where the Commission finds ... that a third country does not ensure an adequate level of protection ... Member States shall take the measures necessary to prevent any transfer of data of the same type to the third country in question.

These are detailed rules but derogations are provided in Article 26 based primarily on the data subject's consent, the data subject's interest or where transfer is from publicly available registers or documents. Given the nature and content of transborder data flow, it seems unlikely, therefore, that there will be many occasions on which the flow of personal data across borders will be restricted under Article 25.

IMPLEMENTATION IN THE UK

The Directive has to be implemented by 24 October 1998. In anticipation of the implementation of the Directive, the Registrar has already considered possible changes to the registration requirements,[88] whereas the previous government had begun a review of the enforcement powers of the Registrar as a consequence of s 5 of the Deregulation and Contracting Out Act 1994 which allows orders to be made modifying enforcement procedures in situations where regulatory provisions are deemed to create an excessive burden on business. It has been suggested that the need for implementation provides the perfect opportunity for a reassessment and reappraisal of the enforcement regime provided under the Data Protection Act 1984.

Questions to Answer: Paper 1 Introduction

... this opportunity to introduce substantial new data protection legislation for the first time in over 12 years should not be used simply as the occasion to apply the Directive to UK law but that a proper examination should be made of the ways in which the current law could be improved irrespective of the

88 See 11th Report of the Data Protection Registrar HMSO 1995.

> Directive ... An opportunity exists to look at the total enforcement package contained in the 1984 Act. Should individuals be left to enforce their rights independently in the courts? To what extent is the criminal law required to secure compliance with data protection rules? Ought the Registrar to carry out audit inspections? Can the Registrar carry out her enforcement functions without more formal investigatory powers? Could enforcement follow the consumer protection model – enforced by local authorities and supervised by a national supervisory authority?

The extent to which the implementation may or may not produce radical change is likely to depend on the form of the implementing measure or measures and, in particular, whether this is effected by primary or secondary legislation.

The current Registrar has made out the case for implementation via primary legislation.[89] One important reason advanced is the need for consistency. The fact that the Directive only applies to areas within Community competence suggests that those areas outside the sphere of legislative activity by the EC would continue to be regulated by the 1984 Act. Operating both regimes in tandem could be both cumbersome and confusing. Primary legislation could instead simplify and streamline the present bureaucracy. Further, the Registrar also suggests that, in view of the express reference to the right of privacy in respect of the processing of personal data, referred to in Article 1(1), such a fundamental change for the UK 'warrants the full consideration which its incorporation through primary legislation would give'. Implementing the Directive in a coherent way would enable the regulatory burden on the user to be reduced. On the other hand, the previous government was of the view that:[90] '[o]ver-elaborate data protection threatens competitiveness and does not necessarily bring additional benefits for individuals'. However, the Queen's speech following the election of the new government in May 1997 contained a proposal for a data protection Bill. It now appears therefore, that the apparent conflict between calls for new primary legislation and proposals for minimal changes may no longer be an issue.

FURTHER ASPECTS OF DATA PROTECTION

With data protection as with other aspects of computer law, there is continual discussion as to whether the law is sufficiently flexible to keep pace with technological change. This has been reflected in successive Reports of the Data

89 See *Questions to answer: Paper 1 Appendix 1 and Consultation Paper on the EC Data Protection Directive (95/46/EC): Response of the Data Protection Registrar.*

90 *Consultation Paper on the EC Data Protection Directive* (95/46/EC) Home Office 1996.

Protection Registrar which include assessments as to how the existing regime might be applied to technological advances.[91] The need to keep abreast of developments is also referred to in Recital 14 of the preamble to Directive 95/46/EC: 'Whereas, given the importance of the developments under way, in the framework of the information society, of the techniques used to capture, transmit, manipulate, record, store or communicate sound and image data relating to natural persons, this Directive should be applicable to processing involving such data.' This reflects the fact that advances in the technology have now made it possible not only for personal data, as such, to be transmitted, manipulated and processed, but also visual and audio material. One major advance during the lifetime of the Data Protection Act 1984, which is also capable of including these features, is the growth in the size and volume of traffic on the Internet; the global network. The original fears expressed about the potential for the abuse of personal data were based on the existence of separate computer networks, a fraction of the size of the Internet. Although quantification of such matters cannot be exact, it is presumed that the magnitude of the risk is likely to increase supralinearly with the size of the network.

ELEVENTH REPORT OF THE DATA PROTECTION REGISTRAR 1995[92]
APPENDIX 6

Data Protection and the Internet

... perhaps the most important thing to understand about the Internet is that its whole purpose is to facilitate the exchange of information. It grew up in an academic and research environment where the ready and open exchange of information is the norm, indeed is the lifeblood. It is an open environment; it exists to publicise information; it encourages browsing.

Today, commercial traffic on the Internet exceeds academic traffic, but the intrinsically insecure nature of the Internet environment has not changed. Protecting information runs counter to the culture. Furthermore, the features which make the Internet so attractive to genuine users and to those whose motive is mere idle curiosity also attract those whose interest is far from innocent. The prospect of being able to roam around the world without leaving your desk, with access to, potentially, a million or more computer systems is an exciting one for any hacker.

Any proposal to use the Internet to provide access to personal data or to communicate personal data from one user to another therefore need to be regarded with caution. Merely connecting a system to the Internet poses a risk for personal data on the system, even if there is no intention to use the Internet to access or communicate those data.

There are risks too for individuals who access services on the Internet. Every time you access a service whether it is to make a contribution to a newsgroup

91 Above, n 36.

92 HMSO 1995.

> or to make a commercial transaction, you are at risk of leaving an electronic trace which can be used to develop a profile of your personal interests and tastes. And who knows through which countries your data has passed and by whom the data might have been captured in transit?

The Internet and, in particular, the growth of the World Wide Web with home pages inviting the browser to 'sign the visitors' book', provides many more opportunities for the capture, retention and subsequent processing of personal data.[93] Photographs may be made available on the Web, identifying particular persons and such images can then be viewed or downloaded across the world. That such data is personal is indisputable, but does it render meaningless the restriction of transborder data flows where there are no guarantees of appropriate safeguards? How can the originator of the material know in which jurisdiction the resultant data might be used? When such information is placed on the Web by an organisation or institution, how should that organisation's registration be framed? If the information is made available on an individual's home page, does that mean that the processing attracts an exemption on the grounds of personal and domestic use? Can the provisions of either the 1984 Act or Directive 95/46/EC cope with this phenomenon? Even if the capability is there, does enforcement and supervision become such a gargantuan task that it becomes impossible for all practical purposes to locate and deal with contraventions?

Increasingly, the Internet is being used for commercial transactions. Completing contracts by electronic means has been happening for some time facilitated by the use of Electronic Data Interchange (EDI).[94] In simple terms, the EDI network is a network developed for business use which provides a more secure environment for data transmission. The increasing amount of commercial traffic on the open network, rather than the dedicated EDI network, is a reflection of the increased access of consumers to the network, resulting in consumer transactions as well as purely business to business contracts, and a consequent increase in the transfer of personal data. Certain techniques for ensuring security and verification have been developed in connection with the EDI network based on encryption, for example,[95] whose use could be extended to the open network and might help to safeguard personal data.[96] This does not address the issue of transfer to third countries which may not provide suitable safeguards. It seems likely that, once Directive 95/46/EC is implemented, such transfer may be legitimate for most commercial transactions where the contract is on behalf of the data subject or

93 See also 'Data Protection and the Internet' available at http://www.open.gov.uk/dpr/guidance.htm and also the discussion on regulation of the Internet in Chapter 8.

94 See Chapter 6.

95 See, eg, International Yearbook of Law, Computers and Technology Volume 6 Carfax 1992, focusing on EDI.

96 See also *The Protection of Personal Data in an Electronic Data Interchange Environment* 12th Report of the Data Protection Registrar HMSO 1996 Annex 7.

in his or her interest. The capability of data protection regulation to cope with the increasing use of the Internet may be more of a problem in relation to its use for other purposes.

DEFAMATION

It is not only a person's privacy that may be compromised by the escalating use of computer networks – the medium provides ample opportunity for propagating scurrilous material about others which may range from the irritating to that which is potentially defamatory or even a form of harassment. This is especially true of the Internet where such activity, known as 'flaming' has been raised almost to an art form with its own brand of rules and etiquette.[97] It is the growth of news groups and bulletin boards which have really facilitated this kind of activity. Easy communication across the globe naturally spawned discussion groups of people interested in similar topics ranging from the serious and scholarly to the frivolous and bizarre. These have been variously organised into newsgroups, electronic bulletin boards and electronic mailing lists for the exchange of views and experiences and the dissemination of information. Although, the way in which they are set up and operated varies, they provide similar scope for the promulgation of defamatory material.[98]

Whatever their subject matter, both bulletin boards and newsgroups may be moderated or unmoderated with a corresponding variation in the integrity of the material available. In particular, those intended for an academic or professional readership are likely to be moderated so that some editorial control is retained. In contrast, it can be the norm for the language used in some unmoderated groups to be somewhat intemperate. The difference being that the normal readership is so different that the use of excessive language does not provoke an avalanche of claims in defamation. In such an environment, Dooley[99] suggests that '... defamation has been elevated to the status of a spectator sport on the information superhighway, with entire bulletin boards being devoted to flaming'.

However, what may be viewed as acceptable by some protagonists may be experienced as 'vituperative literary battles'[100] by those on the receiving end for which, if they believe their reputation to have been diminished thereby,

97 See, eg, JA Inman and RR Inman *Responsibility as an Issue in Internet Communication: Reading Flames as Defamation* (1996) 1 J Tech Law and Policy 5 and references cited therein. This article is also available at http://journal/law/ufl/edu/~techlaw/1/inman.html.

98 See, eg, Nick Braithwaite *The Internet and Bulletin Board Defamations* (1995) 145 NLJ 1216.

99 Stephen Dooley *Defamation on the Internet* (1995) 1 CTLR 191.

100 Nick Braithwaite and Robert Carolina *Multimedia Defamation* (1994) 12 International Media Law 19.

they may wish to seek redress in a court of law. This should be distinguished from invasion of privacy – what is at stake here is the individual's standing in the eyes of his or her peers and the way in which the law can protect it. As in the discussion of privacy, this necessitates balancing the protection of an individual's reputation against the right of others to pass comment on that person's words and actions. Even in a country like the UK, with no written constitution, the law has identified the public interest in the freedom of speech, in the defences available to an action for defamation such as fair comment, absolute and qualified privilege etc.

The Australian case, *Rindos v Hardwick*[101] was the first libel action to arise as a consequence of information posted to a newsgroup. Rindos, an anthropologist, had been refused tenure at the University of Western Australia. A comment, in support of his work was placed on ANTHRO-L, an electronic bulletin board subscribed to by anthropologists. In response, the defendant sent a vitriolic missive about Rindos to the newsgroup, sci.anthropology, another forum frequently accessed by academic anthropologists. Although establishing that, in principle, libel could be committed via electronic media, this case did not really have to address any of the difficult issues which might arise.

Is it libel or slander?

It is important to establish whether defamation by electronic means falls within the category of libel or slander, because libel is actionable per se, whereas slander requires proof of damage. It is generally accepted that defamation which is written and permanent will be libel but that which is audible and purely transient, such as the spoken word, will constitute slander. However, these represent the most clear cut examples and some examples will fall between the two extremes. Most commentators seem to believe that defamation over the Internet, should be viewed as libel and the judgment of Ipp J in *Rindos v Hardwick* assumes that the criteria for libel are made out. There has been some discussion, however, as to whether the medium provides sufficient permanence.[102] What constitutes permanence? *Monson v Tussauds Ltd*[103] concerned an exhibition of waxworks in which an effigy of the

101 Supreme Court of Western Australia No 1994 of 1993 (Unreported Judgment 940164, 31 March 1994), unverified text available at http://mark.law.auckland.ac.nz/cases/Rindos.html. See also Timothy Arnold-Moore, 'Legal Pitfalls in Cyberspace: Defamation on Computer Networks' (1994) 5 Journal of Law and Information Science 165 and Francis Auburn, 'Usenet News and the Law' [1995] Web JCLI available at http://webjcli.ncl.ac.uk/.

102 See, eg, Timothy Arnold-Moore, 'Legal Pitfalls in Cyberspace: Defamation on Computer Networks' (1994) 5 Journal of Law and Information Science 165, Stephen Dooley, 'Defamation on the Internet' (1995) 1 CTLR 191 and Richard Shillito, 'Making Bones of Sticks and Stones Law' Soc Gazette 91/38 19 October 1994.

103 [1894] 1 QB 671.

plaintiff was placed in the entrance to the Chamber of Horrors. Lopes LJ, discussing the various forms that libel could take, pointed out that, although writing or printing was the most usual medium, any other permanent form could suffice including 'a statue, a caricature, an effigy, chalk marks on a wall, signs or pictures'. Clearly, there is no general standard of permanence exhibited in these examples – chalk marks can easily be erased and in this particular case, it was the positioning of the waxwork, a factor which is clearly not inherently permanent, rather than its content, that gave rise to a finding of libel. To what extent can information made available over computer networks be viewed as permanent? Braithwaite and Carolina explain the answer as follows:[104] 'Electronic messages although seemingly transitory, can be both stored for future reference and redisseminated far more readily than the printed word. Their transience and ease of alteration can be overstated, while their damaging effects may be much harder to eradicate.' This not only assesses the level of permanence but also suggests a policy reason why electronic communication should give rise to actions in libel rather than slander as a result of the potential for damage.

In 1975, the Faulks Committee on Defamation recommended that the distinction between libel and slander be abolished.[105] This was never acted upon but it may be that there is a need for statutory clarification in respect of electronic communication. If that were to be the case, it would not be the first time that the law had intervened in this way. Section 166(1) of the Broadcasting Act 1990 provides that, for the purposes of libel and slander 'the publication of words in the course of any programme included in a programme service shall be treated as publication in permanent form'.[106]

Publication

The purpose of the tort of defamation is to protect reputation rather than injury to feelings caused by insults addressed only to the plaintiff, for instance. Thus, there will only be a cause of action where there is *publication* of the libel to a third party.[107] One of the dangers of participation in electronic discussion groups for the unsuspecting defendant is that it can, at times, appear very like a one-to-one interchange; it can be easy to forget that the contents may be mailed to others or available to others who choose to access a particular newsgroup. It is also true that, newsgroups and bulletin boards aimed at academics and professional users are increasingly specialised in

104 Nick Braithwaite and Robert Carolina, 'Multimedia Defamation' (1994) 12 International Media Law 19.

105 Cmnd 5909 HMSO 1975.

106 Section 4 of the See also Theatres Act 1968.

107 But for offensive and insulting e-mail intended only for the recipient a charge under the Malicious Communications Act 1988 may be possible.

content and may attract a significant proportion of readers amongst that particular interest group. Thus the potential for damaging an individual reputation in the eyes of others working in the same field can be high. In the words of Braithwaite and Carolina:[108]

> ... bulletin boards are often the chosen method of correspondence in certain fields of study. Scurrilous bulletin board messages, even if not widely disseminated by conventional mass media standards, may be nicely targeted to achieve maximum damage to professional or business reputations.

They also have this to say in relation to the fact of publication itself:

> When does publication occur? Is information published when data are copied to or stored on individual host computers or is it only when the information is actually communicated to the end user? Principle suggests that the actual communication is necessary, not mere availability, since the gist of defamation is actual or presumed damage to reputation flowing from publication. On the other hand, it would be onerous to expect a plaintiff to prove that stored information had been accessed.

There is old authority which suggests that actual *communication* to the third party may not be necessary to show publication.

R v Burdett (1820) 4 B & Ald 95 at 126

> It is assumed that publication means a manifestation of the contents. I deny that such is the meaning of the word publication. In no part of the law do I find that it is used in that sense. A man publishes an award, but he does not read it. Again, he publishes a will, but he does not manifest its contents to those to whom he makes the publication; he merely desires the witnesses to take notice at the paper to which they affix their different attestations is his will. So in the case of a libel, publication is nothing more than doing the last act for the accomplishment of the mischief intended by it. The moment a man delivers a libel from his hands his control over it is gone; he has shot his arrow, and it does not depend upon him whether it hits the mark or not. There is an end of the *locus pœnitentiæ*, his offence is complete, all that depends upon him is consummated, and from that moment, upon every principle of common sense, he is liable to be called upon to answer for his act. Suppose a man wraps up a newspaper and sends it into another county by a boy; who is the publisher? The boy who perhaps cannot read or is ignorant of its contents, or the man who has put it in the envelope? The boy who carries it is merely an innocent instrument; there can be no other publisher but the person who sent it, and who publishes when he delivers it to the boy. If the sending of a letter by the post be not a publication in the county from whence it is sent, how is a libeller to be punished who sends his libel by the post to some foreign country for circulation?

In *Byrne v Dean*,[109] the person who was in control of the contents of a physical noticeboard in a private club was held to be responsible for the publication of

108 Nick Braithwaite and Robert Carolina 'Multimedia Defamation' (1994) 12 International Media Law 19.

109 [1937] 1 KB 818.

a defamatory notice posted by someone else on the grounds of her failure to remove the offending notice.

***Byrne v Dean* [1937] 1 KB 818 at 837**

Greene LJ

> ... publication, of course, is a question of fact and it must depend on the circumstances in each case whether or not publication has taken place. It is said that as a general proposition where the act of a person alleged to have published a libel has not been any positive act, but has merely been the refraining from doing some act, he cannot be guilty of publication. I am quite unable to accept any such general proposition. It may very well be that in some circumstances a person, by refraining from removing or obliterating the defamatory matter, is not committing any publication at all. In other circumstances he may be doing so. The test it appears to me is this: having regard to all the facts of the case is the proper inference that by not removing the defamatory matter the defendant really made himself responsible for its continued presence in the place where it had been put?

Greene LJ went on to explain that there might be certain cases in which it would be difficult for someone in the position of the defendant to remedy the matter but:

> On the other hand you have a case such as the present where the removal of this particular notice was a perfectly simple and easy thing to do involving no trouble whatsoever. The defendants having the power to remove it, and being able to do it without any difficulty at all, and knowing that members of the club when they came into the room would see it, I think must be taken to have elected deliberately to leave it there. The proper inference therefore, in those circumstances it seems to me is that they were consenting parties to its continued presence on the spot where it had been put up. That being so it seems to me that they must be taken to have consented to its publication to each member who saw it.

This may have relevance to the operators also of electronic bulletin boards which will be considered further in the next section.

Who is liable for the publication?

It is not only the author of a libel who may be liable, but anyone who participates in the publication of the defamatory matter; this might include the publisher, editor, printer and distributor. It may be that mere distributors have no cause to suspect the existence of a libel in the material in question and in such a case, they may be able to avail themselves of the defence of innocent dissemination. This was originally established in the case of *Emmens v Pottle*[110] and applies where the defendant had no reason to believe that the publication

110 (1885) 16 QBD 354.

in question contained a libel and this ignorance did not arise from negligence on the part of the defendant. A particular concern for networked information is the extent of the liability of the bulletin board operator or the service provider. Are they akin to distributors so that the defence of innocent dissemination could be applied or are they, in reality more like editors or publishers? Two cases from the US, where a similar defence is available, illustrate two sides of the coin.

Cubby Inc v Compuserve Inc[111] concerned an on-line service provider that provided access to a bulletin board monitored by an independent company who exerted editorial control. A newsletter called Rumorville was available via the bulletin board. The case arose as a consequence of the development by the plaintiff of a news database which would be likely to be in competition with Rumorville. When certain allegedly defamatory remarks were then made about the plaintiff in the newsletter, a libel action was brought against, *inter alia*, Compuserve, the service provider.

> The requirement that a distributor must have knowledge of the contents of a publication before liability can be imposed for distributing that publication is deeply rooted in the First Amendment, made applicable to the states through the Fourteenth Amendment. '[T]he constitutional guarantees of the freedom of speech and of the press stand in the way of imposing' strict liability on distributors for the contents of the reading materials they carry ... In [*Smith v California* (1959)] ... the court reasoned that 'Every bookseller would be placed under an obligation to make himself aware of the contents of every book in his shop. it would be altogether unreasonable to demand so near an approach to omniscience'.
>
> ... Technology is rapidly transforming the information industry. A computerised database is the functional equivalent of a more traditional news vendor, and the inconsistent application of a lower standard of liability to an electronic news distributor such as Compuserve than that which is applied to a public library, book store or newsstand would impose an undue burden on the free flow of information. Given the relevant First Amendment considerations, the appropriate standard of liability to be applied to Compuserve is whether it knew or had reason to know of the allegedly defamatory Rumorville statements.

The court went on to find that Compuserve were not liable for the defamation, because they 'neither knew nor had reason to know of the allegedly defamatory Rumorville statements'. The issue of whether a database operator exercising editorial control over content might be construed as a publisher, rather than a distributor and, in consequence be unable to avail themselves of this 'distributor's defence' was left open.

111 776 F Supp 135 (SDNY 1991) available at http://epic.org/free_speech/cubby_v_compuserve.txt.

In contrast, the circumstances in *Stratton Oakmont Inc v Prodigy Services Co*[112] were to lead to a different result. Derogatory comments and accusations about the plaintiff company were posted on a bulletin board made available by Prodigy and an action was taken against them for libel.

> A distributor, or deliverer of defamatory material is considered a passive conduit and found liable in the absence of fault ... However, a newspaper, for example, is more than a passive receptacle or conduit for news, comment and advertising ... The choice of material to go into a newspaper and the decisions made as to the content of the paper constitute the exercise of editorial control and judgment ... and with this increased control comes increased liability. In short, the critical issue to be determined by this court is whether the ... evidence establishes a *prima facie* case that PRODIGY exercised sufficient editorial control over its computer bulletin boards to render it a publisher with the same responsibilities as a newspaper.

The court found that Prodigy not only held itself out as controlling the contents of its bulletin boards but also that it implemented this control through an automatic software screening program. The court were therefore 'compelled to conclude that ... PRODIGY is a publisher rather than a distributor' and was therefore liable for the defamatory remarks. The court did, however, point out that they fully agreed with the decision in *Cubby* and that 'computer bulletin boards should generally be regarded in the same context as bookstores, libraries and network affiliates'.

As yet there have been no similar cases which have gone to full trial in the UK. An allegation by a scientist that he had been libelled on Usenet by another academic based in Geneva was eventually settled out of court.[113] Recent changes have been made to the law in the UK as a consequence of the Defamation Act 1996 which includes a statutory version of the innocent dissemination defence.

DEFAMATION ACT 1996

Section 1 Responsibility for publication

(1) In defamation proceedings a person has a defence if he shows that

(a) he was not the author, editor or publisher of the statement complained of;

(b) he took reasonable care in relation to its publication; and

(c) he did not know, and had no reason to believe, that what he did caused or contributed to the publication of a defamatory statement.

(2) For this purpose 'author', 'editor' and 'publisher' have the following meanings ...

112 NY Sup Ct Nassau Co 1995, 1995 WL 323710, 63 USLW 2765, available at http://www.gcwf.com/articles\prodigy.htm.

113 See, eg, John Angel 'Legal Risks of Providing Services on the Internet' (1996) 1 Communications Law 105.

'author' means the originator of the statement, but does not include a person who did not intend that his statement be published at all;

'editor' means a person having editorial or equivalent responsibility for the content of the statement or the decision to publish it; and

'publisher' means a commercial publisher, that is, a person whose business is issuing material to the public, or a section of the public, who issues material containing the statement in the course of that business.

This suggests that service providers may escape liability if they act purely as distributors and, to an extent, this is clarified in the subsequent sub-sections.

DEFAMATION ACT 1996

Section 1 Responsibility for publication

(3) A person shall not be considered the author, editor or publisher of a statement if he is only involved ...

(c) In processing, making copies of, distributing or selling any electronic medium in or on which the statement is recorded, or in operating or providing any equipment, system or service by means of which the statement is retrieved, copied, distributed or made available in electronic form ...

(5) In determining for the purposes of this section whether a person took reasonable care, or had reason to believe that what he did caused or contributed to the publication of the defamatory statement, regard shall be had to

(a) the extent of his responsibility for the content of the statement or the decision to publish it;

(b) the nature or circumstances of the publication; and

(c) the previous conduct or character of the author, editor or publisher.

Although pure distributors may escape liability, the situation is much less clear with respect to bulletin board operators and similar activities. Where there is editorial control over the content, then the defence would fall at the first hurdle in s 1(1)(a). The situation would presumably be similar for a moderated newsgroup. This does not automatically mean that it would be safer to operate an unmoderated bulletin board or newsgroup (in any case, this might be undesirable for other reasons) because a presumption may arise that such a bulletin board operator should be aware of the likely traffic on the board to which they provide access and it could be that they would be unable then to satisfy s 1(1)(b) and/or (c). For an unmoderated newsgroup, in particular, it may, in any case, be difficult to identify any appropriate defendant. This might suggest that there could be policy reasons for allowing liability to fall on the service provider in certain cases. Advances such as the Internet and the World Wide Web have made electronic publishing a very accessible operation, often without the need for any participation by a publishing company, as such. It is entirely possible that the situation could arise where, unlike traditional forms of publishing, only the original author could be liable if the circumstances were such that the service provider could avail themselves of this defence. This could be an undesirable outcome, not least because it may make it difficult to bring an action against the author, if he or she happens to be in a different jurisdiction (see below). Compare the rather stricter view of the liability of distributors in the context of contempt of court, especially where this has arisen in another jurisdiction; this difference appears to emanate from policy considerations.

R v Griffiths and others, ex p Attorney-General
[1957] 2 All ER 379 at 383

Lord Goddard CJ

> ... we are holding that to those who in the way of their trade are responsible for putting the offending matter into circulation the defence of innocent dissemination is not available in cases of contempt ... We accept unreservedly that neither of these respondents ... knew of these scandalous paragraphs and we recognise that they immediately took every step in their power to stop the circulation as soon as their attention was directed to the matter. It is regrettable that in holding them guilty of a contempt we cannot also deal with those who are far more responsible but are out of the jurisdiction. We shall impose a fine ... and we do so to emphasis the risk which is run by dealing in foreign publications imported here but which have no responsible editor or manager in this country. The distributors are the only persons who can in these circumstances be made amenable in the courts of this country. Now that the risk and responsibility have been exposed by this case, should offences occur in the future similar leniency may not be extended. It was argued that, if these two respondents are liable, so every small newsagent or street seller who sells the paper would equally be liable. Logically this may be so, but the court would not regard with favour applications against such persons to whom no real blame would attach. This jurisdiction is discretionary and the court can be trusted not to exercise it except against those who can fairly be said to bear some real responsibility for the publication.

Clearly there are certain important differences between the policy considerations which pertain in cases of libel on the one hand, and contempt of court on the other. It remains to be seen in what manner the statutory defence will be applied if the electronic equivalent of the situation described above occurs in relation to either libel or contempt.

In *R v Griffiths*, above, the distributors of contempt of court were found liable on the basis that they were 'the only persons who can ... be made amenable in the courts of this country'. What is the situation in respect of cross-border libel? Where can the plaintiff bring an action? The decision as to whether the English courts will have jurisdiction depends on matters of some complexity, but one factor may be the existence of agreements between the countries in question. Following *Shevill and Others v Presse Alliance SA*,[114] the

114 Case C-68/93 [1995] All ER (EC) 289.

situation has been clarified as far as those countries which are signatories to the Brussels and Lugano Conventions are concerned.[115] The case concerned a French newspaper, *France Soir*, published by Presse Alliance, that had its major circulation in France but also had a small circulation in England. An article in this newspaper suggested that Ms Shevill, who had worked temporarily at a bureau de change in Paris, together with her employers and others, was implicated in the laundering of the proceeds of drug trafficking. As the plaintiff was English and domiciled in England, an action was brought in England claiming damages for the publication of the libel there.

Article 5(3) of the Convention on Jurisdiction and the Enforcement of Judgments in Civil and Commercial Matters (Brussels Convention) allows a plaintiff to bring an action in 'the place where the harmful event occurred'. The defendants, Presse Alliance, argued that the court had no jurisdiction to hear the case as the harmful event had taken place in France and no damage had actually been shown in England. The English law of libel presumes damage once publication has been demonstrated. The Court of Appeal[116] held that the matter of the damage being presumed was not an issue of jurisdiction as such and that 'the place where the harmful event occurred' could be construed as referring to both the place where the tortious act occurred and the place where the damage was suffered. Thus, where an act was done in one state which caused damage in another, the plaintiff could choose to bring an action in either state.

On appeal, the House of Lords referred the following questions to the European Court of Justice:

Shevill and others v Presse Alliance SA
[1995] All ER (EC) 289

1. In a case of libel by a newspaper article, do the words 'the place where the harmful event occurred' in Article 5(3) of the Convention mean: (a) the place where the newspaper was printed and put into circulation; or (b) the place or places where the newspaper was read by particular individuals; or (c) the place or places where the plaintiff has a significant reputation?
2. If and in so far as the answer to the first question is (b), is 'the harmful event' dependent upon there being a reader or readers who knew (or knew of) the plaintiff and understood those words to refer to him?
3. If and in so far as harm is suffered in more than one country (because copies of the newspaper were distributed in at least Member State other than the Member State where it was printed and put into circulation), does a separate harmful event or harmful events take place in each Member State where the newspaper was distributed, in respect of which such Member State has separate jurisdiction under Article 5(3), and if so, how

115 Incorporated into domestic law by the Civil Jurisdiction and Judgments Acts 1982 and 1991.

116 [1992] 1 All ER 409.

harmful must the event be, or what proportion of the total harm must it represent?

4. Does the phrase 'harmful event' include an event actionable under national law without proof of damage, where there is no evidence of actual damage or harm?
5. In deciding under Article 5(3) whether (or where) a 'harmful event' has occurred is the local court expected to answer the question otherwise than by reference to its own rules and, if so, by reference to which other rules or substantive law, procedure or evidence?
6. If, in a defamation case, the local court concludes that there has been an actionable publication (or communication) of material, as a result of which at least some damage to reputation would be presumed, is it relevant to the acceptance of jurisdiction that other Member States might come to a different conclusion in respect of similar material published within their respective jurisdictions?
7. In deciding whether it has jurisdiction under Article 5(3) of the Convention, what standard of proof should a court require of the plaintiff that the conditions of Article 5(3) are satisfied: (a) generally; and (b) in relation to matters which (if the court takes jurisdiction) will not be re-examined at the trial of the action?

These questions would clearly have relevance in cases where the libel had been perpetrated by electronic means, provided the relevant ingredients such as publication in a particular Member State had been established. The European Court divided the questions into two, according to whether they concerned questions of jurisdiction or assessment of damage.

Shevill and others v Presse Alliance SA
[1995] All ER (EC) 289 at 317

33. ... the answer to the first, second, third and sixth questions referred by the House of Lords must be that, on a proper construction of the expression 'place where the harmful event occurred' in Article 5(3) of the convention, the victim of a libel by a newspaper article distributed in several contracting states may bring an action for damages against the publisher either before the courts of the contracting state where the publisher of the defamatory publication is established, which have jurisdiction to award damages for all the harm caused by the defamation, or before the courts of each contracting state in which the publication was distributed and where the victim claims to have suffered injury to his reputation, which have jurisdiction to rule solely in respect of the harm caused in the state of the court seised.

In respect of the remaining questions, referring to the assessment of damage, the court felt that the matter was one that should be decided by the rules pertaining in the particular Member State in which the action was brought, assuming that the provisions of the Convention were not compromised.

Application of the principles, expounded above in relation to newspaper publishing, to electronic fora presumes that there has been identification of those responsible for propagating the libel. This may be no easy task in relation to media such as the World Wide Web, even where the individuals are named on the page. The computer hosting the pages may not readily be discerned and may be in a completely different jurisdiction from the person producing the Web pages. Where a defendant can be isolated and is in a convenient jurisdiction, to what extent are they deemed to be accountable for all the information which can be accessed from their pages? A particular feature of HTML, 'hypertext mark-up language', which is used for preparing information which is to be made available on the World Wide Web, is that embedded links can be incorporated which will provide access to other related sites when the user 'points and clicks'. Suppose the home site is not, itself, defamatory but provides links to other sites which contain libellous material. Is the host of the home page liable for the publication of this material?

Hird v Wood[117] concerned an individual who pointed continually at a placard so that all who passed by were made aware of the writing on it. The person who had written the placard or placed it in position was unknown. It was held that the act of pointing to the contents was enough to constitute evidence of publication. This seems to provide a remarkably good analogy for the situation occurring when readers of a home page are directed to a page hosted by a third party which may provide further information of interest. The matter is not quite so simple as that, however, because, of course, the process does not stop there and there may then be further links to other pages creating the 'Web'. It seems unlikely that any court would find liability for defamatory material hosted on a site which could not be reached directly from the defendant's home pages. The situation is further complicated by the fact that, unlike traditionally produced works, the information on Web pages (or other networked information) is not static but is continually being refined and updated. If a direct link is provided from one page to another provided by a third party then, whether or not there is liability for material will undoubtedly depend on the particular circumstances of the case. Nonetheless proprietors of home pages might be prudent to check their embedded links at intervals, not only to ensure they are still operative but also that they would continue to be happy to point their readers in that direction.

117 (1894) 38 Sol J 235.

CHAPTER EIGHT

POLICING 'CYBERSPACE'

INTRODUCTION

It has been reported that, since 1993, attacks on the computer systems of banks and other financial institutions, made possible by the use of the latest generation of military weapons which target communications systems, have resulted in losses in excess of £500m as the organisations involved pay 'ransom' money.[1] In the last few years there have been prosecutions for the possession and publication of child pornography both in the UK and the US, this being material that was available either on computer networks or other electronic media.[2] Such examples serve to illustrate how the computer can be used to assist the perpetration of crime. Neither is this a new phenomenon. During the 1980s a number of cases came to court in a number of jurisdictions that could, perhaps, be regarded purely as examples of anti-social behaviour, but caused problems for the law in trying to locate the behaviour within existing legal provisions. A number of these were cases of computer hacking and the outcomes were often inconsistent, even in relation to ostensibly similar facts. In some cases there might be an acquittal because the charge chosen was deemed to be inappropriate or, alternatively, the law was interpreted in novel ways in order to found a conviction.[3] Although computer hacking is often what comes to mind when computer misuse and abuse is referred to, there is a whole spectrum of activity that may be referred to as computer crime[4] or computer-related crime that began to become apparent as the so-called computer or information revolution progressed.[5]

---

1 Peter Warren, *Computing* (1996) p 22.

2 See later discussion at p 369.

3 Compare for instance the cases of *R v Gold and Schifreen* and *R v Whitely* discussed pp 337, 340 below.

4 The use of this term has, itself, led to some controversy. Tapper [1987] Crim L Rev 4, describes the phrase as 'ungrammatical and inelegant' although other writers are rather more dismissive of any perceived semantic difficulties: 'Clearly it is easy to argue over a definition of computer crime. Such an argument seems fruitless, and will not be engaged in here.' (Encyclopedia of Information Technology Law, Volume II, para 12.03, Sweet and Maxwell.) This writer is clearly of a much more pragmatic persuasion: 'The notion of computer crime is retained here merely because it serves as a useful umbrella under which to address a range of quite new and difficult criminal law problems ...'.

5 For an anecdotal account of some of the more high-profile cases and examples see Bryan Clough and Paul Mungo, *Approaching Zero: Data Crime and the Computer Underworld* (1993) Faber and Faber.

Thus August Bequai writing in the preface to the Council of Europe Recommendation on Computer-related Crime[6] suggests that 'In the information society, power and wealth are increasingly becoming synonymous with control over our data banks ... The computer revolution has provided tools with which to steal with impunity, control and manipulate the thoughts and movements of millions, and hold an entire society hostage'.

This clearly underlines the potential for a particular type of abuse of computer systems and to this may be added a number of 'traditional' crimes that may be facilitated by the use of computer systems such as offences of theft, deception and fraud, offences related to obscenity and indecency, criminal breaches of copyright arising from intentional distribution and commercial exploitation of copyright works and criminal damage aimed at the computer systems itself. That these are different in kind both from each other and from the 'new' offences related to or relying on computer hacking goes without saying but, together, they make up a body that has come to be referred to, however inaccurately, as computer crime and, in varying degrees, has caused problems for the interpretation and development of the law in this area. It is not the purpose of this chapter to examine the accuracy of the phrase 'computer crime': whatever the shortcomings of this term, it has become accepted terminology for a particular species of activity that has the common ingredient of computer use.

A coherent response to these problems is difficult, however, because of an absence of homogeneity in the subject matter demonstrated by a lack of consensus both in the definition of and in the severity of the offences and also in identifying the jurisdiction in which the offence occurred. Discrepancies in the type of regulation because of the former, together with the confusion raised by the latter, may inevitably lead to the likelihood of 'forum shopping' in the hope of a favourable hearing in situations where an offence can be deemed to have taken place in one of a number of jurisdictions. An explanation for the apparent increase in computer crime is difficult, although the suspicion is that, like the advent of the motor car, the advent of the computer created more opportunities for crime. This difficulty has been identified by Wasik:[7]

> ... the sheer diversity of behaviour within the context of computer misuse, where the computer may figure at one moment as the instrument of crime, and at the next as the target for crime, and given the importance of non-economic motives in some forms of computer misuse, such as the unauthorised access of computer systems purely for intellectual challenge and some cases of computer sabotage, makes any monolithic explanation of this phenomenon quite implausible.

---

6 Council of Europe Recommendation R(89)9 on Computer-related Crime (1990) p 4.

7 Martin Wasik, *Crime and the Computer* (1990) p 33, Clarendon Press.

Whatever the explanation for the behaviour it is clear that the law has had to respond to these activities and has done so with varying degrees of consistency and success. This chapter will consider the response of the law and will draw conclusions as to the consistency of approach.

COMPUTER FRAUD

Many considerations of the phenomenon of computer crime begin with a study of computer fraud, defined by the Audit Commission[8] as '[a]ny fraudulent behaviour connected with computerisation by which someone intends to gain financial advantage'. Fraudulent schemes are usually devised to create some pecuniary benefit or to relieve the perpetrator of a financial burden. Most studies in this area, in common with the Audit Commission, have identified three species of computer fraud namely input fraud, output fraud and program fraud, of which the last is less common as it requires considerably more knowledge and expertise. Thus, input fraud might include the misuse of cash cards or the creation of accounts for 'ghost employees' whereas theft of pre-signed cheques is an example of an output fraud. Program frauds are necessarily rather more elaborate and include the so-called salami type in which a program is written which automatically 'slices off' small amounts from a number of accounts and transfers them to another account created for the purpose. A small deficit may not be noticed or reported on one account, but, if the process is repeated on a vast number of accounts, a considerable sum can be accrued in the illicit account. Salami and other program frauds can also be activated at a later date creating consequent problems in detection of both the fraud and the perpetrator.

How has the law responded to the issue of computer fraud? The Law Commission concluded that, in general, the existing criminal law was adequate to deal with cases of computer fraud.[9] The exception to this that was identified was for those offences that have proof of deception as an element since this raised the vexed question of whether it is possible to deceive a machine or whether this is an act that can only be performed on humans. A further complication may be that, although an appropriate offence can be identified, the nature of computer technology may make it more difficult to identify both when and where the offence occurred, both of which factors may have important ramifications for the final outcome of the case.

The potential difficulties that may arise in such situations are illustrated by the facts of *Thompson*.[10] Thompson was a computer programmer employed by

8 Audit Commission *Computer Fraud Survey* HMSO 1985, p 9.

9 Law Commission Report on Computer Misuse Cmnd 819 HMSO 1989.

10 [1984] 1 WLR 962.

a bank in Kuwait. He identified five accounts that were both substantial and dormant, ie no transactions had been made into or out of them for a long time. He then opened five accounts in his name at various branches of the bank and transferred money into these accounts from the dormant accounts.

To cover his tracks, the program did not execute until he had left the bank's employment and was returning to the UK. The intention was that the program would erase itself and all records of the transfers after executing. Once in the UK, Thompson opened accounts in UK banks and wrote to the Kuwaiti bank manager asking him to transfer the money now in the five accounts held in his own name. This led to him being found out and he was charged and convicted of obtaining property by deception, contrary to the Theft Act 1968, s 15:

> (1) A person who by any deception dishonestly obtains property belonging to another, with the intention of permanently depriving the other of it, shall on conviction on indictment be liable to imprisonment for a term not exceeding ten years.
>
> (2) For the purposes of this section a person is to be treated as obtaining property if he obtains ownership, possession or control of it, and 'obtain' ... includes obtaining for another or enabling another to obtain or to retain it.

Section 4(1) of the same Act provides:

> 'Property' includes money and all other property, real or personal, including things in action and other intangible property.

The issue in the case itself, was not so much a question of whether or not this offence had been committed, but rather when and where and, in consequence, whether or not the English courts had jurisdiction to hear the case. Section 15(2) of the Theft Act 1968 defines 'obtaining property' for the purposes of the offence of obtaining by deception in s 15(1) as obtaining *ownership, possession or control.* The argument for the Crown was that the offence had occurred in England when the credit balance in the fraudulently created accounts was transferred to the accounts in England, as this was the moment at which Thompson obtained *ownership, possession or control*. The defence argued that, on the contrary, control was obtained in Kuwait at the time when the manipulation of the balances in the respective accounts was made. The court, although recognising the points raised, were anxious not to treat the fraud in any different manner to a similar case of fraud perpetrated by more traditional means.

R v Thompson [1984] 1 WLR 962 at 967
Court of Appeal

> **May LJ** We think, however, that one may legitimately ask: of what property did this appellant in that way obtain control in Kuwait? What was the nature of that property? Mr Caplan's reply, as we understand it, was that the appellant obtained the control of those credit balances on his savings accounts, which were effectively choses in action, and were such until the bank discovered his fraud. With all respect to Mr Caplan's persuasive argument, we think that when it is examined it is untenable. We do not think that one can

> describe as a chose in action a liability which has been brought about by fraud, one where the action to enforce that liability is capable of immediate defeasance as soon as the fraud is pleaded. It is neither here nor there, we think, that the person defrauded, in this case the bank, may not have been aware that one of its employees had been fraudulent in this way until a later time. The ignorance of the bank in no way, in our view, breathes life into what is otherwise a defunct situation brought about entirely by fraud. One has only to take a simple example. Discard for the moment the modern sophistication of computers and programmes and consider the old days when bank books were kept in manuscript in large ledgers. In effect all that was done by the appellant through the modern computer in the present case was to take a pen and debit each of the five accounts in the ledger with the relevant sums and then credit each of his own five savings accounts in the ledger with corresponding amounts. On the face of it his savings accounts would then have appeared to have in them substantially more than in truth they did have as the result of his forgeries; but we do not think that by those forgeries any bank clerk in the days before computers would in law have thus brought into being a chose in action capable either of being stolen or of being obtained by deception contrary to section 15 of the Theft Act 1968.
>
> In so far as the customers whose accounts had been fraudulently debited and who had to be reimbursed by the bank, as Mr Caplan submitted, are concerned, we prefer the approach of Mr Walsh. He submitted that properly considered it was not a question of reimbursement: it was merely a question of correcting forged documents, forged records, to the condition in which they ought to have been but for the fraud.
>
> In those circumstances and for those reasons we agree with the judge in the court below that the only realistic view of the undisputed facts in this case is that the six instances of obtaining charged in the indictment each occurred when the relevant sums of money were received by the appellant's banks in England. Further it seems to us quite clear ... that those sums of money were obtained as the result of the letters which the appellant wrote to the bank in Kuwait. The only proper construction to be put upon those letters is that they contain the representations pleaded in the particulars of offences in the indictment.

Thus, in this case, the decision was arrived at by applying exactly the same principles as would be applied in a more conventional case and, although the use of the computer clearly facilitated the fraud, the existing law was still capable of application. This does not automatically mean that all cases of computer fraud present no problems. The prosecution in *Thompson* was able to identify a human mind which had been deceived by the acts of the accused, namely the bank manager in Kuwait, at the time of receiving the letter of instruction from Thompson. Would the result have been the same if no such person could have been identified? The Scottish Law Commission[11] suggested that there was, in this respect, a distinction in relation to offences involving fraudulent activity between the law in Scotland and that in England and Wales.

11 Scottish Law Commission *Report on Computer Crime* Cmnd 174 HMSO 1987, para 2.4.

Cm 174 para 2.5

> ... in Scotland such activities, even where they involved computers, would be adequately dealt with by the common law crimes of fraud, or in some cases, theft. Referring to the classic definition of fraud given by Macdonald,* we did question whether it could be said that there had been a false pretence if no other human being was involved and the pretence was made solely to a computer. However, we concluded that the concept of 'false pretence' is probably sufficiently flexible to cope even with that sort of case. In this respect, we noted, Scots law may have an advantage over English law, which, in the Theft Act 1968 and elsewhere, uses the concept of 'deception' which, it has been held, requires a human mind to be deceived. Under both systems of law, of course, there will be many cases involving computers where it will nonetheless be perfectly possible to say that a false pretence has been made to a person, or that a person has been deceived.
>
> **Criminal Law of Scotland*, 5th edn, p 52: fraud 'involves a false pretence made dishonestly in order to bring about some definite practical result'.

This difference highlights the fact that the applicability of existing legislative provisions to otherwise 'traditional' offences committed with the aid of computers may depend on the vagaries of language and the capability of that language of being interpreted in such a way as to take into account any special features of computer crime. The nuances of the relevant language were spelled out by Buckley J in *Re London and Globe Finance Corporation Ltd*:[12]

> To deceive is, I apprehend, to induce a man to believe that a thing is true which is false, and which the person practising the deceit knows or believes to be false. To defraud is to deprive by deceit: it is by deceit to induce a man to act to his injury. More tersely it may be put, that to deceive is by falsehood to induce a state of mind; to defraud is by deceit to induce a course of action.

There is, thus, no need to wrestle with the thorny question of whether a machine ie a computer can be deceived on occasions where there has been no communication or intervention by humans.

One recent cause for concern has been the phenomenon of so-called phantom withdrawals from automatic teller machines at banks. A recent example was the case of *R v Munden*[13] involving a policeman who alleged that money had been extracted from his account even though he had made no withdrawals. He was prosecuted for attempted fraud and eventually acquitted but for computer law this is, arguably, more correctly described as an issue of evidence than of fraud.[14]

Although the whole area of so-called computer crime was reviewed by the Law Commissions for both Scotland and England and Wales, it was generally concluded that most cases of computer fraud could be dealt with adequately

12 [1903] 1 Ch 728 at 732.

13 (1996) July, unreported, Bury Crown Court, see comp.risks RISKS DIGEST 18.25.

14 See also Chapter 9.

by the existing provisions except for those rare occasions on which the case might rest on the 'deception' of a machine. In recognition of this, the Law Society made the suggestion that the definition in the Theft Act should be extended by introduction of the wording 'inducing a machine to respond to false representations which the person making them knows to be false as if they were true'.

As far as other types of activity were concerned the application of the criminal law was by no means so certain. This was particularly true in relation to the increasing activity of 'computer hacking', which produced some particular headaches for the courts prior to the passing of the Computer Misuse Act 1990. Attempts were made to use a number of pre-existing statutes. One of the most celebrated cases was that of *Gold & Schifreen*.[15]

Gold and Schifreen hacked for a hobby and had managed to obtain the password for the Prestel System operated by BT which provided subscribers with both e-mail facilities and access to a number of database services. The password they obtained was in fact that issued to BT engineers, so not only did it not charge them for use, but it also gave widespread access to all parts of the system (note, however, that it was not a particularly complex password: 22222222 followed by the user id 1234). By this means they were even able to leave messages in the e-mail box of the Duke of Edinburgh! Their activities eventually aroused suspicion and they were tracked down by monitoring their telephone usage. The question then arose as to what could be an appropriate charge. A prosecution was brought under s 1 of the Forgery and Counterfeiting Act 1981 which provides that: 'A person is guilty of forgery if he makes a false instrument with the intention that he or another shall use it to induce somebody to accept it as genuine and by reason of so accepting it do or not do some act to his own or any other person's prejudice.' For offences under this section, the problems identified in relation to the deception of a machine are overcome by express provision in the Act.

Gold and Schifreen were convicted but appealed on the basis that no false instrument had been made. Instrument is defined in s 8 of the Act and includes discs, tapes etc on which the is material stored by electronic means. The prosecution argument relied on the assertion that the dishonestly obtained password could constitute such an instrument as it generated and was transmitted in the form of electrical impulses.

This contention was rejected for two reasons. Firstly, it was felt that any instrument for the purposes of this Act had to be *ejusdem generis* with the other examples in the statutory definition which were all physical objects and, as the electrical impulses in question were only transient, this did not correspond well with the idea of the creation of an instrument. In addition to the difficulties with the definition of the instrument, the inapplicability of the

15 [1988] AC 1063, [1988] Crim LR 437 (HL), see also Feliks J Kwiatkowski (1987) 4 CL & P 15.

charge was also held to be due to the nature of the offence of forgery. In this case the password was not false, it was genuine, there was just no entitlement to use it. Both the Court of Appeal and the House of Lords were of the view that the use of this statute was inappropriate and not intended to apply to this type of case. Lord Brandon of Oakbrook giving judgment in the House of Lords referred, with approval, to the speech of Lord Lane in the Court of Appeal extracted below.

R v Gold and Schifreen [1987] QB 1116 at 1124: Court of Appeal, Criminal Division.

> **Lord Lane CJ** In our judgment the user segment in the instant case does not carry the necessary two types of message to bring it within the ambit of forgery at all. Moreover, neither the report nor the Act, so it seems to us, seeks to deal with information that is held for a moment whilst automatic checking takes place and is then expunged. That process is not one to which the words 'recorded or stored' can properly be applied, suggesting as they do a degree of continuance.
>
> There is a further difficulty. The prosecution had to prove that the appellants intended that someone should accept as genuine the false instrument which they had made. The suggestion here is that it was a machine (under section 10(3)) which the appellants intended to induce to respond to the false instrument. But the machine (ie, the user segment) which was intended, so it was said, to be induced seems to be the very thing which was said to be the false instrument (ie, the user segment) which was inducing the belief. If that is a correct analysis, the prosecution case is reduced to an absurdity.
>
> We have accordingly come to the conclusion that the language of the Act was not intended to apply to the situation which was shown to exist in this case. The submissions at the close of the prosecution case should have succeeded. It is a conclusion which we reach without regret. The Procrustean attempt to force these facts into the language of an Act not designed to fit them produced grave difficulties for both judge and jury which we would not wish to see repeated. The appellants' conduct amounted in essence, as already stated, to dishonestly gaining access to the relevant Prestel data bank by a trick. That is not a criminal offence. If it is thought desirable to make it so, that is a matter for the legislature rather than the courts.

The whole-hearted and unanimous endorsement of this passage by the House of Lords shows the disdain with which the attempt to squeeze the activity of computer hacking into the framework of an inappropriate statute was treated. The clear message was that, although it might be appropriate in some areas of the law to expand and develop the interpretation of existing legal provisions to take account of advances in technology, such provision had to be consonant with the alleged 'offence' in order not to stretch the law beyond its breaking point.

In an attempt to bring a number of anti-social computer users to book, various persons were charged with offences under the Criminal Damage Act 1971. Was there any greater likelihood of success in these cases or were they to be treated with the same contempt as the charges made under the Forgery Act?

The question for the court in *Cox v Riley*[16] was whether the deliberate erasure, by a disgruntled employee, of a computer program from a plastic card controlling a computerised saw, so as to render the saw inoperable, could be construed as criminal damage for the purposes of s 1(1) of the Criminal Damage Act 1971. It was agreed by all parties that the card was 'property' within the meaning of s 10(1), but had it been damaged? At first instance, damage was found in the fact that the card could no longer be used to operate and control the saw. On appeal, the opposing argument was again placed that, in reality, it was not the card that had been damaged but the program; the physical state of the card was unchanged. As the program was intangible it was argued that it could not, of itself, be construed as property within the meaning of s 10(1).

Stephen Brown LJ found, however, that the card was indeed damaged in that it had been deprived of its usefulness and that it would take both time and money to remedy this situation. In arriving at this conclusion, he relied on *dicta* of Cantley J in the case of *Henderson and Battley*[17] which took the definition of damage from the *Concise Oxford Dictionary* as 'injury impairing value or usefulness'. Both Stephen Brown LJ and Cantley J relied, also, on the much earlier precedent of *Fisher*[18] concerning a discontented employee who put a steam engine out of action in such a way as not to damage the engine as such, but to ensure that considerable time and effort was needed to make it operative again. The use of this reasoning to reach the decision in *Cox v Riley* was later criticised by the Law Commission on the basis that it was decided under the provisions of the Malicious Damage Act 1861,[19] an Act which contained a different concept of damage but, notwithstanding the applicability of this case to the situation in *Cox v Riley*, the inherent pragmatism in this approach and its application to rather more modern technology can be seen in the concluding remarks:[20]

> It has to be said that we are living in the age of computers; not only computers but other magnetised operations. One thinks of articles such as the ordinary bank card which is used to withdraw money from certain machines. There are many methods of operating machinery by stimulating or activating electrical circuits or magnetised contacts, all these are matters which are part of the modern industrial and social scene.
>
> It seems to me quite untenable to argue that what this defendant did on this occasion did not amount to causing damage to property ...

16 (1986) 83 Cr App Rev 54.

17 (1984) unreported, ICA.

18 (1865) LR 1 CCR7.

19 See later discussion at p 350.

20 (1986) 83 Cr App Rep 54 at 58 *per* Stephen Brown LJ.

As will be appreciated, this does not really attack the crux of opposing argument which is directed at where the damage lies[21] and is perhaps more informed by the fact that it was well established that the defendant had the requisite *mens rea* rather than confirmation that the necessary *actus reus* had been proved.

A rather different approach was to be taken to the application of the Criminal Damage Act 1971 in computer-related cases in *R v Whiteley*,[22] but, on any assessment, this was a radically different type of case. In brief,[23] Whiteley's hobby was hacking into computer networks and a particular target of his was JANET, the Joint Academic Network. Whilst engaged in such activities, he assumed the identity of Alan Dolby, the 'Mad Hacker', and deleted and changed data, 'locked out' authorised users by effecting changes of password etc. He was eventually traced following monitoring of the system at Queen Mary College, one of his prime targets, and charged with criminal damage.

Again the argument was put that the damage was not to the tangible parts of the computer system but rather to the information contained on the disk. The manner in which such disks store information is in the arrangement of magnetic particles on the surface – if the information is changed (maliciously or otherwise) then this pattern will be altered and the court found that such a change could be sufficient to found a charge of criminal damage.

R v Whiteley (1991) 93 CR App 25 at 27
Court of Appeal

> ... the discs are so constructed as to contain upon them thousands, if not millions, of magnetic particles. By issuing commands to the computer, impulses are produced which magnetise or demagnetise those particles in a particular way. By that means it is possible to write data or information on the discs and to program them to fulfil a variety of functions. By the same method it is possible to delete or alter data, information or instructions which have previously been written on to the disc. The argument advanced on behalf of the appellant, when reduced to its essence, seems to us to be this. That since the state of the magnetic particles on the disc is not perceptible by the unaided human senses, for instance of sight or touch, therefore the appellant's admitted activities only affected the 'intangible information' contained on the disc itself. Even if the absence of such a change is not fatal to the prosecution, goes on the submission, interference with the particles cannot amount to damage in law.
>
> It seems to us that that contention contains a basic fallacy. What the Act requires to be proved is that tangible property has been damaged, not necessarily that the damage itself should be tangible. There can be no doubt that the magnetic particles upon the metal discs were a part of the discs and if the appellant was proved to have intentionally and without lawful excuse

21 For discussion of these rules in a different context see Chapter 4.

22 (1991) 93 Cr App Rep 25, see also David Cowley (1992) 56 J Crim Law 37.

23 For a more detailed account of events see Bryan Clough and Paul Mungo, *Approaching Zero: Data Crime and the Computer Underworld* (1993) p 42 *et seq*, Faber and Faber.

> altered the particles in such a way as to cause an impairment of the value or usefulness of the disc to the owner, there would be damage within the meaning of section 1. The fact that the alteration could only be perceived by operating the computer did not make the alterations any the less within the ambit of the Act.
>
> ... Any alteration to the physical nature of the property concerned may amount to damage within the meaning of the section. Whether it does so or not will depend upon the effect that the alteration has had upon the legitimate operator (who for convenience may be referred to as the owner). If the hacker's actions do not go beyond, for example, mere tinkering with an otherwise 'empty' disc, no damage would be established. Where, on the other hand, the interference with the disc amounts to an impairment of the value or usefulness of the disc to the owner, then the necessary damage is established.

This reasoning might have provided a suitable avenue for the use of existing legal provisions to deal with cases of computer hacking – particularly of the more anti-social variety which involve rather more than mere browsing in the contents of files. However, by the time this decision had been reached the Law Commission's recommendations for reform of the law in this area had resulted in the passing of the Computer Misuse Act 1990 which effectively removed such cases from the ambit of the Criminal Damage Act 1971.

The Law Commission reviewed the application of the existing criminal law and considered the desirability of criminalising activities such as hacking by the creation of specific offences. In so doing they took into account the findings of the Scottish Law Commission which had already reported on this topic.[24] They also had to come to terms with both the notion of computer crime and whether it was either necessary or desirable to create new criminal offences in this area, especially with regard to the activities of hackers. The Scottish Law Commission had recommended in their report that the problem could be tackled by the creation of an unauthorised access offence although this received a mixed reception in some quarters.

'Computer Crime': Scotch Mist
Colin Tapper
[1987] Criminal Law Review 4 at 8

> **Possible responses**
>
> There seem to be three main possibilities. The first is for the legislature to do nothing, but instead to rely upon the judiciary to interpret the existing rules in such a way as to embrace computer-related crimes. The second is for the legislature to assist the task of the judiciary by modifying the definitions and conditions for liability of existing offences, but without enacting new ones. The third is to enact new offences specifically aimed at computer-related crime. This third alternative should perhaps be further subdivided between new offences which are intended to supplant existing offences in the computer-related area,

24 Scottish Law Commission *Report on Computer Crime* Cm 174 HMSO 1987.

and those which are intended to supplement them. Choice between these various alternatives must largely be determined by some perception of the particular uses or abuses of computers which fall outside the ambit of existing offences. Some general considerations are, however, apposite here.

The principal argument for the first alternative is that it is in many ways the most flexible. Development can proceed by minute steps, and those steps can often be retraced if a new perspective shows them to have started out in the wrong direction. It is also likely to be the method most congenial to the judiciary and so most likely to be accorded a sympathetic reception by them. It is much rarer to find determined opposition and destructive interpretation offered to a new common law development than to a new and unwelcome statute. It has the further advantage that the pace of development automatically reflects the incidence of the relevant situation. If no cases come to court for decision, the law stands still; but if many cases come, then some development, or at least crystallisation, is inevitable. This method is also least likely to foster anomalies, either between different applications of the same offence, or between different offences.

The disadvantages are in some ways the converse of the advantages. Just because the law proceeds in a flexible, and reversible, manner, it may lose some of its deterrent effect. It can be argued that in order to influence conduct, potential actors must have some clear idea of when the law is likely to intervene, and that this will be denied if each new situation gives rise to a new decision. Such an argument can be overstated however. Criminal law is concerned with morally reprehensible conduct, and the effect of uncertainty may be to restrain potential actors from doing anything remotely reprehensible in the area. Nevertheless, there remains a constraint upon the judges in this respect. They will be reluctant to depart very far from established rules. In general it is not the province of the judges to create new criminal offences, and this general policy is embodied in rules requiring all doubts to be resolved in favour of the accused, a maxim just as applicable to the establishment of rules as to the finding of facts. It may also be thought that the process of litigation is unlikely to lead to the development of the best-informed rules, rules of relevance confine lawyers to the proof of facts clearly and closely applicable to the particular facts before the court, and neither counsel nor judiciary may be thought sufficiently computerate to be trusted to understand the subject well enough to develop the best rules.

The third alternative lies at the opposite extreme. New legislation can be moulded to fit the precise delineation of the perceived need. It can come replete with exact definitions and explicit exceptions. The range of procedures, forms of proof and level of penalty are all capable of being adapted to the special problems of the situation. It may also be argued that it is just as, if not more, flexible than common law development, since legislation can always be amended, or, if necessary, repealed and replaced. However true this may be in theory, it is, given the pressure on parliamentary time, less than practically possible.

The principal disadvantages are those of creating anomalies and, by so doing, injustice. It is unlikely to be acceptable if criminality, or even sentence or procedure, depends upon whether a computer happens to have been involved

... Nor is it clear that legislators and draftsmen are so much more conversant with the technology of computing than counsel and judges, though they do have more opportunity to seek expert advice. Even so, the encapsulation of the burgeoning technology within the strait-jacket of the ordinary language and comprehensible structure ideally characterising Acts of Parliament, constitutes a formidable task. It is made more formidable still by the hinterland of presumptions, policies and principles customarily bestowed upon the construction of Acts of Parliament establishing new criminal offences, especially if recourse to anything beyond the words themselves is artificially restricted.

The middle course of tailoring definitions and conditions mitigates both advantages and disadvantages of the two extremes. It is likely to reduce anomalies when compared to the creation of wholly new offences, but it can often achieve this only at the expense of some distortion of the pattern of existing offences. The principal point of engagement in the legislative process is also perhaps the most hazardous in terms of drafting, namely in the casting of definitions.

It can be seen from this account that in the abstract there is no clear choice to be made between these different approaches. All must depend upon the array of conduct which is sought to be suppressed, and the aptitude of application of such crimes as already exist.

It had often been suggested that there was no need for further criminal offences because the reality was that this would create anomalies by criminalising behaviour which would not attract this stigma if the outcome of that behaviour was achieved by more conventional means. To set this discussion in context, the Law Commission for England and Wales pointed out the differences between computers and other information storage and retrieval systems.

The Law Commission
Working Paper No 110
Part VI Reforming the Present Law (3) Hacking

6.3 The possible criminalisation of conduct which is not at present directly covered by the criminal law must involve a consideration of whether it is in the public interest that such conduct should be regarded as criminal. This in turn may involve consideration of whether it can be adequately controlled in some other way, in particular by the civil law.

B SHOULD THE OBTAINING OF UNAUTHORISED ACCESS TO A COMPUTER BY HACKING BE A CRIMINAL OFFENCE?

6.7 .... there are some special features concerning computers and their accessibility to which we think attention must be drawn at this stage.

(i) Computers are capable of storing and processing vast amounts of information. Information which twenty or thirty years ago might have been stored in large rooms full of filing cabinets can now be kept on a single disk smaller than a pocket sized note-book. The computer is a relatively recent invention which we must now accept as a feature of late 20th century life. In general, the benefits which this new technology has brought to members of society are not in doubt.

(ii) Much of the information stored in computers is information of a nature which those who disclose it to the computer owner would not want disclosed to third parties. For example, information relating to individuals of a personal kind, bank accounts, credit ratings, medical records and trade secrets.

(iii) For large computer systems to be effective, and to be of maximum use to legitimate users, including those who supply information to computer owners, they must be readily accessible from 'remote' computer terminals. This necessarily gives rise to problems of security which are of an entirely different kind from those which arise in connection with the safeguarding of manual records ... it is difficult if not impossible to create a totally secure computer system.

(iv) It may be possible for a person to obtain unauthorised access to information stored in the computer without the need for any physical presence other than at a terminal which is connected to the computer system by means of a telecommunication system. Without this physical presence, a person who seeks to obtain unauthorised access will not be exposed to the risk of prosecution for offences such as burglary or criminal damage which might be applicable if physical access were required.

(v) In deciding whether obtaining unauthorised access to information held on a computer should be a crime, analogies with other forms of conduct may be helpful but can be misleading. It is probably better, therefore, to consider the computer for what it is ...

1 The arguments for an offence

6.8 One argument in favour of an offence ... acknowledges the importance of computers for society as a whole and suggests that those who use and rely on computers may be inhibited from making full use of them, if they fear that others might obtain unauthorised access to information held on them. For this reason, it is in the public interest that society must try to deter hacking generally, or at the very least in respect of computers holding certain kinds of information.

6.12... further argument in favour of an unauthorised access offence ... rests on the possible consequences of hacking to a computer system. Where the computer system is especially important, or the information stored on it especially valuable, these consequences will be more serious, but hacking could lead to an inadvertent damaging of any computer system. An offence of obtaining unauthorised access to a computer would signal society's disapproval of those who deliberately set out to breach security measures, and amount to a rejection of the claim that hacking is a harmless intellectual pastime. This rejection would have beneficial consequences beyond the number of successful prosecutions likely to be brought ...

6.13Another positive side-effect of a hacking offence would be that its prohibition may serve to deter conduct which is made possible by the obtaining of unauthorised access to a computer, such as computer assisted fraud or theft, or the corruption of data or programs. An offence which may reduce the number of opportunities for subsequent (illegal) activities is worthy of further consideration.

2 The arguments against an offence

6.15 The main argument against the introduction, in any form, of a criminal offence of obtaining unauthorised access to a computer is that, although such conduct may constitute an invasion of privacy, it is not a matter in which the criminal law should interfere. No general right of privacy exists in English law even in the law of tort, and while obtaining unauthorised access to a computer may appear to be akin to the tort of trespass, such behaviour is generally not subject to criminal sanction without some further aggravating feature. Information is not property in English law ... and it is no offence, as such, to read someone else's correspondence or files ...

6.16 A further argument against the creation of a hacking offence is that the offence may be very difficult to enforce. We understand that it is possible for a hacker to obtain access to data on a computer and to ensure that the fact that he has obtained access remains undetected, or a least can be discovered only after a very time-consuming search ... Sometimes conduct may be so serious and so socially damaging that it clearly merits a criminal sanction whatever the problems of enforcement. In other cases where the harm caused by the relevant conduct is not so great, the case for providing a criminal sanction will be weakened by problems of enforcement. It is arguable that mere hacking falls into the latter category.

Further discussion and debate together with further evidence received following the publication of the Working Paper led to the conclusion that, taking all the circumstances into account, the creation of further criminal offences was in fact necessary.[25]

The Law Commission
Criminal Law
Computer Misuse[26]

1.37 ... the main argument in favour of a hacking offence does not turn on the protection of information, but rather springs from the need to protect the integrity and security of computer systems from attacks from unauthorised persons seeking to enter those systems, whatever may be their intention or motive. It is for that reason that we propose, as a deterrent counter to hacking, two offences: the first, a broad offence that seeks to deter the general practice of hacking by imposing penalties of a moderate nature on all types of unauthorised access; and the second a narrower but more serious offence, that imposes much heavier penalties

25 Whether this outcome is desirable continues to be questioned. See, eg, Martin Wasik, *Misuse of Information Technology: What should the role of the criminal law be?* Yearbook of Law, Computers and Technology, 1991, Vol 5, p 158.

26 Cm 819 HMSO 1989.

on those persons who hack with intent to commit, or to facilitate the commission of, serious crime.

Thus the Law Commission came to the conclusion that the existing criminal remedies were inadequate to deal with many instances of computer crime and misuse although they conceded that a number of charges under the Theft Act might be appropriate in cases of computer fraud. However, despite the completion of the Law Commission report, the government seemed to have no plan to introduce legislation, and the Computer Misuse Act eventually saw the light of day as a consequence of a Private Member's Bill introduced by Michael Colvin. This Bill followed fairly closely the Law Commissions proposals – in particular it took the two-tier approach common in such legislation in other jurisdictions, namely the creation of a basic hacking offence plus an ulterior intent offence to cover situations where there is some intent to commit a further crime.

Computer Misuse Act 1990

Section 1 Unauthorised access to computer material

(1) A person is guilty of an offence if

(a) he causes a computer to perform any function with intent to secure access to any program or data held in any computer;

(b) the access he intends to secure is unauthorised; and

(c) he knows at the time when he causes the computer to perform the function that that is the case.

(2) The intent a person has to have to commit an offence under this section need not be directed at

(a) any particular program or data;

(b) a program or data of any particular kind; or

(c) a program or data held in any particular computer.

Section 2 Unauthorised access with intent to commit or facilitate commission of further offences

(1) A person is guilty of an offence under this section if he commits an offence under section 1 above ('the unauthorised access offence') with intent

(a) to commit an offence to which this section applies; or

(b) to facilitate the commission of such an offence (whether by himself or by any other person); ...

(2) This section applies to offences

(a) for which the sentence is fixed by law; or

(b) for which a person ... may be sentenced to imprisonment for a term of five years ...

(3) It is immaterial for the purposes of this section whether the further offence is to be committed on the same occasion as the unauthorised access offence or on any future occasion.

(4) A person may be guilty of an offence under this section even though the facts are such that the commission of the further offence is impossible.

These sections demonstrate the structure of the offences created. Sections 1 and 2 are hierarchical and, when charges are brought under s 2, it is still possible to convict under s 1, even where the necessary intent for a s 2 offence is not proved. Note, however, that certain activities do not fall within the ambit of the statute, in particular, reading of the contents of files non-interactively, eg unauthorised reading after printing out in cases where the print operation had been performed by an authorised user, or mere reading of information on a computer screen. Depending on the nature of the material such acts could fall within the scope of the Data Protection Act 1984.[27] A potentially more serious omission as the technology becomes ever more sophisticated is computer eavesdropping and it may be that, in the future, action may be needed to remedy this lacuna.[28] The Act does not define the word 'computer' but a lengthy interpretation section demonstrates the wide-reaching scope of some of the other crucial concepts in the Act.

Section 17 Interpretation

(2) A person secures access to any program or data held in a computer if by causing a computer to perform any function he

(a) alters or erases the program or data;

(b) copies or moves it to any storage medium other than that in which it is held or to a different location in the storage medium in which it is held;

(c) uses it; or

(d) has it output from the computer in which it is held (whether by having it displayed or in any other manner);

and references to access to a program or data (and to an intent to secure such access) shall be read accordingly.

(3) For the purposes of subsection (2)(c) above a person uses a program if the function he causes the computer to perform

(a) causes the program to be executed; or

(b) is itself a function of the program.

(4) For the purposes of subsection (2)(d) above

(a) a program is output if the instructions of which it consists are output; and

(b) the form in which any such instructions or any other data is output (and in particular whether or not it represents a form in which, in the case of instructions, they are capable of being executed or, in the case of data, it is capable of being processed by a computer) is immaterial.

27 See Chapter 7.

28 Law Commission Working Paper No 119 *Computer Misuse*, Martin Wasik and Alexandra Piperaki, *Computer Crime: the Scottish Law Commission Proposals* Yearbook of Law, Computers and Technology, 1987, Vol 3, 109 at 112, Ian Beale, *Computer Eavesdropping: Fact or Fantasy* (1986) 1 CLSR 16.

(5) Access of any kind by any person to any program or data held in the computer is unauthorised if

 (a) he is not himself entitled to control access of the kind in question to the program or data; and

 (b) he does not have consent to access by him of the kind in question to the program or data from any person who is so entitled.

(6) References to any program or data held in a computer include references to any program or data held in a removable storage medium which is for the time being in the computer; and a computer is to be regarded as containing any program or data held in any such medium.

(7) A modification of the contents of any computer takes place if, by the operation of any function of the computer concerned or any other computer

 (a) any program or data held in the computer concerned is altered or erased; or

 (b) any program or data is added to its contents; and any act which contributes towards causing such a modification shall be regarded as causing it.

(8) Such a modification is unauthorised if

 (a) the person whose act causes it is not himself entitled to determine whether the modification should be made; and

 (b) he does not consent to the modification from any person who is so entitled.

Thus, as far as access is required, it appears that any sort of activity will suffice other than merely reading a screen and that the Act extends to access to, or modification of, the contents of floppy disks if this occurs while they are in any computer. The interpretation of 'unauthorised' allows for the absence of different levels of authority, the one to access the data or program in question and the other, in relation to s 3, the authority to actually modify and change the data or program. This parallels the practice on computer networks of issuing different types of identifiers or passwords for those people who are permitted access on a read-only basis *vis-à-vis* those who have more extensive authorisation to make changes to the computer contents.

The very first case under the Computer Misuse Act 1990, that of *R v Cropp*,[29] raised questions about the scope of the Act. Cropp was charged with an offence under s 2(1) (which requires the establishment of an offence under s 1(1)) following an incident which occurred when he visited the premises of his ex-employer, a wholesaler, with his new employer. Cropp showed interest in an item, picked up a machine and a salesperson began to enter the details on the storeroom computer. The salesperson was called away during this

29 (1991) unreported, Snaresbrook Crown Court but see case note (1991) 7 CLSR 168.

operation and Cropp, being well-acquainted with the operation of the system took the opportunity to input a discount of 70%. His new employer subsequently paid an invoice for £204.60 plus VAT instead of the correct sum of £710.96 plus VAT. Was this a case of unauthorised access to a computer?

A submission of no case to answer was made on the grounds that in order to contravene s 1(1) (and therefore s 2(1)), it had to be established that the accused had used one computer with intent to secure unauthorised access into another computer. This represents the usual definition of 'hacking' which was popularly supposed to be the activity that was proscribed by this new legislation. The judge upheld this submission saying that:

> It seems to me, doing the best that I can in elucidating the meaning of s 1(1)(a), that a second computer must be involved. It seems to me to be straining language to say that only one computer is necessary when one looks to see the actual wording of the subsection: 'Causing a computer to perform any function with intent to secure access to any program or data held in any computer.'

The Attorney-General sought clarification from the Court of Appeal[30] on the basis that the Act had been drafted so as to deal not only with the situation in which indirect access to a computer system is gained by using another computer, but also with the situation where a person misuses a computer to which he or she has direct (but unauthorised) access. The following point of law was at issue:

> In order for a person to commit an offence under section 1(1) of the Computer Misuse Act 1990 does the computer which the person causes to perform any function with the required intent have to be a different computer from the one into which he intends to secure unauthorised access to any program or data held therein?

The argument on behalf of the Attorney-General was that the vital phrase was 'any computer' at the end of s 1(1)(a). Whilst conceding that the major mischief which had led to the enactment of the Act was that in which persons used one computer to hack into another computer, it was submitted that the scope of this section was not confined purely to that activity.

Attorney-General's Reference No 1 of 1991
[1992] WLR 432 at 437
Court of Appeal

> **Lord Taylor of Gosforth CJ** The ordinary canons of construction require this court to look at the words of the section and to give them their plain and natural meaning. Doing that, we look again at the relevant words. They are, 'he causes a computer to perform any function with intent to secure access to any program or data held in any computer'.

30 *A-G's Reference No 1 of 1991* [1992] 3 WLR 432 at 434 and see Susan Singleton (1993) J Crim Law 181.

> Mr Lassman argued successfully before the judge, and sought to argue before this court, that that final phrase, 'held in any computer', should really be read as 'held in any other computer', or alternatively should be read as 'held in any computer except the computer which has performed the function'.
>
> To read those words in that way, in our judgment, would be to give them a meaning quite different from their plain and natural meaning. It is a trite observation, when considering the construction of statutes, that one does not imply or introduce words which are not there when the plain and natural meaning is clear. In our judgment there are no grounds whatsoever for implying, or importing the word 'other' between 'any' and 'computer,' or excepting the computer which is actually used by the offender from the phrase 'any computer' at the end of the subsection (1)(a).

If the court had not arrived at such an interpretation, the potential usefulness of the Computer Misuse Act 1990 could have been severely curtailed resulting in what has been described as 'total emasculation'.[31] The dramatic effect that this might have had is particularly apparent with hindsight as the majority of prosecutions that have been brought since then have far more in common with the situation in *Cropp* than with hacking.[32]

In its report, the Law Commission had also recommended an offence of unauthorised alteration or destruction of data having come to the conclusion that the interpretation of the Criminal Damage Act 1971 as seen in *Cox v Riley*[33] (which they had appeared to endorse in the Working Paper[34] – '[o]ur provisional view is that this reasoning is correct and in accordance with the wide meaning which damage was intended to bear') was in need of clarification. It should be noted that this was written before the decision in *R v Whiteley*.[35]

The Law Commission
Criminal Law
Computer Misuse[36]

> 2.27 Our provisional view was that the wide meaning attributed by the courts to the word 'damage', including as it did any injury impairing the value or usefulness of the property, had had the effect of extending the law of criminal damage to cover the tangible property ... on which programs or data were stored. On this reasoning any unlawful interference with the data or program would amount to damage to the tangible storage medium, providing that its value was thereby diminished.

31 EA Dumbill, *Computer Misuse Act 1990 – Recent developments* (1992) 8 CLSR 105.

32 See further discussion at p 355.

33 (1986) 83 Cr App Rev 54 and see previous discussion at p 339.

34 Law Commission Working Paper No 110, para 3.38.

35 (1991) 93 Cr App Rep 25 and see previous discussion at p 340.

36 Cm 819 HMSO 1989.

2.28 It does not seem to have been seriously questioned that the unauthorised destruction of data and the reprogramming of operational computers ought to be criminal ... Alteration or erasure of data without authority has, in the absence of specific justifications provided by law, no social value; it involves deliberate interference with the property of others, and not merely trespassing on their premises or looking at their information; ... it can cause substantial loss and, in the case of operational systems, physical danger. While it is clear therefore that these activities ought to be outlawed, it is more controversial whether the present law of criminal damage is an adequate response in the way that we provisionally suggested. Our conclusion on further consideration, which was supported by the weight of opinion on consultation, is that clarification of the law is required. The main reasons for that conclusion are as follows.

2.29 'Property' means, for the purposes of the Criminal Damage Act 1971, property of a tangible nature. In *Cox v Riley*, the deleted computer program had been stored on a plastic circuit card, which latter could be and was identified as the tangible property which had been damaged. Several consultees have made the point that there may be more difficulty in other cases in pointing to a physical medium on which the altered or erased data has been held; indeed it has been suggested to us that in some cases data is stored by means of electrical impulses that are only very notionally attached to any tangible property. For the commission of a criminal offence to depend on whether it can be proved that data was damaged or destroyed while it was held on identifiable tangible property not only is unduly technical, but also creates an undesirable degree of uncertainty in the operation of the law.

2.30 The Divisional Court in *Cox v Riley* in effect held, following the unreported case in the Court of Appeal (Criminal Division) of *Henderson and Battley*, that the circuit card had been damaged because to reprogram it would require more than a minimal amount of time and effort. That analysis looked back to *Fisher*, a case decided on section 15 of the Malicious Damage Act 1861, which unlike the 1971 Act referred to 'damage with intent to destroy *or to render useless*' (emphasis added). While the reasoning in Fisher is somewhat ambiguous, it is possible that the court regarded 'rendering useless' as forming a separate head of 'damage'. It is therefore not entirely clear that the view that damage can occur where there has been no physical impairment of the tangible object has survived the repeal by the 1971 Act of the specific offence discussed in *Fisher*. The problem is that neither *Cox v Riley* nor *Henderson and Battley* squarely address the point that the dictionary definition of 'to damage' requires some injury to a thing; the decisions concentrate on the second limb of that definition, that the injury must lessen or destroy its value. In our view, therefore, those authorities cannot be relied on with sufficient confidence as stating the present law on the meaning of damage.

This recommendation was given effect in s 3 of the Act.

Computer Misuse Act 1990

Section 3 Unauthorised modification of computer material

(1) A person is guilty of an offence if

(a) he does any act which causes an unauthorised modification of the contents of any computer; and

(b) at the time when he does the act he has the requisite intent and the requisite knowledge.

(2) For the purposes of subsection (1)(b) above the requisite intent is an intent to cause a modification of the contents of any computer and by so doing

(a) to impair the operation of any computer;

(b) to prevent or hinder access to any program or data held in any computer; or

(c) to impair the operation of any such program or the reliability of any such data.

(3) The intent need not be directed at

(a) any particular computer;

(b) any particular program or data or a program or data of any particular kind; or

(c) any particular modification or a modification of any particular kind.

(4) For the purposes of subsection (1)(b) above the requisite knowledge is knowledge that any modification he intends to cause is unauthorised.

(5) It is immaterial for the purposes of this section whether an unauthorised modification or any intended effect of it of a kind mentioned in subsection (2) above is, or is intended to be, permanent or merely temporary.

(6) For the purposes of the Criminal Damage Act 1971 a modification of the contents of a computer shall not be regarded as damaging any computer or computer storage medium unless its effect on that computer or computer storage medium impairs its physical condition.

The concepts contained in this section are further amplified in s 17(7) and (8).[37] Section 3 creates an offence of doing any act which causes unauthorised modification of the contents of any computer with the requisite intent and knowledge as defined by the section. Interestingly enough, the new Act does not actually amend the Criminal Damage Act 1971 as originally suggested by the Law Commission but in s 3(6), contains a proviso as to the application of that Act to modification of computer material. It therefore appears that if another case like *Cox v Riley*[38] were to occur it would have to be taken under this section, notwithstanding the successful prosecution argument in the later case of *Whiteley*.[39]

37 Above at p 348.

38 (1986) 83 Cr App Rev 54 and see previous discussion at p 339.

39 (1991) 93 Cr App Rep 25 and see previous discussion at p 340.

Section 3 of the Computer Misuse Act 1990 appears to be capable of catching a wide variety of types of activity. It would be expected to embrace the type of modification and erasure seen in *Cox v Riley* but should also be capable of covering the intentional introduction of viruses, worms, Trojan horses[40] and other programs of a potentially destructive nature. Since the intent need not be directed at any particular computer, the liability of the person who originates the virus or worm should be unaffected if in the event, a virus is introduced to a system by means of an infected disk innocently acquired by a third party. On the other hand, it would appear that anyone knowingly introducing an infected disk has a clear intent to modify the contents of a computer.

Not long before the Computer Misuse Act 1990 was passed, the strange case of Dr Lewis Popp hit the headlines. A large number of people associated with computer use received disks through the post purporting to contain important information about the Aids virus. If, in fact, the disks were used, although they did reveal information on that subject they also contained a 'Trojan horse' which was programmed to activate after the computer had been used about 100 times.[41] Although the contents of the hard disk would have been destroyed, there would have been little action which could have been taken as a result of this particular activity, unless the courts would have been happy to use the reasoning in Whiteley.[42] This incident was referred to in the Parliamentary debates on the Bill and it is also evident that, at this stage, it was intended that the new legislation would cover such activities: '... circulation of an infected disk, such as this is not an offence. However, the Bill will make it one.'[43] Despite this there was some discussion after the statute was enacted as to whether it was suitable for apprehending those who introduced viruses into computer systems for whatever reason.[44] Some of this raised problems of detection and enforcement (see below) but the fact that s 3

40 These and similar terms are sometimes used interchangeably in non-technical parlance. A virus is a self-replicating program which may not be immediately apparent on examination of a system but copies itself into the computer memory and from there to any disks which are subsequently loaded and/or into the memory of other computers attached to the same network as data is exchanged. The type of program commonly referred to as a worm is an example of a program that was developed for exploring the capabilities of computer systems and networks and may adversely affect systems on which it is unwanted by consuming resources. A Trojan horse is a program which appears as a program performing an innocuous function but hides the fact that it also has another, usually more sinister function.

41 See, eg, Yaman Akdeniz *Section 3 of the Computer Misuse Act 1990: an Antidote for Computer Viruses!* [1996] 3 Web JCLI (http://webjcli.ncl.ac.uk/).

42 In fact, Dr Popp was eventually arrested in Ohio and charged with extorting money with menaces as those affected were also directed to transfer sums of money to a bank account in Panama. In the event, there was evidence that Popp's mental condition had deteriorated to such an extent that he was pronounced unfit to plead.

43 Michael Colvin HC Debates (1990) Hansard, Vol 166, col 1139.

44 See, eg, Wasik, below, n 47.

could, in principle, be used in this way was put beyond doubt in the case of *R v Pile*.[45] Pile, who referred to himself as the 'Black Baron', developed two particular viruses, Queeg and Pathogen, and also Smeg a guide to writing viruses. He placed these on bulletin boards with the messages 'That's all there is to it. Have fun. The Black Baron'. Although there is an element of the comic in this, the viruses themselves were extremely sophisticated and capable of masquerading as other innocent programs. He was even successful in incorporating a virus into an anti-virus scan program. This was the first time that a person had appeared in court as a result of intentionally introducing computer viruses to a system and the court had no problems in finding a breach of s 3.

However, it still remains uncertain to what extent the Computer Misuse Act could be applicable where persons write and distribute information detailing computer virus codes but are not themselves responsible for introducing a virus into a system. A possibility might be to charge with an inchoate offence such as incitement or conspiracy, or perhaps, in appropriate circumstances, with aiding and abetting an offence under the Act.[46] Pile was, in fact, charged with, *inter alia*, incitement to breach s 3, but, as his was a guilty plea, the likely success of such charges in other cases remains undetermined.

THE OPERATION OF THE ACT

On first examination it does not appear that the new Act has had any more conspicuous success at deterring or apprehending computer misuse than the hotch potch of offences which were the only ones possible prior to its enactment.

Wasik[47] suggested in 1995 that, in reviewing the operation of the law in this area, attention should be focused on two key issues.

> What is the proper role of the criminal law in this area? Should the continuing trend towards criminalisation of computer misuse be society's main response to that behaviour? What should be the priority between that approach and, say, the development of ethical codes and regulatory structures, which would impinge upon manufacturers and others to ensure compliance with higher levels of security in IT products? Might civil liability and/or regulatory

45 (1995) May, unreported, Plymouth Crown Court. For further details see, eg, Jones *Computer Terrorist or Mad Boffin?* (1996) 146 NLJ 46, Yaman Akdeniz Section 3 of the *Computer Misuse Act 1990: an Antidote for Computer Viruses!* [1996] 3 Web JCLI (http://webjcli.ncl.ac.uk/).

46 EA Dumbill, *Computer Misuse Act 1990 – Recent developments* (1992) 8 CLSR 105 at 107, Ian Walden, *Update on the Computer Misuse Act 1990* [1994] J Bus Law 522 at 523.

47 Martin Wasik, International Yearbook of Law, Computers and Technology, 1995, Vol 9, Introduction, p ix.

> arrangements offer a more subtle, and perhaps more effective approach, than further criminalisation? Do we need more law, or less?
>
> To the extent that criminalisation is appropriate in this area (and few would deny that it does offer an important element within a range of responses) we should be concerned to predict, to identify and to remedy the various shortcomings of the law. Will the criminal law as currently drafted cover, for example, the malicious dissemination of computer viruses? This requires us to look, not just at the substantive criminal law but also at the rules of admissibility of evidence in court and the provisions relating to enforcement, search and seizure of evidential material. We should also be concerned to identify new criminal trends associated with widespread computerisation, such as the organised theft of computer hardware and the spread of pornographic material through IT networks.

The Law Commission reports dealt with some of the reasons for the introduction of criminal offences and their activity was paralleled in a number of other jurisdictions which, on the whole, came to similar conclusions. However, this is not to say that there is no place for other regulatory activity and this subject will be returned to later. But what of the shortcomings in the present law? Findings in other jurisdictions that criminal offences had a necessary part to play in combating computer misuse were, inevitably, followed by observations that the introduction of such offences did not provide a complete solution.[48]

In the UK, statistics show[49] that the total number of cases under this legislation is small[50] and, of these, only a small minority are actually hacking cases – the activity which, arguably, precipitated legislative activity. This observation also correlates with the Audit Commission's findings that the instances of computer misuse can, more often, be associated with the employment relationship. Whilst, as identified by the Law Commission, hacking could not be penalised without the Computer Misuse Act 1990, a number of other legal sanctions might be appropriate in the situations identified by the Audit Commission. These could include dismissal,[51] in addition to a range of theft offences where the abuse occurs in order to obtain a pecuniary advantage, or could be construed as blackmail.

Despite the lack of court cases, popular belief, coupled with anecdotal evidence, suggests that hacking is a widespread activity but that, even though this might indicate a breach of s 1, action would be unlikely to be instigated

48 See, eg, Margaret Jackson, *Computer Crime Laws: Are they really needed? The Australian experience*, International Yearbook of Law, Computers and Technology, 1995, Vol 9, p 47.

49 Rupert Battcock (1996) 6 Computers and Law 22.

50 A fact which has been noted in other jurisdictions with similar legislation: '... in many Western countries where there are computer crime laws, there have been only a handful of computer crime prosecutions.' Klaus Brunnstein and Simone Fischer-Huebner, *How far can the criminal law help to control IT misuse?* International Yearbook of Law, Computers and Technology, 1995, Vol 9, p 111.

51 See also *Denco v Joinson* [1992] 1 All ER 463.

until or unless the activity rose above the nuisance level or became in some way damaging. Part of this is due to the problems inherent in detecting and identifying the hacker – something that was not really addressed by the Law Commission report. Clearly the collection of evidence in such cases is not the same process as for more conventional crimes. However, despite criticisms that the expertise of the police is unable to keep pace with that of the hackers,[52] there have been some conspicuous successes, notably the prosecution of Pile, referred to above.

It is not only the detection and apprehension of offenders that has given rise to problems but also the attitude of the courts. This was made particularly apparent in the case of *Bedworth*.[53] Bedworth was a teenager whose hacking activities started when he was given a computer for his 14th birthday in 1987. By the time he was arrested in 1991, together with fellow hackers who had all communicated under pseudonyms via an electronic bulletin board, he had hacked into an impressively long list of computer systems including the *Financial Times*, a cancer research institute in Brussels, the EC offices in Luxembourg and many others, resulting in significant financial losses being incurred by the institutions involved. At his trial, he made no attempt to deny that he had done the acts of which he was accused. His defence was that he was obsessed; he was subject to compulsive behaviour so that, although he knew that what he was doing was unlawful, his obsession denied him the freedom to stop – in other words he was addicted to hacking. To the surprise of the prosecution, the jury acquitted him, a verdict which was widely referred to at the time as if it drove the proverbial 'coach and horses' through the enforcement of the Computer Misuse Act 1990.

Accepting that it can never be known on what basis the jury came to their conclusion, there seem to be three main possibilities. The first of these was that they were intending to signal their disapproval of the Computer Misuse Act in much the same way as the surprise acquittal of Ponting[54] had discredited parts of the Official Secrets Act 1911. This seems unlikely, although there were certain aspects of the investigation of this case (discussed below) which had perhaps aroused the concern of the jury, the case had not been preceded by the history of criticism and bad publicity surrounding the statute in question which had set the scene prior to *Ponting*.

52 See, eg, Andrew Charlesworth, *Between Flesh and Sand: Rethinking the Computer Misuse Act 1990* International Yearbook of Law, Computers and Technology, 1995, Vol 9, 31 at 36.

53 (1993) unreported, Southwark Crown Court. For further details see also Andrew Charlesworth, *Addiction and Hacking* (1993) 143 NLJ 540, *Legislating against computer misuse: the trials and tribulations of the UK Computer Misuse Act 1990* (1993) J Law & Info Sci 80, C Christian, *Down and Out in Cyberspace* (1993) 90/15 Law Soc Gaz 2, Deborah Fisch Nigri, *Computer Crime: Why should we still care* (1993) 9 CLSR 274, Rupert Battcock, *Computer Misuse Act 5 years on – the record since 1990* available at http://www.strath.ac.uk/Departments/Law/.

54 *R v Ponting* [1985] Crim L Rev 318.

The second possibility is that the jury were persuaded by the defence of addiction to computers, notwithstanding the judge's summing up. For addiction to be a sufficient defence to a criminal charge, the individual should be affected to such an extent that the affliction may be viewed as a 'disease of the mind' sufficient to prevent the formation of the requisite *mens rea*, this would then effectively equate with a defence of insanity. Whether or not there is clinical evidence to support any finding of addiction to computer hacking is not a subject which can be debated here, although supporting evidence had been produced during the trial. It is certainly the case that at the trial Bedworth gave repeated assertions, not only that he had committed the acts at issue, but also that he was aware that these acts were wrong and would not be repeated. If he were truly addicted would he be able to make this latter promise? Charlesworth,[55] citing the case of *Lawrence*,[56] points out that courts are unlikely even to take addiction to account in mitigation. *Lawrence* was, of course, a case in which the offence (of burglary) was committed to feed the addiction rather than being directly related to that addiction. Whilst it can be problematic to draw analogies between such cases and those, such as *Bedworth*, in which the addiction is to the criminal behaviour itself, nonetheless, there is confirmation for the absence of a general defence of addiction in *Kopsch*[57] – '[t]he defence of uncontrollable impulse is unknown in English law'.

Finally, it is entirely possible that what acquitted Bedworth was 'the sympathy vote'. There was evidence at the trial that the police had utilised tactics such as 'dawn raids' on his home in their apprehension of Bedworth and it may be that the jury thought that he was only a young fresh-faced boy and that, in the particular circumstances of the case, the police had over-reacted.

Whilst we can never be sure of the precise reasoning on which this acquittal was based, it is clear that no such sympathy was extended to his co-defendants, Strickland and Woods who, having pleaded guilty, were sentenced to six months' imprisonment – a recognition, perhaps, of the fact that the behaviour in question resulted in significant financial loss, can cause serious damage to the systems affected and should be viewed seriously.

Similarly, in the more recent case of *Pile* (above) the judge clearly took the matter very seriously and in the face of the likely losses to affected users, allowed a defence application to seek an expert opinion on the amount of damage caused by Pile's activities, in advance of deciding on sentence. This led to a sentence of 18 months' imprisonment when the case returned to Exeter Crown Court in November 1995. Neither has there has been much

55 Andrew Charlesworth, *Between flesh and sand: Rethinking the Computer Misuse Act 1990*, International Yearbook of Law, Computers and Technology, 1995, Vol 9, p 31.

56 [1989] Crim L Rev 309.

57 (1925) 19 Cr App Rep 50.

leniency for the latest case involving a schoolboy hacker, *R v Pryce*.[58] Pryce was fined a total of £1,200 for 12 counts of hacking into computer systems including that of the Pentagon whose network was said to be much easier to penetrate than that of a UK University!

Even taking into account the provisions provided in the Computer Misuse Act,[59] a further problem which could have surfaced in the case of both Bedworth and Pryce is that of jurisdictional problems; some of the computer systems into which they hacked were in other countries. The reverse situation is obviously equally likely: hackers in other countries can hack into computers and networks in the UK. How is this problem to be addressed? What of the virus which originates in the former USSR or Eastern Europe? The evidence is that this is being dealt with by co-operation between police forces, at least in Europe, and European Police forces have agreed with Interpol that hackers or originators of viruses can be prosecuted in their country of residence, even if the hack or the virus has wreaked havoc in another jurisdiction. This improved co-operation has now been extended into Eastern Europe and has been finding ways of dealing with organised gangs – particularly in Russia and the Balkans. Indeed the evidence that many viruses originate in Eastern European countries with little regulation of such activities has been used as evidence of the efficacy of computer crime legislation – 'the thesis that lack of computer crime legislation tends to mean different ethical standards amongst citizens is, apparently, borne out by what is reported from Bulgaria. Bulgaria had the highest rate of computer virus production per capita of any country in the world. In Bulgaria, there is no computer crime legislation and there are no copyright laws'.[60]

LEGAL PROBLEMS OF COMPUTER NETWORKS

Thus far, two particular types of activity have been the focus of the discussion in this chapter – the use of computers to obtain pecuniary advantage which may lead to a number of offences under theft and related legislation and unauthorised access, including hacking into computer systems. The Computer Misuse Act and similar statutes in other jurisdictions are a particular example of the laws response to unauthorised access to computer systems and, despite the differences between the jurisdictions, shows, in many respects a remarkable consistency of philosophy and approach. This is especially

58 (1997) March, Bow St Magistrates Court. See *Guardian* (1977) 22 March.

59 Section 4 of the Computer Misuse Act 1990 makes it immaterial (subject to certain conditions detailed in subsequent sections and subsections) (a) whether any act or proof of which is required for conviction of the offence occurred in the home country concerned; or (b) whether the accused was in the home country concerned at the time of such an act or event. See also *Dennis Kelleher International Computer Crime* (1997) 147 NLJ 445.

60 Klaus Brunnstein and Simone Fischer-Huebner, *How far can the criminal law help to control IT misuse?* International Yearbook of Law, Computers and Technology, 1995, Vol 9, p 111.

apparent in relation to the almost universal choice of criminal sanctions as appropriate to penalise such actions.

However, these are not the only activities facilitated by the burgeoning use of computers that have caused discussion and concern. The increase in both the size and the capability of computer networks and, in particular the development of the Internet and the World Wide Web have raised a certain amount of disquiet as to the extent to which these media can be used for the propagation of undesirable material. In order to appreciate some of these problems, it is useful to have a rudimentary understanding of the way in which such systems function. The manner of operation of the Internet was set out in *ACLU v Reno*.[61]

ACLU v Reno
United States Court for the Eastern District of Pennsylvania
11 June 1996

II FINDINGS OF FACT

The Internet is not a physical or tangible entity, but rather a giant network which interconnects numerable smaller groups of linked computer networks. It is thus a network of networks. This is best understood if one considers what a linked group of computers – referred to here as a 'network' – is, and what it does ... Some networks are 'closed' networks, not linked to other computers or networks. Many networks, however, are connected to other networks, which are in turn connected to other networks in a manner which permits each computer in any network to communicate with computers on any other network in the system. This global Web of linked networks and computers is referred to as the Internet.

The nature of the Internet is such that it is very difficult, if not impossible, to determine its size at a given moment. It is indisputable, however, that the Internet has experienced extraordinary growth in recent years. In 1981, fewer than 300 computers were linked to the Internet, and by 1989, the number stood at fewer than 90,000 computers. By 1993, over 1,000,000 computers were linked. Today, over 9,400,000 host computers worldwide, of which approximately 60 percent are located within the United States, are estimated to be linked to the Internet. This count does not include the personal computers people use to access the Internet using modems. In all, reasonable estimates are that as many as 40 million people around the world can and do access the enormously flexible communication Internet medium. That figure is expected to grow to 200 million Internet users by the year 1999.

... The resulting whole is a decentralised, global medium of communications – or 'cyberspace' – that links people, institutions, corporations, and governments around the world. The Internet is an international system. This

61 US District Court of Pennsylvania June 1996 – full text available at http://www.access.digex.net/~epic/cda/cda-opinion.html and see later discussion, p 363. See also *Illegal and Harmful Content on the Internet 2. How does the Internet work* Communication to the European Parliament, the Council, the Economic and Social Committee and the Committee of the Regions COM (96) 47. Full text available at http://www2.echo.lu/legal/en/internet/communic.htm.

communications medium allows any of the literally tens of millions of people with access to the Internet to exchange information. These communications can occur almost instantaneously, and can be directed either to specific individuals, to a broader group of people interested in a particular subject, or to the world as a whole ...

Messages between computers on the Internet do not necessarily travel entirely along the same path. The Internet uses 'packet switching' communication protocols that allow individual messages to be subdivided into smaller 'packets' that are then sent independently to the destination, and are then automatically reassembled by the receiving computer. While all packets of a given message often travel along the same path to the destination, if computers along the route become overloaded, then packets can be re-routed to less loaded computers ...

No single entity – academic, corporate, governmental, or non-profit – administers the Internet. It exists and functions as a result of the fact that hundreds of thousands of separate operators of computers and computer networks independently decided to use common data transfer protocols to exchange communications and information with other computers (which in turn exchange communications and information with still other computers). There is no centralised storage location, control point, or communications channel for the Internet, and it would not be technically feasible for a single entity to control all of the information conveyed on the Internet.

The Findings of Fact in this case then went on to discuss the different routes by which people might gain access to the Internet and the different methods by which they might communicate or retrieve information. These include e-mail, newsgroups, real-time interactions, use of distributed databases and remote information retrieval. The most advanced example of this last category is the World Wide Web which was described as follows:

The World Wide Web

A third approach, and fast becoming the most well-known on the Internet, is the 'World Wide Web.' The Web utilises a 'hypertext' formatting language called hypertext markup language (HTML), and programs that 'browse' the Web can display HTML documents containing text, images, sound, animation and moving video. Any HTML document can include links to other types of information or resources, so that while viewing an HTML document that, for example, describes resources available on the Internet, one can 'click' using a computer mouse on the description of the resource and be immediately connected to the resource itself. Such 'hyperlinks' allow information to be accessed and organised in very flexible ways, and allow people to locate and efficiently view related information even if the information is stored on numerous computers all around the world.

Purpose. The World Wide Web (W3C) was created to serve as the platform for a global, on-line store of knowledge, containing information from a diversity of sources and accessible to Internet users around the world. Though information on the Web is contained in individual computers, the fact that each of these computers is connected to the Internet through W3C protocols allows all of the

> information to become part of a single body of knowledge. It is currently the most advanced information system developed on the Internet, and embraces within its data model most information in previous networked information systems ...
>
> ... The Web links together disparate information on an ever-growing number of Internet-linked computers by setting common information storage formats (HTML) and a common language for the exchange of Web documents (HTTP). Although the information itself may be in many different formats, and stored on computers which are not otherwise compatible, the basic Web standards provide a basic set of standards which allow communication and exchange of information. Despite the fact that many types of computers are used on the Web, and the fact that many of these machines are otherwise incompatible, those who 'publish' information on the Web are able to communicate with those who seek to access information with little difficulty because of these basic technical standards.
>
> ... Running on tens of thousands of individual computers on the Internet, the Web is what is known as a distributed system. The Web was designed so that organisations with computers containing information can become part of the Web simply by attaching their computers to the Internet and running appropriate World Wide Web software. No single organisation controls any membership in the Web, nor is there any single centralised point from which individual Web sites or services can be blocked from the Web. From a user's perspective, it may appear to be a single, integrated system, but in reality it has no centralised control point.

Computer networks thus facilitate communications between both individuals and groups as well as providing the means to access and retrieve extensive information from a variety of sources across the globe. Not surprisingly, this does not only include educational and informative material but also includes information that might be undesirable or anti-social. Such material might be defamatory,[62] obscene or pornographic, racist, malicious, threatening or abusive, or constitute undesirable religious or political propaganda. The following list of areas which might give rise to concern in this respect and are likely to be covered by different national and international legal regimes was provided by the European Commission:[63]

- national security (instructions on bomb making, illegal drug production, terrorist activities);
- protection of minors (abusive forms of marketing, violence, pornography);
- protection of human dignity (incitement to racial hatred or racial discrimination);
- economic security (fraud, instructions on pirating credit cards);

62 See discussion in Chapter 7.

63 *Illegal and Harmful Content on the Internet* Communication to the European Parliament, the Council, the Economic and Social Committee and the Committee of the Regions COM (96) 47. Full text available at ttp://www2.echo.lu/legal/en/internet/communic.htm.

- information security (malicious hacking);
- protection of privacy (unauthorised communication of personal data, electronic harassment);
- protection of reputation (libel, unlawful comparative advertising);
- intellectual property (unauthorised distribution of copyrighted works, eg software or music);

It was suggested that these were 'pressing issues of public, political, commercial and legal interest' which could not be ignored even while recognising that 'the benefits of the Internet far outweigh its negative aspects'. Such comments have fuelled speculation about the extent to which the law might be able to intervene and regulate the actual content of information that is available on the Internet and the World Wide Web.

It may be that the existing law is not tailored appropriately for application to computer networks but, whatever the law may be in a particular jurisdiction, it is clear that there is unlikely to be consensus between jurisdictions over acceptable standards. Certain governments may be sensitive about the expression of some political or religious views and it is evident that acceptable standards and definitions of obscene or pornographic material will vary from place to place. Given the ease of accessing information which originates in another jurisdiction, is it possible to control the propagation of such material or to enforce national laws on a medium which does not recognise national boundaries?

There are also a number of divergent views about the nature of these media that colour the debate surrounding the basis on which the law might intervene. At one extreme is the view that this global network of computers is a fundamentally anarchic medium which is not, nor should be, subject to any type of control or regulation. This has even found expression in such comments as 'no law applies to the Internet'. Notwithstanding the sentiments of those who espouse this view of the Internet, the fallacy behind such a statement should be obvious. Far from there being no law that applies, it is clear that there are a multitude of laws which apply in numerous jurisdictions.[64] However, the application and enforcement of those laws in this area may be so fraught with difficulties as to give the outward appearance that no law applies. Even for those who do not see the Internet as completely anarchic, there is a problem in assessing the appropriate analogy to draw with

64 This was amply demonstrated when, in December 1995, a Bavarian court issued an injunction on the commercial service provider, Compuserve requiring them to suspend access to certain newsgroups containing material deemed unlawful in Germany. The response of Compuserve was to deny access to these newsgroups and to all their subscribers worldwide. Although Compuserve subsequently restored the links and the terms of the injunction were complied with by the supply of blocking software, for a short time, far from no law applying, German standards were being applied across the entire globe. More recently, in March 1997, the head of Compuserve in Germany was charged with facilitating ????? to ?????? material.

other fora for the access and exchange of information. Is an encounter in cyberspace the equivalent to exchanging gossip at the village meeting place or to participating in a high level conference? Should the same standards be applied as are applied to publishing of hard copy, or to television and radio broadcasts? The fundamental difference between the Internet or World Wide Web and these other forms of communication is that the global network is capable of fulfilling all of these functions simultaneously, thus, in some circumstances, it may be appropriate to utilise similar rules as are used for traditional publication, but at other times such an attempt may be felt to be a violation of the right to free speech or even the right to privacy.

Arguably, it is the use of the Internet as a medium for the circulation of various types of pornography that has caused the greatest concern and controversy amongst both politicians and the public and a study of the response to these concerns raises a number of the fundamental issues surrounding regulation of the Internet as a whole. In the US the challenge to the Communications Decency Act of 1996 as being unconstitutional on its face highlighted some of these tensions.

The Communications Decency Act 1996 included provisions aimed at preventing young people from accessing indecent material over computer networks. It made it a criminal offence to engage in communication on computer networks that is either 'indecent' or 'patently offensive' if the contents of that communication can be viewed by a minor. Neglecting the not inconsiderable difficulty of ascertaining the age of those accessing the material, this was regarded by many as an unacceptable intrusion into the right to free speech protected by the First Amendment to the US Constitution. Accordingly, the American Civil Liberties Union (ACLU) filed a legal challenge to the statute and the case was heard in June 1996.[65]

Having discussed both the mode of operation of the Internet and the World Wide Web and the way in which they were used,[66] the court went on to make some observations that related to the way in which analogies might be drawn between the Internet and other methods of obtaining and exchanging information.

ACLU v RENO

United States Court for the Eastern District of Pennsylvania

11 June 1996

Because of the technology underlying the Internet, the statutory term 'content provider',[67] which is equivalent to the traditional 'speaker', may actually be a hybrid of speakers. Through the use of HTML, for example, Critical Path and

65 *ACLU v Reno*. Full text available at http://www.epic.org/CDA/.`

66 Extracted above at p 359.

67 The term 'information content provider' is defined in s 509 of the Communications Decency Act at the new 47 USC s 230(e)(3), as 'any person or entity that is responsible, in whole or in part, for the creation or development of information provided through the Internet or any other interactive computer service'.

> Stop Prisoner Rape link their Web sites to several related databases, and a user can immediately jump from the home pages of these organisations to the related databases simply by clicking on a link ...
>
> Because of the different forms of Internet communication, a user of the Internet may speak or listen interchangeably, blurring the distinction between 'speakers' and 'listeners' on the Internet. Chat rooms, e-mail, and newsgroups are interactive forms of communication, providing the user with the opportunity both to speak and to listen.
>
> It follows that unlike traditional media, the barriers to entry as a speaker on the Internet do not differ significantly from the barriers to entry as a listener. Once one has entered cyberspace, one may engage in the dialogue that occurs there. In the argot of the medium, the receiver can and does become the content provider, and vice-versa.
>
> The Internet is therefore a unique and wholly new medium of worldwide human communication ...
>
> Once a provider posts content on the Internet, it is available to all other Internet users worldwide. Similarly, once a user posts a message to a newsgroup or bulletin board, that message becomes available to all subscribers to that newsgroup or bulletin board ...
>
> Once a provider posts its content on the Internet, it cannot prevent that content from entering any community. Unlike the newspaper, broadcast station, or cable system, Internet technology necessarily gives a speaker a potential worldwide audience. Because the Internet is a network of networks ... any network connected to the Internet has the capacity to send and receive information to any other network ...
>
> ... it takes several steps to enter cyberspace. At the most fundamental level, a user must have access to a computer with the ability to reach the Internet (typically by way of a modem). A user must then direct the computer to connect with the access provider, enter a password, and enter the appropriate commands to find particular data. On the World Wide Web, a user must normally use a search engine or enter an appropriate address. Similarly, accessing newsgroups, bulletin boards, and chat rooms requires several steps.
>
> Communications over the Internet do not 'invade' an individual's home or appear on one's computer screen unbidden. Users seldom encounter content 'by accident'. A document's title or a description of the document will usually appear before the document itself takes the step needed to view it, and in many cases the user will receive detailed information about a site's content before he or she need take the step to access the document. Almost all sexually explicit images are preceded by warnings as to the content ...
>
> Evidence adduced at the hearing showed significant differences between Internet communications and communications received by radio or television. Although content on the Internet is just a few clicks of a mouse away from the user, the receipt of information on the Internet requires a series of affirmative steps more deliberate and directed than merely turning a dial.

The court then moved on to an analysis of the legal issues in the case. Notwithstanding the guarantee of free speech provided by the First

Amendment, it is well-established that this guarantee will be forfeited in the case of obscenity and child pornography and there is Federal law which proscribes such activities.[68] The court observed that the existing law was capable of application to whatever medium was used for the dissemination of this type of material and therefore could equally be applied to propagation via the Internet.[69] Commercial distributors of pornography were unlikely to be caught by the provisions of the Communications Decency Act 1996 as their usual practice was to require credit card validation, thus reducing the likelihood of the material being accessed by minors and, in addition, the target of the Act was not obscene material but that which was 'indecent' or 'patently offensive'. Although 'obscene' had a recognised meaning,[70] this was not the case with regard to 'indecent' and neither was it defined in the statute. Given the criminal penalties attached to breach of the Act and the difficulties in ascertaining what material would be covered and the range of defendants, the court were unanimously of the opinion that the statute was unconstitutional for reasons of vagueness. In arriving at this conclusion, the judges found evidence that the Internet had more in common with telephone conversation than with broadcasting, for instance, and that based on this reasoning, the government had little valid pretext for regulating the content.

ACLU v RENO
United States Court for the Eastern District of Pennsylvania
11 June 1996

Dalzell, District Judge

... The Internet is a new medium of mass communication. As such, the Supreme Court's First Amendment jurisprudence compels us to consider the special qualities of this new medium in determining whether the CDA is a constitutional exercise of governmental power. Relying on these special qualities, which we have described at length in our Findings of fact above, I conclude that the CDA is unconstitutional and that the First Amendment denies Congress the power to regulate protected speech on the Internet ...

---

68 Readers who are interested in pursuing further materials dealing with the conflicts, both perceived and real, between the developing technologies in cyberspace and the First Amendment may be interested in the *Symposium Technology and the First Amendment* December 1994, proceedings reported in (1995) 104 Yale L J 1613–1850.

69 See eg *US v Thomas* 74 F 3d 701 (6th Cir 1995), affirmed by US Court of Appeals for the Sixth Circuit 29 January 1996. Thomas concerned obscene material made available on a bulletin board held on a computer in California, the case came to court in Memphis, Tennessee, where the bulletin board was accessed on the basis that, in cases involving transportation of obscene material between states, the proper standard to apply is that of the community of the geographic area where the materials are sent. It had been suggested that the 'community standard' test for obscenity set out in *Miller v California* (1973) 413 US 15, should be modified in the light of the creation of 'cyber communities' but this was considered irrelevant on the facts of this particular case, as membership was required before the bulletin board was accessed which, in practice, meant that some control could be exerted over the likely destination of the files in question.

70 Above, n 69.

Four related characteristics of Internet communication have a transcendent importance to our shared holding that the CDA is unconstitutional on its face ... First, the Internet presents very low barriers to entry. Second, these barriers to entry are identical for both speakers and listeners. Third, as a result of these low barriers, astoundingly diverse content is available on the Internet. Fourth, the Internet provides significant access to all who wish to speak in the medium, and even creates a relative parity among speakers ...

The CDA will, without doubt, undermine the substantive, speech-enhancing benefits that have flowed from the Internet ... The diversity of the content will necessarily diminish as a result. The economic costs associated with compliance with the Act will drive from the Internet speakers whose content falls within the zone of possible prosecution. Many Web sites, newsgroups, and chat rooms will shut down, since users cannot discern the age of other participants. In this respect, the Internet would ultimately come to mirror broadcasting and print, with messages tailored to a mainstream society from speakers who could be sure that their message was likely decent in every community in the country ...

The CDA's wholesale disruption on the Internet will necessarily affect adult participation in the medium. As some speakers leave or refuse to enter the medium, and others bowdlerise their speech or erect the barriers that the Act envisions, and still others remove bulletin boards, Web sites, and newsgroups, adults will face a shrinking ability to participate in the medium. Since much of the communication on the Internet is participatory, ie, is a form of dialogue, a decrease in the number of speakers, speech fora, and permissible topics will diminish the worldwide dialogue that is the strength and signal achievement of the medium ...

... It is no exaggeration to conclude that the Internet has achieved, and continues to achieve, the most participatory marketplace of mass speech that this country – and indeed the world – has yet seen. The plaintiffs in these actions correctly describe the 'democratising' effects of Internet communication: individual citizens of limited means can speak to a worldwide audience on issues of concern to them. Federalists and Anti-Federalists may debate the structure of their government nightly, but these debates occur in newsgroups or chat rooms rather than in pamphlets. Modern-day Luthers still post their theses, but to electronic bulletin boards rather than the door of the Wittenberg Schlosskirche. More mundane (but from a constitutional perspective, equally important) dialogue occurs between aspiring artists, or French cooks, or dog lovers, or fly fishermen.

Indeed, the government's asserted 'failure' of the Internet rests on the implicit premise that too much speech occurs in that medium, and that speech there is too available to the participants. This is exactly the benefit of Internet communication, however. The government, therefore, implicitly asks this court to limit both the amount of speech on the Internet and the availability of that speech. This argument is profoundly repugnant to First Amendment principles ...

The Internet is a far more speech-enhancing medium than print, the village green, or the mails. Because it would necessarily affect the Internet itself, the

> CDA would necessarily reduce the speech available for adults on the medium. This is a constitutionally intolerable result.
>
> Some of the dialogue on the Internet surely tests the limits of conventional discourse. Speech on the Internet can be unfiltered, unpolished, and unconventional, even emotionally charged, sexually explicit, and vulgar – in a word, 'indecent' in many communities. But we should expect such speech to occur in a medium in which citizens from all walks of life have a voice. We should also protect the autonomy that such a medium confers to ordinary people as well as media magnates ...
>
> Cutting through the acronyms and argot that littered the hearing testimony, the Internet may fairly be regarded as a never-ending worldwide conversation. The government may not, through the CDA, interrupt that conversation. As the most participatory form of mass speech yet developed, the Internet deserves the highest protection from governmental intrusion.
>
> True it is that many find some of the speech on the Internet to be offensive, and amid the din of cyberspace many hear discordant voices that they regard as indecent. The absence of governmental regulation of Internet content has unquestionably produced a kind of chaos, but as one of plaintiffs' experts put it with such resonance at the hearing: What achieved success was the very chaos that the Internet is. The strength of the Internet is that chaos.
>
> Just as the strength of the Internet is chaos, so the strength of our liberty depends upon the chaos and cacophony of the unfettered speech the First Amendment protects.

This decision of the Pennsylvania Court was appealed by the US government and the Supreme Court upheld the judgment in June 1997.[71]

Other jurisdictions have introduced legislation purporting to regulate the content and use of information on the Internet that, although not without some adverse comments being made, have not resulted in such a dramatic reaction as in the US, although it is, as yet, too early to assess how effective these statutes might be in practice. A number of states in Australia, for example, have introduced legislation aimed both at restricting access to certain material on the Internet and controlling content but with little opportunity for public debate on the issue.[72] In Singapore, the preferred method has been to introduce 'a licensing scheme that aims to safeguard public morals, political stability and religious harmony'.[73] Both Internet Service Providers and Internet Content Providers are required to register under the scheme. Both will need to follow certain guidelines – for Internet Service Providers this might include blocking objectionable sites as instructed,

71 Full text of the oral arguments presented to the Supreme Court on 19 March 1997 is available at http://www.aclu.org/issues/cyber/trial/sctran.html and also via http://www.epic.org/CDA/. For Supreme Court decision see http://www2.epic.org/cda/cda_decision.htm.

72 See, eg, *Aussie Internet faces restrictions* Computing 15 September 1994, p 20, Graham Greenleaf, *Law in Cyberspace* (1996) 70 Aust LJ 33.

73 *Internet regulation to start on Monday* (1996) *Straits Times* (Weekly Edition) 13 July.

whilst Internet Content providers will have to submit information about prospective readers and the names of those with responsibility for publication. Administration of the system (and presumably those making decisions on what is or is not objectionable) will be by a National Internet Advisory Committee under the auspices of the Ministry of Information and the Arts. On the other hand, recent reports suggest that France has resiled from plans to regulate content on the Internet and will, instead, encourage voluntary compliance with an, as yet, unwritten international code of conduct for service providers.[74]

In the UK, the debate has centred on the extent to which existing laws are adequate to deal with the distribution of pornography on the Internet[75] and also the extent to which they are capable of dealing with instances in which children are exposed to material intended only for an adult audience as well as instances when the Internet is used to propagate child pornography. Parliament recognised the widespread concern surrounding the perceived proliferation of 'indecent' material available via the Internet and convened a Home Affairs Committee to investigate the matter.[76] The Committee defined pornography as 'obscene and indecent images and sounds which are stored, transmitted or viewed using computer technology'. They were given a wide brief to examine and assess the extent of the problems caused by the use of information technology to disseminate such material, the likelihood of additional problems arising as a result of the development of the relevant technologies and, in particular to ascertain whether any changes in legislation were required to deal with existing and potential concerns relating to computer pornography. In the event, although the possibility of dedicated legislation at some future date was not ruled out, the Committee decided that it was possible to deal with the matter by amending the existing legislation to make it clear that it applied equally to the dissemination of material via computer networks. Their recommendations were given effect in the Criminal Justice and Public Order Act 1994 which amended certain sections of the Obscene Publications Act 1959 and the Protection of Children Act 1978.

Section 1(1) of the Obscene Publications Act 1959 makes it a criminal offence to publish any obscene article. Article is defined as 'any description containing or embodying matter to be read or looked at or both, any sound record, any film etc ...'. Unlike the standard in the US which allows for different standards in different communities, such matter will be obscene if, taken as a whole, it is such as to 'tend to deprave and corrupt persons likely to read, see or hear matter contained or embodied in it'. To avoid any possibility that 'article' could

74 BNA's Electronic Information Policy and Law Report (1996) Vol 1, p 531.

75 See, eg, Colin Manchester, *Computer Pornography* [1995] Crim L Rev 546, Thomas Gibbons, *Computer Generated Pornography* International Yearbook of Law, Computers and Technology, 1995, Vol 9, p 83.

76 HC No 126 *Computer Pornography* 1993–94.

be construed as not including information on computer, this section was amended by the Criminal Justice and Public Order Act 1994 to include the transmission of electronically stored data which, on resolution into user-viewable form, is obscene. As the definition of 'publication' includes distribution, circulation etc, this could have the effect of making a network provider liable for obscene material as well as the originator of that information.

There may be more specific offences applicable to particular types of material, for example, offences under the Children and Young Persons (Harmful Publications) Act 1955 which applies to any book, magazine or other like work which is of a kind likely to fall into the hands of children and young persons. Such publications have to be pictorial in the main to attract the provisions of this Act and include stories portraying, 'the commission of crimes, acts of violence or cruelty or incidents of a repulsive or horrible nature in such a way that the work as a whole would tend to corrupt a child or young person'. In the absence of specific amendments, the application of this statute will rest on whether an interpretation of 'other like work' includes material available on computer.

Provisions that criminalise paedophilia are also likely to be of relevance. The Protection of Children Act 1978 creates offences relating to the display and distribution of indecent photographs of children which also include advertisements suggesting that the advertiser makes such material available (s 1(1)(a)–(d)). These provisions have also been amended by the Criminal Justice and Public Order Act 1994 to include both photographs and pseudo-photographs, the latter referring to computer-generated or partially computer-generated images of children. Data stored on a computer disk or other electronic means that is capable of conversion into a photograph or 'pseudo-photograph' is also included.[77] The interpretation of these sections have been discussed in *R v Fellows and Arnold*[78] in which the Court of Appeal dismissed an appeal against convictions for possessing indecent photographs of a child, having an obscene article for publication and for distributing indecent photographs, the material in question being available over a computer network. The defendants had contended that such computer data did not constitute a photograph for the purposes of s 1 of the 1978 Act and that the data were not, in any event distributed or shown merely by reason of being made available for downloading. Evans LJ decided that[79] 'although the computer disk was not a photograph it was a copy of an indecent photograph. The disk contained data not visible to the eye, which could be converted by appropriate technical means into a print which exactly reproduced the

77 For a review of cases relating to child pornography on the Internet see, eg, Yaman Akdeniz, *Regulation of Child Pornography on the Internet* available at http://www.leeds.ac.uk/law/pgs/yaman/child.htm.

78 [1997] 2 All ER 548.

79 *Ibid.*

original photograph from which it was derived. It was a form of copy which made the original photograph, or a copy of it, available for viewing by a person with access to the disk'.

Notwithstanding the applicability of the offences described above to material made available over the network, a problem may arise where the source of the material is outside the UK jurisdiction. Where the offence is one in which mere possession of the offending material is sufficient then there may be still a defendant who can be apprehended in the UK courts. This may not be the case where the offence is one of 'publication'. In such a case the relevant issue may be whether the offending material can be construed as an 'article' for the purposes of s 46 of the Customs Consolidation Act 1876 which prohibits the importation into the UK of 'indecent or obscene prints, paintings, books, cards, lithographic or other engravings, or any other indecent or obscene articles'. HM Customs and Excise believe that this section would not apply where the offending material was made available in the UK via telephone lines, although it would be expected to apply to pornographic material which entered the country on disk.[80] Manchester, mindful of the wide construction of certain concepts that the courts have used in other cases involving pornography, suggests a possible avenue for judicial creativity in this area which is remarkably reminiscent of arguments voiced in other areas of law, discussed elsewhere in this work.[81]

Computer Pornography
Colin Manchester
[1995] Criminal Law Review 546 at 553

> ... it is not inconceivable for the terms 'articles' and 'goods', as defined [in the section 46 Customs Consolidation Act 1876], to be used to describe intangible matter such as information held on computer disks. Both terms make reference to 'property' and the concept of intangible property is well recognised in law, eg copyright in published works. If the reference to 'property' is widely interpreted, this could encompass intangible information held on computer disk and this could certainly be 'movable property', thereby falling within the definition of 'goods', since it can be moved (electronically) from a computer in one place to a computer in another place. Similarly, the term 'item' in the definition of 'article' might be employed to describe an 'item of information', even though the information is not in tangible form. Further, if particular information is held on computer disk along with other information, the particular information might constitute a 'separate element, member or part of anything' viz part of the information held on the disk. If this article on 'Computer Pornography' had been written abroad on a word processor, saved on computer disk and transmitted electronically to the *Criminal Law Review*, would it really be straining language too far to say that there had been an importation of an article into the country?

80 Colin Manchester, *Computer Pornography* [1995] Crim L Rev 546 at 552.

81 See, eg, the discussion of the decision in *Cox v Riley* at 349 and the discussion of software as goods in Chapter 4.

EUROPEAN INITIATIVES

The so-called Information Society is an important phenomenon for the European Union representing as it does a whole new market in services and products. The Institutions of the European Union have, therefore, not been slow to realise the importance of a suitable legal framework within which the new technology can operate. The major thrust of such initiatives is facilitatory – to enable enterprises within the Union to gain full advantage of new technologies and to ensure that any barriers to the provision of services or threats to competitiveness are removed or minimised.

This does not mean that any negative aspects of the market in information and services available via computer networks have been ignored and the Commission's communication[82] *Illegal and Harmful Content on the Internet* is evidence of this. As there is no competence, as such, to legislate on criminal matters, it is for the Member States to respond as appropriate, although competence will be retained where the regulation of the activity in question might threaten the operation of the Internal Market:

> As regards the distribution of illegal content on the Internet, it is clearly the responsibility of Member States to ensure the application of existing laws. What is illegal off-line remains illegal on-line, and it is up to Member States to enforce these laws ... At another level, the presence of illegal and harmful content on the Internet has direct repercussions on the workings of the Internal market. In particular, the adoption by Member States of regulations of new Internet services intended to protect the public interest may also create risks of distortions of competition (for example, through widely divergent responses to the question of potential liability of Internet service providers), hamper the free circulation of these services, and lead to a re-fragmentation of the Internal market. If unsolved, such problems may justify Community intervention.

The document goes on to advocate a combination of self-regulation supplemented by technical solutions to deal with 'illegal content' on the Internet but encounters problems when considering 'harmful content' due to the potential conflicts with the right to freedom of expression and also with the legal framework of the Internal Market, the competition rules and the principle of the free provision of services. This discussion also implicitly presumes that there is no overlap between what is actually illegal and what might be considered merely harmful either in individual Member States or between Member States and that there will be some consensus about what is included in these terms. In respect of the free movement of goods, the European Court of Justice has already been able to extend a wide margin of appreciation to Member States to enable them to define acceptable standards

82 *Illegal and Harmful Content on the Internet* Communication to the European Parliament, the Council, the Economic and Social Committee and the Committee of the Regions COM (96) 47. Full text available at http://www2.echo.lu/legal/en/internet/communic.htm.

for their own territory, even where this might restrict the free movement of goods.[83] The basic position is set out in the case of *R v Henn and Darby*.[84]

***R v Henn and Darby* [1979] ECR 3795 at 3813**
European Court of Justice

> Under the terms of Article 36 of the Treaty the provisions relating to the free movement of goods within the Community are not to preclude prohibitions on imports which are justified *inter alia* 'on grounds of public morality'. In principle, it is for each Member State to determine in accordance with its own scale of values and in the form selected by it the requirements of public morality in its territory ... Each Member State is entitled to impose prohibitions on imports justified on the grounds of public morality for the whole of its territory ... whatever the structure of its constitution may be and however the powers of legislating in regard to the subject in question may be distributed.

This general statement is subject to the proviso that such measures should not constitute arbitrary discrimination as explained in the later case of *Conegate v HM Customs and Excise*.[85]

***Conegate v HM Customs and Excise* [1986] ECR 1007 at 1022**
European Court of Justice

> ... although Community law leaves Member States free to make their own assessments of the indecent or obscene character of certain articles, it must be pointed out that the fact that goods cause offence cannot be regarded as sufficiently serious to justify restrictions on the free movement of goods where the Member State concerned does not adopt, with respect to the same goods manufactured or marketed within its territory, penal measures or other serious and effective measures intended to prevent the distribution of such goods in its territory. It follows that a Member State may not rely on grounds of public morality in order to prohibit the importation of goods from other Member States when its legislation contains no prohibition as to manufacture or marketing of the same goods on its territory.

This approach has effectively been reiterated by the Commission in relation to the provision of information services: '[w]hat is considered to be harmful depends on cultural differences. Each country may reach its own conclusion in defining the borderline between what is permissible and not permissible. It is therefore indispensable that international initiatives take into account different ethical standards in different countries in order to explore appropriate rules to protect people against offensive material whilst ensuring freedom of expression.' However, in the event of substantial differences in attitude between different Member States, it is more difficult to see how this might be accommodated in practice, in relation to Information Services, without compromising the free market in those services.

83 See Article 30 EC and Article 36 EC.

84 Case 34/79 [1979] ECR 3795.

85 Case 121/85 [1986] ECR 1007.

These issues have recently been taken up by a Council Resolution setting out priorities in this area which concentrates heavily on the measures necessary to ensure the Internal market.

Council Resolution of 21 November 1996 on new policy priorities regarding the information society OJ 1996 C376/1

Whereas the information society and the use of new technologies should contribute to the effective protection and exercise of fundamental rights and freedoms of citizens and consumers;

Whereas the distribution of illegal material adversely affecting public order and morality may damage confidence in and acceptance of the new information society; ...

Whereas it will be necessary for all competent Council compositions to consider and to adopt as soon as possible the necessary regulatory and legal measures ...

4. [the Council] stresses ...
   (d) that the proper functioning of the internal market must be improved, that given the increasing share of services in the economy, the provision and free circulation of services – especially new ones – is of particular importance ...
5. [the Council] emphasises ...
   (h) the importance of protecting fundamental rights and freedoms as well as users' and consumers' rights in the information society ...
9. [the Council] stresses the importance of an appropriate and consistent legal framework for the information society at European and at International level.

The Council requests the Member States and the Commission within their respective competences to ...

15. Look into the problem of the distribution of illegal material adversely affecting public order and morality over electronic networks.

It is clear from this that any legislative activity which might be proposed will be expected to have the minimum perturbation possible on the provision of services. If this seems to be a rather different approach than might have been noted from other jurisdictions, it is perhaps important at this juncture to consider the problem in perspective. Although the issues surrounding the dissemination and propagation of illegal and/or harmful material via the Internet are deserving of resolution, in comparison with the total of all information available on global networks, the proportion that would be likely to fall into these categories is very small. As with access to similar information available on more traditional media, the answer may be based more in a reassessment of society and community values, perhaps backed up by technological methods, than in the drafting of unenforceable legislation.

The current state of play thus seems somewhat confusing and there is an inherent tension emerging between the implementation of self-regulation and the desire of governments to impose external regulation on the Internet. Notwithstanding the apparent attitude of the Council of Ministers, evidenced in the Resolution extracted above, Directorate General XIII/E has commissioned the COMCRIME study[86] with the aim of providing up to date information on the legal issues of computer related crime together with an in-depth analysis of the substantive law aspects in the European Union, United States and Japan. This will involve, not only a comparison of national laws on computer crime but also suggestions for alternative legal solutions, so further action from the European Institutions is envisaged in the future.

On the other hand, a study of sites likely to cause offence appears to suggest that the situation is under control or at least can be left to self-regulation.[87] It is pointed out that, despite successful prosecutions for charges related to offensive material on computer, these represent only a small fraction of the total number of cases brought for obscenity. This fact is used to support the view that external regulation is, at best, unnecessary and, at worst, an unwarranted intrusion, although it could equally illustrate the difficulty of detection or be a result of evidential problems.

Regulation and Control of the Internet: is it feasible? Is it necessary?
Paul F Burton
(1995) 21 Journal of Information Science 413 at 425

> Politicians and others are effectively seeking to bring the Internet back into the institutional framework which they know and understand; at present it is too far from their control for them to be comfortable ...
>
> ... a great deal depends on how we approach the Internet as an information medium. In an anarchic, uncontrolled environment such as the Internet, we should strengthen the freedom of information which it offers and accept as a consequence that some material will be distributed which individuals will find offensive. We then have a duty to endure that the content of such material is made clear, to prevent anyone wandering into it innocently ... If we simply approach the problem as one of suppressing material, we will lose more than we gain ... The Internet has the potential to free up information exchange in an unprecedented way ... and while we are still a long way from an information rich global society, that, it is suggested, is a more important goal than the censorship of a relatively small proportion of the whole.

However, the findings of this study seem to be at odds with some other observations[88] and an outcome that satisfies all protagonists seems unlikely in the near future.

---

86 Further information and minutes of meetings available at http://www2.echo.lu/legal/en/crime/.

87 Paul F Burton, *Regulation of the Internet: is it feasible? Is it necessary?* (1995) 21 J Information Science 413.

88 See, eg, Report of the First European Conference on Combating Violence and Pornography on the Internet February 1997 [1997] 1 JILT, http://elj.warwick.ac.uk/jilt/.

CHAPTER NINE

EVIDENTIAL ISSUES

INTRODUCTION

Information which has been stored or processed on computers is frequently and increasingly a source of evidence in both criminal and civil litigation. The computerisation of business, police and governmental records is already so widespread that many everyday transactions, such as the purchase of groceries, the withdrawal of cash from a bank account or the making of a telephone call, frequently generate computerised data, which is typically recorded and stored automatically, without any human effort or intervention. Such data may be recorded with specific evidential uses in mind, or it may fortuitously acquire an evidential significance which was not envisaged when the recording was made. Test data routinely recorded by the manufacturer of a quality-controlled product, with a view to measuring its specification, may later be found useful as a means of identifying that product following its theft, and may be capable of incriminating a thief or a receiver of stolen goods;[1] sales data recorded on a computerised till roll in a department store may be used to help prove a charge of shoplifting;[2] and a computerised record of telephone calls made from a hotel bedroom may be useful, not only for calculating the customer's bill (as intended) but also for proving, in the course of a criminal prosecution, that the customer made calls to various persons with whom he is alleged to have entered into a criminal conspiracy.[3]

Valuable as it may be, information stored on or derived from computer systems can pose a number of evidential problems for the courts, particularly the criminal courts. This is largely because the English law of evidence developed its basic common law rules and principles long before anyone could ever have envisaged the appearance of computer-generated data; and those rules have not always proved adaptable to new kinds of evidence. Various attempts have been made to draft legislation for the purpose of facilitating the proper use of computer evidence, but these attempts have not always been well-considered or effective,[4] and the progress of reform in the law of criminal evidence lags far behind that on the civil side: hence the higher incidence of evidential difficulties in the criminal courts.

1 *R v Wood* (1982) 76 Cr App R 39.

2 *R v Shephard* [1993] AC 380.

3 *R v Spiby* (1990) 91 Cr App R 186.

4 A particularly inept attempt to legislate for the use of computer evidence can be found in s 5 of the Civil Evidence Act 1968 which has only recently been repealed by the Civil Evidence Act 1995.

A party to a civil dispute or criminal prosecution in which computer evidence may be involved is likely to have at least three specific concerns regarding that evidence, namely: (1) will it be permissible to adduce that evidence at the trial, or in other words, is such evidence legally admissible; (2) if so, how cogent will that evidence be; and (3) to what extent and by what methods may such evidence be open to challenge?

Of these, (1) and (3) raise specific questions of law which will be addressed in this chapter. It is more difficult to deal with (2), because the cogency of computer evidence may vary from near-conclusiveness to total ineffectiveness, depending on the evidence itself and on the circumstances of the case. There are, however, certain recognised procedures which it may be advisable to follow in respect of computerised business records, in order to avoid doubts or objections being raised as to the cogency or integrity of the information stored in them. These procedures do not have any force of law, but courts may take account of commercially accepted 'best practices' when evaluating the cogency of such evidence.[5]

It should be noted that issues of admissibility and cogency cannot always be kept distinct. In some cases, failure to adopt procedures for safeguarding the accuracy and integrity of computerised records may result in a court or judge refusing to recognise the authenticity or admissibility of data derived from them.[6]

CRIMINAL CASES

Rules of admissibility

In criminal proceedings, the English law of evidence remains characterised by complexity and excessive technicality. There is no concept of the 'free appreciation of evidence'. It will not necessarily suffice, in other words, to show that a given item of evidence is relevant to some disputed issue in the case. Relevance is clearly important, because no court will waste time listening to evidence which is manifestly irrelevant to any of the issues in the case; but regard must also be had to questions of classification and formal admissibility. Evidence may be excluded, even where it is clearly relevant, if it falls foul of one of the many exclusionary rules of evidence. Such rules were originally designed to exclude unreliable and prejudicial forms of evidence, but are sometimes interpreted so rigidly that they can lead the exclusion of perfectly reliable evidence as well.

5 See for example the BSI-DISC Code of Practice on the Legal Admissibility of Information Stored on Electronic Document Management Systems (PD0008).

6 See in particular s 69 of the Police and Criminal Evidence Act 1984, below.

The hearsay rule

As far as computer evidence is concerned, the most troublesome rule by far is the hearsay rule. This rule might better be known as the rule against second-hand evidence. It ordinarily requires facts in issue to be proved by the oral testimony of persons who have first-hand (ie personal) knowledge of those facts. It is not ordinarily permissible to prove such facts by the testimony of some other person, to whom the facts have been narrated by the original witness, nor is that witness's written account acceptable in place of his or her oral testimony. Cross-examination of witnesses is considered to be a vital ingredient in the forensic search for truth, but one cannot cross-examine a document!

The hearsay rule was designed to exclude unreliable gossip and rumour; but unfortunately it is not always so discriminating. The danger of reliable evidence being excluded as a result of the hearsay rule is illustrated by the notorious decision of the House of Lords in *Myers v Director of Public Prosecutions*:

***Myers v Director of Public Prosecutions* [1965] 1 AC 1001**

Myers was convicted of a number of offences relating to the theft and dishonest receiving of motor vehicles. His practice was to purchase wrecked cars (insurance write-offs) along with their log books or vehicle registration documents. He would then steal cars of similar make and description, and disguise them with the chassis and engine identification plates, registration plates and log books of the wrecked vehicles. The stolen cars could then be sold on as if they were the vehicles he had legitimately purchased. An important part of the evidence against Myers came from records kept by the Austin factory at Longbridge, where records had been kept of the chassis and engine numbers attached to all new cars when they were completed. The records also showed a third number, the cylinder block number, which was stamped into the cylinder block and was accordingly impossible to change. This was cogent evidence, because the Austin cars resold by Myers invariably had engine and chassis numbers which failed to match the numbers stamped into the cylinder blocks, assuming of course that the records kept at Longbridge were correct. The records were kept on a card index, rather than a computer (as would doubtless be the case today) but the principle was the same ...

Lord Reid

> ... The reason why this evidence is maintained to have been inadmissible is that its cogency depends on hearsay. The witness could only say that a record made by someone else showed that, if the record was correctly made, a car had left the works bearing three particular numbers. He could not prove that the record was correct or that the numbers which it contained were in fact the numbers on the car when it was made. This is a highly technical point, but the law regarding hearsay evidence is technical, and I would say absurdly technical ...

> Counsel for the prosecution sought to support the existing practice of admitting such records by arguing that they were not adduced to prove the truth of the particular records, but only to prove that they were records kept in the normal course of business. Counsel for the accused then asked the very pertinent question – if they were not intended to prove the truth of the entries, what were they intended to prove? If they were not capable of supporting an inference that they were probably true records, then I do not see what probative value they could have ...
>
> In argument the Solicitor-General maintained that, although the general rule may be against the admission of private records to prove the truth of the entries in them, the trial judge has a discretion to admit a record in a particular case if satisfied that it is trustworthy and that justice requires its admission. That appears to me to be contrary to the whole framework of the existing law ... No matter how cogent particular evidence may seem to be, unless it comes within a class that is admissible it is excluded ...

The ruling in *Myers* caused shock waves through the criminal justice system, because it had hitherto been assumed that business records of that kind would always be admissible. Legislation was quickly enacted so as to provide for the admissibility of hearsay business records in future criminal proceedings, but only subject to a series of conditions which would have to be satisfied before such evidence could be admitted. The first such legislation was rushed through Parliament within a year of the decision in *Myers*, but this was eventually replaced, first by provisions contained within the Police and Criminal Evidence Act 1984, and then by the current provisions of the Criminal Justice Act 1988. The conditions attached to the admission of hearsay evidence will be considered later in this chapter; but it is first necessary to consider the circumstances under which computer evidence will in fact amount to hearsay. Where it does not amount to hearsay at all, the various conditions governing the admission of documentary hearsay can safely be ignored.

At first, the courts stumbled to the erroneous conclusion that information stored on computers must necessarily be a form of hearsay. In *R v Pettigrew*,[7] the Court of Appeal held that a trial judge had been wrong to admit in evidence an automatically produced computer printout from the Bank of England, which tended to prove that bank notes found in the accused's possession came from a batch which had been stolen in the burglary with which he was charged. The Court of Appeal considered that, since they were being asked to rely on the accuracy of the printout, and since no witness could claim first-hand knowledge of the information it contained, the contents of the printout must be hearsay. This provoked a short but influential article by Professor JC Smith.

7 (1980) 71 Cr App R 39.

JC Smith, 'The Admissibility of Statements by Computer' [1981] Criminal Law Review 387

Where information is recorded by mechanical means without the intervention of a human mind, the record made by the machine is admissible in evidence, provided, of course, it is accepted that the machine is reliable. An elementary example is a maximum and minimum thermometer. This records two items of information in the course of 24 hours and there is no doubt that a witness could give evidence of the reading he took from it if that was relevant to the issue before the court. *A fortiori,* the instrument itself could be produced, if it were possible to do so while it still bore the relevant readings. It would not be necessary to call a professor of physics to prove how a thermometer works, because that is surely such a matter of common knowledge as to be judicially noticed. The same is true of a camera which photographs an event or a tape-recorder which records a conversation, where the event or conversation is in issue or is relevant to the issue before the court. A radar speedometer similarly makes a record of an event – the speed of a passing vehicle – and is no different in legal principle from the thermometer. The physics is more complicated and less comprehensible to the layman, but we are all so completely convinced by our scientific colleagues that it works that the matter is again judicially noticed.

The computer differs from these other instruments only in that it can perform a variety of functions instead of only one. For that reason, it is necessary to have evidence – such as that which was admitted in *Pettigrew* – to establish the nature of the operations which the computer has been programmed to perform. It performs those operations just as mechanically as the thermometer or the camera. Of course, the programmer may make a mistake but so may the person who, for example, devises the scale on the thermometer. This consideration goes to weight rather than admissibility. In any event it certainly has nothing to do with the hearsay rule.

The information produced by the Bank of England's computer seems to be exactly the same in principle as that produced by a camera, a tape recorder, a radar speedometer or the radar set in *The Statue of Liberty*.[8] When it discards a note, it records that fact. If a movie camera could photograph the rejected notes as they were ejected from the machine, the film would be admissible to prove the number of the rejected notes. The computer has a different and more complex method of recording the same information; but there is no difference in principle. Hearsay invariably relates to information which has passed through a human mind. This information never did so.

The logic of Professor Smith's argument was subsequently accepted by the Court of Appeal, and in *R v Wood* the Lord Chief Justice set out to classify the different kinds of computer evidence that might come before the courts.

8 [1968] 2 All ER 195. This was a civil case in which film of radar traces from a coastguard station was used to prove the cause of a collision at sea. It was held to be admissible as a form of 'real evidence' (ie as an exhibit).

R.v Wood (1982) 76 Cr App R 23

A consignment of valuable metals had been stolen, and certain metals, alleged to have come from the stolen consignment, were found on the appellant's premises. A computer was used by chemists to perform calculations on data obtained from tests on the suspect metals, and the results of these calculations showed them to have an identical chemical composition to those of the stolen metals, which had been similarly tested prior to their disappearance. Because the suspect consignment had been tested for the specific purpose of the criminal investigation, the test results could not have been admissible as hearsay under the provisions of the Criminal Evidence Act 1965 which were then in force, but the Court of Appeal held that this was irrelevant. Evidence had been given by the scientists as to the data supplied by them to the computer, and the calculations subsequently performed were held to be analogous to the reaction of litmus paper when dipped into an acid or alkaline solution, and thus not hearsay at all.

Lord Lane CJ

> The computer in the present case was being used as a calculator. It was argued, because the computer was interposed in the course of the production of the final figures, those figures are hearsay. In our judgment, this argument cannot be accepted. Witnesses, and especially expert witnesses, frequently and properly give factual evidence of the results of a physical exercise which involves the use of some equipment, device or machine [such as] a weighing machine ... None of this involves hearsay evidence ... the accuracy of the machine may have to be investigated. But this does not alter the character of the evidence which has been given. [Counsel for the appellant] suggested that there was a difference in kind between a mathematician who uses a slide rule and one who uses a calculating computer. We do not agree. This computer ... did not contribute its own knowledge. It merely did a sophisticated calculation ... The answers produced by the computer were admissible at common law ...

Information stored on or produced by computers may thus contain admissible or inadmissible hearsay, or in other cases it may constitute real evidence. The crucial thing to look for is the reproduction of factual information keyed in by human agency. This will be hearsay if tendered as evidence of those facts (ie, if the court is asked to rely upon the information as being correct), and the same will be true of material which is derived, albeit in a processed form, from such information. Unless the operator can testify, at first hand, as to the accuracy of the input (as was done in *R v Wood*), the output of a computer will then be hearsay.

Computerised bank records concerning customers' accounts represent typical examples of such evidence. Assuming that the computer printout is being tendered as a true record of relevant transactions, it will be hearsay, except insofar as it shows automatic transactions (direct debits, etc) performed by the computer itself without direct human intervention, or automatically monitored customer transactions, such as withdrawals from automated service tills (or ATMs).

Automatic recordings

Following Professor Smith's exposure of the court's misconception in *R v Pettigrew*, the status of automatic computer recordings is now clearly established by cases such as *Castle v Cross*[9] and *R v Spiby*.[10] In the former case, the Divisional Court held that a printout produced by a Lion Intoximeter breath analysis machine, stating that the motorist had failed to provide a sufficient specimen for analysis, constituted real evidence rather than hearsay, and in the latter case the Court of Appeal similarly categorised a printout produced by a hotel computer, showing details of telephone calls made by hotel guests. The calls had been automatically recorded by the computer in order that guests could be charged for them.

Computer evidence as admissible documentary hearsay

There are many different exceptions to the rule against hearsay. None of those applicable to criminal cases deals specifically with computer evidence. Such evidence (assuming it is indeed hearsay) may however be covered by rules designed to deal with various forms of documentary records, of which the most important, in this context, is s 24 of the Criminal Justice Act 1988 which provides:

> **24 (1) Subject:**
>
> (a) to subsections (3) and (4) below;
>
> (b) ...; and
>
> (c) to section 69 of the Police and Criminal Evidence Act 1984,
>
> a statement in a document shall be admissible in criminal proceedings as evidence of any fact of which direct oral evidence would be admissible, if the following conditions are satisfied:
>
> (i) the document was created or received by a person in the course of a trade, business, profession or other occupation, or as the holder of a paid or unpaid office; and
>
> (ii) the information contained in the document was supplied by a person (whether or not the maker of the statement) who had, or may reasonably be supposed to have had, personal knowledge of the matters dealt with.
>
> (2) Subsection (1) above applies whether the information contained in the document was supplied directly or indirectly but, if it was supplied indirectly, only if each person through whom it was supplied received it
>
> (a) in the course of a trade, business, profession or other occupation; or
>
> (b) as the holder of a paid or unpaid office.

9 [1984] 1 WLR 1372.

10 (1990) 91 Cr App R 186.

This provision applies equally to hand-written documents, tape recorded statements and computer records. Its predecessors, namely s 1 of the Criminal Evidence Act 1965 and s 68 of the Police and Criminal Evidence Act 1984 sought to cover the same basic ground, but were more limited in effect, because they permitted the use of such documents only where it could be proved that the makers thereof were no longer available to testify or where they could not be expected to remember the matters recorded. This made it possible for defence lawyers to hamstring the prosecution in complex fraud trials or other trials involving a large quantity of documentary evidence, by insisting, every time a business document was tendered under one of those sections, on proof that the original maker of any statement contained therein was dead, missing, abroad, or incapable of remembering the matters in question.

Section 24(4) does in fact retain such a requirement in respect of documents which were created for the purpose of a criminal investigation or with a view to use in criminal proceedings (thereby ensuring that written or tape recorded statements made to the police do not automatically excuse the witnesses in question from the need to testify in court), but other business documents can now be proved without any such limitations. They may be proved by producing the original document or by means of a copy (or even a copy of a copy) which has been authenticated to the satisfaction of the court or judge.[11]

Judges do however have a discretion under s 25 of the Criminal Justice Act 1988 to exclude any documentary hearsay tendered under s 24 if it appears to them that the interests of justice would not be served by admitting it. A judge may, for example, conclude in a given case that the admission of a computer printout or other business document, in place of oral testimony from the person who originally produced it, would be unfair on the defendant, especially where the content of that document is highly contentious and where the original maker of the document ought to be made available for examination and cross-examination in front of the jury.[12]

25 (1) If, having regard to all the circumstances, [the court] is of the opinion that in the interests of justice a statement which is admissible by virtue of section 23 or 24 above nevertheless ought not to be admitted, it may direct that the statement shall not be admitted.

(2) Without prejudice to the generality of subsection (1) above, it shall be the duty of the court to have regard

(a) to the nature and source of the document containing the statement and to whether or not, having regard to its nature and source and to any other circumstances that appear to the court to be relevant, it is likely that the document is authentic;

11 Section 27 of the Criminal Justice Act 1988.

12 Statements in documents prepared with criminal proceedings in mind are subject to a somewhat stricter discretionary test, laid down in s 26 of the Act.

(b) to the extent to which the statement appears to supply evidence which would otherwise not be readily available;

(c) to the relevance of the evidence that it appears to supply to any issue which is likely to have to be determined in the proceedings; and

(d) to any risk, having regard in particular to whether it is likely to be possible to controvert the statement if the person making it does not attend to give oral evidence in the proceedings, that its admission or exclusion will result in unfairness to the accused or, if there is more than one, to any of them.

Computer evidence and proof of reliability

Under s 69(1) of the Police and Criminal Evidence Act 1984 no statement contained in a document produced by a computer may be admissible as evidence of any fact stated therein unless it is shown:

(a) That there is no reasonable grounds for believing that the statement is inaccurate because of improper use of the computer; and

(b) that at all material times the computer was operating properly, or if not, that any respect in which it was not operating properly or was out of operation was not such as to affect the production of the document or the accuracy of its contents ...

This imposes on whichever party is seeking to adduce the computer statement in question the burden of proving that the computer's output was not affected or corrupted by malfunction and that any statement therein was not rendered inaccurate by misuse. Note that the standard of proof laid down for the prosecution must be the normal criminal standard, namely proof beyond reasonable doubt, whereas any burden which might be imposed upon the defence under s 69 would always be dischargeable merely by proof on balance on probabilities.[13]

Section 69 is not concerned with the accuracy of any data fed into the computer, nor is it concerned with immaterial programming faults. In a drink-driving prosecution, for example, a time or date error on the printout produced by an 'Intoximeter' breath analysis device (resulting from an incorrectly set internal clock) does not render the printout inadmissible as evidence of the level of alcohol in the subject's breath.[14]

Oral testimony may be called for the purpose of satisfying s 69. Alternatively, it may be sufficient for the court to be furnished with a certificate in accordance with para 8 of Schedule 3 to the Act:

13 In other words, the court or judge must consider it 'more likely than not' that the relevant conditions have been satisfied.

14 *Director of Public Prosecutions v McKeown* [1997] 1 WLR 295.

(a) identifying the document containing the statement and describing the manner in which it was produced;
(b) giving such particulars of any device involved in the production of that document as may be appropriate for the purpose of showing that the document was produced by a computer;
(c) dealing with any of the matters mentioned in section 69(1); and
(d) purporting to be signed by a person occupying a responsible position in relation to the operation of the computer.

Note that, although any certificate adduced under Schedule 3 must be signed by a person occupying a responsible position in relation to the computer, oral evidence may be used instead, and need not come from such a person. The scope of s 69 and its relationship with the supplementary provisions contained in Schedule 3 was examined by the House of Lords in *R v Shephard*. In particular, their Lordships were asked to resolve a controversy which had arisen between the judges of the Court of Appeal, who had ruled on several occasions that s 69 only applied to hearsay evidence, and academic commentators, who had argued that there was no statutory or common-sense basis for any such restriction.

R v Shephard [1993] AC 380

Lord Griffiths

My Lords, the Court of Appeal has certified the following point of law of general public importance:

> 'Whether the party seeking to rely on computer evidence can discharge the burden under section 69(l)(b) of the Police and Criminal Evidence Act 1984 without calling a computer expert, and if so how?'

The point of law falls to be considered against the following background of fact. The appellant was arrested at her home ... on 17 March 1989. In her car were goods from Marks & Spencer worth £78.36 ... including a joint of beef priced at £12.57 and five items of clothing. The appellant had no receipt. In an initial interview she declined to answer questions. She was interviewed again on 29 April when she said that she had bought the goods from Marks & Spencer at St Albans. When she returned to her car the bags had split so she transferred the shopping to a bag of her own. She said she never kept receipts and denied stealing the goods.

The principal evidence for the prosecution was given by a store detective employed by Marks & Spencer at their St Albans branch. She said that at 10 am on the morning of 18 March she removed all the till rolls from the tills and recovered a further two till rolls from a cupboard which bore the date 17 March. She explained that the till rolls were connected to a central computer which fed in the date, time, customer number and till number on each of the till rolls. She further explained that each item of clothing has upon it a seven figure numbered label known as a unique product code or UPC. The UPC numbers are unique to clothing of a particular type, size and colour. The till operator punches in the UPC number on the till which then registers the appropriate price. In the case of food, each item of food has a price upon it and the operator punches in the price of each item on the till. She said that they had had no trouble with the operation of the central computer.

She carried out an examination of all the till rolls which she had recovered from the tills which would have been those in use on 17 March and stamped as such by the central computer and she also examined the two till rolls also stamped and dated 17 March which had been placed in the cupboard where all used till rolls were kept. She thus examined all the till rolls in use on 17 March. She said that there was no trace on the till rolls of the UPCs for the clothing found in the appellant's car. She said there was no record on any of the till rolls of an item of food costing £12.57, the price of the beef. Nor was there any group of prices matching the items of food found in the car.

It was quite apparent from the store detective's evidence that she was thoroughly familiar with the operation of these tills and of the computer, albeit she did not pretend to any technical understanding of the operation of the computer.

The appellant did not give evidence and no evidence was called on her behalf. The jury convicted her. If the till rolls were properly admitted in evidence this is hardly surprising, for they provided the most powerful evidence of guilt. It is however submitted that the till rolls should not have been admitted in evidence because the store detective's evidence did not satisfy the provisions of section 69 of the Police and Criminal Evidence Act 1984 ...

The object of section 69 ... is clear enough. It requires anyone who wishes to introduce computer evidence to produce evidence that will establish that it is safe to rely on the documents produced by the computer. This is an affirmative duty emphatically stated: 'a statement in a document produced by a computer shall not be admissible as evidence of any fact stated therein unless it is shown ...'. Such a duty cannot be discharged ... by the application of the presumption that the computer is working correctly ... as appears to be suggested in some of the cases. Nor does it make any difference whether the computer been produced with or without the input of information provided by the human mind and thus may or may not be hearsay. If the document produced by the computer is hearsay it will be necessary to comply with the provisions of section 24 of the Criminal Justice Act 1988 ... before the document call be admitted into evidence and it will also be necessary to comply with the provisions of section 69 of the Act of 1984. I see no warrant for an interpretation of the Act which limits the operation of section 69 to cases that fall within ... section 24 of the Criminal Justice Act 1988. This however was the construction of the Act adopted by the Court of Appeal in *R v Minors* and which has been followed in a number of subsequent cases, most notably *R v Spiby* and *R v Neville* ...

... It is surely every bit as important that a document produced by computer and tendered as proof of guilt should be reliable whether or not it contains hearsay. In *R v Spiby*, the accused was charged with smuggling drugs into this country. As a part of the proof of his guilt the prosecution wished to show he was in touch with an accomplice in France. They invited the jury to draw this inference from a computer printout that recorded a number of telephone calls made from a hotel in Cherbourg at which the accomplice was staying to the accused's home in England. The computer did not record the contents of the conversations but it did show the date, the time, the number of the hotel room from which the call was made in England, the duration and the cost. It seems to me as important to have an assurance that the computer was recording this information accurately as it would be if the computer had also recorded the conversation. The important link in the chain of evidence was not what these men said to each other but the fact that they were in constant touch with one another and for this the prosecution was relying solely on the reliability of the computer record. In such circumstances, evidence to satisfy section 69 is required and in so far as Spiby holds to the contrary it should not be followed ... In fact there was satisfactory evidence given by the sub-manager of the hotel who was familiar with the operation of the computer and could speak to its reliability.

I therefore approach this question upon the basis that, if the prosecution wish to rely upon a document produced by a computer, they must comply with section 69 in all cases. Proof that the computer is reliable can be provided in two ways: either by calling oral evidence or by tendering a written certificate in accordance with the terms of paragraph 8 of Schedule 3, subject to the power of the judge to require oral evidence. It is understandable that if a certificate is to be relied upon it should show on its face that it is signed by a person who from his job description can confidently be expected to be in a position to give reliable evidence of the operation of the computer. This enables the accused to decide whether to accept the certificate at its face value or to ask the judge to require oral evidence which can be challenged in cross-examination. An accused seeing a certificate signed by a store detective would not necessarily assume that such a person was familiar with the operation of the computer or had any responsibility for it and might well challenge the certificate. It does not however follow that the store detective cannot in fact give evidence that shows she is fully familiar with the operation of the store's computer and can speak as to its reliability.

Documents produced by computers are an increasingly common feature of all business and more and more people are becoming familiar with their uses and operation. Computers vary immensely in their complexity and in the operations they perform. The nature of the evidence to discharge the burden of showing that there has been no improper use of the computer and that it was operating properly will inevitably vary from case to case. The evidence must be tailored to suit the needs of the case. I suspect that it will very rarely be necessary to call an expert and that in the vast majority of cases it will be possible to discharge the burden by calling a witness who is familiar with the operation of the computer in the sense of knowing what the computer is required to do and who can say that it is doing it properly.

The computer in this case was of the simplest kind printing limited basic information on each till roll. The store detective was able to describe how the tills operated, what the computer did, that there had been no trouble with the computer and how she had also examined all the till rolls which showed no evidence of malfunction either by the tills or the central computer. In these circumstances I agree with the Court of Appeal that she was fully qualified to

> give the evidence required by section 69 and that in the light of her evidence the till rolls were properly admitted as part of the prosecution case.
>
> I therefore answer the certified question by saying that section 69(1) of the Police and Criminal Evidence Act 1984 can be satisfied by the oral evidence of a person familiar with the operation of the computer who can give evidence of its reliability and such a person need not be a computer expert.
>
> For these reasons, I would dismiss this appeal.

As Lord Griffiths recognised, compliance with s 69 may often be straightforward, but may in some cases involve serious difficulties for the party concerned. The Law Commission cite as an example the unreported case of *R v Newbury*,[15] at which between 15 and 20 hours of a five week trial were spent satisfying s 69.[16] If there is dispute as to the accuracy or reliability of the computer or as to the correctness of the operating procedure, Schedule 3, para 9, enables the court to require oral evidence in addition to or in place of any certificate; but if there are several computers involved, several witnesses may then need to be called.

In some cases, expert evidence might also be necessary in order to explain how a given computer works and why its records are relevant to the facts in issue. If such matters are not adequately proved, whether by expert evidence or otherwise, the computer printouts will remain inadmissible and the s 69 issue of reliability will never even be reached.[17] In cases involving the alleged misuse of bank cashpoint or ATM cards, which are likely to occur on a fairly regular basis, the Court of Appeal has advised that the Crown Prosecution Service should consider devising a standard form of evidence to explain the relationship between the cards, PIN numbers, central bank computers and individual accounts concerned.[18]

Schedule 3 to the Act contains a number of other provisions relating to computer statements tendered under s 69. These merely seem to remind the courts to do what the courts would hopefully do anyway when assessing the weight and credibility of the evidence.

Paragraph 11 provides:

> In estimating the weight, if any, to be attached to the statement regard shall be had to all the circumstances from which any inference can reasonably be drawn as to the accuracy or otherwise of the statement and, in particular
>
> (a) to the question whether or not the information which the information contained in the statement reproduces or is derived from was supplied to the relevant computer, or recorded for the purpose of being supplied to it,

---

15 (1995) Isleworth Crown Court.

16 *Evidence in Criminal Proceedings: Hearsay and Related Topics* (Consultation Paper No 138) para 14.16.

17 *R v Cochrane* [1993] Crim LR 48.

18 *Ibid.*

contemporaneously with the occurrence or existence of the facts dealt with in that information; and

(b) to the question whether or not any person concerned with the supply of information to that computer, or with the operation of that computer or any equipment by means of which the document containing the statement was produced by it, had any incentive to conceal or misrepresent the facts.

Paragraph 12 provides:

For the purposes of paragraph 11 above, information shall be taken to be supplied to a computer whether it is supplied directly or (with or without human intervention) by means of any appropriate equipment.

Paragraph 14 provides:

For the purpose of deciding whether or not a statement is admissible the court may draw any reasonable inference

(a) from the circumstances in which the statement was made or otherwise came into being; or

(b) from any other circumstances, including the form and contents of the document in which the statement is contained.

In *Sophocleous v Ringer*,[19] the Divisional Court held that s 69 has no application in cases where oral evidence is given by witnesses who have relied on computers when preparing that evidence. It is instead confined to cases in which the computer printout, or some document derived from it, is adduced as evidence in its own right. This decision, although criticised by some commentators, and by the Law Commission[20] was approved in *Shephard* and subsequently followed by the Court of Appeal in *R v Golizadeh*.[21] The distinction can be justified on the ground that, in a case such as *Sophocleous v Ringer*, the witness can be cross-examined as to any matters, including matters relating to the operation of the computer, which may be thought to affect the reliability of his testimony. Section 69 provides a check upon the use of printouts themselves, which cannot of course be cross-examined in this way. In *Sophocleous v Ringer*, a Home Office analyst was therefore allowed to refresh her memory from a computer printout without bringing s 69 into operation. Similarly, in *Golizadeh* an expert analyst was permitted to give evidence based on his interpretation of data obtained from a machine which analysed substances suspected of containing drugs by means of a process called gaschromatography masspechtromotry. The Court of Appeal held that, even assuming the machine to be a computer, the printouts were not themselves tendered in evidence, and therefore s 69 did not apply.

19 [1988] RTR 52.

20 *Evidence in Criminal Proceedings: Hearsay and Related Topics* (Consultation Paper No 138).

21 [1995] Crim LR 232.

Proposals for reform

The Law Commission has provisionally proposed major changes to the rules governing the admissibility of computer evidence in criminal proceedings. One of the main thrusts of the Commission's criticism of the existing law is that s 69 of the Police and Criminal Evidence Act 1984 can be awkward to comply with, and yet it provides very little real protection against the dangers of inaccurate or falsified evidence.

Law Commission Consultation Paper No 138: *Evidence in Criminal Proceedings: the Hearsay Rule and Related Topics*[22]

14.17 We believe that a major problem with computer evidence also arises where incorrect data have been fed into the computer, as opposed to there being a defect in the software. We were not surprised when people told us that this sometimes happened. This evidence lends support to Professor Tapper's view that 'most computer error is either immediately detectable or results from error in the data entered into the machine'. Thus section 69 fails to address the main problem with computer evidence, that is, data errors. Instead it deals with matters which would usually be apparent in any event.

14.18 A further problem with the operation of section 69 is that it may often be the *recipient* of a computer-produced document who wishes to tender it in court; but he or she may be in no position to satisfy the court about the operation of the computer. It may well be that his or her opponent is better placed to do that.

14.19 Another significant criticism that has been made of the present law is that it can be effectively exploited by the defence so as unjustly to undermine a prosecution ... Determined defence lawyers can and do cross-examine the prosecution's computer expert at great length. The complexity of modern systems makes it relatively easy to establish a reasonable doubt in a juror's mind as to whether the computer was operating properly. Bearing in mind the very technical nature of computers, the chances of this happening with greater frequency in future are fairly high. We are concerned about smoke-screens being raised by cross-examination which focuses in general terms on the fallibility of computers rather than on the reliability of the particular evidence. The absence of a presumption that the computer is working means that it is relatively easy to raise such a smoke-screen ...

14.21 For all the above reasons, we maintain the view we expressed in our report on the hearsay rule in civil proceedings, that 'it is not possible to legislate protectively' with regard to computer evidence. We agree with the commentator who said recently that 'the only effective course is to weigh evidence according to its reliability, and to rely upon

22 HMSO 1995. Some footnotes omitted.

specific challenges to the cogency or accuracy of computer evidence in cases where misuse, system failure or operator error is suspected.'[23] Where there are specific reasons to doubt the reliability of a particular document generated by a computer, those doubts should in our view go to weight, and not to admissibility ...

14.28 If there were no pre-condition for the admission of computer records, the parties would be able to rely on the presumption of regularity. According to *Phipson*,[24] in the absence of evidence to the contrary, the courts will presume that mechanical instruments were in order at the material time. This passage was approved by the Divisional Court in *Castle v Cross*[25] where it was observed that *Phipson's* formulation included no requirement that the instrument in question should be of a kind which is commonly known to be in working order more often than not. The principle has been applied to such devices as speedometers, traffic lights and Intoximeters, and we see no reason why it should not apply to computers. The prosecution would not need to lead evidence that the computer was working properly on the occasion in question unless there was evidence that it may not have been – in which case the prosecution would have to prove beyond reasonable doubt that it was ...

14.32 Our provisional view is that section 69 fails to serve any useful purpose. Other systems operate effectively and efficiently without it. We provisionally propose that section 69 should be repealed without replacement.

CIVIL CASES

Introduction

The civil courts in England and Wales have in the past faced problems caused by lack of adequate provision for the admissibility of computer evidence. The most widely publicised difficulties were those connected with collection of the notorious community charge (or 'poll tax') in the early 1990s. The poll tax legislation made the magistrates' courts responsible for the judicial enforcement of unpaid demands for this tax, and local authorities throughout the land relied on their computerised records in order to identify and sue defaulters. A magistrates' court would accordingly be presented with computer printouts showing that defendant D owed so many pounds in unpaid poll tax; but was such evidence admissible? In *R v Coventry Justices,*

23 M Hirst, 'Computer Statements in English Civil Proceedings' (1994) 3 Law Computers and Artificial Intelligence 13.

24 *Phipson on Evidence*, para 23.14.

25 [1984] 1 WLR 1372.

ex p Bullard, the applicants obtained orders from the Divisional Court, quashing liability orders imposed by magistrates on the basis of computer evidence adduced by the local authority. The problem faced by the local authority was that most recognised exceptions to the hearsay rule were at that time inapplicable in civil proceedings heard in magistrates' courts.

***R v Coventry Justices, ex p Bullard* (1992) 95 Cr App R 175**

Mann LJ

The decision in *Myers* led to a statutory abrogation of the hearsay rule in the Criminal Justice Act 1965 and there were later abrogations in the Civil Evidence Act 1968 and in the Police and Criminal Evidence Act 1984. None of these abrogations is available in civil proceedings in magistrates' courts, where, subject to the Evidence Act 1938 and to its own established common law exceptions, the hearsay rule remains fully applicable ...

We know nothing of the operation of the computer which produced the printout. However, it must be the case ... that the outputs are of or are derived from information implanted by a human. They are thus hearsay and inadmissible as evidence of either the amounts which the applicants are liable to pay or of the amounts which are unpaid ...

Hearsay and the Civil Evidence Act 1995

As a result of reforms recently introduced by the Civil Evidence Act 1995, admissibility problems of the Coventry Justices kind will no longer be capable of troubling the civil courts or tribunals.[26] The hearsay rule is, for most practical purposes, abolished insofar as it applies to civil proceedings.

Section 1 of the Act provides:

(1) In civil proceedings evidence shall not be excluded on the ground that it is hearsay.

(2) In this Act

(a) 'hearsay' means a statement made otherwise than by a person while giving oral evidence in the proceedings which is tendered as evidence of the maters stated; and

(b) references to hearsay include hearsay of whatever degree.

(3) Nothing in this Act affects the admissibility of evidence admissible apart from this section.

(4) ... (see below)

Sections 2–6 of the Act set out certain safeguards, considerations and procedures to be observed when adducing or assessing hearsay evidence, one of which requires any party proposing to use such evidence to give advance

26 Although the specific problem of enforcing claims against poll tax and council tax defaulters had already been addressed by the time that this legislation was enacted.

notice of that fact to any other parties involved;[27] but s 1(4) provides that these do not apply where evidence is held to be admissible on some basis other than under the Act, even if that same evidence could equally have been adduced under the Act. This may be significant where automatically recorded computer evidence is concerned. Not all 'statements made otherwise than by a person while giving oral evidence in the proceedings' are properly regarded as hearsay at common law, even if that is how such statements are defined in the Act itself. As the criminal division of the Court of Appeal acknowledged in *R v Wood* and *R v Spiby* (above), statements produced by computers may sometimes be admissible at common law as a species of original evidence, and not as a species of hearsay. In civil cases, the use of such evidence was formerly subject to restrictions imposed by s 5 of the Civil Evidence Act 1968, but now that this provision has been repealed, such evidence would appear to be admissible without any need for reference to statutory provisions.

No special 'reliability' rules for computer evidence

A notable feature of the Civil Evidence Act 1995 is the absence of any provision approximating to s 69 of the Police and Criminal Evidence Act 1984.[28] The reasons for this deliberate omission are, in effect, the same as those advanced by the Law Commission in support of its recommendation that s 69 be repealed,[29] and need not be repeated here.

Proving the contents of documents: originals, copies and business records

Much concern has been voiced in recent years over the problem of providing acceptable evidence of commercial transactions which have been negotiated and concluded by means of EDI, or of transactions which are documented only by electronic records. The logistics of paper-based document storage certainly creates problems for some organisations, and electronic image-processed document storage provides a potentially compact and efficient system with which to replace bulky paper files, provided of course that image processed electronic documents will be treated as acceptable by a court of law.

At common law, admissibility would often be problematic in such cases, particularly where copies of original documents are concerned. The 'primary

27 The sanction for non-compliance with such notice requirements is not that the evidence will be excluded (s 2(4)); instead, the party at fault 'may be penalised by the court in the exercise of its powers with respect to the course of proceedings and costs' and it may treat inadequate advance disclosure as a factor affecting the weight or credence given to such evidence under s 4 of the Act.

28 See above, p 383.

29 See above, p 389.

evidence rule' at common law permits the use of copies (even simple photocopies) only in very limited circumstances, but there have long been exceptions to that rule, notably in the case of banking records, which have for well over a hundred years been provable by authenticated copies under the Bankers' Books Evidence Act 1879.[30] That Act remains in force, but at a more general level ss 8 and 9 of the 1995 Act have now largely eliminated problems of admissibility.

As far as business and official records are concerned, the Civil Evidence Act 1995, s 9, provides:

> (1) A document which is shown to form part of the records of a business or public authority may be received in evidence in civil proceedings without further proof.
>
> (2) A document shall be taken to form part of the records of a business or public authority if there is produced to the court a certificate to that effect signed by an officer of the business or authority to which the records belong. For this purpose
>
> (a) a document purporting to be signed by an officer of a business or public authority shall be deemed to have been duly given by such an officer and signed by him; and
>
> (b) a certificate shall be treated as signed by a person if it purports to bear a facsimile of his signature.
>
> (3) The absence of an entry in the records of a business or public authority may be proved in civil proceedings by affidavit of an officer of the business or authority to which the records belong.
>
> (4) In this section
>
> 'records' means records in whatever form;
>
> 'business' includes any activity regularly carried on over a period of time, whether for profit or not, by any body (whether corporate or not) or by an individual ...
>
> 'officer' includes any person occupying a responsible position in relation to the relevant activities of the business or public authority or of its records; and
>
> 'public authority' includes any public sector or statutory undertaking, any government department and any person holding office under Her Majesty.
>
> (5) The court may, having regard to the circumstances of the case, direct that all or any of the above provisions of this section do not apply in relation to a particular document or record, or description of documents or records.

Subsection (5) gives courts an important measure of flexibility with regard to business records. A judge might not, for example, accept the authenticity of a certified business record or of a signature on a certificate, if he has reasons for doubting that authenticity; and he may accordingly insist on some further and

30 As amended by the Banking Act 1979.

better proof before accepting that document in evidence. Respectable and well-organised businesses which adopt sound and reliable methods for verifying and storing their records (on paper or in electronic form) should have little to fear from this. Accepting the authenticity of such records is not necessarily the same thing as accepting the accuracy of their contents. It may still be open to an opposing party to argue that certain statements in a business document are inaccurate or even fraudulent. This is a matter of factual credibility rather than one of legal admissibility, but in many situations it is probably true to say that establishing the authenticity of the document as a genuine business record will make challenges to its accuracy very difficult to sustain.

The status of copies of original documents is meanwhile dealt with by s 8 of the Act:

> 8(1) Where a statement contained in a document is admissible as evidence in civil proceedings, it may be proved:
>
> (a) by the production of that document; or
>
> (b) whether or not that document is still in existence, by the production of a copy of that document or of the material part of it;
>
> authenticated in such manner as the court may approve.
>
> (2) It is immaterial for this purpose how many removes there are between a copy and the original.

'Documents' for such purposes include anything on which information of any description is recorded.[31] Computer disks, CD-Roms and magnetic tape all come within that definition.[32]

Contractual stipulations

Although the 1995 Act permits the use of authenticated copies in evidence, it is still open to contracting parties to stipulate that original documents must be used for specified purposes. Banks, for example, commonly require production of original documentation in connection with international letters of credit. Stipulations of this kind are primarily matters of contract law or banking law, rather than of evidence,[33] and accordingly fall beyond the scope of this chapter. Questions may, however, arise as to what properly amounts to an original document for such purposes. In the cases of conventional typed or

31 Section 13 of the Civil Evidence Act 1995.

32 Computer databases containing printable information are similarly classed as documents for the purposes of rules relating to discovery and inspection under Ord 24 of the Rules of the Supreme Court: *Derby & Co Ltd v Weldon* [1991] 1 WLR 73.

33 Similarly, contracting parties who rely on EDI may agree to adopt the Uniform Rules of Conduct for Interchange of Trade Data by Teletransmission (UNCID); this is also a matter of contract law.

hand-written documents, it may be possible to distinguish clearly between originals and copies; but the original version of an electronically stored document may be harder to identify. Is it the computer disk onto which the document was first recorded? If so, printouts could only be mere copies, but that would not be a workable system at all. In *Glencore International A-G v Bank of China*,[34] the Court of Appeal held that:

> In the context of modern technology, unless otherwise stipulated ... a bank should accept as an original a document produced or appearing to have been produced by reprographic, automated or computerised systems, provided it was marked as an original.

34 [1995] TLR 617.

INDEX

Abstractions
- United Kingdom, 47–49, 51
- United States, 38–39, 42–44

Adaptations
- errors, 104–05
- European Union, 61, 101–02
- literary works, 27
- software, 24–27
  - contracts, 101

Back-ups
- European Union, 58, 59, 60, 102–03
- licensing, 103
- 'necessary', 102–03
- software, 14
  - contracts, 102–03

Bangemann Report, 302, 303

Bespoke contracts, 75–76
- negligence, 213, 216
- product liability, 203
- supply, 170

Bills of lading

Blackmail, 355

Breach of confidence
- data protection, 273, 279
- electronic data interchange, 244
- licensing, 98
- software, 9

Bugs
- damages, 115
- implied terms, 186
- shrink-wrap licences, 115

Bulletin boards, 318, 319, 322, 323–25

Causation
- negligence, 216–17
- product liability, 207–09

Child pornography, 361, 365, 368, 369–70

Civil liberties
- *See* Human rights

Codes of practice, 255–56, 276

Community charge, 286–88, 390

Comparisons, 40, 42, 49

Compatibility, 41, 54

Compensation
- *See also* Damages
- data protection, 270–71

Compilations, 18–19
- United Kingdom, 46–47, 51
- United States, 44

Computer software
- *See* Software

Confidentiality
- *See also* Breach of confidence

Conspiracy, 354

Contempt, 326

Contracts
- *See also* Development contracts, Software contracts, Unfair contract terms
- acquisition, 107–09
- electronic data interchange,
- evidence, 394–95
- formation, 234–47

Copyright
- Berne Convention, 10
- decompilation, 54, 55
- defective software, 158–61
- errors, 104
- European Union, 56–64, 159
- Japan, 10–13
- originality, 14
- ownership, 96–98
- software, 8–64
  - contracts, 89, 96–98
- United Kingdom, 45–53
- United States, 10–13, 21–22, 28, 31–43

Council of Europe
- criminal offences, 332
- data protection, 256, 258, 299–300, 303, 311

Credit reference agencies, 279–87

Criminal offences, 331–74
- *See also* Fraud
- addiction, 357
- blackmail, 355
- conspiracy, 354
- Council of Europe, 332
- damage, 155–57, 337–50
- data protection, 259, 265–67, 279, 288–96
- defective software, 155–57
- detection, 356
- European Union, 371–74
- evidence, 375–90
- hacking, 155–57, 331, 332, 337–50, 356–58, 362
- incitement, 354

jurisdiction, 358
mental illness, 357
networks, 358–70
viruses, 353–55

Damages
See also Compensation
bugs, 115
defective software, 151
misrepresentation, 82
mitigation, 116
remoteness, 116
shrink-wrap licences, 115

Data protection, 249–318
accuracy, 254
Bangemann Report, 302, 303
breach of confidence, 273, 279
codes of practice, 255–56, 276
community charge, 286–88
compensation, 270–71
Council of Europe Convention, 256, 258, 299–300, 303, 311
credit reference agencies, 279–87
criminal offences, 259, 265–67, 279, 288–96
data, definition of, 258–61
data matching, 250
Data Protection Registrar, 263–69, 278, 286–90, 301–18
Data Protection Tribunal, 275–88
direct marketing, 275–78
disclosure, 263, 292
electronic date interchange, 242, 317
encryption, 317
enforcement, 267–72, 314
errors, 271–72
European Union, 258, 276, 295, 317
exemptions, 296, 305, 311–13
freedom of expression, 313
freedom of information, 258
guidelines, 272–73, 279, 287, 297
human rights, 251, 258, 302
inspection, 268
Internet, 316–18
legitimate expectations, 274
Lindop Report, 255–57, 298
mailing lists, 275–78
manual records, 300–01, 304
national security, 296, 305
notices, 268, 279–87
notification, 311
objections, 310–11
opt-out boxes, 278
personal data, 261–62, 299, 305–06
powers of entry, 268
privacy, 251–54, 297, 298, 300–03
report, 252–54
processing, 279–87, 299, 306, 313
quality, 307
recklessness, 289–90
rectification, 271–72
registration, 262–86, 289, 297, 311
Report of Committee on Data Protection, 250–51, 254–55
right of access, 269–70, 309
rights of subjects, 308–09
sensitive data, 305
transborder data flow, 313–14
transfers, 293
unauthorised access, 252
ultra vires rule, 273
Younger Committee on Privacy, 252
World Wide Web, 317

Deception, 333–37

Decompilation
copyright, 54, 55
European Union, 54, 58–62
software, 20, 54–56
sound cards, 56
United States, 54, 55–56

Defamation, 318–329
bulletin boards, 318, 319, 322, 323–25
contempt, 326
distributors, 324–26
European Union, 327–28
Faulks Committee, 320
freedom of expression, 319
innocent dissemination, 322–23, 326
Internet, 318–24, 362
liability, 322–29
libel, 319–20
mailing lists, 318
news groups, 318, 319, 325
on-line services, 323
permanence, 320
privacy, 319
publication, 320–22
slander, 319–20
third parties, 321
World Wide Web, 329

Defective products
  See Product liability
Defective software, 151–221
  business, 183–85
  consumers, 185
  copyright, 158–61
  criminal damage, 155–57
  damages, 151
  description, 172–81
  errors, 153–54
  European Union, 159
  fit for the purpose, 165, 190–96
  functionality, 157–58
  generic goods, 172
  goods, 161, 163–66
  hacking, 155–57
  hardware, 161–66
  implied terms, 151, 171, 183–87, 197
  information, 154–58, 161
  instructions, 153–54, 162
  intellectual property, 158–60
  licensing, 160
  physical form, 155–56
  pragmatism, 163–66
  product liability, 199–221
  sale of goods, 152–54, 160, 161, 165–97
  samples, 196–97
  satisfactory quality, 165, 182–83, 187–90
  services, 166–71
  shrink-wrap licences, 165
  sui generis rights, 159
  supply, 170–71
  tort, 199–221
  unfair contract terms, 171
  United States, 159–60, 164
Delivery, 86
Derivative works, 35
Description
  defective software, 172–81
  definition, 175–81
  generic goods, 172
  identification, 180–81
  reliance, 174
  sale of goods, 172–81
  samples, 197
  unfair contract terms, 180
Designs, 214–16, 219
Development contracts
  acceptance tests, 87–88
  delivery, 86
  fit for the purpose, 86
  further work, 86
  passing of property, 86
  risk, 86
  software, 84–86
  specifications, 84–85
Direct marketing, 275–78
Disclosure
  data protection, 263, 292
  software, 7
Downloading, 15
Duress
  economic, 94–96
  software contracts, 93–96

Economic loss, 213
Electronic data interchange, 225–47
  bills of lading, 241–42
  breach of confidentiality, 244
  contracts, 229, 230
    formation, 234–47
  damage, 234–35
  data protection, 242, 317
  definition, 225
  documents, 231, 233
  e-mail, 225
  European Model EDI Agreement, 242–47
  evidence, 228
  formalities, 231–34
  information, 227
  interchange agreements, 229, 235
  network provider, 228–30
  network users, 229, 230
  paper, 225–34
  postal rule, 235, 239, 240
  risk, 238, 240
  services, 229
  signature, 232, 233
  storage, 245
  symbolic function, 240–42
  telexes, 235–39
  UNCID rules, 229
  UNCITRAL, 228
  unfair contract terms, 229
  VAN service, 225, 229, 239
  writing, 231–33
E-mail, 224
Encryption, 317
Erasure, 353

Errors
adaptations, 104–05
copyright, 104
data protection, 271–72
defective software, 153–54
European Union, 60–61, 101, 103–06
on-line systems, 104
product liability, 203, 210
software, 60–61
contracts, 101, 103–06
defective, 153–54
source codes, 103–05

European Model EDI Agreement, 242–47

European Union
adaptations, 61, 101–02
back-ups, 58, 59, 60, 102–03
Brussels Convention 1968, 326–28
copyright, 56–64, 159
data protection, 258, 276, 295, 317
decompilation, 54, 58–62
defamation, 327–28
discrimination, 372
errors, 60–61, 101, 103–06
exclusive rights, 100
fair use, 59–61
free movement of goods, 372
freedom of expression, 371
harmonisation, 57
information society, 373–74
Internet, 361, 371–74
licensing, 59, 99–100
literary works, 57
Lugano Convention 1988, 326–28
networks, 371–74
product liability, 220–03, 209–11
rental rights, 58
shrink-wrap licences, 110–11
software contracts, 99–106
Software Directive, 54, 56–64
contracts, 99–106
UK implementation, 60–63
sui generis rights, 63–64
unfair contract terms, 141–49
United States, 63–64

Evidence, 375–95
admissibility, 376, 378, 380–83, 390
automatic recordings, 381
civil law, 390–95
community charge, 390
contracts, 394–95
criminal law, 375–90
documentary, 381–83
electronic data interchange, 228
expert, 387
hearsay, 377–83, 389–92
parol, 80–81
prejudice, 376
reform, 389–90
relevance, 376
reliability, 379, 383–88, 392
software contracts, 80–81

Exclusion clauses
See Exemption clauses

Exclusive rights
European Union, 100
software contracts, 117–50

Exemption clauses
construction of contracts, 117–18
definition, 117
licensing, 98–99
negligence, 118
services, 166
software contracts, 117–50
unfair contract terms, 117, 118–50

Expert systems, 70

Expression
ideas, 30
software, 30
United Kingdom, 50
United States, 31–35

Fair use, 59–61

Faulks Committee, 320

Filtration
United Kingdom, 49
United States, 39–40, 42

Fitness for the purpose
defective software, 165, 190–96
development contracts, 86
implied terms, 89, 190–91, 195–96
particular purposes, 191–96
reasonableness, 191
reliance, 195
satisfactory quality, 183, 190, 191
software contracts, 86, 89

Fraud, 333–54
deception, 333–37
definition, 333
erasure, 353

hacking, 337–50
input, 333
Internet, 361
modifications, 352–53
output, 333
program, 333
unauthorised access, 343–44, 346, 351

Freedom of expression
data protection, 313
defamation, 319
European Union, 371
Internet, 364–65, 371

Freedom of information, 258

Generic goods, 172

Goods
defective software, 161, 163–66
definition, 154
product liability, 202
software contracts, 76–77
supply, 170

Guarantees, 120

Hacking, 331, 332, 337–50, 356–58
criminal damage, 155–57, 337–50
defective software, 155–57
definition, 349
Internet, 362
mens rea, 357

Hardware, 75, 161–66

Hearsay, 377–83, 389–92

Human rights
data protection, 251, 258, 302
freedom of expression, 313, 319, 364–65, 371

Ideas
expressions, 30
software, 30
United Kingdom, 50
United States, 31–35

Implied terms
bugs, 186
business, 183–85
consumers, 185
defective software, 151, 171, 183–87, 197
fit for the purpose, 89, 195–96
relevance, 197
samples, 197
satisfactory quality, 183–87
services, 167
shrink-wrap licences, 111
software contracts, 83–84, 89
viruses, 185
unfair contract terms, 171

Incitement, 354

Information
defective software, 154–58, 161
electronic data interchange, 227
product liability, 201, 202–03

Instructions, 153–54, 162

Intellectual property
See also Copyright, Patents
breach of confidence, 9
competition, 9
contracts, 9
decompilation, 54–56
defective software, 158–60
European Union, 54, 56–64
interoperability, 54
literal copying, 29
reverse engineering, 54–56
scope of protection, 28–53
software, 5–73
United Kingdom, 45–53
United States, 28, 31–45
World Intellectual Property
organisation, 5–10
model provisions, 6–8

Interchange agreements, 229, 235

Internet, 359–70
See also World Wide Web
Australia, 367
bulletin boards, 318, 319, 322, 323–25
children, 361, 365, 368, 369–70
credit cards, 361
data protection, 316–18
defamation, 318–24, 362
description, 359–61
economic security, 361
European Union, 361, 371–74
fraud, 361
freedom of expression, 364–65, 371
hacking, 362
national security, 361
news groups, 318, 319, 325
pornography, 361, 363–71
privacy, 362
registration, 367

self-regulation, 371, 373
Singapore, 367
United Kingdom, 368–69
United States, 363–67
Interoperability, 54, 56
Inventions, 65–68
Investment, 6

Japan, 10–13
Jurisdiction
criminal offences, 358
defamation, 326–28

Libel, 319–20
See also Defamation
Licensing
See also Shrink-wrap licences
back-up copies, 103
breach of confidence, 98
defective software, 160
duration, 98
European Union, 59, 99–100
exemption clauses, 98–99
software, 7
contracts, 76, 83, 88–100, 106–16
transfer, 98
Lindop Report, 255–57, 298
Literary works
adaptations, 27
European Union, 57
patents, 72
software, 15–16, 20, 21–27, 29
United Kingdom, 50
United States, 21–22, 35, 37, 41
London Ambulance Service, 199
Look and feel, 30–31

Mailing lists, 275–78, 318
Merchantable quality, 182–83, 187–90
Millennium problem, 2
Misrepresentation
damages, 82
opinions, 81–92
pre-contractual statements, 81–83
rescission, 82
software contracts, 81–83
Modification
criminal offences, 352–53
software contracts, 88–96

National security, 296, 305, 361
Negligence
bespoke legislation, 213, 216
causation, 216–17
design, 214–16, 219
economic loss, 213
engineers, 215–20
exemption clauses, 118
negligent misstatements, 82–83, 213–14
product liability, 212–25
reliance, 213
standard of care, 217–21
unfair contract terms, 121, 129
Negligent misstatements, 82–83, 213–14
Networks, 358–70
See also Internet, World Wide Web
criminal offences, 358
providers, 228–30
users, 229, 230
News groups, 318, 319, 325
Novelty, 72

On-line services
defamation, 323
errors, 104
software contracts, 89
Operating systems, 37
Originality, 14, 47

Parol evidence, 80–81
Patents
expert systems, 70
invention, 65–68
literary works, 72
novelty, 72
software, 8, 10, 64–73
United States, 66–67
Pornography, 361, 363–71
Powers of entry, 268
Pre-contractual statements, 81–83
Privacy
data protection, 251–54, 297, 298, 300–03
defamation, 319

Internet, 362
Younger Committee, 252

Product liability
bespoke software, 203
causation, 207–09
consumer protection, 200–12
defective software, 199–221
development risks defence, 209–12
errors, 203, 210
European Union, 200–05, 209–11
goods, 202
information, 201, 202–03
London Ambulance Service, 199
negligence, 212–21
products, 200–02
reasonableness, 207
Strasbourg Convention, 206–07, 209–11

Programs
See Software

Promises, 90–93

Public domain, 20–21

Quality
See also Satisfactory quality
software contracts, 77–83

Reliance
description, 174
fitness for the purpose, 195
negligence, 213

Rental works, 58

Rescission, 82

Research, 56

Reverse engineering
research, 56
software, 54–56

Risk
development contracts, 86
electronic data interchange, 238–40

Sale of goods
See also Exemption clauses, Fitness for purpose, Satisfactory quality, Unfair contract terms
defective software, 152–54, 160, 161, 165–97
description, 17–81
services, 166–68

Samples
defective software, 196–97
descriptions, 197
implied terms, 197

Satisfactory quality
defective software, 165, 182–83, 187–90
fitness for purpose, 183, 190, 191
implied terms, 183–87
merchantable quality, 182–83, 187–90
reasonableness, 187–89
services, 166
test, 187–90

Services
defective software, 166–71
electronic data interchange, 229
exemption clauses, 166
implied terms, 167
sale of goods, 166–68
satisfactory quality, 166
software contracts, 76–77
supply, 170

Shetland News, 2

Shrink-wrap licences
acquisition contracts, 107–09
bugs, 115
damages, 115–16
defective software, 165
European Union, 110
implied terms, 111
incorporation by reference, 108–09
lawful users, 110
opening the envelope, 109–16
shops, 106–08
software contracts, 106–16
suppliers, 113

Slander, 319–20
See also Defamation

Software
See also Defective contracts, Software contracts
adaptations, 24–27
back-ups, 14
breach of confidence, 9
competition, 9
compilations, 18–19
copyright, 8–9, 10–30
decompilation, 20, 54–56
definition, 19
development, 84–88
disclosure, 7
downloading, 15
engineers, 215–20

errors, 29
European Union, 54, 56–64
expression, 30
fit for the purpose, 86, 89
ideas, 30
intellectual property rights, 5–73
interoperability, 54
investment, 6
Japan, 10–13
licensing, 7
literal copying, 20
literary works, 15–16, 20, 21–27, 29
look and feel, 30–31
object codes, 17, 21
originality, 14
patents, 8, 10, 64–73
parol evidence rule, 80–81
public domain, 20–21
reverse engineering, 54–56
source codes, 17, 19, 21, 24–27, 103–05
trade, 7
United Kingdom, 45–53
United States, 10–13, 21–22, 28, 31–45
vulnerability, 7

Software contracts, 9, 75–150
See also Defective software
adaptations, 101
back-up copies, 102–03
bespoke, 75–76
consideration, 89–93
copyright, 89, 96–98
custom, 84
duress, 93–96
errors, 101, 103–06
European Union, 99–106
exclusive rights, 100
exemption clauses, 117–50
goods, 76–77
implied terms, 83–84, 89
licensing, 76, 83, 98–100, 106–16
misrepresentations, 81–83
modification, 88–96
on-line systems, 89
pre-contractual statements, 81–83
promises, 90–93
quality, 77–83
services, 76–77
shrink-wrap licences, 106–16
standard, 75–76
suitability, 77–83
terms, 83–84
types, 75
unfair contract terms, 117, 118, 119–50
warranties, 78–79

Sound cards, 56

Standard contracts, 75–76, 170–71

Sui generis rights
defective software, 159
European Union, 53–54

Supply
bespoke software, 170
defective software, 170–71
goods, 170
services, 170
shrink-wrap licences, 113
standard software, 170–71

Telexes, 235–39

Transborder data flow, 313–14

Unfair contract terms
businesses, 126–29
consumers, 123, 128–33, 149
defective software, 171
European Union, 141–49
exemption clauses, 117, 118, 119–50
guarantees, 120
hire-purchase, 121, 129
implied terms, 171
list of terms which may be regarded as, 141–49
negligence, 119, 129
reasonableness, 123–23, 126, 128–29, 133–38, 150
software contracts, 117, 118–19

United Kingdom
abstraction, 47–49, 51
comparisons, 49
compilations, 46–47, 51
copyright, 45–53
expressions, 50
filtration, 49
functional works, 52
ideas, 50
intellectual property rights, 45–53
Internet, 368–69
literary works, 50
originality, 47
software, 45–53
United States, 45–50, 53

United States
  abstraction, 38–39, 42–44
  comparisons, 40, 42
  compatibility, 41
  compilations, 44
  copyright, 10–13, 21–22, 28, 31–43
  decompilation, 54, 55–56
  defective software, 159–60, 164
  derivative works, 35
  European Union, 63–64
  expressions, 31–35
  filtration, 39–40, 42
  functional works, 34
  ideas, 31–35
  Internet, 363–67
  literary works, 35, 37, 41
  operating systems, 37
  patents, 66–67
  software, 10–13, 21–22, 28, 31–45
  United Kingdom, 45–50, 53

Viruses
  criminal offences, 353–55
  implied terms, 185

Warranties, 78–79

World Intellectual Property Organisation, 5–10

World Wide Web, 1, 2, 359
  See also Internet
  data protection, 317
  defamation, 329

Younger Committee on Privacy, 252–54